Monarchy Transformed

This decisive contribution to the long-running debate about the dynamics of state formation and elite transformation in early modern Europe examines the new monarchies that emerged during the course of the 'long seventeenth century'. It argues that the players surviving the power struggles of this period were not 'states' in any modern sense, but primarily princely dynasties pursuing not only dynastic ambitions and princely prestige but the consequences of dynastic chance. At the same time, elites, far from insisting on confrontation with the government of princes for principled ideological reasons, had every reason to seek compromise and even advancement through new channels that the governing dynasty offered, if only so they could profit from them. Monarchy Transformed ultimately challenges the inevitability of modern maps of Europe and shows how, instead of promoting state formation, the wars of the period witnessed the creation of several dynastic agglomerates and new kinds of aristocracy.

Robert von Friedeburg is Reader in History at Bishop Grosseteste University and Member of the Academia Europaea. Among his seven monographs and ten (co-)edited books is most recently *Luther's Legacy: The Thirty Years War and the Modern Notion of 'State' in the Empire, 1530s to 1790s* (Cambridge, 2016), which will appear in a German edition in a series of the Max Planck Institute for European Legal History, Frankfurt.

John Morrill retired in 2013 after forty years teaching British, Irish and European History at Cambridge. A major interest has been the long historical relationship between England, Ireland, Scotland and Wales set in a European comparative context. He has written and edited more than twenty books and published more than 100 essays and articles, and he is a Fellow of the British Academy and an Honorary Member of both the Royal Irish Academy and the Academy of Finland.

Monarchy Transformed

Princes and Their Elites in Early Modern Western Europe

Edited by

Robert von Friedeburg

Bishop Grosseteste University, Lincoln

John Morrill

University of Cambridge

CAMBRIDGE
UNIVERSITY PRESS

CAMBRIDGE
UNIVERSITY PRESS

University Printing House, Cambridge CB2 8BS, United Kingdom

One Liberty Plaza, 20th Floor, New York, NY 10006, USA

477 Williamstown Road, Port Melbourne, VIC 3207, Australia

314-321, 3rd Floor, Plot 3, Splendor Forum, Jasola District Centre, New Delhi - 110025, India

79 Anson Road, #06-04/06, Singapore 079906

Cambridge University Press is part of the University of Cambridge.

It furthers the University's mission by disseminating knowledge in the pursuit of education, learning and research at the highest international levels of excellence.

www.cambridge.org
Information on this title: www.cambridge.org/9781316649633
DOI: 10.1017/9781108225083

First published 2017
First paperback edition 2020

A catalogue record for this publication is available from the British Library

ISBN 978-1-316-51024-7 Hardback
ISBN 978-1-316-64963-3 Paperback

Contents

Figures

Tables

viii

Acknowledgements

The contributions to this volume are heavily revised pieces selected from the contributions to two conferences in Rotterdam in 2008 and 2011. They were funded by Erasmus University Rotterdam, the Dutch Royal Academy of Sciences (KNAW) and the research programme 'Reason of State or Reason of Princes – the New Monarchy and its Enemies', a programme in turn funded by the Dutch Organisation for Research (NWO). We are grateful for the support we received, in particular for the detailed pieces of criticism and suggestions from the two anonymous reviewers of Cambridge University Press.

Notes on the Contributors

ANTONIO ÁLVAREZ-OSSORIO ALVARIÑO is Professor of Modern History in the Department of Modern History, Autonomous University of Madrid, and has been Vice Rector there since 2013. He has written extensively on the Habsburg Dynasty, court studies and Spanish art in the Renaissance and Baroque periods.

RONALD G. ASCH is Professor of Early Modern History at the University of Freiburg. His latest monograph is *Sacral Kingship between Disenchantment and Re-Enchantment: The French and English Monarchies c. 1587–1688* (2014), and he is at present working on a study (to be published in German) entitled *The Hero's Twilight: Models of Heroism in England and France from the Wars of Religion to the Age of Enlightenment*.

LUCIEN BÉLY, Chevalier de Legion d'Honneur, has been Professor at Paris-Sorbonne University (Paris IV) since 1997. His 12 books include *Louis XIV, le plus grand roi du monde* (2005) and *La France au XVIIe siècle. Puissance de l'État, Contrôle de la société* (2009).

NICHOLAS CANNY was Professor of History at the National University of Ireland, Galway, for over 30 years, Director of the Moore Institute for the Investigation of Transnational Encounters (CITE) from 2000 to 2011 and President of the Royal Irish Academy from 2008 to 2011. He has written and edited 10 books, mainly on the history of early modern Ireland and on early British colonialism.

PEDRO CARDIM is Associate Professor, Faculty of Social and Human Sciences, New Univeristy of Lisbon, and the author and editor of 10 books, most recently *Portugal unido y seperado. Felipe II, la union de territorios y el debate sobre la condicion politica del reino de Portugal* (2014).

JAMES COLLINS has been at Georgetown University since 1985 and a full professor since 1992. He is the author of five books, including *The State in Early Modern France* (2nd edn, Cambridge, 2009).

B. J. GARCÍA GARCÍA is Professor in the Department of Modern History at the Complutense University of Madrid.

GUNNER LIND is Professor of History at the Saxo Institute of the University of Copenhagen. His most recent book is *Civilians at War: From the Fifteenth Century to the Present* (2014).

JOHN MORRILL, FBA, is a Life Fellow of Selwyn College Cambridge. He retired as Professor of British and Irish History in Cambridge in 2013. His 20 books concentrate on all aspects of British and Irish history from 1500–1700, and he is a leading expert in the fields of state formation, the British Revolutions of 1638–1660 and radical religion.

DRIES RAEYMAEKERS teaches in the Department of History at Radboud University Nijmegen and has published extensively on the court of Albert and Isabella in Brussels around the turn of the sixteenth and seventeenth centuries.

HAMISH SCOTT, FBA, spent most of his academic career at the University of St Andrews and retired as Professor of History to become Honorary Senior Research Fellow at the University of Glasgow. An expert in eighteenth-century international relations and on early modern nobilities, he has most recently edited the two-volume *Oxford Handbook of Early Modern European History, 1350–1750* (2015).

ROBERT VON FRIEDEBURG is Chair of Early Modern History, with special reference to the History of Politics and Mentalities, at Erasmus University Rotterdam. His most recent project is *Luther's Legacy: The Thirty Year War and the Modern Notion of 'State' in the Empire, 1530s to 1790s* (Cambridge, 2016). He will shortly start a position at Bishop Grosseteste University in Britain.

1   Introduction: Monarchy Transformed – Princes and Their Elites in Early Modern Western Europe

Robert von Friedeburg and John Morrill

Until the 1960s, it was widely assumed that in Western Europe the 'New Monarchy' propelled kingdoms and principalities onto a modern nation-state trajectory. John I of Portugal (1358–1433), Charles VII (1403–1461) and Louis XI (1423–1483) of France, Henry VII (1457–1509) and Henry VIII of England (1509–1553), Isabella of Castile (1474–1504) and Ferdinand of Aragon (1479–1516) were, by improving royal administration, by bringing more continuity to communication with their estates and by introducing more regular taxation, all seen to have served that goal.[1] In this view, princes were assigned to the role of developing and implementing the sinews of state as a sovereign entity characterized by the coherence of its territorial borders and its central administration and government. They shed medieval traditions of counsel and instead enforced relations of obedience towards the emerging 'state'. For example, as it was put with regard to England,

feudal rights ... were exploited more systematically during the years of the 'New Monarchy' (from the restoration of Edward IV to the death of Henry VIII),[2] not only to obtain money for the Crown, a necessary obsession of the kings of this period, but also to curb noble power. The prerogative was, then, 'a means of inculcating a healthy fear of royal power', and it played an important role in the move from the early Lancastrian idea of the king as first among equals to the

---

[1] See for example Arthur Slavin (ed.), *The 'New Monarchies' and Representative Assemblies: Medieval Constitutionalism or Modern Absolutism?* (London, 1964), with contributions from Alfred Pollard (1859–1944), Geoffrey Elton, Henri Pirenne, Francis Carsten, Roland Mousnier and Helmut Georg Koenigsberger.

[2] For some recent work that uses the term 'New Monarchy' quizzically for this period, see A. F. Pollard, 'New Monarchy Renovated: England 1461–1509', *Medieval History*, 2:1 (1992), pp. 78–82; A. F. Pollard, *The New Monarchy: England 1471–1534* (Oxford, 1988); Steven Gunn, '"New Men" and "New Monarchy" in England, 1485–1524', in Robert Stein (ed.), *Power Brokers in the Late Middle Ages* (Turnhout, 2001), pp. 153–163; Steven Gunn, 'Political History, New Monarchy and State Formation', *Historical Research*, 82:217 (2009), pp. 380–392.

Tudor conception of the kings as a lonely being elevated above even the greatest of his lords.[3]

Within the continuous playing field constituted by the relatively stable boundaries of each of the late medieval polities of Western Europe entering this path, the early modern future seemed to rest with the growth of the 'princely state' and with disciplining elites; medieval politics based on consent and cooperation between prince and elites was going to be overwhelmed by princely power. For Italy and the German lands of the Holy Roman Empire, the role of centralizing, and thus of state-making, was assigned to the princes making their 'territorial states'. While the later fifteenth and the sixteenth century saw the successful implementation of the tools of state by the 'New Monarchy', the seventeenth century saw the resistance of noble or parliamentary opposition, again within the rather continuous boundaries of each of the European polities. The political rhetoric of the period was therefore also attributed to this duel, to the rise of the 'princely state' ('reasons of state', 'divine right monarchy') or to the opposition of elites. Only a few countries, such as England and, more obviously, the eventual Dutch Republic, escaped this absolutist future into a republican alternative.[4] According to this narrative, the essential nature of the state, whatever the qualifications necessary to allow for differences in detail, ultimately rested on (princely bureaucratic) power, the power of rulers to coerce subjects and elites within the 'coercion-extraction' cycle of sociological parlance into the framework of a solid bureaucratically governed state, with a bureaucracy and army entirely paid by, dependent upon and loyal only to the prince, securing the principle that 'might is right', as epitomized by Richelieu's alleged emphasis on *'raison d'etat'*.[5]

Since the 1955 congress of European historians at Rome, doubts about these roles and the relation of princes, wars, administration and elites

---

[3] Thomas Poole, *Reason of State: Law, Prerogative and Empire* (Cambridge, 2015), p. 23, with reference to David Starkey, *The English Court: From the Wars of the Roses to the Civil War* (London, 1987), p. 3.

[4] Helmut G. Koenigsberger, *Monarchies, States Generals and Parliaments: The Netherlands in the Fifteenth and Sixteenth Centuries* (Cambridge, 2001).

[5] Most recently Norman Davies, *Europe: A History* (London, 1997), p. 456; his elaboration on the meaning of 'state' for the period of European history from the 1450s to the 1670s. See also Mark Greengrass, *Christendom Destroyed: Europe 1517–1648* (London, 2015), on the 'business of states' (pp. 523–552), with balanced accounts on the many facets of what retrospectively could be addressed as 'state-business'. For the 'power-narrative' see in particular Charles Tilly, *Coercion, Capital, and European States, AD 990–1992* (Cambridge, 1992); Charles Tilly, 'War and State Making as Organized Crime', in Peter B. Evans, Dietrich Rueschemeyer and Theda Skocpol (eds), *Bringing the State Back* (Cambridge, 1985), pp. 169–191, 169, and applied e.g. on the German territorial state by Thomas A. Brady Jr., *German Histories in the Age of Reformations, 1400–1650* (Cambridge 2009), p. 98.

have been increasingly formulated.[6] What is not in doubt is that from the later fifteenth century to the middle of the eighteenth century, under the relentless pressure of war, the number of independent European players was reduced dramatically to a small number of larger powers and that government intrusion was far more felt at the regional and local level.[7]

Nevertheless, the other aspects of this master narrative have been increasingly called into question, both with respect to the characterization of the ensuing polities as 'states'[8] and with respect to the argument that princes established these 'states' in the course of wars, of introducing more intense taxation, of creating a bureaucracy funded by the prince and loyal only to him, and by suppressing elites. While European princes were indeed almost continuously busy with fighting wars during the early modern period and indeed able to collect substantially more taxes during the later seventeenth century than their predecessors during the later fifteenth or early sixteenth century, we now know that this increasing amount of taxation was insufficient to permit them to build a state bureaucracy independent of elites or to allow them to coerce these elites into submission. Rather, the wars of the period put immense, unprecedented and unsustainable financial pressures on princely dynasties, and taxation served not least as security to allow dynasties to carry ever-increasing burdens of debt that made them ever more dependent on those groups in society willing to lend to them.[9] Whatever the very real

---

[6] Kordula Wolf, *X Congresso Internazionale di Scienze Storiche, Roma, settembre 1955. Un bilancio storiografico* (Rome, 2005), http://dhi-roma.it/fileadmin/user_upload/pdf-dateien/Tagungsberichte/2005/tagung_1955.pdf.

[7] H. Schilling, *Konfessionalisierung und Staatsinteressen 1559–1660* (Paderborn, 2007). See also Chapter 13 by Nicholas Canny in this volume. See especially pp.349–56.

[8] Lucien Bély, *La societé des princes* (Paris, 1999). See also J. Elliot, 'A Europe of Composite Monarchies', *Past and Present* 137 (1992), pp. 48–71; R. Bonney, *The European Dynastic States 1494–1660* (Oxford 1991), p. 524; J. Morrill, *Uneasy Lies the Head That Wears a Crown: Dynastic Crises in Tudor and Stuart Britain 1504–1746* (Reading, 2005), p. 11; J. Ohlmeyer, *Civil War and Restoration in the Three Stuart Kingdoms: The Career of Randal MacDonnell, Marquis of Antrim* (Dublin, 1993) 2001; A. Álvarez-Ossorio Alvariño, B. J. García García and M. Virginia León Sanz (eds), *La Perida de Europa* (Madrid 2007); A. Alvarez-Ossorio and B. J. García García (eds), *La Monarquía de las naciones* (Madrid 2004).

[9] R. Bonney (ed.), *Economic Systems and State Finance* (Oxford, 1995), specifically W. M. Omrod, 'The West European Monarchies in the Later Middle Ages', pp. 123–162, in particular pp. 146–155. See also W. Schulze, 'The Emergence and Consolidation of the Tax State I: The Sixteenth Century' and Marjolein t'Hart, 'The Emergence and Consolidation of the Tax State II: The Seventeenth Century', in R. Bonney (ed.), *Economic Systems and State Finance* (Oxford 1995), pp. 261–280 and 281–294, respectively, establish, as do the chapters on Spain (G. Muto) and France (R. Bonney), the continued importance of demesne income, the partly dramatic scale of the sale of offices, of the farming of taxes and of the overall establishment of a chronic and endemic state of indebtedness 'solved' with ad hoc and haphazard means. These problems occurred first for the main combatants, the Spanish Habsburgs and the Valois, but since the seventeenth century also for most other dynasties or republics with active foreign

gains in terms of strengthening princely household government towards the later Middle Ages, the wars since the 1490s forced princely dynasties to make almost every compromise in order to secure credit. Given this state of affairs, it has rightly been concluded that whatever the effects of the increasing amount of warfare from the later fifteenth century onwards, wars 'did not make the state'.[10] Indeed, contemporary specialists on royal finance like Colbert attempted to persuade their monarchs to abstain from warfare to avoid the potentially catastrophic consequences of debt default following from war, though to no avail.[11]

This volume builds on these and other lines of criticism of the established narrative on the relation of princes, elites, state-building and war. It brings together both new syntheses and detailed contributions of research in order to shift our understanding further away from this older argument, mainly with respect to three counts.

First of all, there is the importance of the dynastic agglomerate (see in particular the contributions by John Morrill[12] and Hamish Scott[13]): the players surviving the power struggles of the sixteenth and seventeenth century were not 'states' in our sense, but primarily princely dynasties pursuing not only dynastic ambitions and princely prestige but the consequences of dynastic chance.[14] They pursued these by trying to amass heterogeneous groups of principalities, the 'dynastic agglomerate'. This is not to deny that among the principalities that became part of these agglomerates, some, like the kingdom of England, had a long and distinguished history of increasingly dense government that has been cited, like in the example above, as proof of the coming about of the modern state, certainly in comparison with other European polities.[15] But it had also to find structures that would enable it to govern principalities acquired by dynastic merger (Scotland, 1603 and 1707), conquest (Ireland, continuously from 1542) and agreement with local elites (Wales, 1536–1543).

---

policy. S. Gunn, D. Grummitt and Hans Cools, *War, State, and Society in England and the Netherlands, 1477–1559* (Oxford, 2008) concentrate on an earlier period.

[10] P. S. Gorski, 'How War Did Not Make the State', in P. S. Gorski, *The Protestant Ethic Revisited* (Philadelphia, 2011).

[11] For Colbert's advice on war see H. Scott, 'The Fiscal-Military State and International Rivalry during the Long Eighteenth Century', in C. Storrs (ed.), *The Fiscal-Military State in Eighteenth-Century Europe* (Ashgate, 2009), pp. 23–53, in particular pp. 23–25; P. Sonnino, 'Plus royaliste que le pape: Louis XIV Religious Policy and His Guerre de Hollande', in D. Onnekink (ed.), *War and Religion after Westphalia* (Farnham, 2009), pp. 17–24.

[12] See Chapter 2, pp. 17–43.   [13] See Chapter 3, pp. 44–86.

[14] T. C. W. Blanning, *The Pursuit of Glory: Europe 1618–1815* (London, 2007).

[15] Recently confirmed by Len Scales, 'Rose without Thorn, Eagle without Feathers: Nation and Power in Late Medieval England and Germany', in *Bulletin of the German Historical Institute*, 31 (2009), pp. 3–35.

Other 'agglomerates' had this latter experience but hardly the same pre-history of 'dense government'.[16] The larger units that came to dominate the European scene since the later sixteenth century were precisely *not* individual principalities with long medieval or shorter Renaissance histories of government consolidation, but the larger dynastic agglomerates of a much more recent past and of a much more fragile nature.

The coming together of these dynastic agglomerates meant that the economy of scale of politics and the participating number of players kept changing rapidly in the course of the sixteenth and seventeenth century. Indeed, that change came to some preliminary conclusion only by the end of the Spanish War of Succession (1714) and the Great Northern War (1721). Rapid changes in the number of lands of the emerging dynastic agglomerates and, thus, of the potential players within each emerging dynastic agglomerate, meant that neither princes nor elites were acting on a playing field of continuous size or nature. Rather, the haphazard coming together of the dynastic agglomerates forced both princes and elites to re-orientate their horizon, to seek new alliances and new points of contact. Irish, Scottish, English, Austrian, Bohemian, Silesian, Tyrolian, Aragonese, Catalan, Portuguese, Milanese, Burgundian, Breton or Navarre elites, to name but a few, had to deal with the fact that they found themselves part of the dynamics of the formation of a larger dynastic agglomerate with increasingly complex relations to the centre, relations that needed to be developed and shaped to profit from them (see for example the contributions of B. J. García García,[17] Lucien Bély,[18] Antonio Álvarino-Ossorio Alvariño[19] and Pedro Cardim[20]). And of course, they often had to deal with the undoing of agglomerations, as the Portuguese did in the 1640s, and as the Poles, Danes and others did too, or move from one dynastic agglomerate to another, as the Burgundians did three times across the period. And many elites tried without success to detach themselves – as the Irish did in the 1650s or the Scots at the turn of the eighteenth century. No one knew which would survive and which would not. Elites had to readjust their strategies to pursue their interests within this rapidly changing environment. Even where one could point out that France did indeed incorporate its new

---

[16] For a classic account of state formation that is outstanding on looking at the different forms of development that proceeded at different tempi, but very much in an 'English' and not a 'British' or 'dynastic' context, see Michael J. Braddick, *State Formation in Early Modern England, c.1550–1700* (Cambridge, 2000). But see also the article modelling types of state formation, which has more impact on continental scholarship: Michael J. Braddick, 'The Early Modern English State and the Question of Differentiation from 1550 to 1700', *Comparative Studies in Society and History*, 38:1 (1996), pp. 92–111.

[17] See Chapter 5, pp. 127–163.   [18] See Chapter 6, pp. 164–79.
[19] See Chapter 7, pp. 183–211.   [20] See Chapter 8, pp. 212–43.

provinces Burgundy and Brittany into the incorporated possessions of the Crown, noble and urban elites in France's provinces still had to re-orientate themselves into the vaster political cosmos of the emerging metropolitan France, and French kings had to offer new opportunities to rally them to their service. By the same token, the Spanish army became a source of stability, not only in the sense of capturing and securing lands, but also as a source of opportunity for the heterogeneous elites of the many lands of that dynastic agglomerate. And of course, at least for the Atlantic seaboard elites, opportunities to serve together in colonial ventures came and went, as metropolitan kingdoms opened or closed opportunities to non-metropolitan elites. This experience has little to do with the intensification of administration and the coercion of elites within a continuous political unit existing since the later Middle Ages in more or less unchanged fashion.

What is more, as the opportunities offered by monarchy for service and advancement proved to be more or less attainable by different sections of the elites, an elite aristocracy began to emancipate itself from the ranks of the nobility at large that was not least characterized by its ability to obtain substantial offices and receive lands in turn for services in more than one single province.[21] This new elite aristocracy became clearly visible by the latter part of the seventeenth century. As both John Morrill[22] and Hamish Scott[23] argue, the ability of a given dynasty to shape a working relation-ship with this elite aristocracy as it came about proved to be vital for the success of the dynasty and of its congeries of territories. Despite the very real dependence of this elite aristocracy on lands and offices delivered by the Crown, it had little to do with the Weberian image of a bureaucracy only subsisting on state income, in particular where the monarchy needed to sell offices and farm taxes to meet the financial demands of its wars.[24]

Secondly, co-entrepreneurship between princes and elites: as Lucien Bély put it with reference to Louis XIV, *'les creanciers du roi forment des groupes financiers, et derriere eux, la noblesse et la bourgeoisie qui pretent ses avoirs'*.[25] It is certainly true that the support of nobilies and professionals for a given prince became an important characteristic, at least from the later fifteenth century, but the increasing dependence of major and minor powers on support from their elites, not least on credit, developed into an

---

[21] For an example of this, see the discussion of a new elite aristocracy in John Morrill, 'The English Revolution in British and Irish Context', in Michael J. Braddick (ed.), *The Oxford Handbook of the English Revolution* (Oxford, 2015), pp. 555–576, at pp. 565–568.

[22] See Chapter 2, pp. 22–26.   [23] See Chapter 3, esp. pp. 48–57.

[24] See in particular the contributions of B. J. García García, Lucien Bély, and Antonio Alvariño, Chapters 5, 6, and 7, respectively pp.127–163, 164–79 and 183–211.

[25] Lucien Bély, *La France au XVII siècle* (Paris, 2009), 302.

important feature only over time throughout the sixteenth and seventeenth century. Far from experiencing the eventual disciplining of elites to subject status or their momentous transformation into royal office-holders, dynasties had eventually to persuade the elites of their heterogeneous lands to join a more or less precarious co-entrepreneurship. At the same time, elites, far from insisting on confrontation with the government of princes for principled ideological reasons, had every reason to seek compromise and even advancement through the new channels the governing dynasty offered, if only they could profit from them. As Nicholas Canny puts it in his conclusion,

the chapters in this volume ... confirm that the character of monarchy underwent change everywhere because of the escalating scale and the increasing expense of long-term warfare ... However where the original participants in the debate over the existence and character of a General Crisis drew attention to the political and social polarization that resulted from the crisis, the contributors to this volume make repeated reference to the fact that noble elites achieved considerable success either in keeping the intruding power of central government at arm's length, or in ensuring that they too would benefit from the accretions to monarchical power ... The evidence cited in this volume makes it clear that families from the highest ranks of the nobility usually became reconciled to innovation when they were given the opportunity to become parties to the changes that were being promoted.[26]

This emerging co-entrepreneurship, however, had little to do with the later medieval situation. Due to the massively increased importance of wars, taxes, credit and offices, it began to involve areas and manners of cooperation that only really developed during the period in question and are mapped in several of the contributions below, in particular in those of Bély,[27] Alvariño,[28] Cardim,[29] Dries Raeymaekers[30] and Gunner Lind.[31] The core notion of the new emerging relationship between governing dynasty and elites was certainly not primarily that of the subjection of elites to an emerging bureaucratic state, but that of the dramatically intensified importance of credit, of offices profiting from taxes, and of new networks to recruit support for princes, and for the elites to compete for the privileges and resources that contact to the governing dynasty could provide. As the contributions of Hamish Scott[32] and Gunner Lind[33] show, even where a dynasty could radically recast its elite, this new elite gathered substantial land holdings of its own in the process but

---

[26] See Chapter 13, pp. 359–60.   [27] See Chapter 6, pp. 164–79.
[28] See Chapter 7, pp. 183–211.   [29] See Chapter 8, pp. 212–43.
[30] See Chapter 9, pp. 244–66.   [31] See Chapter 10, pp. 267–86.
[32] See Chapter 3, pp. 44–86.   [33] See Chapter 10, pp. 267–86.

did not become part of a fully salaried bureaucratic class in the sense of the older narrative.

What this amounts to is that any new account of the reformed or transformed monarchies must challenge or at least nuance the rather simplistic political economy argument (in the tradition of Perry Anderson)[34] while allowing for the distinct but very real power and influence of monarchy over highly divided and diverse societies, without mistaking that influence for untrammelled control. Such an account assists to understand the catastrophic and sometimes very fast breakdown or implosion of particular monarchies (for the Stuarts, the 1640s; for the Spanish monarchy, the 1640s; for the Valois, ongoing throughout the 1570s to 1590s; for the Bourbons, 1648–1652), breakdowns that monarchs could then over and again remind their elites about in order to scare them into submission or cooperation, precisely because they could not force them. Moral force always proved stronger than physical force.

Thirdly, political rhetoric: The ubiquity of conflict and the mutual dependence of princes and elites upon each other meant that 'might' did not become 'right', but that there was growing demand for political rhetoric to buttress one's aims and in order to persuade; however, we should not easily take the arguments that were developed as either neat representations of what was going on (as in the rhetoric of '*raison d'etat*' allegedly mirroring the process of the making of the coercive state) or as a priori useful to either 'state-building' princes or of 'liberty preserving' elites. The evolving rhetoric of reason of state, for example, hardly indicated the real development of a modern institutionalized state. 'Rule of law', obedience to those in legitimate authority and the preservation of liberties and privileges against the 'hydra of anarchy', were the rallying cry of all.[35] Military prowess – if victories could be scored – impressed elites and subjects alike.[36] Given the complex relations of conflict and co-entrepreneurship in the steadily shifting environment of the emerging dynastic agglomerate, political rhetoric and imagination had an important place of its own in complex relation to the perception of the changing environment (see e.g. the contributions by James Collins,[37] B. J. García García[38] and Ronald Asch[39]).

---

[34] See Perry Anderson, *Lineages of the Absolutist State* (London, 1974).
[35] See Chapter 4, pp. 118–20.
[36] See Chapter 5, pp. 135–47, and 12, pp. 331–57; see in particular T. C. W. Blanning, *The Culture of Power and the Power of Culture: Old Regime Europe 1660–1789* (Oxford, 2002).
[37] See Chapter 4, pp. 87–126.   [38] See Chapter 5, pp. 127–63.
[39] See Chapter 12, pp. 319–48.

This volume synthesizes the last three decades of research and adds new perspectives. It supports the long drift of research away from anticipating the creation of the coercive bureaucratic nation state. Based on a plethora of dense research produced in the wake of the debate of the 'Crisis of the Seventeenth Century',[40] the contributions of this volume map the changing relations of princes and elites as the economy of scale of their environment kept changing dramatically, from the late medieval polities to the larger dynastic agglomerates of the later seventeenth century. The first two contributions by John Morrill[41] and Hamish Scott[42] focus on two notions crucial for the new synthesis we aim at: in comparative fashion, the notion of the 'dynastic agglomerate' (John Morrill) and the notion of the new 'elite aristocracy' straddling the different provinces of the emerging agglomerate and profiting from its fabric of networks and offices (Hamish Scott).

The other contributions provide different examples of the evolution of 'co-entrepreneurship' between princes and elites as they were emerging in the course of the sixteenth and seventeenth century, partly in relation to the political rhetoric developing and used in this context.

Two address the kingdom of France. As both James Collins[43] and Lucien Bély[44] show, the legitimacy of the French king, directing government himself and organizing the channels of favours and services, became, if anything, more crucial as the kingdom of France incorporated new provinces and found itself (for two centuries) in a mortal struggle with the Spanish Habsburgs. Indeed at the end of the period (1702–1714), there was a real prospect of a Bourbon takeover of the whole Spanish Habsburg monarchia. Therefore, periods with a dramatic lack of the security of dynastic succession triggered the development of a rhetoric of the Crown of France and its possessions in order to provide stability where the dynasty did not. But once such stability was achieved again, as under Louis XIV, the new networks run by personal contact to the king proved for France's heterogeneous elites, which had little cooperative contact but much conflict among each other, to be very important and bolstered the strong position of the personal rule of the monarch. As Bély makes clear, the utter heterogeneity of France's elites and the frequent lack of communication among these elites could made the position of the monarch and his court potentially very strong, though in a very different sense than the model of the 'coercive state' or the court as tool to discipline elites had suggested. Indeed, as Ronald Asch[45]

---

[40] For a convenient summary of this debate, see Geoffrey Parker and Lesley M. Smith (eds), *The General Crisis of the Seventeenth Century* (2nd edn, London, 1997).

[41] See Chapter 2, pp. 17–20, 26–34.   [42] See Chapter 3, pp. 56–99.

[43] See Chapter 4, esp. pp. 116–26.   [44] See Chapter 6, pp. 164–79.

[45] See Chapter 12, pp. 325–32.

stresses, the strong role of the king was only upheld to the extent that Louis did not challenge major limits of his government that provided the basis for the elite support he so very much needed. As Asch, Bély and Collins stress, underlying the evolving argument of the incorporated unity of the rights and lands of the Crown and the emerging rhetoric of *'l'estat'* described in particular by Collins lay reciprocal relationships of dependence between elites and king: the king ever more dependent on the financial support and services of the elites, and the elites dependent on the king in their competition among each other for favours, offices and privileges. Because of this dependency, the judicial elites in particular, in the face of the chaos of the Religious Civil Wars, shifted away from Aristotelian notions based on the virtue and participation (read: elite counsel) of citizens and towards a notion of *'l'estat'* stressing the need to be obedient to royal government for the sake of every subject's welfare and safety.[46]

The next four contributions address the dynastic agglomerate of the Spanish Habsburgs. The term 'Spanish Monarchy', as Pedro Cardim[47] reminds us, only came into more frequent use from the late sixteenth century onwards, as part of a self-conscious move of the Habsburgs to give meaning to and to further consolidate their vast accessions. As B. J. García García[48] shows, given the complexity of so many composite polities (Milan is a good example), monarchy became all the more necessary as a source of unity and 'virtue'. Other contemporary suggestions included to forge family alliances among the various elites of the different nations of the agglomerate and to educate the elites of other nations in terms of Spanish language and customs – to forge a union of elites, rather than establish a unitary bureaucratic state. Underlying this rhetoric was the growth of the Spanish military machine, providing conquest and opportunities for social climbing for the many different elites of the monarchy, and an experience of integration, forging a new, Spanish identity. Underlying this was also the venality of offices, providing much needed financial resources for the monarchy and turning its diverse elites into co-entrepreneurs, as officers in the army and as investors into the offices and titles the monarchy had to sell. But the Spanish monarchy did not only attempt to forge supra-national identities; it also attempted to

---

[46] See Chapter 4, esp. pp. 124–26. On the case of England, see Patrick Collinson, 'The Monarchical Republic of Queen Elizabeth I', in Patrick Collinson, *Elizabethan Essays* (London, 1994), pp. 31–57, This essay generated a huge debate, which can be approached via John F. McDiarmid (ed.) *The Monarchical Republic of Early Modern England: Essays in Response to Patrick Collinson* (Aldershot, 2007) and Peter Lake, 'The "Political Thought" of the "Monarchical Republic of Elizabeth I," Discovered and Anatomized', *Journal of British Studies* 54:2 (2015), pp. 257–287.

[47] See Chapter 8, pp. 226.   [48] See Chapter 5, pp. 139–75.

exploit the diverging interests of the provinces by allowing them to have their own naval squadrons where these could pursue strategic aims to the heart of specific provincial interests.

Antonio Álvarez-Ossorio Alvariño and Pedro Cardim[49] show how massive an intrusion into the government of a European principality or kingdom and into the relations among its elites the integration of a polity into a dynastic agglomerate actually was. Antonio Álvarez-Ossorio Alvariño looks at the responses of Milanese elites as they joined the political cosmos of the Spanish monarchy. They tried to preserve their own resources against the potential threat of the new king to distribute them to other elites, and to compete among each other for titles and fiefs as the king and duke of Milan proceeded to sell or auction them in an attempt to fill his coffers to fight wars elsewhere. In addition, the new channels of purchase opened up by the Spanish monarchy were used by Milanese elites to solve problems of succession, for illegitimate sons could purchase titles and fiefs. Critical comments on the proliferation of titles contrary to primogeniture not only shipwrecked at the financial interests of the Crown to sell titles, but also ran contrary to the interests of local elites to provide for offspring. Indeed, Alvariño can point towards strategic differences between the outlook of Spanish grandees, interested in the preservation of an elite aristocracy based on substantial landholdings that was defended by primogeniture, and the mostly lesser noble families of Milan with very different aspirations.

Pedro Cardim[50] pursues the response of Portuguese elites. They even began to shift towards the Spanish language. While the decisive move to realize Philip's II claim to succession was the invasion of Portugal by his army, once conquest was completed, the interests of local elites had again to be met, not least by restricting Spanish interference. But at the same time, even prior to conquest, significant segments of the Portuguese elites had wishes to join the Spanish monarchy to take part in the opportunities it seemed to offer. However, once the fortunes of Spanish conquests began to decline, while costs climbed, the balance among Portuguese elites shifted again. Although Madrid's response to unrest were attempts at strengthening the Crown at the expense of regional elites and although the integration of Portugal's elites into the larger monarchy had increased over decades, Portugal had not become a modern bureaucratic state itself or had been integrated into a Spanish state. It was still run by its elites under the contingent circumstances of wars and dynastic succession. Spanish defeats overseas persuaded Portuguese elites, not least those with a vested interest in Portugal's own colonial possessions, to seek

[49] See Chapter 7 and 8, pp. 127–63, 212–44.   [50] See Chapter 8, pp. 212–43.

their interest outside the Spanish monarchy. Neither the allegiance of Portugal's elites to the Spanish dynastic agglomerate nor their eventual secession was ever a foregone conclusion. None of that takes away the continued attraction of the various international courts of the Habsburgs for elites from all their lands, as described by Dries Raeymaekers with respect to the Brussels court.[51] Here, even after the separation of the lands of the Spanish and German Habsburgs, the elites of both agglomerates kept meeting and constituted the agglomerate as a network of courts, fuelled by the elite's interest in access to patronage.

Gunner Lind[52] presents a different constellation, more akin to the experience of Sweden. As a consequence of the Danish absolutist 'revolution' of 1660–1665, a new service elite developed and was investigated with land (see the contribution of Hamish Scott). The old noble elite had fully participated in manning the new offices that the army offered in the course of Denmark's wars, but since it was not able to fulfil the rapid increase in the demand of men, immigrants, not least from Germany, were allowed to fill the ranks. Therefore, the army was increasingly manned by foreigners with no specific loyalty or ties to the Old Danish noble elite. Under the experience of defeat, noble privileges were increasingly questioned by segments from the cities. Under the impact of the military catastrophe of 1658, Copenhagen elites supported a coup d'état of the Crown against the old nobility, based on an army manned not least by foreign officers. The Crown moved on to create a service elite of its own and massively supported their own men in acquiring land, to the detriment of the older elite, a process documented by Scott in his contribution. Though the economy of scale of government remained significantly smaller than in the cases of the lands of the Spanish Habsburgs or France, and the grip of the monarchy on its much less complex lands was much more secure, its power rested on the alliance of the monarchy with a new consolidated elite that served the monarchy in offices and also received lands in return – not on landless bureaucrats dependent only on crown salaries.

Against this background on the mutual dependence of princes and elites, and the continued possession of resources independent of the Crown in particular in the hands of the elite aristocracy, the two final contributions concentrate on the importance and the independent dynamics of the rhetoric of monarchy. Ronald Asch[53] compares the representations and rationales of divine right monarchy in England and France during the seventeenth century, not least in the way both monarchies reacted to one another and in terms of the challenge, or lack of

[51] See Chapter 9, pp. 244–66.   [52] See Chapter 10, pp. 267–86.
[53] See Chapter 12, pp. 319–48.

such challenge, to the established privileges of the elites. In both cases, the spectacle of monarchy was meant to provide an umbrella of legitimacy beyond the realities of complex and divided societies in order to create allegiance among elites and subjects – real enough in its potential impact, but tied to complex problems of religion and acceptance. Robert von Friedeburg focuses on those sections of the nobility in France and Germany below the emerging formation of an elite aristocracy and their occasional bitter resentment at being left behind.[54]

In his conclusion, Nicholas Canny[55] offers a wide-ranging reflection on all the previous chapters, so his is no simple summary. Canny would have liked more attention to be given to the emergence of the Catholic monarchy and on how its ability to bring to bear its new Atlantic resources on the war against its enemies in Europe stimulated wars (and hence an arms race) of unprecedented scale, ultimately forcing all its competitors to also follow suit. He is sympathetic to, but not entirely convinced by, the emphasis on dynasticism. His chapter then is not an encomium on the volume, but rather the opening up of a debate on its new perspectives. Have the authors gone too far, or not far enough?

---

[54] See Chapter 11, pp. 299–330.   [55] See Chapter 13, pp. 349–80.

Part I

Dynasties and Monarchies

2　Dynasties, Realms, Peoples and State Formation, 1500–1720

John Morrill

In 1450 Europe was a patchwork of kingdoms, principalities and one grand duchy, 25 in the Latin West if we exclude the much more fragmented territories – duchies, counties, prince-bishops and free cities – in what makes up modern Germany and Italy. By 1750, there were only eight monarchs left, and a few small kingless republics in the Netherlands, Switzerland and northern Italy. What have become the major states of modern Europe appear clearly on the map over this time – most obviously France, Spain, Portugal, Britain, The Netherlands, Sweden and Denmark. To these we can add the vast dual monarchy of Lithuania-Poland, and the Austrian-Hungarian Empire, its frontiers with the Muslim Ottoman Empire ebbing and flowing, with the Turks twice at the gates of Vienna, at other times in full retreat as the Habsburg reclaimed lands in Central Europe. Most current historiography assumes the inevitability and stability of these new monarchies of early modern Europe.

This chapter challenges that assumption and argues that these new super-kingdoms – I will call them dynastic agglomerates – were in fact highly unstable and that all kinds of other configurations remained possible well into the eighteenth century. The early and middle part of my career was spent formulating and defending early modern revisionism, and the essence of that revisionism was challenging Marxist and Whiggish histories that followed methodologies which deployed a high teleology (discovering the roots of modernity in the past) and anachronism (explaining the past in the categories of the present).[1] Now, what greater anachronism can there be than that the modern states lineally descended from the super-kingdoms that formed in the sixteenth and seventeenth centuries were destined to be. Norman Davies's *Vanished Kingdoms*[2] explores the might-have-beens of modern history, and

---

[1] All this is very well explored in Glenn Burgess, 'On Revisionism: An Analysis of Early Stuart Historiography in the 1970s and 1980s', *The Historical Journal*, 33 (1990), pp. 609–627.

[2] Norman Davies, *Vanished Kingdoms: The History of Half-Forgotten Europe* (Reading, 2011).

building on his inspiration, this chapter focuses on the processes of dynastic chance and dynastic calculation that haphazardly and contingently created unstable polities that had no guarantee of permanence. It also emphasises the extent to which royal birth, marriage and death competes with warfare (and with the fiscal-military bureaucracies necessary for the new warfare of the new monarchies) as mechanisms of state expansion and formation. This chapter will focus on the importance of dynasticism both in explaining the emergence of a much smaller number of 'dynastic agglomerates' and on looking at the relationship between patterns of dynastic consolidation and the 'whats' of state formation. This in turn affects the 'hows'.

It builds on an early work entitled *'Uneasy Lies the Head That Wears a Crown': Dynastic Crises in Tudor and Stewart Britain 1504–1746*.[3] That work explored the consequences of 'a time of dynastic takeovers and mergers' resulting in the emergence of kingdoms whose boundaries approximate to those of recognisably modern states in Britain, France, Iberia, the Netherlands and much of northern Europe, specifically Scandinavia, and, to a lesser extent central and eastern Europe. That essay then moved to the British case and explored the role of dynastic design and dynastic chance in converting what was, in 1500, a mélange of territories – over less than half of which monarchs based in Southeast England had any effective control – into a single United Kingdom of Great Britain and Ireland by 1720. This was, however, the essay suggested, a kingdom that was 'a state system that was never a state'.[4]

The essay controversially but playfully looked at many 'what ifs', 'might-have-beens' – that is, at counterfactuals.[5] It is clearly not acceptable to construct alternative histories which require historical actors to behave out of character ('If Charles I had made a deal with his critics in the spring of 1641 . . .'), but I do not feel as squeamish about suggesting that events predicated on natural processes of disease, fatal injury or death could have very profound consequences. Thus I explored the case of the premature death of Francis II of France, who succumbed to an ear infection (germs doing what they do naturally) exacerbated by doctors pouring mercury into the infected ear (something they were trained to do) before he had a chance to impregnate his eighteen-year-old wife, Mary Queen of Scots, with a male child who would have been heir to throne of

---

[3] John Morrill, *'Uneasy Lies the Head That Wears a Crown': Dynastic Crises in Tudor and Stewart Britain 1504–1746* (University of Reading Press, 2005).

[4] Morrill, *Uneasy Lies the Head*, p. 19.

[5] For a positive statement of the case for this approach, see Niall Ferguson, *Virtual History: Alternatives and Counter-Factuals* (London, 1997), esp. pp. 1–90.

France[6] and Scotland, and in French (but not in most English or any Spanish) eyes, the rightful ruler or at the very least heir presumptive to England and Ireland. The almost certain consequence, I suggested, would be that the Habsburg-Valois rivalry would have been fought out in a war of English succession rather than over the future of North Italy or of the Netherlands (as the Dutch think of the Eighty Years' War).[7] Although one cannot speculate beyond that, a French claimant to the thrones of Britain, in every foreseeable scenario, would have resulted in a state formation within Britain and Ireland that would have been radically different from what it actually was. Partition between the superpowers would have been the least of the worries of the people of these islands.

Taking this more generally, most studies of state formation exaggerate the imagined permanency of unstable *monarchia* or *imperia*. Did rulers assume that what they ruled had a permanent shape and identity? Did their subjects see themselves as yoked together forever? The terms most used by historians in recent decades for the polities that were being formed into new monarchies are 'multiple' or 'composite' monarchies.[8] My suggestion hitherto, much more thoroughly explored in this chapter, is that those terms exaggerate the inevitability of the processes they describe. I have therefore replaced the anachronistic terms 'multiple' or 'composite' monarchy with another, 'dynastic agglomerate'. The term focuses on the unstable element of 'dynasty' and links it to 'agglomerate' as defined in the Oxford English Dictionary ('to collect or combine together in a mass or group; to accumulate, cluster … to form a coherent but often unassimilated mass … forming a compact head or cluster but not united'[9]). This bringing together, combining, compacting and clustering but not *uniting* seems entirely appropriate as a description of the process. Given a choice between optimising the particular powers they inherited in each of their kingdoms and imposing a new overall set of structures across a ramshackle agglomerate, most found the former easier. One sign of this is the suppression or non-development of

---

[6] A female child would have complicated things because of the Salic law prevailing in France, and it would have created a different kind of crisis.

[7] Morrill, *Uneasy Lies the Head*, pp. 12–13.

[8] For the classic exposition, see J. H. Elliott, 'Europe of Composite Monarchies', *Past and Present*, 137 (1992), pp. 48–71 and in later iterations in J. H. Elliott, 'The General Crisis in Retrospect: A Debate without End', in P. Benedict and P. Guttman (eds), *Early Modern Europe: From Crisis to Stability* (Newark, NJ, 2006), pp. 31–50.

[9] In 'The Conglomerate State: A Perspective on State Formation in Early Modern Europe', *Scandinavian Journal of History* 23 (1998), pp. 189–213, H. Gustaffsson prefers the term 'conglomerate state'. OED defines 'conglomerate' as 'to form into a ball or (more or less) rounded mass; to heap up, heap together'. This is less effective in my mind than 'agglomerate'.

Estates General but the persistence of regional estates. This is true for all the major Western European dynastic agglomerates.[10]

Thus let us be clear. Whatever the 'new monarchies' were about, it was not the creation of nation-states. In a rather unfashionable and neglected book, *Nations and States: An Enquiry into the Origins of Nations and the Politics of Nationalism* (1977), Hugh Seton-Watson wrote that

> States can exist without nations or with several nations, among their subjects; and a nation can be coterminous with the population of one state, or be included together with other nations within one state, or be divided between several states. There were states long before there were nations, and there are some nations that are much older than most states which exist today ... In the main European languages the words 'international relations' and their equivalent are used to denote the relations between states. The organisation set up at the end of the Second World War with the hope of preventing war and promoting peace between states is called the 'United Nations' and its predecessor had been called 'the League of Nations'. But membership of both these organisations was confined in fact to governments of states.[11]

Far too much history of state[12] formation has focused on the internal governance and the relationship between 'society' and 'government'. Too little attention has been given to the 'shape' of 'states'. For the moment, it is enough that Seton-Watson defines states and nations in a functionalist way. A state, he writes, is 'a legal and political organisation, with the power to require obedience and loyalty from its [subjects]/citizens';[13] and a nation is 'a community of people whose members are bound together by a sense of solidarity, a common culture, a national consciousness'.[14] Both are elaborated as he goes around the globe in focused historical analyses, but they serve him and his readers well (although I would have liked to see some reference to the importance of origin myths, of how a people [in Latin=*gens*] had a single founder [pro***gen***itor] and were bound by an overwhelming blood bond.[15] This in turn deepens the importance of so

---

[10] Most obviously argued for by H. G. Koenigsberger, *Monarchies, States Generals and Parliaments* (Cambridge, 2001).

[11] Hugh Seton-Watson, *Nations and States: An Enquiry into the Origins of Nations and the Politics of Nationalism* (London, 1977), p. 1.

[12] There is an immense literature on the emergence of the concept of 'the state' and the move from 'subjects' to 'citizens'. For an introduction to early modern vocabulary of politics, see Howell Lloyd, Glenn Burgess and Simon Hodson (eds), *European Political Thought 1450–1700* (New Haven and London, 2007), pp. 11–17 and *passim*.

[13] Seton-Watson, *Nations and States*, p. 1. A case study which really demonstrates the complexity of this concept is Michael Perceval-Maxwell, 'Ireland and the Monarchy in the Early Stuart Multiple Kingdom', *The Historical Journal*, 34 (1991), pp. 279–295.

[14] Seton-Watson, *Nations and States*, p. 1.

[15] Rees Davies, 'The Peoples of Britain and Ireland, 1100–1400. Pt. 1: Identities', *Transactions of the Royal Historical Society*, 6th ser., 4 (1994), pp. 1–20.

many of the Anglo-Norman settlers[16] who became Gaelicised in the later medieval period being said to have de*gen*erated.) As it happens, Seton-Watson's accounts are strongest on the pre-modern and recent histories and least strong on the early modern period, but they provide some important clues to the story of new stable monarchies and indeed republics (especially the Netherlands and Switzerland), not least some relatively unexplored aspects of dynasticism that we will return to.

If 'states can exist without nations or with several nations, among their subjects [citizens]', then it follows that there is an *ethnic* dimension to state formation as well as a social dimension. In dynastic agglomerates, the dialectic between centripetal institutional tendencies and centrifugal ethnic reactions needs far more study. A failure to address this is the one weakness in the otherwise magnificent analysis by Michael Braddick, whose study of Britain and of the early modern British diaspora has been widely embraced by European scholars.[17]

Before looking at that limitation, let us consider the great lessons Braddick has taught in his analyses of processes of state formation. He has identified four separate processes, each proceeding at a different pace, which he calls the patriarchal state, the fiscal-military state, the confessional state and the dynastic state. The *patriarchal state* involves the ever-greater involvement of the 'state' – monarchs, their councils and counsellors, their courts and their judges – in the regulation of 'society' (poverty, dearth, disease, social relations and social order).[18] The *fiscal-military state* is self-explanatory – the monopolisation of organised military force, the ever-greater size of professional armies, the expansion of ever-more-expensive technologies of defence and war, and the ever greater fiscal demands made on fragile economies that resulted from the needs of war, demands that led to new bureaucracies to raise and spend money.[19] The *confessional state* resulted from the great schism in Latin

---

[16] By Anglo-Norman I mean the mongrel people made up of the pre-1066 inhabitants of Lowland England, themselves the mongrel consequence of waves of invaders but with predominantly Anglo-Saxon laws, language, institutions who in turn are overwhelming by Norman French settlers and their laws, inheritance customs, institutions in the eleventh century leading to new, flexible hybrid English language by the fourteenth century. As Paul Langford has pointed out, in the eighteenth century the 'mongrelism' of the English was considered an advantage: see P. Langford, *Englishness Identified: Manners and Character 1650–1850* (Oxford, 2000), pp. 17–22 and *passim*.

[17] Laid out by Michael J. Braddick, 'State Formation and Social Change in Early Modern England: A Problem Stated And Approaches Suggested', *Social History*, 16:1 (1991), pp. 1–17; and fully developed in Michael J. Braddick, *State Formation in Early Modern England c.1550–1700* (Cambridge, 2000).

[18] For which cf. Steve Hindle, *The State and Social Change, 1550–1640* (Basingstoke, 2000).

[19] The classic statement is John Brewer, *The Sinews of Power: War Money and the English State 1688–1783* (London, 1989). For a full set of essays working with the idea, see C. Storrs, *The Fiscal-Military State in Eighteenth-Century Europe* (London, 2009).

Christendom, the development of a unitary and mandatory pattern of beliefs, practices and regulations together with the creation of political structures necessary to enforce the confessional state in the long age of confessional wars.[20] The *dynastic state*, in Braddick's formulation, is about the expansion of the Tudor dynasty into Wales, Ireland, and the Americas, and the quite separate merger of crowns (1603) and (through legislative union) of kingdoms (1707). For Braddick this is a process that he sees as intimately connected with elite formation in England and then in the 'peripheral' regions – the Principality of Wales, the Lordship (later dependent kingdom) of Ireland, the congeries of separate colonies in North America and the Caribbean. But it is made to seem inexorable and inevitable.

Braddick's four analytical categories, each with its own variations in its timeframes and consequences, help us to understand the processes that produce, in the course of the early modern period, what became 'France', 'Spain', Lithuania-Poland or the Scandinavian Kingdoms that reconfigured themselves after the collapse of Union of Kalmar. The same processes were also at work within the Holy Roman Empire, in its heartland and in many of the reshaped principalities. I highlight these because in arguing for the early modern period as witnessing new forms of monarchy, one of the most striking things is that the outcome was the creation of much more stable and fixed complex polities, what I have elsewhere called 'dynastic agglomerates' that were becoming 'united kingdoms' of Britain, France, Spain, Denmark and Sweden, all of which took a shape across the sixteenth and seventeenth centuries that is recognisable today.

But, if indeed 'states can exist without nations or with several nations, among their subjects [citizens]', then it follows that all the ways that the early modern states 'form' in a scheme such as that proposed by Braddick will be in relation not only to a process of 'social interaction', especially the relations between kings and elites and between kings and non-elites, but also in relation to dialectic processes among the various peoples ['nations'] that made up their 'states': ethnic interaction. Here the work of John Pocock is important, not only for the 'British' composite monarchy or dynastic agglomerate but also for most of the others discussed in this volume.[21] At very much the same time as Seton-Watson was developing

---

[20] For (an English-language) discussion of the concept of confessionalisation, especially in German historiography, see Susan R. Boettcher, 'Confessionalisation: Reformation, Religion, Absolutism and Modernity', *History Compass* online, first published 21 December 2005 [DOI: 10.1111/j.1478-0542.2004.00100.x]. The key case study, obviously is Heinz Schilling, *Konfessionalisierung und Staatsinteressen* (Paderborn, 2007), which provided a model much followed in a study of the county of Lippe.

[21] The classic statement is 'British History: A Plea for a New Subject', *Journal of Modern History*, 47 (1975), pp. 601–628.

his world survey of *Nations and States*, Pocock was developing his new British history as a synecdoche of the relationship of state formation and nationhood. This is the kernel of his writing on the topic of immediate concern to us:

the premises must be that the various peoples and nations, ethnic cultures, social structures, and locally defined communities, which have from time to time existed in the area known as 'Great Britain and Ireland', have not only acted so as to create the conditions of their several existences but have also interacted so as to modify the conditions of one another's existence and that there are processes here whose history can and should be studied.[22]

This is a very carefully worded (if very long) sentence. A whole paper could profitably be devoted to unpacking it. But let us consider just three examples from the seventeenth century, all relating to the relationship between state formation and élite transformation.

The first is the fullest and most significant. In Tudor England (and Stewart Scotland) there was a tight-knit elite of peers holding hereditary titles granted by the Crown that were passed by strict rules of primogeniture from one generation to the next. It was of a type common in the feudal and post-feudal nobilities that had evolved everywhere in the Latin West except in Gaeldom.[23] This system was indeed replicated even in the areas of Ireland under English control (the 'Pale', barely 10 per cent of the land of the island of Ireland in 1500). But beyond the English Pale lay a very different type of elite formation: political leadership was conferred upon men 'elected' by an elite, bound together by a common male ancestor, gathered beneath the open sky on top of a hill at the site of some ancient stone, an elite living in dwellings made of wood and earth, and with the absence of a more rigid gradation between nobles.[24] One task the Tudors set themselves was to transform these Gaelic Lords into peers whose standing integrated them – gave them parity of esteem with, as we would say nowadays – into the European-wide society of orders. They began to incorporate them into the Anglo-Irish peerage with privileges that were particular to Ireland. The best known were the O'Brien Earls of Thomond and the O'Neill Earls of Tyrone.[25] But it was a policy

---

[22] J. G. A. Pocock, 'The Limits and Divisions of British History: In Search of the Unknown Subject', *American Historical Review* 87:2 (1982), pp. 311–336, at p. 317.

[23] Ronald Asch, *Nobilities in Transition 1550–1700* (London, 2003), Chapter 1 and *passim*. By Gaeldom, I mean primarily the people of shared culture, language, law and inheritance who were spread across Ireland and Highland Scotland and its islands. I use Celt when I include the linked but distinct language areas of Wales and Cornwall.

[24] This sentence closely follows Christopher Maginn, 'The Gaelic Peers, the Tudor Sovereigns and English Multiple Monarchy', *Journal of British Studies* 50 (2011), pp. 579–580.

[25] Ibid., pp. 574–575, Tables 1 and 2. For the wider implications of English remodelling of the powers and privileges of the elite in Ireland see also Christopher Maginn, '"Surrender

that stuttered, so that there remained still only seven peers of Gaelic lineage by 1641. In its place, the early Stuarts developed a policy, at once bolder and more significant, for the development of identities of all Irish peers. Instead of integrating the elite of Ireland into a nobility for the *patria* of Ireland, the Stuarts sought to homogenise the elites of all their kingdoms through actively promoting intermarriage and even by granting individuals titles in more than one kingdom which promoted loyalty not to a *patria* but to the *imperium* of Charles I, King of Great Britain and Ireland. By the 1630s, many Scots could speak of themselves as 'we, Your Majesty's *British* nobility'.[26]

As I have written elsewhere, in 1641 there were just over 300 peers across the three Stuart kingdoms, about half of them barons and viscounts, and the other half earls, with between six marquises and three dukes. About 10 per cent of the upper tier had titles in more than one kingdom (and seats in two of the three Parliaments), and many of them were at the heart of Charles's government as the crisis broke. Both the Scottish dukes (Hamilton and Lennox) had English titles (Earl of Cambridge, Duke of Richmond) and English wives (a niece and a daughter of the assassinated royal favourite, George Villiers, Duke of Buckingham). The greatest surviving Gaelic lord in Ulster, Randal Macdonnell, Earl of Antrim,[27] was married to the daughter of the English Earl of Rutland, who was also and more importantly the widow of the Duke of Buckingham. Ulick Burke, 4th Earl of Clanricarde and the greatest Catholic landowner in Connacht, was a half-brother of the 3rd Earl of Essex (by his mother, wife of the 3rd Earl of Clanricarde and also the widow of both Sir Philip Sidney and the 2nd Earl of Essex) and he was married to the only daughter of the earl of Northampton. He sat in the English House as Lord Burgh, and then as earl of St Albans. He was a major landowner in Kent as well as counties Galway and Roscommon. The greatest Catholic landowners in Leinster and Munster all had English wives or English mothers. So did a simple majority of the Protestant nobility of Ireland, especially the earls, most notably James Butler, 12th earl (later 1st marquis and 1st duke) of Ormonde, who was, in the 1640s and at the Restoration, the King's Lord Lieutenant in Ireland. His mother was a Gloucestershshire heiress and he in turn married the heiress of the earl of Desmond who was Lady Dingwall in the Scottish peerage in her own right and the daughter of a Scottish settler in Ireland. There may have been no British state in the 1630s. But there

---

and Regrant" in the Historiography of Sixteenth-Century Ireland', *Sixteenth-Century Journal* 38 (2007), pp. 955–974.

[26] John Morrill, *The Scottish National Covenant in British Context* (Edinburgh, 1990), p. 15.

[27] Earl (since the death of his father, the 1st earl, in 1636), marquis from 1645.

was rapidly becoming a British peerage. Perhaps the ultimate proof that blood-ties mattered for many at least as much as religious affiliation is that Robert Devereux, 3rd earl of Essex and soon-to-be Parliamentarian Captain General (1642–1645), a stern and principled protestant, persuaded Charles I, as one of his 'bridge appointments' in 1641, to make his Catholic half-brother Ulick Burke, earl of Clanricarde, a member of the English privy council, under his English title, earl of St Albans.[28]

But yet again there are asymmetries. Between 1600 and 1649, 60 per cent of all Irish peers took Irish brides (many of course 'Old English' or even second or third generation New English or New Scottish), and 40 per cent took brides born in Britain.[29] The figure for Scotland has not been so authoritatively determined, but (for earls and above) those who married into English or Irish peerage families cannot have been less than fifteen to twenty per cent.[30] The figure for England was negligible, perhaps one to two per cent. Indeed one of the most remarkable things about the period down to 1688 is that while many English peers willingly gave up their daughters to Scottish and Irish lords, they did not offer their sons to the daughters of Scottish peers, not even to wealthy Scottish heiresses.

When a Scottish monarch inherited England, and more particularly moved to England, the Scottish nobility moved south in large numbers and many took English wives and established themselves as major landowners on both sides of the border.[31] But there is an even greater asymmetry here. Not a single English peer married a Scottish heiress and not a single English peer acquired land in Scotland at any point before 1688. This is surely a direct consequence of James VI inheriting England and not a descendant of Edward VI inheriting Scotland.[32]

It is true that a handful of Englishmen acquired Scottish titles (without Scottish lands), the most prominent of whom was the grandfather of Lord

---

[28] All references in this paragraph are from *Oxford Dictionary of National Biography*, Oxford University Press, 2004, online edn, January 2008 [http://www.oxforddnb.com/view/arti cle/7566, accessed 12–20 December 2012] and from J. McGuire and J. Quinn (eds), *Dictionary of Irish Biography* (Cambridge, 2009).

[29] J. Ohlmeyer, *Making Ireland English; the Irish Aristocracy in the seventeenth century* (2012), p. 184. By 'Old English' I mean those who self-consciously saw themselves as the descendants of the English settlers in Ireland between the late twelfth and early sixteenth centuries.

[30] This is a subject largely ignored by Keith Brown in his otherwise outstanding *Noble Society in Scotland: Wealth, Family and Culture from Reformation to Revolution* (Edinburgh, 2000) and even in his discussion of political elites in *Kingdom or Province: Scotland and the Regal Union 1603–1715* (Basingstoke, 1992), pp. 33–35.

[31] Brown, Noble Society in Scotland.

[32] The preceding paragraphs include material from an article by John Morrill, 'The English Revolution in British and Irish Context', in Michael J. Braddick (ed.), *Oxford Handbook to the English Revolution* (Oxford, 2015), pp. 555–576, at pp. 565–566.

General Thomas Fairfax, but this was not a political issue in either country. On the other hand, the swamping of the Irish peerage with Englishmen did have significant consequences. Between 1603 and 1641, fifty-one English families acquired Irish titles. Twenty-two of these were men without titles in England who had been planters or servitors (former army officers), mainly post 1580 in Munster or post 1590 in Ulster, and they were a solid New English Protestant bloc in the Irish Parliament (to which can be added a further six peers from among the Scottish settlers, Protestant and Catholic).[33] But there were also twenty-nine non-resident English peers. Some of these had some family connection with Ireland. Thus one was the grandson of an Elizabethan Lord Deputy, and others had fathers who had served with Essex between 1597 and 1601 and who were still owed money. But most were friends or suitors of Buckingham, rewarded or fobbed off with an Irish title.[34]

Central to the new super monarchies or dynastic agglomerates, as this whole book argues, is the social cohesion of new elites. My contribution here is thus to emphasise not so much 'vertical' cohesion (a concept of 'nobility' that extended to new service nobilities and the conversion of old landed, feudal, and military nobilities into service nobilities) as 'horizontal' cohesion, as the distinctive peerages of three kingdoms began to knit together in the ways just shown.[35] For it is from the integrated elements of this 'Britannic' nobility that the executive government on the ground, especially in the outlying kingdoms, was formed. If the 'British state system' operated through a single decision-making council in London and enforcing/implementing councils in London, Edinburgh and Dublin, then this development was of the first importance, as indeed is the even less studied and poorly understood atrophy of the process of creating a Britannic nobility after 1660. Perhaps this as much as anything explains why the British state system never really became a British state.

Returning to my three comments on Pocock's complicated sentence: a second and yet more dramatic aspect is the phenomenon of Irish Catholic royalism in the 1640s. The motto of the Confederate Irish, rebels in the eyes of almost all Englishmen and, above all, of the English Protestant settlers in Ireland whom they slaughtered by the thousands, was *Pro Deo, rege et patria, Hiberni unanimis* – 'Irishmen united for God, King and Homeland' – that is, for a Catholic God and a Protestant

---

[33] Ohlmeyer, *Making Ireland English*, p. 35.

[34] C. R. Mayes, The Early Stuarts and the Irish Peerage, *EHR* 73 (1958), pp. 227–251.

[35] For the important but different point about those changes in the changing nature of 'nobility' within the component parts of a dynastic agglomerate, rather than across them, see chapters in this volume by Garcia, pp. 136–44; Lind, pp. 269–73; Alvariño pp. 183–8; and Scott, pp. 75–80.

King.[36] This is because they hoped against hope that Charles would allow them to create a kingdom under Catholic control, loyal to him but completely independent of English control – English Parliament, English colonial administrators, English religion. They believed that what he had granted to the Scottish Presbyterians, he would also grant to Irish Catholics in order to secure the resources he needed to defeat his puritan English subjects.[37] They had a highly developed sense of the kind of monarchical republic they would create in Ireland in a very loosely federated Stuart dynastic agglomerate. What they wanted was an Irish *patria* within a British *monarchia*. As John Pocock has suggested, there are elements of three different kinds of civil war in the 1640s, three kinds of civil war known to the Romans and therefore to early modern readers of Roman History: a *bellum civile*, which is to say a *bellum into cives*, a war among citizens or subjects, a war for control of the institutions that controlled the Commonwealth; a *bellum sociale*, which is to say a *bellum inter socios*, a war in which the outlying parts of the Roman state claimed equality and rights of full citizenship; and a war of independence or secession, like the Jewish revolt that led to such catastrophe in AD 70. My own gloss on this is that in the 1640s the English had primarily a *bellum civile*; Scotland had a *bellum civile* and a *bellum sociale;* and Ireland had all three.[38]

And thirdly and even more briefly, let me just note that one excellent way to understand British History from 1688 and 1746 is to call it the 'war of two dynasties', with on the one hand lowland England, lowland Scotland and the English plantations in Ireland committed to the victory of princely houses from first the Netherlands and later from Hanover, and on the other hand with Highland and Celtic Britain and Ireland pretty solidly behind the exiled House of Stuart. A victory for the Stuarts (and with France, Spain, Rome and Sweden at various points willing to fund

---

[36] The best recent accounts of the political and religious ideas of the Confederation of Kilkenny (1642–1649) are M. O Siochru, *Confederate Ireland 1642–9: A Constitutional and Political Analysis* (Dublin, 1999) and T. Ó hannrachain, *Catholic Reformation in Ireland: the Mission of Rinuccini* (Oxford, 2002).

[37] John Morrill, 'The English Revolution'.

[38] J. G. A. Pocock, 'The Atlantic Archipelago and the War of the Three Kingdoms', in Brendan Bradshaw and John Morrill (eds), *The British Problem c.1534–1707: State Formation in the Atlantic Archipelago* (Basingstoke, 1994) and for evidence that there were more radical (separatist) understandings of the relationship, see Ian Campbell, 'Catholic Revolution and Holy War in Seventeenth-Century Ireland', forthcoming. For my own take on this, see John Morrill, 'The Reign of Saint and Soldiers: The Wars of Religion in Britain and Ireland 1638–1660', in J. Wormald (ed.), *A Short History of the British Isles: The Seventeenth Century* (Oxford, 2008), pp. 83–116; and John Morrill, 'Rethinking Revolution in Seventeenth-Century Britain', in Kazuhiko Kondo (ed.), *State and Empire in British History* (Tokyo, 2003), pp. 39–57.

major international expeditions to support them, it was never a foregone conclusion that the Jacobite cause was hopeless) would not have broken up the British *monarchia*, but a king who had regained his throne with Gaelic and Catholic help would hardly have founded his regime on the calculated destruction of their social and cultural worlds as the Hanoverians did.[39]

Thus I think the external physical boundaries and internal mental boundaries and 'shapes' of the new monarchies – 'French', 'Spanish,' 'Danish', 'Swedish', 'British' or for that matter a 'Dutch' republic' – have been too readily taken for granted as being embryonically modern. In 1500 none of these were aspirational or imagined. Who could have imagined a Spain with Navarre but without Portugal? In John Pocock's *tour d'horizon* 'Two Kingdoms and Three Histories? Political Thought in British Contexts', surely the most brilliant of all his essays on the subject of what constitutes British history, he speaks of British political thought as 'a discourse directed at the "matter of Britain", that is at the problematics of conceiving and realising a political entity to be known by that name'.[40] In the course of the essay, he demonstrates that this is no simple matter. In the early modern period (certainly down to at least 1707), 'Britain' existed but only in a limited sense as a political entity, and the ways in which the same man acted as king in each of his kingdoms remained bound by separate legal prescriptions and cultural proscriptions. This is emblematically demonstrated by the way that James VI had a spiritual identity in England by virtue of the English Reformation by Act of State (Crown and Parliament) and in Scotland by virtue of an act of noble and popular rebellion in defiance of the Crown.[41] In what ways these malleable frontiers on maps and in the mind would develop and morph was far from predetermined.

The British dynastic agglomerate became what is recognisably the modern United Kingdom between Henry VIII's schism and claim to imperial sovereignty in the 1530s and the constitutional completion and articulation of the 'United Kingdom' by the 1720s, just as a Spanish

---

[39] For the best recent work on the international dimensions of Jacobitism, see Edward Corp, *A Court in Exile: The Stuarts in France, 1689–1718* (Cambridge, 2003); Edward Corp, *The Stuarts in Italy, 1719–1766: A Royal Court in Permanent Exile* (Cambridge 2011); Daniel Szechi, *The Jacobites: Britain and Europe, 1688–1788* (London, 1994); and for the more obscure Swedish angle, see A. Francis Steuart, 'Sweden and the Jacobites, 1719–1720', *The Scottish Historical Review*, 23: 90 (January, 1926), pp. 119–127.

[40] Pocock's essay begins with a frank confession: 'A Center for the History of British Political Thought Must Sooner or Later Pay Attention to Its Own Title', in J. G. A. Pocock (ed.), *A Discovery of Islands* (Cambridge, 2005), pp. 58–76, at 58.

[41] Pocock, 'Two Kingdoms and Three Histories', pp. 66–68.

dynastic agglomerate became recognisably modern Spain between 1469 and 1714, and the French dynastic agglomerate became recognisably modern France between 1453 and 1660. In the process, ancient kingdoms and principalities vanished – a process brilliantly perceived and analysed by Norman Davies.[42] Who in 1450 would have foreseen the disappearance of the kingdom of Navarre, or the Duchy of Burgundy, or the Lordship of the Isles, a kingdom in all but name that straddled the Western Highlands and Islands of Scotland and the North Eastern tip of Ulster? For example, the kingdom of Navarre [Pamplona], straddling the Pyrenees, had been an independent kingdom since the ninth century.[43] Who would predict that by 1650 the kings of Spain would be kings of Navarre but not of Portugal (especially after it had been absorbed by the kings of Spain in 1580, only to break free in 1640)?

In every century since the fifth century, the political and constitutional shape of Britain and Ireland, and the relations of the peoples within them, has experienced a seismic shock. For reasons of space, I will speak here only of the last 500 years. Between 1536–1543, Wales was incorporated into England, the lord of the Pale became the king of Ireland, and plans were laid for a dynastic union of England in Scotland. In 1603–1608 a union of the Crowns of England and Scotland was made and defined, but a legislated union of the kingdoms was abandoned or at least deferred. In 1707, the Union of the Crowns became the Union of the Kingdoms, and thereabouts a radical new political relationship was formed between the English and Irish kingdoms (through the Irish Penal Laws).[44] This in turn was transformed by the Act of Union of 1801 and by Catholic Emancipation. The Partition Treaty of 1921 that created the two jurisdictions unpacked a century of integration, which was the only time there was really a British state. And the devolution of power to a re-established Scottish Parliament and to Wales and Northern Ireland Assemblies in 1998 and the Good Friday Agreement of 1999 were turning points as significant as anything since the reforms of 1536–1543. None of these can be treated as teleological in the strong sense[45] – in the sense that it is 'the

---

[42] N. Davies, *Vanished Kingdoms: The History of Half-Forgotten Europe* (2011).

[43] Jean-Francois Berdah, 'Pyrenees without Frontiers: The French-Spanish Border in Modern Time, Seventeenth to Twentieth Century', in Steven G. Ellis and Reingard Esser (eds), *Frontiers, Regions and Identities in Europe* (Pisa, 2009), pp. 163–169, building on Peter Sahlins, *Boundaries: The Making of France and Spain in the Pyrenees* (Berkeley, 1989), pp. 25–60.

[44] For this, see John Morrill, 'The Causes of Penal Laws: Paradoxes and Inevitabilities', in J. Bergin, Eoin Magennis and Lesa Ni Mhunghaile (eds), *New Perspectives on the Penal Laws* (Eighteenth-Century Ireland, special issue no.1 [Dublin, 2011]), pp. 55–75.

[45] See Glenn Burgess, 'On Revisionism', *Historical Journal* 33 (1990), pp. 609–627, at pp. 614–616.

self-authenticated history of a self-perpetuating polity or culture'.[46] It is the history of a might-have-been (or better, of a might-become, of an aspiration),[47] and it is a history of those who sought to subvert that might-become, that aspiration. Since what is imagined as might-becoming changes over time, so does that history mutate.[48] French history is the history of what became France; Spanish history of what became Spain (without Portugal, but with the Basques); British history is something different. For in British history, Ireland was integrated into a state system which then, in 1922, unravelled into the United Kingdom of Great Britain and Northern Ireland and into the Irish Free State. It is very striking that there is not and never has been a geographical term to describes the islands of Britain and Ireland in the way that 'Britain' means the island of Britain. The term 'British Isles', seen as neutral in many parts of the world, has been and remains offensive to a great many Irish people.[49] And across 1,000 years of British-Irish political interaction, there persisted a range of origin myths that sought to define the common origin of the peoples of Britain (most obviously the 'Brutus' myth of the peopling of Britain by the Trojan exile Brutus who divided up his kingdom between his three sons, conferring England on the eldest, Scotland on the middle and Wales on the youngest son, laying the foundation for a feudalised sense of English overlordship. But no such origin myth, no sense of a progenitor (pro-*gen*-itor = founder of a 'race' or 'people', as we have seen) existed for the peoples or polities of Britain and Ireland. English claims to Ireland could only rely on conquest and papal grant before 1534, and solely on conquest after 1534, a very incomplete conquest at that.

Just as one marriage, that of Isabella and Ferdinand in 1469, defined the future of the Iberian monarchies (but as we shall see, it might not have done), so the marriage of James IV of Scotland and Margaret, elder

---

[46] Pocock, 'Two Kingdoms and Three Histories', p. 311.

[47] Unless one considers 1800–1922 as being the multi-national state that the subject yearns to find – a period with one head of state, one sovereign legislature, one imperial system, but more than one legal system, several religious systems and several self-consciously separate nations.

[48] For a fuller discussion of this, see John Morrill, 'Thinking about the New British History' in David Armitage (ed.), *British Political History in History, Literature and Theory, 1500–1800* (Cambridge, 2006), pp. 23–46. This includes a section on how the teaching of History in England, Scotland, (Northern) Ireland and Scotland has hermetically sealed off the histories of the local part of the archipelago from the rest.

[49] Robert von Friedeburg wisely counsels me not to overstate British exceptionalism. There are plenty of examples of possible dis-agglomeration elsewhere in Europe that could succeed – Basque separatism in Spain and Corsican separatism in France are current examples, let alone modern historical attempts at dis-agglomeration such as Bavaria (1918–1920).

daughter of Henry VII of England and sister of Henry VIII in 1503, was to define the future of the British monarchies when – a full century later – James VI of Scotland, the great-grandson produced by Henry VIII's elder sister Margaret Tudor and her husband James IV of Scotland, claimed to be king of England and Ireland as the closest by blood (in a compounded uterine succession, his claim being via his mother and his great-grandmother) to the childless Elizabeth I. That a Scot inherited the English throne was central to the social, cultural and constitutional relationship between the three kingdoms. How different would have been the succession of a child of Edward VI and Mary of Scotland if the marriage treaty of 1543 had been honoured? Would English nobles have spurned Scottish heiresses as they did after 1603? Would the Scottish Parliament have survived until 1707? (We might also ask: what if a Castilian king had married an Aragonese Queen and not vice versa?) I have already alluded to what could have happened if Francis II of France had had a child by Mary Stewart instead of succumbing to an ear infection, but what if Mary Tudor and Philip II of Spain had had a male child – which had been prevented by Mary's cervical cancer – especially since the marriage treaty barred any child from inheriting the Spanish Crowns but provided for any child of the marriage to receive the Netherlands, thus uniting the two great Northern European trading and colonising nations of the ensuing century? What if Charles II had had one legitimate child as well as at least fourteen illegitimate ones?[50] What if William III and Mary II had had children, opening up the prospects of a British-Dutch Union? Or if any of Anne's 17 pregnancies had resulted in a child to keep a Protestant Stuart dynasty going?

Everywhere the shape of the agglomerates that were to be transformed by state formation were determined by dynastic chance and dynastic roulette. This affects *what* was transformed and *how* it was transformed. The most obvious and most spectacular examples are the Habsburgs, so let us remind ourselves of their story before we move back to the Tudors and Stewarts.

The Emperor Charles V (1500–1558)[51] inherited Burgundy and what we would now call the Netherlands from his father; the kingdoms of Spain and its dependencies from his mother; and central Europe and the

---

[50] George Edward Cokayne, *The Complete Peerage of England, Scotland, Ireland, Great Britain*, Vol. 6 (London, 1910), p. 706.

[51] There is a slightly incorrect list of all Charles V's titles towards the end of https://en .wikipedia.org/wiki/Charles_V,_Holy_Roman_Emperor. An anonymous Cambridge University Press reader says that the French Wikipedia corrects the errors in the English entry. For a discussion of 'the twenty-two kingdoms', see Alvariño's chapter in this volume, pp. 183–211.

Habsburg lands in Austria from his paternal grandmother. All this was the result of rather fuzzy dynastic calculation, but it required the failure of both Charles the Bold (1433–1477) and Ferdinand and Isabella to leave any male issue (John [1478–1497] their only son to survive infancy died without issue). Their eldest daughter died in childbirth in 1498, having been married to two successive kings of Portugal. If she or the male child she bore who died at one year old had survived, then there would have been no union of Burgundy-Spain, but one of Spain-Portugal. And if the second daughter Joanna (who married Charles V's father) had died before giving birth, the thrones of Spain would have passed through her younger sister, again to the Crown of Portugal or most dramatically of all, to Mary I of England through her mother Catharine of Aragon, yet another daughter of Isabella. So although Charles V's inheritance can be said to be by dynastic calculation, it was also a result of dynastic chance, the failure of both the Burgundian and Spanish monarchies in the male line at crucial moments. All this inbreeding was to lead eventually, upon the failure of the Portuguese line, to the succession of the grandchild of Isabella's fourth child through her marriage to Miguel I to the Portuguese throne in 1580 and to the short-lived union of whole of Iberia for the only time in its history (1580–1640). But who, until the eve of 1640, could have foreseen that union unscrambling?[52]

What dynastic chance and dynastic calculation had joined, they could put asunder. It is very important that when Charles came to bequeath his vast empire, he had only one surviving son, who was to become Philip II of Spain and of its European and extra-European dependencies and of the Burgundian inheritance. But the Habsburg lands across central and Eastern Europe went to his elder daughter and to her husband, who also happened to be Charles's brother. Would that have been what happened if Charles had had a second son and a brother who predeceased him?

However, Charles's dynastic flexibility can be seen in the way that he was willing to see a variety of ways of dividing up his empire in order to further his strategic goals. In the treaty of Crépy between Charles and the French King Francis I in 1541, for example, it was agreed that Charles and Francis would each abandon their various conflicting claims and restore the *status quo* of 1538; the Emperor would relinquish his claim to the Duchy of Burgundy and the King of France would do the same for the Kingdom of Naples, as well as renouncing his claims to Flanders and Artois. The Duke of Orléans would marry either Charles's daughter Mary

---

[52] See Cardim's chapter in this volume, pp. 212–43; D. Birmingham, *A Concise History of Portugal* (2nd edn, Cambridge, 2003), pp. 33–43.

or his niece Anna; the choice was to be made by Charles. In the first case, the bride would receive the Netherlands and Franche-Comté as a dowry – i.e. the lands of Charles's birth; in the second, Milan. Francis, meanwhile, was to grant the duchies of Bourbon, Châtelherault and Angoulême to his son; he would also abandon his claims to the territories of the Duchy of Savoy, including Piedmont and Savoy itself. Models of state formation that start from the need to consolidate and integrate what in fact came to be consolidated and integrated over the centuries are inadequate.[53] All great landowners constantly purchased and married into new property and rationalised their holdings by selling some, settling some on their children and consolidating. Why should monarchs, all great landowners in their own right, not follow the same practices into their state-building?

At the other end of the period, we can look at the dynastic ambitions of Charles, younger son of the Emperor Leopold I, who began his adult life as king of Spain and ended it as a Hispaniolized central European emperor. That there was a succession crisis in Spain was itself largely the result of the incessant inbreeding among the Habsburgs, resulting in the sad and depressing figure of Charles II, who was physically and mentally handicapped, impotent and sterile.[54] The French and Austrian royal houses had almost equally good claims through multiple female lines, with the French deriving their claims through several sisters older than the Austrian females and with the Austrians relying on disclaimers by French monarchs in marriage treaties which the French retorted were null and void because of the non-payment of dowries. Anticipating the crisis, the major powers agreed to two Partition Treaties, the first offering the Crowns of Spain and its transoceanic dependencies itself to the six-year-old Electoral Prince of Bavaria, the Italian territories to the Dauphin (except for Milan which would go to the Duke of Lorraine), while the Archduke Charles would get the Southern Netherlands. But following the highly inconvenient death of the Prince, a second treaty gave Spain (but not its European dependencies) to the Archduke Charles.[55] This piecemeal dismantlement of his inheritance so infuriated the enfeebled Charles II that he made a will leaving *everything* to Philip of Anjou, younger grandson of Louis XIV.[56] Louis XIV

---

[53] K. Brandi, *The Emperor Charles V: The Growth and Destiny of a Man and of a World-Empire* (London, 1939), pp. 519–522.

[54] G. Alvarez, F. C. Ceballos, C. Quinteiro, 'The Role of Inbreeding in the Extinction of a European Royal Dynasty', *PLoS ONE* 4:4 (2009), e5174, doi:10.1371/journal. pone.0005174 (available free online).

[55] H. Kamen, *The War of Succession in Spain 1701–14* (London, 1969).

[56] For a neat summary of Carlos II's frailties and catastrophic decisions, see William D. Phillips and Carla Rahn Phillips, *A Concise History of Spain* (Cambridge, 2010), pp. 168–171.

accepted the will and rejected the Partition Treaty. Understandably, most of Europe did the opposite. For the next ten years, there was a French king of Spain based in Madrid and an Austrian king of Spain based in Barcelona. And it ended in Austrian tears. Spain and its empire was secured by the French ruling house (but only with a guarantee that the thrones of France and Spain would not be united), while the Austrian Habsburgs had to make do with adding the kingdom of Naples and Sardinia, the Duchy of Milan and also the Spanish Netherlands (the core of the old medieval Duchy of Burgundy) to the Austrian Habsburg portfolio. There was much else in the Treaty of Utrecht, but the dynastic consequences were long-lasting.[57]

This has much to tell us about the natural instability of the dynastic agglomerates down to the end of the period. First, there was the sheer pragmatism on show. In order to get the Spanish Empire for their *families*, in the 1690s both Louis XIV and the Emperor Leopold were willing to pass their claims to their second sons – Philip and Charles, respectively. Yet, as dynastic chance would have it, in both cases, subsequent deaths left Philip as the next in line to France and Charles as the successor to his father and elder brother. Charles's unwillingness to forego either the Spanish or Austrian agglomerates weakened the resolve of his allies to keep the French out of Spain. They no more wanted a new Charles V than an even more bloated Louis XIV.

Second, in the period around 1707–1711 (prior to the death of Charles's elder brother, Emperor Joseph I), with war-weariness spreading, there was surely a possibility that the powers might have sought to partition Spain itself, with Castile going to Philip, and Aragon and the Americas to Charles (and with Italy and the Netherlands also being parcelled out). What Ferdinand and Isabella had put together, persistent inbreeding might have put asunder. Even with the Northern Powers losing their commitment to Charles as a probable future emperor and as simultaneously king of Spain, and with Charles himself in Vienna obsessing over his central and Eastern European inheritance, it took an almighty effort to dislodge his supporters from Barcelona. Thus even in the early eighteenth century, Spain could have reverted to separate kingdoms of Castile and Aragon.[58]

Thirdly, there was the impact of Charles VI's time in Spain on his subsequent government in Germany and the Balkans. It was very unusual

---

[57] Trevor Dadson and J. H. Elliot (eds), *Britain, Spain and the Treaty of Utrecht 1713–2013* (London, 2014).

[58] I am grateful to the anonymous Cambridge University Press reader who pointed out that in 1709/1710, at the nadir of Louis XIV's military fortunes, France itself was in danger of dismemberment, a point s/he added would be grist to my mill!

but not unknown for a ruler to gain experience in one kingdom and then to transfer to another. James VI of Scotland, who became James I of England and Ireland, is the most obvious example, but Henri III of France, the third son[59] of Henri II, was for 15 months the elected king of Poland before abdicating upon unexpectedly inheriting the French Crown in 1575, with the result that Poland left rather less of a mark on him than he left on Poland.[60] But in the case of Charles VI, his Spanish experience underpinned everything he aspired to and attempted during his long reign as a Habsburg ruler based in Vienna (1711–1740). When he returned from Barcelona, he brought with him much of the Catalan nobility and bureaucracy and gave them a disproportionate role in his new agglomeration of territories – 2,874 officials of Spanish origin (among a total of 16,000 he had to provide for in one way or another). He built himself a palace/monastery at Klosterneuburg to mirror the Escorial and to underline the coming together of *regnum et sacerdotium* (handing the Frenchified Palace at Schonbrunn to his brother's widow); Spanish musical styles and art also came to dominate a court that introduced Spanish court ceremonial and etiquette. His early military successes against the Ottomans allowed him to reclaim large parts of what is now Hungary and the Balkans, and he planted Spanish exiles. His plans were very consciously adapted from the Spanish *Reconquista* 200 years earlier. One of his earliest reforms in Spain had been to remodel the *Consejo* of the Indies; this was reproduced in Vienna with ambitious plans to create an Atlantic trading Empire based on Ostend, and new port cities (funded by the Crown) in Trieste and Fiume, with the express intention of taking on the great trading cities of Valencia and Catalonia. His new Company of the Indies was to explore the possibility of establishing a colonial/trading presence in Madagascar, Bengal, the Solomon Islands or Tobago. As William O'Reilly has pointed out, all this was predicated upon his dream of recreating the empire of his great-great-great grandfather Charles V or even recreating the empire of Charlemagne. He never let go of his hopes of one day getting back Spain and its European and American colonies. But the point is that his

---

[59] Or fourth son if we include Prince Louis, who died in infancy.

[60] The Henrician Articles or King Henry's Articles were a permanent contract between the 'Polish nation' (i.e. the *szlachta* (nobility) of the Polish-Lithuanian Commonwealth) and a newly elected king upon his election to the throne that stated the fundamental principles of governance and constitutional law in the Polish-Lithuanian Commonwealth. While *pacta conventa* comprised only the personal undertakings of the king-elect, the Henrician Articles were a permanent statute that all king-elects had to swear to respect. The articles functioned, essentially, as a first constitution for Poland until the Constitution of May 3, 1791. (Jacek Jędruch, *Constitutions, Elections, and Legislatures of Poland, 1493–1977: A Guide to Their History* [Washington, DC, 1998] pp. 84–86.)

six years in Spain in vain pursuit of a dynastic ambition had a huge and lasting impact on state formation in the wholly separate lands that the grim reaper gave him instead.[61] The dynastic chances that made him first Charles III King of Spain and then the Emperor Charles VI, ruler of much of central and Eastern Europe, where and when they did, profoundly affected the kind of state formation experienced by the peoples of Spain and Austria.

And so to my final case study: Great Britain. In 1500, the House of Tudor claimed to rule the whole of England and Wales, although in fact the king's writ did not run in much of Wales and much of the North of England. Only about one-third of Wales was shired (in the basic administrative unit of counties), and the rest was under the control of men who were fiefs of the King but who exercised private jurisdiction in their marches; none of Wales and parts of the Northern England returned no MPs to Parliament and were thus not liable to taxation. The Tudors were 'lords' not 'kings' of Ireland, and their writs ran in less than 10 per cent of Ireland. Another 30–40 per cent were again marcher territories under the descendants of Late Norman settlers, and the rest was completely outside the control of the Crown, governed by more than 100 tribal leaders (tribes=septs or clans) who were native, Gaelic Irish or Old English lords who had de-*gen*-erated, or unraced themselves. Scotland was an independent monarchy with little influence north and west of the Highland line, with kings who had regularly acknowledged the feudal suzerainty of kings of England but who were effectively independent. And in the southwest highlands and western islands of Scotland and the northeast of Ireland there was the remnants of the old Norse kingdom now known as the Lordship of the Isles, under the control of the Clan Macdonald or Macdonnell. As we now know, state formation in Britain and Ireland in and after the 1530s was to see kings in South East England establish effective control over the whole of the archipelago, imposing English as the language of law and government, imposing English land law and inheritance customs, and seeking unsuccessfully to impose English Protestantism as the religion of the archipelago. This might look like a great success story, and it can be told as a story about how each governmental core in London, Edinburgh and Dublin expanded its power across its own periphery, and the English core extended its authority over the other cores. But it was in fact a messier process than this might sound.[62]

---

[61] This paragraph draws extensively on W. O'Reilly 'Lost Chances of the House of Habsburg', *Austrian History Yearbook* 40 (2009), pp. 53–70.
[62] Morrill, *Uneasy Lies the Head*, pp. 19–22.

For by 1750 there was within the archipelago one monarch, but two parliaments and legal systems, three confessional systems, four major languages and five nations (of whom four recognised themselves as additionally being British and one did not).[63] And I want to suggest that the shape state formation took was a result of the particular form of dynastic history within the Tudor-Stewart state system.

We have seen that Habsburg state formation was determined by inbreeding, constantly thwarted dynastic plans for growth through family marriage, the instabilities created by the way Charles V had inherited an empire as big as Charlemagne's and the way he had divided it in 1555 between his son and his brother. It remained an aspiration that was to haunt and transform Charles VI's life and that of his subjects 200 years later. For in Spain, as in England, the survival of the Spanish branch had always hung by a thread. Neither Philip II, nor Philip III, nor Charles II had a younger brother,[64] one effect being that there was no great extended family to feed and worry about. In France, state formation was conditioned by the existence of many cadet branches and, at key moments, in the centralisation of the French state, especially in the 1610s and 1640s and 1650s, resistance to the growth of the state was led by cadet branches of the royal family that the Crown could not easily control or eliminate. France, again unlike Spain, was bedevilled by long minorities (in the 1560s and 1570s, and from 1610–1626, 1643–1660, 1715–1723) during which state formation went into reverse (e.g. the creation of the Huguenot state-within-the-state, the *soulevements populaires*, the *Frondes*). In fact, six of the eight monarchs of France between 1547 and 1774 were minors at the time of their succession, compared with one of the 15 in England. And in addition to cadet or agnatic branches, the French monarchy also had to provide for many bastards, again a thorn in the flesh to their successors.

The extreme example of a dynastic state which suffered from long minorities was Scotland. Look at the lower part of Table 2.1. Scotland was in minority for 76 or the 115 years from 1488 to 1603, with royal lands and jurisdiction parcelled out among the nobility. A major task of each monarch once he or she was of age was the restitution of royal power lost during their minority. And cadet branches of the royal family, especially the Hamiltons and the Lennox-Stewarts, were always snapping at the heels of monarchs. Although the Stewarts managed to weaken and then eliminate the Lordship of the Isles, there was little royal presence in the localities down to 1640.

---

[63] English, (New) Irish, Anglo-Irish, Scots, Welsh (Ulster Scots). English, Welsh, Scots and (Ulster Scots) were all willing to call themselves British too, but meant different things by it.

[64] The exception is Philip IV, who had two younger brothers that died childless.

Table 2.1 *The Tudor and Stuart Dynasties, 1485–1727*

Monarch regnal dates	Children alive at time of death	Age at time of death	Relationship to predecessor	Age at accession	Acknowledged bastards	Nationality of spouse(s)
England 1485–1603, Great Britain 1603–1727						
Henry VII 1485–1509	1s 2d	52	remote cousin	28	0	English
Henry VIII 1509–1547	1s 2d	55	son	17	1	4 English, 1 Sp 1 Germ
Edward VI 1547–1558	0	15	son	9	0	unmarried
Mary 1553–1558	0	42	sister	37	0	Spanish
Elizabeth 1558–1603	0	70	sister	25	0	unmarried
James VI 1603–1625	1s 1d	58	1st cousin twice removed	36	0	Danish
Charles I 1625–1649	3s 3d	48	son	24	0	French
Charles II 1649/1660–1685	0	54	son	18 or 29	14+	Portuguese
James II 1685–1688	1s 3d	67	brother	51	3	English, Italian
[Mary II 1689–1695]	0	32	daughter	28	0	Dutch]
William III 1689–1702	0	51	nephew of J II	38	0	English
Anne 1702–1714	0	49	brother-in-law/cousin	37	0	Danish
George I 1714–1727	1s 1d	67	2nd cousin	44	2	German
Scotland (to 1603)						
James IV 1488–1513	1s	40	son	15	3	English [si. of HVIII]
James V 1513–1542	1d	30	son	12 days	2×	French
Mary 1542–1568	1s	42	daughter	7 days	0	1 French, 2 Scots
James VI 1568–1625	1s 1d	58	son	18 months	0	Danish

First, only one king was a minor when he acceded to the throne (i.e. Edward VI),[65] and for that matter there were no dotages. The ages at accession of English rulers between 1485 and 1727 was almost always 25–40 (the only outliers being Henry VIII, who was on the brink of 18; George I at 44; James II at 51), and all but three died before their sixtieth birthday, again the exceptions being Elizabeth I (just after her seventieth birthday), James II and George I (both at 67). Most died between 48 and 58. So in terms of state formation, new monarchs (however insecure their title or unclear the line of succession) never had to claw back powers lost or centrifugal forces in spate, as a result of long minorities or senilities.

Secondly, no king between Edward IV in the 1470s and Charles II in the 1670s had a younger brother. Imagine the problems Henry VII's eldest son Arthur would have had if he had lived to be king with the wilful Henry VIII as his younger brother and as Duke of York? Or James VI's puritan elder son would have had with Charles I as a crypto-Catholic Duke of York? And just look at what happened (especially in and after 1678) when Charles II *did* have a younger brother!

Thirdly, staggeringly seven of the 13 rulers from Henry VII to George had no legitimate issue to succeed them. The 13 monarchs were survived by only 20 legitimate children, six of them born to Charles I and Henrietta-Maria (four of whom, by the way, died as Catholics). Thus 12 monarchs across the period 1485–1727 were survived by only 14 children.

Fourthly, one striking fact is that of these 13 monarchs, only one – James VI and I – lived to see any grandchildren born, and only one monarch between 1485 and 1720 had more than one son alive at the time of his/her death (Charles I). Of the 13, only four were succeeded by their children. Where would monarchical republicanism have been without such chronic dynastic insecurity?

Fifthly no ruler between 1485 and 1660 left a bastard to confuse the succession. When Henry VIII got into marital difficulties in the 1520s and began to panic about the succession, he transformed the education of his bastard son by Elizabeth Blount, Henry Fitzroy, Duke of Richmond (1519–1536) into that of an heir to the throne.[66] So, if Richmond had not died in 1536, what would Henry have done in his Acts of Succession? And during the succession crisis of the 1670s, when Charles II had no legitimate issue and his heir presumptive was his Catholic brother, James Duke of York (himself son-less until 1688), there was a party willing to consider Charles II's senior bastard, James Duke of Monmouth (1649–1685).

---

[65] Henry VIII came to throne just before his eighteenth birthday, but there was no regency or minority.

[66] This is thoroughly explored in Aysha Pollnitz, *Princely Education in Early Modern England* (Cambridge, 2015) Chapter 3.

Sixthly, only one ruler, James VI and I, was succeeded by an adult male son. That might seem ironic, since it was the first really secure succession since 1399, and it ended in civil war and regicide. Of course, that is *why* it ended in civil war and regicide! If Charles I had had a brother or a grown-up son or even a cousin who was an over-mighty subject – a Condé figure – there would almost certainly been a campaign to depose and replace Charles, an abolition of Charles I and not of monarchy itself.[67]

Seventhly, there was no inbreeding in the English royal house. The 13 English monarchs of the period contracted 16 marriages. Two never married and one married six times. Only one of the marriages (William of Orange to Mary II) was a marriage within the laws of consanguinity of the Reformation Churches, a marriage of first cousins, and it was childless. From the death of Henry VIII to the Glorious Revolution, the age of confessional wars, every spouse of a monarch regnant died a Roman Catholic.[68]

All this leaves open that series of counterfactuals discussed above, to which we might add one or two that are bit freer: what if the Scots had honoured the treaty of Greenwich and delivered the infant Mary Queen of Scots to be educated in England and eventually married to the young Edward VI, making Scotland a dependent kingdom of England? Or what if Henry Prince of Wales had not succumbed to smallpox in 1612? He was a prince likely to have been a friend to puritans (unlike his brother Charles) and also one all too likely to plunge himself headlong into the Thirty Years' War as a British Gustavus Adolphus (causing huge [unsupportable?] strains on the British fisc). Or what if James II had died in 1688, leaving his kingdoms to a Catholic prince and regency and hence, in the half century after 1689, state formation in Britain and Ireland had taken place in the context of internal wars fuelled by international arms and supplies between the legitimate heirs of a British Stuart royal house that was Catholic and the much more remote claims of a Protestant German ducal dynasty, descended from the daughter of James VI and I? Or what if Henry VIII had died at any point before 1534; or if the Duke of Northumberland, watching the gravely ill teenage Edward VI and desperate to prevent the accession of the Catholic Mary and to promote

---

[67] In a lecture c.1990, never published, Conrad Russell argued that Charles I took with him when he went to the House of Commons in January 1642 to arrest five MPs for treason the Earl of Hertford and Prince Charles-Lewis of the Palatinate. Hertford had a remote claim to the throne through his grandmother and great-great grandmother, the younger daughter of Henry VII; Charles-Lewis was the eldest son of his sister Elizabeth, Electress of the Palatinate and Winter Queen of Bohemia. Russell argued Charles wished to implicate them since he saw a remote possibility that they might seek his thrones.

[68] I.e. King Philip and Queens Anne of Denmark, Henrietta Maria, Catherine of Braganza and Mary of Modena. In addition, James II's first wife, Anne Hyde, converted to Catholicism before James did.

the cause of the Protestant Grey sisters, had had time to follow up on his offer to Henri II to cede the Kingdom of Ireland to France in return for military support for his plans?[69] Or what if the Scots had accepted the offer of the Commonwealth of England and Ireland to become once more, as before 1603, a freestanding monarchy[70] – just as Portugal had in ceding from 'Spain' a decade earlier? There were powerful forces driving the Tudors and Stuarts to create a single state-system throughout the archipelago, of which dynastic insecurity (and the lack of the kind of adamantine principle of succession that helped France through its crises in the late sixteenth century)[71] was one. The Reformation and the drive for a single confessional identity throughout the monarch's dominions was another such force, but the Achilles' heel of the Tudor/Stewart *monarchia* was the unassimilable Catholic majority in Ireland. Catholics still made up more than 75 per cent of the population in 1720, even after 150 years of Protestant settlement, although by then they owned less than 10 per cent of the land.

All that said, the English monarchy was in constant chronic or acute distress from 1399 to 1714, with the single exception of 1631–1641. And how does this affect state formation?

We have seen how it affects intellectual history. There is a huge literature on monarchical republicanism[72] in England, which sees it as a response to the pervasiveness of Christian Humanism in the sixteenth century and neo-classicism in the seventeenth century, but most authors have missed an obvious point: that there were chronic dynastic crises which were exacerbated by a series of acute crises over the succession, and the greatest of all fears among the elites – a collapse into anarchy – made working politicians and their advisers seek solutions. Too much political thought obsesses about threats of royal tyranny and fails to recognise that this was more than balanced by greater fears of the anarchy that resistance to tyranny could produce. There was no great

---

[69] Morrill, *Uneasy Lies the Head*, p. 13, citing *Calendar of State Papers Domestic of the reigns of Edward VI and Mary*, ed. Robert Lemon (1856), p. 45.

[70] Morrill, 'The English Revolution', pp. 555–557.

[71] One of the many lessons of the essay in this volume by James Collins is that France had had its dynastic time of troubles in the fourteenth century and had emerged with that very adamantine commitment to the Salic law of succession via a pure male line. But note also his analysis of the extreme fragility of the French royal line in the early 1590s (what if the 1594 assassination attempt had succeeded, he asks) and he goes on to point out that neither son of Henri IV fathered a male child until 1638). See Chapter 4, pp. 40–43.

[72] J. McDiarmid (ed.), *The Monarchical Republic of Early Modern England: Essays in Response to Patrick Collinson* (Aldershot, 2007) brings this debate up to date. It was begun by Patrick Collinson, 'The Monarchical Republic of Elizabeth I', *Bulletin of the John Rylands Library* 69:2 (1987), pp. 394–424. But n.b. Collins' discussion of a discourse of 'a monarchical commonwealth' in late medieval France, see Collins, Chapter 4, pp. 101–116.

breakthrough in 1584 or 1679.[73] The same solutions were found then as were found in 1461 or 1543.[74] And it was pragmatism, not principle, which made the accession of Elizabeth I in 1558 (positive law [her father's will and Acts of Succession] trumping natural law)[75] compatible with the accession of James I in 1603 (natural law trumping positive law [that same will and series of Acts]).[76] No wonder James I spoke so powerfully about divine right – he stressed the divine right to *be* king rather than what he could *do* as king. In 1688 there was a fudge – had James abdicated, been deposed or abandoned his throne? Parliament regulated the succession, as it had in 1461 and 1543 and as it had attempted to do in 1679, but in doing so, it then strove to restore the natural law of succession in the heir general (i.e. in the closest male or female by blood and then via the nearest male, followed by female by blood) which had been violated in more half the successions since 1066 – Anne and any children of hers or descendants of those children would succeed ahead of the children by any second marriage William III might contract following the death of Mary.[77] The supreme irony is that finally in 1701, the British succession became elective, in the gift of Parliament, and, setting aside the claims of 48 Catholics, was offered to the House of Hanover. At that moment the Crown became elective. Since then it has remained absolutely in the line of succession as laid down by the Anglo-Norman law of inheritance.

This state system – which was never a state and could have been reshaped into a number of different shapes, with Scotland and/or Ireland within a French *imperium*; a Jacobite Ireland under French, or Spanish or indeed Swedish protection alongside a Hanoverian Britain; or even quite separate Anglo-Irish and Scottish monarchies – is not, in my view, helpfully called a multiple or composite monarchy or even, until the eighteenth century, a federal or confederal monarchy. There is a clear implication of permanence and solidity about these terms. All are anachronistic, of course, and none existed in the seventeenth century. There was an English *imperium*, there was a British *monarchia*, but there was not

---

[73] P. Collinson, 'The Elizabethan Exclusion Crisis and the Elizabethan Polity', *Proceedings of the British Academy*, 84 (1994), pp. 51–92.

[74] M. Levine, *Tudor Dynastic Problems 1461–1570* (London, 1973), pp. 17–22, 71–72, 127–131 and 161–165.

[75] Ibid., pp. 66–67, 74–80 and 167–173. Elizabeth was bastardised by Henry but succeeded by virtue of his 3rd Succession Act 1543 and his final will and testament.

[76] That same succession Act and will excluded the Scottish line from the throne and the Act had never been repealed and nothing in Elizabeth's will superseded Henry's. All these issues will be transformed by Susan Doran and Paulina Kewes (eds), *Doubtful and Dangerous: The Question of Succession in Late Elizabethan England* (Manchester, 2014).

[77] John Morrill, *The Nature of the English Revolution* (Abingdon, 1994), pp. 430–432.

a British state. Both *imperium* and *monarchia* imply a heterogeneous rather than a homogenous political entity, and if we need an anachronistic modern term to convey the instability of the way these entities form and de-form, then I would continue to favour 'dynastic agglomerate'. Early modern state formation is not part of the making of the modern world. It is a product of dynastic calculation and dynastic chance. It is a working out of the Reformation, not an anticipation of the Enlightenment.

3   Dynastic Monarchy and the Consolidation of Aristocracy during Europe's Long Seventeenth Century

Hamish Scott

Introduction: The 'Crisis' Debate and the Nature of Monarchy

This past generation has seen a welcome revival of interest in the nature of early modern polities, particularly in Anglophone scholarship, and with it a recognition of the clear limitations upon institutional authority even on the eve of the French Revolution.[1] Historians have come to recognise that monarchical states were far from unitary, instead consisting of a series of subordinate kingdoms, provinces and other dependent territories. Rulers stood in quite separate and often different relationships to each of these areas, exercising authority through distinct titles and governing through separate institutions and even in diverse ways. The territories and especially their influential elites appreciated the complex historical and legal bonds which bound them to their monarch, and they skilfully exploited the opportunities these bonds provided to strengthen and even enhance their own power.[2] All retained and defended their traditional political culture and sense of identity, sometimes expressed in a distinctive language, together with their own law code, separate administration, (in many cases) territorial assembly, and ruling elite, which dominated the territory's government and political and social life. Individual provinces and kingdoms defended their own *patria*, and periodically mounted

[1] I am grateful to Robert von Friedeburg and Thomas Munck, who both read a draft of this chapter and made valuable suggestions for its improvement. A much earlier version was given as a seminar paper at the German Historical Institute in London, and subsequently published as '"Acts of Time and Power": The Consolidation of Aristocracy in Seventeenth-Century Europe, c.1580–1720', *German Historical Institute London: Bulletin* 30 (2008), 3–37. I am indebted to its Director, Professor Andreas Gestrich, for permission to re-publish parts of that essay here and for the invitation to address the seminar, which was its origin. Much of the material for this article was collected during my tenure as a Leverhulme Major Research Fellow, and I thank the Trust for its support.
[2] A process examined, for France, by William Beik in an important review article, 'The Absolutism of Louis XIV as Social Collaboration', *Past and Present* 188 (2005), pp. 195–224.

resistance – often notably effective – against the centralising intentions of dynastic monarchy throughout the early modern period. This phenomenon was a legacy of previous historical developments and has variously been labelled 'composite state' (H. G. Koenigsberger), 'composite monarchy' (J. H. Elliott), 'multiple kingdoms' (Conrad Russell), 'conglomerate state' (Harald Gustafsson) and, most recently, 'dynastic agglomerate' (John Morrill).[3]

Concern with the composite nature of all early modern polities grew out of one of the most celebrated debates in the study of early modern history, that surrounding the 'General Crisis of the Seventeenth Century', variously portrayed as the product of the incessant fiscal demands of monarchical governments almost permanently at war, the result of worldwide climatic change and the birth pangs of capitalism.[4] This has not been fully appreciated, though one of the participants in that debate, Sir John H. Elliott, has recently drawn attention to this exact link, writing that his 'insight into the importance of the patria ... [which] became the rallying-point for resistance to the

---

[3] H. G. Koenigsberger, '*Dominium Regale or Dominium Politicum et Regale*: Monarchies and Parliaments in Early Modern Europe' [1975], reprinted in *Politicians and Virtuosi: Essays in Early Modern History* (London, 1986), pp. 1–25, esp. pp. 12ff.; J. H. Elliott, 'A Europe of Composite Monarchies', *Past and Present* 137 (1992), pp. 48–71; Conrad Russell, 'Composite Monarchies in Early Modern Europe: The British and Irish Example', in Alexander Grant and Keith Stringer (eds.), *Uniting the Kingdom? The Making of British History* (London, 1995), pp. 133–146; the articles on 'Multiple Kingdoms' in *Transactions of the Royal Historical Society 6th series*, vol. 2 (1992), pp. 153–94; Harald Gustafsson, 'Conglomerates or Unitary States? Integration Processes in Early Modern Denmark-Norway and Sweden', in Thomas Fröschl (ed.), *Föderationsmodelle und Unionsstrukturen: Über Staatenverbindungen in der frühen Neuzeit von 15. zum 18. Jahrhundert* (Vienna and Munich, 1994), pp. 45–62; Harald Gustafsson, 'The Conglomerate State: A Reflection on State Formation in Early Modern Europe', *Scandinavian Journal of History* 23 (1998), pp. 189–213; John Morrill, '*Uneasy Lies the Head that Wears a Crown*': Dynastic Crises in Tudor and Stewart Britain, 1504–1746 ('The Stenton Lecture, 2003'; Reading, 2005), esp. pp. 10–11. M. Perceval-Maxwell, 'Ireland and the Monarchy in the Early Stuart Multiple Kingdom', *Historical Journal* 34 (1991), pp. 279–295, is a valuable discussion of the legal, constitutional and practical complexities of a 'composite monarchy', while there is much of interest on this theme in Mark Greengrass (ed.), *Conquest and Coalescence: The Shaping of the State in Early Modern Europe* (London, 1991); and the more recent collection edited by Jon Arrieta and John H. Elliott, *Forms of Union: The British and Spanish Monarchies in the Seventeenth and Eighteenth Centuries* (Donostia, 2009).

[4] For the debate, which raged between the 1950s and the 1970s, see the essays conveniently reprinted in T. S. Aston (ed.), *Crisis in Europe 1560–1660* (London, 1965), and Geoffrey Parker and Lesley M. Smith (eds.), *The General Crisis of the Seventeenth Century* (London, 1978; 2nd expanded ed., London, 1997), together with two recent retrospectives in special issues of journals: *American Historical Review* 113:iv (2008), pp. 1029–1099; and *Journal of Interdisciplinary History* 40 (2009), pp. 145–303. A major contribution renewing the debate has now appeared: Geoffrey Parker, *Global Crisis: War, Climate Change and Catastrophe in the Seventeenth Century* (New Haven, CT, 2013).

demands of central governments bent on introducing fiscal, administrative and constitutional change was [his] most useful contribution to
the general crisis debate'. It focused attention, he continued, on 'the
intentions of the state and resistance to the state', and so encouraged
historians to explore the structure and nature of Europe's dynastic
monarchies.[5]

This is an important reminder that the debate over the 'General Crisis',
while often viewed as inconclusive, had an important and positive impact
on the study of early modern Europe that can all too easily be
overlooked.[6] Above all, it focused attention on the chronological seventeenth century, often seen as the poor relation of early modern history
since it seemingly lacked a unifying central development such as the
Renaissance or the Reformation, the Enlightenment or the French
Revolution, which commanded attention and around which scholarship
could coalesce.[7] The notion of the 'General Crisis' appeared for a time to
offer a master narrative hitherto lacking. The debate also drew attention
to the important transition during the century's middle third, which
prepared the way for the political stability and, before long, economic
expansion that were to characterise Europe in the hundred years before
the French Revolution of 1789.[8]

Both the concern with 'composite monarchy' and the debate over the
general crisis have contributed to the growing scholarly interest in the
traditional elite, the military nobility, which was in any case beginning to
revive. A recognition of the limitations upon institutional bonds within
monarchical polities and of the diversity which these contained focused
attention upon the leading families, who were credited with a central role
in the creation of the stability everywhere evident by the 1680s and

---

[5] J. H. Elliott, 'The General Crisis in Retrospect: A Debate without End', in
Philip Benedict and Myron P. Gutmann (eds.), *Early Modern Europe: From Crisis to
Stability* (Newark, NJ, 2005), pp. 31–51, at p. 37; see also Elliott's 'Revolution and
Continuity in Early Modern Europe', initially published in *Past and Present* 62 (1969),
pp. 35–56, and reprinted in Parker and Smith (eds.), *The General Crisis of the Seventeenth
Century*, pp. 110–133, at pp. 121ff., and his recent *History in the Making* (New Haven,
CT, 2012), Chapter 2 *passim*.

[6] An astute historiographical guide is provided by Jonathan Dewald, 'Crisis, Chronology,
and the Shape of European Social History', *American Historical Review* 113:iv (2008), pp.
1031–1052; see also the discussion in Francesco Benigno, *Mirrors of Revolution: Conflict
and Political Identity in Early Modern Europe* (1999; English translation, Turnhout, 2010),
pp. 87–136.

[7] The Scientific Revolution of the seventeenth century was the most obvious contender
for this role, but when the 'General Crisis' debate flourished, the history of science
occupied a less central place within historical scholarship than it would subsequently
assume.

[8] An argument most effectively advanced in an important book by Theodore K. Rabb,
The Struggle for Stability in Early Modern Europe (New York, 1975).

1690s.[9] This present chapter re-examines the position of Europe's nobilities during the long seventeenth century. It points to an important but often neglected consolidation of the status and authority of the prominent lineages, which was both a product of and a contribution to growing monarchical stability, and does so from the perspective of 'composite monarchies' or 'dynastic agglomerates'.

One particular value of Professor Morrill's proposed term, is that it once again focuses attention on the contingent, on the importance of short-term events and political developments for Europe's historical evolution, in addition to the structures, economic trends and longer-term developments which have recently received more prominence.[10] In the significant consolidation of noble power which took place during these decades, the actions of rulers and the opportunities created by political upheavals were to be important and, at times, decisive. Yet an exclusively 'top down' perspective on state formation must be avoided.[11] Provincial elites saw potential gains as well as undoubted challenges in the new ambitions of centralising monarchical regimes. They welcomed the enhanced prospects of careers and material gain, together with the increased political and social stability which rulers promised and sometimes achieved. They also made gains, moreover, within their own locality. The nobility secured greater control over the key resource, that of peasant labour, as rulers facilitated formal restrictions on peasant mobility and an extension of seigneurial privileges, and tacitly acknowledged, over much of Europe, their own inability to intervene on noble estates. This authority was further strengthened by the social elite's key role in the local administration of justice and, in parts of Europe, in military recruitment too. There came to be real synergy and an unexpected degree of overlap between the aims of rulers and their elites which was fundamental

---

[9] Elliott, 'A Europe of Composite Monarchies', p. 57 and *passim*; Rabb, *Struggle for Stability*, pp. 20, 118–119 and *passim*; H. G. Koenigsberger, 'The Crisis of the Seventeenth Century: A Farewell?', in *Politicians and Virtuosi*, pp. 149–168, at pp. 164ff. The growing strength of the nobility and its importance had earlier been emphasised in a wide-ranging and acute survey by Ivo Schöffer, 'Did Holland's Golden Age Coincide with a Period of Crisis?', originally published in *Acta Historiae Neerlandica* 1(1966), pp. 82–107, and reprinted in Parker and Smith (eds.), *The General Crisis of the Seventeenth Century*, pp. 83–109, at pp. 100ff. William Beik, *Absolutism and Society in Seventeenth-Century France: State Power and Provincial Aristocracy in Languedoc* (Cambridge, 1985), is a model study of the local elite's role in the achievement of stability in the southern French province of Languedoc, while Steven G. Ellis, 'Tudor State Formation and the Shaping of the British Isles', in Steven G. Ellis and Sarah Barber (eds.), *Conquest and Union: Fashioning a British State, 1485–1725* (London, 1995), pp. 40–63, is a parallel demonstration of how the Tudor monarchy depended upon local nobles in the border regions both within Britain itself and in Ireland.

[10] Morrill, *'Uneasy Lies the Head That Wears a Crown'*, p. 11.

[11] See the comments of Mark Greengrass, *Conquest and Coalescence*, p. 7.

both for the extension of monarchical authority at this period and for the growing social power of the nobility itself.[12]

Consolidation and Differentiation within the Social Elite

This emphasis upon a seventeenth-century consolidation of the social elite incorporates a second and quite fundamental shift in historical scholarship during this past generation. Until the 1970s and even 1980s, historians of early modern Europe viewed the nobility as a group which was declining socially, economically and politically, and had even experienced a 'crisis' of its own. Here the influence of Lawrence Stone's *The Crisis of the Aristocracy, 1558–1641*, a study of England's peerage and its supposed decline before the outbreak of the English Civil War, was quite central.[13] First published in 1965, it launched the notion of a 'Crisis of the Early Modern Nobility', which flourished particularly during the 1970s. This too was encouraged by and perhaps rooted in the debate over the 'General Crisis'. Building on Stone's book and embracing his central metaphor, the French historian François Billaçois proclaimed a full-blown 'crisis of the European nobility' between 1550 and 1650 in 1976, by which time it had already been applied to Denmark, Castile, Sicily, France and Muscovy; it would subsequently be extended to Bohemia and may have been canvassed even more widely.[14]

This 'crisis' incorporated established assumptions about the nobility's early modern decline. Politically it was believed to be losing out to the absolutist state. The strengthening of monarchical authority was supposed to have been achieved largely at the expense of the traditional elite. The new, supposedly absolutist regimes, headed by Louis XIV's personal government (1661–1715) in France, were believed to rest upon the triumph of monarchy, as leading noblemen lost their traditional influence and even status, exemplified by the great open prison of Versailles where, on one fashionable interpretation, they were detained

---

[12] Nicholas Henshall, *The Zenith of European Monarchy and Its Elites: The Politics of Culture, 1650–1750* (Basingstoke, 2010), explores the cultural dimension of this process.

[13] (Oxford, 1965). For its impact, see Hamish Scott, 'The European Nobility and Its Contested Historiographies, c.1950–1980', in Matthew P. Romaniello and Charles Lipp (eds.), *Contested Spaces of Nobility in Early Modern Europe* (Farnham, 2011), pp. 11–39.

[14] 'La crise de la noblesse européenne (1550–1650)', *Revue d'histoire moderne et contemporaine* 23 (1976), pp. 258–277; four years earlier, Henry Kamen had argued in very similar if more nuanced vein: *The Iron Century: Social Change in Europe, 1550–1660* (London, 1971), pp. 129–165. An immediate and influential echo of Stone's book was E. Ladewig Petersen, *The Crisis of the Danish Nobility, 1580–1660* (Odense, 1967).

at the king's pleasure.[15] The nobility's principal function – that of 'warrior-elite' – was eroded by near-simultaneous developments in land warfare: primarily the emergence of standing armies, the greatly enhanced role of infantry and the adoption of gunpowder weapons, which along with the new-style fortifications were the central elements in what has been labelled the 'Military Revolution'. Its very existence appeared to be imperilled by the loss of its traditional role, as the mounted cavalry suffered eclipse on the battlefield. These changes were also integral to the second strand in the 'noble crisis': an ideological challenge to its traditional pre-eminence, which was rooted in Renaissance ideas of honour and virtue as the main source of social esteem, rather than the claims of birth and ancestry advanced by noble propagandists, at exactly the point at which the nobility's established claim to be the 'men on horseback' and so the dominant social group was itself becoming more and more difficult to sustain.

Finally and perhaps most importantly, the elite was believed to have experienced severe economic problems, which weakened it fatally. The idea of an economic 'crisis' of the early Stuart peerage had been central to Stone's arguments and one upon which his numerous critics focused, in the process delivering some fatal blows to his overarching thesis. In the wider European context it has probably stood up rather better than the ideological or political strands, though whether these undoubted economic problems affected the entire nobility or merit the description 'crisis' is far less certain. These difficulties resulted from two linked developments. The sixteenth-century Price Revolution had created problems for individuals and families whose income, above all rents from long-term leases, could not keep up with the rapidly rising prices. When the period of expansion ended in the decades around 1600 (and the chronology has been hotly contested and clearly varied not merely from country to country but from region to region), many nobles found it difficult to keep their heads above water during a phase of recession and contraction, with falling prices, unstable markets and a general slowdown in the economy. This was particularly true of families in the middle and lower ranks of the nobility who lacked the direct access to the monarchical court and its opportunities and patronage which the leading families enjoyed. This advanced the process of differentiation within the elite, which was to be such a feature of the period.

---

[15] The argument is most famously set out in Norbert Elias, *The Court Society* (1969; English trans.; Oxford, 1983); its shortcomings are made clear by Jeroen Duindam, *Myths of Power: Norbert Elias and the Early Modern European Court* (Amsterdam, 1994).

Though the impact of such economic difficulties was greatest upon the lesser nobility, some better-off lineages also experienced real problems. One striking example was the Spanish Count of Benavente, whose income from his estates fell by one-fifth in only five years (1638–1643), at the outset of the midcentury economic collapse.[16] Expenditure was simultaneously being forced up by 'conspicuous consumption', as the elite were expected to build expensive country residences and town palaces, and generally to bear the costs of a more opulent lifestyle which centred on the burgeoning courts now maintained by rulers. The spiralling level of debt confronting many families appeared the most obvious evidence of these economic difficulties. Yet while individual lineages undoubtedly experienced real financial problems, such borrowing should not be viewed as evidence of more general problems, much less decline, while the argument for a generalised economic 'crisis', like the wider thesis, remains unproven. Stone himself, in a book published two decades later, retreated from many of his own earlier arguments and instead emphasised the peerage's resilience together with the continuation and consolidation of its dominance.[17]

With hindsight each of these challenges can be recognised to have been a far less serious threat to the wider nobility than was once believed. While individual families experienced real difficulties, and some declined as a result, the elite as a whole managed to ride out the contraction of the European economy. Historians of the nobility are now much more cautious about using aristocratic debts – which had featured prominently in Stone's analysis – as evidence of difficulties. Instead they now recognise that such borrowing was frequently a symptom of economic strength, not weakness, and that it could be a way of surmounting short-term problems.

In a similar way, it is now clear that the military changes did not reduce the nobility's role so much as change it fundamentally. The social elite was actually re-militarised during the seventeenth and eighteenth centuries, as it came to provide the officer *corps* in Europe's

---

[16] I. A. A. Thompson, 'The Nobility in Spain, 1600–1800', in H. M. Scott (ed.), *The European Nobilities in the Seventeenth and Eighteenth Centuries* (2 vols.; 1995; 2nd ed., Basingstoke, 2007), i.225; see C. J. Jago, 'The "Crisis of the Aristocracy" in Seventeenth-Century Castile', *Past and Present* 84 (1979), pp. 60–90, and Bartolomé Yun Casalilla, 'The Castilian Aristocracy in the Seventeenth Century: Crisis, Refeudalisation, or Political Offensive?', in I. A. A. Thompson and Bartolomé Yun Casalilla (eds.), *The Castilian Crisis of the Seventeenth Century: New Perspectives on the Economic and Social History of Seventeenth-Century Spain* (Cambridge, 1994), pp. 277–300, for other examples of leading Spanish noble families which experienced economic difficulties at this period.

[17] Lawrence Stone with Jeanne C. Fawtier Stone, *An Open Elite? England 1540–1880* (Oxford, 1984).

enlarged armies.[18] The spectacular expansion of the French armed forces
has received most attention from historians, but it had its parallels in the
scarcely less rapid growth of the military forces maintained by
Brandenburg-Prussia, Denmark, Russia and Sweden.[19] Everywhere,
the military hierarchy came to resemble the hierarchy within the nobility.
The middle and lesser nobilities secured colonelcies and captaincies,
while members of leading families dominated the higher ranks of
Europe's armies. There were important differences from earlier epochs:
the level of training and expertise required was greater, as was the commitment of time involved, while nobles served not as a matter of right but
because of the qualities which they could bring to the service of the
monarchical state. But overall the nobility's role was actually strengthened by the 'Military Revolution', as it became the indispensable backbone of the enlarged armies created during this period, and this would
continue until the First World War.[20] This was especially important for
large numbers of poorer provincial noblemen, who secured status, prestige and careers along with some income, which enabled families to
retrieve their economic fortunes, which had been damaged by the sixteenth-century rise in prices.

Though it is clear that increasing numbers of noblemen were serving in
royal armies, providing statistical evidence is much more difficult. One of
the few detailed investigations is Jean-Marie Constant's study of the
Beauce, an area lying to the south and west of Paris, where the number
of noble families sending at least one son into the army almost doubled in
the course of the sixteenth and seventeenth centuries, rising from 97 to
186. During the same period, the percentage of noblemen undertaking
a military career rose between three- and fourfold: from 4.45 per cent
(1500–1560) to 5.98 per cent (1560–1600), 8.78 per cent (1600–1660)
and finally 16.10 per cent (1660–1700: the period of greatest growth in
the size of the French royal army).[21] Overall the suggestion that by
the second half of Louis XIV's reign approaching half of all French
noblemen may have been undertaking military service may not be too

[18] See Gunner Lind in Chapter 10 in this volume for a striking national example of this
trend.
[19] For the Hohenzollern case, see Peter-Michael Hahn, 'Aristokratisierung und
Professionalisierung: Der Aufstieg der Obristen zu einer militärischen und höfischen
Élite in Brandenburg-Preussen von 1650–1725', Forschungen zur Brandenburgischen und
Preussischen Geschichte N.F. 1 (1991), pp. 161–208
[20] Christopher Storrs and H. M. Scott, 'The Military Revolution and the European
Nobility, c.1600–1800', War in History 3 (1996), pp. 1–41; reprinted in Jeremy Black
(ed.), Warfare in Europe 1650–1792 (Aldershot, 2005), pp. 3–43.
[21] J.-M. Constant, Nobles et paysans en Beauce aux XVIe et XVIIe siècles (Lille, 1981),
Table 51, p. 159 bis, p. 160 and Chapter 8 passim.

wide of the mark. In a broader sense, absolute monarchy in Europe is now generally recognised to have rested not on confrontation but on coopera- tion with the social elite: in the expanded armies, as we have seen, in both central and local government, and in more specialised areas such as the enlarged diplomatic services which rulers were now maintaining and which were overwhelmingly staffed by aristocrats from the end of the seventeenth century onwards.[22]

The 'crisis' theory was important in directing attention to nobility as a topic and in encouraging detailed research, which began to be published during the second half of the 1970s. This quickly revealed the 'crisis' metaphor to be simplistic in the extreme, and replaced it with an emphasis on resilience and adaptability to changing circumstances, which con- tinues until the present time. The key word to describe the seventeenth- century nobility became and remains not 'crisis' but 'consolidation'. What is now impressing its historians – and the study of the social elite is extremely fashionable, in all countries and many languages – is the resilience, the adaptability, the sheer continuity of its social and political power in modern European history.[23] Its obituary, so confidently written 30 years ago, is recognised to have been premature, for the seventeenth as for the eighteenth and even the nineteenth centuries.

One group which clearly had declined during the early modern centu- ries, was the numerically preponderant lesser nobility, some of whose members had abandoned the unequal struggle to retain their privileged status. Their fate focuses attention upon the internal structure of the Second Estate, which was much more stratified and differentiated than often realised. There was a fundamental and growing distinction between 'nobility' and 'aristocracy', which became increasingly evident during the seventeenth century but can too easily be overlooked by historians. 'Nobility' was a privileged legal status enjoyed by a small secular elite in return for the services, above all military, which it provided for rulers. It had solidified across much of Western and Southern Europe

---

[22] Lucien Bély, *Espions et ambassadeurs au temps de Louis XIV* (Paris, 1990), especially Part Two, demonstrates this growing dominance from the later seventeenth century onwards; see more generally, Hamish Scott, 'Diplomatic Culture in Old Regime Europe', in Hamish Scott and Brendan Simms (eds.), *Cultures of Power in Europe during the Long Eighteenth Century* (Cambridge, 2007), pp. 58–85, especially pp. 70ff.

[23] The best introductions to the early modern nobility are the two overlapping syntheses by Ronald G. Asch, *Nobilities in Transition 1550–1700: Courtiers and Rebels in Britain and Europe* (London, 2003) and *Europäischer Adel in der Frühen Neuzeit* (Cologne, 2008); while H. M. Scott (ed.), *The European Nobilities in the Seventeenth and Eighteenth Centuries* (2 vols.; 1995; 2nd ed., Basingstoke, 2007), contains national surveys and a full and up-to-date bibliography of the subject. In what follows, I have not provided anything like full references to the abundant secondary literature on which the arguments of this article rest.

between the thirteenth and fifteenth centuries, and became a central component of aristocracy. In several European languages, the term 'nobility', meaning both a quality possessed by an individual of high status and a description of the collective body of nobles, came into use during the Later Middle Ages: this was the case with *noblesse* in French and *Adel* in German.

Noble status was characterised primarily by the possession of hereditary privileges, which were both social and legal in nature. The Second Estate (as it was styled) derived from the celebrated, if largely theoretical, medieval tripartite division of society into those who prayed, the First Estate (*oratores*), those who provided defence and military muscle (*defensores* or *bellatores*), and those who worked (that is to say everyone else who made up the Third Estate, the *laboratores*) to provide for the first two estates in their more important functions. Such social divisions were always more imagined than real, but the idea of a trifunctional division of society was always an important myth, particularly for nobles, who long regarded themselves as the fighting caste, the men on horseback, a role which had been the principal origin of their privileged status and remained their most important role within Europe's dynastic monarchies.

By contrast the term 'aristocracy' denoted the leading families within the nobility, lineages which were not quite royalty but were often related to the ruling dynasty by ties of blood and marriage. These aristocratic houses, which had become more and more numerous and prominent since the Later Middle Ages, possessed enhanced social status, a monopoly of the higher titles of nobility, considerable social and political power, and economic resources primarily in the form of land, and so constituted a small but influential elite within the wider nobility. All aristocrats were noble, but only a tiny minority of nobles were aristocrats. Though social differentiation was accelerated at certain periods by the disappearance of large numbers of poorer families who were unable to maintain their noble status, it was primarily developments within prominent lineages which produced a more stratified and hierarchical Second Estate.

There was a similar but rather later linguistic change than had been the case with 'nobility'. Traditionally the term 'aristocracy' designated 'rule by the best', a usage which went back to Ancient Greece and long remained important within political theory. It continued to be employed in this sense, designating a particular form of government, into the early modern period and even beyond. But after 1600, the meaning of 'aristocracy' began to correspond to the modern usage: a description of the leading families comprising the very top layer of the nobility. It was a relatively easy transition for the term, which described the possession of political authority by an elite group, to be applied to that group itself, as it increasingly was during the seventeenth century. In Castilian Spanish, in Italian and in English the word 'aristocracy' can be found during the earlier decades of the century to have described the noble elite, while the third edition of the English polymath John Selden's celebrated *Titles of Honour* also employed the noun in this sense.[24] The term 'aristocrat', however, was far from ubiquitous as a description of what was a widespread social evolution: in seventeenth-century France the magnates were known collectively as '*les grands*', a term which had first been used in the previous century, while in Russia, during the first half of the following century, contemporaries designated the noble elite which had become consolidated by the term '*znatnye*', meaning 'distinguished', or 'known' in the sense of celebrated.[25]

The social construction of this elite had begun during the Later Middle Ages, when first in England; then in the Iberian Peninsula, particularly the dominant Kingdom of Castile; and finally in the lands ruled over by the Kings of France and their great rivals the Dukes of Burgundy, leading families gained in status and in social, economic and political power, coming to form something approaching an 'aristocracy'. Elsewhere in Europe many of the same developments took place during the long seventeenth century, leading to a more complete stratification of the nobility in Central, Northern and Eastern Europe, at a period when earlier changes were being completed and redirected in the countries along the western periphery.

Three further preliminary points must be made about the internal structure of the early modern nobility. In contrast to twentieth- and twenty-first-century society, and even in the nineteenth century to some extent, wealth followed status and not the other way round. Many high status aristocrats would either inherit wealth or acquire it, primarily from

---

[24] Martín Alonso, *Enciclopedia del Idioma: Diccionario histórico y moderno de la lengua española (siglos XII al XX)* (3 vols.; Madrid, 1947), i.474; Carlo Battisti and Giovanni Alessio (eds.), *Dizionario Etimologico Italiano* (5 vols.; Florence, 1950–1957), i.288; Manlio Cortelazzo and Paolo Zolli (eds.), *Dizionario etimologico della lingua italiana* (5 vols.; Bologna, 1979–1988), i.72; *The Oxford English Dictionary* ed. J. A. Simpson and E. S. C. Weiner (2nd ed., 20 vols.; Oxford, 1989), i.630; John Selden, *Titles of Honour* (1614; 3rd ed.; London, 1672), p. 437.

[25] Alain Rey (ed.), *Dictionnaire historique de la langue française* (2 vols.; Paris, 1992), i.910; cf. ibid., i.110 on the way in which 'aristocracy', and 'aristocrat' (which came to mean both the nobility and a single nobleman) came into widespread use only in the final years of the eighteenth century and were linked to the French Revolution. See Thomas E. Kaiser, 'Nobles into Aristocrats, or How an Order Became a Conspiracy', in Jay M. Smith (ed.), *The French Nobility in the Eighteenth Century: Reassessments and New Approaches* (University Park, PA, 2006), pp. 189–224; Brenda Meehan-Waters, 'The Russian Aristocracy and the Reforms of Peter the Great', *Canadian-American Slavic Studies* 8 (1974), pp. 288–304, at p. 289.

their ruler, sometimes from other nobles through marriage or succession. Wealth alone did not create the kind of status possessed by prominent individuals and leading families: it was perfectly possible, if uncommon, to be an impoverished aristocrat. In contrast to the later modern era, social status still rested upon esteem, upon the value and therefore the respect and approbation which other members of society felt towards an individual's function and role, and not in the mere possession of wealth. Seventeenth-century Europe was a deeply traditional society, despite the undoubted progress of national and international trade and of manufacturing, a world within which deference and traditional values still dominated. Foremost among such attitudes was respect for social superiors and for the aristocracy most of all.

This society differed from that of later modern Europe in a second way. The individual was always less important than the wider social group of which he or she formed part. The key analytical units were families, lineages and houses, which were enduring, unlike the human beings they contained, who were transient. Noblewomen, and even many noblemen, lacked much in the way of what would now be called 'agency'. Decisions about upbringing and education, career and marriage or lack of it, would be made for them, often by a council consisting of the senior members of the lineage, which existed in many aristocratic families. Some individuals refused to follow the dictates of the family strategy and followed their own chosen paths, sometimes with considerable success. But these were unusual and almost certainly exceptional, and in hindsight it is the degree of compliance which is striking and significant.

One final preliminary point is quite fundamental. Noble status theoretically descended through the legitimate male line, that is to say primarily by means of the succession from father to son. Other forms of descent were possible, but much less common. Since nobility was an essentially male attribute in almost all European countries, that made the birth of a male child, or preferably several, crucial to dynastic continuity. Yet the statistical probability of legitimate male children who survived into adolescence being born to any married couple was no more than 60 per cent, and in periods of dearth or disease, it might be significantly less.[26] Survival for more than four or five generations in the direct male line

---

[26] See the comments of Michel Nassiet, 'Parenté et Successions dynastiques au 14e et 15e siècles', *Annales HSS* 50 (1995), pp. 621–44, especially p. 621; for the original calculation, E. A. Wrigley, 'Fertility Strategy for the Individual and the Group', in Charles Tilly (ed.), *Historical Studies of Changing Fertility* (Princeton, NJ, 1978), pp. 135–154, esp. pp. 139ff; cf. Jack Goody, 'Strategies of Heirship', *Comparative Studies in Society and History* 15 (1973), pp. 3–20, for a rather different method of calculating such probabilities which yields broadly similar results.

was unusual, while a third of all lineages were likely to become extinct every hundred years.[27] Significant numbers of ennoblements were needed simply in order to maintain the number of noble families at a constant level, much less bring about expansion. Many 'new' lineages emerged during the seventeenth century and some even joined the aristocracy, though on closer inspection the families which were becoming part of the noble elite usually turned out to be established lineages rising in status and wealth. Such replenishment was always under way within the European elite, though during these decades it was probably more extensive than at other times. The opportunities for rapid social and political ascent were more numerous, and so the numbers of families joining the Second Estate or rising within it were correspondingly larger.

An important and neglected consolidation of aristocratic power took place across much of Europe during the 'long seventeenth century', the decades from – very broadly – the 1580s to the 1720s. Long-established lineages and other families of more recent – occasionally very recent – creation rose in status, creating an expanded and reinforced aristocracy and, in so doing, establishing the European social elite which would endure at least until the First World War. Four factors together brought this about. The first was the availability of land on a quite new scale in many, though not all, countries, as a result of the major political upheavals and near-permanent warfare of these decades. Secondly, the seventeenth century saw important changes in inheritance practices and, to a lesser extent, in marriage patterns, and these together created a larger, more influential and more integrated group of families at the head of the nobility. The third development was state-formation, the creation of more powerful domestic regimes brought about primarily by the frequent and extensive international and civil wars of the period: regimes which depended upon cooperation with this aristocracy and, in return, fostered its consolidation. Finally, and building on these developments, there was a stratification and diversification of the nobility, with the continuing decline of some families in the lesser nobility, the recovery of others and, much more importantly, the emergence of a larger, more coherent and, above all, more powerful noble elite, distinguished by titles and enhanced status and wealth. What Stone styled the 'inflation of honours', the proliferation of titles at this time, both contributed to and highlighted this stratification. The long seventeenth century thus saw a completion of the synergy between family organisation and monarchical power which

---

[27] One example would be the comtes de Belin, the subject of a notable recent monograph by Elie Haddad, *Fondation et ruine d'une 'maison': Histoire sociale des comtes de Belin (1582–1706)* (Limoges, 2009).

had been under way in Western and Southern Europe since the Later Middle Ages, together with its expansion into other regions of the continent. Behind these national variations the same basic processes can be identified, though particular geographical and historical circumstances imposed individual time-scales and produced rather different outcomes. It completed the social construction of an aristocracy in most European countries.

Political Strife and Elite Consolidation

Seventeenth-century Europe was dominated by international conflicts and civil wars to a quite exceptional extent. There were only four complete calendar years between 1600 and 1700 when fighting was not taking place somewhere in Europe, while certain leading polities – the Spanish Habsburg Monarchy, the Dutch Republic, France, Sweden – were on a war footing for over half of the entire period.[28] The Thirty Years' War (1618–1648) dominated the first half of the century, and the wars of Louis XIV the decades from the 1670s onwards, with the Dutch War (1672–1679), the Nine Years' War (1688/9–1697) and the War of the Spanish Succession (1701/2–1713/4). There was serious and widespread fighting around the Baltic in the 1650s, 1670s and from 1700–1721, while Russia was engaged in extended if usually informal warfare against Poland-Lithuania to the west and against the Ottoman Empire and its allies to the south and southwest throughout the century. It was also, and to an unprecedented extent, a period of rebellions and civil wars, often attracting external intervention: the British Civil Wars of 1637–1652 and of 1688–1691, in France the conflicts of 1617–1629 and the *Frondes* of 1648–1653, the Bohemian Revolt of 1618–1620, the so-called 'Time of Troubles' in early seventeenth-century Muscovy (1598–1613), Portugal's revolt against Spanish rule which began in 1640 and finally restored independence in 1668, and the other revolts within the scattered lands of the Spanish Monarchy during the 1640s, to mention only the major domestic conflicts. Though warfare was ubiquitous in early modern Europe, the struggles of the seventeenth century were on a quite new scale both in their continuity and extent, and especially in their decisive outcomes, something which is quite central to the broader argument of this chapter.

These decades, and particularly the century's second half, also saw sustained and mostly successful efforts at state-building. Though the

---

[28] This was first pointed out by Sir George Clark, *The Seventeenth Century* (1929; 2nd ed., Oxford, 1947), p. 98.

outcomes of these initiatives varied significantly, reflecting individual historical circumstances, the motives behind them were much more uniform. Rulers sought to extend their authority primarily to support warfare, and the enlarged military establishments this made essential, to facilitate the taxation and conscription this entailed, and to increase control over outlying provinces and regions. The seventeenth century saw efforts to construct a 'British state', following the accession of the Stuart rulers of Scotland to the throne of England in 1603, and eventually, an Anglo-Scottish parliamentary union in 1707, together with growing English control over large areas of Ireland. It witnessed an expansion of central government authority in France from the 1630s onwards, and identical developments in smaller states such as Denmark, where a form of 'absolutism' was established by a military coup in 1660; in Sweden where Karl XI (1660–1697) followed suit in 1680; and in the northern Italian polity of Savoy-Piedmont, where a significant extension of Turin's authority took place during the reign of Victor Amadeus II (1675–1730).

The seventeenth century also saw the creation of a 'composite monarchy' in Brandenburg-Prussia and the consolidation of one in the Austrian Habsburg territories, with the extension of Vienna's authority first over the Kingdom of Bohemia, as a result of the defeat of the Bohemian rebels, and then large areas of Hungary, reconquered from its Ottoman occupiers between the 1680s and 1718. Further east, between Ivan IV's reign (1533–1584) and the early decades of the eighteenth century, the lands nominally governed by the ruler of Russia were dramatically extended through conquests and annexations. Russian territory expanded eastwards into Siberia; southeastwards into Central Asia; southwards into the borderlands which separated the Ottoman Empire and its satellite Khanate of the Crimea from the rich farming territories of southern Russia; westwards against Poland-Lithuania, from which large swathes of territory were seized; and finally, in the years immediately after 1700, it gained territories in the eastern Baltic. During the century after the 1580s the tsar's territories probably trebled in extent; over the longer period c.1450–1721 this growth was even more remarkable, and unparalleled in early modern Europe.[29]

These domestic and international conflicts, and the efforts at state-formation which accompanied them, were quite fundamental for the

[29] See the estimates of Richard Hellie, 'The Expanding Role of the State in Russia', in Jarmo Kotilaine and Marshall Poe (ed.), *Modernizing Muscovy: Reform and social Change in Seventeenth-Century Russia* (London, 2004), pp. 29–55, at p. 30.

consolidation of Europe's aristocracies. They made land available on a wholly new scale, as estates were confiscated from rebels or other opponents, or became available in recently incorporated provinces or newly conquered regions. These struggles simultaneously created a need for soldiers and administrators who could be rewarded with that same land, while these decades also witnessed an unusual number of changes of dynasty, exemplifying Professor Morrill's underlying point. New regimes struggling to establish themselves, notably the Bourbons in France after 1589, the Romanovs in Muscovy after 1613 and the Braganzas in Portugal after 1640, and sought to win political supporters by distributing these windfalls. The fourth such change of dynasty and in many ways the best known, the accession of the Stuart King of Scotland, James VI, to the English throne on the death of Elizabeth I in 1603, had less impact upon the nobilities of his Anglo-Scottish Kingdoms. Scotland's frequently impoverished noblemen hoped that the reverse would be true and looked south expectantly, but only a minority of families benefitted to any great extent from the Union of the Crowns.[30]

The escalating costs of warfare and the resulting financial problems monarchies faced, together with the wider economic difficulties of the period, led governments all over Europe to distribute not pensions or other cash gifts to their elites, but landed property and, particularly where this was in short supply, titles and honours of all kinds. The Spanish King Philip IV (1621–1665) was quite explicit about this. 'Without rewards and punishments [he wrote] no monarchy can be preserved. Now rewards may be either financial or honorific. We have no money, so we have thought it right and necessary to remedy the fault by increasing the

---

[30] This emerges clearly from the work of Keith Brown on the Scottish nobility at this period: see in particular 'Courtiers and Cavaliers: Service, Anglicisation and Loyalty among the Royalist Nobility', in John Morrill (ed.), *The Scottish National Covenant in its British Context* (Edinburgh, 1990), pp. 155–192; 'From Scottish Lords to British Officers: State Building, Elite Integration, and the Army in the Seventeenth Century', in Norman MacDougall (ed.), *Scotland and War AD79–1918* (Edinburgh, 1992), pp. 133–169; *Kingdom or Province?: Scotland and the Regal Union 1603–1715* (Basingstoke, 1992); *Noble Society in Scotland: Wealth, Family and Culture from Reformation to Revolution* (Edinburgh, 2000); *Noble Power in Scotland from the Reformation to the Revolution* (Edinburgh, 2011); 'The Origins of a British Aristocracy: Integration and its limitations before the treaty of Union', in Ellis and Barber (eds.), *Conquest and Union*, pp. 222–249; 'The Scottish Aristocracy, Anglicization and the Court, 1603–38', *Historical Journal* 36 (1993), pp. 543–576. A final and important example of dynastic change would be the accession of a branch of the Swedish Vasa family to the elective Polish-Lithuanian throne in the persons of Sigismund (1587–1632) and his son Wladyslaw IV (1632–1648); Sigismund had also been King of Sweden from 1592 until 1599, when he was deposed by his uncle. But this dynastic union seems to have had less enduring impact upon both countries' social elites than in any similar case.

number of honours.'[31] Existing nobles and a rather smaller number of newly ennobled lineages were the principal beneficiaries of this largesse.[32]

The question of landholding remains a crucial but elusive subject for the study of the nobility, since we are still very poorly informed about the details of which individual or family, or what institution, held a particular estate and the precise terms on which they did so. Early modern governments made repeated unsuccessful efforts to establish reliable surveys or cadasters of landholding, usually in order to facilitate a land tax, but in the leading monarchies the results were always disappointing and incomplete. As late as the 1780s and with the combined apparatus of the bureaucracy and the army to carry out the work, the Emperor Joseph II could not complete a survey of landholding even in part of the Austrian Habsburg Monarchy, and his failure paralleled that of similar attempts in states of any size. Within medium-sized polities – Denmark, Savoy-Piedmont, Sweden – greater precision was possible than in larger countries such as the French, Spanish and Austrian Habsburg monarchies, to say nothing of the vast Russian empire. The kind of detailed and remarkably precise survey of landholding that the first Norman King of England, William the Conqueror, had produced in the late-eleventh century when Domesday Book was compiled, was extremely unusual in early modern Europe, where reliable and detailed information of this kind remained and still remains scarce.

Landed property, however, was the principal basis of noble status and power, apparent in the fact that in some countries certain estates were formally designated as reserved for the nobility – what was known as a *Rittergut* in early modern Germany – and their acquisition by a commoner theoretically prohibited. The nobility was collectively the leading landowner in almost every European country. Land was a source of social and even political authority, as well as an economic resource, and any would-be nobleman, or poorer noble who wished to rise in status, set about acquiring as much as he – or, very occasionally she – could secure. Within a traditional economy such as that of early modern Europe, land was also the principal economic resource. If farmed directly, it yielded agricultural produce which could be either consumed or sold to generate cash; or it could be leased out to tenants, either for short or more extended periods of time. It also generated revenues in the form of seigneurial dues and a variety of other payments which were collected by the local lord. Land was a far more reliable and also far more important economic resource than either trade or manufacturing, which in some countries nobles were supposedly prohibited from undertaking on pain of

---

[31] Quoted and translated by Kamen, *The Iron Century*, p. 163.   [32] See Table 3.5.

'derogation': the loss of their privileged status. Within a traditional and deeply deferential society landed property was also an important source of authority, whether formally in the legal powers which many nobles held and frequently exercised, or less formally in the shape of social leadership and dominance in their immediate locality. By the early modern period, extensive landholding – 'rolling acres' in the English phrase – was seen as the essential accompaniment to the privileged status of aristocrat throughout Europe.

Despite the lack of precise information, it is clear that the seventeenth century was exceptional in the amount of land which was transferred from one noble family to another, mainly as a result of the widespread civil strife of these decades. The French Religious Wars between the 1560s and the 1590s, together with the continuing if more intermittent fighting during the next generation saw significant changes to landholding in France, though the impact remains to be investigated in any detail. In Bohemia, more than half of all noble estates changed hands as a result of the defeat of the Rebellion of 1618–1620 and the wider outcome of the Thirty Years' War.[33] In seventeenth-century Ireland, even more property changed hands, with the extension of English control over large areas of the island and the accompanying decline of Gaelic lordship, together with the upheavals brought about by the civil wars of the midcentury and of 1688–1691.[34] Two simultaneous processes can be detected. The proportion of land controlled by Protestants rose significantly: from 30 per cent (1641) to 67 per cent (c.1670); that of Catholic landowners fell by approximately the same proportion over the same period, from 66 per cent to 29 per cent. At the same time, however, these figures reveal that the leading families

---

[33] The latest and most authoritative surveys are those by Petr Mat'a, *Svet Ceské Aristokracie (1500–1700)* (Prague, 2004), pp. 125ff. and Chapter III *passim*; and Thomas Winkelbauer, *Österreich Geschichte 1522–1699: Ständefreiheit und Fürstenmacht: Länder und Untertanen des Hauses Habsburg im Konfessionellen Zeitalter* (2 vols.; Vienna, 2003), esp. vol. 1. I owe my knowledge of Dr Mat'a's fundamental work to Ms Jitka Perinova, who digested it for me. This study mainly focuses on the 'Kingdom of Bohemia'; the 'Lands of the Bohemian Crown' also included neighbouring Moravia, Silesia and the two Lusatias. See also Tomâs Knoz, 'Die Konfiskationen nach 1620 in (erb)länderübergreifender Perspektive: Thesen zu wesentlichen Wirkungen, Aspekten und Prinzipien des Konfiskationsprozess', in Petr Mat'a and Thomas Winkelbauer (eds.), *Die Habsburgermonarchie 1620 bis 1740: Leistungen und Grenzen des Absolutismusparadigmas* (Stuttgart, 2006), pp. 99–130. The wider context is provided by the classic study of R. J. W. Evans, *The Making of the Habsburg Monarchy, 1550–1700* (Oxford, 1979).

[34] The recent study by Jane Ohlmeyer, *Making Ireland English: The Irish Aristocracy in the Seventeenth Century* (London, 2012), transforms our knowledge of this subject; a model examination of one dimension is John Cunningham, *Conquest and Land in Ireland: The Transplantation to Connacht, 1649–1680* (Woodbridge, 2011).

of both faiths increased their overall share of Ireland's total landholding by around a half: from 18 per cent to around 26 per cent.[35] In both Ireland and Bohemia, decisive political change and unsuccessful rebellion, with the losers being expropriated, were fundamental to the massive redistribution of property which took place. A rather different pattern, but one with a similar outcome, is evident in the case of Russia, where it was primarily the extensive lands conquered to the south and east which were awarded by successive Romanov rulers to their leading supporters and servants, thereby endowing the aristocracy emerging in Russia with estates in the rich agricultural lands of the so-called Black Soil regions.[36]

Analogous, though not identical, developments took place in Sweden, which dramatically emerged from political obscurity to become a leading European power during the first half of the seventeenth century. The Swedish economy remained an economy of barter, and this, together with the country's own relative poverty and backwardness, inhibited the development of taxation on the scale evident elsewhere. Instead successive rulers funded their seventeenth-century wars primarily by alienating the substantial crown estates which were largely acquired as a result of the Protestant Reformation a century before, together with the vast new territories in the eastern Baltic which were conquered by Swedish armies during the period before 1629. Once again the main beneficiaries were the high nobility, as the Crown attempted to secure its cooperation in the imperial venture.[37] Donations of this kind to favoured royal servants had begun during the sixteenth century, but after 1600 they reached quite unprecedented levels. These alienations took two forms. Some crown estates were sold outright to raise cash, or granted as security for loans, which a bankrupt monarchy was often unable to repay. Other properties were leased out for extended periods on very favourable terms, in order to pay overdue wages or settle debts.

The scale of these alienations was quite remarkable. By 1650 the number of farms (the primary unit of land division in Sweden) directly controlled by the nobility had doubled since the beginning of the century; a handful of leading families, the so-called Council Aristocracy, had gained most of all. By the 1660s the nobility controlled no less than

---

[35] Ohlmeyer, *Making Ireland English*, p. 301 and Chapter 6 *passim*.

[36] The best Western-language guide to developments remains Robert O. Crummey, *Aristocrats and Servitors: The Boyar Elite in Russia 1613–1689* (Princeton, NJ, 1983).

[37] Peter Englund, *Det hotade huset: Adliga föreställningar om samhället under Stormaktstiden* (Stockholm, 1989), a major study of the seventeenth-century elite, is primarily concerned with changing attitudes; there is much valuable information in Kurt Ågren, 'Rise and Decline of an Aristocracy', *Scandinavian Journal of History* 1 (1976), pp. 55–80.

63 per cent of all the land in Sweden and Finland.[38] The aristocracy also secured substantial estates on the other side of the Baltic Sea, in the vast territories acquired during the decades before 1660. In the eastern Baltic lands (Ingria, Kexholm and Livonia) conquered during the 1610s and 1620s they secured large donations which probably eclipsed those within Sweden itself. By around 1680 in Livonia the leading Swedish families controlled approaching half of the estates (45 per cent), while the lesser nobility owned a further 12 per cent.[39] The greatest gainer in Livonia was none other than the Council magnate Axel Oxenstierna, Sweden's chancellor for four decades, Gustav Adolf's closest political collaborator and the uncrowned ruler for more than a decade after the king's death, during the regency for Queen Kristina (1632–1644). The Oxenstierna family gained even more land in Ingria, where their main overseas estate was located. Subsequent campaigns in Germany during the Thirty Years' War brought further landed booty to the Swedish elite.

It is of course true that the absolute monarchy set up after 1680, recovered some of this property through Karl XI's celebrated *Reduktion*.[40] During the 1680s and 1690s, in an initiative without parallel in early modern Europe, royal commissioners carried out a detailed investigation into noble landholding, seeking to recover alienated estates for the Vasa monarchy by exploiting the mid-fourteenth-century Land Law, the country's fundamental point of political reference. Many families handed over at least part of their recent gains, and one or two were completely ruined: notably the de la Gardie. Magnus Gabriel de la Gardie, for a time the favourite of Queen Kristina and then the dominant figure in the regency for the boy-king Karl XI after 1660, had secured vast landholdings through inheritance and crown donations, but he lost almost everything in the *Reduktion* and in his old age was reduced to living on royal handouts in straitened circumstances.[41] His case was exceptional, and the most prominent families seem to have retained a significant proportion of their gains into the eighteenth century and far beyond. Exactly how much remains uncertain: the detailed impact of the *Reduktion* remains to be studied. But the one province which has been

---

[38] In 1665 noble families controlled 39,632 *hemman* out of 60,750 in metropolitan Sweden and 14,323 out of 24,539 in Finland: Claude Nordmann, *Grandeur et liberté de la Suède 1660–1792* (Paris, 1971), p. 41. The rest was either controlled directly by the Crown or in the hands of the peasantry.

[39] Edgars Dunsdorfs, *The Livonian Estates of Axel Oxenstierna* (Stockholm, 1981), p. 4.

[40] A. F. Upton, *Charles XI and Swedish Absolutism* (Cambridge, 1998), Chapter 4, is a good brief guide.

[41] His career is sketched by Göran Rystad, 'Magnus Gabriel De la Gardie', in Michael Roberts (ed.), *Sweden's Age of Greatness 1632–1718* (London, 1973), pp. 203–236.

Table 3.1 *Landed Power of 'New' Nobility in Denmark after 1660*

	Zealand		Funen		Jutland	
	1680	1717	1680	1717	1680	1717
Old Nobility	37.6%	23.9%	58.8%	–	48.0%	32.5%
New Nobility	20.2%	17.9%	4.0%	38.8%	10.8%	25.1%
Counts/Barons	9.6%	19.5%	17.1%	51.0%	13.8%	18.1%

Source: Based upon E.L. Petersen, 'Poor Nobles and Rich in Denmark, 1500–1700', *Journal of European Economic History* 30 (2001), Table 5, p. 119.

examined in depth – the rich farming province of Uppland, north of Stockholm – suggests that the aristocracy retained the most productive estates. There the nobility had secured 60 per cent of the farms during the seventeenth century; by the end of the reign of Charles XII in 1718, these families retained at least two-thirds of these gains, corresponding to the wider European pattern.[42]

The consolidation of aristocracy and the accompanying redistribution of land could be the result of changes of political *régime*, as the examples of Denmark, Portugal and Russia all demonstrate in different ways. In the Danish Monarchy, the Crown, which had seized full authority in 1660, set out quite deliberately during the following decades to create a service nobility, which soon began to acquire the landed possessions which its status required.[43] Military and administrative service were the principal routes into this elite, within a monarchy which had become far more meritocratic than a generation earlier. Developments before 1660 both anticipated and prepared the way for what was a fundamental change. One important outcome was the emergence of a new elite of administrators, granted for the first time formal titles of nobility ('count' and 'baron'), which came to the fore during the closing decades of the seventeenth and the earlier-eighteenth century. Table 3.1 highlights the success of these nobles, with important assistance from the Crown, in securing lands to match their status.

Portugal's recovery of political independence after 60 years of Madrid's rule during its War of Independence (1640–1668) and the accession of the plutocratic Duke of Braganza as John IV (1640–1656) also saw a new

---

[42] Figures from Upton, *Charles XI*, p. 67.

[43] See Gunner Lind in Chapter 10 of this volume, and the briefer account by Knud J. V. Jespersen, 'The Rise and Fall of the Danish Nobility, 1600–1800', in H. M. Scott (ed.), *The European Nobilities in the Seventeenth and Eighteenth Centuries, vol. II: Northern, Central and Eastern Europe* (1995; 2nd ed., Basingstoke, 2007), pp. 53ff.

aristocracy take shape. In 1640 there were 56 titled Portuguese lineages, after a notable 'inflation of honours' during the period of Spanish rule (1580–1640). No fewer than 24 of these families – almost half – remained loyal to the Spanish crown, which in many cases had granted them their newfound eminence. Their disappearance and the accompanying loss of land and income facilitated a reconstitution of the elite. The court aristocracy, which took shape under the early Braganzas, was reinforced by lineages drawn from the untitled but frequently venerable nobility.

The Portuguese kingdom provides an example of a country where formal possession of land was less important than control over the wealth it yielded. The country's earlier history meant that the three Military Orders of Avis, Christ and Santiago controlled large estates, but these were all under royal control since by the seventeenth century the Portuguese monarch was hereditary Grand Master of each. The new Braganza rulers distributed commanderies in these orders and the accompanying income to the families which had supported the rising against Madrid. One outcome was the creation of a powerful and wealthy aristocracy, but one unusually dependent upon the Crown. A century later, in the mid-1750s, the titled nobility controlled two-thirds (66.4 per cent) of this revenue; in the early 1610s this figure had been less than one-fifth (18.4 per cent), underlining the scale of the consolidation which had taken place. By the third quarter of the eighteenth century over half of aristocratic income (on average) was derived either directly or indirectly from the Crown.[44] Though the direct control and exploitation of land was less important in Portugal than the revenue it yielded, the outcome was essentially similar: the creation of a wealthy aristocracy who exercised authority and possessed the resources needed to support the Crown.

This was also true in Russia, though developments there were distinctive in one important respect. In the vast expanses ruled over by the Romanov dynasty after 1613, control over an exiguous and thinly scattered population and the villages in which it lived was at least as important as dominance over land per se. The Russian elite at exactly this period was undergoing important changes analogous to the wider continental pattern, based its power not merely on their extensive landholdings but also on enhanced control of peasants, consolidated by the formal imposition of serfdom by the Law Code of 1649. The reigns of Alexis (1645–1676) and especially Peter I (1682/89–1725) saw further decisive changes to the Russian elite, with a vast increase in landholding

---

[44] Nuno Gonçalo Freitas Monteiro, *O Crepúsculo dos Grandes: A Casa e o Património da Aristocracia em Portugal (1750–1832)* (1998; 2nd ed., Lisbon, 2003), Table 4, pp. 50–51, and Table 27, pp. 261–263.

and a shift towards hereditary ownership of property, together with a sharp increase in the numbers in the boyar Duma.[45] By the eighteenth century it was exhibiting features which were more distinctly 'European', with the introduction of the titles of 'count' and 'baron', and even an unsuccessful attempt to facilitate the adoption of primogeniture through the Law of Single Inheritance, introduced in 1714 but rescinded in 1731.[46]

The Inheritance of Landed Property

This leads naturally to the second major development at this time: significant changes in how landed property was passed on to the next generation. Inheritance arrangements were fundamental to aristocracy, which depended upon the transmission of social and political authority, together with the human and economic resources needed to sustain this, from one generation to the next. The nobility as a caste sought to perpetuate itself through legitimate father-to-son succession. An exaggerated emphasis upon such direct descent and the distinguished ancestry it conferred was always part of aristocratic self-representation and became a founding myth of its ideology, yet it was difficult to reconcile with demographic realities.[47] The French elite, the *ducs-et-pairs*, provides a striking example of this fragility.[48] For lay peers, excluding Princes of the Blood, the average lineage survived for little more than three generations in direct male descent, which was required in order to retain the rank of *duc-et-pair*. Fifty-nine *duchés-pairies* had been created between 1297 and 1642; only 27 of these were still in existence when Louis XIII died in 1643. During the next half-century a further dozen died out, leaving no more than 15 of the pre-1642 creations extant, though simultaneously a significant number of new *duchés-pairies* were created. Over the period from 1519 to 1790, the average lifespan of all *duchés-pairies* was some 66 years. Figures such as these underline the scale of the demographic challenge confronting all families and individuals in the social elite as they struggled to secure the succession.

---

[45] These have been painstakingly charted by Marshall T. Poe, *The Russian Elite in the Seventeenth Century* (2 vols.; Helsinki, 2004). The earlier study of the Petrine impact upon the Russian social elite by Brenda Meehan-Waters, *Autocracy and Aristocracy: The Russian Service Elite of 1730* (New Brunswick, NJ, 1982), remains valuable.

[46] Lee A. Farrow, 'Peter the Great's Law of Single Inheritance: State imperatives and noble resistance', *Russian Review* 55 (1996), pp. 430–447.

[47] See above, pp. 55–56.

[48] Christophe Levantal, *Ducs et Pairs et Duchés-Pairies Laïques à l'Époque Moderne (1519–1790)* (Paris, 1996), pp. 227–228, for the figures which follow; cf. Appendix, pp. 381–392, on the transmission of *duchés-pairies* between 1519 and 1789.

The transmission of resources presented similar pitfalls. By the early modern period there were, broadly speaking, two possibilities: partible inheritance, where all the legitimate male children of a noble father, and sometimes the daughters too, secured a proportion of his property and wealth; and primogeniture, where the first-born son secured the major part of the landed property in particular. The first was obviously a threat to the survival of aristocratic patrimonies, since repeated divisions would lead to the atomisation of the all-important landholding, undermining the lineage's status and reducing its resources. One reason why this article says next to nothing about the Reich, is that it was one principal area – the other two were Poland-Lithuania and Russia – where partible inheritance was widely practised by the higher nobility. Despite family agreements to keep the estates together and share the revenues, it was one factor militating against the creation of substantial territorial aristocracies there during the long seventeenth century. The extent of political fragmentation within the Holy Roman Empire and its distinctive constitutional structure, which together limited the resources available to any single ruler for distribution, constituted a second important reason for the absence of any development towards the creation of a more powerful noble elite apparent elsewhere.

The one group of territories in which a form of primogeniture became established was altogether improbable: the Catholic ecclesiastical states which huddled together in southwest Germany and were headed by the three ecclesiastical electorates of Mainz, Trier and Cologne. These and various neighbouring bishoprics headed by Münster were scattered across the Rhineland and, by the early modern period, they were controlled by enclosed, tightly knit and self-perpetuating oligarchies. Since formal hereditary succession – son succeeding father – was obviously precluded by Church law, these lineages had developed an ingenious system of lateral inheritance by which the holder of the prebend was succeeded by his nephew, ideally his brother's son, in each generation. This enabled the same lineage to retain one ecclesiastical office, and crucially the substantial resources it controlled, and to exercise what was in effect hereditary possession. It permitted the maintenance of family dynasties of bishops and archbishops in wealthy and important prebends, while nominally observing Church law.[49]

---

[49] See the pioneering Heinz Reif, *Westfälischen Adel, 1770–1860: Von Herrschaftsstand zur regionalen Elite* (Göttingen, 1979), which in spite of its title contains a great deal of information and analysis of the period 1648–1770, on the nobility of Münster, together with the subsequent and more wide ranging study by Christophe Duhamelle, *L'Héritage Collectif: La noblesse d'église rhénane, 17e-18e siècles* (Paris, 1998).

During the Later Middle Ages and the early modern period there had been a distinct shift across much of Europe towards male primogeniture, that is to say a system of inheritance in which the eldest son – or more accurately, the eldest surviving son – secured the bulk of the landed property and sometimes all of it, with the other children being provided for out of the family's moveable wealth, if at all. The assumption always was that any nobleman of any standing, and certainly all aristocrats, required either an establishment of their own or help in launching a career: usually in the army, in Roman Catholic countries also in the Church, or in rather fewer cases in government. Noblewomen were granted a dowry – which could be very considerable – if they married – or a 'spiritual dowry' if they entered the Church. Failing these destinations, they were maintained within the extended family and expected to help with the upbringing of its younger members.

The move towards male primogeniture had been accompanied, particularly in Southern Europe, by the emergence of formal arrangements by which family property was placed within an enduring entail, that is to say a formal legal trust was created, with each eldest son in succession enjoying the income but more or less unable to touch the landed and other resources within it.[50] An entail was, in the most general sense, a bequest

---

[50] The most comprehensive guide to this crucial development is still the remarkable article by J. P. Cooper, 'Patterns of inheritance and settlement by great landowners from the fifteenth to the eighteenth centuries', in Jack Goody, Joan Thirsk and E. P. Thompson (eds.), *Family and Inheritance: Rural society in Western Europe 1200–1800* (Cambridge, 1976), pp. 192–327; the recent collection of essays edited by Anne Bellavitis, Jean-François Chauvard and Paola Lanaro, 'Fidéicommis: Instruments juridiques et pratiques sociales (Italie/Europe, Bas Moyen Âge/XIXe siècle)', which was published in *Mélanges de l'École Française de Rome: Italie et Méditerranée* 124:2 (2012), provides a valuable Franco-Italian perspective on the subject. There are some important national studies: see, for the Iberian Peninsula, especially Bartolomé Clavero, *Mayorazgo: Propriedad feudal en Castilla 1369–1836* (1974; 2nd ed., Madrid, 1989), in a notably legal idiom, and Maria de Lurdes Rosa, *O Morgadio em Portugal secs. XIV–XV: Modelos e practicas de comportamento linhagístico* (Lisbon, 1995). For Naples, see the chapter 'Strategie successorie e regimi dotali', in Maria Antonietta Visceglia, *Il bisogno di eternità: I compartamenti aristocratici a Napoli in età moderna* (Naples, 1988), pp. 13–105, esp. pp. 16ff., an informative and exemplary study: this first appeared under the title 'Linee per uno studio unitario dei testamenti e dei contratti matrimoniali dell'aristocrazia feudale Napoletana tra fine quattrocento e settecento', in *Mélanges de l'École Française de Rome: Moyen Âge, Temps Modernes* 95 (1983), pp. 393–470; and Gérard Delille, *Famille et Propriété dans le Royaume de Naples (XVe-XIXe siècle)* (Rome-Paris, 1985), which provides a penetrating examination of inheritance within the wider system of kinship, with particular attention to demographic factors: see esp. pp. 23–85. For France, there are helpful introductions by Paul Ourliac and Jean-Louis-Louis Gazzaniga, *Histoire du droit privé français, de l'An mil au Code civil* (Paris, 1985), and Jean-Marie Augustin, *Les substitutions fidéicommissaires à Toulouse et en Haut-Languedoc au XVIIIe siècle* (Paris, 1980), together with the same author's brief but informative survey, 'Successions', in Lucien Bély (ed.), *Dictionnaire de l'Ancien Régime* (Paris, 1996),

which an individual made by 'begging' his legatee to transfer something –
the thing bequeathed – to a third person, and so on throughout the
generations. Its ultimate origin was the system of *fide commissum* in
Roman law. By establishing a legal trust containing the family lands and
moveable property, together with any other valuable assets, this sought to
ensure the survival of a secure material base for future generations.
Succession to this trust was precisely laid down. Usually it was restricted
to the eldest son or nearest male relative in each generation, who would
enjoy the income during his lifetime but have no access to the capital or, at
most, a very limited right to draw upon the resources protected by the
trust.

Both primogeniture and entail very often required that the provisions of
a provincial law code be set aside, which only a ruler was able to do, and so
these practices rested upon and, at the same time, deepened cooperation
between social elite and dynastic monarchy. Entails normally required
specific royal assent, or general enabling legislation, and could usually be
broken only with the ruler's explicit permission. They were most often
included in wills or set up as part of marriage settlements. These trusts
varied widely both as to specific provisions and as to duration: they might
be for two or three generations, or they could be permanent as in the case
of the Spanish variant, the *mayorazgo*, which was a peculiarly rigid legal
trust and could only be amended with considerable difficulty. Though
there was no such thing as a 'standard' entail, there was a template which
could be adjusted to cover the contours of a particular family situation
and the scale of available resources. The device provided a flexible solution to the myriad possible permutations within an aristocratic lineage.
In both the Iberian Kingdoms and the French monarchy, leading families
had first created an accepted social and family mechanism, and then
a formal legal means, by which the greater part of a father's property
could be transmitted to successive generations of eldest sons or, where
these were lacking, to other close male relatives, and in this way stabilised
its landholding.

Arrangements of this kind had become widespread in late medieval
Castile and, on a smaller scale, in fifteenth-century Portugal (the *mayorazgo* in the former, the *morgadio* in the latter) and during the sixteenth
century had been adopted within the Italian peninsula, particularly in the
south where Spanish influence was strong (the *fedecommesso*). Some
entails had also been created in France, though noble inheritance
arrangements there are both highly complex and notably obscure.

pp. 1178–1186; while the old study by Charles Lefebvre, *L'histoire du droit civil français:
L'ancien droit des successions* (2 vols.; Paris, 1912–1918), esp. vol. 1, remains informative.

The French kingdom was juridically divided twice over, and the striking legal pluralism which resulted persisted throughout the early modern era. There was an area, broadly the northern two-thirds of the kingdom, where traditional *coutumes*, regional customary laws which had solidified by the mid-thirteenth century, applied, and a southern zone where Roman law gradually became dominant. It was also fragmented between a plethora of rival and overlapping jurisdictions, and particularly those of the Parlement of Paris and the various provincial *parlements*, each with its own area of legal authority, which the King alone could override.

Where it existed, the device of entail created an enduring material base for the lineage, and insured against a spendthrift heir squandering its wealth. It also created a secure line of succession, which was at least as important though it has attracted less attention from historians. The permanent demographic threat to noble power was clear: the like-lihood was that the average family might survive for as little as three or four generations in direct male descent. One important function of an entail was to provide a series of substitutes from among brothers, nephews, uncles and even female heirs, if the direct male line failed. Though it could not ensure against the extinction of individual noble houses, it could make dynastic survival considerably more likely. Portugal was one southern European country where entails had gained only a limited foothold at an earlier period, but it now came into line with its Spanish neighbour. The early decades of the seventeenth century, during the period of union with Madrid (1580–1640), saw the majority of Portuguese aristocratic families establish such trusts, encouraged by a law code which sought to standardise their form with the Castilian *mayorazgo* as the prototype.

During the long seventeenth-century arrangements of this kind spread north of the Alps and became a defining characteristic of the aristocracies taking shape there: as they had long been in most Mediterranean countries. The creation of a dynastic elite in the Austrian Habsburg Monarchy mentioned earlier was in many ways the classic demonstration of the potential of entail: what is known in German as a *Fideikommiss*. Bohemian families traditionally practised partible inheritance, and during the sixteenth century many estates had been divided to provide for younger sons, with a consequent atomisation of landholding. Now, however, many Bohemian and Austrian aristocratic families established such entails. Though co-ownership of family property was traditional, during the Later Middle Ages lineages had actually begun to divide their landed possessions. In the sixteenth century, however, primogeniture gained ground, and some entails had even been created. In Austria the first formal *Fideikommiss* seems to date from 1527, while a family agreement which aimed to entail its estates, survives from as early as 1501.[51] During the later-sixteenth century several families had begun to adopt the device, as the Dohna did in 1600.[52] The turning point was the establishment of a *Fideikommiss* in August 1605 by Count Johan von Khevenhüller, former Austrian ambassador in Spain and so personally familiar with the *mayorazgo*. The Liechtenstein, who had concluded its own first entail three years earlier, now created a more extensive and enduring one, and a few other families followed their lead before the outbreak of the Thirty Years' War.

The main period of foundation was the generation after 1620, and the principal founders were the families who had been the greatest beneficiaries of the share-out of estates in Bohemia and, to a lesser extent, Austria, where less property changed hands.[53] The scale of the land transfers in the Kingdom of Bohemia was quite remarkable. Slightly more than half of *all* noble estates and many more of the larger ones changed hands during the 1620s and 1630s, with profound and enduring consequences. Most leading families simultaneously adopted the device of entail.[54] Exactly as was the case elsewhere, Habsburg monarchs exploited the approval which the creation or variation of a *Fideikommiss* required to exert leverage over the social elite. But the principal importance of entails was their central role in securing the succession and stabilising landholding, and in this way they became fundamental both to the creation of the magnate caste which took shape in the Bohemian and Austrian territories and to the establishment of the vast estates over which they ruled. By 1787 there were to be no fewer than 62 *Fideikommisse* in Bohemia alone.[55]

A similar though far less complete evolution took place in the Kingdom of Hungary, as the Habsburgs extended their authority during the seventeenth century. Here the lead was taken by native families who supported the extension of Vienna's authority, securing lands and titles in return.

---

[51] Otto Fraydenegg und Monzello, 'Zur Geschichte des Österreichischen Fideikommissrechts', in B. Sutter (ed.), *Reformen des Rechts* (Graz, 1979), pp. 777–808, at p. 781.

[52] Details in L. Pfaff and F. Hoffmann, *Zur Geschichte der Fideikommisse* (Vienna, 1884), p. 26, n. 91. The leading Bohemian family of Rosenberg was another lineage which moved away from dividing its lands.

[53] Pfaff and Hoffmann, *Geschichte der Fideikommisse*, p. 28, lists many of these.

[54] Pfaff and Hoffmann, *Geschichte der Fideikommisse* is an informative if legalistic introduction, while Karl Theodor von Inama-Sternegg, 'Die Familien-Fideicommisse in Oesterreich', *Statistische Monatschrift* (1883), pp. 465–481, contains valuable information and attempts to provide a welcome degree of statistical precision. (I am grateful to Dr William D. Godsey, Jr., for drawing this latter article to my attention and sending me a photocopy.)

[55] P. G. M. Dickson, *Finance and Government under Maria Theresia, 1740–1780* (2 vols.; Oxford, 1987), i.95. This figure is for the 'Kingdom of Bohemia', that is to say Bohemia but not Moravia or the Lusatian or Silesian territories.

The Pálffy were the first to establish a *Fideikommiss* in 1653, and the following hundred years saw a handful of arrangements of this kind, such as those founded by the Eszterházys in the mid-1690s, as the Kingdom's elite emulated their counterparts in the Austro-Bohemian territories by adopting rigid male primogeniture and establishing trusts. In Hungary too entails stabilised landed power and were one foundation of the vast estates which existed by the eighteenth century.

Impartible inheritance among the high nobility also spread into Scandinavian countries at this period. In Sweden the titles of count and baron which had been introduced during the second half of the sixteenth century and proliferated after 1600, when a titled aristocracy evolved, had made the accompanying landed property impartible, that is to say indivisible, and provided for it to descend by male primogeniture, and these provisions were confirmed in 1604.[56] If a family failed in the male line, the fief reverted to the Crown. In Denmark families granted titles in the new aristocracy established after 1660 were specifically required to establish an entailed estate (the so-called *stamhus*), and this privilege was made more widely available to the nobility some years later; its impact is evident in the fact that by 1800 one-fifth of Denmark's agricultural land lay within estates of this kind.[57]

A similar form of inheritance arrangements also became much more common among leading families in France. The vehicle for this was the *duché-pairie*, until the mid-sixteenth century reserved for high churchmen, royal relatives and the *princes-étrangers*, but opened to traditional military houses from the 1560s onwards. These dignities were in practice hereditary in the male line, though the Crown formally retained the right to appoint each new holder. They were impartible and descended through primogeniture, reverting to the Crown when male heirs failed. Between the twelfth and sixteenth century, French noble families had made significant use of entails, but these had been subjected to restrictions during the 1560s, when both their duration and the degrees of kinship to which they could extend had been limited. By contrast *duchés-pairies* could be made subject to permanent 'substitutions', as the practice of entailment was widely known in France. Though in a number of provinces, 'substitutions' were formally prohibited, the Crown could and did allow favoured individuals who were not *ducs-et-pairs* to create perpetual entails, in the process overriding local legal codes.

---

[56] Michael Roberts, *The Early Vasas: A History of Sweden, 1523–1611* (Cambridge, 1968), pp. 220ff., 243ff.
[57] Jespersen, 'Rise and Fall of the Danish Nobility', pp. 43–71, provides a brief introduction.

The new Bourbon monarchy, as it struggled to establish its authority and restore domestic peace, employed the dignity of *duc*, usually but not invariably accompanied by a *pairie*, to reward its own supporters and win over key magnates. Between the family's accession in 1589 and the end of the regency for Louis XV in 1723, their numbers rose from 40 to 76. Within these totals, the ecclesiastical peers and the royal relatives remained a relatively constant figure, around 15 in total.[58] The growth was overwhelmingly in families in the higher nobility; their numbers increased almost fivefold, from 11 (1589) to 62 (1723). The laws governing succession to this dignity were identical to those governing the Crown itself: strict male primogeniture applied, the lands reverted to the king if the direct line of descent failed, though in certain circumstances and with specific royal approval female succession was permitted in order that a title might survive.[59] The need to preserve the landed base of such dignities, and thus their wealth and social pre-eminence, led to the widespread adoption of the practice of *substitution* both among the peerage and within rising lineages.[60] These entails were included in marriage contracts or, less commonly, took the form of separate agreements, and rigidly upheld strict male primogeniture and the inalienability of the estates. Though detailed investigation remains to be conducted into the Bourbon aristocracy's use of such devices, it is clear that many leading families adopted the practice of substitution and that contributed to the increasing stability of France's social elite and its landholding at this time.

The same intention was evident in seventeenth-century Ireland, though it was not to be fully realised in practice. The so-called surrender-and-regrant agreements concluded by the English government with native Gaelic lords, from the early 1540s onwards, and the English titles which sometimes accompanied them, involved the obligation to accept male primogeniture at least by the midpoint of Elizabeth I's reign (1558–1603).[61] This was directed against the native custom of tanistry, by which a successor was elected or even designated by the chief, a system with considerable disruptive potential. During the seventeenth century the new and largely Protestant English elite in Ireland embraced primogeniture, though far from completely, and some entails were even

---

[58] See Labatut, *Ducs et pairs*, p. 69.

[59] Levantal, *Ducs et Pairs*, pp. 199–200, 202, 382. Where a family held two *duchés-pairies*, the junior line of the lineage could be permitted to hold the second: ibid, p. 199, n. 250.

[60] Labatut, *Ducs et pairs*, pp. 240–243 *passim*, provides a list of some of the more important of these, though it is far from comprehensive.

[61] See most recently Christopher Maginn, '"Surrender and Regrant" in the Historiography of Sixteenth-Century Ireland', *The Sixteenth-Century Journal* 38 (2007), pp. 955–974; Christopher Maginn, 'The Gaelic Peers, the Tudor Sovereigns, and English Multiple Monarchy', *Journal of British Studies* 50 (2011), pp. 566–586.

established. Remarkably the celebrated 'Act to Prevent the Further Growth of Popery' (1704), a centrepiece of the so-called penal laws of eighteenth-century Ireland, imposed partible inheritance on Roman Catholic landed families, or such as survived, but not on their Protestant counterparts, who had secured social and political mastery during the seventeenth century. The intention was quite clear: to destroy Catholic landholding and create an enduring Protestant ascendancy, underlining the intimate connection now recognised throughout Europe to exist between the practice of primogeniture and the continuity of a landed elite.[62]

The adoption of the Strict Settlement in Later Stuart England, which was fundamental to the significant social and political recovery of the landed classes after the midcentury upheavals, was even more extensive.[63] After 1660 the Strict Settlement – so-called because it was usually restricted to one individual and his sons – spread swiftly among the peerage. In its essentials and impact the English Strict Settlement resembled continental entails, but it was more comprehensive and differed in one important respect: it made specific provision for widows and younger sons, and sometimes for daughters too, in addition to the heir to the title and property.[64] Such agreements, often drawn up in wills or included in marriage settlements, were highly individualistic: their contours reflected the circumstances of a particular family. But their essentially dynastic aim was clear: to provide a secure landed patrimony to support a title in perpetuity. The Earl of Westmorland, who placed his lands within a Strict Settlement in 1668, spoke for his fellow peers when he declared that he did so in order that his estate 'might continue in his name and blood and may descend within the Earldom to the heirs male of the family'.[65]

---

[62] Ian McBride, *Eighteenth Century Ireland: The Isle of Slaves* (Dublin, 2009), pp. 195ff.

[63] See James M. Rosenheim, *The Emergence of a Ruling Order: English Landed Society 1650–1750* (London, 1998), for the wider evolution.

[64] This has inspired a substantial and, at times, controversial literature. The most detailed examination is Sir John Habakkuk, *Marriage, Debt and the Estates System: English Landownership 1650–1950* (Oxford, 1994), but see also J.V. Beckett, *The Aristocracy in England 1660–1914* (Oxford, 1986), esp. Chapter 2; Lloyd Bonfield, *Marriage Settlements 1601–1740* (Cambridge, 1983); Barbara English and John Saville, *Strict Settlement: A Guide for historians* (Hull, 1983); Stone and Stone, *An Open Elite*; Eileen Spring, *Law, Land and Family: Aristocratic Inheritance in England, 1300–1800* (Chapel Hill, NC, 1993); and Ralph Trumbach, *The Rise of the Egalitarian Family: Aristocratic Kinship and Domestic Relations in Eighteenth-Century England* (New York, 1978), pp. 69–117 *passim*; together with the list of journal articles in which the debate was initially carried on conveniently provided by Susan Staves, *Married Women's Separate Property in England, 1660–1833* (Cambridge, 1990), p. 276, n. 5, and the summary of that debate, *ibid.*, pp. 199–205.

[65] Quoted by Habakkuk, *Marriage, Debt and the Estates System*, p. 52.

By the close of the seventeenth century there were very few peerage families in England which were not safeguarding their landholding in this way. While historians have debated the precise extent to which it alone was responsible for the rise of larger estates in many English counties at this period, its undoubted and major contribution seems undeniable. It has been suggested that, by the middle of the eighteenth century, as much as half of all noble-held land may have been placed within settlements, and a hundred years later this figure may have been between 70 per cent and 90 per cent.[66] The great estates, which had been created in the later-seventeenth century, would survive for the next two centuries. Once again the adoption of such inheritance arrangements facilitated the creation and then ensured the survival of great landed patrimonies which were becoming common across Europe during the seventeenth century, as they had long been in Castile and some parts of France.

The practice of strict endogamy – which strengthened within the aristocracy at this period – could play the same role, particularly where primogeniture did not prevail, as in Russia.[67] The expansion of the aristocracy itself contributed to this, since families with whom the most important lineages intermarried were themselves entering the highest level of the nobility. This is clear from a detailed study of the *ducs-et-pairs* over the period 1589–1723, which reveals that their marriages were overwhelmingly with other peerage families or lineages which were themselves part of the high nobility or rising into it. This was so in over four-fifths of instances: 129 out of 162. Less than one-fifth were with *robe* dynasties or other ministerial families.[68] As in other countries, marriage within such a relatively narrow circle of aristocratic houses together with the established vagaries of succession and inheritance, strengthened the existing trend for most landed property to remain within the wider family, albeit at the price of extensive and often prolonged litigation over disputed inheritances. A shrewd and successful marriage strategy and a concentration upon intermarrying with other high-ranking lineages, which appears to be on the increase during the long seventeenth century, further consolidated aristocratic power throughout Europe.

New Opportunities and Elite Consolidation

The consolidation of the social elite and the extension of monarchical authority went hand in hand; there was an essential synergy between

---

[66] These estimates come from Habakkuk, *Marriage, Debt*, p. 48.
[67] See above, pp. 67–8.   [68] Figures from Labatut, *Ducs et pairs*, pp. 187–188.

aristocracy and what came to be styled absolutism.[69] Specialised personnel were needed in increasing numbers to officer the enlarged military forces and to staff the agencies of central and local government, and the traditional nobility were the principal – indeed almost the only – source from which these could be drawn. The old idea that the modern state rested on teams of bureaucrats of middle-class origin who had studied Roman law has been discredited. On the contrary: it is now abundantly clear that monarchical authority depended, in the seventeenth century and beyond, on partnership with the social elite. This was why the dying Cardinal Mazarin told the young Louis XIV in March 1661 that his regime must be based on the traditional alliance with the French nobility, which was his 'right arm'.[70] It was also one further reason – in addition to financial exigency – why the sale of offices, which usually led to the acquisition of noble status sooner or later, flourished during these decades. This practice became most formalised in Bourbon France, leading to a great expansion of the *robe* nobility.[71] Aspects of it were to be found in several countries, however, and further strengthened the bonds between ruler and elite. Monarchs both possessed the resources – abundant available land or, where this was lacking, pensions together with an effective monopoly on the provision of titles – to endow the new aristocracy, while a royal licence or tacit permission was needed to establish or amend an entail. Such arrangements required the ruler's permission, whether that was specific to a particular entail or generalised through enabling legislation. Over time the second became more usual than the first. Seventeenth-century rulers were happy to facilitate arrangements of this kind, which not merely created a pool of younger sons available for state service but also established the kind of powerful and enduring aristocracies upon which monarchical power depended, as it had always done.

The high nobility had always played a central role in the workings of central and local government. Control over more distant territories was accomplished primarily by winning over and cooperating with the local

---

[69] This is underlined for England by the seminal study of Michael J. Braddick, *State Formation in Early Modern England c.1550–1700* (Cambridge, 2000), p. 337 and Chapter 8 *passim*; for Europe as a whole, the articles by Robert Descimon, 'Power Elites and the Prince: The State as Enterprise', and Antoni Maczak, 'The Nobility-State Relationship', in Wolfgang Reinhard (ed.), *Power Elites and State Building* (Oxford, 1996), pp. 101–122 and 189–206, respectively, provide a wider perspective.

[70] Quoted by Richard Bonney (ed.), *Society and Government in France under Richelieu and Mazarin, 1624–61* (Basingstoke, 1988), p. 76.

[71] The best guide is now Robert Descimon and Elie Haddad (eds.), *Épreuves de Noblesse: Les experiences nobiliaires de la haute robe parisienne (XVIe-XVIIIe siècle)* (Paris, 2010).

elite.[72] The Spanish Monarchy was the outstanding example of this, with mutual dependence shaping relations between the Crown and the leading families; the persistence of such bonds was one important reason why Castile and other regions in the heartlands were unscathed during the 1640s, when many outlying provinces were wracked by rebellion.[73] The aristocracy, however, had a much wider role than merely serving as conduits between centre and periphery. Leading noblemen dominated the army's high command and went on military campaigns; they acted as councillors and also administered justice: upholding law, and maintaining civil peace, were always the principal objectives of monarchs within their own realms, while the nobility constituted almost the only substantial and available pool of personnel to discharge these tasks. The sixteenth-century Reformation, together with an increasing secularisation of political life, reduced the role of leading Churchmen within royal government during the early modern centuries, and this too increased the importance of the nobility as potential state officials. Such service had always been one source of status and advancement, and it became more important during this period, as the activities of monarchical governments and thus their size increased.

The evolution of the French provincial governorship during the seventeenth and eighteenth centuries demonstrated the aristocracy's continuing importance for royal administration. Before 1600 the office had been primarily military in nature. A governor's main duty had been to assemble and to lead the province's contingent to the king's forces when war threatened. The slow establishment of a royal army during the first century of Bourbon rule had weakened and, eventually, removed that role, though many great aristocrats remained important in the enlarged military establishment of the French State. During the seventeenth century the provincial governorships became part of the new administrative structure slowly constructed from the 1630s onwards. The central element in this was the post of royal provincial intendant, employed to supervise the raising of the necessary resources for warfare. It was an important innovation, and created what had hitherto been lacking: agents

---

[72] A valuable demonstration of this is J. H. Elliott, 'A Provincial Aristocracy: The Catalan Ruling Class in the Sixteenth and Seventeenth Centuries', reprinted in his *Spain and Its World 1500–1700: Selected Essays* (London, 1989), pp. 71–91.

[73] I. A. A. Thompson, *War and Government in Habsburg Spain, 1560–1620* (London, 1976), Chapter 5; Ignacio Atienza Hernández, *Aristocracia, poder y riqueza en la España moderna: La Casa de Osuna siglos XV-XIX* (Madrid, 1987), pp. 53–54 and *passim*; J. H. Elliott, 'A Non-Revolutionary Society: Castile in the 1640s', in his *Spain, Europe and the Wider World 1500–1800* (New Haven, 2009), pp. 74–91; Luis R. Corteguera, 'Loyalty and Revolt in the Spanish Monarchy', in Benedict and Gutmann (eds.), *Early Modern Europe*, pp. 80–99.

in the localities who were directly responsible to the Crown and would respond quickly and unquestioningly to royal commands. But the new system always worked in partnership with the established authorities. Crucially, the number of provincial intendants and the relatively small numbers of subordinate officials who aided them, were never sufficient to carry out all the duties which the Crown expected them to discharge. France was an extremely large country, and the number of administrators inadequate. The consequence was that the intendants everywhere cooperated with the established figures, above all the royal governors.

The House of Condé provides a particularly striking example of the continuing importance of the high nobility in government. Between 1632 and the French Revolution it provided six governors of the province of Burgundy, and was only ousted from that position – and then temporarily – during the 1650s, when the Great Condé was in revolt against the Crown and fighting on the side of the Spanish Monarchy.[74] This dynastic continuity was nearly unique: son succeeded father on five successive occasions, with the son often having already served an apprenticeship to familiarise him with the province and its administration. Most sons were formally involved in governing the province from the age of 16 or 17, in order to gain experience before they themselves assumed full authority upon head of the family.

Aristocratic siblings were one important source of military and administrative personnel. This was in part a consequence – at times quite deliberate – of changed inheritance arrangements. The adoption of strict primogeniture created a reservoir of younger sons denied much wealth of their own and so anxious to serve the monarchical state, which might provide both a career and, if they were fortunate, a degree of independent wealth which their own lineage's economic circumstances or family strategies could deny them. In many aristocratic houses a strategy of restricted marriage was the essential corollary of primogeniture, as younger sons were prevented from marrying because of the financial implications for the lineage as a whole. Within Catholic monarchies – and most countries where such arrangements flourished were Catholic – male siblings would be packed off to a career in the Church or the army, with such financial support as the lineage could provide from its own resources and, perhaps, from loans contracted for the purpose. Even in the post-Counter Reformation Church there were bishoprics and even archbishoprics, and monasteries as well, which were in practice permanently controlled by a single lineage and integrated into its family

---

[74] The governors are listed in Jean Duquesne, *Dictionnaire des Gouverneurs de Province sous l'Ancien Régime (novembre 1315 – 20 février 1791)* (Paris, 2002), pp. 178–179. The first Condé governor was appointed in September 1631, but does not seem to have assumed office until the following year.

strategy.[75] But even in Catholic monarchies usually only one son would be launched on a career in the Church, and in Orthodox Russia and Protestant Denmark, Sweden and England a rather different pattern prevailed.

Everywhere, however, younger sons were increasingly becoming drawn to a military or administrative career in state service. This was one reason behind Peter the Great's attempt to introduce primogeniture into Russia through the Law of Single Inheritance and would inspire an identical attempt – half a century later – by Prussia's Frederick the Great to establish the *Fideikommiss* among the Junkers.[76] Both iniatives were unsuccessful, because the Junkers and their Russian counterparts were devoted to partible inheritance, which was long established, and perhaps more importantly, because of the relative poverty of landed estates in both countries. The trouble and expense involved could be justified only if there was sufficient landed and other wealth worth placing within a legal trust: it is striking that in the Austrian Habsburg Monarchy the *Fideikommiss* flourished primarily in the rich farming areas of Bohemia, Styria, Lower Austria and, to a lesser extent, Upper Austria, and seem to have been far less widely adopted in more mountainous regions such as Carinthia or the Tyrol.[77] It would be the nineteenth century before entails were adopted at all widely in either Prussia or Russia.

This period thus saw a synergy between a series of developments, the chronology and detailed nature of which varied from region to region and even province to province, but in their essentials were similar. Political upheavals and foreign wars made land available on a wholly new scale; individual families organised their affairs in ways which concentrated resources increasingly upon the eldest son and his first surviving male heir, and in this way fostered the development of aristocracies across much of Europe; while rulers deliberately encouraged this evolution by distributing lands and, less commonly, other forms of wealth to their elites, and facilitating its concentration upon the first-born male child in each generation. To adapt Charles Tilly's celebrated aphorism about the essential interdependence of war and state power: during the seventeenth century the monarchical State and family practices together made aristocracy, and the aristocracies in turn made States. The consequence was

---

[75] For the way in which papal families were able to exercise neo-hereditary authority, see Maura Piccialuti, *L'immortalità dei beni: Fedecommessi e primogeniture a Roma nei secoli XVII e XVIII* (Rome, 1999), pp. 40, 183; cf. above, p. 67, for an identical situation in the Catholic Rhineland.

[76] See above, p. 66; cf. the Prussian King's comments in the 'Political Testament' of 1768: Richard Dietrich (ed.), *Die politischen Testamente der Hohenzollern* (Berlin, 1986), p. 500.

[77] This seems to be one implication of the statistical information provided by Inama-Sternegg, 'Die Familien-Fideicommisse in Oesterreich'.

that Europe's noble elite, by the decades around 1700, was defined to a far greater extent than a hundred years before by its proximity to monarchical power.

Profiting from Change: Social Elites and the Transformed Monarchy

The fourth and final theme is the question of who were the beneficiaries of these developments? What kind of individuals received the lands taken from defeated rebels, alienated from crown demesne or acquired as new provinces were conquered and annexed? What was the composition, in other words, of the aristocracy which resulted? Undoubtedly some were genuinely 'new' men with origins outside the nobility, individuals who by their own efforts and, perhaps, a large slice of luck, simply being in the right place at the right time, secured lands and the status to match. Richard Boyle, who rose from being a younger son of a Cambridgeshire yeoman farmer to become the First Earl of Cork, exemplified such a trajectory.[78] He built up a large landholding in southern Ireland by highly dubious if quasi-legal means during the period when English authority was being expanded (he was a member of the Dublin government), bought the title of 'Earl of Cork' for £4,000 from the Duke of Buckingham, James VI and I's all-powerful favourite, and successfully established aristocratic lineages on both sides of the Irish Sea. But men like Cork, though they can be identified in most countries, were everywhere in a minority, and usually a very small minority at that.

Relatively few individuals made such a spectacular ascent and rose into the aristocracy within one generation from outside the nobility. The spectacular emergence of the Hungarian family of Eszterházy, the greatest success story of seventeenth-century aristocratic Europe, was rather more typical. Originally impoverished lesser nobles, their ascent had begun during the more socially fluid decades before 1600.[79] Subsequently the family prospered through skilful marriage and fortunate succession followed by faithful service to the Habsburg dynasty, to become the kingdom's greatest magnate lineage, with landholdings which at their eighteenth-century peak may have been more than one million acres in extent. Two individuals played central roles: Miklós Eszterházy (1583–1645) and his son Pál (1635–1713). Miklós, who

[78] See the notable study by Nicholas Canny, *The Upstart Earl: A Study of the Social and Mental World of Richard Boyle, First Earl of Cork, 1566–1643* (Cambridge, 1982).

[79] The articles in the 1995 exhibition catalogue *Die Fürsten Esterházy: Magnaten, Diplomaten und Mäzene*, eds. Jakob Perschy and Harald Prickler (Eisenstadt, 1995) provide a helpful introduction.

became palatine – the head of the kingdom's government and representative of the Habsburg ruler – in 1625, secured vast estates mainly in the northwest of the Kingdom of Hungary, around Eisenstadt in the Burgenland which became the centre of the family's power, together with the impressive castle of Forchtenstein. Himself a convert, he played a key strategic role in winning over Protestant magnates to Catholicism. The marital arrangements through which he aimed to retain this patrimony were even more remarkable and constitute a quite extreme example of endogamy. Miklós married, as his second wife, the widow of Imre Thurzó, Krisztina Nyáry, by whom he had a son Pál. He then married the son of his own first marriage to the daughter of Krisztina Nyáry's first marriage to Thurzó. These shrewd marital alliances enabled the Eszterházy to benefit from the extinction of the Thurzó in the male line in 1636. But Miklós's dynastic operations were far from finished: even more remarkably Pál, his son by Krisztina Nyáry, was then married to the granddaughter of his own first marriage! Subsequently Pal Eszterházy would be the brother-in-law of Ferenc Nádasdy, who himself was the son-in-law of none other than: Miklós Eszterházy![80]

The point about these incestuous marriages, both figuratively and literally, was that they aimed to preserve and extend the family patrimony, and did so very effectively indeed. They were undertaken long before the family created a *Fideikommiss*, and aimed at the same broad goal: that of preventing the break-up of the family's estates. Pál Eszterházy was in his turn Palatine (1681–1713), skilfully balancing Hungarian patriotism with Habsburg dynastic loyalism, and secured further extensive estates for the family as the Ottoman occupiers were driven back by successive military campaigning. By the 1690s, when a series of *Fideikommisse* were concluded – by this point his fecundity had led to the establishment of a series of collateral branches – the Eszterházy latifundia was close to its greatest extent. His magnate status was signalled in two further developments: the award of the title of Imperial Prince (the first Hungarian to be so honoured) in 1687, and the building of an impressive palace at Eisenstadt, which would remain the centre of the family's power until the construction of the fabled residence of Esterháza during the later eighteenth century.

Analyses of Europe's new aristocracy reveal that the gainers were almost always established lineages in the nobility or, in England, the gentry. Members of middle-ranking and even lesser-noble families benefitted, along with younger sons from the aristocracy itself, securing lands and status and founding major new lineages. Developments in Bohemia,

---

[80] For these marital arrangements, see Evans, *Making of the Habsburg Monarchy*, especially pp. 241, 247.

referred to earlier, provide the best example. The greatest beneficiaries from a redistribution of land during the Thirty Years' War were a group of around ten families drawn from the country's old nobility, who consolidated their power impressively and by the mid-seventeenth century constituted the first and most important element in a new magnate elite which would dominate the region for three centuries to come. The latest calculation is that native Bohemian families secured over half (53 per cent) of the confiscated estates redistributed during the Thirty Years' War.[81]

Denmark provides a rather different pattern, though one which was quite compatible with wider European developments. After 1660 the monarchy recovered the sole right to ennoble, hitherto shared with the aristocratic council and in practice exercised largely by the elite, which had resulted in relatively few ennoblements as the oligarchy closed ranks: little more than one a year over the entire period since 1536. This opened the way for a wide-ranging reconstitution of the nobility. Titles were awarded for the first time in 1671, and proved to be the first of a wide-ranging series of changes, which established what was in practice a Table of Ranks, as social distinction was closely tied to the acceptance of service to the Crown. Such service was to be overwhelmingly administrative in nature: the new elite primarily comprised the central government officials of the absolute monarchy. By the end of the eighteenth century, 62 comital titles and 58 baronial ones had been awarded. Many of these men were now either courtiers or army officers, as the pattern of ennoblements began to change.[82]

The composition of Europe's aristocracies was changing in this way. At the same time, however, and perhaps more importantly, the nobility was itself becoming more compressed and stratified, with a much larger aristocracy both proportionately and in numerical terms. One dimension of this wider development lies beyond the subject of this article: the widespread decline of many families in the lesser nobility, trapped by the sixteenth-century Price Rise in the vice of static or near static incomes, with rents fixed in long-term tenancies and no access to court patronage of the kind which enabled leading families to prosper, and rising prices, exacerbated by the demands of conspicuous consumption which imposed new levels of expenditure on even poorer members of the Second Estate. In some countries the persistence of partible inheritance among the lesser nobility (in contrast to the aristocracy) and the consequent fragmentation of estates was a further reason for this group's increasing difficulties.

---

[81] Mat'a, *Svet České Aristokracie*, p. 147.

[82] There is considerable information on this in Albert Fabritius, *Danmarks Riges Adel: Dens Tilgang og Afgang 1536–1935* (Copenhagen, 1946).

Table 3.2 *Rise of Titled Nobility and Decline of the Lesser Nobility in the Early Modern Kingdom of Bohemia, with Their Share of All Landholdings (expressed as a percentage of the total number of peasants under their control)*

	1557	1603	1615	1656	1741
Estate of Lords	184 (49%)	216 (45%)	197 (45%)	293 (60%)	279 (?)
Estate of Knights	1,438 (34%)	1,131 (35%)	977 (31%)	587 (10%)	238 (?)
Total	1,622	1,347	1,174	880	517
Proportion of Lords in Nobility	11%	16%	17%	33%	54%

Source: Petr Mat'a, *Svet Ceské Aristokracie (1500–1700)* (Prague, 2004), p. 159.

Table 3.3 *Nobles and Lords in Early Modern Lower Austria*

	Estate of Lords		Estate of Knights		Combined Totals	
Year	Families	Individual members	Families	Individual members	Families	Individual members
1415	43	67	167	222	210	289
1580	56	119	197	281	253	400
1620	87	243	128	224	215	467
1720/27	160	280	105	111	265	391

Source: Karin J. MacHardy, *War, Religion and Court Patronage in Habsburg Austria: The Social and Cultural Dimensions of Political Interaction, 1521–1622* (Basingstoke, 2003), p. 134.

Throughout Europe these decades saw a clear and at times marked decline in the numbers of poorer noble families, as many simply abandoned the unequal struggle to maintain their status. Tables 3.2 and 3.3 demonstrate this for Bohemia and for Lower Austria, with the clear rise of the Estate of Lords (*Herrenstand*) and within it the emergence of an aristocratic tier of counts and princes: the two highest titles of nobility.

Everywhere these decades saw a noted expansion of the aristocracy. One guide to this, which reinforced the process which was under way, was the 'inflation of honours', the rapid expansion evident throughout seventeenth-century Europe in the numbers of titled nobles and even in the range of dignities which could be granted. The awarding of more and more titles, and the resulting rise of a lineage through the various ranks, which in German-speaking Europe went from baron to count and then prince, was a central dimension of this process. Tables 3.4, 3.5 and 3.6 provide three national examples of the way in which the numbers of titled

Table 3.4 *The Rise of the* Ducs-et-Pairs *in Bourbon France*

Date	Ecclesiastical Peers	Royal Relatives	(a) Princes-Étrangers	Aristocrats	Total
1589	5	10	14	11	40
1610	6	9	14	17	46
1643	6	8	14	28	56
1661	6	12	8	38	64
1715	8	6	11	48	73
1723	8	7	9	52	76

Source: Jean-Pierre Labatut, *Les ducs et pairs de France au XVIIe siècle: Étude sociale* (Paris, 1972), p. 69.

Table 3.5 *Expansion of the Titled Nobility in the Spanish Monarchy, 1500–1700*

	Títulos	Dukes	Marquises	Counts
1506	53	10	7	36
1557	64	11	10	43
1577	105	22	37	46
1597	127	23	46	58
1615	193	26	73	94
1630	212	27	81	104
		[41 grandees 1627]		
1665	236	[93 grandees 1659]		
1700	533	[113]	334	171

Source: Based upon I. A. A. Thompson, 'The Nobility in Spain, 1600–1800', in H. M. Scott, ed., *The European Nobilities in the Seventeenth and Eighteenth Centuries* (2 vols.; London, 1995), vol. 1, p. 191. Though slightly different totals are given in the earlier study by Ignacio Atienza Hernández, *Aristocracia, Poder y Riqueza en la España Moderna: La Casa de Osuna siglos XV–XIX* (Madrid, 1987), p. 41, cf. p 17, the two sets of figures reveal an identical trend.

families and their equivalent in Russia, the members of the boyar Duma, increased significantly at this time. Whether it is the expansion of the *ducs et pairs* in France, or the *títulos* and the *grandeza* in the Spanish Monarchy, or the creation of a titled aristocracy in Sweden; the creation of non-royal dukes in later Stuart England, the emergence of an imperial elite of princes, counts and barons in the Austrian Habsburg Monarchy, the introduction of a titled aristocracy in post-1660 Denmark, or the expansion of the boyar Duma in seventeenth-century Russia, the European trend is identical and always sharply upwards.

Table 3.6 *Seventeenth-Century Expansion of Boyar Duma Cohort*

Year	Overall Size	Boyars	Okol'nichie	'Aristocracy' (Boyars plus Okol'nichie)
1613	37	24	8	32
1645	41	23	14	37
1676	96	39	32	71
1682	151	73	46	119
1694	154	63	48	111

Source: Compiled from Marshall T. Poe, *The Russian Elite during the Seventeenth Century* (2 vols.; Helsinki, 2004), ii.52, 63, 64.

Monarchs played a crucial role in this process by granting lands to their leading subjects, thereby facilitating that lineage's rise. The other principal commodity they had to bestow, was honours and dignities of all kinds, such as habits of the Military Orders in the Iberian Peninsula and the accompanying incomes, and titles most of all. Status preceded wealth, though in the socially fluid seventeenth century, it could also accompany enhanced economic well being. Only a very small minority of nobles actually possessed a title, even after the 'inflation of honours'. Those who did were clearly marked out as members of the social elite. The award of a dignity such as that of 'count' or 'duke' confirmed the hierarchical nature of society, at the head of which stood the monarch himself, and reinforced the stratification which was under way. It identified the various strata of which a particular noble elite consisted: by the later seventeenth century the hierarchy of titles had become effectively the hierarchy of the aristocracy.

This was one reason – another was the growing importance of court society and the development of its own protocols – for the proliferation of reference works such as the *État de la France*, often officially or semi-officially inspired, which delimited precedence and resolved whether, on formal occasions, the son of a duke preceded a marquis and tricky questions of this kind.[83] The award of a title also could also change a family's relative position within that same hierarchy, and for that reason such dignities were avidly sought both by individuals and by the lineages of which they were part. All noble families were engaged in a permanent competition not merely to maintain their own standing, but if possible to rise in the hierarchy and to secure more status than their aristocratic rivals: as the more formalised court societies which emerged from the seventeenth-century revealed.

[83] See Jeroen Duindam, *Vienna and Versailles: The Courts of Europe's Dynastic Rivals, 1550–1780* (Cambridge, 2003), esp. Chapters 6.

Titles were a significant index of success, as well as an indication of the extent to which aristocratic society – like the wider nobility of which it formed the most important part – was now more and more hierarchical.

Aristocratic Consolidation and Its Legacies

These developments were crucially important in the longer perspective. Historians of the modern European nobility – taking their cue from Arno Mayer's seminal *The Persistence of the Old Regime: Europe to the Great War*, published a generation ago – have made clear just how successfully the aristocratic elite sustained its power into the nineteenth century and even beyond.[84] Many of the families whose endurance is highlighted by Mayer had first secured real prominence and the lands and status to support this, during the early modern period. It is striking that the three principal examples which he employs for the Austrian Habsburg Empire – the Liechtenstein, Schwarzenberg and Eszterházy families – all secured their extensive landholdings during the seventeenth century: the Liechtenstein benefitted notably from the redistribution of estates during the Thirty Years' War, particularly in Moravia; the Schwarzenberg, originally from Franconia, had risen by skilful family strategy and service to the dynasty before buying vast estates in Bohemia to add to their existing landholding; while the Eszterházy, as we have seen, gained from the recovery of Habsburg control over Hungary at this period.[85] All three families benefitted from their continuing support of the Habsburg dynasty, as well as from their own successful opportunism and shrewd family strategies. Each lineage retained these estates down to the First World War and did so, revealingly, by continuing to employ family *Fideikommisse*.

This encapsulates the longer-term significance of the developments sketched in this chapter. Europe's aristocracy, which further consolidated its position during the eighteenth century, was sufficiently strong to survive the twin challenges of political revolution and economic transformation after the 1780s, and to preserve its status and influence largely intact into the very different world of later modern Europe. That it was able to do so was due, in no small measure, to the firm and deep roots which it had established in Europe's social, political and economic life through its partnership with dynastic monarchy during the long seventeenth century.

---

[84] (New York, 1981). There are good syntheses of the abundant recent literature by Dominic Lieven, *The Aristocracy in Europe 1815–1914* (Basingstoke, 1992) and Ellis Wasson, *Aristocracy and the Modern World* (Basingstoke, 2006).

[85] Mayer, *Persistence of the Old Regime*, p. 27; cf. above, p. 80, for the Eszterházy.

4   Dynastic Instability, the Emergence of the French Monarchical Commonwealth and the Coming of the Rhetoric of '*L'état*', 1360s to 1650s

James Collins

Introduction: Commonwealth, State, and Kingship

> The office of kings because of their royal dignities is to govern and administer all of the *chose publique*, not to put part of it in good order and leave other parts without proper provision. Charles V, ordinance on regencies, October 1374.[1]

The famous entry of Henry II and Catherine de Medici into Rouen in October 1550 symbolically displays the French monarchy near the end of its Commonwealth days. The centrepiece of these 'pleasant spectacles and magnificent theatres' offered to 'the sacred Majesty' of the king by the 'citizens' of Rouen was the legendary dance of 300 men completely naked, *hallez et herissonez* – 50 Brazilian 'savages' 250 Rouennais pretending to be Brazilians – which so astonished Catherine that she 'forgot to eat or drink'.[2]

This dazzling display of early colonialist visual rhetoric has outshone the entry's other elements of nakedly royalist discourse of splendour and obedience: in the first chariot, Renown, represented by a woman of 'incomparable beauty', illustrated the victory of famous kings, like Francis I or Henry II, over Death. In the third chariot, Fortune put on Henry II's Caesar-coiffed head an imperial crown or tiara of fine gold, well burnished and closed on top by two crossed hemi-circles in the form of two *colures*,[3] to

---

[1] *Ordonnances*, VI, 45. [*Ordonnances des rois de France de la troisième race*, 22 vols. (Paris, 1723–1847).]

[2] *La Deduction du somptueux ordre plaisantz spectacles et magnifiques theatres dressés et exhibés par les Citoiens de Rouen ville Metropolitain du pays de Normandie A la sacrée Maiesté du Treschristien Roy de France, Henry second leur souverain Seigneur et à Tresillustre, ma Dame Katherine de Medicis La Royne son espouse* (Paris, Rouen, 1551). One can find the Brazilian ball image online at: https://upload.wikimedia.org/wikipedia/commons/5/5b/Brazilian_ball_for_Henry_II_in_Rouen_October_1_1550.jpg.

[3] The '*colures*' were two circles that split the equator or the zodiac into four equal parts, and which stood for the four seasons. (From the *Dictionary of the Académie Française*, 1762.)

Figure 4.1 'Brazilian ball' at Henry II's 1550 entry into Rouen, contemporaneous French painting, anonymous. Online at: https://uplo ad.wikimedia.org/wikipedia/commons/5/5b/Brazilian_ball_for_Henry _II_in_Rouen_October_1_1550.jpg

declare that the sovereign majesty of the Kings of France held only of God. The 1550 Rouen entry, like that of 1549 in Paris, thus marked a profound iconographic shift with respect to the royal-imperial crown.[4] The traditional image was the one provided in the Grandes Chroniques de France with respect to the Emperor Charles IV's 1378 visit to Paris, showing both King Charles V and Wenceslas, King of the Romans, wearing royal (open) crowns: only the emperor wore a closed, imperial one.[5]

---

[4] I. D. McFarlane, *The Entry of Henri II into Paris 16 June 1549* (Binghamton, NY, 1982), which reproduces *C'est l'ordre qui a este tenu a la nouvelle et ioyeuse entrée ... Henry deuzieme ... 16 juin 1549* (Paris, 1549). Angels carry 'an Imperial crown [...] signifying that the King of the French does not recognize any superior on earth, but is monarch in his land, which he holds only of God and the sword' (7).

[5] The closed imperial crown had slowly crept into French ceremonials during the reign of Francis I. See M. François, 'Le pouvoir royal et l'introduction en France de la Couronne fermée', *Comptes-rendus des séances de l'Académie des Inscriptions et Belles-Lettres* 106:2 (1962), pp. 404–413. La deduction du sompteux ordre can be found online at: http://bibliotheque -numerique.inha.fr/collection/952-c-est-la-deduction-du-sumptueux-ordre-p/. The Good Fortune image is on p. 63. The Grandes Chroniques de France, Bibliothèque Nationale de France (BNF), Manuscrit Français 2813, is available at the Bibliothèque Nationale's online resource, Gallica. The image of the emperor and the two kings is found on folio 470, in glorious full color.

Royal entry ceremonies, going back at least to the fourteenth century, invariably had this element of asserting the King of France's *puissance absolue*, that is, his independence from earthly authority, whether through the colour of the horse or the shape of the Crown. We anachronistically assume this concept had to do with the king's subjects, whereas, in fact, it targeted the emperor and the pope. By the seventeenth century, *puissance absolue* focused on the king's independence from the pope, as the controversy over the Third Estate's first article at the Estates General of 1614 made clear: the deputies wanted the king to declare a 'fundamental law of the kingdom' on the 'independence' of the Crown, such that the king was recognized as 'sovereign in your state'.

That article came from the cahier of the city of Paris, although a similar one appeared in other cahiers, even at the castellany level in Champagne. The second element of the article held that no earthly power could strip the king of the Crown or declare that his subjects no longer had to obey him. The king held his crown from God alone, and 'no power [*puissance*] on earth', had any right over his kingdom. Anyone attacking his 'sacred person', in deed or word, was to be declared guilty of *lèse-majesté*.[6] This article, and the various discussions about it, harkened back to the assassinations of France's two previous kings and to strident political debates about the king's relationship to the pope in 1588–1595 and in 1610, with the publication of Cardinal Bellarmine's response to the Anglo-French legist William Barclay.

The author of this article was none other than Antoine Arnauld, father of the famous Jansenist. Arnauld had represented the University of Paris in its lawsuit against the Jesuit Collège de Clermont in 1593, and his attacks against the Jesuit order had a direct connection to the failed assassination attempts against Henry IV in 1593 and 1594. Unsurprisingly, given the role of Parlementaires in the local assembly of Paris, the judges sided with this article: 'your Parlement supplicates Your Majesty not to permit that the sovereignty he holds nakedly and immediately of God be submitted to another power [*puissance*] for whatever pretext there might be'.[7] The other power in question was, of course, the Pope: this initiative at the Estates General intertwined completely with the contemporaneous controversy between Bellarmine and Barclay about the nature of papal power.[8]

---

[6] C. Lalource and C. Duval (eds.), *Recueil des cahiers généraux des trois ordres aux États-généraux: d'Orléans en 1560, sous Charles IX.; de Blois en 1576, de Blois en 1588, sous Henri III.; de Paris en 1614, sous Louis XIII* (Paris, 1789), v. VIII, p. 85, taking the wording from the procès-verbal of the Third Estate.

[7] Remonstrances of Parlement of Paris, 22 May 1615: BNF, M Fr 15,536, fols. 193r and ff.

[8] On Bellarmine, see the recent books by Stephania Tutino, *Empire of Souls: Robert Bellarmine and the Christian Commonwealth* (Oxford: Oxford UP, 2011). For far more

This insistence on the temporal independence of the King of France had a long visual history. Perhaps the most famous such image remained the iconography of Emperor Charles IV's 1378 ceremonial entry into Paris. In the *Grandes Chroniques de France* [*GCF*] of Charles V, the images and the written text emphasized the colour of the horses: Charles V rode a white horse; his guests, who had arrived at Saint-Denis on white horses, switched to black horses, which he had sent to them for the entry into Paris.[9] Jean Fouquet's magnificent mid-fifteenth-century illustrations for a new manuscript of the GCF similarly emphasized the white-black horse contrast.[10] Christine de Pizan, following closely the text of the *GCF*, explained why it mattered: 'and this colour was not chosen without counsel; for the emperors, by their right, when they entered into walled towns of their lordship (*seigneurie*) were accustomed to be on white horses; the King did not wish this to be done in his kingdom, in order that there would not be noted any sign of domination'.[11] The identification of the white horse with royal supremacy long endured, whether in the colour of Francis I's steed in Taddeo Zuccaro's fanciful *Francis I Leading Emperor Charles V and Cardinal Farnese into Paris*, or in Rubens' equally imaginary *Triumphal Entry of Henry IV into Paris*, with the king's chariot pulled by magnificent white steeds.[12]

detail on the interplay of the two, see the relevant chapters in my *Republicanism and the State in Early Modern France* (Cambridge, forthcoming). William Barclay's response to Bellarmine appeared posthumously, published by the efforts of his son, John, then living in England. William Barclay, although English, lived in France; he taught at the law school of the University of Angers. He studied with the leading French legal scholar, Jacques Cujas, who had also taught many of the principal jurists of late sixteenth-century France, including the First Presidents of several of the Parlements. On Cujas, see the new biography by Xavier Prévost, *Jacques Cujas (1522–1590). Jurisconsulte humaniste* (Geneva, 2015).

[9] A. Hedeman, 'Valois Legitimacy: Editorial Changes in Charles V's *Grandes chroniques de France*,' *Art Bulletin* 66:1 (1984), pp. 97–117, shows that the royal government quite specifically used the *Grandes chroniques* for political purposes.

[10] The *Grandes chroniques de France* [GCF] mentions this privilege; Christine de Pizan, in her biography of Charles V, reproduces verbatim the description from the GCF. E. Inglis, *Jean Fouquet and the invention of France* (New Haven and London, 2011), pp. 172–74 (and Illustrations 75 and 76), notes that eight of the 53 illustrations in Fouquet's *GCF* cover this event. François Avril, in his edition of the Fouquet manuscript, discusses the production of various copies of the GCF: F. Avril, M. -T. Gousset and B. Guenée, *Les Grandes chroniques de France. Reproduction intégrale en fac-similé des miniatures de Fouquet. Manuscrit français 6465 de la Bibliothèque nationale de Paris* (Paris, 1987).

[11] C. de Pizan, *Le livre des fais et des bonnes meurs du sage roy Charles V*, Chapter XXXV. Oddly, the copy of the GCF created at Paris in the 1390s in the 'Bohemian' style, initially owned by Jean, duke of Berry, contains not a single image of the 1378 visit. BNF, M Fr 2608, available on Gallica. Royal workshops created four copies at this time, based on the original of Charles V.

[12] Image of Zuccaro's painting online at https://en.wikipedia.org/wiki/Villa_Farnese; for the Rubens, it can be viewed at the virtualuffizi.com website. Francis I did not, in fact, meet Charles V outside Paris; he sent his sons. As for Henry IV entering Paris, the famous 1606

In the Rouen entry, just before the three triumphal chariots rode a group of 50 men, representing famous captains from the *pays* of Normandy, who had defended the French Commonwealth; these men 'faithfully [...] served the kings of France their natural seigneurs'. Then came 57 men, representing the kings of France back to Pharamond, 'who, by their magnanimity, virtue, solid prudence, and penetrating providence have so ruled and maintained their subjects in good peace and justice, that the renown of these kings, spread to all the climates of the universe, will be crowned with immortal glory'.[13] We get here a litany of the attributes of the good king, who allows his subjects to live in peace and rules with justice. The elements of the political discourse of the previous 200 years are all present: the importance of the *pays*, the service to the Commonwealth, and the virtues of the good king, who rules through justice.[14]

Henry II's coronation, in 1547, had marked a decisive symbolic moment in the evolution of the French royal Commonwealth: for the first time, in the coronation oath, the king 'married' the kingdom. As a 'husband', he obtained the usufruct of his 'wife's' immoveable possessions, but not ownership: he could not sell, alienate or exchange lands 'she' brought.[15] In February 1566, chancellor Michel de l'Hospital had Charles IX issue the Edict of Moulins, which forbade the alienation or selling any part of the royal demesne, except to provide an apanage for a royal son or, on a temporary basis (with permanent right of repurchase), to raise money for war. The edict restated these principles because 'some of the ancient rules and maxims about the union and conservation of our demesne are badly known, and others little known'.[16] Many contemporaries took this edict to be one of the three fundamental laws of the kingdom: the Salic Law; the inalienability of the royal demesne; and the *puissance absolue* [exclusive right to make public law] of the king.

---

engraving based on Nicolas Baullery accurately shows him on a horse. The heavily romanticized 1817 version of François Girard shows Henry astride a cream-coloured steed.

[13] Later as 'La Deduction du somptueux ordre', consulted at archive.org: https://archive .org/stream/cestladeductiond00unkn#page/n37/mode/2up.

[14] I am using the English 'Commonwealth' for the French *'Respublique'* in order to avoid confusion with 'Republic' in the sense of a polity without a monarch. On the complexities of 'commonweale' in fifteenth-century England, see D. Kern, 'Comparative Political Legitimacies: Representative Institutions and Political Conflict in England and Castile, 1450–1520', PhD thesis, Georgetown University, 2012, Chapter 2.

[15] R. Jackson, *Vive le Roi!* (Chapel Hill, NC, 1984), 85ff.; on inalienability, G. Leyte, *Domaine et domanialité publique dans la France medieval (XIIe-XVe siècles)* (Strasbour, 1996), 324ff. None of Henry II's sons seems to have used this part of the ceremony; Henry IV did.

[16] Relevant edicts in *Ordonnances*, I, 665; I, 762; VI, 45ff. See Leyte, *Domaine*, pp. 329ff. for a full discussion.

The edict offered a fine example of the usage of the term '*estat*' in the mid-1560s: Charles called the demesne 'one of the principle sinews (*nerfs*) of our state'.[17]

All three of these principles came into being in the fourteenth century; not surprisingly, the coherent idea of a French Commonwealth (*respublique françoise*) also came into being at that time. These three laws unequivocally gave pre-eminence to the Crown and Commonwealth over the king, to the king's eternal body over his temporal one.[18] The changes of the mid-sixteenth century paved the way for the transformation of Commonwealth to state, which transpired in the coming half century, that is, precisely during the massive increase in government personnel.

How massive was this increase? Normandy, in 1500, had a single general receiver, controller general, treasurer of France, chief clerk, and 'general' of finances, along with 15 local districts (*élections*), each staffed by an overseer (*élu*), a receiver, and a controller: roughly 50 officers of finances.[19] After the creation of the *généralités* of Rouen and Caen in 1542, it had two treasurer-generals, general receivers, and general controllers. Normandy still had only 17 *élections* and 20 *élus* in 1570. By 1620, Normandy had 200 *élus*, double the number the entire kingdom had held in 1500.[20] The Norman central financial personnel grew from five in 1500 to ten in 1542, to roughly 75 by 1620.[21] The growth was as great in Norman law courts.[22]

---

[17] Isambert, *Recueil*, XIII, 185ff. The League sought to make 'Catholicity' a constitutional law of France. The edict offers an unusual Renaissance gloss on Cicero's maxim that taxes were the sinews of the *res publica*; the more common usage was 'taxes are the *nerfs* [sinews] of war', which Richelieu changed, precisely as we would expect, to 'taxes are the sinews of the State'.

[18] E. Kantorowicz, *The King's Two Bodies* (Princeton, 1955).

[19] The 'general' of finances oversaw the collection of taxes; the treasurer of France looked after demesne revenue: in practice, the two men often worked together. Individual parishes collected their own direct taxes and paid them to the local receiver, at the *élection*. He passed about 85 per cent of the money to the general receiver.

[20] J. Collins, *Fiscal Limits of Absolutism* (Berkeley, 1988), pp. 39–42 and Appendix A. France had about 85 *élections* in 1500, each with an *élu*; by 1620, it had about 125 *élections* and over 1,000 *élus*. Those numbers jumped sharply after 1620 due to the extension of *élections* into the southwest. We have excellent statistics for the later *généralité* of Montpellier: 111 royal officers in 1500, 124 in 1550, and 441 in 1600, with the increase roughly balanced between judges and financial officers. The *gages* paid rose from 14,885 l. in 1500 to 257,091 l. in 1600. F. Irvine, 'From Renaissance City to Ancient Régime Capital: Montpellier, c. 1500–c. 1600', in P. Benedict (ed.), *Cities and Social Change in Early Modern Europe* (London, 1989), pp. 105–133.

[21] Normandy had many other royal offices: in the 41 warehouses of the *gabelle* (salt monopoly) system, import-export duty administrations, woods and waters, etc.

[22] J. Dewald, *The Formation of a Provincial Nobility: The Magistrates of the Parlement of Rouen, 1499–1610* (Princeton, 1980). Z. Schneider, *The King's Bench* (Rochester, 2008).

Under Louis XIII, a flood of officers such as 'commissioners of the *tailles*' and keepers of the petty seals watched over the *pays d'élection*: in most cases, these were small fries, buying a share of royal debt as much as an office.[23] As Georges Pagès pointed out 80 years ago, this policy gave the monarchy a solid base among a broad social group, who not only shared in authority (becoming Aristotelian citizens by executing the law) but also in the monarchy's financial well being.[24] Real administrative costs remained modest – a typical *élection* cost about 7 per cent of the amount collected – but disguised borrowing, like the *droits aliénés*, took a far greater share: they reached 52 per cent of gross revenue in 1633.[25]

When we look at political discourse in the sixteenth century, we must remember that it took place within a relatively small apparatus of royal officers, but that contemporaries (rightly) sensed the explosive growth of that apparatus after 1550. First President Achille de Harlay, of the Parlement of Paris, told the king in 1597 about an edict related to heredity of offices: 'It's a horrible and incredible thing to see 1500 or 1600 people employed doing that which 10 or 12 handled in the times of kings Louis XII and Francis I.'[26] The transformation from a discourse of Commonwealth to one of state took place in the midst of this revolution in the size of royal officialdom. For authors like Jean Bodin, 'respublique' [Commonwealth] meant one of the three Aristotelian legitimate models of legitimate government: monarchy; aristocracy; timarchy. Consider Bodin's first sentence in *Les Six Livres de la République* (1576): 'Commonwealth' [*respublique*] was a 'legitimate government' (*droit gouvernement*) holding sovereign power. In this Commonwealth, the king ruled all, including his closest relatives and the great aristocrats, but they, in turn, ruled their 'subjects'. The king's men, drawn largely from

---

[23] R. Descimon, 'La vénalité des offices comme dette publique sous l'Ancien Régime français. Le bien commun au pays des intérêts privés', in J. -P. Grenier (ed.), *La dette publique dans l'histoire* (Paris, 2006), pp. 177–242. Some of the *droits aliénés* went to receivers, who were often men of considerable means. Collins, *Fiscal Limits*, Table 17, gives the list of *droits aliénés* created between 1616 and 1634. In theory, between 1616 and 1633, the king sold about 15 to 20 new minor offices in each *élection*, so, in Normandy, about 500 offices. In many cases, the same man bought multiple offices, such as the three commissioners of the *tailles* created in each *élection*.

[24] G. Pagès, 'Essay sur l'évolution des institutions administratives en France du XVIe à la fin du XVIIe siècle', *Revue d'Histoire Moderne* 7 (1935), pp. 8–57; 113–138. Pagès did a series of remarkable articles on the officers, in the late 1920s and 1930s in this journal and in *Revue Historique*.

[25] Collins, *Fiscal Limits*, on the *droits aliénés*, surtaxes sold to existing and newly created officers, a classic example Descimon's point that the state viewed offices as a form of public debt.

[26] BNF, M Fr 3888, fol. 129. Harlay, on behalf of a delegation of presidents and councillors, presenting remonstrances to Henry IV, January 1597.

those elements of the urban bourgeoisie with legal training, shared governance through the execution of the law, by means of royal offices.[27]

Although we take France as the model for the state, from the time of Charles V (1364–1380) to the reign of Henry IV (1589–1610), France was a monarchical Commonwealth. The men of Rouen certainly thought they lived in the 'respublique françoyse', a place where free men governed themselves and were governed in turn, in a kingdom built on laws and justice.[28] Just as nobles believed the king governed them, and they governed their 'subjects', so, too, urban elites felt the same way about their *civitas*, although they did 'consult' the community of men of substance before taking important decisions. Even the Duke of Feria, Philip II's ambassador to the League Estates General of 1593, speaking to the deputies, said that his master urged them not to break up until they had elected a Catholic king who would restore the splendour of the Commonwealth. Philip's letters referred to the restoration of the 'kingdom', perhaps recognition that 'respublique' increasingly had to mean a polity without a monarch.[29]

Before we dismiss the 'respublique françoyse' as an empty rhetorical flourish, we might consider the judgment of Niccolò Machiavelli, who believed the 'countless laws' of France 'limited' the kings and 'guaranteed the security of all their people'.[30] Machiavelli here describes the Bodinian 'Commonwealth', in which the king, while keeping the right to make public law, in fact is bound to obey existing law, and is restricted by

[27] Schneider, *King's Bench*, shows how the seventeenth-century legal system worked at the local level, where royal and seigneurial courts overlapped, often using the same personnel. The term 'republique' had multiple meanings: I am focusing here on the primary usage at any given moment. All of this political terminology had diverse meanings: 'patrie' could refer to one's town, to the town and its hinterlands, to a province (like Brittany), or to the kingdom.

[28] J. Collins, 'Noble Political Ideology and the Estates General of Orléans and Pontoise: French Republicanism', *Historical Reflections/Reflexions Historiques*, 27: 2 (2001), pp. 219–40. J. Bodin, *Les Six Livres de la République* (Paris, 1576, 1583). Several years after doing 'Noble Political Ideology' article, my colleague Jo Ann Moran Cruz introduced me to Patrick Collinson's use of the same term for England; several of his articles are reproduced in *Elizabethan Essays* (London, 1994), above all pp. 31–58, 'The Monarchical Republic of Elizabeth I'. See also J. McDiarmid (ed.), *The Monarchical Republic of Early Modern England* (Aldershot, 2007), for a fine collection of essays on this topic. Some articles in Q. Skinner and M. van Gelderen (eds.), *Republicanism: A Shared European Heritage* (Cambridge, 2002) lay out the particulars for other European polities.

[29] *Procès-verbaux des États généraux de 1593*, ed. A Bernard (Paris, 1842), p. 118. At that point, his daughter Isabella, being proposed as Queen of France, was Philip's private secretary.

[30] N. Machiavelli, *The Portable Machiavelli*, ed. and trans. P. Bondarella and M. Musa (New York, 1979), 221. Chapter XVI of Book I of *The Discourses*: 'In esemplo ci è il regno di Francia, il quale non vive sicuro per altro che per essersi quelli re obligati a infinite leggi, nelle quali si comprende la sicurtà di tutti i suoi popoli'.

reason and justice. The French monarchy always remained highly legalistic, although, like our contemporary governments, it often sought to
interpret the law to its own ends.[31] Aside from a blatant tyrant like Louis
XI, French monarchs generally held to the idea that the legitimate king
acted, and had to act, according to laws built on reason, and thus reflecting Divine order and justice.[32] We might consider that the image of the
France as a 'royal monarchy' contrasted with England's 'political and
royal monarchy', which comes to us from John Fortescue, probably stems
from the fact that Fortescue lived in France precisely in the period of
Louis XI's tyranny, the early 1460s.[33]

The credential given to the French negotiators at Bruges in 1376
explicitly referred to Charles V's obligation to render justice to vassals
in Guyenne who had sought his justice; it stated unequivocally 'that
he would not be worthy [digne] to be called King if he did not do
justice'. The credential went on: 'The first reason is that the King at
his origin and consecration swore in the presence of his people not to
alienate the rights of his crown. [...] had he done the contrary, he
would have been a perjurer and, by consequence, infamous, and
would not be worthy to be King'.[34] Even Louis XI, after the War of
the Bien Public (1465), changed his tune, as is clear from the letter of
dedication he wrote to his son in the *Rosier des guerres*: 'I send you this
present *Rosier* touching upon the guardianship and defence of *la chose
publique*'.[35]

As Charles V's white horse made clear, the king of France's right to
make public law was 'absolute', that is, 'independent' in the sense of not
having to refer to an earthly superior, neither emperor nor pope. Royal
documents, starting at least in 1297, made regular use of the term '*pleni-
tudo potestatis*', mimicking the pope, or the emperor, to define the range of

---

[31] When (1661) Louis XIV disgraced Nicolas Fouquet, *surintendant* of finances, and named
   a panel of 21 judges to try him, he gave the presiding judge, Henri Pussort, clear
   indications that he wanted Fouquet executed. The trial ended in 1665, the judges voting
   13–8 for banishment; Louis could not order the execution, but he could, and did, change
   their sentence to life in prison. D. Dessert, *Fouquet* (Paris, 1987).

[32] In calling Louis XI a tyrant, I use the term as his contemporaries understood it; I do not
   mean to reprise the evil spider caricature of Louis so effectively dismantled in J. Favier,
   Louis XI (Paris, 2000). See below on Louis XI and the War of the Bien Public.

[33] My thanks to Jo Ann Moran Cruz for this insight: Fortescue distinguishes between
   '*dominium regale*' (France) and '*dominium politicum et regale*' (England). In the former,
   the king may himself make the law and levy taxes without consent.

[34] E. Perroy, *The Anglo-French Negotiations at Bruges, 1374–1377*, Camden Miscellany
   (London, 1952), vol. XIX, p. 57. The credential cites a maxim of Roman law: *Quia
   infamibus non porte dig[nita]tum*. See below, n. 85.

[35] Cited in Y. Labande-Mailfert, *Charles VIII* (Paris, 1986), p. 21. Louis enjoined his son to
   make sure he 'did nothing' without consulting his conscience to see that he acted
   'according to God and reason'.

their power.[36] The Christian king, and, even more so, *rex Christianissimus* had to rule, as the oath of 'coronation and consecration' put it, according to God's law, reason and justice; a legitimate king had to 'govern according to the statutes and laws and ordinances left to him' (Nicole Oresme). The king made public law, as Fortescue said, but he did not make custom, which he was bound to 'guard'. The 'will of the prince' may have been 'law', but any king who regularly violated existing law lost his status as a king and became a tyrant.[37]

In the well-ordered Christian kingdom – like Christine de Pizan's *Cité des Dames* – law, reason, and justice were inseparable. She and her contemporaries generalized the term *cité*, a community of citizens, from Nicole Oresme's glossary to *The Politics*: 'all of a kingdom or a country is a large *cité*, which contains many partial *cités*'.[38] Those citizens ruled, and were ruled in turn, in a polity based on reason and justice. In his *Remonstrances for Peace*, written for the Estates General of 1576, the young Huguenot Philippe Duplessis-Mornay glossed Oresme: 'All this kingdom is only one *Cité*, one house, one body, which has only one King, one Father of the family, one head, which ruins itself, burns itself, dies all together'.[39]

Charles V's propaganda emphasized the image of the just king as *princeps*. He commissioned the 'sceptre of Charlemagne', which long remained important in ceremony. In his speech to Louis XIII, after his coronation in 1613, First President Harlay opened with a comment on its meaning: 'Sire ... the royal sceptre [for the state] is presented to you, to be held in your right hand, so as to teach you that God gave you royal power to defend your subjects from oppression and to oppose yourself by force

---

[36] The use of *plentitudo potestatis*, and the simultaneous doctrine of the king as 'Emperor in his own kingdom', entered French practice when there was no emperor, and had not been one for half a century. J. Krynen, *L'Empire du roi: Idées et croyances politiques en France, XIIIè–XVè siècles* (Paris, 1993), establishes the important role of Évrard de Trémaugon, author of the *Songe du Vergier*, in establishing the principle that the king had unique authority to make public law, without interference of pope or emperor. In late medieval or early seventeenth-century French, '*absolu*' literally meant '*indépendant*', which remained the first definition of the term even in the 1694 dictionary of the Académie Française.

[37] Jean, duke of Burgundy had Louis, duke of Orléans, assassinated in 1407; Jean hired Jean Petit to justify it, on grounds of tyrannicide. Jean Gerson led the universal condemnation of Petit; tyrannicide did not develop as a key part of French medieval constitutionalism, in part due to this incident.

[38] A. Menut, *Maistre Nicole Oresme Le Livre de Politiques d'Aristote. Transactions of the American Philosophical Society*, New Series, vol. 60:6 (1970), pp. 1–392, at p. 119. This definition follows logically from Oresme's comment to Book III, part 3, that 'the men, not the place make the city'. [le lieu ne fait pas la cité, mes la gent] Reason, Right (*Droitture*), and Justice were the three Ladies who established Christine's '*Cité*'. Ambrogio Calepino's dictionary gave *cité* as the French equivalent of *civitas* and *polis*.

[39] *Remonstrance aux États pour la Paix* (Paris, 1576), p. 40.

to the evil intentions of enemies of your state'. The king's left hand then received the 'hand of justice' [the Commonwealth] 'to represent to you that good Kings reign by justice, and that without justice Kingdoms are no longer Kingdoms, Kings are no longer Kings, exchanging the beautiful name of King for other odious names; Justice is the firm column on which rests a state, which alone can reassure the good and make the evil fear'.[40]

The preceptors of French kings from Philip IV to Louis XIV inculcated Harlay's lesson into them, both in their religious training and in their study of history. Giles of Rome, preceptor of the future Philip IV, composed *De regimine principum*, to teach his pupil the importance of reason restraining appetite. The goal of his prince was to bring 'himself and citizens to virtues and good manners', as Giles' fifteenth-century English translator put it. When Giles welcomed Philip IV to Paris, on behalf of the university and community, he emphasized justice as the fundamental obligation of a king. A century later, Charles V ordered a French translation of *De regimine principum* for the use of the future Charles VI.[41] Jean Gerson, writing to the preceptor of the dauphin Louis, Duke of Guyenne, c. 1409, listed *De regimine* as one of the books the young man should read.[42]

Hardouin de Péréfixe, preceptor of Louis XIV, in his *Histoire du roi Henri le Grand* (public edition, 1662), composed as part of Louis' French history textbook, noted his pupil's 'particular affection' for his grand-father; the young king wished to take him 'for his model'. Péréfixe tells readers he had gathered 'all that might serve in forming a great Prince, and to make him capable of reigning well'. Péréfixe extols many of Henry's qualities, such as his courage and his unflappable demeanor, not changed by misfortune: Henry was 'always a King and a Sovereign,

---

[40] Arsenal, Ms 4058, f. 136v. Harlay made this speech in the immediate aftermath of Bellarmine's controversial writings about tyrannicide. We see the importance of this duality as late as 1775, when the famous Boston silversmith, Paul Revere, made a new seal for Massachusetts: it showed a patriot with a gun in his right hand and a copy of Magna Carta in his left hand, and carried a couplet from the seventeeth-century English radical Algernon Sidney (executed in 1683). See the fourth seal down on http://www.sec .state.ma.us/pre/presea/sealhis.htm. Massachusetts is one of four American states still officially called a 'Commonwealth': the others are Pennsylvania, Virginia and Kentucky (which was part of Virginia in 1787).

[41] C. Briggs (ed.), *Giles of Rome's De regimine principum: Reading and Writing Politics at Court and University c. 1275–c. 1525* (Cambridge, 1999), p. 146 on the goal. This emphasis on reason restraining passion received an important theoretical foundation with William of Moerbeke's Latin translations of Aristotle, c. 1260, and, of course, through subsequent commentary by Thomas Aquinas and others.

[42] A. Thomas, *Jean de Gerson et l'éducation des dauphins de France; étude critique* (Paris, 1930), pp. 41ff. *De regimine* was the first secular book mentioned by Gerson. He also cited Oresme's translations of Aristotle and Raoul de Presle's translation of Augustine's *City of God*, both funded by Charles V, c. 1370.

without recognizing superiors other than God, reason, and justice'.[43] Hardouin de Péréfixe might well have been calling to mind Gerson's admonition to the royal preceptors about the importance of reading: prospective kings must learn that without sapience, men are mere brutes.[44]

From the 1370s onward, the French took their definitions of king and of tyrant from Oresme's glossary. 'Monarchy is the polity or princedom held by one person': its two varieties were kingdom and tyranny. Oresme gives a specific definition of the tyrant: 'First of all, it is one person who holds the princedom and the monarchy for his own profit [*propre profit*] and against the public good [*bien publique*].'[45] Mornay's 1576 *Remonstrance* (p. 45) followed Oresme here, too: kings relied on 'the love of their people', tyrants on their 'fear'.

The lawyers who did all the groundwork for the royal council in France, from the fourteenth century onward, defended the interests of the king, but within the framework of the law. Royal lawyers had three clients: the individual king; the Crown; and the Commonwealth, what Charles V's lawyers, like chancellor Pierre d'Orgemont, called the '*bien de la chose publique*', a phrase later rendered more succinctly as the '*bien public*'.[46] The lawyers and the political philosophers, like Oresme or Gerson, however, disagreed about the balance of the three elements: lawyers focused on the Crown, not Oresme's '*bien public*'.[47]

The Commonwealth vocabulary largely died out with the Valois. In the sixteenth century, whether in a Parlement or a meeting of estates, speakers invariably spoke of defending the king, the Crown, and the *bien public*. In private meetings with deputies arriving for the Estates General of Blois in 1588, Henry III told each little delegation that he 'did not wish to be a tyrant', but wanted 'to devote what remains of his life to the *bien public*'. In the face of the living embodiment of the 'respublique françoyse' – an

---

[43] Hardouin de Péréfixe, *Histoire du roi Henri le Grand* (Paris, 1776 edition), p. 7.

[44] Thomas, *Jean Gerson*, p. 41.

[45] Menut, *Nicole Oresme Le Livre de Politiques d'Aristote*, pp. 371–372.

[46] M. S. Kempshall, *The Common Good in Late Medieval Political Thought* (Oxford, 1999) on the fundamental distinction between common good and public utility. Charles V, in the regency ordinance, used the term '*bien publique*' in one section.

[47] Oresme was clear on the primacy of the common good: 'Car le bien publique est a preferer devant la propre volente de chescun' (103). See Krynen, *L'Empire du roi*. I disagree with Krynen's argument that medieval lawyers were laying absolutism's foundations. The old idea of the Parlement as the defender of the *bien public* survived even in 1754, when Barthélemy Rolland, in his *Lettres d'un Magistrat à Monsieur. F. Morenas* (pp. 12–13) claimed *Unigenitus* attacked 'religion, the state, and the inviolable faith due to the sovereign'. The forced registration made the magistrates, 'zealous for the *bien public*', unable to preserve 'the Church and the State' from this 'monster'. We see here a typical eighteenth-century conflation of state and *bien public*.

Estates General (1576, 1588) or an Assembly of Notables (1583) – Henry III might use the vocabulary of Commonwealth, but in everyday administration his council opted for a new, somewhat awkward phrase: '*le bien du service du roi*'. He shied away from the '*bien public*' even in the convocation letters for the Estates Generals of 1576 and 1588. In his letters to the *baillis*, Henry III emphasized that deputies needed to speak freely, to help preserve '*mon Estat*'. Henry's opening speech to the deputies on 6 December 1576 used the language of Commonwealth, but avoided the term *bien public*: 'there is no one who does not know the causes {for calling Estates} [...] nor anyone who has not brought the zeal and affection that a good and loyal subject owes to his King and the salvation of his fatherland [*patrie*]'.[48]

The preface of Louis Le Roy's *De l'excellence du gouvernement monarchique*, (1575)[49] offers a splendid example of the confusion of vocabulary of that time: he wrote because 'I hope they will serve for the honour of God, salvation of the Kingdom, public good and public peace [*repos*], maintenance of the communion and mutual good will of natural {i.e., native-born} French people among themselves.' Le Roy brings forward most of the key elements of the political debates of the time, from the emphasis on the 'honour of God' and peace (*repos*) to the mention of the public good (*bien public*), to the appeal to native Frenchmen. In his translation of Aristotle's *Politics* (1576), Le Roy's dedicatory epistle to Henry III described '*Politique*' as the 'science of governing public states', which consisted primarily in actual practice. Le Roy regularly used the term 'state', but, as was typical of Henry III's time, in two distinct ways: 'affairs of state' and 'his [Henry's] state'. He largely avoided the term '*bien public*', yet defined '*republique*': 'Commonwealth is the life of the *cité* and the *cité* is a multitude of citizens'.[50]

---

[48] BNF, Mss Fr 16,250, fol. 4 and ff., diary of Pierre de Blanchefort, deputy to the Estates for the nobility of the Nivernais. Blanchefort is also the source for Henry III's opening speech. On Blanchefort, see A. Boltanski, *Les Ducs de Nevers et l'État Royal. Genèse d'un compromise (ca 1550 – ca 1600)* (Geneva, 2006). On the Commonwealth thought of Henry III's time, see the splendid work of M. Greengrass, *Governing Passions. Pacification and Reformation in the French Kingdom* (Oxford, 2007), the fine article by M. Holt, 'Attitudes of the French Nobility at the Estates-General of 1576', *Sixteenth Century Journal*, 18 (Winter 1987), pp. 489–504, and M. Orlea, *La noblesse aux États généraux de 1576 et de 1588* (Paris, 1980), which contains interesting biographical details on the deputies.

[49] Le Roy, aka Regius, was best known for his translation (1576) of Aristotle's *Politics* from the Greek; it immediately supplanted Oresme's version. Like Oresme, Le Roy used '*cité*' for polis, but his commentary made extensive use of the word '*Estat*' in the sense of the French polity, and '*république*' for the general political community.

[50] Le Roy's translation of Aristotle's *Politics*, p. 150. Le Roy here follows Ambrogio Calepino's dictionaries, which defined a *cité* as an 'amas de citoyens'.

Henry III and his councillors also revived the old formulae of 'public utility' and '*repos public*', the latter a phrase meaning not simply peaceful tranquility but social immobility, that is, everyone remaining in his or her place.[51] Given that the second half of the sixteenth century was one of the most active periods of ennoblement,[52] we can understand why the monarchy wanted to emphasize '*repos*' in its dealings with subjects. The oath of the Catholic League used the term, too: they acted for 'the singular zeal and entire devotion that they have for the honor of God, service of His Majesty, public peace [*repos*] and conservation of their lives, goods, and fortunes, and those of their wives and children'. Henry III, in a letter of 2 December 1576, gave a slightly different version of the oath: 'the honour of God, the service of the king, and the good [*bien*] and peace [*repos*] of the *patrie*'.

Henry IV dropped Henry III's awkward replacement, employing a new phrase, '*le bien de l'Estat*', the good of the state.[53] Henry IV borrowed it from his chief opponent, the duke of Mayenne, who styled himself '*lieutenant general de l'Estat et royaume de France*'. Henry IV abandoned the phrase '*le bien public*' after the Peace of Vervins (1598).[54] With a few exceptions, '*le bien de l'Estat*' became the normative phrase not only of the government, but even of its opponents: during the *Fronde*, for example, the Mazarinades virtually never mention '*le bien public*', but regularly cite Mazarin's attacks on '*le bien de l'Estat*'.

We can well understand why Henry III and Henry IV both wanted to move away from '*le bien public*': the Catholic League invariably framed its goals in terms of protecting the '*bien public*', particularly 'the honour of God'.[55] Jean Chastel, the Parisian student who stabbed Henry IV in 1594, claimed no one had put him up to the deed, and that 'what he

---

[51] A. Jouanna, *Le devoir de révolte* (Paris, 1989), shows that the nobility also took up the public utility phrasing in the 1580s. J. Nicot, *Thrésor de la langue françoyse* (Paris, 1606), consulted on artfl.com. All studies of the rhetorical shift of late sixteenth-century France begin with M. Fumaroli, *L'age de l'éloquence* (Paris, 1980), and with his insights into the movement from Ciceronian to Tacitean rhetoric. S. Daubresse, *Le Parlement de Paris ou la voix de la raison* (Geneva, 2005), offers a rigorous examination of the Parlement's rhetoric in the critical years of the Wars of Religion.

[52] E. Schalk, 'Ennoblement Ennoblement in France from 1350 to 1660', *Journal of Social History* 16:2 (Winter, 1982), pp. 101–110.

[53] Isolated usages of this term can be found in the 1580s, for example in the private writings of some secretaries of state, like Bellièvre and Villeroy, but I have not found it in public documents.

[54] J. Collins, 'La Guerre de la Ligue et le Bien Public', in J. -F. Labourdette (ed.) *Autour du traité de Vervins, guerre et paix en Europe à la fin du XVIe et au début du XVIIe siècle* (Paris, 2001), pp. 81–96. My thanks to Olivier Poncet for pointing out Mayenne's usage of the term.

[55] N. Le Roux, *Un Régicide au nom de Dieu. L'assassinat d'Henry III* (Paris, 2006) makes the case for the assassination of 1589.

had done, was for the sole motive of his conscience, and for the zeal for the honour of God'. Fifteen years later, Henry's assassin, François Ravaillac, testified that 'one must prefer the honour of God to all things'.[56] Little wonder that the *'bien public'* would soon disappear from public political discourse in France, the Commonwealth giving way to the state.[57]

We might posit two termini in the evolution of a French political unity built around a collective identity independent from the individual king, in 1316–1373 and in 1589–1593. The first of those crises led to a monarchical Commonwealth; the second one led to the state. In our rush to seek out institutional elements of the monarchy, we should not lose sight of the fact that dynastic issues created these two crises. The initial crisis came about because of the first collateral succession in the Capetian dynasty; the last one combined the threat of religious innovation with a collateral inheritance so far outside normal legal channels that it would have shocked the fourteenth- and fifteenth-century lawyers who invented the Salic Law fiction. Henry IV's Protestantism *and* his lack of an heir led French elites to embrace the state as the new focus of their loyalty; the monarchical Commonwealth had proven to be unworkable.

Dynastic Chaos and the Birth of the Monarchical Commonwealth

'ad coronam regni Franciae mulier non succedit'
Chronicle of Saint-Denis, reporting the decision reached by
a council of barons and prelates, February 1317.

The extraordinary events of 1316–1317 created unprecedented dynastic chaos that had two lasting effects: 1) the exclusion of women from succession; and 2) the affirmation of the unity of royal possessions.[58] After 300 years of successions from father to son, the Capetians suddenly had to cope with a collateral succession in November 1316, followed rapidly by two more, in 1322 and 1328.[59] The new Valois dynasty had

---

[56] Bibliothèque Sainte-Geneviève, Mss 827, fols. 70–87, trial transcript of Ravaillac, from a copy made c. 1640. I also consulted multiple other copies of this document. An online version can be found in the Mémoires de Condé, v. 6, supplement (London, 1743), interrogation starts on p. 261.

[57] Urban governments continued to use this phrase with respect to local affairs, but even there it became relatively rare.

[58] R. Cazelles, *La société politique et la crise de la royauté au temps de Philippe de Valois* (Paris, 1958), long ago pointed out the centrality of this second principle.

[59] After Philip I, only Saint Louis (12) was not a legal adult; unsurprisingly, his 'uncle' – Philip, count of Boulogne, son of a dubious marriage of Philip II, born legally illegitimate, although later legitimized by the Pope – immediately revolted against the Regent, Blanche of Castile.

the miraculous good fortune that its first two kings, Philip VI (1328–1350) and John II (1350–1364), passed the throne to an adult son. After John II, the Valois managed that trick only twice: in 1461, to a son in exile and *persona non grata*, and again in 1547. The Bourbons did worse: none of the five Bourbon kings passed the throne to an adult son, and the first three transitions involved extended regencies.

The failure of four successive kings (1316, 1316, 1322, 1328) to leave the throne to a viable descendant, the dynastic wars of the 1340s through 1370s, followed soon afterwards by the agony of 30 years (1392–1422) of rule by an intermittently mad king, who signed a treaty leaving the king-dom to Henry V of England and his heirs,[60] made French elites urgently and continuously aware of the need for a unifying principle that did not depend on a single man. Their solution was to promulgate two related conceptions of political unity: the Crown and the Commonwealth. Unhappy, as ever, with a binary authority, the lawyers, above all those working for the central government, eventually sought to merge these two entities into a new one, the state, at the end of the sixteenth century.

The succession crises of 1316 mandated a new form of collective action to preserve the unity of the polity.[61] French medieval kings always claimed to act, and usually did act, in consultation with the leading members of the political community. Royal ordinance preambles stated that the king had consulted, often in official assemblies, leading barons, prelates, learned men and bourgeois of Paris, and that the 'better part' of this group had reached a consensus opinion which was reflected in the ordinance. The noble uprisings of 1314–1315, which forced Louis X to issue charters of rights to nobles in Normandy, Champagne and Burgundy, were surely fresh in the mind of his brother, Philip of Poitiers, when he convoked such an assembly in Paris in July 1316, and another one in February 1317, to provide legitimacy for his resolution of the question of the successions of Louis X and John I.

Philip, count of Valois, followed the same procedure in 1328 when Charles IV died without a male heir. French elites uniformly believed that an 'Estates General' had elected Philip as King of France in 1328. At his speech on behalf of the child king Charles IX, to the Estates General of 1561, chancellor Michel de l'Hospital specifically stated that the *election*

---

[60] The Treaty of Troyes (1420) specified that Henry V and his heirs would rule England and France; it made no mention of any inheritance rights of Catherine of France, although it did protect her rights as wife and widow.

[61] Here I consciously use the term explained so superbly in J. Watts, *The Making of Polities, Europe 1300–1500* (Cambridge, 2009). Contemporaries often spoke of the 'kingdom', a term with a long historical tradition, but one closely tied to an individual king. As the fourteenth century wore on, they would speak of the 'Crown of the Kingdom of France'.

of Philip VI had been the ultimate expression of the power of an Estates General.[62] When Leaguers wanted to rally around a Catholic king, the Duke of Mayenne, who styled himself 'lieutenant general of the kingdom and State of France', called an Estates General in 1593, to decide which French princess would marry the new king. Even King Philip II of Spain recognized that an Estates General had the right to 'elect' a Catholic king of France. The early-arriving deputies, writing to encourage others to hurry to Paris, claimed the Estates would deal with 'the greatest and most important affair that could present itself for the good of our religion and the State'. Henry IV outflanked Mayenne by negotiating directly with the deputies, that is, with the members of the Commonwealth.

The neat little formula of the Salic Law provided an *ex post facto* justification of the three decisions of 1316, 1317 and 1328, but aside from the anachronism of speaking of Salic Law before anyone had heard of it, the fact of the matter is that any man inheriting the throne by collateral succession had to deal with the potential claims of the key royal women, and their husbands.[63] From the death of Louis X (1316) to the accession of Henry IV (1589), the royal family consistently followed a policy of neutralizing the claims of any woman who might serve as the basis for a claim to the throne. Louis X's daughter married into a royal line (Evreux); Philip V's daughters did the same (and their heirs intermarried), as did Blanche, posthumous daughter of Charles IV, who married Philip, Duke of Orléans, younger brother of King John II. In 1498, Louis XII divorced his predecessor's (infertile) sister to marry his widow, Anne of Brittany. His cousin-successor, François d'Angoulême, married the royal daughter, Claude. In 1589, Henry IV had long been married to Marguerite, sister of his three predecessors.

The shift of dynasty in 1328 has gotten most of the historiographical attention, but the real crisis took place in 1316–1317. Philip of Valois faced little serious opposition in 1328; Philip of Poitiers [Philip V] had to deal with armed opposition and symbolic affront in 1316. Louis X left a pregnant second wife and a four-year-old daughter, Jeanne, by his first

---

[62] R. Descimon (ed.) *Discours pour la majorité de Charles IX et trois autres discours* (Paris, 1993).

[63] The first references to Salic Law come during the reign of John II; it developed under Charles V but became a normative doctrine only between 1400 and 1420. J. Barbey, *La fonction royale. Essence et légitimité d'après le Tractatus de Jean de Terrevermeille* (Paris, 1983) and E. Viannot, *L'invention de la loi salique (V^e – XVIe siècle)* (Paris, 2002). The Salic Law stated that no woman could inherit in the lands of the Salian Franks: as invented in the late fourteenth century, it meant the eldest male in direct line of male descent became king of France. In England, Parliament knew perfectly well the dangers of a queen on the loose. They passed (1428) legislation to prevent Catherine's remarriage after Henry V's death. Catherine struck up a relationship with Owen Tudor; their grandson became Henry VII.

wife, Margaret of Burgundy, whose involvement in the Tour de Nesle infidelity scandal led to her imprisonment and suspicious death in the Château Gaillard.[64] Philip of Poitiers, in Lyon at the time of his brother's death, on his return to the Paris area organized a unique ceremony: the only second funeral carried out for a king of France. Philip had been in Lyon trying to get the cardinals to elect a new pope.[65] Informed of his brother's demise, he immediately consolidated his position in the south of France, seeking and getting oaths of loyalty from major nobles, clerics and towns; he styled himself 'governor' of the kingdom and even stated openly his claim to be heir to the throne, as closest heir to Louis.[66] Philip carefully marginalized the other potential regents – his uncle Charles of Valois; Queen Clémence; and Duke Eudes II of Burgundy, Jeanne's uncle.[67] The *Ancient Chronicle of Flanders* – which tells us Philip obtained the title of 'gouverneur' of the kingdom by 'love' and by force – relates the story that men-at-arms loyal to Charles of Valois and Charles de la Marche had a confrontation with those loyal to constable Gaucher de Châtillon, on the grounds of the royal palace.[68] No other chronicle

[64] In 1314, Margaret of Burgundy and her cousins, Blanche and Jeanne, wives of the royal brothers Louis, Charles and Philip, ended up in the Château Gaillard because of the suspected liaisons between Margaret and Blanche and two Norman knights (both executed after torture), and Jeanne's supposed complicit silence. Louis X could not get an annulment, because there was no Pope from 1314 until after Louis' death; contemporaries believed Louis had Margaret poisoned. When Charles became king in 1322, Pope John XXII annulled Charles' marriage to Blanche, who died four years later, still in prison. Philip V helped exonerate Jeanne: she became queen of France in 1316 and passed her fiefs, the counties of Burgundy and Artois, to her daughter Jeanne.

[65] In August 1316, the cardinals selected a French client of the Angevin family, Jacques d'Euse, as John XXII. E. A. R. Brown, 'The Ceremonial of Royal Succession in Capetian France: the Double Funeral of Louis X', *Traditio* 34 (1978), pp. 227–271. G. Mollat, 'L'élection du pape Jean XXII', *Revue d'histoire de l'Église de France*, 1 (1910), pp. 34–49 and 147–166.

[66] Juan Lopez, writing from Lyon, to King James II of Aragon, on 30 June 1316, informed him of Philip receiving 'multiple homages of fidelity'; he says Philip was already using the title 'regni et patrie gubernator'. H Finke (ed.), *Acta Aragonensia*, I (Berlin and Leipzig, 1908), p. 208. Lopez viewed Philip's seizure of the regency, over Clémence, to be the fundamental act. Pope John XXII, in a letter of 6 September 1316, calls Philip 'regna Francie et Navarre regentis'. [G. Mollat (ed.), *Lettres communes de Jean XXII*, v. I, letter 2; letter 145, to Philip.] Brown, 'Double Funeral', p. 245, n. 77, cites the letters read at Nîmes in mid-July 1316 : 'heredis jure proximitatis' of the said Louis.

[67] Charles of Valois claimed the right, as senior prince of the royal blood, to be regent; Clémence could cite the example of Blanche of Castile, regent for Louis IX; Eudes, as the senior male maternal relative of the orphaned Jeanne, claimed to protect her rights. Charles of Valois' son, Philip (later Philip VI), did not participate in either the Paris assemblies or the coronation (Cazelles, *Société politique*).

[68] Dom Martin Bouquet (ed.), *Recueil des historiens des Gaules et de la France*, t. 22; new edition by L. Delisle and N. de Wailly (Paris, 1860) *Rerum gallicarum et francicarum scriptores*, t. 22, 329ff. When the constable threatened to break down the door and decapitate those inside, they capitulated. Brown argues that the evidence suggests that Charles of Valois and Philip had already come to an agreement before Philip reached

reports this incident, but, as Brown suggests, the story indicates the public awareness of princely conflict.

Philip orchestrated a deal at an assembly of barons and prelates, on 17 July 1316, which formally made him regent during the pregnancy; he was to keep this title for a male child, until the boy reached 18.[69] This decision followed the principles of '*garde noble*', in which the presumed heir protected the property of a noble child: Philip, as senior uncle, trumped Clémence, a stepmother (and a foreigner, as some chroniclers noted). If Clémence had a girl, the assembly posited two scenarios: 1) the girls would renounce their royal rights, but Clémence's daughter would get Champagne and Jeanne, Navarre; Philip would become king; or 2) Philip would act as 'gouverneur' until the younger princess reached the age of puberty (13), when a decision would be taken (presumably by the great barons and prelates) as to who would get a princess and the Crown.[70] The agreement specifically reserved the rights of a prospective male child, for whom Philip would also be regent.

Some contemporaries immediately grasped the meaning: King Sancho of Majorca wrote to King James II of Aragon, on 5 September 1316, and predicted that Philip's seizure of the regency, and exclusion of the Queen, meant that Philip would become king, if the Queen had a daughter.[71] At precisely this moment, Philip seems to have cemented a deal with Pope John XXII, elected by a conclave Philip had supervised: Philip got the right to a *décime* (clerical tenth) over four years, to pay for a proposed crusade, and annates for a year. The pope openly supported Philip, calling him 'king of France' as soon as he heard news of John II's death, and interceding with major French princes, such as Charles of Valois and Charles de la Marche, to back Philip's claim: the pope even promised to intercede with Philip to get him to pay some of Valois' debts, if the count went along with Philip's coronation.[72] Philip also compromised Jeanne's

Paris, but she also cites a statement by Philip to the envoy of Aragon in 1317, that Charles had opposed him in 1316.

[69] Philip was the first person to use this official title in France; he had been calling himself '*gouverneur*', although the Pope already referred to him as '*regentis*'.

[70] In *garde noble*, the guardian relinquished control when a boy attained knighthood or when a girl reached the age of marriage, precisely as was done here. Standard practice had shifted the norm to the age of majority, at least for boys, again as was done here. On *garde noble*, J. Bart, *Histoire du droit privé de la chute de l'Empire romain au XIXe siècle* (2nd ed., Paris, 2009), pp. 306–307.

[71] *Acta Aragonensia*, I, 465–66

[72] See the discussion in G. Tabacco, *La Casa de Francia nell'azione politica di Papa Giovanni XXII* (Rome, 1953), Chapter IV. John XXII wrote to Robert of Artois in November 1316, to encourage him to desist from rebellion against Philip; in April 1317, he wrote to Eudes and Agnes to urge them to swear fidelity to Philip, and he later provided the necessary dispensation for the proposed marriage of Philip's daughter and Eudes. John XXII's letters are published in several sources; the ones

chief champion, Eudes of Burgundy: on 29 September, he announced the engagement of his daughter (another Jeanne, then age nine) to Eudes.

Baby John did not live out a week; as King Sancho had predicted, Philip became king in lieu of a daughter. The decision involved three successions: France; Navarre; and the county of Champagne, the latter two of which Louis X had inherited from his mother (Jeanne de Navarre). Should the inheritance be broken up, as the July 1316 deal had envisioned? The short life of John voided the agreement of July 1316; the issue was now the inheritance of John I. Right after Christmas, Eudes of Burgundy wrote to Count Robert of Flanders that Philip had invoked the clause in the treaty of July 1316 that voided the arrangements for Louis X's daughters in case of the birth of a boy.[73] Eudes insisted that 'common law and usage' made Jeanne heir to Champagne, Navarre and even France. Agnès wrote to Robert (also in December) that she had consulted wise men and lawyers and that they all agreed Jeanne was heir to France, Navarre and Champagne, both from her father and from her brother. She went further than Eudes, appealing to Robert on the grounds of his 'faith and loyalty' to the 'Crown of France' to oppose Philip's coronation: she informed Robert that she had written to the other peers, demanding that they, too, oppose the coronation.

Jeanne could no longer claim to be a descendant of the previous king, but simply one among the collateral relatives. Philip insisted he was king, and organized a coronation at Reims in January 1317. In effect, he again followed the rules of 'garde noble', which presumed the guardian was the heir of the child under care. Most of the lay peers boycotted the coronation: Eudes of Burgundy; Jean III, Duke of Brittany; Edward II of England, Duke of Guyenne; and Robert III, Count of Flanders.[74] Charles de la Marche came with his brother to Reims, but demanded,

specific to France in A. Coulon, *Jean XXII Lettres secrètes et curiales relatives à la France* (2 vols., Rome, 1902). On Charles de Valois, J. Petit, *Charles de Valois* (Paris, 1900), pp. 173–174, citing papal letters from Coulon's edition. The Pope sweetened the pot for Charles by giving him (9/1316) the annates of all bishoprics in his lands: he used this money to pay the dowry of his daughter Marguerite, who married Gui de Chatillon, count of Blois. We might see this arrangement as part of an early deal among Pope John XXII, Philip V, and Charles of Valois: the Pope granted Philip the annates of the entire kingdom of France for four years, excepting only those of the bishoprics in Charles of Valois' lands.

[73] G. Servois, 'Documents inédits sur l'avènement de Philippe le Long', *Bulletin-Annuaire de la Société de l'Histoire de France* (1864), pp. 44–79, document 1 (66); Agnès' letter is document 2.

[74] Of the original six lay peerages, Normandy and Toulouse were part of the royal demesne, and Champagne was in limbo (did it belong to the king or to Jeanne?). Philip IV had created (1297) new lay peerages for Anjou (held by Charles de Valois), Artois, and Brittany, in part because he had stripped the count of Flanders of the designation, moving it to Artois (originally part of the same fief). The two other major royal princes, Philip of

on the eve of the coronation, a better apanage and, in all likelihood, a peerage.[75] When Philip told him to wait, Charles, unable to leave through the locked gates, climbed down the city walls, made his way across a marsh and fled the city. The only two lay peers who came were Charles de Valois, Count of Anjou, and Mahaud, Countess of Artois and Philip's mother-in-law.

The coronation ceremony had the Crown of France held by the lay peers as a group, prior to the archbishop of Reims taking it and placing it on the king's head. The description of the ceremony indicates that Charles of Valois did not hold the Crown, so Mahaud did so alone: Géraud de Frachet, continuator of Guillaume de Nangis' chronicle, claims that this fact 'excited the indignation of some'.[76] We might wonder at the contradiction of a succession and coronation that took a hard line against women with respect to the royal succession, yet allowed a woman to have a ceremonial role in the coronation, as a peer of France. The illustrations of Philip V's coronation in the various manuscripts of the *Grandes Chroniques de France* do not show a woman among the peers surrounding the king. Surely those present at the coronation might have suppressed a smile at the spectacle of Mahaud, who 'held' her peerage because of closer degree of affinity, holding the Crown aloft, so that Philip could become King by overriding that principle.[77] Mahaud also held the dubious distinction of having been accused, by Charles de la Marche, of

---

Valois (the later Philip VI) and Robert, count of Clermont, did not come; Robert stayed away due to ill health; he died soon afterward. Brown, 'Double Funeral'; P. Lehugeur, *Histoire de Philippe le L`ong, roi de France (1316–1322)* (Paris, 1897), Chapter 2, which must be corrected on some details by Brown. P. Desportes, 'Les pairs de France et la couronne', *Revue Historique*, 282 (1989), 305–340, has useful details on the peerages.

[75] In theory, Philip IV gave Charles the counties of la Marche and Angoulême, from the lands formerly held by Guy I de Lusignan, who died in 1308. In practice, Guy's death touched off a protracted and complicated lawsuit and Charles did not get La Marche until after the death of Guy's sister, Yolande. In December 1316, Philip V united all possessions he held within France, prior to being king, to the demesne; he 'reunited' the seneschalsy of Angoulême with that of Saintes. (*Ordonnances*, XI, 444.) The discussions of January 1317 surely focused on Angoulême and on the question of a peerage, because Philip, on the very day of the coronation, made Louis, count of Evreux, a lay peer. Philip V later made la Marche into a peerage and did the same for the county of Angoulême, which he gave to the dispossessed Jeanne in February 1318, making her the first woman for whom a peerage was created.

[76] H. Géraud (ed.), *Chronique latine de Guillaume de Nangis, de 1113 à 1300, avec les continuations de cette chronique, de 1300 à 1368* (Paris, 1843), p. 1, 396. The usual assumption that their objection revolved around Mahaut's gender does not make sense. The count(ess) of Champagne was one of the six lay peers. Jeanne de Navarre, countess of Champagne, wife of Philip IV, had been one of the peers holding the Crown during her husband's coronation in 1286, so there was ample precedent for a woman to act at the coronation. After Philip's coronation, Jeanne received a crown as queen of France.

[77] The county of Artois was being held in trust by the Philip's uncles, pending a decision as to whether Mahaud or her nephew Robert was rightful heir. The male usually had

poisoning the infant king: Philip had to convene a special tribunal to clear her of the charges, and he enlisted Pope John XXII to write letters to Charles urging him to retract his charges.

One person protested: Philip suffered the embarrassment of the spokesman for Agnès, dowager Duchess of Burgundy, daughter of Saint Louis, stepping forward and insisting that the rights of Agnès' granddaughter, Jeanne, had not been respected. In Agnès' name, he called on the peers, and 'above all on the prelates who assisted at the coronation' (Frachet), not to crown Philip until they had fully examined Jeanne's rights. Eudes and Agnès finally signed a 'treaty' on Jeanne's behalf in March 1317.[78] Eudes was ultimately bought off with the dowry of Philip's daughter, Jeanne: in 1330, she brought the counties of Artois and Burgundy to her husband, giving him control of two peerages.[79] Philip V created new peerages to reward his followers, like Louis d'Evreux, or to buy off his opponents: Charles de la Marche's county became a peerage two months after the coronation, and the young Jeanne received, in February 1318, a peerage for the county of Angoulême, which Philip had forced her to accept in exchange for Champagne. She married Philippe d'Evreux, son of the Louis who had been made a peer in 1317.[80]

preference in similar degrees of affinity, thus a brother over a sister, but gender did not override degrees of affinity. The exclusion of Jeanne in 1316 violated this principle. As child and sibling, she was closer than Philip V to Louis X and to John I. The ruthless pragmatism of the king of France is obvious: when the last Capetian duke of Burgundy died, in 1361, King John II claimed the duchy, by personal right of inheritance, citing his closer degree of affinity of Philippe de Rouvres, and rejecting the claim of Charles of Navarre that, on the principle of primogeniture, he deserved to be duke. Charles was the great-grandson of duke Robert's elder daughter; John was the grandson of Robert's younger daughter.

[78] D. -F. Secousse, *Recueils de pièces servant de preuves aux Mémoires sur les troubles excités par Charles II dit le Mauvais* (Paris, 1755), document 2. Many of the major French princes and princesses witnessed the document and affixed their seals to it: Charles de Valois, Louis d'Evreux, Charles de la Marche, Mahaut d'Artois, Blanche of Brittany (granddaughter of Henry III of England, and sister-in-law of Mahaut), Louis and Jean de Clermont, cousins (descendants of Robert de Clermont, youngest son of Louis IX), Charles de Valois the younger (later count of Alençon), Guy de St-Paul, Jean, Dauphin of Viennois, Amez, count of Savoy, Gaucher de Chastillon, constable, Mille de Noyers, Henri de Sully (who held the keys to the royal treasury), Guillaume de Harcourt, Ansel de Gienville, sgr de Rinel, and Harpin de Arqueri, chevaliers.

[79] Eudes IV's sister, Jeanne, was the wife of Philip of Valois (later Philip VI), son of Charles of Valois. The close relationship with 'Saint Louis' was so important that Philip V, in his ordinances, regularly claimed to restore the good laws and practices of 'our great-grandfather, our lord Saint Louis'.

[80] Philippe d'Evreux's sister, Jeanne, later became Charles de la Marche's third wife: she was the pregnant queen whose delivery everyone awaited in 1328. Jeanne de Navarre's guardians made these exchanges in her name; when she came to adulthood, she had to ratify their actions.

Philip sent commissioners all over France to take oaths of loyalty.[81] He also presided over an assembly of barons, prelates and leading bourgeois of Paris in February 1317; they unanimously decided 'a woman does not succeed to the kingdom of France'. Had an assembly taken this decision in July 1316, the principle would have violated the normal practice of inheritance, which was that property went first to descendants, before going to a collateral relative, like a brother.[82] But John had succeeded Louis, so Princess Jeanne herself was now a collateral relative. Should the throne go to a half-sister or a full uncle, brother of the previous king? Philip left them no choice: Jeanne's guardians later complained in a letter to Philip that he had allowed no discussion at the assembly.

The assembly similarly leaned to the interpretation that the royal inheritance should not be broken in parts, the way a family lordship might be, so they accepted Philip's claims to Navarre and Champagne, while recognizing Jeanne de France had rights to them that she did not have with respect to France. In 1322, when Philip died without a male heir, Charles de la Marche, relying on the precedent of 1316, claimed the two thrones. The many manuscripts of the *Grandes Chroniques* show us that royal succession remained tenuous: instead of Charles' coronation (illustrated for other fourteenth-century kings), they illustrate his second marriage.

In 1328, Charles IV left a pregnant wife, so, once again, a 'gouverneur' had to be appointed; Philip of Valois, as senior royal prince, took the job.[83] Clearly Philip of Valois understood, just as Philip of Poitiers and Sancho of Majorca had understood in 1316, that getting the position of regent meant, absent the birth of a boy, the regent would become king. When Queen Jeanne d'Evreux had a girl, French elites faced a new dilemma: having established the precedent of excluding women, should they go with the usual principle of affinity of degree, in which case the nephew of Charles IV, King Edward III of England, was the closest relative?

The ruling of February 1317 offered a precedent for exclusion based on gender; if the King of France was 'emperor in his own kingdom', it was a short step to the principle that since no woman could be emperor, no woman could inherit the kingdom of France.[84] Eudes IV made a brief claim on behalf of poor Jeanne (now 16), but Philip VI was his brother-in-

---

[81] Brown, 'Ceremonial', gives multiple examples of these oaths.

[82] Bart, *Histoire du droit privé*, pp. 319–320.

[83] Pope John XXII used the term 'regentis' for Philip of Valois, just as he had for Philip of Poitiers.

[84] In fourteenth-century Europe, a woman inheriting a throne could take the title of 'king'. In Poland, for example, Jadwiga, daughter of King Louis [a member of the Anjou branch of the French royal family], inherited the throne when he died (1382). Her charters refer to her as '*rex*', not '*regina*'. When she married Jagiełło, Grand Duke of Lithuania, he took the title of King of Poland, but Jadwiga retained her title as '*rex Poloniae*'.

law, too.[85] The *Grandes Chroniques* say that Robert III of Artois, who had lost Artois to his aunt Mahaud, was a key supporter of Philip: he supposedly argued that Philip was regent precisely because he was the senior male royal measured in descent in the male line only, so that he should be king on that basis, too. Even the *Grandes Chroniques*[86] say several doctors of civil and canon law agreed with the English position that affinity of degree should decide the issue. The French elite could do nothing about Navarre, a separate kingdom, which now fell to Jeanne; the new king had to recognize her rights to Champagne, too, but in keeping with the principle of not letting the original peerage fiefs slip out of royal hands, he forced her to exchange it for lesser fiefs.

Géraud de Frachet tells us that the French elite at the assembly did not relish (*non æquanimiter*) the prospect of being 'subjects' of the king of England. As late as 1365, the Valois took so seriously Jeanne's claim, that they made her son Charles 'the Bad' of Navarre formally renounce his rights to France. Six years later, Charles' brother Louis, in renouncing his claims to Champagne and Burgundy, promised not to make war on Charles V or on 'his descendants in Royal line by paternal agnation'. Charles the Bad ultimately failed in his efforts to get not only the kingdom, but Champagne and Burgundy, to which he had excellent legal rights. The policies pursued by him and by Edward III in the 1350s and 1360s, however, show that they were perfectly willing to settle for a share of the family inheritance. Both of them thought less in terms of kingdoms and more in terms of fiefs they viewed as family possessions: Normandy, Anjou, Maine and Aquitaine for Edward; Normandy, Champagne and Burgundy for Charles the Bad.

A Patchwork of Apanages and the Practice of the Monarchical Commonwealth

> The kingdom must remain united without any dismemberment or excessive dividing up (*partage*).
>
> Anseau Choquart, royal lawyer, 1375.

In the Treaty of Brétigny-Calais (1360), Edward III renounced his rights to the throne in return for the old duchy of Aquitaine and the restoration of the county of Ponthieu.[87] The treaty process, and the text

---

[85] Eudes IV's actions on behalf of Jeanne may have helped her regain Navarre and compensation for Champagne.

[86] BNF, M Fr 2608, 410v.

[87] Edward III inherited Ponthieu from his grandmother, Eleanor of Castile, wife of Edward I. Eleanor inherited Ponthieu from her mother, Jeanne de Dammartin. Earlier versions of the treaty also gave him Normandy.

itself, show that Edward understood France to be a monarchical Commonwealth: he insisted on oaths and signatures from members of the immediate royal family and 'others of his [John's] close lineage, from the peers of France, all dukes, counts, barons, and great land-owners ("*grands terriers*"), and all royal officers, who, at the moment of their institution, were to swear to the treaty'. He further insisted that the members of town governments swear to it. Edward took hostages from each group, including Paris and 19 others towns.[88] Henry V insisted on the same procedure in the Treaty of Troyes (1420). The two French kings explicitly cited the larger good as the reason for their actions: John II claimed, in the preamble, that he signed the 1360 treaty for the '*bien de pais*'; Charles VI said he acted in 1420 for '*le bien de la chose publique*'.

French elites generally stood against such a division, illustrating a process identified 30 years ago by Gerard Oestreich.[89] In 1359, John II had agreed to the Second Treaty of London, which had given Edward most of the old Plantagenet lands: not just Aquitaine, but Normandy, Anjou and Maine. Charles, Duke of Normandy, acting as regent, brought the matter to an assembly of the great men of France, who unanimously rejected it. 'The said treaty was quite displeasing to "all the people of France" and after hearing and deliberating, they responded to the said regent that the said treaty was not passable nor doable, and for that reason ordered war to be prepared against the English'.[90]

The large fiefs, above all the peerages, formed the principal 'members' of the Commonwealth's body politic, and in line with elite opinion, in the aftermath of Brétigny, John II and Charles V quickly moved to tie permanently and irrevocably those 'members' to the French body politic. John II issued letters patent in November 1361 which permanently codified a law of his father that attached the duchies of Burgundy and Normandy, and the counties of Champagne and Toulouse to the Crown.[91] Charles added a unity clause to the coronation ceremony – '[We swear] to watch over the superiorities, laws, and nobilities of the Crown of France, and neither to transport nor to alienate them' – to bind all future kings of France to

---

[88] Many of the urban hostages, including those of Paris and Rouen, died from an outbreak of plague in England. Towns rotated their hostages: English documents show the last rotation for hostages from Caen and Lyon in 1369. Rymer, *Foedera*, III, p. 871.

[89] G. Oestreich, *Neostoicism and the Early Modern State* (Cambridge, 1981), argued that elites, not princes, preserved political unities.

[90] *Grandes Chroniques*, copy in BNF, M Fr 2608, fol. 479r.

[91] John had so stated in the edict granting Burgundy to his son Philip in 1361. He promulgated a specific edict on these fiefs in November 1361, *Ordonnances*, IV, p. 212.

the principle.[92] Charles here reiterated promises he had made as regent, in 1357, to a meeting of Estates General of Languedoïl: he would hold, guard, and defend with all 'our power, the highnesses, nobilities, dignities, franchises of the said crown, and of all the demesnes belonging to it ... and that we will never alienate nor suffer to be alienated or estranged from our power, the said demesne'. Charles had his brother Louis, duke of Anjou, whom he named (1374) as potential regent, promise that he would guard and defend 'the demesne, the nobilities, the rights and seigneuries of this kingdom, against all living men, without alienating or suffering them to be alienated in any possible manner nor for any possible cause, color, or occasion that there might be'.[93] The *Grandes Chroniques* report a large council of great men in 1375 telling the king he could not 'surrender any of his sovereign rights or powers without breaching his coronation oath, and thus imperiling his honor and his soul'.[94]

John II and Charles V issued an unending stream of charters to towns, lordships and even villages who demanded that the king recognize them as permanently attached to the royal demesne and, often, to either the 'kingdom of France' or 'our kingdom'.[95] St-James-de-Beuvron's letters had the usual formula: 'without division, transfer or separation ... from Us, from our own demesne, Sovereignty, Jurisdiction, obedience and Seigneurie in all cases and in all the things, rights and Sovereignties that our Predecessors and Us [had from all ancient times]'. After 1369, Charles always issued a letter of permanent liaison to the Crown for each major town and fief he regained. The letters for the city of Limoges spoke of 'the immense utility that will come to Us and the

---

[92] *Coronation Book of Charles V*, p. 12: 'superiorates jura et Nobilitates Coronae Franciae custodiam, et illa nec transportabo nec alienabo': this clause was new to the royal oath in 1364. 'Superiorates' in Latin invariably became 'souverainetés' in the French version of a document. Text in the invaluable R. Jackson (ed.), *Ordines Coronationis Franciae*, v. II (Philadelphia, 1995, 2000), p. 476; in n. 47, Jackson reveals that this phrase was added by the scribe, who erased the segment of the oath based on earlier *ordines*. Jackson argues that the change was certainly not in a different hand, and represents a change perhaps implemented for the ceremony. In *Vive le Roi*, he gives a detailed explanation of the lack of hard evidence that any king actually took this oath. Kings from Charles V through Francis I invariably made explicit reference to having done so, but no text of actual ceremonies has this clause. Henry IV did not take such an oath. I would agree with Leyte, *Domaine*, that the regular reference to such an oath by kings from Charles VI through Francis I made universal the belief in such a clause in the coronation oaths. '*Ressort*' meant ultimate jurisdiction, and implied in all such documents the jurisdiction of the Parlement of Paris, as the king's chief court. On what that meant in practice, see the splendid maps in L. Dauphant, *Le royaume des quatre rivières* (Seyssel, 2012), which provide details on which areas actually did appeal cases to the Parlement in the late Middle Ages.
[93] *Ordonnances*, VI, p. 45ff.   [94] *Grandes Croniques*, II, p. 176.
[95] *Ordonnances*, III, p. 490 (April 1362).

commonwealth [*rei publice*] of our Kingdom. No individual king had the right to give away the Crown's *ressort* in any region or town'.[96] At his death in 1380, a dense network of legal connections bound the kingdom of France into a single entity. On the theoretical level, we can contrast the theory of unity, laid out most clearly in Jean de Terrevermeille's writings, with the statement by Charles V, in a letter to the town government of Montpellier in 1364, that he had succeeded to the throne by '*droite paternelle*', as if it were simply a piece of ordinary property.[97]

Between 1316 and the 1370s, two separate issues were at play: who should succeed to the throne, absent a male descendant; and what should happen to fiefs inherited by members of the royal family other than the designated king? The Parlement of Paris had made a key ruling on this second issue, with respect to Philip V's daughter, Jeanne, who claimed to inherit his county of Poitou. The Parlement ruled for Charles IV, not because they decided an apanage should be returned to the Crown in the absence of a male heir, but because they sided with the king's *procureur*, who argued that once Philip became king, he held the county of Poitou as king, not as count.[98] Charles IV, having succeeded Philip as king, received all of the lands Philip V had held as king. Philip IV had issued specific letters stating that, absent male heirs from legitimate marriage, the county of Poitou would revert to the Crown, because he did not want the County to be '*en main de femelle*', but the Parlement's *arrêt* makes no reference to that point. Louis X had apparently contradicted his father's reasoning: 'reason and natural rights [*drois naturez*] give out that in default of male heirs females must also inherit and have succession of the goods and possessions of fathers' if born in loyal marriage.[99] Moreover, the dispossessed Jeanne de France obtained from Philip

---

[96] *Ordonnances*, III, p. 140, cited in Guillaume Leyte, *Domaine et domanialité publique dans la France médiévale* (Strasbourg, 1996), p. 336. Philippe de Beaumanoir (1283, *Customs of Beauvaisis*) clearly stated the principle that any fief in the kingdom of France, by definition, had to be within the *ressort* of the King of France and his Parlement. Evrard de Trémaugon, in his *Songe du Vergier* (1370s), agreed. Charles V took this position in negotiations with the English in the 1370s; when he consulted John of Legnano and three other law faculty of Bologna, they ruled that 'iura superioritatis et ultimo ressorti' were owed to the king of France, by all in the kingdom, and that the king could not be deprived of these rights (*iurium*). Trémaugon studied with John of Legnano.

[97] The theory that the king succeeded to the throne by specific law, and not by simple paternal right, had taken root in the 1370s, as many documents attest. Terrevermeille created a fully elaborated statement of it in his *Tractatus* (1419): J. Barbey, *La Fonction royale. Essence et légitimité d'après les Tractatus de Jean de Terrevermeille* (Paris, 1983). Terrevermeille's *Tractatus de iure futuri successoris legitimi in regiis hereditatis* laid out the principle that the king was the usufructuary of the kingdom, not its owner.

[98] Philip V had, in fact, issued an ordinance to this effect, *Ordonnnances*, XI, p. 444.

[99] Petit, Charles de Valois, citing a document in the archives at Calais; he does not specify its nature.

V the promise that if he died without male heirs, she would regain the
county of Champagne, as a peerage, for her and her heirs.[100]
The principle of exclusive male inheritance of apanages became royal
law under Charles V, as part of a series of ordinances he issued in the
1370s to establish clear rules related to succession to the throne and
government during royal minorities. He also established the principle
that any personal possession of the King of France, within the kingdom,
inherited separately from the Crown, became a permanent part of the
royal demesne at the death of that king.[101] We might consider his rules
about male line only for the inheritance of an apanage to be part and
parcel of both his understanding of the female exclusion from the throne
(what came to be called Salic Law) and his understanding that the fiefs
were the 'members' of the body politic of the Crown: the king was its
head.

Charles V's regulation of the apanage process in the 1360s and 1370s
entailed the revocation of all grants of 'Nobilities and Seigneuries, *rentes*
and revenues from the royal demesne and *propre* heritage of the Kingdom
and Crown of France'.[102] Charles V made the female succession rever-
sion clause normative in all apanage grants. The rules for royal minorities
and regencies he created in 1374, were struck down in 1380, after
a debate between the chancellor and a royal lawyer, by an assembly of
the leading men of the kingdom, supervised by his brothers. They
declared Charles VI to be king at the age of 12. Little wonder that elites
worried about the stability of a system built around one man.

In their eyes, the body politic consisted of the king, as the head, and the
'members', of which the nobility were the most distinguished (the arms
and hands, as Christine de Pizan put it). The most important members
were, of course, those related to the royal family. Many of these lines
died out quickly, often in the first generation, but a steadily increasing
number lingered on. Even in a single lifetime, an apanage like the duchy
of Berry, given to John II's eponymous son, could reduce the monarchy's
resources for over half a century. Between Louis VIII (d. 1228) and
Charles V (d. 1380), kings of France gave away as apanages that remained
in existence in 1380: the duchy of Burgundy; the duchy of Anjou; the
county of Maine; the duchy of Berry; the county of Alençon; Bourbon

---

[100] Secousse, *Recueil*, pp. 6ff., agreement of 27 March 1317. If Philip V lived and had heirs,
Jeanne was to get 50,000 l. to purchase lands that would be made into a peerage fief.
[101] Under this principle, once Louis X had inherited Champagne from his mother, at his
death it would have passed permanently into the royal demesne. Navarre, as a separate
kingdom, would be bound by its own rules. The principle did not apply to territories
owned by the king's wife, such as the duchy of Brittany during the reigns of Louis XII
and Francis I.
[102] *Ordonnances*, IV, pp. 466–467, July 1364.

lands; and the Orléannais. Members of the royal family held other fiefs, like Artois, but that grant long antedated the apanage rules, so Artois passed several times to women. Unlike the duchy of Burgundy, which Louis XI claimed as soon as Duke Charles of Burgundy died in 1477, Artois remained in Mary of Burgundy's hands.[103]

A patchwork of apanages and peerages had to be a Commonwealth, in the sense of a federation in which these powerful princes had considerable authority. They usually collected all the tax revenues in their apanages, and they had de facto power to name the 'royal' officers (the king had to approve). A prince like Jean, Duke of Berry, or his brother, Philip, Duke of Burgundy, created elaborate governing structures of their own.[104] The dukes of Burgundy called meetings of estates, without seeking royal permission, and they minted coins. The king kept very limited rights in an apanage: *ressort* (final jurisdiction); 'sovereignty' (meaning he was *souverain seigneur*, highest lord); and protection of churches and abbeys holding letters of royal safeguard (a cathedral, for example, automatically remained under the king's protection). Kings in a relatively weak bargaining position, like Philip V in 1317, might grant explicit letters foregoing jurisdiction, to a prince like the duke of Brittany.

When the king violated the principle of this body politic, as Louis XI did in the first years of his reign, the political community rose in revolt, the War of the Bien Public. Historians tend to dismiss that conflict as one in which the princes fought on behalf of selfish interests – which they also did, and which Louis used to his advantage – but they did defend the '*bien public*'.[105] Louis recognized the legitimacy of the accusation: he issued an ordinance protecting life tenure of royal officials, backed off his interference in town

---

[103] John II's letters specifically say that he personally had inherited Burgundy from Philip de Rouvre and gave his **personal** inheritance to Philip. The letters for the apanages of John's sons Louis and Jean both specifically state that only male heirs may succeed, and that the lands revert to the Crown absent a male heir born in legitimate marriage; the letters for Philip say only heirs in legitimate marriage, and make no reference to gender. Mary's grandson, Emperor Charles V, always believed he was the rightful duke of Burgundy; he made the 'restoration' of 'his' duchy of Burgundy one of the terms of the Treaty of Madrid (1529).

[104] R. Favreau, *La ville de Poitiers à la fin du Moyen Age. Un capital régional* (2 vols., Poitiers, 1977–1978); J. Rauzier, *La Bourgogne au XIVe siècle : Fiscalité, population, économie* (Dijon, 2009); A. Leguai, 'De la seigneurie à l'État: le Bourbonnais pendant la guerre de Cent ans', *Bulletin de la Société d'émulation du Bourbonnais, lettres, sciences, arts* 54 (1968), pp. 28–58; J.-P. Leguay, *Fastes et malheurs de la Bretagne ducale, 1213–1532* (Rennes, 1996); Bertran Schnerb, *L'État bourguignon, 1363–1477* (Paris, 1999). Both the dukes of Brittany and of Burgundy developed seals showing them seated in majesty, rather than the traditional ducal motif of the mounted knight.

[105] Here I disagree with Favier, *Louis XI*, who rejects any broader dimensions to this conflict for an inter-princely battle: 'Le Bien public was a formula, but it was not a program' (p. 484).

governments and, de facto, restored the Pragmatic Sanction of Bourges. He specifically enjoined his successors not to repeat his mistakes. His daughter, Anne de Beaujeu, regent, followed his advice: the first act of the child Charles VIII was to confirm all the judges of the Parlement of Paris.[106] No French king after Louis XI ever carried out a wholesale purging of royal officers upon his succession.[107] As for the argument that Louis XI sought to destroy the princes to strengthen the central 'state', it makes no sense in dynastic terms: he left a sickly son (who died childless at 28) and deliberately married Louis d'Orléans, second in line to the throne, to his own handicapped daughter, Jeanne, so that Orléans could not reproduce. For whom precisely was Louis XI building this strong monarchy? Thomas Basin, Louis' disgruntled contemporary, had it right: Louis wanted to make sure no one could revolt 'against *him*' [emphasis added] or have the audacity to oppose his will.

Religion and Dynastic Instability: The Birth of the State

> We have for a certain and ordinary law that no one can be King nor command a Catholic people, if he is not Catholic.
>
> François Cromé, Dialogue entre le maheustre et le manant

The Commonwealth arrangement established by Charles V lasted until the Wars of Religion, when an obvious issue created tension between the king and the *bien public*: how could a king of different religion be serving the *bien public*? If one accepted – as French elites did – the principle that the 'honour of God' was a key part of the *bien public*, then no Protestant could believe a Catholic king defended the *bien public*, nor, in 1589, could many Catholics believe a Protestant king did so. A king who failed to defend the *bien public* was, by definition, a tyrant: what rights did loyal subjects have against a tyrant?

Unsurprisingly, in the aftermath of the St Bartholomew's Day Massacre, Huguenot authors like Mornay, in his *Vindiciae, contra Tyrannos* (1579), argued the 'people' [i.e. the citizens] had the right to overthrow a tyrant.[108]

---

[106] *Ordonnances*, XIX, p. 125. Commynes' testimony (Chapter 10), that Louis repented his 'folly and error', rings true.

[107] Individual counsellors, of course, often suffered disgrace upon the change of monarch. The official royal historian of Louis XIV, François de Mézeray, in his *Histoire de France depuis Faramond jusqu'au règne de Louis le juste: enrichie de plusieurs belles & rares antiquitez & de la vie des reynes* (Paris, 1685), p. II, 681, castigated Louis XI for removing the 'best officers' of the Crown.

[108] J. Collins, 'De la république française à l'état français: Duplessis-Mornay et la transformation de la citoyenneté en France', H. Daussy and V. Ferrer (eds.), *Servir Dieu, le roi et l'État. Philippe Duplessis-Mornay (1549–1623), Albineana 18* (Niort, 2006), pp. 325–339.

Later, when Mornay's friend Henry of Navarre became Henry IV, Mornay changed his tune: subjects owed loyalty to the king. The hard-line Catholics, so ardent for supreme royal power when a Catholic sat on the throne, now turned into the Monarchomachs, who picked up the old Huguenot refrain about the right to kill a tyrant. One of the most extreme Monarchomachs, Jean Boucher, in his *Apology for Jean Chastel* (1595), claimed the poor lad never said that it was legitimate to kill a king, but only a tyrant. Boucher recognized the person of the king as sacrosanct, having been anointed by God. Henry of Navarre, however, was an ex-communicant, a relapse, a profaner of sacred things, a declared public enemy, an oppressor of Religion, and as such excluded from all right to succeed to the crown, and moreover a tyrant instead of a King [...] who [...] had lost all sense [...] of humanity and love toward God, toward the Church, and toward his *patrie*.[109] Fifteen years later, arguing against the Englishman William Barclay, Cardinal Bellarmine insisted that while a legitimate prince had to be obeyed, one who had been excommunicated, and was thus illegitimate, did not. He drew a strong conclusion: 'Christians are not obliged to tolerate, indeed they must not tolerate a heretic King [...] when divine right and human right are in contrast [*pugnant*], it is necessary to maintain the divine right, neglecting the human one.'[110] Not surprisingly, the Parlement of Paris condemned Bellarmine's work to the fire.

This new attack on the royal person – and, given that Henry III and Henry IV were the only two French kings to be assassinated, we may consider the discourse of tyrannicide to be speech *acts* – mandated a new definition of the polity.[111] Building on many sources, and responding to

---

[109] J. Boucher, *Apologie pour Jehan Chastel, Parisien, exécuté à mort & pour les pères et escolliers de la Societé de Jesus, bannis du Royaume de France, contre l'arrest du Parlement, 29 décembre 1595* (Douai, 1595), p. 15.

[110] Cited in Stefania Tutino, *Law and Conscience. Catholicism in Early Modern England, 1570–1625* (Ashgate, 2007), p. 149, Latin original in footnote. The Latin title differs from its usual English one: *Tractatus de Potestate Summi Pontificis in rebus temporalibus adversus Gulielmum Barclaium*. Bellarmine published first in Rome (1610), then in Cologne (1611), the edition usually cited in France and England. '*Pugnant*' carries more the sense of being in combat or conflict, not just in contrast.

[111] J. L. Austin, *How to Do Things with Words* (Cambridge, MA, 1975, revised second edition), laid the theoretical foundation for thinking about the context of 'utterances' of given words: the place, time, intonation, audience, etc. affect the meaning and purpose, turning what might be an abstract musing in one setting into a call for action in another. Michèle Fogel's innovative Les cérémonies de l'information dans la France du XVIᵉ au XVIIIᵉ siècle (Paris, 1989), demonstrates conclusively, in my view, that the monarchy itself was extraordinarily conscious of context for its speech acts. Fogel illustrates (Chapter 1, 'Rituel et espace de la publication') that the monarchy used different public places in Paris to post up notices based on the content of the poster. Nor has this practice disappeared: American politicians, including presidents, regularly choose Georgetown University's Gaston Hall to signal to interested parties a major address on foreign policy.

the model proposed by the nobility, the French judicial elite came up with the new theoretical entity, the state. As was the case with the rise of the monarchical Commonwealth, this transition took place in a moment of extreme dynastic fragility.

French political discourse needed a new term to take the place of the '*bien public*', with its emphasis on the 'honour of God'. From 1560 to 1626, five French kings tried to consult with various bodies about the most effective means to run the kingdom, and to settle the religious dispute: Estates General in 1560, 1561, 1576, 1588 and 1614; Assemblies of Notables in 1583, 1596, 1617 and 1626; an unnamed but important meeting at Moulins in 1566; an aborted attempt to call the Estates General in 1573; to say nothing of the League Estates of 1593. Given that kings of France made virtually no such efforts between 1507 and 1560 or again after 1626, we cannot help but look at this interval as exceptional.[112] The consultation model reflected the effort of French political elites, including the king, to create a new political system. They emerged with a state, in which elites could share power through implementation of policy, rather than in a representative body. Some within the elites did craft the policies, but they reached decisions in camera, as it were, and then sought cooperation from elites to carry out the new laws and policies. The sovereign courts, beginning especially in the Regency of Marie de Medici, complained incessantly that the persistent use of *lits de justice* to force registration of royal edicts deprived them precisely of their legal right to modify legislation, that is, in essence, to consult on its formulation. The phrase they used again and again was that they had been deprived of the 'liberty of their opinions' [*voix*] and the 'liberty of their suffrages'.[113]

Why did French elites go along with this change? Why did they give up rights they believed fundamental to their identity as free men? Simply put: France in 1589 was a society in chaos;[114] the order we historians create

Why? Georgetown has a world-renowned School of Foreign Service, where many US diplomats get their education, and where former ambassadors often teach after retirement. Politicians rarely make major domestic policy speeches in Gaston Hall.

[112] Anne of Austria and Mazarin called an Estates General for 1649. Some local assemblies met, but Anne cancelled the Paris meeting due to the *Fronde*. Roland Mousnier, J.-P. Labatut, and Yves Durand published two of the *cahiers* drawn up by local noble assemblies: *Deux Cahiers de la noblesse* (Paris, 1965). J. Russell Major's many books called it a 'Renaissance Monarchy', lasting from Charles VII to Henry IV, but that broader formulation, stimulating as it might be for research, does not entirely fit the evidence.

[113] BNF, M Dupuy 646, f. 202, in 1622 First President Nicolaï of the Chamber of Accounts, protesting the forced registration of financial edicts, offers one example among many.

[114] M. Bernard, *Écrire la peur à l'époque des guerres de Religion. Une étude des historiens et mémorialistes contemporains des guerres civiles en France (1562–1598)* (Paris, 2010), p. 339: historians of the time, above all, 'wanted to restore order, absolutely necessary to a France wiped out by decades of civil war'.

enables us to classify, to analyse and to narrate, but that essential service should not blind us to the fact that we create the order whose narrative we chronicle. Is 'chaos' too strong a word? Loménie de Brienne, archbishop of Toulouse, at his 1771 inauguration into the *Académie Française*, chose it: 'How many others have celebrated the elevated and profound views by which he {Cardinal Richelieu}, so to speak, pulled politics from the void, and the monarchy from chaos.'[115] From the 1590s to the 1780s, the image of Henry IV slaying the Hydra of Anarchy was a staple of royalist art in France.[116]

'Pulled politics from the void, and the monarchy from chaos': many in the days of Henry III, Henry IV and Louis XIII shared those sentiments. In November 1586, president Pierre II Séguier, royal commissioner sent to the Estates of Provence, told them that Henry III governed not the 'entire ship [of state]. It was the remainder of past shipwrecks'. Worse could follow: 'And if it does not please God to conserve for many years the life of him who he has given us for King, it will be worse. Our fate, our heredity, our share of the inheritance then will be murder and blood.'[117] Seven years later, during the civil war Séguier predicted, the rump Parlement of Paris, holding sessions at Tours told the king: 'we do not doubt that on the conservation of your generous soul depends the public salvation. [...] society is no farther from its ruin and subversion than the length of your life'.[118] In 1595, after Henry IV survived Chastel's attempt on his life, the Parlement came back to this theme, using one of Séguier's metaphors:

God has by this means {saving the king's life} cast a pitying eye on us and deployed his veil of mercy, because a second shipwreck would have immediately seen this Kingdom bloody with murders, filled with sacking (of cities), pillaging, brigandage, the state of the Monarchy suddenly changed, and in a moment would be born as many Sovereignties as there are towns and fortresses. In short, the bottom of our unhappiness would be to survive the calamities of this State, which we have long foreseen not to be farther distant from its ruin than the length of your life.[119]

---

[115] He used the same argument to the Assembly of Notables in May 1787, when he was head of royal finances. Brienne descended directly from one of Richelieu's secretaries of state. Speech online at: http://www.academie-francaise.fr/node/1553.

[116] http://www.musee-chateau-pau.fr/pages/page_id18052_u1l2.htm: Augustin Pajou's 1785 *Henri IV Trampling Underfoot the Hydra of Anarchy*, a fine example of the genre.

[117] BNF, M Fr 16,517, fol. 263, Pierre II Séguier, président à mortier of the Parlement of Paris, was the son of Pierre I Séguier, famous avocat of the mid-sixteenth century and himself a président à mortier. The later chancellor, Pierre Séguier, was the nephew of Pierre II.

[118] BNF, Dupuy 3888, fol. 106.   [119] BNF, Dupuy 3888, fol. 114v.

The religious question of 1589 is so obvious that it has often obscured the second dimension of the crisis: dynastic insecurity. The death of Henry III made the unthinkable real: Salic Law made a twice relapsed heretic, Henry of Navarre, king of France. Did educated people actually believe in Salic Law? Public speakers made constant reference to it; historians like Étienne Pasquier touted its immemorial sway in France; the successions of 1498 and 1515 seemed to follow its principles.

Yet if we scratch beneath the surface, we see matters were not so simple: let us take the cases of 1498 and 1515. Louis XII was married to his predecessor's sister; he immediately divorced her and married the widowed Anne of Brittany to make sure her duchy did not move out of the royal hands. The couple had two daughters, the elder of whom was to get Brittany: her mother, who had been betrothed to Maximilian of Habsburg prior to her forced marriage to Charles VIII, engineered a betrothal of Claude to Maximilian's grandson, Charles of Ghent (the later Emperor Charles V): the prospective 'spouses' were four years old.

When his political position improved, Louis XII convoked a special assembly at Tours in 1506 to 'demand' of him that he break the engagement of Claude with Charles, and betroth her instead to his cousin and Salic Law–designated heir, François d'Angoulême. The Parisian assembly ordered their delegates to look after the 'good, peace and union of the Commonwealth of the Kingdom [*bien, paix et union de la chose publicque du Royaulme*]'.[120] Lyon sent three deputies to Tours, for the '*bien*, profit, and utility . . . of the kingdom of France and its *chose publique*'. The chief deputy, Claude Le Charron, doctor in law, chief judge of the bailiwick, reported back that the king had approved the towns' 'request' that he arrange the marriage and that François d'Angoulême 'had now been created Dauphin [*créé dauphin*] and declared successor to the Crown of France'.[121] Here we have a highly trained lawyer, the chief judge in the third largest city in the kingdom, telling his constituents that Francis had been '*created*' dauphin, a phrase that suggests that, at least in 1506, the Salic Law had precious little to do with the succession as a practical matter, even in lawyers' eyes.

Let us stop a moment to consider the possible 'kings' of 1590. After the death in captivity of the 66-year-old Cardinal of Bourbon, the Leaguers

---

[120] RDHV Paris, I, 117ff. The deputies included members of all three estates, beginning with two royal officers (one of them *prévôt des marchands* as well); two doctors of theology, regents of the University; a merchant; a lawyer (*avocat*); the town receiver, and two nobles (one of them also an officer, Master of *Eaux & Forêts*). Louis XII made it clear to the towns that he wanted the 'request' to come from them; he went through the charade of debating two days at the assembly about whether to accede.

[121] AM de Lyon, BB 25, fol. 18v, consulted online [image 19].

had to find a new 'king'. The Duke of Lorraine, Charles III, had married Claude de France, daughter of Henry II.[122] Claude's older sister, Elizabeth, had married Philip II of Spain; taking into account seniority, their daughter Isabella, 23 and single in 1589, was the obvious female heir. Charles, Duke of Guise, son of the assassination victim of 1588, was the obvious popular choice for her spouse, and the kingship. His father, Henry of Guise, was the great-grandson of Louis XII; both of Charles of Guise's parents descended from a female Bourbon.[123] In Le Roy Ladurie's famous phrase, they were 'all cousins'.[124]

Salic Law may have precluded inheritance through a female line, but Mayenne convoked an Estates General in 1593 precisely on the grounds of the precedent of 1328: that in the absence of a clearly legitimate heir, the Estates General had the right to elect a new king. Long-standing practice would have given precedence to someone with close ties to the previous king. Remove the Bourbons from the equation, and the Isabella of Spain-Charles of Guise couple look like the obvious choice. The key lawyers among the Leaguers, men like the royal counsellor Villeroy or the later Guard of the Seals, Guillaume du Vair, however, by this time took seriously the need to uphold the law as they understood it: that meant Henry IV was king. This legal reality, in 1593, greatly facilitated Henry's direct negotiations with the Estates and with key figures like Villeroy. The correspondence of the time shows that all of these men deeply resented Spanish interference in the French succession.

Isabella and Charles were also 'foreigners'. Throughout the 1570s to the 1590s, pamphlet literature in France, to say nothing of speakers at the Estates General of 1576 and 1588, denounced 'foreign' influence in France. They insisted on the need to promote 'natural born Frenchmen', and to get rid of the perfidious Italians (1570s especially) and Spaniards (post-1585). Throughout the period, those attacking the Guise family never failed to mention their 'foreign' origins: Lorraine, after all, lay within the Holy Roman Empire.[125]

---

[122] Their only son, Henry, later (1599) married Catherine of Bourbon, sister of Henry IV

[123] The Guise family had other royal connections: Mary of Guise was the mother of Mary, Queen of Scots, who had briefly been Queen of France (1559–1560). Mary of Guise's grandson, James, inherited England in 1603. On the Guise family, S. Carroll, *Martyrs and Murderers: The Guise Family and the Making of Europe* (New York, 2009). Renée, second daughter of Louis XII and Anne of Brittany, married Ercole II d'Este; their daughter, Anne d'Este married François of Guise, father of Henry of Guise. François of Guise was the son of Antoinette de Bourbon; Catherine of Cleves, Charles' mother, was the daughter of Marguerite de Bourbon, an aunt of Henry IV.

[124] E. Le Roy Ladurie, *L'État royal, 1460–1610* (Paris, 1987), chart on pp. 306–307.

[125] For perspectives on this dimension of propaganda from the time, see X. Le Person, *'Practiques' et 'Practiqueurs'. La vie politique à la fin du règne de Henri III (1584–1589)* (Geneva, 2002); J.-F. Dubost, *La France italienne. XVIe-XVIIe siècle* (Paris, 1997);

What about the possible heirs on Henry IV's side: Henri de Condé, the infant son of the king's cousin; the prince of Conti, the king's childless, 41-year-old first cousin; and more distant cousins in the Soissons and Montpensier branches. According to law, the infant prince of Condé was Henry's heir; alas, life was not so simple. Louis II, prince of Condé had died of 'poisoning' (1588); Henry IV, like almost all of his contemporaries, believed Condé's wife, Charlotte de la Trémouïlle had murdered him to cover up a love affair.[126] He further believed the young child was a bastard born of that liaison. Henry kept Charlotte imprisoned in a convent on suspicion of murder for years after he became king.

Pierre de l'Estoile, in his journal for 1609, reports a famous incident between Condé, then 21, and Henry IV. The king had fallen in love with the 15-year-old Charlotte de Montmorency, whom de l'Estoile assures us was not simply the most beautiful woman at Court, but the most beautiful woman in France. Henry engineered her marriage to his cousin, so she would stay at Court. When the king began to make obvious advances, Condé decided he and his wife should take their leave of Court. In the acrimonious exchange about this issue, Condé responded 'a bit haughtily, and mixing into his utterances this word, tyranny'. The king harshly replied: 'never in his life had he committed an act of a tyrant except when he had recognized him [Condé] as what he was not; and when he wished it, he would show him his father in Paris'.[127]

Had Henry IV died leading his famous charge at Ivry in 1590, or under Jean Chastel's knife in 1594, would the Salic Law have made the two-year-old or six-year-old Condé king? The idea is laughable. Go back to 1589: Salic Law says that Henry of Navarre, 46 years old, with no legitimate children and estranged from a wife who was universally believed to have borne an illegitimate son in 1583, is now king. What sort of dynasty did he represent in 1589 or in 1593? Quite aside from his religion, Henry IV was a highly problematic king because he looked to be the last of his line, and the second Bourbon-Condé line would surely have been ruled extinct, had it come to that. Salic Law was all well and good, but reading the correspondence of men like Villeroy or Jean Bodin, no one took the prince of Conti – who should have been next in line after Henry

---

A. Tallon, *Conscience nationale et sentiment religieux en France au XVIe siècle : essai sur la vision gallicane du monde* (Paris, 2002).

[126] De l'Estoile's journal for 1588 mentions that the '*commun bruit*' had it that Condé had been poisoned by a page in his household, under orders from Charlotte de la Trémouïlle. He does not mention the infidelity.

[127] Henry used the stronger *ne ... point* construction, rather than the simple *ne ... pas*: 'jamais il n'avoit fait acte de tiran en sa vie que quand il l'avoit fait reconnoistre pour ce qu'il n'estoit point'. De l'Estoile goes out of his way to insist that he has this story from reliable sources.

IV, if the young Condé were eliminated on grounds of illegitimacy – to be a serious candidate; they cited his unkingly demeanour (which included a speech impediment). They all discussed Soissons and Montpensier as the potential candidates, and we know that the politics of Henry IV's consideration of prospective husbands for his sister, Catherine, focused on Soissons (her choice), Montpensier (Henry's choice), and even on Charles of Guise (for whom his mother negotiated with Henry in 1593). Marrying Catherine de Bourbon would have fit the pattern noted above of getting control of the royal woman who presented the greatest potential threat to a collateral male heir.[128] The fear of dynastical instability, so evident in the speeches we have seen above, lay behind all political debates in France in the 1580s and 1590s. Law provided an important buttress to Henry in 1593, but the fragility of the solution strongly encouraged the legal elite to seek out a new source of loyalty and unity: they came up with the state.

That prior to 1638 neither of Henry IV's sons had produced a son, and that the same Henry of Condé (or his son), looked almost certain to inherit the throne, brought the old nightmares to life, especially in moments like Louis XIII's near death from illness in September 1630. The narrative of history seventeeth-century French elites believed was one in which Richelieu saved the political nation from chaos, just as the *Académie Française* he founded saved the French language from barbarism and disorder.[129] By the early eighteenth century, a confirmed 'patriot' like marshal Vauban would regularly write of the need of someone who loved his '*patrie*' to serve the '*bien de l'Estat*'.

We look back and see the Bourbons ruled France from 1589 to 1792, so we see stability; they lived instead a narrative of instability, sometimes descending, in their eyes, into chaos. The narratives we historians have

---

[128] Salic Law, legitimately interpreted, would also have placed the Courtenay family, direct descendants, in male line only, of Louis VI, in line of succession after the Bourbons. The family regularly filed petitions – down to 1715 – to have their status as 'princes du sang' recognized by the king (or, in 1715, Regent). The Bourbons used the excuse that Saint Louis [Louis IX] had supposedly 're-issued' the Salic Law, so it applied only to **his** descendants. Other contemporary sources show that the aristocracy believed the Courtenay family had been eliminated from the succession rights because no one in the family had been a ruling prince in over a century. Be that as it may, when the duke of Montpensier showed up for Henry IV's coronation, one of the members of his retinue was the scion of the Courtenay family. The 1662 petition is available on Gallica: http://gallica.bnf.fr/ark:/12148/bpt6k5658049j.r=Courtenay%2C%20Louis%20de.

[129] The succession remained tenuous until the 1680s and became so again after the deaths in the royal family in 1711–1712. For Vauban's use of 'patrie' and 'Estat' see the remarkable collection of his short writings for Louis XIV: M. Virol, dir., *Les Oisevetés de Monsieur Vauban* (Seyssel, 2007). For Richelieu, see, for example, the speeches he gave at the Assembly of Notables of 1626: http://gallica.bnf.fr/ark:/12148/bpt6k469670.r=assemblee%20des%20notables%201626.

created become, consciously or unconsciously, teleological. Rather than seeing the 'state' as a royal imposition, we need to understand that the French judicial elite consciously made the choice to share power with the king through the royal administration itself; they disliked representative assemblies, from which their members were, as individuals, excluded by longstanding practice.

Where late medieval French elites agreed to a polity based on Crown and Commonwealth, the elites of the 1590s, above all the lawyers who dominated the royal administration, combined those two elements to insist on loyalty to a new unifying concept, the state: the monarchs were just along for the ride. In France, where landed nobles dominated representative assemblies, it made sense for the legal elite to share power (and balance royal power) from within the government, not by means of trying to wrest power from the nobles in those assemblies. By Louis XIV's time, this 'nobility of state' (a term we associate with Pierre Bourdieu, but a concept really laid out by Henri See, who called them the 'noblesse administrative') had completely taken over the central administration.[130] We have a bizarre idea of the relationship of the Parlements and the Crown: we focus on their disagreements. Most of the time, they worked together hand-in-glove. Provincial Parlements were a key instrument of royal power's implementation.

L'État

> Estat, *m.* [...] disposition, ordre, succes, police, et cours, conduict et maniement des affaires, ainsi dit-on, Tel estoit ou est l'Estat du Royaume.
>
> Jean Nicot's Thrésor de la langue françoyse (1606)

French dictionaries show the rapid progress the new meaning of 'state' made in the seventeenth century. Nicot first defined *'estat'* in terms of 'status', but added the second meaning of conduct of government affairs. By the end of the century, Antoine Furetière (1695) codified the new usage: *'L'intérest particulier cède à la raison d'Estat'*. Giovanni Botero's formula had now become the clearest way to define the concept of 'state' itself. During the course of the seventeenth century, two terms – Commonwealth and state – began to be used as synonyms: Hobbes does so in the introduction to *Leviathan*, claiming that the English word for the Latin *civitas* is 'state'. A century later, in his *Dictionary of the English*

---

[130] P. Bourdieu, *Noblesse d'État. Grandes écoles et esprit de corps* (Paris, 1989), discusses the roots of the modern system in the eighteenth century; H. Sée, *La France économique et sociale au XVIIIe siècle* (Paris, 1925), Chapter V, where he rightly identifies the Conseil d'État as the 'center of the administrative nobility'.

Language, Samuel Johnson gives, as his sixth definition of 'state': 'The community; the publick; the commonwealth'. His ninth definition is even more confusing: 'A republick; a government not monarchical'. By that standard, virtually none of the 'states' of eighteenth-century Europe could be called a 'state'.[131]

The same linguistic shift took place in France, but in the early seventeenth century. During the *Fronde* (1648–1653), when opponents of the government took up the timeless theme of reforming a corrupted monarchy, they spoke in defence not of the '*bien public*' or the 'honour of God' but of the '*bien de l'Etat*'. Paul Pellisson's remarks on his induction as a special member of the *Académie Française* at precisely that moment (1652) show that the campaign to equate the Commonwealth and the state had succeeded: Kings, Conquerors, and even several of those Heroes that Antiquity made its Gods, formerly took a great honor from being made citizens [*bourgeois*] of certain Republics. [. . .] a State, however flourishing and however illustrious it might be, is it anything other than a group of people [*amas de gens*], which interest and necessity alone joins together, where sometimes reigns riches, sometimes force and violence, sometimes intrigue and chicanery, and very rarely merit and virtue?[132] In one breath Pellisson speaks of the honour of becoming a citizen of the 'republic', while in the next he explains that a 'state' is an '*amas de gens*', a group of people brought together by common interest and necessity, a paraphrase of the description of the *polis* in the opening paragraph of Aristotle's *Politics*. Pellisson here also paraphrases the definition of *civitas* (*cité; polis*) given by the most widely consulted multi-language dictionary of his time, that of Ambrogio Calepino: '*amas de citoyens*', group of citizens. Pellisson, unconsciously I think, provides us with a critical distinction of our two terms: a state is a given political unit in which people live under a common rulership (as Turgot put it in the 1770s, 'an

---

[131] Q. Skinner, 'The State', in T. Bell, J. Farr and R. Hanson (ed.), *Political Innovation and Conceptual Change* (Cambridge, 1989), places this development in England squarely in the seventeenth century, with roots in the Florentine discourse of Machiavelli and Guicciardini. The French use of 'state' from the 1570s onward, and particularly after 1589, seems to me to have a different context, in part because the actual state apparatus of the French monarchy was so large. I believe the French discourse had an important impact in England, but that issue needs to wait for another day.

[132] *Recueil des Harangues prononcées par Messieurs de l'Académie Françoise dans leurs receptions, & en autres occasion, depuis l'establissement de l'Académie jusqu'à present*, 2ᵉ édition, reveuë et augmentée t. 1 (Paris, 1714). Pellisson had written a history of the Académie; they rewarded him by making him a supernumerary member, with the right to sit in their assembly, and the right to the next available seat. Later a client of Fouquet, he spent four years in the Bastille. Released from jail, he went to work for Louis XIV, for whom he helped draft the famous *Mémoirs pour l'Instruction du Dauphin*. My thanks to the Bibliothèque de l'Institut de France and to my friend and colleague Jean-Pierre Babelon for their assistance in getting access to this collection.

assemblage of men united under a single government'); a Commonwealth is a group of citizens. People have legal rights; citizens have political rights. Jean Bodin (*République*, I, 6) makes that clear: when the head of the family leaves his household, where he is the sovereign power, to confer and negotiate with the other heads of families about public matters ['de ce qui leur touche à tous en général ... laissans sa famille, pour entrer en la cité: et laissans les affaires domestiques, pour traitter les publiques'], he becomes a 'citizen', that is, 'the free subject holding of the sovereignty of another'. ['Et au lieu de seigneur, il s'appelle citoyen: qui n'est autre chose en propres termes, que le franc subiect tenant de la souveraineté d'autruy'.]

Pellisson moves to a fascinating juxtaposition of the two entities: some states, he tells us, are run by the wealthy (oligarchy, an Aristotelian category of illegitimate polity); some are run by force; and some by intrigue. Force is not an Aristotelian category of polity, legitimate or illegitimate; it is a state of fact. Intrigue has to do not with forms of political organization, but with the practice of government. Pellisson then returns to more familiar ground: few states, he says, are run by merit and virtue, categories that take us back to Aristotle's 'common good', whose pursuit is the purpose of the polity itself. From Henry IV's day to our own, those ruling every manifestation of the state in France have sought to convince those whom they ruled that the 'common good' of the medieval and Renaissance champions of the Commonwealth and the state invented in the days of good king Henry are one and the same. Blinded by the master narratives of nineteenth-century Republican historians, historians have too often done the same.

5   Setting Limits to Grandeur: Preserving the Spanish Monarchy in an Iron Century

B. J. García García

The Consolidation of a Vast Dynastic Conglomerate: A Globalized Imperial System

At the dawn of the seventeenth century, the Spanish monarchy appeared to have reached its moment of plenitude in the processes of aggregation, expansion and consolidation that it had implemented with policies of conquest, pacification and accord since the reign of the Catholic Kings Ferdinand of Aragon and Isabella of Castile.

This trend had been favoured, in particular, by the ambitious universalist vocation of Charles V.[1] The emperor had chosen to maintain the kingdoms that capricious dynastic fortune had given him as one heritage, and also to champion the cause of a fervent 'Catholic' confessional militancy, making this the cohesive element uniting the territories that had been incorporated into the monarchy. His decisions reinforced their overall sense of being part of a well-established collective identity; links were forged not only between the subjects and the long-standing 'Catholicity' of the sovereigns of Spain that had been acknowledged since 'the time of the Visigoths',[2] but

This study was undertaken as part of the project: 'Cultura política y mecenazgo artístico entre las cortes de Madrid, Viena y Bruselas (1580-1715)', ref. HAR2009–12963-C03-03; and 'Estrategias de comunicación y cultura política en la red familiar de los Austrias (1570-1725)', ref. HAR2012-39016-C04-03 financed by the Dirección General de Investigación del Ministerio de Economía y Competitividad.

[1] J. M. Headley, 'The Habsburg World Empire and the Revival of Ghibellinism', *Medieval and Renaissance Studies* 7 (1978), pp. 93–127; A. Pagden, 'Monarchia Universalis', in A. Pagden, *Señores de todo el mundo. Ideologías del imperio en España, Inglaterra y Francia (en los siglos XVI, XVII y XVIII)* (Barcelona, 1997), pp. 45–86; J. H. Elliott, 'Monarquía compuesta y monarquía universal en la época de Carlos V', in F. Sánchez Montes-González and J. L. Castellano Castellano (eds.), *Carlos V, europeísmo y universalidad* (Madrid, 2001), V, pp. 699–710; and M. Rivero Rodríguez, *Gattinara: Carlos V y el sueño del imperio* (Madrid 2005), pp. 83–89 and 129–148.

[2] See, for example, texts such as Gregorio López Madera, *Excelencias de la Monarquía y Reino de España* (Madrid, 1999), ed. J. L. Bermejo Cabrero, Chapter VI, 'De la religión y christiandad del reyno de España, su antigüedad en la fe; la excelencia de sus apóstoles, la de su continuación y augmento, y cómo primero uvo reyes christianos

also with the *Pietas Austriaca*. The monarchy constantly demonstrated its commitment to defending the faith and to evangelization across borders and overseas, since these actions provided the justification that legitimized its 'imperial mission' and hegemonic role.[3]

During his reign, loyalties to the monarch were built up in the various territories and nations eventually making up the emerging dynastic agglomerate, and a more plural network of courts was brought closer together. The ways and means of exercising royal patronage to reward service were strengthened, as were procedures for supervising the management of the administration. Organizational mechanisms for joint government were developed, along with the delegation of powers necessary for this asymmetric 'confederate' system with feudal-vassal foundations (which were, nonetheless, basically negotiated), and consisting not of one, but of various composite monarchies, such as the Crown of Aragon, or conglomerates of a complex diversity, like the Seventeen Provinces of the Low Countries and their links between the Holy Roman Empire and the Burgundian legacy. Fiscal and financial resources were also multiplied to meet the challenges arising from the combination of the vast dynastic and patrimonial interests of the House of Austria and the growing confessional division within Europe, the impact of Ottoman expansion and the demands imposed by the recent transoceanic globalization. Moreover, the prevalence of an accessible and highly regarded system of justice in the Spanish monarchy and its colonial dominions – from local tribunals and *corregimientos* to councils, royal assizes (*audiencias*) and chancelleries – underpinned a real 'empire of municipalities' and 'urban republics'.[4] The legal, judicial and representative system, which was developed from that time to resolve conflicts and for political negotiations, worked well enough and created a lasting climate of internal stability.[5]

After Charles V's legacy was divided up between the two branches of the House of Austria, Philip II took on the task of shaping and defining the new

y cathólicos en ella que en ningún reyno de los de agora', pp. 76–98. (This was first published in Valladolid in 1597.)

[3] A. Pagden, 'Desposeer al bárbaro: derechos y propiedad en la América española', in A. Pagden, *El imperialismo español y la imaginación política. Estudios sobre teoría social y política europea e hispanoamericana, 1513–1830* (Barcelona, 1991), pp. 31–65.

[4] A. Espinosa, *The Empire of the Cities: Emperor Charles V, the Comunero Revolt and the Transformation of the Spanish system* (Leiden and Boston, 2009), pp. 10–12 and 275–276; X. Gil Pujol, 'Republican Politics in Early Modern Spain: The Castilian and Catalano-Aragonese Tradition', in M. van Gelderen and Q. Skinner (eds.), *Republicanism. A Shared European Heritage* (2 vols., Cambridge, 2002), pp. I: 263–288; and F. J. Aranda Pérez and P. Sanz Camañes, 'Burgués o ciudadano en la España moderna: una conceptualización historiográfica', in F. J. Aranda Pérez (ed.), *Burgueses o ciudadanos en la España moderna* (Ciudad Real, 2003), pp. 21–67.

[5] See, for example, the collected contributions of the F. J. Guillamón Álvarez and J.J. Ruiz Ibáñez (eds.), *Lo conflictivo y lo consensual en Castilla. Sociedad y poder político, 1521–1715* (Murcia, 2001).

Catholic Monarchy which, as a result of the incorporation of the Crown of Portugal and its overseas empire from 1580, completed a political, territorial, military and socioeconomic network that had never been seen before.[6] It is no surprise that Charles V's motto *Plus Ultra* should have been transformed into the new motto of the Spanish monarch, *Non sufficit orbis* (the world is not enough).[7] A composite dynastic agglomerate of global dimensions and interests had been assembled whose members were differentiated from each other. Each of these members retained its own institutions, legislation and privileges, and contributed resources through negotiated forms of cooperation, networks of interests (family, client, economic, confessional, national and so forth) or mechanisms of patronage and promotion; each could count, nevertheless, on the multinational ramifications of a colonial empire overseas of dual Hispano-Portuguese construction.[8]

The greater organization and increased political, military, economic and cultural interdependence between the different parts of the Spanish monarchy in this new phase of its development led to its being defined as an 'imperial system',[9] more aware of its overall strategic priorities and able to give a regional treatment to its policies because it had more resources available, although there was no lack of resistance from, or rivalry and competition among, its various parts. It has, however, also been referred to as a 'negotiated empire',[10] for there were noticeable differences between the policies of the 'centre' and the periphery, or between various 'centres and peripheries'.[11] Fraud, corruption, the

[6] B. Yun Casalilla, *Marte contra Minerva. El precio del Imperio español, c. 1450–1600* (Barcelona, 2004); and A. M. Bernal, *España, proyecto inacabado. Los costes y beneficios del Imperio* (Madrid, 2005).

[7] F. Bouza, 'Retórica de la imagen real. Portugal e la memória figurada de Felipe II', *Penélope* 4 (1989), pp. 20–58.

[8] S. Gruzinski, *Las cuatro partes del mundo. Historia de una mundialización* (México, 2010); and B. Yun Casalilla, 'Las instituciones y la economía política de la Monarquía Hispánica (1492–1714): Una perspectiva trans-nacional', in F. Ramos Palencia and B. Yun Casalilla (eds.), *Economía política desde Estambul a Potosí. Ciudades estado, imperios y mercados en el Mediterráneo y en el Atlántico ibérico, c. 1200–1800* (Valencia, 2012), pp. 140–144.

[9] J. A. Maravall, *Estado moderno y mentalidad social, siglos XV a XVII* (Madrid, 1972), pp. I:235–240; G. Galasso, 'Il sistema imperiale spagnolo da Filippo II a Filippo IV', in P. Pissavino and G. Signorotto (eds.), *Lombardia borromaica, Lombardia spagnola, 1554–1659* (Rome, 1995), I:14–15; A. Musi, 'L'Italia nel sistema imperiale spagnolo', in A. Musi (ed.), *Nel sistema imperiale, l'Italia spagnola* (Rome, 1994), pp. 51–66; A. Musi, 'Sistema imperiale spagnolo e sottosistemi: alcune verifiche da studi recenti', *L'Acropoli*, 4 (2005), 406–422; and M. Merluzzi, 'Impero o monarchia universale? Il caso della Castiglia tra XVI e XVII secolo', in G. Sabatini (ed.), *Comprendere le monarchie iberiche. Risorse materiali e rappresentazioni del potere* (Rome, 2010), pp. 73–106, and especially, pp. 94–99.

[10] B. Yun Casalilla, 'Entre el imperio colonial y la monarquía compuesta. Élites y territorios en la Monarquía Hispánica (ss. XVI y XVII)', in B. Yun Casalilla (ed.), *Las redes del Imperio. Élites sociales en la articulación de la Monarquía Hispánica, 1492–1714* (Madrid, 2009), pp. 29–35.

[11] See R. Vermeir, D. Raeymaekers and J.E. Hortal Muñoz (eds.), *A Constellation of Courts: The Courts and Households of Habsburg Europe, 1555–1665* (Leuven, 2014).

'patrimonialization' of office, non-compliance with royal commands, rivalries and conflicts between different jurisdictional courts, factional infighting and client networks that prioritized their private interests over the common good or royal policy – all these phenomena were constant features of this imperial system, not to mention the simple difficulties of coordinating more effectively or a stubborn resistance to change, shown by the reluctance to implement more innovative reforms and solutions.

The cosmographer and chief chronicler of the kingdom of Portugal, João Baptista de Lavanha, provides one of the images that best reflects the vast dynastic conglomerate of the Spanish monarchy, the essential foundation for legitimizing royal power and the key to the organization of its patrimony and territories. Around 1600, he handed the young Philip III in those early years of his reign his *Libro de la descripción e historia de todos los reynos y estados de S.M. y de la genealogía de los reyes y príncipes dellos*.[12] This was a kind of genealogical and geographical history, composed of some 17 drawings among maps and coats of arms of each one of the Catholic monarch's possessions, and a series of genealogical allegories (such as the forest, the rose bush and so on), which detailed the extensive and complex dynastic ties of the 'Spanish' branch of this *Felix Austria*. The work was never published and, although the original manuscript has been lost, there are at least two surviving examples of one of the pieces that formed part of the set, which was engraved by Juan Schorquens and known as the *Silva genealógica de los fundadores y príncipes de la monarquía española* (Figure 5.1).[13]

In this engraving, we can see the forest formed by the descendants of the 15 main lineages or family trees making up the full title of the Spanish monarch. The image does not address a number of states assembled together into a composite whole, but a number of dynasties joined into the dynastic agglomerate. The central axis of the scene is the main trunk of the House of Austria, the straightest of those that form the forest. On its right, the genealogy of the kings of Portugal appears, from the House of Avis until they join the Trastamaras and the Habsburgs, and they are

---

[12] See the catalogue of *Grabadores extranjeros en la Corte española del Barroco*, ed. by J. de Blas, M.ª C. de Carlos Varona and J.M. Matilla (Madrid, 2011), no. 259, pp. 250–251.

[13] This large engraving (176.4 cm × 141 cm) printed from eight plates was made after the marriage of the Prince of Asturias, the future Philip IV, to Princess Isabella of Bourbon. It is likely that the engravings were made in the context of the heir to the throne taking the oath and being presented in the kingdom of Portugal, since Lavanha and Schorquens collaborated with each other on the edition of the chronicle of Philip III's journey to that kingdom in 1619, compiling a magnificently illustrated book of the royal entry into Lisbon (printed in 1622, in both a Spanish and a Portuguese edition). One of these copies is kept in the Biblioteca Nacional de España, with a cloth backing, and the other, brightly coloured, is in the Schloss Ambras in Innsbruck.

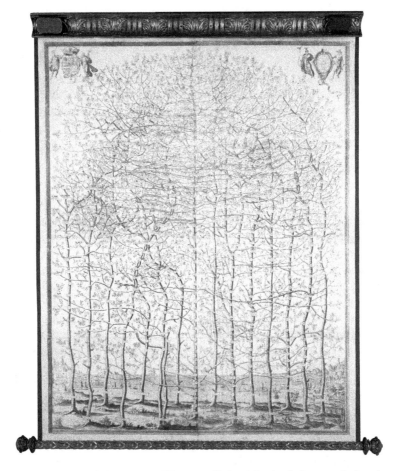

Figure 5.1 J. Schorquens, *Silva genealógica de los fundadores y príncipes de la monarquía española*, after a design by J.B. Lavanha, *c.* 1619–1620. Biblioteca Nacional de España, Invent. 80056.

followed by the House of the Dukes of Burgundy and Brabant, and the Counts of Hainault, Flanders, Holland and Burgundy (Franche-Comté). On its left, the lineages of the Kings of Jerusalem, Castile, Leon, Aragon, Navarre, Sicily and the Counts of Barcelona are shown. The upper branches of each of these trees finally converge in the treetops in the Prince and Princess of Asturias, Philip and Isabella, the heirs to the Spanish monarchy. King Philip III's coat of arms presides in the top left hand corner, while the Crown that tops it off is being held by the allegories

132 B. J. García García

of Mars (*Armis* or military power) and *Pietas* (the power of devotion or *pietas austriaca*); and in the top right hand corner, the console that identifies this genealogical forest is being held up by the goddess Minerva and the god Mercury, symbols of wisdom and ingenuity, mastery of the arts and, especially, prudence, the most important virtue of any good ruler. The background to this image of a leafy wood is a seascape with a city on either side, representing the well-known territorial dispersion of a monarchy whose vast dominions could only be united by the seas.

Government of Harmony and Temperance: Unity Amid Diversity

After the terrible decade of the 1590s,[14] marked in the Spanish monarchy by the onerous costs of simultaneous wars on various fronts, persistent plague epidemics, lost harvests, famine and obvious signs of exhaustion, the change of reign and turn of the century seemed an appropriate moment to put new ideas into practice and introduce corrective measures to halt the apparent 'decline' that was being perceived in the peninsular kingdoms. Gaspar de Pons, Agustín Álvarez de Toledo, González de Cellorigo, Álamos de Barrientos, Pedro Franqueza, Antonio Pérez and many other authors, both well known and anonymous, analysed the priorities of the new government and proposed a wide variety of solutions, in writings addressed to the young king, Philip III, or his favourite, the Duke of Lerma. This was undoubtedly one of the most intense and prolific periods of reflection on what the Spanish monarchy was and what kind of future lay in store for it in the middle of that new 'Iron Age' between 1550 and 1660 that marked the history of Europe,[15] or the one between 1580 and 1680 that Spanish historiography re-baptized as the 'Age of the Quixote'.[16]

---

[14] For this period of crisis analysed in a wider European context, see P. Clark (ed.), *The European Crisis of the 1590s: Essays in Comparative History*, London 1985; and the monograph directed by F. Bouza Álvarez on *Felipe II: El ocaso del reinado. Madurez, crisis y juicio del gobierno de la Monarquía en la década de 1590*, in *Studia Historica. Historia Moderna* 17 (1997), pp. 5–143.

[15] Here I am using the expression 'Iron Century' or 'Iron Age' in the meaning spread from the Classical Culture (a period of war, disorders, crime and injustice; see Ovid, *Metamorphoses*, Book 1) and reused by H. Kamen, *The Iron Century: Social Change in Europe 1550–1660* (London, 1971) to label the European Crisis of that period.

[16] For works defined in this way, see those of J. M. Jover Zamora (ed.), *El Siglo del Quijote. Historia de España* (Madrid, 1988), tome XXVI, vols. 1–2; and P. Sanz Camañes (ed.), *La Monarquía Hispánica en tiempos del Quijote* (Madrid, 2005); or those specifically covering the period of Cervantes' lifetime (1547–1616), such as those by A. Feros and J. Gelabert (eds.), *España en tiempos del Quijote* (Madrid, 2004); or M. Rivero Rodríguez, *La España de Don Quijote. Un viaje al Siglo de Oro* (Madrid, 2005).

It seemed that the time had arrived to consider more far-reaching reforms – even going as far as to alter the model of aggregation on which the Spanish monarchy was based – that would strengthen the collaboration of the kingdoms in maintaining the whole.[17] It was essential to bind the parts together more firmly and develop a much greater union and correspondence between them by favouring the circulation and promotion, not only of the 'Spaniards' in the different kingdoms, but also of elites of a transnational character who were interested in preserving this territorial conglomerate. And that 'time of peaces' in the early 1600s[18] offered an excellent opportunity to implement policies to redeem the royal revenues and put them back on a sound footing, to promote a more active involvement of 'parliamentary' representations or their standing committees, and to increase the collaboration of rising groups.

During a large part of this decade, Baltasar Álamos de Barrientos – who was in prison for helping the fugitive secretary, Antonio Pérez – spent his sentence conscientiously studying the work of Tacitus and translating it into Spanish. He then used it as the basis for compiling *Suma de preceptos justos, necesarios y provechosos en Consejo de Estado* for the future king, Philip III.[19] This was a guide to government in the form of 502 aphorisms, which he had selected from the writings of the celebrated Roman historian, whose work was to have so much influence on the political and courtly thought of those generations. His purpose, as he let it be known in the preamble, was to instruct the sovereign in the preservation of 'great domains' like the Spanish monarchy, which could be compared to a sophisticated instrument with many strings, keys and sounds, and required its player to have skill, ability, knowledge and gentleness.[20]

Among the allegories that best respond to this conception of a well-tempered, prudent and harmonic government that Philip III should invoke in order to manage the complex structure and enormous resources

[17] J. I. Fortea Pérez, 'Entre dos servicios: La crisis de la Hacienda Real a fines del siglo XVI. Las alternativas fiscales de una opción política (1590–1601)', *Studia Historica. Historia Moderna*, 17 (1997), pp. 63–90, esp. 89–90; and I. A. A. Thompson, 'Castilla, España y la Monarquía: La comunidad política, de la *patria natural* a la *patria nacional*', in R. Kagan and G. Parker (eds.), *España, Europa y el mundo atlántico. Homenaje a John H. Elliott* (Madrid, 2001), pp. 195–199.

[18] B. J. García García, *La Pax Hispanica. Política exterior del Duque de Lerma* (Leuven, 1996), pp. 185–203; and B. J. García García (eds.), *Tiempo de paces (1609–2009). La Pax Hispanica y la Tregua de los Doce Años*, exhibition catalogue (Madrid 2009), pp. 17–35.

[19] B. Álamos de Barrientos, *Tácito español ilustrado con aforismos* (Madrid, 1614); and Antonio Pérez, *Suma de preceptos justos, necesarios y provechosos en Consejo de Estado al Rey Felipe III siendo príncipe. Aforismos sacados de la Historia de Publio Cornelio Tácito*, ed. by M. Santos (Barcelona, 1991).

[20] Pérez, *Suma de preceptos*, p. 22.

Figure 5.2 Francesco Villamena, *Allegory of the Temperance of Philip III (Allegory of the Pax Hispanica)*, Rome, 1603. Biblioteca Nacional de España, Invent. 14.740.

of the Spanish monarchy, is an engraving made by Francesco Villamena, published in Rome in 1603 (Figure 5.2).

In a majestic vestibule in the style of a classical palace, reminiscent of the Roman basilicas where justice was mainly administered, we see the medallion of the young Spanish sovereign, Philip III, portrayed as king of the 'Spains' and the Indies. The composition is symmetrical and opens out at the back towards other rooms and courtyards of the palace until it finishes at a door topped by an obelisk or pyramid, which reinforces the symbology of good government and lasting peace. It is, without doubt, a magnificent emblem illustrating the policy of his reign, known as the *Pax Hispanica*.[21]

Occupying the centre of the scene is a table covered with a cloth on which a spear, the symbol of fortitude, rests on top of a viol, the symbol of harmony and temperance, and underneath a quotation from Horace (*Carminum*, book III, ode 4): 'VIM TEMPERATAM DII QUOQ. PROMOVENT' (The gods themselves advance temperate power).

---

[21] García García, *Tiempo de paces*, cat. 18, pp. 283–284.

Thus, the exercise of force (the spear) is subject to the temperance and harmony of good government (the viol). To represent the well-ordered republic or harmoniously arranged social body, treatises on education for princes often make use of the simile of polyphonic or multi-stringed instruments, as in this case, the viol.[22] The allegory of good government derives from the harmony resulting from its various strings, and corresponds to the harmony of the prince who acts justly, like a good player who knows how to temper and tune the disparate elements of which his diverse dominions are composed. Let us not forget that Philip III himself enjoyed music and dancing from a very early age and spent hours playing the viol, hence the appropriate choice of that instrument for an allegory intended to define his style of government.

The emblem of a lute on a table, symbolizing concord and the alliances between his subjects and their neighbours that the prince should watch over, already appears among those published by Andrea Alciato (*Emblematum liber*, Augsburg 1531, emblem X, *Foedera*, dedicated to the Duke of Milan, Massimiliano Sforza). If the principles and laws agreed between the prince and his subjects, or the terms of an alliance were broken, concord was shattered and peace destroyed. Consequently, since the time of the Romans, a multi-stringed instrument like a lyre (which over the centuries would be replaced by a lute or viol) was taken as a symbol of concord, to signify that if, while it was being played, just one string should snap, harmony would be lost and uncertainty and confusion would ensue.

The monarch's shields are on either side of the table, one held by a Turkish Janissary and the other by an American Indian (to convey the idea that his possessions stretch as far as the boundaries of the East and West Indies). Two vanquished figures are lying at their feet: Argos (on the left, with many eyes in his head), an allegory of the excess of zeal and futile vigilance, conquered by Mercury, the god of prudence, eloquence and ingenuity; and the giant Geryon (on the right, with three heads), the symbol of discord and fratricidal conflict, defeated by the guile of Hercules in his tenth labour. About 50 female figures representing the different kingdoms and dominions of Philip III's possessions are standing around the table and holding their respective shields (Galicia, Granada, Naples, Sicily, Portugal, Biscay, Seville, Castile and Leon, the Canary Islands, Milan, and the Seventeen Provinces of the Low Countries). Each one, moreover, bears other symbolic attributes that reinforce the allegory

---

[22] L. Robledo Estaire, 'El clamor silencioso: la imagen de la música en la literatura emblemática española', *Edad de Oro* XXII (2003), pp. 373–423, at pp. 391–392.

of the sovereign's good government: religion, justice, fortitude, concord, abundance, prudence, wisdom and intelligence.

Álamos de Barrientos also wrote *Discurso político al rey Felipe III al comienzo de su reinado*, whose main purpose was to analyse the state of his kingdoms and dominions, offering advice on how the monarch should proceed and conduct himself with each one of them. The entire discourse revolved around the dispersed, asymmetric structure of the states and realms that comprised the Spanish monarchy, and the way they had been incorporated into it. Among the *inherited* dominions, he included the kingdoms and feudal lordships of the Crown of Castile, its colonial territories in the West Indies and the dominions of the Crown of Aragon, together with the islands it possessed in the Mediterranean. They also included the States of Flanders, since – despite the recent cession of sovereignty agreed in favour of Infanta Isabella Clara Eugenia in 1598 as part of her dowry[23] – the 'superiority' and 'protection' of those states remained in the hands of the Catholic monarch. The solution to the conflict with the 'rebel' provinces continued to be one of his main dynastic and international commitments, because it directly concerned the royal authority, the political and military reputation of the monarchy itself and the strategic control that it could exercise over other neighbouring states.[24]

Álamos considered as *conquered* all those dominions that had been incorporated into the monarchy as a result of military action against the will of the inhabitants, such as the kingdom of Portugal and its colonial empire, the tiny kingdom of Navarre and, in Italy, the State of Milan and the kingdoms of Naples and Sicily.[25] He established this distinction so that he could later recommend to the young sovereign the different means and remedies that these diverse nations called for because of the way they had been aggregated to the monarchy.[26]

The king's powerful inner circle knew how to instil into this varied collection of kingdoms and nations the role of the sovereign as the necessary arbiter and main common source of grace and favour, despite

---

[23] The fullest and most recent study of the cession of the sovereignty of the Low Countries and the Franche-Comté as the dowry for the marriage between Infanta Isabella Clara Eugenia and Archduke Albert in the strategy to pacify the Wars in Flanders is provided by A. Esteban Estríngana, 'Los Estados de Flandes: reversión territorial de las Provincias leales (1598–1623)', in J. Martínez Millán and M. A. Visceglia (eds.), *La Monarquía de Felipe III, vol. IV: Los Reinos* (Madrid, 2008), pp. 593–640. See also, L. Duerloo, *Dinasty and Piety. Archduke Albert (1598–1621) and Habsburg Political Culture in an Age of Religious Wars* (Farnham, 2013), pp. 61–67.

[24] B. Álamos de Barrientos, *Discurso político al rey Felipe III al comienzo de su reinado*, ed. by M. Santos (Barcelona, 1990), p. 5.

[25] Ibid., pp. 8–9.   [26] Ibid., p. 9.

the fact that he was an 'absentee sovereign' in many of these territories. Nevertheless, the development of the system of 'favourites' (*validos*) with their special privileges, enjoyed by the Duke of Lerma and the Count-Duke of Olivares, substantially altered the distribution mechanisms of the royal grace and split some of the functions of the office of sovereignty. This enabled the royal favourites to act as intermediaries or privileged filters, managing political priorities, the monarch's agenda and access to him while they set up their own networks of clients and factions, enriched their own families and increased their personal wealth. Even so, we must stress that royal power paid special attention to the legitimization of its authority, by reconstructing the past (in genealogies, written or drama-tized chronicles, legends, iconographic series of histories in the form of paintings, prints, sculptures and tapestries, etc.), appropriating customs and traditions, developing or adapting forms of representation (private devotions, public festivities and ceremonies, rites of passage, chivalric games and courtly leisure, and so on), creating new symbolic languages and paying careful attention to legal and judicial procedures in relation to the subjects of the Crown.[27]

The Spanish monarchy's successful capacity for conquest and expan-sion between the end of the fifteenth century and the beginning of the seventeenth forged a military reputation that was a key factor in preser-ving this conglomerate of territories, not least by offering opportunity for social advancement within the army, which suffered scarcely any significant revolts in the zones that had been taken by force.[28] The defence of each territory was conceived as a part of the whole. In fact, it is not unusual to find treatise writers, diplomats and council-lors of State making allusions *avant la lettre* to the domino theory, to emphasize the interdependence of the different 'provinces' of the mon-archy; according to this, if one province fell, the rest could fall one after the other. For that reason, strongholds, citadels and garrison towns were built at strategic points, but organized using the ordinary contribution of each realm's own resources, noble cavalries and the forces of the vassals or the local, territorial and national militias.[29] Multiple human, material

---

[27] See, for example, F. Checa Cremades and L. Fernández-González (eds.), *Festival Culture in the World of Spanish Habsburgs* (Farnham, 2015).

[28] J. H. Elliott, 'A Formula for Survival: The Spanish Monarchy and Empire', in *17° Congreso Internacional de Ciencias Históricas* (Madrid, 1992), II, pp. 722–726; and J.J. Ruiz Ibáñez and G. Sabatini, 'Monarchy as Conquest: Violence, Social Opportunity, and Political Stability in the Establishment of the Hispanic Monarchy', *The Journal of Modern History*, 81:3 (September 2009), pp. 501–536.

[29] A. Jiménez Estrella, 'Los nuevos bellatores de Su Majestad. Reflexiones en torno al servicio militar al rey en los siglos XVI y XVII', and A. J. Rodríguez Hernández, 'Servir al rey con hombres. Recompensas concedidas a élites y representantes del rey por su

and financial resources were coordinated in pluri-national campaigns and military enterprises in the continuous drive to build a sense of identity and encourage forms of integration, cooperation and emulation among their units.

The involvement of the militia in the armies and navies of the Spanish monarchy helped create an elite of soldiers, bureaucrats and 'adventurers' that expanded the opportunities for promotion and *merced* [favour] among subjects in the various territories and was one of the key means of keeping the parts of the whole together.[30] But this capacity for cohesion and participation depended on how regularly they were paid, how satisfied they were with the way recognition of their achievements, loyalties and services was formalized, and on the degree of rivalry that existed between the commands or nations that supplied the armies and navies.[31] Armies on campaign and troops billeted in wretched conditions because of a shortage of finance also created situations of extreme vulnerability, such as long-running mutinies, indiscriminate looting, desertions and the use of coercive violence in the surrounding territory, which endangered the sovereign's authority and reputation and demonstrated the fact that military service depended on contracts and agreements.[32] However, in spite of the Spanish monarchy's possible flaws and the titanic efforts that it made to meet its global strategic and military commitments, it did succeed in conveying to its own subjects and other nations and foreign princes, a powerful idea of service through arms that opened the way to a prestigious international reputation, social advancement and ennoblement, remunerated offices and governments of different rank with local,

colaboración en el reclutamiento (1630–1700)', in A. Esteban Estríngana (eds.), *Servir al rey en la Monarquía de los Austrias. Medios, fines y logros del servicio al soberano en los siglos XVI y XVII* (Madrid, 2012), pp. 387–413 and 415–443, respectively; and J.J. Ruiz Ibáñez, 'Introducción: Las milicias y el rey de España', in J.J. Ruiz Ibáñez (eds.), *Las milicias del rey de España. Sociedad, política e identidad en las Monarquías Ibéricas* (Madrid, 2009), pp. 9–32.

[30] A. Jiménez Estrella, 'Mérito, calidad y experiencia: criterios volubles en la provisión de cargos militares bajo los Austrias', in J. F. Pardo Molero and M. Lomas Cortés (eds.), *Oficiales reales. Los ministros de la Monarquía Católica, siglos XVI–XVII* (Valencia, 2012), pp. 241–264.

[31] See, for example, A. Esteban Estríngana, 'Cabos de guerra: satisfacción de la oficialidad y eficacia bélica en el Ejército de Flandes, entre los siglos XVI y XVII', in ibid., pp. 265–293.

[32] A good example of this can be found in studies such as G. Parker, 'Mutiny and Discontent in the Spanish Army of Flanders', *Past & Present* 58 (1973), pp. 38–52 (reprinted in G. Parker, *Spain and The Netherlands, 1559–1659. Ten Studies* (New York, 1979); T. Piceu, *Over vrybuters en quaetdoeners: terreur op het Vlaamse platteland, eind 16de eeuw* (Leuven, 2008); or J. J. Ruiz Ibáñez, 'Vivir en el campo de Marte. Población e identidad en la frontera entre Francia y los Países Bajos, siglos XVI–XVII', in M. Bertrand and N. Planas (eds.), *Les sociétés de frontière: de la Méditerranée à l'Atlantique: XVIe-XVIIIe siècles* (Madrid, 2011) pp. 165–175.

regional or colonial responsibilities.[33] The fact that military officers moved about the Spanish possessions so much during their careers was instrumental in their experience, training, reputation and conduct being extended throughout the territories of the monarchy and had a great influence on allies and enemies alike. Nor should we forget that the historical memory of the peoples and kingdoms of the monarchy was shaped especially by the contemporary interest in the 'historical' narrative of military events and news of this type, presented more or less in the form of novels, illustrating the heroic iconography of their monarchs and generals on medallions, crockery and in prints, in the ephemeral decorations of public entries and funeral rites, in the paintings in galleries, state rooms or in majestic sets of tapestries.[34] This collective historical memory about common enterprises and shared successes also secured the ties uniting their territories and generated confidence in the face of future challenges.

In general, the monarchy succeeded in remodelling the 'conquered' societies by turning them into populations that were participants in a common project. They made constant use of local structures and practices that involved the new subjects, not only in the management mechanisms and provision of material and economic assistance, but also in the paths to promotion and the recognition of services and loyalties. This was, certainly, one of the main foundations of the strength and durability of the Spanish monarchy.

One of the most viable solutions that the Crown adopted to strengthen the monarchy's naval capacity and increase the participation of some provinces in the burdensome economic and human effort that the naval security of its frontiers and its strategic routes required, was the development of provincial squadrons and small navies.[35] This model made use of 'national' interests in the partial control, at least, of the very mechanisms of defence, by employing commanders-in-chief recruited from among notables or influential families of the provinces in question. It also solved the problem of financing and equipping new squadrons. Although these were ordinarily devoted to coastal security tasks, they could also contribute to the common enterprises of the monarchy, in much the same way as the great *armadas* brought together between 1588 and 1597, or the habitual *juntas de galeras* [joint enterprises of the galley squadrons of the

---

[33] D. Centenero de Arce, 'Una Monarquía de lazos débiles? Circulación y experiencia como formas de construcción de la Monarquía Católica', in Pardo Molero and Lomas Cortés (eds.), *Oficiales reales*, pp. 137–161.

[34] In this regard, see the collected contributions in ed. B. J. García García, *La imagen de la guerra en el arte de los antiguos Países Bajos* (Madrid, 2006); but also Checa Cremades and Fernández-González, *Festival Culture*.

[35] García García, *La Pax Hispanica*, pp. 177–182.

Spanish monarchy and its allies] convened for the expeditions to North Africa, the Mediterranean Levant or to face the deployments of the Ottoman navy and other enemy squadrons within its spheres of influence.

On its Atlantic seaboard, provincial squadrons were formed by means of *asientos* [credit loans] negotiated with the lordship of Biscay, Guipuzcoa and the Four Towns of Cantabria, as well as small squadrons of galleons that later became part of the so-called Cantabrian Squadron of the Armada of the Ocean Sea. In 1617, when the Marquis of Alenquer was viceroy of Portugal, he succeeded in putting together an *Armada da Costa*, or Armada of Portugal, consisting of Portuguese ships, crews and officers, financed entirely by the Crown of Portugal. In 1619, the kingdom of Galicia, for its part, negotiated the supply and equipping of a small fleet of six ships, paid for by lords with possessions on the coast, the bishops and prelates of the kingdom and an extraordinary donation of 100,000 ducats, in exchange for Galicia obtaining the nineteenth vote in the *Cortes* of Castile. The Crown approved its creation and granted the seat in the *Cortes* in 1621. To these squadrons should be added those that were created with finance from mercantile activities to protect the ocean routes, namely the Indies Fleets, the *Armada de Barlovento* in the Caribbean Sea and the Armada of the South Sea, or to act against piracy and harass the economic resources of the enemy, such as the Admiralty's fleet in the Low Countries, the Strait Guard squadron or the Mediterranean Armada promoted by Anthony Sherley and later taken over by the Duke of Osuna. Furthermore, squadrons of galleys from Spain, Sicily, Naples and occasionally from Catalonia, Valencia or Denia also operated in the Mediterranean. Galleys from Genoa and Malta and other private squadrons, sponsored by viceroys or Italian princes, usually collaborated with them under contract.

There is no doubt that Spanish soldiers and officers formed the backbone of the Spanish monarchy's armies and navies, not only among the troops involved in campaigns, but also for their role garrisoning strongholds and strategic ports in Italy, Flanders, Portugal and North Africa, or deployed abroad on missions in France, to the war in Hungary, to Transylvania or the Indies. Difficulties in recruitment to cope with all those tasks meant that the monarchy inevitably had to rely on the collaboration of other nations (Flemish and Walloons, Burgundians, Neapolitans, Sicilians, Sardinians, Lombards, and Portuguese), as well as hire the services of soldiers, entrepreneurs and 'adventurers' from other territories 'allied' by dynastic links to the House of Austria (Tyroleans, Bavarians, Alsatians, Austrians and so on), or for religious reasons, such as the Irish, Scottish or English Catholics, those from the Graubünden, French exiles, Germans from the Rhineland bishoprics, and subjects of other Italian principalities. Even so, the pluri-national character of the Spanish monarchy meant that it had such a variety of resources of its own at its disposal that the percentage of mercenary troops and hired units was always quite limited.[36] The award of the Golden Fleece, the habits of the Spanish Military Orders, noble titles, or the rank of 'grandee' of Spain and many other mechanisms of the system of royal patronage also served to reward the services that non-Spanish subjects or foreigners provided in this sphere; in this way, strong links were forged between the Crown and the lineages of those military men who could recruit troops and co-finance campaigns with their own credit, or use personal or national client networks, serving as a model for others to emulate.[37]

A particular case is offered by the Irish exiles after the Battle of Kinsale (1602). The English occupation and confiscation of their lands led the Gaelic lords and their clans to emigrate to other Catholic states in search of protection and succour. The main destination was the Spanish monarchy. Since the 1580s, the Irish had served occasionally as soldiers and sailors, but from 1603 onwards, the arrival en masse of these exiles and their petitions to the monarch forced the councils of State and War to designate a 'protector of the Irish nation' in 1604, and to create the first Irish infantry regiment the following year (Irish *tercio*). The development of this active military participation of the Irish in the Army of Flanders and the infantry of the squadrons of war continued to increase throughout the reigns of Philip III and Philip IV, and subsequently extended to other fronts, such as the wars in Extremadura and Catalonia, eventually forming dynasties of service, whose integration and importance in the armies of the Spanish monarchy would become apparent in the ensuing centuries.[38]

---

[36] L. Ribot, 'Las naciones en el ejército de los Austrias', in A. Álvarez-Ossorio Alvariño and B. J. García García, *La Monarquía de las naciones. Patria, nación y naturaleza en la Monarquía de España* (Madrid, 2004), pp. 653–677; and O. Recio Morales, 'La gente de naciones en los ejércitos de los Austrias hispanos: servicio, confianza y correspondencia', in E. García Hernán and D. Maffi (eds.), *Guerra y sociedad en la Monarquía Hispánica. Política, estrategia y cultura en la Europa moderna, 1500–1700* (2 vols., Madrid, 2006), pp. I: 651–679.

[37] See, for example, the studies of the main military bases in the Spanish Monarchy carried out by D. Maffi, *Il baluardo della Corona. Guerra, esercito, finanze e sotietà nella Lombardia Seicentesca, 1630–1660* (Florence, 2007); and D. Maffi, *La cittadella in armi. Essercito, società e finanza nella Lombardia di Carlo II, 1660–1700* (Milan, 2010); also the numerous studies collected in García Hernán and Maffi, *Guerra y sociedad*.

[38] R. A. Stradling, *The Spanish Monarchy and Irish Mercenaries. The Wild Geese in Spain, 1618–1668* (Dublin, 1994); E. García Hernán and O. Recio Morales (eds.), *Extranjeros en el Ejército. Militares irlandeses en la sociedad española, 1580–1818* (Madrid, 2007); E. de Mesa Gallego, 'The Irish "Nation" and the Councils of State and War, 1603–1644', and P. Williams, 'The Irish in the Spanish Royal Armada, 1650–1670: Community and solidarity in the Irish Tercio', in O. Recio Morales, *Redes de nación y espacios de poder:*

The complex and heterogeneous system of territorial division that existed in a monarchy of a composite nature like the Spanish one[39] was based on the legal principles of Roman-canonical tradition and was held together by pacts and accords between the common holder of the sovereignty and each one of its parts, which ranged from monarchies and kingdoms, to provinces, fiefs and lordships, cities and corporations. Depending on the circumstances in which the incorporation of a part had come about, and on the importance of that part and its aspirations, the accord was stipulated in terms of equality or inequality. In some cases, union could mean the full integration of a territory into another one, which then assumed the government and management of both; this is what is known as 'accessory union'. The most frequent formula, however, was the '*aeque et principaliter*' union, or 'main union and between equals', in which each part retained its institutions and system of laws and government. In such a case, the union was verified through the holder of sovereignty, which was recognized by means of the swearing of the laws, privileges and traditions of each kingdom.[40] The construction and establishment of the *lex regia* – the body of laws – of each of the monarchy's territories, as well as their study and systematization, was the work of jurists and judges, who, for the most part, came from the main councils and tribunals in the kingdom.[41] The publication at that time of specific studies improved theoretical knowledge, debate and university teaching of those *leges regiae*. These works, together with the experience accumulated through judicial practice in the courts and during the careers of many of the lawyers, contributed significantly to more 'royalist', or more limited and conditioned, interpretations of the legal framework on which

La comunidad irlandesa en España y la América española, 1600–1825 (Valencia, 2012), pp. 155–170 and 171–182, respectively; E. de Mesa, 'Soldados de "naciones" para la Armada del Mar Océano: las compañías irlandesas de los tercios embarcados, 1604–1639', in *Obradoiro de Historia Moderna* 24 (2015); and E. de Mesa Gallego, *The Irish in the Spanish Armies in the Seventeenth Century* (Martlesham, 2014).

[39] F. J. Gil Pujol, 'Visión europea de la Monarquía española como monarquía compuesta, siglos XVI y XVII', in C. Russell (ed.), *Las monarquías del Antiguo Régimen, ¿monarquías compuestas?* (Madrid, 1996), pp. 65–95; and J. H. Elliott, 'Una Europa de monarquías compuestas', in J. H. Elliott, *España. Europa y el mundo de Ultramar, 1500–1800* (Madrid, 2010), pp. 29–54.

[40] J. Arrieta, 'Las formas de vinculación a la Monarquía y de relación entre sus reinos y coronas en la España de los Austrias. Perspectivas de análisis', in Alvariño and García García, *La Monarquía de las nacion*, pp. 303–326; and J. Arrieta, 'Forms of Union: Britain and Spain, a Comparative Analysis', in J. Arrieta and J. H. Elliott (eds.), *Forms of Union: the British and Spanish Monarchies in the 17th and 18th Centuries. Revista Internacional de los Estudios Vascos, cuad.* 5 (2009), pp. 23–52, in particular, pp. 36–37.

[41] J. Arrieta, 'La dimensión institucional y jurídica de las cortes virreinales en la Monarquía Hispánica', in J. L. Palos and P. Cardim (eds.), *El mundo de los virreyes en las monarquías de España y Portugal* (Madrid and Frankfurt, 2012), pp. 45–55.

the relations between the Crown and its subjects in each territory of the monarchy were established.

At the same time, the development of territorial councils (Castile, Aragon, Italy, Flanders, Portugal, the Indies) and royal assizes (*Audiencias*) meant that existing instruments for interpreting the laws and traditions of the kingdoms could be strengthened in the sovereign's entourage, as could the representation of the kingdoms in the ambit of the royal court, mediation in negotiations between the king and his subjects, the resolution of many jurisdictional and patrimonial conflicts, and the distribution of royal patronage. Through these senatorial and national institutions, the monarchy could develop a common, more widely shared space of justice[42] at the same time as the sovereign made his presence felt in each territory by means of viceroys, governors, judges and other officials who exercised delegated powers.

Another essential mechanism in this relationship, in the particular case of the monarchy's Italian territories, was provided by the 'general visits' to the kingdoms between 1517 and 1679. They helped to underscore the monarch's interest in the application of justice and in the supervision of the work that the kingdoms' institutions and royal officers carried out, but they also supplied abundant information on the practical reality of the problems that they perceived and documented in the administrative, fiscal and political management of those states.[43]

Besides the diverse nature of the incorporation of each territory, Álamos de Barrientos also examined in his *Discurso* the geographical shape of the monarchy, which showed some kingdoms united in the peninsula of Spain and other far-flung dominions, such as the States of Flanders and Italy, 'hemmed in by secret and public enemies, or unsafe, greedy friends', or those of the Indies 'separated by such a vast expanse of sea, which in a certain way seem to be dismembered from the others, the former being the masters in the present state of arms, and the latter the source of the money, the main foundations of the monarchy'.[44]

This differentiation would enable him to defend a model of 'peninsular unity' in Spain that would broaden and strengthen the 'head of the monarchy' – identified with the royal court and the Crown of Castile – enhancing collaboration and creating common interests among the native population, but which would simultaneously improve the interrelationship and interdependence of the Crown of Castile with the *far-flung*

---

[42] M. Rivero Rodríguez, *La edad de oro de los virreyes. El virreinato en la Monarquía Hispánica durante los siglos XVI y XVII* (Madrid, 2011), pp. 123–131.

[43] M. Peytavin, *Visite et gouvernement dans le Royaume de Naples, XVIe–XVIIe siècles* (Madrid, 2003), pp. 72–87 and 409–413.

[44] Álamos de Barrientos, *Discurso político*, p. 9.

territories. Preserving the monarchy, particularly its head, the Crown of Castile, did not seem viable in the medium term without addressing reforms to redistribute the fiscal and military burdens more proportionately among the different kingdoms that constituted the body politic of this pluri-national system. The expansion and construction model of this 'warrior monarchy' had to be reviewed, as did the leading role exercised by Castile and Spain. The alternatives involved dealing simultaneously with economic recovery at the centre and promoting genuine cohesion between the kingdoms of the Iberian Peninsula, as well as greater collaboration, or 'correspondence', with the monarchy's other European territories. Safeguarding the centre depended on this effort being shared, so that the burden of the dynamic leading role that Castile had played in the preceding century could be lightened by the progressive development of a broader-based and much more participatory model.[45] These conceptions are clearly formulated in the writings of Álamos de Barrientos, Pedro de Herrera and the Count-Duke of Olivares, although they reflect a more widespread state of opinion in those early decades of the 1600s.

Despite the proposals to *castilianize* the monarchy, there is also in this period a noticeable process of '*dehispanicization* or *peripheralization* of Castile',[46] at least among various sectors of the urban elites. On some occasions, it is manifest in the yearning for that golden age that was attributed to the reign of the Catholic Kings Ferdinand and Isabella; on others, it appears as a rejection of the 'imperial' or dynastic commitments to fighting at such high cost in conflicts that were felt to be not theirs or too remote, but increasingly it was to defend policies to redeem revenue obligations and ensure the social, moral and economic restoration of Castile. This vein of criticism was especially marked during the final years of Philip III's reign and the first decade of Philip IV's, hence the insistence on the need to demand greater cooperation from the other peninsular kingdoms, which apparently were not involved so much in the general policy of the monarchy and were more protected in their relation with the Crown on account of their own constitutional traditions.

The Calabrian Dominican Tomasso Campanella[47] – who would identify 'this Monarchy of Spain that embraces all nations and takes in the

---

[45] Ibid., pp. 29–30. See B. J. García García, 'Precedentes de la Unión de Reinos: La unión de las Españas en tiempos de Felipe III', in Alvariño and García García (eds.), *La Monarquía de las naciones*, pp. 385–419.

[46] I. A. A. Thompson, 'Castilla, España y la Monarquía: La comunidad política, de la patria natural a la patria nacional', in Kagan and Parker (eds.), *España, Europa y el mundo atlántico*, pp. 177–216, at 178–179.

[47] See L. Díez del Corral, 'Campanella y la Monarquía Hispánica', *Revista de Occidente* 54 (1967), pp. 159–180 and 313–335.

world' with 'the universal Monarchy of the Messiah'[48] – also valued the challenges that the very diversity of the Spanish monarchy involved. Hostility from its many enemies and competitors or disunity and separation among its own territories might eventually undermine its continuity. The Ottoman imperial model, by contrast, seemed much more solid and long-lasting, since it kept its kingdoms 'in extremely close union', would attack neighbouring states as a way of acquiring new dominions and kept the children of its enemies close, training them in religion and war, in order to keep their possessions secure.

To govern different regions and maintain them under a single sovereign, Campanella recommended making them similar to each other, as far as possible. To this end, he distinguished three types of union between men: the confessional community, the mixing of lineages and sharing common economic interests.

He considered the first of these as the strongest, since it guaranteed a common set of beliefs and way of thinking, ensuring strong ties between nations that were otherwise very different from each other. The Spanish monarchy was exemplary in this sense, because its kingdoms were united in their commitment to the defence of the faith and the preservation of the Catholic Church, even though they were so geographically scattered and disparate.[49] This commitment had turned into a key characteristic of a monarchy that called itself 'Catholic' and a dynasty like the House of Austria that sought to project an image of devotion and piety.[50] Its leadership and grandeur made the Catholic Monarchy the principal world power, which attracted many 'adventurers' and exiles trying to gain the political, military and financial aid that would enable them to liberate their own peoples from foreign or confessional oppressors. This commitment to intervention and providing refuge, which bound the Catholic monarch in conscience, has been referred to as 'reason of religion'.[51] One has only to recall the help given to Catholic leagues, in both France and the Holy Roman Empire, to Irish Catholics and the development of the 'Ireland Mission' during the

---

[48] T. Campanella, 'Discorsi ai principi d'Italia', in *Opere di Tommaso Campanella*, ed. d'Ancona, cited in Díez del Corral, 'Campanella', p. 167.

[49] T. Campanella, *La Monarquía Hispánica*, ed. P. Mariño (Madrid, 1982), p. 150. We should consider the content of this work by Campanella with care because the edited texts include many interpolations by Giovanni Botero.

[50] J. Martínez Millán, 'La formación de la monarquía católica de Felipe III', and A. Sarrión Mora, 'Identificación de la dinastía con la confesión católica', in J. Martínez Millán and M. A. Visceglia (eds.), *La Monarquía de Felipe III. La Casa del Rey* (4 vols., Madrid, 2008), vol. I, pp. 118–122, 187–197 and 246–302.

[51] J. M. Iñurritegui, 'Hércules y el Minotauro. La paz de Flandes y la Razón Católica de Religión', in L. Ribot García and E. Belenguer Cebriá (eds.), *Las sociedades ibéricas y el mar a finales del siglo XVI* (Madrid, 1998), pp. V: 233–252.

seventeenth century,[52] or the numerous Balkan projects that were presented to the three Philips[53] to liberate those territories from Ottoman
dominion and open the way to recovering the Holy Land. There were
even plans of varying degrees of audacity to conquer one of the great
empires of the East.

Religious intolerance and the war against the infidel certainly constituted essential features of the Spanish monarchy, and served to forge
a most intense and rigorous social, political and confessional cohesion,
albeit not without very high costs, such as those arising from anti-Spanish
propaganda, the persecution of converted minorities and, above all, the
expulsion of the Moriscos (1609/10 and 1614). Nonetheless, there were
recurring conflicts of jurisdiction – especially significant in the Italian
dominions of the monarchy – between the royal power, or its representatives, and the authority of the Church. And when international policy
made it expedient, peace treaties and alliances with infidel princes or
heretics were concluded and respected, and merchants of other nation-
alities and confessions were guaranteed the protection of the royal authority against the actions of the inquisitorial courts.

The Habsburg dynasty strove to reaffirm the pious charisma of its
members and particularly of the sovereign himself. This devotion was to
propitiate the favour of God and the protection of the Virgin and saints to
confront Evil in any of its forms and to secure the peace, prosperity and
salvation of the dynasty and its subjects.[54] Religious zeal, the promotion
of public devotions, the persecution of heresy, the spread of evangelization, support for the Catholic Church, the war of crusade and purity of
blood were all habitual elements of this 'new monarchy', which took up
a hegemonic role in a divided Christendom and exercised its influence all
over the world when the very concept of Catholicism was being completely transformed as a result of the Reformation, overseas expansion and
the new resources of written culture and image.

It is another Dominican, Fray Juan de la Puente, a royal chronicler and
prior of the monastery of Santo Tomás in Madrid, who produced

---

[52] E. García Hernán, *Ireland and Spain in the Reign of Philip II*, Dublin 2009; O. Recio
Morales, *Ireland and the Spanish Empire 1600–1825* (Dublin, 2010); O. Recio Morales
(ed.), *Redes de nación y espacios de poder: la comunidad irlandesa en España y América
española, 1600–1825* (Valencia, 2012); and the PhD Dissertation of C. Bravo Lozano,
*Tierras de Misión. La política confesional de la Monarquía de España en las Islas Británicas,
1660–1702* (Madrid, 2014).

[53] P. Bartl, *Die Westbalkan zwischen spanischer Monarchie und osmanischen Reich*
(Wiesbaden, 1974); and J. M. Floristán Imízcoz, *Fuentes para la política oriental de los
Austrias, 1571–1621* (2 vols. Leon, 1988).

[54] A. Esteban Estríngana, 'El mito de Gedeón y la noción de servicio. De soberanía
y sujeción política entre los siglos XVI y XVII', in Esteban Estríngana (ed.), *Servir al
rey en la Monarquía*, pp. 87–118.

a voluminous work whose purpose was to show the similarity that existed between those which he considered to be the two greatest Catholic monarchies in the world: the 'ecclesiastical monarchy' of the Roman Church and the Monarchy of Spain, so as to defend the precedence of the Catholic monarch over all the rest of the temporal kingdoms.[55] According to the author, the four characteristics common to both monarchies – one of a spiritual nature and the other temporal – were: their *unity* under one prince, one law, one religion and one and the same government; their *holiness*, because of the number of 'just men and friends of God' that they had produced; their *Catholicity*, or universality, which was so enduring, the fact that they embraced so many nations, the obligation of their laws, and the perfection of their government; and their *apostolic* commitment, both in their origins and in their ends.[56]

The grandeur of this Catholic Monarchy, for the first time truly universal, surpassed in extent and diversity all the ancient empires (Egyptian, Assyrian, Persian, Macedonian and Roman) and the modern ones (Turkish, Muscovite, Chinese and Mongol).[57] What seemed to be most miraculous, however, was that this entire collection of nations and territories, which were so disparate and scattered across the globe, should obey one and the same sovereign under one common religion:

> such a miraculous unity, as if the soul of a human body were giving life to limbs separated from each other and from its head, a rare and prodigious thing, which was not read about in the ancient Monarchies, nor do we know that in the Empires that sovereign Princes possess today is there this division of kingdoms, this unity of one king and one obedience.[58]

The perception of the sheer grandeur and diversity of the Spanish monarchy became even more obvious with the development of cartography in printed form, which helped inculcate and disseminate identification with a defined geographical space by means of the maps of kingdoms and provinces and the popularization of maps of the continents and the world. It should be remembered that one of the rooms in the royal apartments in the Monastery of El Escorial was decorated with Gerard Mercator's maps showing the monarchy's possessions,

---

[55] Fray J. de la Puente (O.P.), *La conveniencia de las dos Monarquía católicas, la de la Iglesia Romana y la del Imperio Español, y defensa de la Precedencia de los reyes Católicos de España* (4 tomes, Madrid, 1612), Chap. I, p. 4.

[56] Ibid., 6–7.   [57] Ibid., in 'Declaración del blasón que está en la cabeça deste libro', n.d.

[58] 'unidad tan milagrosa, como si el alma de un cuerpo humano animasse miembros discontinuados entre sí y de su cabeça, cosa rara y prodigiosa, que no se lee en las antiguas Monarquías, ni sabemos que en los Imperios que oy poseen los Príncipes soberanos, aya esta división de reynos, esta unidad de un rey y de una obediencia', ibid., 9–10.

and cartographical elements of this kind were also to be found in the Royal Library of the Escorial and other rooms of the Real Alcázar in Madrid.

In the autumn of 1602, the secretary to the Florentine embassy to the Spanish court, Orazio della Rena,[59] sent the Grand Duke of Tuscany a very full report about the *Monarchia Spagnuola*, which he subtitled *Osservationi della Spagna et della potenza et stati del Rè Cattolico et della sua Casa et Corte.*[60] In this report, he briefly outlined the geography of the Iberian Peninsula, its main cities, economic resources and customs, accompanying these brief sketches with a manuscript map and another printed one by J. Hondius, as well as a description of the American possessions of the West Indies, with their corresponding manuscript map, and of the East Indies, explaining in both cases the sea routes taken and the commercial exploitation of the fleets. As was customary with such reports of State drawn up by diplomats, he added a lengthy explanation of the main government institutions of the Crowns of Castile, Aragon and Portugal, of the Indies and of Italy. The most detailed parts dealt with the main offices and territorial governments of the monarchy, the fiscal system and the royal revenues, together with a list of all the titles, perquisites, benefices and *encomiendas* provided by royal patronage, as well as the ordinary and extraordinary expenditure incurred by the Spanish monarch. In the second section, apart from Philip III's genealogy, Della Rena offered a comprehensive account of all the states that the king of Spain possessed in Europe, Asia, Africa and the New World. He went on to report on the strongholds, the troops in the armies and navies, to present the structure of the royal households, with summaries of various aspects of their court etiquettes and to add personal biographical sketches of the king, the queen and their most important counsellors. He ended with listings of kinship relations between the various noble houses,

---

[59] Orazio della Rena was the secretary to Florentine legations in Ferrara (1589–1590) and Spain (1593–1605), as well as secretary to the Grand Duchess Christina of Lorraine, ambassador to Rome (1607–1611) and secretary to the Grand Duchess Maria Maddalena of Austria (1614–1624). See D. Toccafondi Fantapiè, 'Orazio della Rena', in *Dizionario biografico degli Italiani* (Turin, 1989), vol. 37, pp. 250–253; E. Golberg, 'State Gifts from the Medici to the Court of Philip III. The Relazione segreta of Orazio della Rena', in J. L. Colomer (ed.), *Arte y Diplomacia de la Monarquía Hispánica en el siglo XVII* (Madrid, 2003), pp. 114–133; and P. Volpini, 'Orazio della Rena fra diplomazia e storiografia. Sulla "publicazione manoscritta" del *Compensio della vita di Filippo Secondo re di Spagna*', in E. Fasano Guarini and F. Angiolini (eds.), *La prattica della Storia in Toscana. Continuitàe mutamenti tra la fine del '400 e la fine del '700* (Milan, 2009), pp. 101–120.

[60] O. della Rena, *Monarchia Spagnuola, cioè Osservazioni della Spagna, et della potenza, et stati del re Cattolico et della sua Casa et Corte* (Valladolid, 4 October 1602), in Biblioteca Nazionale Centrale de Florencia (BNCF), Mgl. Cl. xxiv, Cod. 223.

enumerating the surnames of the principal families and of the ministers with posts of responsibility in the government of the monarchy. It would certainly have made an overwhelming impression on its distinguished reader.

In spite of its strength and size, the 'ruin of Spain', according to the opinion of Campanella, could come about because of the obstacles and limitations that were imposed on the 'union of bodies' and lineages (*natural union*) between the subjects of the monarchy's different kingdoms. In his view, this had been one of the major successes of the Ottoman Empire, which used it as a basic instrument for its prosperity and preservation, employing the *devshirme* system to bring up the children of the peoples that it subjugated to be soldiers and settlers, and dignifying them with important posts and other honours, while disarming and weakening those who retained their religious difference.[61]

Finally, Campanella considered that the 'union of money and riches' was an essential source of cohesion for the monarchy; its strength, in fact, depended on it. He gave as an example the 'dominion' exercised by the king of Spain over the financial capital of the Genoese, who provided the Crown with abundant credit, underwritten by the royal revenues and the constant influx of silver from the Indies, and obtaining in exchange, *mercedes*, titles and privileges in the monarchy's dominions.[62] And, following the Genoese economic model, this interrelationship and common interest could be further cemented by encouraging the active participation of other nations of the monarchy in the colonial and mercantile business of the Indies: 'attract all the other nations or invite them to sail to the New World to accumulate treasure in their lands, as we see being done in Genoa'.[63] This same idea of co-participation in profits, benefits and common interests is present in the *Discurso* that Anthony Sherley dedicated to the Count-Duke of Olivares with the title *Peso político de todo el mundo* at the beginning of November 1622:

... but [if] all ([are] linked to interests and profits) it is to bind them together for life and lives [i.e. generations], because the obligation is general: in no particular favour, nor particular satisfaction is the general contentment of all secured; but

---

[61] Campanella, *La Monarquía Hispanica*, p. 151.

[62] Ibid., pp. 152–153. Of particular interest in this respect are M. Herrero Sánchez, 'Génova y el sistema imperial hispánico', in Alvariño and García García (eds.), *La Monarquía de las naciones*, pp. 528–562; the monograph also coordinated by M. Herrero Sánchez, 'La República de Génova y la Monarquía Hispánica (siglos XVI–XVII)', *Hispania*, LXV/1:219 (2005), pp. 9–20; and the studies collected in M. Herrero Sánchez, Y. R. Ben Yessef Garfia, C. Bitossi and D. Puncuh (eds.), *Génova y la Monarquía Hispánica, 1528–1713* (2 vols., Genoa, 2011).

[63] Campanella, *La Monarquía Hispanica*, p. 153.

profits, benefits and common interests are those that generally work on everyone, interest everyone and oblige everyone.[64]

So, the way to preserve the cohesion of the separate dominions in a composite monarchy was firstly to encourage the *natural union* of the vassals of the various territories, in order to address true *political union* later. According to Campanella and other contemporary treatise writers, it was precisely the constitution of a 'mixed' *natural society* – by means of the union of lineages and patrimonies of the families of the nations making up the Monarchy of Spain – that was the best way to increase its size and strengthen its dominion. The members of that society would be bound by ties of kinship and affinity, sharing a common space, under the same sky, laws, customs, common uses and desires, with a common language and dressing the same way. These numerous shared links would make the society stronger and enable the dominion that the sovereign exercised over it to be asserted.[65]

In the case of the Spanish monarchy, Campanella considered it advisable for these unions to be consistent with the greater affinity existing between its principal nations (Spaniards, Italians and Belgians),[66] and

[64] '. . . pero a todos (vinculados con interes y provechos) es encadenarlos para vida y vidas, por ser la obligazion general: en ninguna particular merced, ni particular satisfacción se asegura el general contento de todos; pero probechos, beneficios y intereses comunes, son los que generalmente, obran en todo y interesan a todos, y obligan a todos', A. Sherley, *Peso político de todo el mundo del conde D. Antonio Xerley*, ed. C. Viñas Mey (Madrid, 1961), p. 3. See also A. Amadori, *Negociando la obediencia. Getsión y reforma de los virreinatos americanos en tiempos del conde-duque de Olivares (1621–1643)* (Madrid, 2013), pp. 33–244.

[65] Ibid., p. 149. See for this P. Fernández Albaladejo, 'Common Souls, Autonomous Bodies: The Language of Unification under the Catholic Monarchy, 1590–1630', *Revista Internacional de Estudios Vascos*, cuad. 5 (2009), pp. 73–81.

[66] The question arises whether Campanella deliberately excluded the Portuguese from this nucleus of 'principal nations' of the Spanish Monarchy or whether they might have been included within that more plural definition of the 'Spains' (typical of the designation '*Hispaniarum Rex*' for example, that appeared on consoles, inscriptions, medallions, seals, and coins), whose origin conceived of a common homeland with the ancient Lusitanians forming part of Roman and Visigothic Hispania prior to the conquest by the Moors and the loss of that original 'unity'. For the plurinational organization of the Spanish Monarchy, see relevant contributions such as those collected in the volume alluded to earlier: Alvariño and García García, *La Monarquía de las naciones*, in which I should like to make particular mention of the illuminating chapter by X. Gil Pujol, 'Un rey, una fe, muchas naciones. Patria y nación en la España de los siglos XVI y XVII', pp. 39–76. Another indispensable work on this issue is T. Herzog, *Vecinos y extranjeros. Hacerse español en la Edad Moderna* (Madrid 2006), and I would particularly like to highlight the references to *naturaleza* [nationality], understood as the *comunidad del reino* [community of the kingdom], pp. 107–143, and the relations of nationality between Castile and America, pp. 145–175. See also T. Herzog, 'Naturales y extranjeros: sobre la construcción de categorías en el mundo hispánico', and O. Recio Morales, 'Los extranjeros y la historiografía modernista', in O. Recio Morales and T. Glesener (eds.), *Los*

proposed using the Spaniards as the common model, recommending that the other nations in the monarchy should assimilate their customs to them and learn their language: 'it is necessary for the rest to change to their customs, like trees that are grafted on to others'.[67] Campanella's purpose was 'to Hispanicize the world' by making the rest of the nations participants in the same prerogatives and particularities of ceremonial that the Spanish were so proud of.

The assimilation of customs ought to be accompanied not only by the encouragement of mixed marriages at certain levels[68] – especially among military personnel serving in the defence of territories different from their places of origin and among the middle-ranking and high nobility – but also by granting access to offices to worthy and qualified people irrespective of their nationality.[69] In this respect, and leaving aside the training of the Janissaries in the Ottoman Empire, Campanella recalled the example of the seminaries and religious orders of the Catholic Church, which admitted 'to the rank of priest, bishop and cardinal all men from all nations without distinction, be they poor or rich, barbarians or Latins'.[70]

The fact is that long before the aggregation of the different kingdoms that comprised the Spanish monarchy took place, there already were wide-ranging networks of dynastic ties between noble or common families, which contributed to the existence of kinship relations, patrimonial and financial interests, pathways to promotion and service, shared cultures and practices that helped, no doubt, to give a structure to the monarchy. The system of rewards contributed to the circulation of people and practices, and so increased interaction between the different parts of the whole. Among these rewards were the sale of offices and the 'market in favours' (with the transnational extension of recognition in the form of the rank of grandee of Spain, the habits of the Spanish Military Orders, meritorious service decorations with gold chains and medals carrying the effigy of the king, the grant of expense allowances and other vantages, and so on); the leasing of rents and the management of taxes; investment in the monarchy's military or colonial enterprises; education in colleges or universities; the patronage of 'national' corporations (brotherhoods, churches and hospitals);[71] careers that involved moving from province

---

extranjeros y la nación en España y la América española, Supplement X of Cuadernos de Historia Moderna (Madrid, 2011), pp. 21–31 and 33–51, respectively.

[67] Campanella, La Monarquía Hispanica, pp. 152–153.

[68] A. Álvarez-Ossorio Alvariño, 'Naciones mixtas: los jenízaros en el gobierno de Italia', in Álvarez-Ossorio and García García (eds.), La Monarquía de las naciones, pp. 597–649, especially pp. 597–600.

[69] Campanella, La Monarquía Hispanica, pp. 80 and 153.   [70] Ibid., p. 95.

[71] See B. J. García García and O. Recio Morales (eds.), Las corporaciones de nación en la Monarquía Hispánica (1580–1750) (Madrid, 2014).

to province (lawyers, cofferers, officers of the quill, etc.); mercantile activities; and service to religion or the armed forces.

The territorial elites held everything together, while also providing the driving force behind this dynastic agglomerate.[72] So, we are able analyse the horizontal relations established between the elites, who acted as agents and intermediaries or benefited from the possibilities of circulation, promotion and upward mobility that the system offered, yet who also entered into competition and conflict (keeping offices for natives, differences of nation, favouritism, corruption and fraud, endogamy, and so on).[73]

The venality of offices, privileges, honours and titles was an alternative source of liquidity for the Crown, and the sales increased considerably as its financial needs grew.[74] The trend had already started in the reign of Charles V and had benefitted those whose main merits had been the cash they paid when these resources of the royal patrimony were auctioned off, or those who had rendered other non-pecuniary services to the monarchy and were rewarded with alienations of this kind. The various waves of sales of municipal posts and the leasing of public rents and offices of the quill favoured the political and social advancement of the new municipal and national elites, by building family and client networks with bonds of interests and kinship that extended from the court (or provincial courts) to those places where their families resided.[75] It was not so much the salaries that made these offices and titles so lucrative, but the opportunities for preferment and social recognition that they afforded, and the political power and influence that went with them. The system favoured the 'patrimonialization' and perpetuation of posts in a lineage, forming dynasties of officers who used bonds of kinship and endogamous practices to consolidate these areas of service and power.[76] A secondary

---

[72] J. M. Imízcoz Beunza, 'Las redes de la monarquía: familias y redes sociales en la construcción de España', in F. Chacón and J. Bestard (eds.), *Familias. Historia de la sociedad española desde la Edad Media hasta nuestros días* (Madrid, 2011), pp. 393–444, especially pp. 406–431.

[73] See, for example, the collected studies of the volume mentioned earlier: B. Yun Casalilla (ed.), *Las redes del Imperio* (Madrid, 2008); and G. Muto and A. Terrasa (eds.), *Estrategias culturales y circulación de la nueva nobleza en Europa (1570–1707)* (Madrid, 2015).

[74] A. Jiménez Estrella, 'Poder, dinero y ventas de oficios y honores en la España del Antiguo Régimen: un estado de la cuestión', *Cuadernos de Historia Moderna*, 37 (2012), 259–271.

[75] F. Burgos Esteban, *Los lazos de poder. Obligaciones y parentesco en una élite local castellana en los siglos XVI y XVII* (Valladolid, 1994); and E. Soria Mesa, 'Los estudios sobre las oligarquías municipales en la Castilla moderna', *Manuscrits. Revista d'Història Moderna*, 18 (2000), pp. 185–197.

[76] Good examples of this are the studies devoted to the subject of the Basque and Navarrese elites by ed. J. M. Imízcoz, *Élites, poder y red social. Las élites del País Vasco y Navarra en la Edad Moderna* (Bilbao, 1996); J. M. Imízcoz, 'Las élites vasco-navarras y la monarquía hispánica: construcciones sociales, políticas y culturales en la edad moderna', *Cuadernos*

market also existed among private individuals, which was beyond the control of the Crown.

Venality of offices was especially important in the Indies[77] and the Italian dominions,[78] and affected every type of office. An analysis of the impact of the sale of 'magistracies' and subaltern posts in the inquisitorial courts, royal assizes and other judicial bodies revealed that numerous problems and conflicts were caused in the administration of justice because of the essential role that these officers had in processing trials. Moreover, although there were significant obstacles to the sale of military offices, ranks and honours – in view of the possible implications for the functioning of the units and because the military had its own jurisdiction – there were private contractors and recruiters who enlisted in the offices of the militia and obtained special recognition for their services. From the end of the sixteenth century we find cases of captains of companies who acquired their commission in return for financing the cost of recruiting the troop, and various posts in the commands of coastal defence or in the militias also began to be the patrimony of a few families.[79] The venality of honours spread to the sale of *hidalguías* [low-ranking nobles without titles], lordships and jurisdictions, habits of the Military Orders and titles of nobility, so opening the door to wealthy bourgeois groups, officers in the administration, lawyers, military men and the new financial and mercantile aristocracy.[80] Resorting to the sale of offices was one of the key means of raising finance during the War of

---

de Historia Moderna, 33 (2008), pp. 89–119; and R. Guerrero Elecalde, *Las élites vascas y navarras en el gobierno de la monarquía borbónica. Redes sociales, carreras y hegemonía en el siglo XVIII* (Bilbao, 2012).

[77] J. H. Parry, *The Sale of Public Office in the Spanish Indies under the Habsburgs* (Berkeley, 1953); M. A. Burckholder and D. S. Chandler, *De la impotencia a la autoridad. La corona española y las Audiencias en América, 1687–1808* (Mexico, 1984); and A. Sanz Tapia, *¿Corrupción o necesidad? La venta de cargos de gobierno americanos bajo Carlos II, 1674–1700* (Madrid, 2009).

[78] See, for example, the studies by A. Álvarez-Ossorio Alvariño, 'La venalidad de las magistraturas en el Estado de Milán durante el reinado de Carlos II', *Archivio Storico Lombardo*, CXXVI (2000), pp. 111–261; '¿El final de la Sicilia española? Fidelidad, familia y venalidad bajo el virrey marqués de los Balbases (1707–1713)', in A. Álvarez-Ossorio Alvariño, B. J. García García and V. León Sanz (eds.), *La pérdida de Europa. La Guerra de Sucesión por la Monarquía de España* (Madrid, 2007), pp. 831–912; and 'La venta de magistraturas en el reino de Nápoles durante los reinados de Carlos II y Felipe V', *Chronica Nova*, 33 (2007), pp. 57–94.

[79] See some of the collected studies in F. Andújar Castillo and M. del M. Felices de la Fuente (eds.), *El poder del dinero. Ventas de cargos y honores en el Antiguo Régimen* (Madrid, 2011).

[80] E. Soria Mesa, *La nobleza en la España Moderna. Cambio y continuidad* (Madrid, 2007), pp. 213–260. On the evolution of the concepts of nobility in the treatises and the processes of ennoblement in Castile and Portugal, see also the work of J. A. Guillén Berrendero, *La Edad de la Nobleza. Identidad nobiliaria en Castilla y Portugal, 1556–1621* (Madrid, 2012).

the Spanish Succession and the practice continued to expand during the Bourbon administration.[81]

According to Campanella, in order to bring about *political union* between the different dominions of the monarchy, *religious union* between its nations should be encouraged by the activity of preachers and theologians, and 'the admiration for great power' be fostered by the cultivation of 'distinguished arts, sciences and languages'.[82] An analysis of the Spanish monarchy's development of 'soft power' really deserves greater attention. There have been studies of the effects of public ceremonial and festivities,[83] for example, and some notable contributions about the artistic and cultural patronage of the Habsburg sovereigns and their relatives, and we are beginning to find out more about the patronage of the high nobility and the clergy; there remain, however, many aspects that are worthy of closer examination and we still do not have an overall view of the main elements that constituted that 'soft power', which was capable of generating a common memory and a positive and powerfully attractive image of the Spanish monarchy among so many of its contemporaries.[84]

Despite the fact that most writers of political treatises considered that tight-knit, united empires were better able to defend and preserve themselves in the long run, they did not underestimate the unquestionable might of the Spanish monarchy, whose global reach was backed by its powerful armies, its extraordinary financial capacity and the combination of its navies of galleys and galleons that enabled it to link up its broad dominions and keep them secure. The best-known example of this argument is the one offered in the influential work by Giovanni Botero, *Della ragion di Stato*. For him, even though the states that belonged to the Spanish monarchy were so obviously scattered across the globe and distant from each other, they were in practice more secure and enduring, because each one had sufficient resources that it had no need to fear the

---

[81] F. Andújar Castillo, *El sonido del dinero. Monarquía, ejército y venalidad en la España del siglo XVIII* (Madrid, 2004).

[82] Campanella, *La Monarquía Hispanica*, p. 153.

[83] See, for example, the studies collected in M. L. Lobato López and B. J. García García (eds.), *La fiesta cortesana en la época de los Austrias*, Valladolid 2003; K. De Jonge and B. J. García García (eds.), *El legado de Borgoña. Fiesta y ceremonia cortesana en la Europa de los Austrias, 1454–1648* (Madrid, 2010); and Checa Cremades and Fernández-González, *Festival Culture*.

[84] A good example of this is the recent work about the typology and political and ceremonial use of portraits and statues of the Spanish sovereigns in the Monarchy, published by D. Bodart, *Pouvoirs du portrait sous les Habsburg d'Espagne* (Paris, 2012); the studies in J. L. Palos and D. Carrió-Invernizzi (eds.), *La historia imaginada. Construcciones visuales del pasado en la Edad Moderna* (Madrid, 2008); or the inaugural address delivered to the Royal Academy of History by F. Marías, *Pinturas de historia, imágenes políticas. Repensando el Salón de Reinos* (Madrid, 2012), to quote just a few examples.

sabre-rattling of its neighbours and was able, if necessary, to repel attacks by enemy armies or navies; also thanks to the monarchy's naval power, its dominions were always within reach and connected to each other by sea. It could be said that it was a global monarchy whose hegemony rested in large part on the maintenance and control of strategic routes and navies capable of 'lording it' over the seas.[85]

Government of Restraint and Moderation: Measuring Strength and Preserving the Monarchy

However, the providential momentum of the Spanish monarchy that had swept all before it as it expanded in the course of the sixteenth century appeared to be reaching its limit. The opinion of many statesmen and political treatise writers of the latter years of that century and the early decades of the following one – schooled in the instructive experience of ancient and medieval empires – was that the expected rapid decline awaiting the Spanish monarchy could only be avoided or delayed by setting stable limits to the size of its empire and giving it 'state' to ensure its preservation. Undertaking and accepting further increases in size would only be justified for reasons of security and should be minor ones.[86]

In the tract on *Virtudes reales* (1626), written for the political education of the Cardinal-Infante Ferdinand of Austria, his Lord Steward, Alonso Carrillo Lasso de la Vega, alluded to the concepts of preservation and increase when considering the 'size of Empires'. He asserted that *limit* and *extend* were complementary terms that affected different situations and sets of circumstances through which the provinces of a *'lordship'* or dominion passed. Thus, after an expansion or increase in the monarch's sovereignty (*empire*), this should be limited by giving the resulting territorial entity a form of 'state' (or government) that would provide it with more lasting stability and secure its preservation. This idea was also present in Pedro Fernández de Navarrete's *Conservación de Monarquías*, published by the Royal Printers in Madrid, also in 1626, when all the threats that were hanging simultaneously over the Spanish monarchy after the *Annus mirabilis* of 1625 – and subsequently illustrated among the paintings of epic deeds on display in the Hall of Realms in the Palace of the Buen Retiro – appeared to have been exorcised with unprecedented success and without significant risks. In his *Discurso VIII*, he analysed the causes of Castile's depopulation, emphasizing the constant departure of

---

[85] G. Botero, *Della ragion di Stato libri dieci, con tre libri delle cause della grandezza e magnificenza delle Città* (Venice, 1589), p. 15.

[86] Alonso Carrillo Lasso de la Vega, *Virtudes reales* (Cordoba, 1626), p. 19.

Spaniards who left to serve in the administration and settlement of remote colonies, and the countless strategic and military commitments of a monarchy that waged wars a long way from Spain. He considered it necessary for Spaniards to be actively involved in the Indies trade, in military deployment in Flanders – which he judged to be essential so as not to lose what they had put so many years of effort into gaining – and to keep the control of strategic strongholds and garrison towns (in Italy and Africa) in the hands of Spanish officers and soldiers, because: 'Stationing soldiers of other nations in the garrisons would be giving foreigners the keys to the Empire, exposing it to the known risk of the strongholds being taken over.'[87]

Extending or expanding a monarchy was justifiable as long as it was based on 'reason of justice', or by right of lineage and descendants, although a region could also be conquered for reasons of security or as a precaution, and guaranteeing its security would be essential when an empire had reached its peak or maximum extent. It would be folly to try and extend its dominions in all directions and be faced, almost simultaneously, with numerous enemies, and to intervene at the same time in provinces that were quite remote from each other, which would end up with them strengthening their alliances against the common adversary and threatening the monarchy with ruin. It was essential, therefore, to establish limits to the size of the empire, and for these to be agreed by using all the prudence of good government, rather than them being imposed by necessity.[88]

A sovereign prince should set limits to the conquest of new territories, not on the basis of fear or lack of material resources, but for reasons of justice and advantage. And of the two, advantage should take precedence over the justice of a cause, unless the fame or reputation of the sovereign and the 'law of God' were compromised to the extent that the very nature and constitution of his 'state' were altered. Not all the evils of the world could be remedied, nor all just causes be protected in the defence of virtue or the faith, since one of the basic precepts dictated by divine wisdom and the laws of nature was that men should first take care of their own children and dependants before strangers; the responsibility of princes was to watch over the preservation and prosperity of their subjects and provinces, so that they were protected from great evils, instead of risking their perdition in the name of justice and good intentions, by exceeding the bounds of humanity and political prudence.[89]

---

[87] Pedro Fernández de Navarrete, *Conservación de Monarquías y discursos políticos sobre la gran consulta que el Consejo hizo al señor rey don Filipe Tercero* (Madrid, 1626), p. 58.

[88] Pagden, *Señores de todo el mundo*, pp. 137–164.

[89] Carrillo Lasso de la Vega, *Virtudes reales*, pp. 18–20.

Fernández de Navarrete thought it best to send a contingent of troops from other 'auxiliary nations' to help the allied princes 'on the grounds that, if the wars are in their provinces, they won't take place in ours' and so keeping the Spanish soldiers in reserve.[90] At that critical juncture in Europe marked by the Thirty Years' War and other related conflicts, the need was stressed for the Spanish monarchy to gauge its own strength and to manage its external commitments by limiting them of its own accord, so as to guarantee its continuity in the medium term:

It is right for Spain to come to the aid of the needs of the Empire, and as the arbiter of peace in Italy, to curb those who would disturb it, as it has done and continues to do so daily; but this should be done by ensuring that Castile, as head of this Monarchy, does not become so feeble and weak that it is overcome by those who today are nourished in her shadow. To prevent the Spaniards from wasting away and perishing, it would make sense to set limits and draw a line round its extensive Empire; because, by fully extending itself at the beginning, its riches increased, which awakened ambition, and ambition sought out greed, which is the root of all evils, with the result that people are experiencing in Spain the same as in all other monarchies, whose ruin normally originates from its very size.[91]

In the opinion of the authors of these political treatises, the very size and scattered nature of a monarchy without stable or well-defined limits entailed extraordinary risks in the long term, not only because of the apprehension generated in other friendly states, but also because the disproportionate size of a 'superpower' led to alliances of greater quality and range. This occurred in European politics when Portugal was aggregated to the monarchy of Philip II from 1580 onwards.[92] In the face of this apparently unlimited capacity for expansion, not even the providential support of God could be guaranteed indefinitely, since He would correct ambition, abuses, bad government and excess by giving rise to divided opinions, revolts and war, and so jeopardizing the survival of the whole.[93]

Faced with the first symptoms of decline that many detected in the economic structures at the heart of the monarchy of Castile, and the resistance jointly offered by the rebels in the Low Countries allied to

---

[90] Fernández de Navarrete, *Conservación de Monarquias*, p. 60.

[91] 'Justo es, que España socorra las necessidades del Imperio, y que como arbitra de la paz de Italia, enfrene a los que la quisieren perturbar, como lo ha hecho, y haze cada dia; pero esto deve ser teniendo atencion a que Castilla, que es cabeça desta Monarquia, no quede tan enervada y flaca, que venga a ser presa de los que oy se sustentan a su sombra. Para evitar el consumirse y acavarse los Españoles, seria cordura poner limite y raya a su estendido Imperio; porque con la demasiada extension crecieron al principio las riquezas, y ellas despertaron la ambicion, y la ambicion solicitó la codicia, que es la raiz de todos los males, con que se va experimentando en España lo que en todas las demas monarquías, cuya ruina suele originarse de la misma grandeza ... ', ibid., pp. 60–61.

[92] Rivero Rodríguez, *La España de Don Quijote*, p. 409.

[93] Carrillo Lasso de la Vega, *Virtudes reales*, p. 24.

other northern powers, policies of preservation and containment had to be adopted to safeguard the reputation and wealth of the monarchy. These policies meant that the obligation to maintain peace and prosperity within its own states had to take priority over its commitment to defend religion beyond its frontiers.

When Philip III succeeded to the throne in 1598, the Catholic Monarchy remained in a parlous state. Several years of epidemics and abject poverty in the Iberian Peninsula had taken their toll. Added to this there was the current delicate and complicated transition towards a new peace with France and its implications in northern Italy, which was set against the permanent background of war with Elizabeth I's England, fluctuating between a costly continuation of hostilities and bringing them to an end, and the offensives of the United Provinces, in a conflict that was slowly beginning to have an impact on the strategic colonial routes of the hegemonic Spanish-Portuguese system and which, two decades later, would assume global proportions.[94]

In the final years of his reign, Philip II and his key ministers (Moura, Idiáquez, Zúñiga, Chinchón, Poza, Cardinal-Archduke Albert) made a titanic effort to improve this situation, in which there would inevitably be a change of government in this superpower committed to defending Catholicism against heresy by increasing evangelization and civility, and by preserving and expanding the dynastic and global patrimony of the House of Austria, not only within its own borders but also as a safeguard for allies, relatives and clients.

The enormous volume of economic resources obtained from the extraordinary order suspending payments in 1596[95] were deployed very

---

[94] As can be seen from the studies by J. Israel, C. Rahn Phillips and P. C. Emmer, Dutch activity on routes outside of Europe did not yet represent a serious threat to fleets from Iberia and the major bases of its ocean-going traffic. For this, see the assessment of P. C. Emmer, 'La primera guerra global. Los holandeses contra los ibéricos en Asia, África y el Nuevo Mundo, 1590–1609', in A. de Béthencourt Massieu (ed.), *Canarias y el Atlántico 1580–1648. IV Centenario del ataque de Van der Does a Las Palmas de Gran Canaria* (Las Palmas de Gran Canaria 2001), pp. 479–501, which concluded that, with the exception of the exploitation of the salt flats of Punta de Araya on the coast of Venezuela and of Brazilian sugar, the level of investment in this kind of enterprise was very low, and the damage caused by the Dutch merchants on the Iberian trade routes outside Europe barely made an impact before 1621. This Dutch expansion had scarcely any military worth. The same could be said of the English settlements in Virginia and the Bahamas, and the French in Marañon and Canada.

[95] García García, *La Pax Hispanica*, pp. 205–208 and 360–364; and C. Sanz Ayán, 'La estrategia de la Monarquía en la suspensión de pagos de 1596 y su medio general', in *Actas del Congreso Internacional Las sociedades ibéricas y el Mar a finales el siglo XVI, in tome II: La Monarquía, recursos, organización y estrategias* (Madrid, 1998), pp. 81–97; see also the version published as 'Procedimientos de la Monarquía ante la suspensión de pagos de 1596', in C. Sanz Ayán, *Estado, monarquía y finanzas. Estudios de historia financiera en tiempos de los Austrias* (Madrid, 2004), pp. 21–37.

unequally on internal expenses and developing a military response on a good number of these war fronts, while diplomatic efforts directed towards obtaining peace agreements, and, in particular, lengthy truces in the conflicts between the monarchy and its major enemies, were redoubled. It is hardly surprising that in the summer of that year, Philip II should write to all archbishops and bishops, the cathedral chapters, abbots and priors, generals and provincials of the religious orders and chaplains of all the royal chapels, with an extraordinary plea to them to offer up prayers with urgency and devotion, and for them to redouble their efforts and correct and reform the bad habits among their parishioners, so as to make divine providence more propitious at that crucial moment. At the beginning of his reign, Philip III also made an appeal for general prayers to be said for him, so that he should be successful in taking decisions, and to ask for divine favour in the accomplishment of his mission: 'so that it may help prepare and ensure the good success of my intentions, so that my motives and resolution are the effects of His Holy Service and the glorification of the Holy Apostolic Church of Rome'; and again, at the beginning of 1602, to obtain significant achievements in the battle against heretics and infidels in the *política de efectos* that Philip III had undertaken on all fronts (Ireland, Algiers and Ostend) in those early years of his government.[96]

With the Treaty of Vervins (1598),[97] Spanish intervention in French political and confessional hostilities came to an end and, although the economic and military balance sheet of the Catholic Monarchy at the end of that intervention was considered disastrous, the Anglo-French alliance had been broken and a path towards the much needed peace in the North had opened up. The main objective of that agreement and of the cession of sovereignty to Infanta Isabella Clara Eugenia, ratified by Philip III, was to create the most appropriate conditions for restoring the Southern

---

[96] Archivo Histórico Nacional (AHN), Consejos, Cámara de Castilla, Patronato Eclesiástico, Libros de Iglesia, book 4, fol. 27r. These letters are dated in Villamiel, 17 August 1596 (in this book they appear registered in fols. 27r–31r). Those of Philip II are dated in Barcelona, 29 June 1599, AHN, Consejos, book 4, fol. 351r–v, and in Leon, 31 January 1602, AHN, Consejos, book 5, fols. 133r–135r.

[97] See, in particular, the studies collected for the commemorative conferences organized by C. Vidal and F. Pilleboue (eds.), *La paix de Vervins 1598* (Laon, 1998); and J. -F. Labourdette, J. -P. Possou and M. -C. Vignal (eds.), *Le Traité de Vervins* (Paris, 2000), as well as those by N. G. Goodman, *Diplomatic Relations between England and Spain, with Special Reference to English Opinion, 1597–1603* (Philadelphia, 1925), pp. 12–21; A. E. Imhof, *Der Friede von Vervins 1598* (Aarau, 1966); R. B. Wernham, *The Return of the Armadas: The Last Years of the Elizabethan War against Spain, 1595–1603* (Oxford, 1994), pp. 210–249; V. Vázquez de Prada, *Felipe II y Francia, 1559–1598. Política, religión y razón de Estado* (Pamplona, 2004), pp. 411–446; and J. J. Ruiz Ibáñez, *Esperanzas y fracasos de la política de Felipe II en Francia (1595–1598): la historia entre la fe y las armas jornaleras* (Murcia, 2004).

Provinces of the Low Countries, both politically and economically, and thereby ensuring a better climate for reunification with the Northern Provinces. It formed part of a policy of reconciliation and the design of it anticipated a government that was closer to its Flemish subjects and more broadly accepted by the elites, which would, at the same time, be capable of protecting the strategic and dynastic interests of the Spanish monarchy in this space, which was regarded as vital to the preservation of its domestic and international prestige because it was able to exert the necessary pressure on its main adversaries and create more favourable conditions for completing the general peace-making process with the Franco-Spanish treaty of Vervins. Hence, once the change of regime was consolidated with sovereigns linked to both France and the House of Austria, this could open up a new way of moving closer to and under-standing the United Provinces, with a view to negotiating a lasting peace and sealing a reunification agreement with the Seventeen Provinces gov-erned by these new princes and their successors.

I should like to conclude by recalling a third image published in this context. It is an anonymous Dutch engraving (Figure 5.3) based on an anthropomorphic map known as *Europa regina* (after 1537), the work of the famous German cartographer and cosmographer, Sebastian Münster, who included it among the illustrations of his *Cosmographia* (Basel, Heinrich Petri, 1544).[98] The earlier versions show Europe in the glorious times of Charles V as a united *res publica Christiana*; the map takes the form of a woman, whose features resemble those of Empress Isabella of Portugal, holding the imperial insignia, the sceptre and orb, in her hands, and wearing the Crown of the Holy Roman Empire. *Hispania* is the ruling head of Europe and the waters surrounding the continent are calm, suggesting that the government is stable and peace-loving. On the other hand, the Dutch print, entitled '*Het Spaens Europa*' (Spanish Europe) shows a continent being buffeted by the more turbulent waters on the side facing the ocean, in which the Dutch Republic – represented on an island by the figures of a *gueux* and a lion (the emblem of the Low Countries, the *Leo Belgicus*), protected by a wooden palisade and a group of small fishing boats – is fighting an unequal battle against the Ship of the Catholic Church, captained by a figure with three heads: the pope, the King of Spain Philip II, and a Jesuit or Spanish Inquisitor. They are resisting the treacherous peace that the Spaniards are keen to promote because it will bring with it the forced re-catholicization of the Low Countries and the establishment of a false religion.

[98] M. A. McLean, *The Cosmographia of Sebastian Münster: Describing the World in the Reformation* (Aldershot, 2007).

Figure 5.3 Anonymous Dutch engraving of August 1598, *The Spanish Europe against the Dutch Rebels*, based on Sebastian Münster's map *Europa regina*. Nuremberg, Germanisches Nationalmuseum, H.B. 296.

Off the coast of *Hibernia*, the defeat of the Armada is portrayed, recalling not only the shipwreck of the Spanish fleet in the autumn of 1588, but also the more recent dispersal of another fleet under the command of the *adelantado* of Castile in the middle of October 1597. The Spanish monarchy, as head of the continent, is trying to assert its authority and preserve its hegemony by brandishing a sword in her left hand as a threat to the island of the Dutch Republic. The latter appears to have completely broken away from the domains controlled by the Spaniards. Spain's face seems to be clearly portraying that of Infanta Isabella Clara Eugenia.[99] This is an allusion to the Dutch rejection of the cession of sovereignty (approved in 1598, the date that appears in

---

[99] For the image of the Infanta Isabella Clara Eugenia, see the contributions collected in C. van Wyhe (ed.), *Isabel Clara Eugenia. Soberanía femenina en las cortes de Madrid y Bruselas* (Madrid, 2011).

the legend beneath the engraving), which was designed not only as a means of bringing peace to the Low Countries after more than 30 years of war, but also to favour the negotiation of an agreed reunification of the Seventeen Provinces by means of the reconciliation and reconstruction of consensus within the framework of the States General.[100]

This initiative aimed at resolution and peace-making was undertaken at the end of that final decade of the sixteenth century;[101] nonetheless, we may regard the *Pax Hispanica* policy overall – from the ratification of Vervins and the cession of the Low Countries in 1598 to the peace concluded in Madrid in 1617 – as a genuine commitment by King Philip III, supported by his favourite and chief minister, the Duke of Lerma, to the cause of peace in Christendom, to ensure the preservation of the Catholic Monarchy without giving up its hegemonic position, yet also aware of its own limitations, strategic priorities and the balance necessary to avoid or contain new conflicts.[102] This, certainly, had been the way marked by his father. Tackling the task and facing the challenges involved would call for the new sovereign and his favourite to adopt a demanding political and negotiating role. They would have to be able to exercise prudence, strengthen the mechanisms of royal patronage, resort to arms with efforts calculated to maintain the monarchy's military reputation and ensure the cohesion of a scattered system. It would also require some degree of religious tolerance as the lesser of two evils, because of the need to prioritize the public utility of harmony, restoration and prosperity, and to respond with novel and pragmatic defensive solutions to the commercial and maritime expansion of the northern powers.

The main device and impresa of King Philip III,[103] displayed at the funeral rites held in the Real Monasterio de los Jerónimos in Madrid,

---

[100] A. Esteban Estríngana, 'La Tregua de los Doce Años: fracaso del principio de reunión pactada de los Países Bajos bajo el dominio de los Archiduques', in the *Dossier* coordinated by X. Gil Pujol, *1559, 1609, 1659: conflictes religiosos, minories i relacions internacionals*, in the journal *Pedralbes. Revista d'Història Moderna*, XIX, 29 (2009), pp. 95–157, and particularly, pp. 100–132.

[101] F. Braudel, *El Mediterráneo y el mundo mediterráneo en la época de Felipe II* (2 vols., Madrid, 1976), II, pp. 784.

[102] García García, *La Pax Hispanica*, pp. 27–88; B. J. García García, 'La *Pax Hispanica*: una política de conservación', in J. Martínez Millán and M. A. Visceglia (eds.), *La Monarquía de Felipe III. vol. IV: Los Reinos* (Madrid, 2008), pp. 1215–1276; and B. J. García García (ed.), *El arte de la prudencia: La Tregua de los Doce Años en la Europa de los Pacificadores* (Madrid, 2012), pp. 11–40.

[103] See S. López Poza, 'Empresas o divisas del rey Felipe III de España', in A. Martínez Pereira, I. Osuna and V. Infantes (eds.), *Palabras, símbolos, emblemas: las estructuras gráficas de la representación* (Madrid, 2013), pp. 323–332.

in May 1621, was *Ad utrumque* (Ready for Either Course), taken from Virgil's *Aeneid* (2, 61). The emblematic image that accompanied it presented a golden lion rampant on an azure field, holding a spear in its right paw and a cross crowned with laurels in the left, signifying that it was prepared to demonstrate its fortitude and determination with arms, or to serve as an example, through its Christian devotion, to go to war or safeguard religion and peace.

6   The New Monarchy in France, the Social Elites and the Society of Princes

Lucien Bély

The Crown, the Society of Princes and the Elite Aristocracy

The French monarchy seemed to become more absolute during the seventeenth century, especially during the personal rule of Louis XIV. Historians have shown that this was a gradual evolution rather than a total metamorphosis.[1] Some time ago, Pierre Goubert underlined the limits of royal power: 'On n'en finirait pas d'énumérer les textes législatifs d'une précision extraordinaire, menaçant les contrevenants d'amendes énormes, du pilori, du fouet, de la marque (infamante) ou des galères, tranquillement ignorés du public, bien qu'ils fussent âprement rappelés de temps à autre.'[2] ['There is no end to enumerating the legislative texts with extraordinary precision, threatening the offenders with enormous fines, the pillory, the whip, the brand (infamante) or the galleys; quietly ignored by the public, they were bitterly recalled from time to time.']

The system was still based on negotiations between the king, his counsellors and his ministers on the one hand[3] and, on the other, on cooperation with the main social forces.[4] For example, the links between the monarch and the nobility were complex, and war had an important place in this relationship. One could almost argue that a sort of principle regarding war and the monarchy had been established since the late

---

[1] Lucien Bély, *La France au XVIIe siècle. Puissance de l'État, contrôle de la société* (Paris, 2009). See also Fanny Cosandey and Robert Descimon, *L'absolutisme en France. Histoire et historiographie* (Paris, 2002).

[2] Pierre Goubert, *L'ancien régime, 2, les pouvoirs* (Paris, 1973), p. 16. See also Pierre Goubert and Daniel Roche, *Les Français et l'Ancien Régime* (Paris, 1984).

[3] Thierry Sarmant and Mathieu Stoll, *Régner et gouverner. Louis XIV et ses ministres* (Paris, 2010).

[4] To consider the French society in a comparative approach, see Annie Antoine and Cédric Michon (eds.), *Les sociétés au XVIIe siècle. Angleterre, Espagne, France* (Rennes, 2006); Michel Cassan (ed.), *Les sociétés anglaise, espagnole et française au XVIIe siècle* (Paris, 2006). For a European approach to the nobility: Hamish M. Scott, *The European Nobilities in the Seventeenth and Eighteenth Centuries* (London, 1995).

Middle Ages and during the sixteenth century. The French monarchy had to wage war abroad in order to avoid civil war at home and to satisfy the thirst of the nobility for prestige, offices and war-related gains.[5] The Italian wars provided plenty of scope for engagement of the main noblemen in the kingdom. However, the strength of Spain's Catholic Monarchy put an end to those adventures. The Wars of Religion of course had religious roots, but they also had a social basis: the nobility was divided into two main parties, and they saw civil war as a means of finding new areas of conflict. The ambitious foreign policy of France in the seventeenth century was a way to give the nobility honours, riches and dreams through war outside rather than inside France. Foreign wars were the main way to maintain the nobility under the king's control. Louis XIV has integrated this necessity in his bellicose policy.

In fact, the monarchy needed powerful middlemen from the aristocratic elite to maintain social order, but those very middlemen were not always faithful. The princes of the royal family and the princes of the blood had to support the king in his endeavours, but they often pursued their own agendas and even opposed royal government. Sustained periods of dynastic instability made the situation more difficult, for instance during 1610 to 1638, when Louis XIII had no son as heir. Thus, Gaston, Louis XIII's brother, was the heir to the Crown. But he also appeared as an opponent to the political choices of the king and of the king's first minister. A large part of the nobility agreed to enter into rebellion behind Gaston by plotting to assassinate Cardinal Richelieu. He was even involved in negotiations with the king of Spain, who gave his support to such plots. During the *Frondes* (1648–1653), the prince of Condé thought that he should be head of government instead of Mazarin, and a part of the nobility followed him when he rebelled, again with support from Spain. In effect, the government had to organise military campaigns within France against Condé, Louis XIV's cousin, who maintained his own troops within the kingdom. And both Gaston d'Orléans and Condé negotiated with foreign powers while opposing royal government.[6] That shows that they considered themselves as members of the European society of princes,[7] each prince being entitled to communicate with the

---

[5] Jean-Marie Constant, *La noblesse en liberté, XVIe-XVIIe siècles* (Rennes, 2004); Laurent Bourquin, *La noblesse dans la France moderne (XVIe-XVIIIe siècles)* (Paris, 2002).

[6] Caroline Bitsch, *Vie et carrière d'Henri II de Bourbon, prince de Condé (1588–1646). Exemple de comportement et d'idées politiques au début du XVIIe siècle* (Paris, 2008); Katia Béguin, *Les princes de Condé. Rebelles, courtisans et mécènes dans la France du Grand siècle* (Seyssel, Champvallon, 1999).

[7] Lucien Bély, *La Société des princes. XVIe-XVIIIe siècle* (Paris, 1999). See also Christof Dipper and Mario Rosa (ed.), *La Società dei principi nell'Europa moderna (secoli XVI-XVII)* (Bologna, 2005).

others, and not as subjects in any sense. The temptation to rebel disappeared during Louis XIV's personal government. There were some plots, but the highest nobility would not dare to have contacts with foreign powers during Louis' wars.

During political crises, the princes of the blood led aristocratic rebellions against royal power, too. The justification for such movements was often the usurpation of royal authority by a courtier, for example Concini in Maria de Medici's day and, later, Richelieu and Mazarin.[8] For decades, from the late sixteenth to the mid-seventeenth century, the absence of an adult dauphin increased the problems. Under Louis XIII, first the minority of the king himself, then the absence of a dauphin (until 1638) and then the minority of that successor actually became a platform from which the high nobility questioned the politics of queen mothers, regents and advisors. Under Louis XIII, they fell into step with the king's brother, Gaston. These facts bring home how utterly important the continued presence of the personal rule of an adult king actually was. The consolidation of royal power that historians have perceived during the seventeenth century was thus not primarily or entirely due to the building of a bureaucratic state or the eventual suppression of elites, but due to the fact that with the accession of Louis XIV, for the first time since the middle of the sixteenth century, after a long row of minorities, the long term personal rule of a king became possible again. Thus, it was only from the reign of Louis XIV onwards that this situation ceased to exist; the elites subsequently lost the will to discuss the king's political choices and the main decisions, prepared by the ministers. However, the monarchy maintained some channels of communication and dialogue with the traditional elites. This dialogue remained in a large part secret and did not appear in the public sphere. Behind the façade of perfect obedience, the government tolerated permanent negotiation, especially so as to succeed the ambitious foreign policy of the reign. This ambitious foreign policy not least satisfied demands of the nobility, but in turn it kept the monarchy dependent on its elites.

New Channels of Communication

Not least from the experience of the 1570s to the 1580s, the French monarchy thought that the Estates General were not useful and could indeed turn out to be dangerous. As the various parts of society could

---

[8] Arlette Jouanna, *Le devoir de révolte. La noblesse française et la gestation de l'État moderne, 1550–1661* (Paris, 1989). About Concini, see Hélène Duccini, *Faire voir, faire croire. L'opinion publique sous Louis XIII* (Seyssel, 2003). About Richelieu, see Françoise Hildesheimer, *Richelieu. Une certaine idée de l'État* (Paris, 1985).

have antagonistic interests, only the king could and should judge what was best for the kingdom.[9] During the international negotiations for peace during the congress in Utrecht (1712–1713), the English government thought that the Estates General could approve the decision to separate definitively the Crown of Spain and that of France. Louis XIV refused, asserting that his own oath had a higher value than the engagement of the estates.

The monarchy tried to create other intermediary bodies to communicate with its noblemen. The peers of the realm, the marshals of France and the Knights of the Holy Spirit were faithful supporters of the Crown. Their situation was comparable with that of the Grandees of Spain, who were appointed as governors or viceroys of Spanish territories (Sicily, Naples, Milan or the Netherlands), or with the Knights of the Golden Fleece in the Spanish Netherlands, who were members of the highest nobility (though the *toison d'or* was not restricted to Burgundian elites). Most of these dignitaries had their own contacts, a network of kin, friends, vassals and servants. Louis XIV also created a new order, the Knights of Saint Louis, to reward courageous warriors. The French monarchy succeeded by establishing strict and limited frameworks for social dialogue. As a result of almost constant foreign wars, the army grew significantly and the proportion of noblemen serving in the army also rose: captains and colonels were recruited from the nobility and had to buy their own regiment or company; they were responsible for the recruitment of their own soldiers under royal supervision.[10] The succession of wars had an important social impact, and, in fact, the whole French economy depended on this military stimulus through the construction of warships, the provision of munitions for the armies and the building of fortresses on the frontiers.[11]

In spite of the failure of the Estates General in 1614–1615, dialogue remained crucial between the Crown and the provincial states in a number of border provinces such as Languedoc.[12] The nobility took part in this type of dialogue. That was essential to ease the collection of taxes.[13]

---

[9] See the contribution in this volume by James Collins on the change of rhetoric from 'bien publique' to 'l'estat' in this period (Chapter 4).

[10] Hervé Drévillon, *L'impôt du sang. Le métier des armes sous Louis XIV* (Paris, 2005); Guy Rowlands, *The Dynastic State and the Army under Louis XIV: Royal Service and Private Interest, 1661–1701* (Cambridge, 2002).

[11] Lucien Bély, *Louis XIV. Le plus grand roi du monde* (Paris, 2005).

[12] William Beik, *Absolutism and Society in Seventeenth-Century France: State Power and Provincial Aristocracy in Languedoc* (Cambridge, 1985).

[13] See the contribution in this volume by Robert von Friedeburg on the case of Brittany as described by James Collins (see below at p.292).

Dialogue also existed with the agents of the Crown, the 'officers' whose number increased, especially as regards tax collectors. In 1515, there were approximately around 7,000 to 8,000 people working for the Crown, approximately one royal agent for 2,000 inhabitants. By 1559, that number had tripled, and, during the early personal reign of Louis XIV in 1661, there was one agent of the king for every 250 inhabitants of the kingdom. According to another evaluation, the king's servants represented 0.4 per cent of the population in 1515 and 3 per cent in 1665, so it had increased five- or six-fold.[14]

The Parlement of Paris, the highest court of law in the land, could lead resistance against royal decisions, as it did during the *Frondes*.[15] Although Louis XIV seemed to succeed in the control of 'sovereign courts', there were in fact always negotiations between servants of the king and the parliaments,[16] for example when passing the great decrees prepared by Colbert or for the dynastic renunciations at the end of the reign.

Dialogue was also necessary with the Church of France. The king himself took care of the *feuille des benefices* (or list of ecclesiastical benefices) personally, with assistance from his confessor, and he had the power to nominate persons to fill the offices of bishops and abbots. How this secret reflexion worked when it came to the main members of the church remains unclear, but it was an essential part of the king's power. Benefices were very important for noble lineages. Via these benefices, essentially allocated by the king, younger sons could enter the church, obtain religious and ecclesiastical authority, and enhance their family's reputation.[17] For his part, the king could rely on a hierarchy which corresponded to the social hierarchy. Bishops and abbots headed the complex organisation of curates and monks, themselves providing leadership for their flocks. The assemblies of the clergy, which took place every five years, were the framework of this

---

[14] Pierre Chaunu, *La Civilisation de l'Europe classique* (Paris, 1966); Pierre Chaunu and Richard Gascon, *Histoire économique et sociale de la France, I/1, 1450–1660. L'Etat et la ville* (Paris, 1977).

[15] A. Lloyd Moote, *The Revolt of the Judges. The Parlement of Paris and the Fronde, 1643–1652* (Princeton, NJ, 1971).

[16] Albert N. Hamscher, *The Parlement of Paris after the Fronde* (Pittsburgh, 1976); Hamscher, *The Conseil Privé and the Parlements in the Age of Louis XIV: A Study of French Absolutism* (Philadelphia, 1987); Hassen El Annabi, *Le Parlement de Paris sous le règne personnel de Louis XIV: l'institution, le pouvoir et la société* (Tunis, 1989); John J. Hurt, *Louis XIV and the Parlements: The Assertion of Royal Authority* (Manchester, 2002). See also about the parliament of Bordeaux, Caroline Le Mao, *Les fortunes de Thémis. Vie des magistrats du Parlement de Bordeaux au Grand Siècle* (Bordeaux, 2006).

[17] Joseph Bergin, *The Making of the French Episcopate 1589–1661* (New Haven and London, 1996); Bergin *Crown, Church and Episcopate under Louis XIV* (New Haven and London, 2004).

institutional dialogue.[18] An elaborate financial organisation collected the *don gratuit* (literally, the 'free gift'), which provided significant input into the royal coffers.[19]

Royal government was designed to show that the kingdom was well administered, with everybody obeying an authoritative king. In fact, the French monarchy was still an accumulation of provinces and *pays* (localities), companies and various *corps* or corporations, and various social and spiritual forces: the king's agents had to discuss matters with them, and the monarchy still needed the support of the lord on his estate and the curate in his parish. This system was able to integrate new provinces during the eighteenth century such as Artois, Roussillon, Flandres, Franche-Comté and Alsace.[20]

Louis XIV and His Court: The Distribution of Favours

In the reign of Louis XIV, the court provided the main, if not the only, scope for such discreet negotiations. Norbert Elias has shown how court society may have influenced the whole society,[21] but historians must also describe how society is represented in such a small community.

For most members of the nobility, attendance at court was used to access the king's favour.[22] A position at court provided a means of achieving an ambition to live close to the king and have opportunities to have access to the king.[23] For example, Polignac, who later became one of the negotiators of the Peace of Utrecht (1713), had wanted a position at court to pursue his career. Therefore, he agreed to become Master of the Chapel despite the fact that, at the time, he was already a cardinal. For this 'second' position, he should have taken an oath in the hands of the

---

[18] Pierre Blet, *Le clergé de France et la monarchie. Etude sur les Assemblées du clergé de 1615 à 1660* (Rome, 1959); Blet, *Les assemblées du clergé et Louis XIV de 1670 à 1693* (Rome, 1972); Blet, *Le clergé de France, Louis XIV et le Saint-Siège de 1695 à 1715* (Archivio vaticano, 1989); Blet, *Le clergé du Grand Siècle en ses assemblées, 1615–1715* (Paris, 1995).

[19] Claude Michaud, *L'Église et l'Argent sous l'Ancien Régime. Les receveurs généraux du clergé de France (XVIe-XVIIe siècle)* (Paris, Fayard), 1991.

[20] Marie-Laure Legay, *Les États provinciaux dans la construction de l'État moderne aux XVIIe et XVIIIe siècles* (Geneva, 2001).

[21] Jeroen Duindam, *Myths of Power: Norbert Elias and the Early Modern European Court* (Amsterdam, 1994); Daniel Gordon, *Citizens without Sovereignty: Equality and Sociability in French Thought, 1670–1789* (Princeton, NJ, 1994).

[22] Jean-François Solnon, *La Cour de France* (Paris, 1987); Emmanuel Le Roy Ladurie and Jean-François Fitou, *Saint-Simon ou le système de la Cour* (Paris, 1997); Jeroen Duindam, *Vienna and Versailles: The Courts of Europe's Dynastic Rivals, 1550–1780* (Cambridge, 2003).

[23] Leonhard Horowski: '"Such a great advantage for my son": Officeholding and Career Mechanisms at the Court of France, 1661–1789', *The Court Historian* 8, 2 (2003) 125–177.

grand maître. Instead, he took advantage of the grand maître's temporary absence from court to take the oath in the hands of the king himself.[24] For officers of the court, attendance was an obligation, part of their required service, and cases of negligence or failure were very quickly sanctioned. The Marquis of Courtenvaux, Louvois' son and Captain of the Cent-Suisses, was brutally stripped of his pavilion in Marly, for example, after being absent without leave.[25] In all cases, for officers or simple 'courtiers', the monarch seems to have been sensitive to attendance, and he had plenty of means at his disposal to reward it. The monarch could list the gentlemen in his service – to review the elite troops figuratively, as well as literally if one thinks of the military household[26] and of the importance of 'reviews' until the end of the king's life. The king thus had the opportunity to get to know the top echelons – the 'elite' to use a modern word – of French society very well.

Presence at court provided opportunities to find out in time about vacancies in bishoprics, abbeys, governorships and even embassies. It also left time to apply for the position in question, using appropriate channels to reach ministers and confidants, or even the king's confessor, especially since the court incorporated the servants of the state, ministers and secretaries of state working with the king. Their place remained marginal, because often, in the days of Louis XIV, they were not members of ancient noble families. For example, in 1707 the king became very angry with the Marquise of Torcy, wife of the Secretary of State (a member of the Colbert Dynasty), because, by mistake, she was placed before a titled lady and occupied a more honourable place.[27] If osmosis was therefore relative between nobility and families in the service of the king, the contacts that could be developed at court were nevertheless very useful for the courtiers, as is evident from the friendship of Saint-Simon with ministers. Advantageous marital connections for the sons and daughters of ministers completed their integration.

Records of the *bienfaits du roi* (the king's graces and favours), which are kept at the Bibliothèque nationale de France, summarise the many individual decisions taken by the king in terms of distributing favours. For example, in January 1696, he bestowed an ecclesiastical benefice on Noailles, the Bishop of Chalons, and on a monastery at the request of the

---

[24] Louis, duc de Saint-Simon, *Mémoires*, Arthur de Boislisle (ed.) (Paris, 1879–1828), XXIII, p. 407–408.

[25] Ibid., XXVI, p. 244–245.

[26] Jean Chagniot, 'Le régiment des gardes du roi d'après les rôles de montres conservés à la Bibliothèque nationale de France (1584–1643)', in Bernard Barbiche and Yves-Marie Bercé (eds.), *Etudes sur l'ancienne France offertes en hommage à Michel Antoine* (Paris, 2003), pp. 101–114.

[27] Ibid., XV, pp. 243–251.

Duke of Orleans, who had it in his prerogative. He also permitted an exchange between a vicarage and a priory. He accepted an Italian duke as a knight of his orders. He gave the position of *lecteur du roi*; he confirmed the situation of the captain of the Fontainebleau Castle; he gave a duchy to the son of the Marshal-Duke of Luxembourg. In the same way, as it was wartime, he appointed a large number of general officers (17 *lieutenants généraux*, 43 *maréchaux de camp*, 35 *brigadiers de cavalerie*, 35 *brigadiers d'infanterie*). He appointed a surveyor general of the navy, an intendant of the navy in Dunkirk, four captains of the guards who could then purchase regiments, and he appointed naval captains. He allocated 50 warships to *lieutenant général* Château-Renaut and gave Renau d'Eliçagaray, called 'Petit Renau', a few vessels for America. He also had to appoint various officers for the army in Italy. The monarch distributed three governorships. He named his friend Dangeau as *conseiller d'État d'épée*, appointed an intendant for the county of Nice and named one *commissaire général* for Lorient. He added an annuity for the Cardinal of Arquien, father of the queen of Poland, and made a gift of a diamond cross for the wife of the ambassador of Venice.[28] Of course, ministers and their clerks prepared the decisions, but the last word came from Louis XIV. A courtier was in a better position to apply for a job or a promotion for himself, a relative, a client or even a vague acquaintance. In turn, the successful courtier who had secured an appointment for a client could himself expect some reward in return.

For the traditional elites, it became necessary to have an access to this favour in order to maintain the financial and social situation of their families. As monarchy transformed and the distribution of favours increased, simply staying in the province and administrating one's estates proved insufficient even in order to only defend one's position relative to other families, let alone to improving prestige and resources. The king's favour was the major avenue for finding new opportunities in the armies, in the church or in the embassies. Some new elites were also created by the royal administration and by the financial operations of the monarchy. They also needed some access to the circles of the royal court, even to the secondary ones, to help their social ascension and their affairs.

Change in the Nature of Networks

From the sixteenth to the seventeenth century, this transformation in the relation of the Crown and elites was accompanied by a change from

---

[28] Bibliothèque nationale de France, Manuscrits Français 7662 Bienfaits du roi de l'année 1696. Manuscrit de Louis de Courcillon, abbé de Dangeau. See Irène de Vulpian, 'Les Bienfaits du roi. Le système des nominations royales d'après le journal de l'abbé de Dangeau', mémoire de maîtrise de l'Université Paris-Sorbonne, 2004–2005.

networks based on friendship to networks based on the centralised clienteles that increasingly characterised relations between the provinces and the court in France.[29] The court had changed. When the king's favourites had centralised the granting of favours, gentlemen became afraid of being excluded from the distribution of such favours, offices and other opportunities. Louis XIV rejected the idea of favourites and reclaimed for himself the whole distribution process. In fact, he knew how to master the distribution of his favours and to legitimate this practice. The great nobles, far from simply being subjected to absolutist kingship, found compensation for the increasing need to juggle for the king's favours in the new importance they themselves received in turn as intermediaries between the king and the provinces. Aristocrats with access to king and court were supposed to develop links with their provincial estates; they could recommend men and build their own network of clients. Their power could be useful in protecting vassals or peasants from the demands of the Crown by using their influence. In any case, the court itself was the place of negotiations between the king, his ministers and his government on the one hand, and the nobles and elites on the other.

The court was also the setting for the ever more important financial negotiations. Some *donneurs d'avis* managed to find influential courtiers to present their financial projects to members of the government, guaranteeing a percentage in case of success. More generally, the financial system of the monarchy depended on the elites in its broadest meaning – not just the princes of royal blood and the aristocracy, but also the lower nobility and the bourgeoisie. They all lent money to the king through the *financiers*; all their contributions proved necessary to keep royal finances afloat, and they were reimbursed through the taxation of the whole population.[30]

While the need for contacts among the elites thus rather grew, not least with respect to the ever increasing financial hunger of the Crown to finance its wars, it was by no means easy to create links between the broader spectre of social elites on the one hand and the much more narrow elite aristocracy, let alone the princes of the blood. For example, the latter wanted to contract marriages only within their own small world, to keep their royal blood pure.[31]

---

[29] Arlette Jouanna has studied very deeply this change in her works.
[30] Daniel Dessert, *Argent, Pouvoir et Société au Grand Siècle* (Paris, 1984); Françoise Bayard, *Le Monde des financiers au XVIIe siècle* (Paris, 1988). See also, Katia Béguin, *Financer la guerre au XVIIe siècle. La dette publique et les rentiers de l'absolutisme* (Seyssel, 2012).
[31] Lucien Bély, *La Société des princes*; See also, Bartolomé Bennassar, *Le lit, le pouvoir et la mort. Reines et princesses d'Europe de la Renaissance aux Lumières* (Paris, 2006); Isabelle Poutrin and Marie-Karine Schaub, *Femmes et pouvoir politique. Les princesses d'Europe, XVe-XVIIIe siècle* (Paris, 2007). Among recent studies, see Loïc Bienassis,

The French experience of 'foreign princes' was an attempt to create intermediate levels at court, but it was not a success.[32] These lineages came from reigning houses in Europe, possessed several duchies in France and held a rank that placed them between the princes of the blood and duke-peers.[33] Jonathan Spangler, who focuses primarily on the princes of the House of Lorraine, shows that, if the Guises are well known for their part in the Wars of Religion, the presence of multiple branches of the House of Lorraine has been neglected by historians even though they still had a prominent place during the seventeenth century. For Spangler, the question is whether there was solidarity between members of these branches, as suggested by some authors of the time. Their roots were based on recent history, through the power of the Guises at the court of the last Valois, but also on a legendary history of the House of Lorraine, in particular with the idea of a Carolingian origin. Spangler examined the fate of the different branches of the House of Lorraine, describing the extinction of the lineage of Guise, the decline of the Elbeuf family and the rise of the Armagnac and Marsan lines. In the course of his analysis, he described the development of the 'dynastic identity' of the various branches and of the house itself.

The Lorraines held a central place among the nobility, with two prominent figures: the count of Armagnac, who dominated the entire house from the 1680s onwards, and the Chevalier of Lorraine, a lover of Monsieur, the king's brother. Spangler goes one step further by studying the matrimonial strategies, the marriage contracts and the status of widows. These foreign princes were kept at a distance by the princes of the blood with two exceptions – the Duke of Guise married an Orleans princess and Duke Leopold of Lorraine married the niece of Louis XIV (but he was a sovereign prince). By investigating these developments, Spangler provided an original study of the involvement of Lorraine-Guise in the endless litigation that characterised pre-Revolutionary society. Margaret Chabot, Duchess of Elbeuf, for example, spent fifty years of her life in legal disputes to double her fortune.

'Le mariage franco-anglais: politique étrangère et rivalités de cour (1624–1625)', *Revue d'histoire diplomatique* (2006), pp. 205–226; Géraud Poumarède, 'Mazarin, marieur de l'Europe. Stratégies familiales, enjeux dynastiques et géopolitique au milieu du XVIIe siècle', *XVIIe siècle, 243*, 61ᵉ année (2009), pp. 201–218; Anna Blum, 'Un mariage manqué: la Grande Mademoiselle et le duc Charles-Emmanuel II de Savoie', *Revue d'histoire diplomatique* (2009), pp. 255–277.

[32] Jonathan Spangler, *The Society of Princes: The Lorraine-Guise and the Conservation of Power and Wealth in Seventeenth-Century France* (Farnham, 2009).

[33] On the duke-peers: Jean-Pierre Labatut, *Les ducs et pairs en France au XVIIe siècle* (Paris, 1972); Labatut, *Noblesse, pouvoir et société en France au XVIIe siècle* (Limoges, 1987).

The Lorraines remained bound to the House of Lorraine, but they did not access the small world of sovereigns. They represented a stratum of French nobility. They were fully part of this nobility, but the Lorraine-Guise lineage was not part of the society of princes. We can find, nevertheless, other examples which could be seen as successes in terms of straddling different camps among the elite. Marie-Jeanne-Baptiste of Savoy belonged to the Nemours branch, *princes étrangers* living in France. By marriage, she became Duchess of Savoy. When a widow, she governed in Turin for the young Victor-Amadeus and kept Savoy and Piedmont in the wake of France. Her sister, Marie-Françoise-Elisabeth, married first King Alphonse VI of Portugal and so played a prominent part in the revolution in 1667: the brother of the sovereign became prince regent, and the king was exiled in the Azores. The marriage of Alphonse was annulled, and the queen married her brother-in-law, the future Peter II.[34] There was also an attempt during Louis XIV's reign when the king decided to legitimate his illegitimate offspring. These children were born of love affairs with some women of the nobility, the Duchess of La Vallière and the Marquise of Montespan. The king also decided to organise the marriage of royal princes and princesses with those legitimated ones and further to admit his legitimated sons as his possible successors after all the princes of the blood. This revolution showed the royal will to discard all succession problems, but it showed also that the king used his absolute power to create some new princes of the blood against all the rules of the church and of society. After his death, these decisions were, however, not followed.

Some court functions created a special position within the entourage of princes from which it was possible to get influence and power. Princess Orsini was a preeminent figure at the court of Philip V of Spain as *camarera mayor* to the queen, and she served as a vital link between the courts of France and Spain. Marie-Anne de la Trémoïlle, born in 1642, who came from a great family in her own right, was the widow of a member of the Talleyrand-Périgord family. She took refuge in Rome, was admired by the Cardinals and married Flavio Orsini, Duke of Bracciano. When the surname was transformed into a French term, she became the *Princesse des Ursins*. She knew how to be helpful to French

---

[34] The two sisters planned the marriage of the Infanta of Portugal with Victor-Amedeus, but it failed. The sisters acted in that case more as Savoyard princesses than as French ones. See Toby Osborne, '"Notre grand dessein": O projecto de casamento entre o Duque Victor Amadeu e a Infanta Isabel Luisa e a politica dinastica dos Saboia (1675–82)', in M. Antonia Lopes and B. Alice Raviola (eds.), *Portugal e o Piemonte: a casa real portuguesa e os Sabóias. Nove séculos de relações dinásticas e destinos políticos (XII-XX)* (Coimbra, 2012), pp. 211–238.

interests in Rome, and that brought her close to Madame de Maintenon. As a result she was appointed to train and advise the new queen of Spain: she took with her knowledge of European courts and the international networks of modern Europe, her regular contacts with princes and cardinals and complete mastery of the rules of ritual with a view – and mission – to give more flexibility to a Spanish court that was considered too formal and stuffy. She also had long experience of life, excellent writing skills and real political intelligence. She maintained essential correspondence with Madame de Maintenon, and especially with Torcy. Until her downfall in 1714, she imposed not her political views (this was not part of her duties), but a form of relationship between two princes: a dynastic solidarity that recognised the differences and disputes between the two countries and sought to blur them. The presence of a Bourbon in Madrid created a unique relationship, but it resembled the earlier relationship between the branches of the House of Habsburg.[35] The role of the princess depended on the court, and she gained influence by following the example of the Marquise of Maintenon who knew how to further her plans in a roundabout manner. The path was discreet, informal and mysterious, quite the contrary of all that was official and public. Yet the monarchy needed this element of secrecy and its state secrets, and the fact that women were in charge of it is quite revealing in itself.[36]

By occupying positions at court, it became possible for members to approach the princes of the royal family, especially the future king and queen, thereby paving the way for interesting future career opportunities. Competition among elites for these opportunities proved fierce when it came to appointments, especially the establishment of 'households', a significant step up in administrative terms. During the creation of a princess's household, for example, activities reached fever pitch at court, as reported by Saint-Simon on the arrival of the Duchess of Burgundy in 1696:

Sa Maison fut plus longtemps à être déterminée. La Cour était depuis longtemps sans reine et sans dauphine : toutes les dames d'une certaine portée d'état ou de faveur s'empressèrent et briguèrent, et beaucoup aux dépens les unes des autres; les lettres anonymes mouchèrent, les délations, les faux rapports. Tout se passa

---

[35] In the eighteenth century, a Bourbon Europe gradually emerged in Versailles, Madrid, Naples and Parma, recreating and installing, in another area around the western Mediterranean Sea, the links that had existed in Habsburg Europe.

[36] Lucien Bély, 'La présence et l'action des ambassadeurs de France dans le gouvernement de Philippe V d'Espagne: conduite de la guerre et négociation de la paix', *L'Espagne et ses guerres*, under the direction of Annie Molinié and Alexandra Merle (Paris, 2004), pp. 183–201; Molinié and Merle, 'Élisabeth Farnèse et la princesse des Ursins: un coup de majesté?', *Elisabetta Farnese, principessa di Parma e regina di Spagna* (Rome, 2009), pp. 71–89.

uniquement là-dessus entre le roi et Mme de Maintenon qui ne bougeait du chevet de son lit pendant toute sa maladie, excepté lorsqu'il se faisait voir, et qui y était la plupart du temps seule. Elle avait résolu d'être la véritable gouvernante de la Princesse, de l'élever à son gré et à son point, de se l'attacher en même temps assez pour en pouvoir amuser le Roi sans crainte qu'après le temps de poupée passé, elle lui pût devenir dangereuse.[37]

The Duchess of Burgundy would have one *chevalier d'honneur*, the Marquis of Dangeau, a friend of Louis XIV; one *dame d'honneur*, the Duchess of Lude, whom Saint-Simon accused of having bribed a servant of Madame de Maintenon; one *dame d'atours*, the Countess de Mailly; and a *premier écuyer*, Tessé, who had negotiated the marriage. Six *dames du palais* completed this first group, which also included a first maid, a confessor, a first chaplain (Bossuet) and a first butler. This select group of men and women were to serve, advise and guide a princess in a country which was foreign to her: on her success also depended their wealth, and this ambition was evident behind the fierce competition at court.

The nomination of the governor and the tutor of a young king or a dauphin was also quite important. We can think of men such as Bossuet for Louis XIV's son and Fénelon for his grandson. Families tried to retain and defend such positions. Thus, the court was characterised by the long-term presence of the same lineages occupying the same positions: a Condé as *grands maître*, a Bouillon as *grand chambellan* and a Lorraine as *grands écuyer*. For the office of governor and governess of the Children of France, there was the same concern to keep the job in the same family, which also then held a place in the heart of the king and of his family and fulfilled the same role. Madame de Lansac, daughter of Souvré, governor of Louis XIII, was appointed *gouvernante* in 1638. She had to resign upon the death of the king, but her granddaughter, the Marshal of la Motte-Houdancourt's wife, became governess in 1664. In 1704, Louis XIV chose the Duchess of Ventadour, her daughter, to assist and succeed her. And the position was retained into the eighteenth century, passed down from mother to daughter, grandmother to grand-daughter, aunt to niece. Saint-Simon, who had seen some examples of these long chains of family members holding a certain position, wrote: 'Ainsi le maréchal de Souvré, Mme de Lansac, la maréchale de la Motte, la duchesse de Ventadour, et les deux belles-soeurs, petites-filles de celle-ci, font cinq générations de gouverneurs et gouvernantes des enfants de France, dont trois rois et plusieurs dauphins'.[38] Madame de la Motte and her daughter raised twenty-three Children of France.

---

[37] Saint-Simon, *Mémoires*, III, pp. 157–158.   [38] Ibid., XVII, p. 12.

Ambassadors were concerned with the personal affairs of the princes. They negotiated marriages. They could even laugh about the strange arrangements. One such ambassador was Abel Servien, amused in 1647 about the idea of a marriage between Maria-Theresa of Spain and Louis XIV, who were twelve years old : 'Il est vray qu'il fut parlé des chiens de chasse, sur ce que je dis, en riant, que nos maistres estoient desjà assez proches parens et que les chasseurs observoient, pour avoir des chiens vigoureux, de mesler des races différentes'.[39] Diplomats had to keep a watchful eye on the young princes and princesses to discern their good qualities, their health and their appearance. Sometimes, an ambassador represented the husband in a wedding by proxy. It is commonly asserted that the only case of a woman acting as an ambassador and obtaining for herself the title of 'ambassadrice' is the Marshal of Guébriand's widow, who accompanied the new queen of Poland, Maria Gonzaga, to her new kingdom in 1646.[40] Her mission was noteworthy because a princess should have been chosen to travel with a queen. A princess, however, would not have received this title, having a rank too high for it.

Some of the prelates belonged to the court whether or not they had official titles. They acted as the king's advisors in important theological issues such as the disputes over Jansenism or Quietism. Bishops were rarely employed in foreign countries. Cardinals and abbots still travelled abroad as ambassadors and so participated in royal affairs. In fact, embassies were the way for churchmen to approach the society of princes and influence it by negotiating royal weddings and joint actions in Roman Catholic Europe.[41]

Cardinal d'Estrées represented Louis XIV in Rome and afterwards in Madrid in the reign of Philip V. The French ambassador provided a link between the grandfather and the grandson, an ambassador of the house. It had worked well in the Habsburg dominions, but this time it was not a success, and Abbot Jean d'Estrées, his nephew, took over from him for a short time. The two men had to counter the action of Princess Orsini, and they were unable to win over the royal couple of Spain.

Abbot Melchior of Polignac, ambassador in Poland, had a good, strong relationship with John Sobieski and his French wife Marie-Casimire, and after Sobieski's death, he supported the Prince of Conti's candidacy as King of Poland. His significant financial promises allowed for the election

---

[39] *Acta Pacis Westphalicae, II B, Die Französichen Korrespondenzen*, 5/1, Guido Braun (ed.), Münster, Aschendorff (2002), n° 78, Servien à Lionne, 21 janvier 1647, pp. 390–391.

[40] Bély, *L'Art de la paix en Europe. Naissance de la diplomatie moderne, XVIe-XVIIIe siècle* (Paris, 2007), pp. 213–224.

[41] About the *cardinaux protecteurs*, see Olivier Poncet, *La France et le pouvoir pontifical (1595–1661). L'esprit des institutions* (Rome, 2011).

of the French prince, but the Elector of Saxony imposed himself as sovereign and Conti came back to France. Polignac was forced to retire to his abbey of Bonport in Normandy as a punishment.[42]

Conclusion

The links between the broad spectre of social elites and the upper elite of France's aristocracy, in particular the society of princes and the princes of the blood, remained rather thin: the latter remained a family of kings who wanted to preserve the purity of their blood line. By and large, the bulk of the French nobility had no international networks. Only prelates could intervene in Roman Catholic countries. Merchants and bankers belonged to classes which were not given access to the secret affairs of the Crown, to 'matters of state'. Apart from the small group of ambassadors, there were very few social actors upholding political dialogue throughout Europe in a context of frequent wars. This is why it is important to study this world of diplomats as intermediaries between sovereigns and European societies.[43]

For the higher French nobility, the king himself remained at the focus of interest: Since royal service was often onerous, the high nobility expected to be reimbursed for expenses made, for example, in the armies or in the embassies. The king was expected to be generous to those who served him faithfully and who were present near him. The circumstances of obtaining royal generosity, however, had changed, both in terms of the nature of contact and the amount of offices and opportunities to be dispersed.

Crucially, obtaining offices, government positions or other favourable financial opportunities had become, if anything, more important to defend and consolidate a family's prestige and fortune, and in order to obtain these favours, access to the king and to central government had become more vital than it was ever before. The king and elites had become more regularly dependent on each other: As stressed above, the

---

[42] Lucien Bély, *La diplomatie et les compromis dans l'Europe centrale et orientale* (Viterbo, 2002), pp. 11–28.

[43] Bély, *Espions et ambassadeurs au temps de Louis XIV* (Paris, 1990) and also recently Lucien Bély and Géraud Poumarède, *L'Incident diplomatique, XVIe-XVIIIe siècle* (Paris, 2010). About this field of research see Lucien Bély, 'Les relations internationales des Temps modernes: essai de bilan historiographique pour la France', 'Les relations inter-nationales' (with Georges-Henri Soutou), *Les Historiens français à l'œuvre, 1995–2010*, Jean-François Sirinelli, Pascal Cauchy, Claude Gauvard (eds.) (Paris, 2010), pp. 261–275; Bély, 'Histoire de la diplomatie et des relations internationales des Temps modernes: un état de la recherche en France', *Sulla diplomazia in età moderna. Politica, economia, religione*, Renzo Sabbatini and Paola Volpini (eds.) (Milan, 2011), pp. 19–34.

financial system of the transformed monarchy depended ever more on the elites at large – aristocracy, lower nobility, bourgeoisie – to fund its foreign politics. These elites needed to lend money to the king through the 'financiers' and were reimbursed through the taxation of the whole population. But to obtain the major profitable offices or to get access to profitable financial transactions and to get direct access to the court and the king was key. Against this background, key advisors received a fundamentally new and problematic role.

The experience of 'First Ministers' such as Richelieu and Mazarin had been very problematic. Many appointments depended on them. Simultaneously, once there was such a chief counsellor, he tried to fortify his own situation by gathering for himself a large wealth as well as abbeys, duchies or provincial governments. Clients of the advisor profited as well. This led to considerable frictions with the elites.[44] With Louis XIV's reform in 1661, all the main appointments were dependent on him and of course of his ministers and counsellors. The French Court offered goods as a way to enter into financial affairs or to obtain a rich marriage. Such paths did not exist for the provincial and lower nobility, who had no access to the court. The later claim of Colbert, that Louis' personal rule was precisely what the elites had actually demanded, was not entirely mistaken. Though the legitimacy of Louis' personal rule, not least based on the avoidance of the criticism against the distribution of favours by First Ministers, had little to do with the establishment of an absolutist state in the older sense of the term, it was not least a reaction to the demands of the larger kingdom of France of distributing favours and keeping contact between monarchy and elites.

The aristocracy who could have access to the king had also deep roots in the provinces. Often, the petty nobility acted as clients of the aristocratic families. Colonels or captains, of noble origin, recruited friends and vassals to serve with them in the royal army. But in fact and over time, more and more, the leading aristocrats and courtiers lived in Versailles, in Paris or in the main towns. For given the fact that the Estates General did not meet again, the Royal Court did become the most important and perhaps the only place where the elites could negotiate with the king and his ministers, to obtain a regiment, an embassy, the government of a province or of a fortified place, and of course an office in the court itself. The king could facilitate some marriages between the highest and oldest nobility and the rich new one: the three Colbert daughters married three dukes. As such offices and opportunities and the incomes depending on

---

[44] See the contribution by Robert von Friedeburg in Chapter 11 of this volume (See particularly below, pp. 292–7).

them became ever more important in the framework of the transformed monarchy, the ability to access them at court remained vital. It separated the elite aristocracy, which profited from such opportunities, even more from the lesser nobility in the provinces, who did not.

The gap between this elite aristocracy (and their way of life) and the lower nobility who lived like wealthy farmers, if anything, widened. For the lesser nobility, even military service could become a problem, for they might lack even the resources to participate in the wars; military service rather became a burden on their shoulders.

The monarchy tried to create new links with the provinces. The intendants became administrators with a large scope of competence: they were the eyes and the ears of the king in the kingdom. They helped the government to be aware of the provincial realities. The royal power asked also the main towns to send deputies to the court – *deputés de commerce* – to defend the local and regional interests and to help government to define a coherent political line for international commerce. The whole monarchy tried to gather information from the provinces as well as from the foreign countries. The ministers, since Colbert's time, organised new archives, especially for foreign affairs and war.[45] The French court was also a main piece in the network of European courts where more and more the same way of life, the same customs, the same garments and the same wigs can been seen. Of course war was still very present in Europe. Nevertheless, the European society of princes adopted similar ways of living. and those convergences helped to prepare negotiations during wartime. That set them even more apart from the broader lesser nobility.

---

[45] Jacob Soll, *The Information Master: Jean-Baptiste Colbert's Secret State Intelligence System* (Ann Arbor, 2009).

Part II

Elites, Rhetoric and Monarchy

7 The King and the Family: Primogeniture and the Lombard Nobility in the Spanish Monarchy

Antonio Álvarez-Ossorio Alvariño

Profound changes took place in the relationship between the sovereign and the elites of Milan, when it became part of Charles V's empire and subsequently a part of the monarchy of Philip II.[1] The War of Flanders and Spanish involvement in the Religious Wars in France forced the monarch to find new sources of income to finance the Army, including the sale of titles of nobility. At the beginning of the seventeenth century, Philip III imposed a transformation in the system of succession of these noble titles among the Lombard families. Instead of the father's title passing to all his sons, which was the custom in the empire, the system changed to one of male primogeniture, as in Castile and in the Spanish kingdoms. This change initiated prolonged negotiation and conflict between the Court of Madrid, where the Spanish king held the title of Duke of Milan, and the Lombard elites.

The Monarchy of the Twenty-Two Kingdoms

The Countess of Aulnoy wrote in her *Relation du Voyage d'Espagne*, published in 1691, that in 1679 everywhere she went, whenever the Catholic King's courtiers spoke of the new queen, Marie Louise of Orleans, they boasted: *'qu'elle va être Reine de vingt-deux Royaumes'*.[2] That glittering array of sceptred realms, however, was actually quite heterogeneous, embracing honorific kingdoms like Jerusalem, and others

This study was undertaken as part of the project 'Sociedad cortesana y redes diplomáticas: la proyección europea de la monarquía de España', ref. HAR2015-67069-P, financed by the Dirección General de Investigación del Ministerio de Economía y Competitividad-FEDER, UE.
[1] This study uses the term 'Milan', to refer to the territories which, in the sixteenth and seventeenth centuries, included the Duchy of Milan, the Principality of Pavia and the counties of Cremona, Lodi, Novara, Como, Alessandria, Tortona and the Marquisate of Vigevano. Milan formed part of the Holy Roman Empire.
[2] *Relation du Voyage d'Espagne*, ed. La Haye (Paris, 1705), t. III, p. 187.

that lacked institutional strength, such as some forming part of the Crown of Castile. There were even a number of politico-legal networks with their own courts and parliaments, like Aragon, Valencia, Sardinia, Navarre, Sicily and Naples. Such an accumulation of crowns was quite unusual in seventeenth-century Europe, where very few territories, in fact, were recognized as kingdoms. Within the confines of the Holy Roman Empire, the Germanic princes frequently tried, without success, to acquire a kingly title to bolster their claims to power and reputation. Something similar also happened in northern Italy where, under the jurisdiction of the empire, Spain or the pope, princes and republics competed for the title of king, implying as it did ceremonial precedence and strategic projection.[3]

During the sixteenth and seventeenth centuries, the Spanish monarchy added numerous kingdoms and dominions to its European and overseas territories. In its European dimension, the monarchy brought together a variety of kingdoms: the Crowns of Aragon, Castile, Portugal, Navarre, the kingdom of Naples and Sicily, the State of Milan and the royal Low Countries or Spanish Netherlands, as well as various garrison towns in the western Mediterranean. The sovereign's powers were different in each territory. To some extent, relations between the prince and each dominion were dependent on both the formula used to integrate the kingdom into the monarchy and the legal and historical discourses and readings that paved the way for that integration, which on occasions involved conflict.[4] 'Inheritance', 'pact' and 'conquest' were not clearly separated categories which determined how much absolute authority would be exercised in territorial government, but were often used in various combinations in the dynamic process of interaction between the dynasty and each territory.[5]

In what way was the shaping of the political society of a European territory altered by belonging to the Spanish monarchy? Was the Catholic King able to modify the family structure of the provincial elites? It is from this perspective that we propose to approach the

---

[3] For the importance of the royal title in the north of Italy, see Daniella Frigo, *Principi, ambasciatori e 'jus gentium'. L'amministrazione della politica estera nel Piemonte del Settecento* (Rome, 1991), pp. 269–281.

[4] With regard to the processes of integration of the kingdoms in the monarchy, see the comparative studies brought together in Alfredo Floristán Imízcoz (ed.), *1512. Conquista e incorporación de Navarra* (Barcelona, 2012).

[5] Jon Arrieta Alberdi, 'Las formas de vinculación a la Monarquía y de relación entre sus reinos y coronas en la España de los Austrias', in A. Álvarez-Ossorio Alvariño and B. J. García García (eds.), *La monarquía de las naciones. Patria, nación y naturaleza en la monarquía de España* (Madrid, 2004), pp. 303–326.

relations, in times of peace and war, between the king of Spain and the nobility of the State of Milan from the mid-sixteenth century until the first third of the seventeenth, as the Crowns of Spain and France strove for European hegemony.

During the first half of the sixteenth century, the main kingdoms of Europe were involved in the different phases of the wars in Italy. The presence of French and Spanish soldiers, ministers and diplomats in the Italian peninsula, as well as their interactions with the oligarchies of each principality or territory, opened up a new period that shaped the social identity of Mediterranean Europe. The experience of the aggregation of the State of Milan, first by the kingdom of France and then by the empire of Charles V, was one reason for the influx of *barbarian* or Transalpine nobles into the cities and courts of northern Italy. The European dimension of Charles V's empire involved an intense process of mutual recognition of local hierarchies within a universal space. As the dynamics of ennoblement spread across Europe, so there was a corresponding need to move beyond the distinctions of ranks and honours recognized in microspaces to compare them on a wider scale against similar titles and honours in the great European monarchies.[6]

The integration of Milan into Charles V's empire and, from 1555 onwards, its absorption into the Spanish monarchy ruled by Philip II created a twofold dynamic. On the one hand, the oligarchies of the main cities in Lombardy organized a reserved space, known as the patrician system, to protect themselves against the new families and the interference of the absent sovereign. On the other hand, these same patrician families and the newcomers needed attributes of distinction that were recognized both inside and outside the borders of the *Stato*.

The Sale of Noble Titles in the Time of Philip II

The elites of the city of Milan made sure that they secured control of the city's administration and certain strategic corporations, such as the college of noble jurisconsults, by means of a variety of restrictive measures between 1541 and 1586. These mechanisms, the preserve of the oligarchy, made it difficult for families who had not been resident in the city for three generations beforehand, or had been engaged in occupations

---

[6] On the significance of the distribution of ranks and honours in the interaction between Italian princes and the Spanish monarchy, such as the accolade of the Golden Fleece, grandeeships of Spain and titles, see Angelantonio Spagnoletti, *Principi italiani e Spagna nell'età barocca* (Milan, 1996), pp. 51–127.

considered undignified, to enter the patriciate.[7] As a result, Philip II could not include newly rich Spaniards or Lombards in the Milanese patriciate.

In parallel with the process in which the patriciate tended to close ranks against the newcomers in the main cities of the State of Milan, there was a growing practice in Lombard society of competing for titles of nobility as a way of accrediting family honour, both inside and outside Milan. During the reign of Philip II the titles of marquis and count became the blazon of glory of a lineage. The nobility of the kingdom of Castile underwent a similar process between the second half of the fifteenth century and the sixteenth century, when it shifted from a system based on the public recognition of the honour and power of each lineage to a hierarchy that depended on titles granted by the sovereign. By means of noble titles, the King of Spain – who was also the Duke of Milan – assumed the role of arbiter of honour and kept the balance of pre-eminence in the social arena. To adopt a metaphor used by the writers of political treatises, the monarch was a 'potter prince', able to mould the rank of his subjects.[8]

In contrast to the small number of nobles created in Milan by the Dukes Visconti and Sforza, and even the Emperor Charles V, the second half of the sixteenth century and the seventeenth century saw a gradual and steady increase in the families who received a noble title from the king of Spain. The mechanism for granting a title of nobility in Milan usually began with the intervention of the *Magistrato Straordinario* or Extraordinary Court, a Lombard court entrusted with managing the fiefs and revenues that devolved to the Chamber in the case there was no successor. This same court also administered patrimonial assets, confiscations and monetary penalties, the concession of licences to export cereals and for the care of waters in the public domain, and those of the *navigli*, or canals.[9]

---

[7] For the patrician system see Cesare Mozzarelli, 'Struttura sociali e formazioni statuali a Milano e Napoli tra '500 e '70', *Società e storia*, 3 (1978), pp. 431–463. See also Giulio Vismara, 'Le istituzioni del patriziato', in *Storia di Milano, tome XI* (Milan, 1958), pp. 225–282; and Elena Brambilla, *Il 'sistema letterario' di Milano: professioni nobili e professioni borghesi dall'età spagnola alle riforme teresiane*, in G. Barbarisi et al. (eds.), *Economia, istituzioni, cultura in Lombardia nell'età di Maria Teresa*, vol. III (Bologna, 1982), pp. 79–160.

[8] For the image of the potter King, see my study 'El Favor Real: liberalidad del príncipe y jerarquía de la república (1665–1700)', in Chiara Continisio and Cesare Mozzarelli (eds.), *Repubblica e Virtù. Pensiero politico e Monarchia Cattolica fra XVI e XVII Secolo* (Rome, 1995), pp. 393–453.

[9] The activity of the Extraordinary Court is analysed in Marco Ostoni, 'Prassi amministrativa e abusi del Magistrato Straordinario nella visita di Don Felipe de Haro (1606–1612)', *Studi e fonti di storia lombarda. Quaderni milanesi*, 33–34 (1993), pp. 5–42. A detailed list of the competences of the Extraordinary Court is found in Giuseppe Benaglio, *Relazione istorica del Magistrato delle Ducali Entrate Straordinarie* (Milan, 1711), pp. 205–235.

The noble titles had to have a feudal 'support', requiring a candidate for a title to possess or acquire a fief of particular characteristics in terms of its value and the number of dwellings or people who lived on it.[10] Auctioning feudal revenues and fiefs was a common practice from the mid-sixteenth century onwards. The sale of honours in Lombardy was based on the close link between fief and title, and hence between the market in the sale of fiefs organized by the Extraordinary Court and the granting of titles. Examples of this process are the clarifications concerning the value and qualities of a list of fiefs that the president of the Council of Italy, Count of Miranda, requested of the Governor of the State of Milan, the Constable of Castile, in 1599. On the list of lands and fiefs that the Extraordinary Court could sell in aid of the Exchequer, was 'the land of Mortara, and Voghera with their jurisdictions and revenues, with the title of Marquis', and with the title of Count 'the land of Mandrino, Annone, Monte Acuto, Mondondone, Loino, Brignano, Conturbia and Mazenta with their jurisdictions and revenues', as well as other fiefs without titles.[11]

In addition to the Extraordinary Court, the Governor of Milan, the most important figure in the government of Lombardy, also played a significant role in the concession of titles of nobility. On the one hand, he was the institutional figure who oversaw the functioning of the main tribunals, such as the Senate and the Ordinary and Extraordinary Courts; on the other, the governor had, on particular occasions, extraordinary powers to sell fiefs with titles. As well as the sales processes in Milan, it should be borne in mind that the Madrid court could also be involved. The concession of noble titles was a regalian right that could be exercised, not only by the king's representatives and ministers in Milan, but also under the supervision of the Council of Italy in Madrid. Thus, in December 1599, the king, through the Council of Italy, sought explanations from the Constable of Castile about the sale of fiefs, with and without titles attached. The Council of Italy's aim was to increase its control over the sale of fiefs with titles, and stipulated that Madrid should

---

[10] Katia Visconti, 'Feudo e società nel contado milanese tra sei e settecento', *Annali di storia moderna e contemporánea*, 9 (2003), pp. 193–263. The feudal lord acquired the right to receive regalian rights such as the *dacios* [tax] on wine, meat, bread, possible fishing and water rights, and milling and baking privileges. The jurisdictional powers of 'merum et mixtum imperium ac potestas gladii' were very limited because of the competences of the Senate and the tribunals. The feudatories could appoint a feudal praetor for the administration of justice. Giovanni Muto compares the restrictive measures of the feudal jurisdiction adopted in the State of Milan in the mid-fifteenth century with the strengthening of the barons' jurisdiction in the kingdom of Naples in the same period. G. Muto, 'Problemi di stratificazione nobiliare nell'Italia spagnola', in E. Chiosi (ed.), *Dimenticare Croce? Studi e orientamenti di storia del Mezzogiorno* (Naples, 1992), pp. 81 and 93.

[11] Archivio di Stato di Milano (henceforth, ASMi), Feudi Camerali parte antica (henceforth, p.a.), cart. 2.

henceforth be kept informed about the auctions of these fiefs, the bids and the qualities of the possible purchasers. The Lombard tribunal resisted this attempt, alleging that the process would be excessively protracted, causing the bids to be reduced. At the same time, the Grand Chancellor and the Extraordinary Court tried to justify their work in this particular matter, citing as an example the sale of the fief of Annone. The Extraordinary Court reported the details of the sale of this fief and how the buyer, Giovanni Antonio Beccaria, was a 'foremost knight of the City of Pavia, descendant of nobles families, and among the most ancient of Italy, and, according to the information we have, he has ten thousand scudi per year of income, and has served as a mercenary in the wars of Savoy having a great number of people with him at his expenses'.[12] In any case, the Council of Italy's point was to establish that the granting of titles had of necessity to be approved by the king in Madrid, after consulting the council.

In addition to the Governor, another prominent figure at the highest level of the government of the State of Milan was the Grand Chancellor; in specific circumstances, such as during the 1580s, he also played a crucial role in the sale of titles and fiefs, after the monarch granted him extraordinary powers to do so.[13] Danese Figliodoni, Grand Chancellor between 1579 and 1592, and his successor, Diego Salazar, who occupied the post from 1592 to 1617, were both actively involved in the sale of fiefs and titles.

During Philip II's reign, the concession of noble titles in the State of Milan ceased to be simply a way of recognizing services and became a means of raising revenue for the Exchequer. The impact of the revolt in the Low Countries was a decisive factor in this dynamic, although war was nothing new for Philip II, as it had not been for his father either, since most of the reigns in the sixteenth century were spent waging open warfare on various fronts. The factor of change was the new role of the State of Milan within the Spanish monarchy. In contrast to the periodic journeys that Charles V and his son had made until 1559, Philip II never returned either to Milan, Italy or the Low Countries. The system of the absentee figure of the remote prince involved the distribution of competences between the Council of Italy in Madrid, and the governor and

---

[12] Report of December 1599 signed by the Grand Chancellor Diego Salazar and the president of the Extraordinary Court Giacomo Menocchio. ASMi, Feudi Camerali p. a., 2. The Pavian patrician, Beccaria, had paid the Chamber 35,100 lira for a fief that theoretically brought in only 120 lira per year.

[13] For the figure of the Grand Chancellor in the Lombard administration, see my study 'La sombra del gobernador y cuello de la República: el Gran Canciller del Estado de Milán', in G. Mazzocchi (ed.), *El corazón de la Monarquía. La Lombardia in età spagnola* (Pavía, 2010), pp. 15–41.

tribunals in Milan. As time passed, the oligarchies in the cities of Lombardy adapted to the new scenario and, after the Dutch revolt, Lombardy became a crucial part of the route taken by the Spanish infantry on their way to Flanders.

The critical juncture that accelerated the process of selling titles of nobility in Milan was reached in 1573, after the Duke of Alba's failed attempt to put down the revolt of the nobles in the Low Countries. Philip II ordered Governor Luis de Requesens to leave for Flanders to replace the Duke of Alba. In response to Requesens's complaints about the lack of means to take on this thorny task, the king granted him extraordinary powers to alienate fiefs and revenues belonging to the Chamber. The whole process of the sale was carried out in Milan, and confirmed later by the royal court. The sales realized that year were substantial. In 1573 Agostino and Giovanni Battista Litta were actively involved in the purchase of fiefs, *dacios* [tributes] and regalian rights. In March 1573, the Milanese patrician Agostino Litta purchased from Governor Requesens the fief of Gambolo, situated in the territory of Vigevano, and the title of marquis, for 61,100 imperial lira. That same month, Agostino Litta acquired the fief of Valle, located in the province of Lomellina, and the title of count from the governor.[14] In May 1574, Philip II confirmed the sale of the two fiefs and the noble titles attached to those lands.[15] Other Milanese families took advantage of the sale of fiefs and titles to add lustre to their pedigree. Marco Antonio Rasini, who became wealthy as a result of the commercial activity of his father and uncles, bought the title of count attached to the fief of Castel Novetto in Lomellina in March 1573 for 43,000 lira. In addition, the governor sold the countship of Busto Arsizio, situated in the province of the duchy, to the Milanese patrician, Paolo Camillo Marliani, a member of the Decurion Council and son of Pietro Antonio Marliani, who was president of the *Magistrato Ordinario* or Ordinary Court. The governor also sold the countship of the Corte de Dovera to Guido Cusani, while Costanzo d'Adda was sold the power to appoint an heir to succeed him in the countship of Sale in the province of Pavia.[16] Costanzo was the brother

---

[14] ASMi, Araldica p.a., 1.

[15] A. González Vega and A. M. Díez Gil (eds.), *Títulos y privilegios de Milán*, Catálogo del Archivo de Simancas (Valladolid, 1991), pp. 197–198.

[16] The price paid for these acquisitions and those mentioned later, which took place during the reign of Philip II, are detailed by the heirs to the titles in ASMi, Araldica p.a., 1. For confirmation of these sales by means of royal privileges signed and sealed by Philip II in March 1575 (Marliani), November 1579 (Cusani) and January 1573 (D'Adda), see respectively González Vega and Díez Gil, *Títulos y privilegios de Milán*, pp. 217, 122 and 317. Governor Requesens probably also helped Camillo Landriani acquire the title of Count of Pandino in 1573.

of the decurion Agostino, who had obtained the countship in 1549. Costanzo's marriage to Bianca Beccaria produced no issue, so that when Costanzo d'Adda died of the plague in 1576, his legitimized natural son, Francesco, inherited the countship. In this way, the power to appoint an heir to the title enabled this Milanese patrician family to avoid a serious succession crisis.

Consequently, the cycle of sales of noble titles in 1573 was closely associated with mobilizing resources to put down the Dutch revolt. The main characteristics of this process of selling honours were, on the one hand, the leading role played by the governor of the State of Milan, and, on the other, the link between the market in fiefs and the acquisition of the titles of marquis and count. By the same token, the families, like the Litta and the Marliani, who competed for fiefs and titles, belonged in the main to the Milanese elites. This phenomenon demonstrates the interest of the old families of the patriciate in acquiring new attributes of nobility in order to reinforce their pre-eminence in the north of Italy and the territories of the Spanish monarchy. Family ambitions of this kind are apparent in the career of Agostino Litta, who, in 1573, purchased two titles with two fiefs attached. Agostino was a member of the Decurion Council – a patrician corporation in the city of Milan on which his father Gerolamo had also sat – from 1567.[17] This branch of the Littas belonged to the old families of the Milanese patriciate. The noble titles served to lend authority to the power and reputation that had been built up in the city and duchy over the centuries.

During the remainder of Philip II's reign, noble titles attached to fiefs continued to be sold. These sales were largely channelled through the governors, who received extraordinary powers from the monarch. In December 1578, Cesare Cuttica purchased the title of marquis attached to the fief of Cassine Alessandrino from the governor, the Marquis of Ayamonte, for 60,900 imperial lira.[18] Between December 1579 and May 1580, for the price of 38,085 imperial lira, the Chamber sold Cardinal Bartolomeo Gallio the title of Count of the *Tre Pievi* – Gravedona, Sorico and Dongo – above Lake Como, with the power to appoint one of his three nephews as his heir.

---

[17] The data about the posts held by the Lombard families appear on the now classic lists drawn up by Franco Arese, published recently in the volume *Carriere, magistratura e stato*, ed. Cinzia Cremonini (Milan, 2008). For Agostino Litta in particular, see p. 97. Likewise, the genealogical tree of this branch of the Litta family, as well as the other two branches closely tied to Agostino, can be found in the *Teatro genealógico delle Famiglie Nobili Milanesi*, ed. Cinzia Cremonini, vol. II (Mantua, 2003), p. 51.

[18] This is what his grandson Cesare Cuttica declared when he appeared before the Extraordinary Court in 1633 (ASMi, Araldica p.a., 1). Philip II confirmed this sale in November 1579. González Vega and Díez Gil, *Títulos y privilegios de Milán*, p. 104.

Between 1580 and 1581, the new Grand Chancellor of the State of Milan, a native of Piacenza, Danese Figliodoni, took on a prominent role in the sale of titles and fiefs when Philip II granted him power of alienation. In January 1581, Giovanni Battista Serbelloni, the illegitimate son of the famous soldier Gabrio Serbelloni and his partner Catterina Belingeri, purchased the title of count attached to the fief of Castiglione Lodigiano for 71,000 lira from the Grand Chancellor. Figliodoni also realized the sales of other titles, for example, the countship of Desio in the province of the duchy, acquired by Jorge Manríquez de Lara for 63,000 imperial lira.[19]

As a consequence, during Philip II's reign the purchase of a noble title could sometimes be an important way to overcome a succession crisis caused by the families of the Milanese elites not having legitimate male heirs. Illegitimate sons tried to strengthen their questioned position in Lombard society by acquiring a title, as happened with Francesco d'Adda and Giovanni Battista Serbelloni. Sons who were 'naturali bastardi spuri' – whether legitimized or not by the Senate and the apostolic counts palatine of the college of jurisconsults – found it difficult, if not impossible, to gain access to public office and certain corporations, such as the colleges of jurisconsults.[20]

In order to complete this overview of the sale of noble titles in Milan during the reign of Philip II, it should be pointed out that in 1588 the governor, the Duke of Terranova, sold the fief of Binasco to Pedro González de Mendoza, who obtained the title of count the following year. In May 1598, and for a price of 18,000 ducats, the last governor of the reign, the Constable of Castile, sold Cardinal Alessandrino the title of count attached to the fief of Bosco del Campo Alessandrino, with the authority to leave it, after his death, to his nephew, the Marquis of Casano.[21] During the second half of Philip II's reign, the governors and the Grand Chancellor sold at least eight countships and two marquisates with fiefs for prices ranging from 38,000 to 71,000 imperial lira. During the seventeenth century, the Extraordinary Court and the Royal Exchequer reviewed these titles and questioned the

---

[19] For this sale in particular, see González Vega and Díez Gil, *Títulos y privilegios de Milán*, p. 213. The enfeoffment of Desio has been analysed by Visconti in 'Feudo e società', pp. 206–211.

[20] For the rights to paternal inheritance of natural sons whether legitimized or not, see Chiara Porqueddu, *Il patriziato pavese in età spagnola* (Milan, 2012), pp. 43–58. Only in exceptional cases, such as Ersilio Majno's and always in the absence of direct legitimate male succession, did legitimized natural sons also inherit the father's feudal property. Although the professional colleges excluded natural sons, in certain cases they did manage to enter such corporations.

[21] González Vega and Díez Gil, *Títulos y privilegios de Milán*, p. 7.

legitimacy of some of the sales made by the governors and the Grand Chancellor, for instance, the titles of nobility acquired by the Rasini and Serbelloni families.

At the end of the sixteenth century, the sale of noble titles spread to all the Italian territories belonging to the monarchy, and the number of titles sold steadily increased throughout the following century.[22] From the second third of the seventeenth century, the sale of titles of nobility spread from Italy to the kingdoms of the Crowns of Aragon and Castile. At the beginning of the eighteenth century, the system of sales of noble titles was reinforced and expanded in Spain and America.[23]

The beginning of Philip III's reign, in 1598, had repercussions on the market of titles and fiefs in Milan. Juan de Zúñiga, Count of Miranda and President of the Council of Italy, let the governor know that he wished to be fully informed of any transactions that were made in Milan. In March 1600, the king commanded that no more titles of marquis or count should be granted without the parties involved presenting themselves in Madrid to seek royal approval through the Council of Italy. This line of approach was continued by the Count of Miranda's successor to the presidency of the council, the Constable of Castile, who progressed from being governor of Milan to presiding over the council with the same authority and power as his predecessor. Shortly after taking office as president, and with the support of the king's favourite, the Duke of Lerma, the Constable forcibly reformed the council, strengthening his leading role in deliberations and reducing the provincial regents' scope for action.[24]

'The Abuse That Resulted in Italy from Many Farmers, Lackeys and Others of Lowly Office Calling Themselves and Being Counts and Marquises': The Establishment of Male Primogeniture in the Succession to Titles of Nobility

Between 1592 and 1600, Juan Fernández de Velasco, the Constable of Castile, held the post of Governor of the State of Milan.[25] In 1601, he

---

[22] For the sales of titles of nobility in the kingdom of Sicily during Philip III's reign, see Fabrizio D'Avenia, 'Il mercato degli onori: i titoli di Don nella Sicilia spagnola', *Mediterranea. Ricerche storiche*, a. III (2006), pp. 268–288.

[23] María del Mar Felices de la Fuente, *La nueva nobleza titulada de España y América en el siglo XVIII (1701–1746). Entre el mérito y la venalidad* (Almería, 2012).

[24] Manuel Rivero Rodríguez, 'Los Consejos territoriales', in José Martínez Millán and Maria Antonietta Visceglia (eds.), *La monarquía de Felipe III: la Corte*, vol. III (Madrid, 2008), pp. 406–420.

[25] For the government of the Constable in Milan and his development as a scholar, including his relationship with Lipsio, see Cesare Mozzarelli, 'Nella Milano dei re cattolici.

assumed the presidency of the Council of Italy, making use of his experience in Italy to promote new lines of action from Madrid with respect to the political government of Milan, Naples and Sicily. With regard to the concession of titles and fiefs, the Constable was determined to impose the principle of male primogeniture on the Lombardy oligarchies. He was backed in this endeavour by the lawyer, Miguel Lanz, the Spanish *regente* or councillor for the State of Milan on the Council of Italy. From 1583, Lanz had occupied the posts in Milan of prosecuting counsel, quaestor of the Ordinary Court and, finally, senator, from 1591 to 1595, when he was promoted to regent on the Council of Italy. Both the Constable and Lanz were resolute in their shared objective of establishing male primogeniture in the succession of families with titles of nobility, in opposition to the custom in Lombardy. The attempt was not new; in fact, it resumed a practice that was current in the final years of Philip II's reign, although this time the intention was quite explicit and admitted of no exceptions.

In 1618, the Council of Italy reminded Philip III of the late Constable's programme:

In the State of Milan it is established by ancient custom that any fief or title of Count or Marquis is divided among all the descendants of the first acquirer, so that on a single fief there are fifty lords, and as many Counts and Marquises of it, to the considerable detriment of the subjects and contempt for the honour of the titles. And so, in the year 1601, the Constable of Castile, shortly after he took possession of the Presidency of this Council, sought a remedy for the titles that were being granted, by again declaring that, in the privileges, only the first-born son could inherit the title of Count or Marquis, and some years later the same thing was done in the privileges or sales of newly granted fiefs.[26]

Even though male primogeniture was the habitual practice regulating succession when granting titles at the end of Philip II's reign, this approach was reinforced from 1601 onwards. Ottavio Visconti asked the monarch for the title of count attached to the ancient family fief of Gamarelo, situated in the county of Alessandria. The Court, the Secret Council and the governor examined the services of the pretender to the title in detail and endorsed the petition provided that 'only the first-born son of the said Ottavio Visconti succeeded him, and so on successively,

---

Considerazioni su uomini, cultura e istituzioni tra Cinque e Seicento', in Paolo Pissavino and Gianvittorio Signorotto (eds.), *Lombardia Borromaica, Lombardia Spagnola, 1554–1659* (Rome, 1995), vol. I, pp. 421–456. For the State of Milan under Philip III, see Pablo Fernández Albaladejo, 'De llave de Italia a corazón de la monarquía: Milán y la monarquía católica en el reinado de Felipe III', in Pissavino and Signorotto (eds.), Lombardia Borromaica, vol. I, pp. 41–91.

[26] Legal opinion of the Council of Italy addressed to Philip III. Madrid, December 23, 1618. Archivo General de Simancas (henceforth, AGS), Secretarías Provinciales (henceforth, SP), legajo (henceforth, leg.) 1801, no. 226.

maintaining the order of primogeniture'. In 1601, the Council of Italy considered this clause fundamental 'in order to avoid the problem of all of someone's sons adopting the title of count as they are wont to do in the State of Milan'. The Council's legal opinion or *consulta* added that: 'Your Majesty should know that in that State it is not customary to serve by paying for titles, because there would not be any [title] that would be esteemed [if obtained] by those means.'[27] If this were so, either the sales realized between 1573 and 1599 were being concealed, or they were considered to have been sales of fiefs with a title, not titles without a fief attached.

The month after the Council had issued their opinion, it became clear how interested the king and his favourite were in the cash revenues associated with the sale of titles. The Count of Fuentes endorsed Giovanni Antonio Beccaria's request for a title of count, mentioned earlier. This patrician, a native of the city of Pavia, offered 4,200 lira for the title, after having already bought the fief of Annone in Milan, which did not come with a title. The Council of Italy insisted on the primogeniture clause and added 'that he should serve for this title with one thousand five hundred Castilian ducats'; this money was allocated to pay the expense allowances of the regents and secretaries of the Council, occasioned by the 'moving of the court' from Madrid to Valladolid, that the king's favourite had decided on. In the decree based on the Council's legal opinion, the monarch raised the sum to 3,000 ducats in exchange for the title of the Count of Annone.[28]

The urban patriciate families in Lombardy put up resistance to the imposition of the principle of male primogeniture. In the State of Milan, as in most of northern Italy and in the empire, the paternal inheritance was divided equally among all legitimate sons. Even in the statutes of the city of Milan, any discrimination among male descendants in favour of the first-born was expressly forbidden.[29] The growing interest of patrician families in the main towns of Lombardy in acquiring noble titles to add lustre and pre-eminence to their houses collided head on with the principle of male primogeniture. This imposition ran counter to the customs of the land and it was considered that it could provoke civil unrest among the patrician houses, endangering the harmony of economic discipline.

In June 1602, the Council of Italy received several petitions for the monarch to be less intransigent, allowing brothers to share the honours of the title in accordance with Lombard custom. Abbot Giovanni Battista

---

[27] Legal opinion or *consulta* of 13 August 1601. AGS, SP, leg. 1798, no. 296.
[28] Legal opinion of 14 September 1601, AGS, SP, leg. 1798, no. 290.
[29] Porqueddu, Il patriziato pavese, p. 15–16.

Arcimboldi, together with his brothers, Angelo and Luigi, sought to obtain the title of count attached to the fief of Candia. Mention was made of a cardinal and two archbishops of Milan related to their lineage by marriage, in particular Giovanni Angelo Arcimboldi, who was Archbishop of Milan between 1550 and 1555. The Council's legal opinion included details of the dwellings on the fief, the annual income that the patrician family received and the public offices held by the petitioners' father, Giovanni Arcimboldi, a member of the Council of the Sixty Decurions and of the Tribunal of Twelve of Provision of Milan. While the *merced* [favour] was being processed, Luigi Arcimboldi had died and in view of the achievements listed, the Council of Italy was inclined to recommend that the title be granted to both brothers, 'for even though it is now understood that the title is for both, once the abbot's days are over, it will only remain with the one [surviving brother] and his first-born successors'. The price proposed by the Council was 2,000 Castilian ducats. In his decree, Philip III remained adamant that the earlier regulations were to be applied: 'Only one of these will be given the title (whoever they decide between them) by paying the 2,000 ducats.'[30]

At the same time, one of the families that formed part of the Pavia patriciate also tried to circumvent the court in Madrid's determination with regard to primogeniture. The brothers, Alessandro and Ottavio Mezzabarba, pointed out to the monarch that their father, Carlo, had negotiated the acquisition of the title of count attached to the fief of Corvino 'in the form and manner that was usual in the State of Milan'. In return, they had discovered that the title

only passes to the first-born, and being that, in the State of Milan the property of the parents is shared equally between the sons, the petitioners find themselves with a very great problem which could happen often, that the person who inherits the title is left without the fief, and consequently the [other] one with the fief [is] without the title, something prejudicial that Your Majesty might take into consideration, apart from the discord that could arise between said brothers, the property being divisible, as has been said, and one seeing himself with the title and the other one without it.

The Mezzabarba brothers made some cogent points about the disparity in the criteria governing succession between two elements so closely linked to each other: the title and the fief. While male primogeniture was imposed on the succession to the title, the fief formed part of the divisible portion of the paternal inheritance, which produced divergent outcomes: either the feudal inheritance was divided up or it was concentrated in one male line.

[30] Legal opinion of 27 June 1602. AGS, SP, leg. 1798, no. 285.

The Lombard nobility's discourse of internal discord was a rhetorical device used against an innovation – led by Spanish aristocrats and lawyers in Madrid and Valladolid – that attacked the custom of the local territory. The Mezzabarba brothers added that the principle of primogeniture should be applied only to gratuitous titles granted by the king, not to onerous ones. Given that his father had had to make a donation for the title, either the clause should be changed or the money reimbursed. The Council of Italy's legal opinion reiterated that 'for some years now' both Philip II and the monarch had granted titles that included the primogeniture clause,

but because until now they have always been gratuitous grants and this new form of primogeniture has not been established by order, and it may not have come to the notice of everybody, and, in addition to this, in that state, titles are not held in such high esteem as they are elsewhere because no authority or pre-eminence is acquired with them. It appears that in consideration of these matters, the petitioners have right on their side in this petition ... [and] so that the discord that might arise between these two brothers be avoided, let it be well and good that they both share the grace and concession of the title of count, but on condition that it be passed down only through their eldest male heirs.[31]

Should this proposal not be accepted, the Council reminded the king that the 2,000 ducats handed over for the title should be returned.

As had been the case with the legal opinion on the Arcimboldi brothers, the Council inclined towards a compromise solution, without rigidly imposing primogeniture. Nevertheless, not every member of the Council of Italy ratified the ruling. The regent, Miguel Lanz, distanced himself from the ruling of his fellows and opted to issue a dissenting opinion setting out his arguments for the king. The Spanish lawyer re-examined Carlo Mezzabarba's negotiations from 1597 onwards and the gift of 2,000 ducats offered in 1601. The Council had advised Mezzabarba's agent that he should pay it at 'Milan values', so that the amount was set at a rate of exchange of 20,000 *reales*. The agent had received the dispatch after handing over the agreed sum.

Regent Lanz set out the reasons that had led the sovereigns to impose primogeniture:

[In] past years the King Our Lord resolved and commanded that each and every time a title of Count was granted in that State, it was to be only for the first-born sons, even if the property upon which the title was founded were divided among many siblings, and this was because of the problem and abuse that resulted in Italy from many farmers, lackeys and others of lowly office calling themselves and being Counts and Marquises.

---

[31] Legal opinion of 12 June 1602. AGS, SP, leg. 1798, no. 269.

From the Spanish lawyer's point of view the proliferation of titles devalued the decorum of the nobility.

The lawyer went on to attack the legal bases of the Mezzabarba family's petition, emphasizing the superiority of *potestas absoluta* over the customs and statutes of the territory:

Furthermore, because saying and adducing that it was the custom of Milan that when one was granted the title of Count then all one's sons and descendants were [too], the response is that the people introduce custom but do not give titles, because that is the prerogative of the Prince alone, and he does not make custom but Law, besides which, for custom to create an obligation it has to be tested at least twice in court in accordance with it, which has never ever been done in a case like this. And if it were to be said that the Dukes of Milan were accustomed to granting titles for all the sons of the person to whom they granted the title of Count, this cannot be adduced as custom, or law, to try to oblige Your Majesty who is not a descendant of the Dukes. Apart from the fact that granting titles with more or less authority depends solely upon the will of the Prince, and this reason militates all the more because since that State has become part of Your Majesty's crown, no title has ever been granted in this manner for sixty-six years.[32]

Miguel Lanz's dissenting opinion echoed the arguments of the Castilian lawyers who had maintained since the mid-sixteenth century that the State of Milan had not been aggregated to the Crown by inheritance but by conquest during the Italian wars and that, therefore, it was not necessary to respect the local privileges or customs, but that the supreme authority of the sovereign could mould the constitutions of the territory and impose new systems of government.

Finally, the regent recalled the case of another patrician who was a native of Pavia, Giovanni Antonio Beccaria, who had just paid more money for a title on which primogeniture was established. Lanz did not consider that the donation had to be paid back. In any case, it seems significant that the other regent on the Council of Italy representing the State of Milan, the Cremonese, Giacomo Mainoldi, did not second his Spanish colleague's stance. The lawyer Mainoldi had been a regent since 1597 and eventually became president of the Senate. When Philip III settled the legal ruling by decree in July 1602, he decided to accept regent Lanz's opinion, disregarding the proposal of the majority of the Council and the plea of the patrician brothers. The king decreed that 'only the first-born was to succeed to the title, and since nothing else was requested when I granted the *merced,* and since the recent titles have been dispatched with the primogeniture succession clause [included], I do not know what objections can be made against this'.[33] In short, the monarch

---

[32] AGS, SP, leg. 1798, no. 270.   [33] AGS, SP, leg.1798, no. 269.

indicated that if they appealed, the case could be tried in the court of justice with the involvement of the Royal Exchequer. As had happened with the Arcimboldi brothers, the Mezzabarba brothers also failed in their attempt to re-establish Lombard custom in the face of the designs of the court in Valladolid.

'Many Lords on the Same Land': The Controversy over Enforcing Primogeniture in the Succession to Fiefs

The various petitions addressed to the court in Madrid by patrician families such as the Arcimboldi and Mezzabarba brothers highlighted the deep-rooted inconsistency of the rulings in favour of male primogeniture. Given the close link between a title and the fief attached to it, it did not seem to make sense for succession to the title to be restricted to the eldest son, whereas the fief was divided up and passed from hand to hand. At the royal court, instead of rescinding or mitigating the measures adopted up until then, those in favour of pushing ahead with reforming the system of inheritance – the most prominent being the Constable of Castile, President of the Council, and the regent Miguel Lanz – carried the day. Lanz, in fact, was the doyen of the regents on the Council and had led the Council in the president's absence, when the Constable travelled to London to conclude the peace treaty with England. Halfway through 1609, the Council of Italy addressed the nub of the issue head-on and suggested that the monarch should bring more pressure to bear.

On 2 June 1609, at the monastery of San Lorenzo el Real, Philip III signed and sealed a letter addressed to the governor, the Count of Fuentes, concerning feudal succession. The monarch decreed that

Some years ago I resolved that the titles of marquises and counts granted by me in that State should pass only to the eldest sons, so that only one should be called Marquis or Count, notwithstanding the fact that other descendants were living who inherited part of the fief on which said titles were placed and settled. And lest anything should be overlooked in this matter, it is my wish to order and command you (as I do) to decree and give the order to the Senate and the Courts, that in every case they should ensure that it is observed in the concessions of similar titles authorized by me since the year six hundred and one until now, and those which from now on may be granted, notwithstanding any words and tenor that there may be in the privileges of them [i.e. the concessions], and that this order be recorded in the Chancelleries of all the tribunals, so that it be known and observed by everyone inviolably always.[34]

---

[34] ASMi, Feudi Camerali, p.a., 3

In this way, the provisions concerning male primogeniture in the succession to titles were given the force of law, dispelling all doubts that had been raised in the Council itself about the absence of an express, positive order, known to all the Lombard subjects, which would settle the matter once and for all. Even though this form of succession was already the prevailing practice at the end of Philip II's reign when the privileges of the titles were drawn up, it seems significant that, in the 1609 letter, the year 1601 was taken as the foundational moment of the new paradigm, associating the beginning of the Constable of Castile's presidency with the unequivocal directive to impose the successional model on the Lombard titles.

After establishing succession by primogeniture for titles granted from 1601, the royal letter then addressed the question of earlier titles:

And because it appears that the problems arising from the same land having many Counts have not been properly resolved with this order, with the result that these titles are coming to be despised and held in low esteem because of the various titles granted before said year of six hundred and one, I charge and command you that, with the Senate's opinion, you advise me if it would be better to decree without distinction, and not touching those who, by the death of their forebears would have succeeded to the fief and title in accordance with the wording of the feudal investitures, whether the same should be observed with those who succeed henceforth; namely, it is meet that [of] the descendants of anyone who will be in possession of said title, only the first-born may use it, and not any other descendants of those who may be alive at present with regard to the same fief [for] they will die out sooner and come to an end as the lines of those who now have said title in their possession are slowly extinguished until they are reduced to just one in any fief.[35]

Thus the king and the Council of Italy were demanding a Senate report in order to proceed to a far-reaching measure that meant radically altering the successional structure of the most ancient and reputable lineages in the territory of Lombardy. The figure of the counts *condivisi* was integral to the structure of the State of Milan's nobility. In the seventeenth century, titles of count were shared among the brothers of numerous illustrious aristocratic houses, such as the Borromeos, some branches of the Visconti, the Barbiani di Belgioioso, the Castiglioni, the Cavazzi della Somaglia and the Bolognini, as well as patriciate families from Pavia, like the Pietra, the Malaspina (who were marquises) and the Gambarana – who were of extremely ancient stock – among many other distinguished houses. A large number of these families had acquired their titles and privileges of counts during the second third of the fifteenth century, in

---

[35] Ibid.

particular in the early years of Francesco Sforza's rule. Other houses, such as the Malaspina and the Pietra received theirs in the third decade of the sixteenth century and the Visconti of Cavaglio and Vaprio in 1551, granted by Emperor Charles V.[36] The schema of a single title linked to one fief represented a challenge to the successional rights of the principal houses of the old feudal nobility of the State.

After proposing the progressive extinction of the *condivisi* titles in the royal dispatch, the crucial question was tackled: the market in fiefs. Although there were quite a few shared titles before the middle of the sixteenth century that belonged to very influential families, their number was substantially smaller than the number of shared fiefs, which affected a significant section of the old Lombard nobility who were merely landed gentry without a title.

It is also understood that since the fiefs are divisible according to the custom of that State, and all male descendants succeed equally, there will continue to be many lords on the same land, to the detriment of the subjects, such that its remedy can brook no delay. For which purpose, with the Senate's opinion, you will make me an official record of what can be done in this regard, and whether it is advisable that henceforth fiefs be granted on the condition that they are only passed on to the first-born son, and [whether] it will be possible for the concessions already made to be remedied and [whether] they will have to be, by ordering the same thing [i.e. having the primogeniture clause included], and adding that the first-born should compensate the others who would have jointly succeeded by virtue of the ancient investitures, and at the same time, you will advise me if other means, which over there are judged to be more just and advantageous for the public good, are offered.[37]

In the seventeenth century, among the Lombard families that would have been affected by the hypothetical extinction of shared succession to fiefs were the Arrigoni, the Azzanelli, the Barzi, the Beccaria, the Bentivoglio, the Biglia, the Caraffini, the Casati, the Estes, the Fantoni, the Giorgi Vistarino, the Marino, the Mezzabarba, the Seccoborella, the Genoese Spinola, the Taverna, the Tornielli, the Tortona, the Villani and various branches of the Visconti. This was how both the *condivisi* counts and the feudal lords came to hold a significant number of posts in the civic administration of the principal cities in Lombardy, as well as posts as Supreme Court judges of the State, Church dignitaries and military commanders.[38]

---

[36] Apart from the studies mentioned and the genealogical *Teatro*, see the detailed accounts of grants of titles and fiefs offered by Franco Arese, 'Feudi e feudatari nello Stato di Milano alla morte di Carlo II (1700)', in *Storia di Milano, tome XI* (Milan, 1958), pp. I–XIX.

[37] ASMI, Feudi Camerali, p.a., 3.

[38] A broad view of the political reach of the patriciate can be found in Stefano D'Amico, *Spanish Milan. A City within the Empire, 1535–1706* (New York, 2012), pp. 133–150.

Finally, Philip III strengthened the role of the Council of Italy in the transactions involving fiefs:

And finally it seems advisable that, in the alienations of fiefs, on no account should they be sold with the titles of Marquis or Count, notwithstanding the order that I gave on this, because for these titles the parties will later have to come to me so that, once their quality and achievements are understood, I can deny or grant them [i.e. the titles]. And it is also judged very necessary that in said sales no condition whatsoever be admitted outside those that are wont to be ordinarily placed on them, but rather the customary form be kept. You will advise me later what you think about this, and likewise of the people or tribunals to whom it would be deemed appropriate to entrust the care of these sales in order to regulate them firmly and properly, ordering the Extraordinary Court that in the meantime it should not proceed with making said sales. Because everything that you are commanded here has appeared appropriate to my service and the welfare of my subjects in that State, so it proceeds from my will.[39]

In Defence of the *uguale et popolare* Nobility: The Resistance of the Patrician Tribunals

The Count of Fuentes, the Governor of the State of Milan, ordered the king's letter to be read out in the Secret Council. The letter was then immediately sent to the Senate and the Ordinary and Extraordinary Courts, so that they could submit their reports to the governor on the matters raised in the royal order. Most of the ministers who sat in these tribunals belonged to the Lombard patriciate. Many of the patrician houses were wary of the innovations imposed by Spanish ministers at the royal court designed to reshape the titled nobility and feudal succession. In the early stages, the tribunals adopted delaying tactics. Even though the monarch's letter indicated that the Senate was expected to issue a report on some of the measures proposed, the tribunals did not do so. Neither did they issue a report when the Constable of Castile returned to Milan to take up the position of governor of the state for a second time while also retaining the presidency of the Council of Italy; it was unheard of to have a governor-president of the Council and the situation was not repeated anywhere else in the Habsburg domains. This second governorship was known for its brevity and for the deterioration in the Constable's health, which prevented him from carrying out his duties with any regularity.

Almost three years after the dispatch of the royal letter in 1609, the monarch once more had to urge the authorities in Milan to report to him

---

[39] Letter from Philip III to the governor, the Count of Fuentes. San Lorenzo el Real, 2 June 1609. ASMi, Feudi Camerali p.a., 3.

on the issues raised. In April 1613, the new governor, the Marquis of Hinojosa, put pressure on the Ordinary Court 'che non ritardi più la risposta della lettera di Sua Maestà' on the matter of titles and fiefs. The king's attorney issued a ruling on which the authority of the prince was based, in order to decree legislative changes for the public good, imposing primogeniture in feudal succession, even if some might consider this modification 'odious and *contra legem*' and '*contra pietatem*'. On 23 July, the Ordinary Court submitted its opinion to the governor, once the vote of the college of public prosecutors on the matter had been examined. The tribunal focused its legal opinion on the question of whether 'it would be convenient to reduce with a general law all future successions in the feuds of this state to a matter of primogeniture', so as to avoid the damage caused by the multiplicity of lords on the same land. The nub of the controversy was that the main argument in support of primogeniture, is usually considered to be that it was good for the dignity of the Prince to have more illustrious and powerful vassals. Primogeniture also guaranteed that the head of the house would have more resources to maintain the prestige of families.

Against this measure the Ordinary Court highlighted 'the custom of this Province, in favour of equality among descendants of a same person'. On this basis, the municipal laws of the city and Duchy of Milan were invoked, which expressly forbade giving one heir preferential treatment, even with regard to allodial property. The peer share was a very old custom of the Province, that always liked to privilege an equal and common condition among its citizens, instead that an eminent power and strength in some among them. This was the Ordinary Court's way of extolling the virtues of the Lombard model of succession, by associating it with a specific typology of nobility.

The tribunal's opinion represented an explicit political commitment to the *uguale et popolare* proliferation of *cittadini* nobles to guarantee the social harmony of a stable order, safe from magnates so powerful that they might come to eclipse the supreme sovereign power.

Concerning the appearance of a Prince having vassals of higher condition, it is evident that His Majesty does not act for this reason, but only in the interest of his subjects. Moreover, if one would look at the interests of the Prince, maybe not few would suggest him [to maintain] equality among the vassals, instead of eminence in authority and power for some of them.[40]

---

[40] Part of this paragraph is crossed out in the original opinion of the Ordinary Court. ASMi, Feudi Camerali p.a., 3, where the opinion of the king's attorney on the matter is also to be found.

Perhaps, by 1613, there was a clear contrast between the aspirations of this middle-ranking nobility, identified with the urban patriciate, and the political consequences of the accumulation of resources through primogeniture among the Castilian aristocracy and *grandees* of Spain, the beneficiaries of the new system of royal favourites.[41] The primogeniture option was associated with a powerful aristocracy, capable of threatening the sovereign's interests. Significantly, the tribunal's report had to be handed over to the governor, a Mendoza, and a prime example, like his ancestors and immediate successors (the Enríquez, the Velasco, the Toledo y Ossorio and the Fernández de Córdoba), of that very same Castilian aristocracy.

Furthermore, the Ordinary Court considered that obliging the firstborn son to compensate the other possible heirs to the fief would be a cause of litigation and family discord. The tribunal questioned the damage caused to the subjects from having '*più padroni*', given that when the government was divided, the feudatories normally came to an agreement about the election of the *podestà*, or official, who was to administer justice, either by concurring with the appointment or 'allocate among them the years of the elections'.[42] The tribunal also mentioned the limits of feudal jurisdiction in Milan, where citizens and tenants were exempt from it: 'In civil causes, if so is requested by one of the parts, the Council called Wise acts as Judge confident of the nearest town, and in the criminal all that is sudden is referred to the Senate, to whom always one appeals, and from whom one obtains provision in case of rise, and oppression.'[43]

After these deliberations, the Ordinary Court concluded its opinion by recommending 'that could His Majesty be served in not changing anything in regard to past investitures, providing instead in granting future successions in feuds as it will appear more convenient'. So, the tribunal's political priority was to neutralize the proposal of the 1609 letter, aimed at remedying without delay the question of succession in the divisible fiefs by means of the eldest son compensating the others with successional

---

[41] For the role of the favourite in the times of Philip III, see Francesco Benigno, *La sombra del rey. Validos y lucha política en la España del siglo XVII* (Madrid, 1994); Antonio Feros, *Kingship and Favoritism in the Spain of Philip III, 1598–1621* (Cambridge, 2000); and Patrick Williams, 'El favorito del rey: Francisco Gómez de Sandoval y Rojas, V Marqués de Denia y I Duque de Lerma', in J. Martinez and M. A. Visceglia (eds.), *La Monarquia de Felipe III: La Casa del Rey* (4 vols., Madrid, 2008), vol. III, pp. 185–259.

[42] This question was largely resolved by the Senate when it ruled, in 1616 and 1624 that in shared fiefs the lords should exercise jurisdiction for two years at a time, beginning with the eldest son. Cesare Magni (also drawing on the *Dizionario feudale* by E. Casanova) in *Il tramonto del feudo lombardo* (Milan, 1937), p. 136.

[43] ASMi, Feudi Camerali, p.a., 3

rights under the ancient investitures. Who formed part of the Ordinary Court in 1613? The tribunal was largely made up of Milanese patricians, such as the quaestors, Luigi Melzi, Giovanni Tomaso Gallarati, Filippo Pirovano and Giovanni Battista Fagnani, together with two Spanish ministers, Gaspar Suárez de Ovalle and Fermín López. Some of those quaestors, like Gallarati, owned fiefs that had been granted in the middle of the fifteenth century. The president of the Ordinary Court, Giulio Arese, was an outstanding representative of the most powerful family in the Milanese patriciate throughout the seventeenth century until the death of his son, Bartolomeo.[44] Six years after putting his signature to the report on feudal succession, Giulio Arese would attain the presidency of the Senate.[45]

Halfway through 1613, the Senate and the Courts opposed the attempt to impose primogeniture in the order of succession to divisible fiefs that were regulated by the ancient investitures. The tribunals reminded the governor, the Marquis of Hinojosa, that 'the custom not only of this State, but of all of Italy, according to the Doctors, that all feuds and surely those with the dignity of Count and Marquess are by immemorial custom split among all descendants'. The tribunals joined forces to defend the Italian and Lombard custom.[46]

Besides, the scenario had changed with respect to 1609, when Philip III had signed the letter about the succession to titles and fiefs. After half a century of peace – during which the State of Milan had been a base for military operations, sending resources to Flanders or taking part in occasional actions in the French civil wars – the outbreak of the Monferrato war of succession and the Duke of Savoy mobilizing his troops led to fighting along the borders of the state. Open war altered the perceptions of the court in Madrid in regard to relations with the Lombard elites. The need to mobilize resources and increase the tax burden were the arguments that the Council of Italy employed with the monarch to recommend strengthening ties with the local nobility in times of war emergency.

The treaty of Madrid signed in September 1617 brought hostilities to an end. In September 1618, Philip III once more reminded the then governor, the Duke of Feria, of the content of the 1609 letter and ordered

---

[44] Gianvittorio Signorotto, *Milano spagnola. Guerra, istituzioni, uomini di governo (1635–1660)* (Milan, 2001), pp. 141–156.

[45] For the family history and ministerial career of Giulio Arese, the son of a senator and grandson of the regent of the Council of Italy, Giulio Claro, see my study 'El gobierno de Milán', in Martínez Millán and Visceglia (eds.), La Monarquia de Felipe III vol. IV, pp. 445–466.

[46] ASMI, Feudi Camerali, p.a., 3

him 'as soon as possible to have the report that is asked for therein sent to me, without further delay', and enjoined him, in the meantime, to arrange for devolved fiefs to be sold off, in view of the pressing needs of the Exchequer. In October, the Duke of Feria gathered together the reports of the tribunals and sent the Senate's legal opinion to Madrid.[47]

The Council of Italy met on 23 December 1618 to present the opinion to the monarch for him to settle a controversy that had dragged on for almost a decade. The main standard-bearers of the measures in favour of primogeniture in Lombardy, the Constable of Castile and Miguel Lanz, had died. With respect to affairs regarding the State of Milan, the most influential figure at that time was Gerolamo Caimi, a Milanese patrician and regent since 1606, who enjoyed the confidence of the royal entourage. Together with Caimi, another outstanding minister with experience in Lombard affairs was Felipe de Haro, who was visitor-general in the State between 1606 and 1612. The view of ministers in favour of finding an amicable solution to this thorny problem was the one that finally prevailed in the opinion issued by the Council of Italy. After reviewing the regulations governing titles and fiefs between 1601 and 1609, the Council of Italy informed the king that

seeing that with this judicial procedure the problem of the titles and ancient fiefs, which are many, was not being resolved, a report was sought from the Governor of Milan with the opinion of the Senate about how this might be remedied, and because no reply was ever received, the order was renewed for the Duke of Feria, the present governor of said State, and the Duke in a letter of 24 October of this year sent the report that the Senate had given him on this matter. [The Senate] says that interfering with the ancient titles and fiefs would be something that would be felt deeply in Milan, alleging other objections, and so it should not be done, but that it will be very useful for the public to grant them in future under the rule of Primogeniture, so that there is only one lord to a fief, and only one count or marquis of it, and that continuing in this way, in time, this will eventually remedy the abuse of titles and ancient fiefs, because in that State when there is no male line, the fiefs devolve to Your Majesty and when they are granted again, it will be to the first-born sons only.[48]

The Council of Italy proposed this compromise solution of gradual change, which respected what was laid down in the ancient feudal investitures at the same time as it reaffirmed the principle of primogeniture in the feudal succession of new grants.

And having dealt with it in Council with the proper attention, it has not appeared that anything new should be done for now in this matter against the opinion of the

---

[47] On 19 October 1618 the Duke of Feria ordered the Senate to present the report and on October 24 he sent it to the royal court. ASMi, Feudi Camerali p.a., 3.

[48] AGS, SP, leg.1801.

ministers over there, and so [the Council] is in agreement with the one [i.e. opinion] the Senate gives, that is, not to talk of the ancient titles and fiefs, but only of those that will be newly granted, with the order that neither here nor over there will fiefs or titles be granted in any other form than that in the clause stating that there must always be only one feudatory and only one bearer of the title, and that it should be the first-born male when the deceased leaves only one fief, but it he were to leave two or three, then let those be divided among the descendants as before, namely, that in one fief and title, one may succeed, and in the other the other, it being sufficient for the public benefit that no more than one may succeed in a single fief or title, rather it being advisable if there are many fiefs that they be divided, and not be together, because the State is very narrow, and it is not advisable for many fiefs to be kept together for a long time in one house, either for Your Majesty's service or for the general benefit of your subjects.[49]

Thus, at the end of the legal opinion, the Council of Italy had accepted part of the arguments that the Lombard tribunals had put forward against the concentration of resources in a single branch of the family bloodline. The recent war was whipping up a climate of distrust, to such an extent that the Lombard magnates who possessed strategic fiefs might be tempted into joining forces with the princes bordering on the State of Milan. This question would be crucial when war broke out in Europe and also a source of disquiet among the royal ministers during the decades of war with France and her allies in the north of Italy.[50] Consequently, a single powerful house was not in accord with the prince's interests, whereas an extensive *egalitarian* nobility that was identified with the urban patriciate was presented as a guarantee of loyalty and peace in the domain.

Philip III was convinced by the Council of Italy's opinion. As a result, in January 1619, the long-drawn out process that had begun in 1601 – and had ever since cast its shadow over the shaping of political society in Lombardy – was finally concluded.

At other junctures during Philip III's reign, various measures associated with the transmission of property were proposed that affected the way order within the family was organized. Among the *arbitrios* [discretionary taxes] that the Count of Villamedina proposed to the monarch in 1615 for raising extra revenue in the State of Milan, was the question of extending the institution of entails to Lombard estates. The Duke of Lerma ordered the Council of Italy to pronounce on this matter. Villamedina explained that 'in the State of Milan there are no entails, and this is why houses come to an end, and it would be possible to give

---

[49] Legal opinion of the Council of Italy to Philip III. Madrid, 23 December 1618. AGS, SP, leg. 1801, no. 226. The king's resolution was published on 18 January 1619.

[50] Gianvittorio Signorotto, 'Stabilità política e trame antispagnole nella Milano del Seicento', in Yves-Marie Bercé and Elena Fasano Guarini (eds.), *Complots et conjurations dans l'Europe moderne* (Rome, 1996), pp. 721–745.

permission for them to be instituted, without prejudice to the children already born, by giving Your Majesty two half-annates of the fruits'. The Council of Italy reported to the king on this affair:

It is true that in the State of Milan there are but very few Entails; however it is also true that there is no law to prevent them, leaving their *legítima* [legitimate portion] to the children in accordance with common law, and if there are none, the reason is that the dwellers there are not inclined to make Entails. Only in the city of Milan is it forbidden for the ascendant to leave more to one descendant than to the other, and Your Majesty sometimes allows a waiver and, even though it is free, in ten years only once has it been sought for a house with no other property, so it is obvious that the *arbitrio* will serve no purpose, for they have no need of permission, except in a case where, even though free, it is not taken up.[51]

In 1615, the Council of Italy decided that there was not sufficient space in Lombard political society for the institution of the entail to be applied along the lines of the Castilian model. Family trusts had been established in the State of Milan since the mid-sixteenth century as a way of keeping family patrimony indivisible and inalienable for generations.[52] Family trusts privileged the will of the testator and ensured that it was impossible to alienate property subject to those conditions in order to preserve the family. As a general rule, the *favor agnationis* meant that women were excluded from the provisions of the trust. The Senate acted as a *paterfamilias* and could grant waivers by examining the pleas and allegations of the members of the family, case by case.

The importance of this type of trust perhaps explains why the entail barely existed in the State of Milan, even though its use gradually increased throughout the seventeenth century. In any case, it appears that the entail as *usus Hispaniae* was most widespread in the kingdoms of Naples and Sicily.[53]

In both Spanish and European legal treatises, the institution of the entail had, to a certain extent, been identified with male primogeniture.[54]

---

[51] AGS, SP, leg. 1800, no. 197. The king accepted the Council's opinion and the resolution was published in December 1615.

[52] Maria Carla Zorzoli, 'Della famiglia e del suo patrimonio: riflessioni sull'uso del fedecommesso in Lombardia tra Cinque e Seicento', *Archivio Storico Lombardo*, 115 (1989), pp. 90–147. With regard to the Senate's involvement in trust waivers, see Annamaria Monti, *Iudicare tamquam Deus. I modi della giustizia senatoria nel Ducato di Milano tra Cinque e Seicento* (Milan, 2003), pp. 199–216.

[53] A. Romano, 'Successioni e difesa del patrimonio familiare nel Regno di Sicilia', in L. Bonfield (ed.), *Marriage, Property and Succession* (Berlin, 1992), pp. 71–154. For entail, see Bartolomé Clavero, 'Favor maioratus, usus Hispaniae: moralidad del linaje entre Castilla y Europa', in Bonfield (ed.), *Marriage, Property and Succession*, pp. 215–254.

[54] A detailed approach to the relationships between entail and primogeniture before and after the passing of the laws in Toro in 1505 can be found in Bartolomé Clavero, *Mayorazgo. Propiedad feudal en Castilla, 1369–1836*, 2nd expanded edition (Madrid,

It should be remembered, however, that there were also entails for second sons, daughters, nephews and nieces. Nevertheless, Law 40 of Toro, imposing the principle of primogeniture on succession by entail, had been approved by Ferdinand the Catholic in 1505. A pragmatic sanction, signed and sealed by Philip III in April 1615, decreed that succession to entails should comply with the provisions of the laws of *Partidas*, putting an end to the doubts generated by Law 40 of Toro.[55] It seems significant that it should be in 1615 when the Castilian model of succession by entail was finally clarified. The spread of entail in Castile by means of the laws of Toro of 1505 constituted a basic process in the interaction between the Crown and the nobility; the entail was a means of stabilizing and strengthening noble lineages by concentrating resources in particular family lines.

Primogeniture, Equal Nobility, Trade and the Happiness of the Citizens

During Philip III's reign, the royal court was fully committed to establishing and strengthening the principle of male primogeniture, firstly in the succession to titles of nobility and later in the succession to fiefs. These measures were supported and encouraged by very influential Spanish aristocrats and lawyers among the sovereign's entourage, such as the Constable of Castile and the regent, Miguel Lanz. It was a matter of extending practices that prevailed among the Castilian nobility to Lombardy, as well as ending or curtailing customs considered indecorous for those of noble rank, such as shared or *condivisi* titles.[56] The change in succession to title ended up spreading to fiefs that were newly granted. These provisions were justified by disparaging the proliferation of noble titles and the scarcity of resources available to some *condivisi* titleholders. This process coincided with the Council of Italy's interest in controlling the sale of noble titles and increasing revenues from this quarter by raising the prices for titles of marquis and count.

The urban elites of the State of Milan and the patrician ministers opposed this interference in the shaping of political society by defending

1989), pp. 211–221. Clavero amplifies the perspective on entail and primogeniture in the European dimension in the appendix 'La institución del mayorazgo entre Castilla y Europa' (pp. 435–473).

[55] Ibid., p. 213.

[56] The process of strengthening male primogeniture and forcing it on the Castilian nobility has been analysed by Marie-Claude Gerbert, *Las noblezas españolas en la Edad Media, Siglos XI–XV* (Madrid, 1997), pp. 340–346. The functions of the first-born son (moral guardianship of the family and religious, political, military and economic roles) have been detailed by Rafael Sánchez Saus, *Caballería y Linaje en la Sevilla medieval* (San Fernando, 1989), pp. 55–65.

the model of an extensive middle-ranking nobility. The tribunals drew attention to the danger of patrimonial resources being concentrated in a single line of a house and so increasing its authority and power to the extent that it could pose a risk to civil harmony and the prince's interests. Although the Crown needed nobles with resources so that they could provide assistance, the accumulation of wealth within a single family could become a threat to the sovereign's *maiestas*. The successional system and primogeniture were the means that enabled the *potter* king to mould the scale of the provincial nobility. Finally, a compromise agreement was reached between the Council of Italy and the Senate, maintaining the shared fiefs in accordance with the ancient investitures and accepting primogeniture as the general principle for granting new titles and fiefs, including the old ones that devolved to the Chamber. This was the practice that prevailed during the reigns that followed.[57]

The discourse of an *equal* nobility is associated with the Lombard patriciate. The Lombard patricians presented themselves to the King of Spain and the court in Madrid as guarantors of peace in the domain in times of war emergency. The patricians assumed the mantle of spokesmen for their land against the royal court and at the same time succeeded in keeping the domain peaceful, so that the State of Milan was one of the few territories in the Spanish monarchy in Europe that did not experience significant revolts or plots by the nobility during the seventeenth century. However, the discourse of an equal nobility was becoming increasingly fractured. On the one hand, the families were competing, not only for patrimonial and economic resources, but also for offices and magistracies, military commands or appointments as ecclesiastical dignitaries, extending their influence as far as the courts in Madrid, Rome and Vienna. On the other hand, the system of honours that had built up in the Spanish monarchy was the very antithesis of an egalitarian nobility. The habits of the Spanish military orders, the noble titles, the rank of grandee of Spain and the accolades of the Golden Fleece were all instruments of inequality in the noble hierarchy, designed to multiply the steps on the 'pyramid of honour' of the nobility in Europe. The Lombard lineages competed for and achieved these honours, even the highest ones, such as the rank of grandee of Spain and the Golden Fleece.

From the early years of the seventeenth century, the change in the successional system for new titles and fiefs gradually began to leave its imprint on the shape of the Lombard elites.[58] Until then the major form of

---

[57] As Cesare Magni points out (also drawing on the Casanova *Dizionario*) in *Il tramonto del feudo lombardo* (Milan, 1937), pp. 136–139.

[58] Dante E. Zanetti, *La demografia del patriziato milanese nei secoli XVII, XVIII, XIX* (Pavia, 1972), pp. 49–51.

property inheritance was by succession in equal parts among the sons. There was no sudden change;[59] nonetheless, it was more common in the seventeenth century than in the preceding one, in families belonging to the elites, for the eldest son to benefit in inheritance.[60] From the early decades of the seventeenth century, the practice of primogeniture trusts spread throughout Lombardy.[61]

During the seventeenth and eighteenth centuries, the tension between the principle of male primogeniture as a strategy for preserving patrimony, and the rights of the other male siblings persisted within Lombard patrician families. At the height of the Enlightenment in Lombardy, the controversy found echoes in the scholarly circle of *Il Caffè*, among whose most prominent members were Pietro Verri and Cesare Beccaria. The periodical, *Il Caffè*, was published between 1764 and 1766.

Among the topics dealt with in *Il Caffè*, the patrician Alfonso Longo put forward a variety of *Osservazioni su i fedecommessi*. Abbot Longo wondered 'what is the point of trusts and primogenitures? Of, one will tell me, keeping families rich and illustrious.' The order of succession in noble families ought to be governed by different principles from those of reigning dynasties:

In matters of kingly succession, it is right for the sovereign to regard State provinces as inalienable, and government, which is to remain undivided, should go to the first-born, in order for the monarchy not to dilute itself, from mighty as it is to small principalities, sure game for a bigger neighbour. Things go otherwise for private families, on the other hand. Ridiculous laws leave younger siblings as victims in misery for the happiness of the first-born. So how would that be a means to keep a family's lustre? I believe that the name of the family must be understood as pertaining to all family members. And as to wealth and status, they should be distributed among all family members. Are we to keep a family's lustre by making younger siblings unhappy, by enriching those who were born earlier only by chance? One should only call a family rich and illustrious when wealth is as equally distributed as possible among all family members; when all siblings are in put in a position to live comfortably, to pick each a bride, and to supply their country with citizens (their offspring: note the use of the word 'citizens'). It looks like primogeniture is incompatible with the goal of caring for the people, which ought to be the primary one.[62]

---

[59] Porqueddu, *Il patriziato pavese*, pp. 15–26.

[60] Examples of cooperation between the first-born and the *cadetto* in the case of the Crivelli family are set out in C. Cremonini, *Le vie della distinzione. Società, potere e cultura a Milano tra XV e XVIII secolo* (Milan, 2012), pp. 90–92.

[61] Zorzoli, 'Della famiglia', pp. 115–119.

[62] A. Longo, 'Osservazioni su i fedecommessi', in G. Roverato (ed.), *Il Caffè* (Treviso, 1975), pp. 73–74.

The attack on primogeniture was extended to the practice of celibacy among the younger siblings, or *cadetti*, who were deprived of noble titles, fiefs and most of the patrimony.

In the 1760s, the principle of male primogeniture was rejected in Milan on the basis of new paradigms in political economy. According to enlightened Lombards, the happiness of the citizens, trade and the increase in the population were incompatible with primogeniture and *maiorascato* [entail]. Abbot Longo maintained that the public good required 'la maggiore felicità possibile divisa colla maggiore egualità possibile'. Once again, an egalitarian nobility was associated with the Lombard right of shared inheritance among male siblings. In contrast, the exclusion of women via the *favor agnationis* established in primogenitures, entails and trusts was not addressed.

During the second half of the eighteenth century, the question of primogeniture continued to cause discord and conflict within the Lombard patriciate. On certain occasions, family solidarity was shattered and feuding between brothers became particularly intense. One such example was the case of the Verri brothers; the provisions of their father, Gabrielle's will in favour of primogeniture in the future to preserve the family's honour, was the source of lengthy and bitter disputes between Pietro, Alessandro, Carlo and Giovanni in the last 20 years of the eighteenth century.[63]

To sum up, the implementation of male primogeniture in the succession to noble titles and fiefs in the State of Milan is an example of the impact of political and social processes intrinsic to the aggregation of a territory to the Spanish monarchy. During the seventeenth century the absolute authority of the king and the custom of the territory interacted until they brought into being complex ways of shaping a political society in which both Imperial-Lombard and Spanish components eventually combined to acquire a new social dimension.

---

[63] The feud between brothers over the paternal inheritance, seen from the point of view of a *cadetto*, Carlo, is in Elena Riva, *Carlo Verri. Patrizio, prefetto e possidente* (Milan, 2006), pp. 61–81.

8 Portugal's Elites and the Status of the Kingdom of Portugal within the Spanish Monarchy

Pedro Cardim

The incorporation of the Portuguese crown into the Monarchy of Philip II of Spain, in 1581, was the culmination of a multifaceted dispute over royal succession. As is well known, the Portuguese succession crisis began in 1578 with the unexpected death of King Sebastian I in the battle of Alcacer Kibir. The king of Portugal had no direct successor, and for that reason a major juridical dispute took place, in which several candidates participated. One of them was Philip II of Spain. However, what began as a juridical dispute soon degenerated into a swift military operation of conquest carried out by Spanish forces, which included confrontations and even some violence against the population. At the same time, the emissaries of Philip II negotiated with the Portuguese noble, administrative and ecclesiastical elites, and were able to satisfy many of their immediate demands. This settling of affairs resulted in the traditional affirmation that Philip II of Spain 'gained Portugal' by *inheritance*, by *conquest*, and by *negotiation*.

Six decades passed between the moment of Portugal's *aggregation* to the Spanish Monarchy in 1581 and its subsequent *disaggregation* and return to independence beginning on 1 December 1640. During this period, the Portuguese were subjected to an experience that to them was unprecedented: namely, the condition of sharing the same monarch with many other peoples. Being part of a dynastic conglomeration was something relatively common in Europe for that period.[1] To the subjects of the Portuguese crown, however, the first time they found themselves in this situation was, precisely, in 1581, and this situation necessitated some adaptation, given that they had to become used to relying upon a king who lived primarily outside of Portuguese territory, a fact with significant political implications.

---

[1] John Elliott, 'Introduction – Forms of Union: the British and Spanish Monarchies in the Seventeenth and Eighteenth Centuries', *Revista Internacional de Estudios Vascos*, 5 (2009) pp. 13–19.

Besides this, it did not take long for the Portuguese to realise that, hereafter, they would have to manoeuvre within a political universe that was far more complex than the one they were used to. As subjects of a 'monarch', a sovereign who governed several kingdoms, the Portuguese began to live alongside the subjects of Castile, Aragon, Catalonia, Valencia, Granada, Navarre, Naples, Milan, Flanders, and the *Criollos* from the *Indias de Castilla* as well as others who all shared the condition of being subject to the same ruler.

As for Philip II of Spain, the incorporation of Portugal into his monarchy further accentuated the heterogeneity of the conglomeration he governed. In virtue of this, the king and his counsellors had to find the most appropriate position in which to situate the Portuguese within this hierarchy of territories. They also had to establish a form of government that was likewise befitting of Portugal, for it was evident to all that this was in large measure essential to maintaining the political stability of Habsburg Portugal.

This delicate political necessity rose from the fact that Portugal had become part of a dynastic conglomeration composed of such varied territories that the ruling groups of each region were led to compare their situation with that of their counterparts. Portugal was no exception, and shortly after Philip II made his oaths in the *Cortes* of Portugal (the representative assembly) held in Tomar in May 1581, the elites of Portugal began to examine their status in respect to the other territories also part of the Spanish monarchy. At the same time, the ruling groups from other territories turned their attention to this new member and began to position themselves against the Portuguese elites and their ambitions.

This study therefore examines the 60-year Portuguese affiliation with the Spanish monarchy and considers the impact of this situation on the kingdom of Portugal. This analysis will focus on the discourse produced, beginning in 1581, about the political status of the Portuguese kingdom. It will focus, to a large extent, on the many contemporary political treatises that discussed the status of Portugal within the Spanish monarchy. As I am about to show, parallel to debating this subject matter, such treatises also addressed key issues of the late sixteenth and early seventeenth-century political debate.

In this sense, I will begin by tracing the Iberian debate over the union of the kingdoms in order to contextualise the 1581 controversy and the way in which the Portuguese crown was incorporated by the Spanish monarchy. Then, I will examine what this incorporation into the Spanish monarchy signified to the Portuguese, and I will give special attention to the deliberations over Portuguese territorial status. I will then evaluate the controversy surrounding the status of Portugal during the reign of Philip III at the very moment when Castile's political influence was increasing. Then, I will assess the debate generated by the reforms implemented from 1624 onward by Philip IV's favourite, the Count-Duke Olivares, a debate in which once again the status of Portugal figured prominently. Finally, coinciding with the period of rupture between Portugal and Philip IV, in 1640, I will demonstrate that the propaganda supporting the 'Portuguese rebels' took up again many of the questions that had been at the centre of political debate in the preceding decades, in particular the political status of Portuguese territory and its elites.[2]

As we will see, there were essentially three foci in the production of discourse over the political status of Portugal: first, the Portuguese, who were constantly vigilant in protecting their rights; second, the other subjects of the Spanish monarchy, who endeavoured to ensure that their positions would not be affected by the incorporation of this new territory; and third, the royal circle itself, which strove to respect the Portuguese royal condition while simultaneously ensuring the governability of the ensemble of territories under its rule.

***

Beginning at the end of the fifteenth century, political entities endowed with unprecedented vastness and complexity emerged across the Iberian world. As is well known, the expansion of political horizons occurred first in the Iberian Peninsula at the end of the 1400s due to the union of the Crowns of Castile and Aragon, the conquest of the Muslim kingdom of Granada, the possibility of a unified Iberia under the rule of Miguel da Paz (the prince of Portugal), the Portuguese and Castilian expansion beyond Europe, and, already in the sixteenth century, the conquest of part of Navarre and its incorporation into Castile.

This widening of political horizons led to the production of a vast literature dedicated to the new challenges of governing clusters of

---

[2] For an overview of the six decades (1581–1640) during which Portugal was part of the Spanish Monarchy, see John H. Elliott, 'The Spanish Monarchy and the Kingdom of Portugal, 1580–1640' in Mark Greengrass (ed.), *Conquest and Coalescence. The Shaping of the State in Early Modern Europe* (London, 1991), pp. 48–67. The best in-depth analysis of the so-called Habsburg Portugal is Fernando Bouza Álvarez's *Portugal en la Monarquía Hispánica (1580–1640). Felipe II, las Cortes de Tomar y la Génesis del Portugal Católico* (Madrid, 1987). See also Mafalda Soares da Cunha, Leonor Freire Costa and Pedro Cardim (eds.), *Portugal na Monarquia Espanhola. Dinâmicas de Integração e Conflito* (Lisbon, 2013); and Ronald Cueto, '1580 and All That ... Philip II and the Politics of the Portuguese Succession', *Portuguese Studies*, vol. 8, Special Issue supported by the Comissão Nacional para as Comemorações dos Descobrimentos Portugueses (1992), pp. 150–169.

territories and peoples. Likewise, many works were specifically devoted to the uniting of territories.[3]

As Jon Arrieta Alberdi notes in his several works on this topic, the governing doctrine of the period distinguished two kinds of territorial union: one was called '*aeque principaliter*', literally 'of equal importance'; the other was 'conquest'.[4] The first one referred to the process of incorporating new territories fairly, in which united kingdoms were allowed to preserve their institutional frameworks. Such were the circumstances of the union of Castile and Aragon, which was in contrast to the cases of Granada and Navarre, where territorial expansion occurred via 'conquest', that is, an 'unequal' and 'vertical' union in which the conquering territory was left in a position of clear supremacy over the conquered kingdom.[5] As for the incorporation of Castile and Aragon into the Habsburg's domains, the political personality of the two Iberian crowns and their institutional framework was largely respected.

---

[3] See Anthony Pagden, 'Fellow Citizens and Imperial Subjects: Conquest and Sovereignty in Europe's Overseas Empires', *History and Theory*, 44:4 (December, 2005) pp. 28–46; Joan-Lluís Palos and Pedro Cardim, 'El Gobierno de los Imperios de España y Portugal en la Edad Moderna: Problemas y Soluciones Compartidos' in Joan Lluís Palos and Pedro Cardim, *El Mundo de los Virreyes en las Monarquías de España y Portugal* (Madrid, 2012), pp. 11–31. For a comparative perspective, see John Morril, 'State Formation and Nationhood in the Atlantic Archipelago 1500–1720' in I. Burdiel and J. Casey (eds.), *Identities: Nations, Provinces and Regions (1550–1900)* (Norwich, 1999), pp. 135–170; and John Robertson, 'The Conceptual Framework of Anglo-Scottish Union', *Revista Internacional de Estudios Vascos, Cuad.* 5 (2009), pp. 125–137; Nicholas Canny, 'La Incorporación de Irlanda y Escocia a Inglaterra. Una Comparación con la Península Ibérica' in Alfredo Floristán (ed.), *1512. Conquista e Incorporación de Navarra. Historiografía, Derecho y otros Procesos de Integración en la Europa Renacentista* (Barcelona, 2012), pp. 453–468; Frederick Cooper and Jane Burbank, *Empires in World History: Power and the Politics of Difference* (Princeton, NJ, 2010), pp. 122 ff.

[4] Jon Arrieta Alberdi, 'Las Formas de Vinculación a la Monarquía y de Relación entre sus Reinos y Coronas en la España de los Austrias' in Bernardo García and Antonio Álvarez-Ossorio Alvariño (eds.), *La Monarquía de las Naciones. Patria, Nación y Naturaleza en la Monarquía de España* (Madrid, 2004), pp. 303–326; Jon Arrieta Alberdi, 'La "Lex Regia" en la Obra de Francisco Martí Viladamor: Recepción y Evolución del Concepto', *Pedralbes. Revista d'història moderna*, I:28 (2008), pp. 103–140. One of the first historians to address this topic for the early modern Iberian context was John H. Elliott in 'A Europe of Composite Monarchies', *Past and Present*, 137 (November 1992), pp. 48–71; see also António M. Hespanha, '*El Espacio Político' in La Gracia del Derecho. Economía de la Cultura en la Edad Moderna* (Madrid, 1993), pp. 85–121.

[5] Alfredo Floristán, 'Lealtad Personal, Fidelidad Nacional y Fe Religiosa. Reflexiones Morales en torno a la Conquista de Navarra' in Pablo Fernández Albaladejo (ed.), *Monarquía, Imperio y Pueblos en la España Moderna. IV Reunión Científica de la Asociación Española de Historia Moderna (Alicante, 27–30 de Mayo de 1998)* (Alicante, 1997), pp. 343–352; see also Alfredo Floristán, 'Las Incorporaciones de Navarra y de Portugal a la Monarquía Española y la Posibilidad Irlandesa' in E. García Hernán (ed.), *Irlanda y la Monarquía Hispánica: Kinsale, 1601–2001. Guerra, Política, Exilio y Religión* (Madrid, 2002), pp. 341–355.

The fact that the Iberian Peninsula was brought into the realm of Charles of Habsburg incited even further reflections on the terms of territorial unions. Beginning in 1520, interest in the history of each territory increased significantly as a way of defining, via historical perspective, the political status of each of the dominions of Charles V in respect to each other.[6] The foundational agreements made at the inauguration of each kingdom's independence were subject to intense scrutiny, a fact that also led to debates over royal power and the way by which each of the territories that were now part of the vast and diversified dominion of the Habsburgs had been established.[7]

In the Iberian context, this reflection was conditioned by a series of deeply ingrained cultural issues common to the peninsular territories.[8]

First was the idea of continuity between, on one hand, the former Visigoth and Suevi kingdoms, and, on the other, the Iberian kingdoms born through the course of war against the Muslims.[9] Castile insisted on its link with the Visigoths, whereas Portugal claimed to be the direct successor of the Suevi kingdom. Implicit to this claim was the fact that the Suevi kingdom was the first to convert to Christianity.

Second were the memories of the 'reconquest', memories that varied from region to region. On this point, a persistent tension existing between two contrasting understandings of the reconquest should be noted: on one hand were those who maintained that each kingdom had fought, per se, the Muslims and was 'conquered' alone. On the other were those who promoted a unified vision of the reconquest, which had been led mostly by the efforts of Castile (and also the ancient kingdom of León).

Third was the dimension of divine right, a quality nearly always associated with the foundational moments of political entities. All of the Iberian kingdoms promoted more or less legendary histories, which

---

[6] John H. Elliott, 'Monarquía Compuesta y Monarquía Universal en la Época de Carlos V' in AA. VV., *Carlos V. Europeísmo y Universalidad. Vol. V – Religión, Cultura y Mentalidad* (Madrid, 2001), pp. 699–710; Bernardo García (ed.), *El Imperio de Carlos V. Procesos de Agregación y Conflictos* (Madrid, 2000). For a comparison with the English expansion, see Ken MacMillan, *Sovereignty and Possession in the English New World. The Legal Foundations of Empire, 1576–1640* (Cambridge, 2006).

[7] Xavier Gil Pujol, 'Imperio, Monarquía Universal, Equilibrio: Europa y la Política Exterior en el Pensamiento Político Español de los Siglos XVI y XVII', *Lezione XII del Seminario de la Università di Perugia. Dipartimento di Scienze Storiche* (1996), pp. 3–23; Ana Isabel Buescu, *Imagens do Príncipe. Discurso normativo e representação (1525–49)* (Lisbon, 1996).

[8] Ricardo García Cárcel, 'Introducción' in Ricardo García Cárcel (ed.), *La Construcción de las Historias de España* (Madrid, 2004), pp. 20 ff.

[9] Pablo Fernández Albaladejo, 'Entre 'Godos' y 'Montañeses'. Avatares de una Primera Identidad Española' in A. Tallon (ed.), *Le Sentiment National dans l'Europe Méridionale aux XVIe et XVIIe siècles* (Madrid, 2007), pp. 123–154.

included transcendent moments of divine providence in their political origins. In the case of Portugal, one is referred to the so-called miracle of Ourique, a mythical narrative that attributed a divine origin to Portugal's political founding on the twelfth century.

Fourth, and finally, was the recollection of foundational moments that were characterised by treaties and pacts, moments that asserted that the body politic was born through a process of voluntary subjection of the community to a ruler, thus giving birth to a limited royal authority. Such occurred in Catalonia (the voluntary subjection to Charlemagne) or in Aragon (the *fueros* of Sobrarbe).[10] As for Portugal, the interest in these agreements are related to representative assembly which supposedly was held in the town of Lamego, in the first moments of Portugal's independence.

Between 1578 and 1581, the dispute over royal succession of the Crown of Portugal occurred in this milieu of debate and, in reality, it was strongly influenced by the arguments that for some decades had already been developed in various regions of the Iberian Peninsula.[11]

As indicated above, the Portuguese succession crisis was resolved following a swift and intimidating military campaign by which Philip II of Spain imposed his will above the claims of the remaining candidates. The specific targets of the military action were the supporters of Dom António, Prior of Crato, one of the candidates to the Portuguese throne. As is widely known, the bulk of the supporters of Dom António were aldermen coming from the main Portuguese urban centres. Only a small number of Portuguese aristocrats and a minority of the major clergymen supported him. Anticipating that Philip II would eventually succeed, the majority of the Portuguese nobles and bishops awaited for the result of the brief confrontation that took place in 1580. At the same time, they kept constant contact with the envoys Philip II sent to Portugal, in order to make sure that they would be able to maintain their status under the likely Spanish rule in Portugal.

After his actions were concluded, Philip II and his counsellors were faced with deciding Portugal's status in the hierarchy of Spain's

---

[10] Alfredo Floristán, "Ex Hostibus et in Hostes'. La Configuración de Identidades Colectivas como Confrontación Múltiple: Navarra entre Sobrarbe y Cantabria' in Bernardo García and Antonio Álvarez-Ossorio Alvariño (eds.), *La Monarquía de las Naciones. Patria, Nación y Naturaleza en la Monarquía de España* (Madrid, 2004), pp. 327–354.

[11] Fernando Bouza Álvarez, 'De un fin de Siglo a Otro. Unión de Coronas Ibéricas entre Don Manuel y Felipe II' in AA.VV., *El Tratado de Tordesillas y su Época. Congreso Internacional de Historia* (Valladolid, 1995), pp. 1453–1463; Mafalda Soares da Cunha, 'A Questão Jurídica na Crise Dinástica' in Joaquim Romero Magalhães (ed.), *História de Portugal. No Alvorecer da Modernidade* (Lisbon, 1997), pp. 552–559.

dominions. At this moment, there arose a slight hesitation: on one side were those in favour of *assimilation*, that is, the full integration of Portugal as a 'conquered' territory, with the subsequent conversion of the kingdom into a *province* and loss of royal status such an action would entail; on the other side were those who defended *aggregation*, in which Portugal's royal status would be somewhat preserved.[12]

This was a hesitation stemming from the aforementioned distinction between horizontal ties (*aeque principaliter*) and vertical ties, the latter being typical of 'conquest' situations. Nevertheless, although the circumstances of 'conquest' were present in 1580, a decision was made to exempt Portugal from this relationship to the Monarchy of Philip II according to the following terms: without causing the structure of the kingdom to suffer significant changes, Portugal would be given a horizontal relationship of quasi-equality to the other territories of the Spanish monarchy.

Philip II agreed to adopt the title of Philip I of Portugal and to create the Council of Portugal at the court in Madrid, an organ that was due to become the symbol of the Portuguese royal status within the Habsburg conglomerate. In addition, the king also promised that Portugal would be governed by a viceroy (and not by a mere governor), when possible belonging to the royal family. As for Portuguese government and administrative institutions, the king promised that only Portuguese-born dignitaries would be appointed to them, and a similar commitment was established regarding the granting of Portuguese noble titles and ecclesiastical offices. Philip gave all guarantees to the nobility and the clergy regarding the preservation of their sphere of influence. Additionally, it was also decided that the Portuguese language would continue to be used in all administrative affairs, and the monarch agreed to maintain a Portuguese royal house. Finally, Philip II also made the decision to keep the separation between the Portuguese and the Castilian overseas possessions. As Fernando Bouza Álvarez has ably demonstrated, Portugal in this way preserved its personality within the Spanish Habsburg conglomeration.[13]

When compared to other territories also ruled by Philip II, the Portuguese ruling groups were undoubtedly more successful in establishing limits to the interference, within the Portuguese sphere, of people coming from other territories that were also part of Philip II's

---

[12] Fernando Bouza, 'Introdução' in *Cartas para Duas Infantas Meninas. Portugal na Correspondência de D. Filipe I às suas Filhas (1581–1583)* (Lisbon, 1998).

[13] Fernando Bouza Álvarez, *Portugal en la Monarquía Hispánica (1580–1640). Felipe II, las Cortes de Tomar y la Génesis del Portugal Católico* (Madrid, 1987).

conglomerate.[14] However, the events of 1580–1581 left a controversial legacy, resulting in at times diametrically opposed interpretations. Especially virulent was the disagreement surrounding the political significance of the oath made by Philip II in the Portuguese *Cortes* in May 1581 in what would have been his first official act as King Philip I of Portugal: was this a sign of royal favour? Or was Philip II obliged to swear by Portuguese law and custom before his new subjects would in turn make an oath of fidelity?

On the other hand, it must be recalled that only a short time after Portugal entered into the dominions of Philipp II, the Genoese chronicler Girolamo Franchi Conestaggio published his *Historia dell'unione del Regno di Portogallo alla Corona de Castiglia* (1585) in which he offered a fairly raw perspective of the entire process, characterising it as a *conquista* and referencing a *unione* of the kingdom of Portugal, not as a newly affiliated member of the Spanish monarchy but specifically '*alla Corona de Castiglia*'. As is known, this book garnered a negative reception, not only for showing the violence of the process but also for representing the incorporation of Portugal as a conquest carried out by Castile. In the years that followed, several treatises were published, written both by Portuguese and non-Portuguese participants, in which Conestaggio's views were intensely disputed.[15]

***

It is important to note that the Portuguese population, and especially its ruling groups, did not wait long to align themselves with the Spanish monarchy's political project. In reality, even prior to 1581 there were many Portuguese who imagined themselves joined to the political-religious project being carried out under the Catholic sign, headed by Philip II of Spain, and these Portuguese elites – which included a significant part of the nobility and the clergy – welcomed the fact that the Portuguese crown would be incorporated into the wider universe of the 'Catholic Monarchy'. As this very name indicates, the political conglomeration that Portugal joined in 1581 was principally

---

[14] On this topic, see Ana Isabel López Salazar, *Inquisición y Política. El Gobierno del Santo Oficio en el Portugal de los Austrias (1578–1653)* (Lisbon, 2011), available at http://hdl .handle.net/10316.2/25266. See also Antonio Terrasa Lozano, 'The Last King's "Naturais": Nobility and "Naturalidade" in Portugal from the Fifteenth to the Seventeenth Century', *e-Journal of Portuguese History*, 10:2 (2012).

[15] Giacinto Manuppella, 'A Lenda Negra de Jerónimo de' Franchi Conestaggio e da sua "Unione del Regno di Portogallo alla Corona di Castiglia"', *Revista da Universidade de Coimbra*, 31 (1984) pp. 53–148; Rafael Valladares, *A Conquista de Lisboa. Violência Militar e Comunidade Política em Portugal, 1578–1583* (Lisbon, 2010).

united by its Catholic identity.[16] This fact brought about several important consequences.

First and foremost, Habsburg Portugal found itself in a space where religious homogeneity under the sign of Catholicism was an unavoidable imperative.[17] Such an imperative manifested itself in a strong overlap between political and religious policy, in the constant vigilance against heterodox positions and lastly in the thorough conviction that Catholicism was the correct creed and that the various Protestant currents were misconceptions that needed to be combated whether by repression or by the spread of Catholic orthodoxy.[18]

As a member of this Catholic monarchy, Portugal found itself joined to the fight waged by the Habsburgs, Spanish and Austrians against the Protestant world, which was symptomatically classified as 'heretic'. It should be remembered that Protestantism had little impact on the majority of the Portuguese population and that the primary quarrels the Portuguese had had up to that point were with Reformed religions not so much in Europe, but rather outside of it, namely in the Atlantic with the French Huguenots who were searching for new opportunities in South America. Additionally, as subjects of a monarchy that defined itself above all as 'Catholic', the Portuguese became equal participants in the antagonism between Christians and Muslims, who were commonly classified as 'infidels'.

Another aspect of the 'Catholic' character of the political environment the Portuguese now found themselves bound to was the fact that they were now governed by a king who, at the end of the sixteenth century was more and more systematically referred to as a 'monarch', i.e. a ruler who exercised his power over a conglomeration that was classified as a 'monarchy'. These terms – 'monarch' and 'monarchy' – had special meaning to the political sensitivities of the day. This was primarily because the title of 'monarch' was not within reach of just anyone, given that it referred to the dominion one ruler exercised over a vast and heterogeneous grouping of territories, many of which held the status of

---

[16] Pablo Fernández Albaladejo, 'Católicos antes que Ciudadanos: Gestación de una "Política Española" en los Comienzos de la Edad Moderna' in José Ignacio Fortea Pérez (ed.), *Imágenes de la Diversidad. El Mundo Urbano en la Corona de Castilla (s. XVI–XVIII)* (Santander, 1997), pp. 103–127.

[17] Xavier Gil Pujol, 'Un Rey, una Fe, Muchas Naciones. Patria y Nación en la España de los Siglos XVI y XVII' in Bernardo García and Antonio Álvarez-Ossorio Alvariño (eds.), *La Monarquía de las Naciones. Patria, Nación y Naturaleza en la Monarquía de España* (Madrid, 2004), pp. 39–76.

[18] María José Rodríguez-Salgado, *Felipe II, el 'Paladín de la Cristiandad' y la Paz con el Turco* (Valladolid, 2004); Xavier Gil, 'Spain and Portugal' in H. A. Lloyd, G. Burgess and S. Hodson (eds.), *European Political Thought, 1450–1700. Religion, Law and Philosophy* (New Haven and London, 2007), pp. 416–456.

kingdoms. Consequently, a monarch was a king of kings who exercised his power broadly, not so much out of greed or ambition but rather motivated by the goal of accomplishing the ancient yearning of Christianity: to establish universal dominion under the sign of Catholicism. This is what the term 'catholic' evokes after all – universal power.[19]

In essence, the status of a monarch was much closer to the condition of an emperor, a political leader whose domain was accompanied by a special political and moral responsibility.[20] Like an empire, a monarchy was also viewed as a political conglomeration characterised by clear transcendental resonances, for the monarch was viewed by many as the instigator of a project of domination with strong religious significations. Therefore, the monarch did not exercise merely secular dominion, given that he was entrusted with concretising the desire for a *Republica Christiana*: the return of all Christian peoples to a single kingdom.

In this light, many Portuguese viewed it as an honour to participate in this political and Catholic undertaking with its universal ambitions. Prior to 1581, the Portuguese were already accustomed to the extremely wide limits of their crown, in Europe and outside it, and their sense of national identity was becoming more and more tied to their overseas explorations and discoveries.[21] The same can be said about the religious overtones of the conquests carried out by the Portuguese in Africa, Asia and America.[22] However, after 1581, and in contrast to what might be

---

[19] Jesús Lalinde Abadía, 'España y la Monarquía Universal (en torno al Concepto de "Estado Moderno")', *Quaderni Fiorentini per la Storia del Pensiero Giuridico Moderno*, 15 (1986) pp. 109–166.

[20] About this topic, see Anthony Pagden, 'Afterword: from Empire to Federation' in Elizabeth Sauer and Balachandra Rajan (eds.), *Imperialisms. Historical and Literary Investigations, 1500–1900* (New York, 2004), pp. 257ff.; also by A. Pagden, 'Conquest and the Just War. The "School of Salamanca" and the "Affair of the Indies"' in Sankar Muthu (ed.), *Empire and Modern Political Thought* (Cambridge and New York, 2012), pp. 30–60. On the close connection between politics and Catholicism in late sixteenth and early seventeenth century Iberia, see Harald Braun, 'Conscience, Counsel and Theocracy at the Spanish Habsburg Court' in H. Braun and E. Vallance (eds.), *Contexts of Conscience in Early Modern Europe, 1500–1700* (Houndmills, 2004), pp. 56–66; also by H. Braun, *Juan de Mariana and Early Modern Spanish Political Thought* (Aldershot, 2007); and Erin Rowe, *Saint and Nation. Santiago, Teresa of Avila, and Plural Identities in Early Modern Spain* (University Park, 2011); José Javier Ruiz Ibáñez, 'The Baroque and the influence of the Spanish Monarchy in Europe (1580–1648)' in Harald Braun and Jesús Pérez-Magallón (eds.), *The Transatlantic Hispanic Baroque. Complex Identities in the Atlantic World* (London, 2014), pp. 114ff.

[21] Giuseppe Marcocci, *L'invenzione di un impero. Politica e cultura nel mondo portoghese (1450–1600)* (Rome, 2011).

[22] Pedro Cardim, 'La Aspiración Imperial de la Monarquía Portuguesa (siglos XVI y XVII)' in Gaetano Sabatini (ed.), *Comprendere le Monarchie Iberiche: Risorse Materiali e Rappresentazione del Potere* (Rome, 2010), pp. 37–72.

expected, a Portuguese identity tied to an extra-European projection not only did not disappear but, in fact, increased. In reality, Portuguese maritime achievements continued to be exalted, but only now they were integrated into the broader efforts that Catholics – Hispanic and otherwise – were expending in order to establish a universal dominion under the sign of Christ. A good example of this can be found in the statement made by a Portuguese chronicler named Pedro de Mariz in his *Diálogos de Varia Historia* (1594): 'Donde claramente fica concluido, que ajunte Deos o poder de Hespanha en huma só cabeça, principalmente estas duas naçoens Portugueza, Castelhana, he pera alguma notável obra de seu serviço'. [Let it be clearly surmised that God by gathering the power of Hispania under a single head, namely these two nations, the Portuguese and the Castilian, was aiming to accomplish some notable work in His service.]

Nevertheless, it cannot be denied that there were many Portuguese who did not hide their dissatisfaction over the fact that Portugal had become bound to the Catholic Monarchy. First of all, as much as the Portuguese kingdom was already a multi-continental reality before its entrance into the Spanish Habsburg dominion, the truth is that after 1581 the Portuguese found themselves involved in complex political matters that they had never before faced. As members of a monarchy with global ambitions, Portugal's horizons were suddenly and exponentially expanded, and although this situation offered some positive promise – for many nobles and merchants the Spanish monarchy revealed itself to be a space of extraordinary opportunities, either in service to the Crown, or in terms of one's career or business prospects – it was also viewed negatively.

As was noted at the beginning of this text, one of the changes that most perplexed the Portuguese elite was the fact that Portugal had lost its independence and had begun to be governed by a king who spent most of his time outside of Portuguese territory. Since the founding of the kingdom of Portugal, this was the first time that this had happened. Although this royal distance was not always seen as an inconvenience, given the fact that it allowed for a great deal of autonomy and self-governance, there is no doubt that for Portugal, the absence of a king was viewed as a demotion, in the same way that Castile welcomed the fact that the monarchs were spending more and more time in their territory and were establishing the central institutions of the monarchy there.[23]

---

[23] Fernando Bouza Álvarez, Fernando, 'Lisboa Sozinha, Quase Viúva. A Cidade e a Mudança da Corte no Portugal dos Filipes', *Penélope. Fazer e Desfazer a História*, 13 (1994) pp. 71–94.

Furthermore, to many the great expanse of the Habsburg dominions raised some fears and doubts regarding the governability of such a vast and heterogeneous grouping of territories. Even before 1581 many Portuguese expressed doubts over the viability of governing the territories then held by Portugal, dispersed over four continents and extremely far between. Nevertheless, from the moment that Portugal became part of the Catholic Monarchy, the global projection of this conglomeration gave added strength to the voice of those who doubted the viability of these enormous political constructions.

Another motive for discontent had to do with the fact that the Portuguese began to be called upon, with increasing frequency, to contribute – especially in fiscal terms – to the causes promoted by the Spanish monarchy with which Portugal had little or no interest. As a political construct, the Spanish monarchy was somewhat abstract and struggled in the short term to foster feelings of loyalty, belonging, and solidarity towards peoples so different and distant from Portugal.

On the other hand, there were many who feared that through its incorporation into such a broad conglomerate Portugal might be dissolved as a political and cultural community, with the accompanying loss of prerogatives inherent in such dissolution. There is no doubt that Portugal, when compared with other territories also ruled by the Spanish monarchy, was more successful in establishing limits to the interference of people coming from other Philip II's dominions. As mentioned before, in 1581 this monarch granted a series of concessions to the Portuguese, thus preserving, to a significant extent, the royal status of the realm. Nevertheless, besides all this, many regarded Castile as a threat to the Portuguese political status. Additionally, the Portuguese continued to feel a great amount of pride for their own history, especially concerning the fight against the Muslims on the Iberian Peninsula, their maritime exploits and their linguistic individuality. Because of this, the fact that Portugal was deprived of its independence and had become a member of the Spanish monarchy led some voices to appeal to patriotic sentiment and complain about the situation the Portuguese crown had been placed in. Whenever tensions arose between Portuguese institutions and the monarchy, there were soon after complaints over the fact that Portugal was being governed from Castile. The same thing happened whenever the Portuguese suffered some military setback in extra-European areas.

And in spite of the galvanising force of Catholic identity, a complete consensus did not exist even on the religious plane. The decades-long war between the Spanish Monarchy and the secessionist provinces of the Netherlands affected the business dealings of some of Portugal's principal merchants. Since the late-medieval period, Flanders had been a traditional market for Portuguese products – notably salt – and it is consequently understandable that many Portuguese merchants became disgruntled with the fact that, beginning in 1581, they were prevented from dealing with the Netherlands because of the war the monarchy was waging against the 'rebellious' provinces of the Low Countries.

In any event, in the field of cultural and political identity there also existed a certain ambivalence as well, for many Portuguese saw them-selves as members of a community that transcended the borders of their royal space, a community that many viewed as the successor to the ancient *Hispania*, the Iberian world from which Portugal had emerged. Beginning in 1581, several works were published that perfectly illustrate this point, in which pride over Portugal's particular history was viewed as being compatible with the condition of membership in the Spanish monarchy.[24]

The feeling of belonging to a cultural, economic, and political reality common to the Iberian Peninsula was reinforced by the interaction between the Portuguese and the other Iberian peoples since the Middle Ages. Consider, for example, the intense interaction between the Portuguese nobles and the nobility from all parts of the Peninsula, or the collaboration between the Portuguese crown and the other Iberian kingdoms in defending the attacks made by the powers of North Africa. Regarding Iberia's expansion beyond Europe, it should be remembered that there were many Portuguese who participated in the conquest of America and in the construction of the so-called Spanish America.[25] Additionally, many Portuguese circulated throughout the Iberian Peninsula or between Portuguese America and the 'Indias de Castilla', speaking Castilian with nearly the same fluency as they did Portuguese.[26]

[24] Eugenio Asensio, 'España en la Épica Portuguesa del Tiempo de los Felipes' *in Estudios Portugueses* (Paris, 1974), pp. 455–493; Miguel Martínez, 'A Poet of Our Own: The Struggle for "Os Lusíadas" in the Afterlife of Camões', *The Journal for Early Modern Cultural Studies*, 10:1 (Spring/Summer 2010), pp. 71–94; Rafael Valladares, 'Vasallos que se Observan. Opinión y Escritura Imperial bajo la Unión de Corona (1580–1640)' in Margarita Rodríguez et al. (eds.), *Descrição Geral do Reino do Peru, em Particular de Lima* (Lisbon, 2013), pp. 55–68.

[25] Daviken Studnicki-Gizbert, *A Nation upon the Ocean Sea. Portugal's Atlantic Diaspora and the Crisis of the Spanish Empire, 1492–1640* (New York, 2007); see also Francisco Bethencourt, 'The Iberian Atlantic: Ties, Networks, and Boundaries' in Harald Braun and Lisa Vollendorf (eds.), *Theorising the Ibero-American Atlantic* (Leiden and Boston, 2013), pp. 15–36.

[26] Lewis Hanke, 'The Portuguese and the Villa Imperial de Potosí' in AA. VV., *III Colóquio Internacional de Estudos Luso-Brasileiros* (Lisbon, 1960), pp. 266–276; Rafael Valladares, *Castilla y Portugal en Asia (1580–1680). Declive Imperial y Adaptación* (Leuven, 2001); Maria Manuel Torrão, 'Formas de Participação dos Portugueses no Comércio de Escravos com as Índias de Castela: Abastecimento e Transporte' in AA.VV., *A Dimensão Atlântica da África, II Reunião de História de África, 30–31 de Outubro a 1 de*

At this same time, in the literary world there was a profound miscegenation, a phenomenon that was closely related to the bilingualism of a substantial part of Portuguese population. During these years, many Portuguese writers opted to write in Castilian, conscious of the fact that by using this language they would reach an even greater audience. And this occurred because of a long-standing reality of multilingualism in the royal courts of Portugal, Castile and Aragon.[27] As would be expected, after Portugal entered the monarchy, this cultural and intellectual miscegenation intensified.[28]

As is well known, Spanish literature was experiencing a moment of particular flourishing and so it is especially understandable that the Spanish literary world would have been so attractive to men of Portuguese letters in that period. A substantial part of the books published in Portugal between 1581 and 1640 was in Castilian, and most of the nobles and clergymen could read, write and speak such language in a fluent way.

Thanks to the cultural similarity to Castile, a great deal of Portuguese therefore adapted themselves easily and took advantage of the political and ecclesiastical resources of the monarchy. In fact, from 1600 onwards a number of Portuguese aristocrats held government posts in several Habsburg territories, and the same can be said about clergymen. Some Portuguese aristocrats, like the Marquises of Castelo Rodrigo, succeeded in becoming high counsellors of the Spanish monarch, thus demonstrating that, for some, the Monarchy became an outstanding space of opportunities.[29]

And concerning the absence of the king, although this question may have frequently been taken up as a way of amplifying resentment against measures that impacted the established interests of Portugal, the truth is that for many Portuguese the distance of the monarch was frequently viewed positively as an opportunity to develop autonomy that probably would

Novembro de 1996 (Lisbon, 2002), pp. 203–222; Maria da Graça Ventura, *Portugueses no Peru ao Tempo da União Ibérica. Mobilidade, Cumplicidades e Vivências* (Lisbon, 2005).

[27] Ana Isabel Buescu, 'Aspectos do Bilinguismo Português Castelhano na Época Moderna', *Hispania*, LXIV/1:216 (2004) pp. 13–38; Xavier Gil Pujol, 'Las Lenguas en la España de los Siglos XVI y XVII: Imperio, Algarabía y Lengua Común' in AA.VV., *Comunidad e Identidad en el Mundo Ibérico* (Valencia, 2013), pp. 81–120.

[28] On the interaction between the Castilian and the Portuguese juridical milieus, see Bartolomé Clavero, 'Lex Regni Vicinoris. Indicio de España en Portugal', *Boletim da Faculdade de Direito de Coimbra*, 58 (1983), pp. 239–298.

[29] On the Marquises of Castelo Rodrigo, see Santiago Martínez Hernández, '"Fineza, Lealtad y Zelo". Estrategias de Legitimación y Ascenso de la Nobleza Lusitana en la Monarquía Hispánica: Los Marqueses de Castelo Rodrigo' in Manuel Rivero Rodríguez (ed.), *Nobleza Hispana, Nobleza Cristiana: la Orden de San Juan* vol. 2 (Madrid, 2009), pp. 913–960.

have been impossible to achieve had the king and the central institutions of the Crown been permanently established in Portuguese territory.

***

Portugal was brought into the conglomerate ruled by Philip II at a time in which the Habsburgs were already feeling some fatigue after decades of more or less constant military expansion. As indicated before, it was precisely at this juncture that the notion of a 'monarchy' emerged as a way of characterising the dominion of the Spanish Habsburgs. I. A. A. Thompson has shown that by adopting the status of 'monarchy', the Habsburgs appropriated for themselves the privilege of directing universal Christianity, an idea that had enormous power as an element of unity and collective identity.[30]

In the late sixteenth century, the expressions 'Catholic Monarchy' and/ or 'Spanish Monarchy' became much more present in royal discourse. And although both expressions bore a desire for universal rule, at that point in time they still seemed compatible with the plural nature of Spain and with the imperative to respect the personality and specific characteristics of each of its parts.

Likewise, at this point in time, the centrality of Castile within the Habsburg Empire became even more distinct, a phenomenon that was not unrelated to the growing diffusion of the expression 'Spanish monarchy'.[31] Gregorio López Madera's chronicle, *Excelencias de la monarquía y reino de España* (1597), contributed to strengthening the relationship between Castile and the idea of 'Spain'. Besides this, at the end of Philip II's reign numerous histories of Spain were published that privileged a Castilian point of view and conveyed an ever-stronger Spanish patriotism.[32]

The 'Castilian resonance' of the term 'monarchy' caused a certain degree of controversy and some of the other territories of the Habsburgs who felt most threatened by the growing pre-eminence of the Castilian crown even formally claimed their own right to use this designation. Such was the case with Portugal, where the noun *monarquia* [monarchy] became fashion at the end of the 1500s, the moment when friar Bernardo de Brito, a Cistercian chronicler, published his history of the

---

[30] I. A. A. Thompson, 'La Monarquía de España: la Invención de un Concepto' in F. J. Guillamón Álvarez et al. (eds.), *Entre Clío y Casandra. Poder y Sociedad en la Monarquía Hispánica durante la Edad Moderna* (Murcia, 2005), pp. 31–56.

[31] I. A. A. Thompson, 'La Respuesta Castellana ante la Política Internacional de Felipe II' in AA. VV., *La Monarquía de Felipe II a Debate* (Madrid, 2000), pp. 121–134.

[32] María José Rodríguez-Salgado, 'Patriotismo y Política Exterior en la España de Carlos V y Felipe II' in Felipe Ruiz Martín (ed.), *La Proyección Europea de la Monarquía Hispánica* (Madrid, 1996), pp. 49–104.

origins of the Portuguese kingdom, entitled *Monarchia Lusytana* (1597). The adoption of the term *monarquia* was, after all, a form of expressing Portugal's pretension to maintain its particular status within the heart of the Spanish conglomerate. But it was also a way of recalling that the Portuguese kingdom was very ancient and continued to be the head of a vast multi-continental conglomerate of territories, whose individuality had been expressly guaranteed by Philip II in 1581.

Reactions to the growing political weight of Castile led to an even more intense commemoration of the origins of each of the Iberian kingdoms. At about this same time, the Portuguese chronicler Pedro de Mariz published his work *Diálogos de Varia Historia* (1594), which gives special attention to the founding of the kingdom and, above all, to the mythical narrative of the already mentioned 'miracle of Ourique', the mythical narrative that spoke of a divine intervention in Portugal's political founding.[33] Besides this, Mariz defended the idea that Portugal descended from the ancient Suevi kingdom, and thus had been the first Iberian territory that had become Christian. Such a claim was related to the intense rivalry during the sixteenth and seventeenth centuries between the archbishops of Toledo (the episcopal primate of Castile) and Braga (the primate of Portugal). As is evident, underlying this episcopal rivalry was another and greater political tension between Portugal and Castile.

Initially, the Spanish patriotism referred to previously, even with its Castilian expression, coexisted without major difficulties among the other Hispanic patriotisms (including the Portuguese) that flourished at the time, both in Europe and in America. However, beginning in the first years of the 1600s, this issue became more and more controversial as complaints emerged over the fact that the king was spending increasing amounts of time in Castile, which accentuated his absence from the remaining territories.[34] This situation only intensified in the following years.

Debates over the absence of the king led to numerous substantive questions of a 'constitutional' nature. The discussion caused by the various times in which Philip III delayed his visit to Portugal shows well how politicised the atmosphere had become. Between 1598 and 1619, Philip III's visit was repeatedly postponed, causing several questions to be raised: did the fact that Philip III had opted to put off his

---

[33] Francisco Bethencourt, 'La Sociogénesis del Sentimiento Nacional', *Manuscrits*, 8 (January, 1990), pp. 17–40.

[34] Bernardo García, *La Pax Hispanica. Política Exterior de Felipe III* (Lovaina, 1996); Antonio Feros, *Kingship and Favoritism in the Spain of Philip III, 1598–1621* (Cambridge, 2000).

journey to Portugal signify that this territory was being 'demoted' from kingdom to province? Was Philip III already king of Portugal even before setting foot in this territory as a royal individual to make his royal oaths? Was Philip III obligated to convoke the *Cortes* (the representative assembly) on the first occasion in which he as king should come to Portugal?[35]

As can be seen, the delay of the royal visit caused the topic of the royal oaths to become the centre of debate in Portugal during the first two decades of the seventeenth century. Nonetheless, it is important to note that questions similar to these were being raised, at the same time, among the other territories of the monarchy. For example, in Aragon the political implications of the royal oaths were also widely debated,[36] leading to the following questions: could Philip III exercise his jurisdiction in Aragon before making the royal oaths? Did Philip III have an obligation to go and swear to the *fueros* of Aragon after having already done so as a prince? In essence, what this reveals is the degree to which these preoccupations had become widespread, not merely as a reaction to the prolonged absence of the king, but also in response to the growing weight that Castile held within the monarchy.

In the Portuguese context, the terms of Portugal's incorporation into the Spanish Monarchy, along with the meaning of the oath sworn in 1581, were heatedly discussed. The debate about the limits of royal authority became so strong that some dignitaries were forced to come out in defence of monarchical power. In January 1613, Don Diego de Silva, Count of Salinas and a prominent member of the Council of Portugal, expressed his view about the prerogatives of the king and the parliament of Portugal, in which he discussed at length the agreement of 1581 and defended the royal prerogative. Furthermore, the Count of Salinas vehemently rejected the idea that the king was obligated to swear the *foros* of Portugal before the representative assembly of this kingdom.[37] In 1613

---

[35] Santiago de Luxán Meléndez, *La Revolución de 1640 en Portugal, sus fundamentos sociales y sus caracteres nacionales. El Consejo de Portugal. 1580–1640* (Madrid, 1988), p. 237; Jean-Frédéric Schaub, 'Dinámicas políticas en el Portugal de Felipe III (1598–1621)', *Relaciones*, revista del Colegio de Michoacán, México, 73 (1998), pp. 169–211.

[36] Eliseo Serrano, 'No demandamos sino el modo. Los juramentos reales en Aragón en la Edad Moderna', *Pedralbes*, 28 (2008), pp. 435–464.

[37] Claude Gaillard, *Le Portugal sous Philippe III d'Espagne. L'action de Diego de Silva y Mendoza* (Grenoble, 1982), pp. 107ff.; Erasmo Buceta, 'Dictamen del Conde de Salinas en que se examinan las prerrogativas de la Corona y de las Cortes de Portugal', *Anuario de Historia del Derecho Español*, 9 (1932), pp. 375–385, at pp. 378–379; Trevor Dadson, 'The Duke of Lerma and the Count of Salinas: Politics and Friendship in Early Seventeenth-Century Spain', *European History Quarterly*, 25 (1995), pp. 5–38; T. Dadson, 'Conflicting views of the Last Spanish Viceroy of Portugal (1617–1621): Diego de Silva y Mendoza, Count of Salinas and Marquis of Alenquer',

Francisco de Sosa, Bishop of the Canaries, defended a similar position after a visit he made to Portugal as Philip III's envoy, maintaining that the oath sworn in 1581 had been a sign of royal favour and not the fulfilment of an obligation.[38]

***

During the subsequent reign of Philip IV and under the oversight of his powerful favourite, the Count-Duke Olivares, from 1624 onward war and economic pressures aggravated the debate over these and other questions of a 'constitutional' nature.[39] At this juncture of pressure, there arose a new interest in the rights of each territory of the Spanish monarchy, and the timing and circumstances of the constitutive act of each of its kingdoms came to the centre of the political debate.

A great interest in history, above all medieval history, swept through the peninsula, especially the period of the so-called 'reconquest', that is, the fight against the Muslims and the foundational moment of each Christian territory as an independent entity. As mentioned above, initially the purpose of verifying this historical knowledge was to extract from the particular history of each kingdom the greatest amount of information possible to justify a pre-eminent territorial status within the Spanish Monarchy. Under Philip IV, however, the recovery of historical knowledge became a way of defending against the reformist ambitions of Olivares.

At this point in time, the notion of *lex regia* gained widespread currency, leading to treatises dedicated to the process of transmitting power from the community to the prince. Among the principal questions taken up in these treatises on *lex regia* were the following: in what circumstances was the conquest of the territory to the Muslims accomplished? Who was the original holder of the power to create governing authority? Was this power transmissible or not? In the event that it was, what were the limits and conditions of such a transmission?[40]

It was in the last years of the reign of Philip III that the Aragonese jurist Pedro Calixto Ramírez published his paradigmatic text on the topic. In *Analyticus Tractatus de Lege Regia, qua, in Princeps Suprema & absoluta potestas translata fuit: cum quadam corporis politici ad instar phisici, capitis; &*

Portuguese Studies, 7 (1991), pp. 28–60 ; and also by T. Dadson, *Diego de Silva y Mendoza. Poeta y Político en la Corte de Felipe III* (Granada, 2012).

[38] Pedro Cardim, 'Felipe III, la Jornada de Portugal y las Cortes de 1619' in José Martínez Millán and María Antonietta Visceglia (eds.), *La corte de Felipe II y el gobierno de la Monarquía Católica (1598–1621)*, vol. IV (Madrid, 2008), pp. 900–946.

[39] António M. Hespanha, 'O Governo dos Áustria e a 'Modernização' da Constituição Política Portuguesa', *Penélope. Fazer e Desfazer a História* 2 (February 1989), pp. 55ff.

[40] Arrieta Alberdi, 'Las Formas de Vinculación'.

membrorum conexione ... (1616), Calixto Ramírez discusses the origins of the kingdom of Aragon and the contribution that each Christian community of the Iberian Peninsula had made to the fight against the Muslims. Calixto rejects the idea that the 'reconquest' had been a sole Castilian initiative originating in Asturias. Instead, he argues that there was a plural response to the Muslim invasion, a thesis that had concrete implications regarding the political status of each territory. This was primarily because defending a plural response to the Muslim rule signified rejecting the idea that it was Castile who had brought independence to each of the peninsular kingdoms, an argument that complicated Castilian pretensions of supremacy in the internal hierarchy of the Spanish Monarchy. Furthermore, by emphasising the specific origin and trajectory of each territory, this argument endowed each kingdom with its own particular notion of *lex regia* that the monarch would have to respect.

In Portugal there was a similar renewed interest in the specific history of the kingdom and its *lex regia*. In 1627, a jurist named João Salgado de Araújo published a treatise entitled *Ley Regia de Portugal*, in which he traces the main moments of Portugal's political founding, including a thorough examination of the legendary 'miracle of Ourique'. It is important to note that such event had become the object of new critical evaluations since the beginning of seventeenth century, namely by chroniclers like Duarte Nunes de Lião, Bernardo de Brito and other erudite defenders of the status of the Portuguese kingdom.

In any event, and with respect to the 'reconquest', various contradictory positions emerged: Luís Coelho Barbuda, in his *Empresas Militares de Lusitanos* ... (1624), defended the proposition that the Portuguese had priority in the 'reconquest', while João Salgado de Araújo, in his *Ley Regia de Portugal* ... (1627), argued that León and Castile had conquered the Portuguese territory to the Muslims and had granted independence to the Portuguese. The jurist António de Sousa de Macedo, in *Flores de España Excelencias de Portugal* ... (1631), in turn affirmed that 'es Portugal Monarchia soberana independiente, y sin reconocer superior alguno ...' [Portugal is a sovereign and independent Monarchy and does not recognise any superior] thereby defending Portugal's role in the 'reconquest'. This brief enumeration shows that a consensus did not exist within the Portuguese regarding the view of the 'reconquest', a situation that was replicated in other parts of the Iberian Peninsula.

As might be expected, Olivares' reform efforts were frequently associated with Castile's primacy within the Spanish Monarchy. Because of this, the tension generated by his measures caused many of the books being published on the debate of Iberia's past to express a tone of xenophobia. Several treatises emphasised historical episodes of hostility between the Portuguese and the Castilians, for example, during the time of the 'reconquest', though also throughout the rest of the medieval period and even through the course of their overseas expansion. These books, in turn, provoked reactions in defence of a harmony between Portugal and Castile, many of them in treatises authored by Portuguese. Good examples of this counterreaction are found in the works of Luís Coelho Barbuda and Lourenço de Mendonça, the latter a clergyman who lived several decades in Spanish America.

On the other hand, the Spanish monarchy began to face increasing military, financial, and economic difficulties. In Portugal such difficulties were strongly felt: since the second decade of the seventeenth century the Dutch had begun challenging many Portuguese possessions in Asia, and from 1630 onwards a great deal of Brazil was conquered by the Dutch West Indian Company forces. This event was considered a major setback because the American part of the Portuguese overseas rule was already the most prosperous of all its overseas possessions. In the years that followed the failure of the Spanish monarchy's attempts to expel the Dutch from Brazil eroded the allegiance of many Portuguese to Philip IV.

The Spanish Monarchy therefore began to lose the ground it had won during the fair weather of the sixteenth century. The Crown progressively referred to the resources it appropriated from its various territories as belonging to 'Spain', and these resources themselves became increasingly scarce and fought over. It was also at this time that Philip IV's subjects coming from outside Castile acknowledged that 'Spain' was the status which afforded the most advantages within the monarchy.[41]

Accordingly, a series of debates unravelled over the Spanish identity of the diverse Iberian territories. For example, discussions arose over which kingdom had the oldest claims to Spain and which territory was most intensely 'Spanish'.[42] Castile became increasingly associated to Spain, and it was also regarded as the Iberian territory where royal supremacy was more intense. Typical of this debate, similarities with Castile became one of the most frequently invoked criteria of 'Spanishness'. This was the case in Pedro Barbosa de Luna's *Memorial de la preferencia, que haze el Reyno de Portugal, y su Consejo, al de Aragon, y de las dos Sicilias* (1627), in

---

[41] I. A. A. Thompson, 'Castile, Spain and the Monarchy: The Political Community from "Patria Natural" to "Patria Nacional"' in R. Kagan and G. Parker (eds.), *Spain, Europe and the Atlantic World. Essays in Honour of John H. Elliott* (Cambridge, 1995), pp. 125–159.

[42] Tamar Herzog, 'Être Espagnol dans un Monde Moderne et Transatlantique' in A. Tallon (ed.), *Le Sentiment National dans l'Europe Méridionale aux XVIe et XVⁿ Siècles* (Madrid, 2007), pp. 1–18; see, also, John H. Elliott, 'Rey y Pátria eⁿ Hispânico' in Victor Mínguez and Manuel Chust (eds.), *El Imperio Sub' y Naciones en España e Hispanoamérica* (Madrid, 2004), pp. 17–35.

which he presented a series of reasons for the pre-eminence of Portugal over Aragon within the Spanish monarchy. Luna's primary criterion was the degree of sovereignty held by the king, and he argued that within the Iberian Peninsula, it was in Castile where the king was more sovereign. He therefore argued that the status of Aragon was inferior to that of Portugal because in the latter the king enjoyed greater authority, thereby approximating the situation in Castile.[43]

The Portuguese clergyman Lourenço de Mendonça, in his *Suplicacion a su Magestad Catolica del Rey nuestro señor, que Dios quarde. Ante sus Reales Consejos de Portugal y de las Indias, en defensa de los Portugueses* ... (1630), also elaborated a vehement defence of the Spanish identity of the Portuguese based on historic and cultural affinities between Castile and Portugal. Mendonça's aim was to demonstrate to Philip IV that the Portuguese were at least as Spanish as his other Iberian subjects, and, precisely for that reason, they should be allowed to settle down in Spanish America and take advantage of its business opportunities and resources.[44] As for García de Góngora y Torreblanca, in *Historia apologética y descripción del reino de Navarra* (1628), he likewise appealed, instead, to antiquity, affirming that Navarre had an unquestionable Spanish identity because it was even more ancient than Castile or Aragon. And regarding America, Juan de Palafox y Mendoza echoed '*criollo*' claims of Spanishness.

Besides contributing to the establishment of a more rigid notion of the Spanish monarchy, Olivares' reforms also occasioned proposals for ways of restructuring the institutional apparatus in order to reinforce the king's supremacy over the various territories and simplify certain administrative processes. In Portugal, as in other regions of the monarchy, writings that supported Olivares' politics reaffirmed the king's supremacy and expressed an unfavourable opinion over the role of the *Cortes* (the representative assembly) in the political system, precisely because it was seen as an institution that limited royal power. It should also be remembered that power to convoke such an assembly was exclusively held by territories that had royal status. The *Cortes* was a symbol of the Portuguese royal status. For this reason, an attempt to limit the power of the Portuguese

---

[43] Emilia Salvador Esteban 'Integración y Periferización de las Coronas de Aragón y de Portugal en la Monarquía Hispánica. El Caso Valenciano (1580–1598)' in L. Ribot and E. Belenguer (eds.), *Las Sociedades Ibéricas y el Mar a Finales del Siglo XVI, vol. III, El Área del Mediterráneo* (Madrid, 1998), pp. 159–180, at p. 174; Xavier Gil, 'Parliamentary Life in the Crown of Aragon: Cortes, Juntas de Brazos, and other Corporate Bodies', *Journal of Early Modern History*, 6 (2002), pp. 390ff.

[44] Pedro Cardim, '"Todos los que no son de Castilla son yguales". El Estatuto de Portugal en la Monarquía Española en el Tiempo de Olivares', *Pedralbes. Revista d'Història Moderna*, Any XXVIII, Núm. 28 vol. I (2008), pp. 521–552.

representative assembly, at this point in time, was the equivalent of an attack on Portugal's status as a kingdom.

Among the many examples of these writings that could be cited is a text written in the 1620s by the aforementioned Portuguese jurist João Salgado de Araújo, which discusses the legitimacy of organising, in Madrid, councils to more quickly address Portugal's affairs. Salgado de Araújo, who had previously written about Portugal's 'ley regia', defended in this text the formation of such councils. No sooner did this news arrive, that a rumour spread which indicated that plans were being made to suppress the Portuguese representative assembly. This was considered to be a sure sign that Portugal's royal status was soon to be revoked.

In response to these invectives, several texts were published that reiterated the factuality of the 'miracle of Ourique' as a way of reinforcing Portugal's divinely appointed royal status. On the other hand, the 'minutes' of a representative assembly which had supposedly been held in the town of Lamego during the initial moments of Portugal as an independent kingdom, were conveniently 'discovered' during the 1630s and divulged by the Portuguese chronicler António Brandão in his *Terceira parte da Monarchia Lusitana: que contem a historia de Portugal desde o Conde Dom Henrique, até todo o reinado del Rey Dom Afonso henriques* ... (1632). Brandão intended to prove that from the time of its founding as a royal entity, in the twelfth century, Portugal had retained the right to determine its own administrative affairs. Furthermore, this same document offered historical arguments to those who stood for the representative assembly and defended a limited conception of royal power in Portugal. In this light, we can see why the minutes of the assembly of Lamego served to galvanise all those who had been affected by the policies of Olivares and his authoritarian way of governing.

Those who opposed the reforms of the count-duke were hereafter called *'repúblicos'* [republicans] or *'populares'* [populars]. At this point in time the word 'repúblico' began to refer to those who defended the liberties of the commonwealth against the 'authoritarian' measures of the Crown. It should be noted as well that in June 1640, Catalan leaders, who were already in a pre-revolution condition, were referred to by royal officers as 'republicos'.

In 1638, following the rebellions which had occurred the previous year in the south of Portugal,[45] the Crown took measures that clearly pointed to the strengthening of royal authority in Portugal: in Madrid the monarch's

---

[45] J. Romero Magalhães, '1637: Motins da Fome', *Biblos*, 52 (1976), pp. 319–333; António de Oliveira, *Poder e Oposição Política em Portugal no Período Filipino (1580–1640)* (Lisbon, 1991), pp. 161ff.; António de Oliveira, *Movimentos Sociais e Poder em Portugal no Século XVII* (Coimbra, 2002), pp. 423ff.

favourite convened a restricted special meeting intended to substitute the representative assembly of Portugal, and a short time later dissolved the Council of Portugal, the institution that, until that moment, asserted the royal status of Portugal at royal court. At the same time, several proposals – some of them authored by Portuguese – circulated regarding the definitive reconfiguration of Portugal's status within the Spanish Monarchy: the Portuguese clergyman Agostinho Manuel de Vasconcelos proposed a solemn joint-meeting in Madrid between the representative assemblies of the two crowns – Castile and Portugal – or, as an alternative, a gathering of dignitaries from the nobility, the clergy, and representatives from Portugal's principal cities.[46] In essence, Olivares intended for the Portuguese representative assembly to cease to be a symbol of regional royalty and become instead a sign of loyalty to the collective governed by the monarchy.[47]

Without question, one consequence to this veritable wave of debates regarding Portugal's political condition was the work of Juan Caramuel Lobkowitz, *Philippus prudens Caroli V. Imp. Filius Lusitanae Algarbiae, Indiae, Brasiliae legitimus rex demonstratus ...* (1639). Caramuel Lobkowitz, a theologian and mathematician of Bohemian ascendancy, was a fierce supporter of the royal prerogative and of Philip IV of Spain. The cover of his book portrays an allegory that suggests, in a rather restrictive manner, that Portugal had been 'conquered' by Philip II in 1581. In other words, this image suggests that Habsburg authority over Portugal did not have a limited scope, mostly because the Portuguese territory had been conquered and allegedly shared, since 1581, the status of 'conquest'. As for the work itself, Caramuel Lobkowitz examines the founding of Portugal and asserts the initial submission of the Portuguese to the kingdom of León and Castile. He also affirms that centuries earlier, Portuguese nobility participated at the *Cortes* of León, a sure sign of an early submission by Portugal to this kingdom.[48]

***

The outbreak of war between the Spanish Monarchy and France (1635) and, five years later, the appearance of revolts in Catalonia and Portugal were events that exposed the failings of the Habsburg political model.

---

[46] Jean-Frédéric Schaub, *Le Portugal au Temps du Comte-duc d'Olivares (1621–1640). Le Conflit de Juridictions comme Exercice de la Politique* (Madrid, 2001), pp. 130ff.

[47] Pablo Fernández Albaladejo, 'Common Souls, Autonomous Bodies: the Language of Unification under rhe Catholic Monarchy, 1590–1630', *Revista Internacional de Estudios Vascos, Cuad.* 5 (2009) pp. 78ff.

[48] Fernando Bouza Álvarez, 'Retórica da Imagem Real. Portugal e a Memória Figurada de Filipe II', *Penélope. Fazer e desfazer a história*, 4 (Abril de 1990), pp. 45ff.

The revolt and the subsequent secession of Portugal from the Spanish monarchy, in 1640, took place at a moment when the integration in the monarchy of both the Portuguese nobility and high clergy was reaching its maximum level.[49] In spite of the aforementioned political tension, a considerable number of Portuguese high dignitaries was spread in all parts of Philip IV's territories, taking advantage of the career opportunities granted by the Habsburg.[50] This explains why the protagonists of the revolt were mainly second rank nobles, members of the lower clergy, several magistrates, representatives of the main city councils and some merchants. In other words, the initial support to the rebellion that took place in Lisbon on 1 December 1640, came from the groups most affected by Olivares' policy, and also from sectors that had not benefited greatly from the Spanish monarchy. As for the aristocracy, due to the fact that a great deal of its most prominent members was outside Portugal, it cautiously awaited for the course of events and only gradually declared its allegiance to the newly enthroned dynasty of the Braganzas. Nevertheless, some nobles ended up maintaining their loyalty to Philip IV, and for that reason never returned to Portugal.

The Catalan and the Portuguese revolts also exposed the failings of the strictly Catholic conceptions of political action.[51] The traditional appeals to a 'holy war' faced the hard reality of the conflict between the disaffected subjects of Philip IV: it was an all-out battle among Catholics. As for the notion of a 'just war', Catholic authorities began to suggest that it was necessary to break the peace in order to achieve certain fundamental objectives. The principle of *necessitas* [necessity] was increasingly invoked by political counsellors and governors alike as a justification for political action.

Even so, traditional political concepts continued to exert a powerful influence, especially in the visceral repugnance provoked by the gestures of rebellion and betrayal.[52] This in turn explains the propagandistic campaign waged by the Catalans and the Portuguese, after 1640, to

---

[49] Fernando Bouza Álvarez, 'A Nobreza Portuguesa e a Corte de Madrid entre 1630 e 1640. Nobres e Luta Política no Portugal de Olivares' in *Portugal no Tempo dos Filipes. Política, Cultura, Representações (1580–1668)* (Lisbon, 2000), pp. 207ff.

[50] For two recent assessments of this topic at the level of the 'lower groups', see Jean-Frédéric Schaub, *L'Île aux Mariés. Les Açores entre Deux Empires (1583–1642)* (Madrid, 2014); and Tamar Herzog, *Frontiers of Possession. Spain and Portugal in Europe and the Americas* (Cambridge, 2015).

[51] Maria de los Ángeles Pérez Samper, *Catalunya i Portugal el 1640: dos Pobles en una Cruïlla* (Barcelona, 1992); Joan-Lluís Palos, 'Les Idees i la Revolució Catalana de 1640', *Manuscrits*, 17 (1999), pp. 277–292.

[52] John H. Elliott, 'Una Sociedad no Revolucionaria: Castilla en la Década de 1640' in *España en Europa. Estudios de Historia Comparada. Escritos Seleccionados* (Valencia, 2002), pp. 193–213.

justify secession and to mollify the stigma of being called 'rebels'. The protagonists of the two rebellions spared no efforts to justify their actions and, similar to what had happened in the United Provinces, in both Portugal and Catalonia neo-scholastic thinking with its theories about the 'popular' origin of power provided ample fodder to those who opposed Olivares.

From the perspective of those who supported the two revolts, the obligations of 'love for country' were presented as stronger than ever, superseding fidelity to Philip IV. In Catalonia, the justification for revolt appealed to themes such as the natural right to self-defence and to self-preservation, just cause, *necessitas*, and even the idea of the 'voluntary princedom', which was argued for in treatises by Covarrubias, Vázquez de Menchaca, Suárez and other doctrinaires of the late sixteenth and early seventeenth century. Additionally, the Catalan propaganda spread the conviction that, during the medieval period, the Catalans had liberated themselves from Muslim rule. Accordingly, the Christian 'reconquest' of the Iberian Peninsula again returned to the centre of political debate.

As for Portugal and its rebellion, João Pinto Ribeiro, Francisco Velasco de Gouveia, and many other jurists elaborated arguments regarding the theory of transfer of sovereignty, 'popular sovereignty', and the right to resist tyrants. Juan Caramuel Lobkowitz's aforementioned book was the target of varied reactions, many of which returned to the notion of the election of kings and also to the moment in which Portugal had entered into the Spanish monarchy.[53] Defenders of the Portuguese rebellion rejected Caramuel's interpretation that Philip II of Spain had conquered Portugal and furthermore asserted that in the Portuguese context royal power had always been negotiated and agreed upon rather than seized. They also rejected the existence of an original dependency of Portugal on León and Castile, a good example being the book published by António Pais Viegas, *Principios del Reyno de Portugal, con Vida y Hechos de Don Alphonso Henriquez su Primero Rey y con los Principios de los otros Estados Christianos de España* ... (1641). Once again the 'reconquest' and the founding moment of the kingdom became the centre of polemics.

Various arguments were mobilised to legitimate the Portuguese revolt. Some of these arguments appealed to a limited conception of royal power, like Francisco Velasco de Gouveia's paradigmatic juridical and political treatise, *Iusta Acclamação do Serenissimo Rey de Portugal Dom Ioão o IV. Tratado Analytico Diuidido em tres partes. Ordenado, e Divulgado em nome do mesmo Reyno, em justificação de sua acção* ... (1644). A good part of the

---

[53] Fernando Bouza Álvarez, '1640 perante o Estatuto de Tomar. Memória e Juízo do Portugal dos Filipes', *Penélope. Fazer e Desfazer a História*, 9–10 (1993), pp. 17–27.

post-1640 propaganda likewise opted towards arguments in favour of 'popular sovereignty'. Similarly to what was happening in other parts of Western Europe, Portugal was also the stage for an 'explosion of print', and that resulted in the politicisation of increasing sections of society.[54] The names of some great Castilian thinkers – Suárez or Molina – were invoked both to justify Portuguese separatism and to support a limited royal prerogative, and this also explains the protagonist role played by the Portuguese parliament during the period immediately following the rupture of 1640 (the *Cortes* met in 1641, 1642, 1645 and 1653).

The Portuguese and Catalan revolts greatly expanded the notion of a supposed pact that united the king and the community. This idea appeared, for example, in various sermons and numerous pamphlets. In Portugal and throughout its overseas territories, dozens of preachers took up this theme as well as the miraculous and messianic nature of Portugal's reclaimed independence on 1 December 1640, portraying the events of that day as a 'restoration' of a situation that had been interrupted in 1581.[55] Apart from asserting that the secessionist Portugal was undoubtedly protected by divine providence, the propaganda disseminated various examples of godly protection of Portugal throughout history.[56] And in 1674 an expanded version of Pedro de Mariz's chronicle *Diálogos de Varia Historia* was republished, in which the mythical narrative of the 'miracle of Ourique' was once again celebrated.

With the exception of the northern African city of Ceuta, all the Portuguese extra-European territorial possessions ended up supporting the rebellion that took place in Lisbon in December 1640, although in some cases with some hesitation. As already said, the defeats of the previous decades eroded the trust in the military capacity of the Spanish Monarchy. In South America the richest part of Brazil – Pernambuco and the surrounding captaincies – remained occupied by the Dutch, and for the thousands of Portuguese who lived in Spanish America life was becoming increasingly difficult, due to the constant pressure of

---

[54] On this topic, see Diogo Ramada Curto, *O Discurso Político em Portugal (1600–1650)* (Lisbon, 1988); see, also, D. Ramada Curto, *Cultura Política no Tempo dos Filipes (1580–1640)* (Lisbon, 2011). For a comparative perspective, see Jason Peacey, *Print and Public Politics in the English Revolution* (Cambridge, 2013).

[55] João Francisco Marques, *A Parenética Portuguesa e a Restauração 1640–1668. A Revolta e a Mentalidade* (Porto, 1989).

[56] Huges Didier, "'Lusitaniae est imperare orbi universo". El Padre António Vieira y los Autores Austrohispanistas de Castilla', *Literatura Portuguesa y Literatura Española* (Cuadernos de Filología, anexo XXXI) (Valencia, 1999), pp. 143–153; Luís Filipe Silvério Lima, *O Império dos Sonhos. Narrativas Proféticas, Sebastianismo e Messianismo Brigantino* (São Paulo, 2010); Gaetano Sabatini and Pedro Cardim, 'António Vieira e o Universalismo dos Séculos XVI e XVII' in AA.VV., *António Vieira, Roma e o Universalismo das Monarquias Portuguesa e Espanhola* (Lisbon, 2011), pp. 13–28.

authorities. These facts in part explain the support of Portuguese colonial elites to the rebellious movement.

Nevertheless, there is no doubt that propaganda was crucial to gain support to the revolt, both in Portugal and in its overseas territories. Contrarily to the Catalans, the Portuguese rebels rapidly decided to have their movement headed by the Duke of Braganza, enthroned as King John IV.[57] This decision also contributed to legitimise the split from the Spanish Monarchy, to make the rebellion less despicable, and to assert Portugal's royal status. The enthronement of the Duke of Braganza was presented as a 'restitution', given the fact that the Crown had returned to the grandson of D. Catarina de Bragança (one of the candidates to the Portuguese throne in 1581, defeated by Philip II). The imminent separation of several parts of the Spanish monarchy also stimulated debate regarding the causes of the phenomenon, which once again brought attention to the events of 1581.

At this point in time it also became equally urgent to disseminate the view that this secession from the Spanish monarchy constituted an action that was unanimously supported by all social groups within Portugal. For this reason, feelings of Portuguese national identity became deeply politicised and were tinged with elements of a transcendent and providential character. Several topics of the so-called black legend were appropriated by some to denigrate Philip IV and demonise Castile. Consequently, anti-Castilian xenophobia flared up again, which is related to the already mentioned Castilian connotation of many of Count-Duke Olivares' actions.[58]

In terms of the rest of Europe, Portuguese propagandists also gambled on the strategy of demonising the Habsburg government. Interestingly enough, the books aimed at the European public did not insist much in the topic of limited royal prerogative, in order not to affect the reputation of the newly enthroned king of Portugal. Instead, they seek to ennoble Portugal, its new dynasty, its overseas possessions and its political status. Besides trying to assert that Portuguese territory had never been subject to León-Castile, Portuguese defenders promoted on the European diplomatic stage the image of a Portugal that, in its founding, had been blessed by divinity, having fought alone against the Muslims and established on

---

[57] Xavier Gil Pujol, 'El Discurs Reialista a la Catalunya dels Àustries fins al 1652, en el seu Context Europeu', *Actes del IV Congrés d'Història Moderna de Catalunya: Catalunya i Europa en l'Edat Moderna, Pedralbes*, II:18 (1998), pp. 475–487.

[58] See Pedro Cardim, 'História, política e reputação no *Discurso del duque de Alba al Catolico Felipe IV sobre el consejo, que se diò en abril passado, para la recuperación de Portugal ...* (1645), de Braz da França' in David Martín Marcos, José María Iñurritegui and Pedro Cardim (eds.), *Repensar a identidade. O mundo ibérico nas margens da crise da consciência europeia* (Lisbon, 2015), pp. 91–130.

its own a great multi-continental empire, thereby become worthy to be qualified as a 'monarchy' itself.

As for the Spanish Monarchy, its supporters also turned to moral arguments and pamphlets while promoting a version of the 'black legend' against the Portuguese, who were systematically identified as rebels and portrayed as traitors and ungrateful persons.[59] The Portuguese defects included instability, the breaking of oaths, and a natural inclination towards rebellion. The Portuguese were furthermore criticised for their behaviour throughout history. For example, in reference to the conquest of America, the chronicler Cristóbal Acuña detailed in his *Nuevo Descubrimiento del Gran Rio de las Amazonas* ... (1641) the cruelties committed by the Portuguese in South America, alleging that because of their greed, the Portuguese thought only about enslaving Indians.

The internal convulsions that affected the Spanish monarchy beginning in 1640 exposed the failings of the Catholic political paradigm.[60] The most fundamental premises of the Catholic understanding of politics not only were no longer the centre of concern, but they were reduced to mere instrumentality. This is what happened with the oath between the king and his subjects. At one point viewed as almost a 'sacrament of power' because of its religious implications, the oath became an instrument manipulated by the Portuguese 'rebels' soon after the revolt of 1640. On the other hand, Catholic authorities did make alliances with Protestants who until then had been branded as 'heretics': after 1648 the Spanish Monarchy drew closer to the United Provinces,[61] which until then had been their natural enemies, and the Bragança of Portugal looked for support from the Protestant world, and to obtain it, Portugal did not hesitate to 'offer' parts of its overseas empire to its former Protestant rivals.

The serious conflict between the newly established Braganza dynasty and the papacy also served to deepen the crisis regarding Catholic political notions. This conflict radicalised the opposing positions regarding the supremacy of the Crown's jurisdiction over the Church, a theme

---

[59] María Soledad Arredondo, *Literatura y propaganda en tiempo de Quevedo. Guerras y plumas contra Francia, Cataluña y Portugal* (Madrid, 2011); Pedro Cardim, '"Portugal unido, y separado". Propaganda and the discourse of identity between the Habsburgs and the Braganza' in Flocel Sabaté and Luís Adão da Fonseca (eds.), *Catalonia and Portugal: the Iberian Peninsula from the periphery* (Bern, 2015), pp. 395–418.

[60] José María Jover Zamora, 'Sobre los Conceptos de Monarquía y Nación en el Pensamiento Político Español del XVII', *Cuadernos de Historia de España*, 12 (1950), pp. 101–150; Fernando Bouza Álvarez, 'Felipe IV sin Olivares. La Restauración de la Monarquía y España en Avisos' in AA.VV., *Actas de las Juntas del Reino de Galicia*, vol. VI: 1648–1654 (La Coruña, 1999), pp. 49–74.

[61] Manuel Herrero Sánchez, *El Acercamiento Hispano-neerlandés (1648–1678)* (Madrid, 2000).

minutely analysed by the Portuguese jurist Domingos Antunes de Portugal in *Tractatus de donationibus, jurium et bonorum regiae coronae* (1673). In this treatise Antunes de Portugal revisited the debate that had begun at the beginning of the seventeenth century in which Francisco Salgado de Somoza and Gabriel Pereira de Castro, both jurists, figured prominently.[62]

A decidedly intense climate of political debate developed in which some defended the positions of 'popular sovereignty' while others reaffirmed royal authority. It is notable that appealing to one position or the other became extremely situational and relative, depending primarily upon the criteria for political opportunity at the moment. One thing is certain: the capacity of the Catholic creed to generate political allegiance diminished dramatically in this case.

As mentioned before, initially the Portuguese propaganda insisted on the negotiated nature of royal authority. Nevertheless, in the years that followed, and due to the pressures of war, the governing practice of the Crown became markedly authoritarian, both in Portugal[63] as well as in Spain: in Castile, the *Cortes* was even no longer called to assemble beginning at the end of the 1660s. At the same time, there emerged new articulations in favour of the prerogatives of the Crown, like, for example, the work of Diego de Tovar Valderrama, *Instituciones políticas, en dos libros dividias, es a saber, de republica, i principe; al serenisimo Senor don Baltasar Carlos* ... (1645).

In the Portuguese context, traditional conceptions were coupled with more pragmatic political approaches, as demonstrated by the treatise of Sebastião César de Meneses, *Summa Política, oferecida ao Príncipe D. Teodósio* ... (1649), and the writings of the Jesuit António Vieira, who stands out as an ardent defender of royal entitlement. Notwithstanding, Catholic conceptions of government continued to play a role, in part because they were so deeply intertwined with the culture and sensitivities of the period, but also because they provided a way of dealing with the crises affecting the Iberian world, which was becoming more and more pronounced. It was a period in which the distance between politics and moral philosophy narrowed significantly, and one of the best examples of this is the work of Baltazar Gracián.[64]

---

[62] Luís Reis Torgal, *Ideologia Política e Teoria do Estado na Restauração*, vol. II (Coimbra, 1981–1982), pp. 55ff.

[63] Pedro Cardim, 'La gobernación de Portugal: de los Austrias a los Braganza (1621–1667)' in David Martín Marcos (ed.), *Monarquías encontradas. Estudios sobre Portugal y España en los siglos XVII-XVIII* (Madrid, 2013), pp. 11–64.

[64] Xavier Gil, 'Baltazar Gracián: Política de "El Político"', *Pedralbes*, 24 (2004), pp. 117–182.

The jurisdictional understanding of politics and the 'cultural' aversion to authoritarian government remained very much present, and a good representative is Diogo Henriques de Vilhegas and his *Leer sin Libro. Direcciones acertadas para el govierno éthico, económico y político. Dirigido al Señor Principe D. Pedro el Felice* ... (1672).

Another good example of the climate during this time of crisis is the book by the Portuguese jurist António de Sousa de Macedo, *Eva, E Ave ou Maria Triunfante. Theatro da Erudiçam, & Filosofia Christãa, Em que se representão os dous estados do mundo Cahido em Eva e Levantado em Ave* ... (1676). Before writing this book Sousa de Macedo had a long juridical and political career under the Spanish monarchy and the Bragança, first as a magistrate and later on as secretary of state. His treatise is based on two central ideas: in the beginning, everything was good and favourable to religion; later, and with the passing of time, humans became responsible for the decline that has made the establishment of an artificial order necessary. A pessimistic anthropological notion therefore runs throughout this book that focuses on the malicious nature of man and the difficulties caused by this nature.

The political crises that emerged after 1640 gave rise to debates that, for the most part, were already well worn. These debates took place not only in Peninsular Portugal, but also across the Portuguese ruled by the Portuguese in Asia, Africa and South America. The Portuguese victory in Pernambuco (in northeast Brazil) over the Dutch led the '*criollos*' of Portuguese America, and in particular Pernambucans, to call for a reconfiguration of their territorial status. Similar to what had taken place in the Iberian Peninsula and in Spanish America at the end of the 1500s,[65] after 1654 many Luso-Brazilians took advantage of the moment of Pernambuco's re-entry into Portuguese rule. By acknowledging that Pernambuco was, unequivocally, a 'conquest' (with all of the implications entailed by such a political status), many Pernambucan maintained that the 1654 victory over the Dutch 'heretics' had transformed the nature of Pernambuco's tie to Portugal, seeing that the victory had come about, in great measure, because of the efforts made by those born and/or living for a long time in America. In other words, the Pernambucans changed from

---

[65] Bernard Lavallé, 'Peut-on Parler d'un Projet Créole au XVIIème Siècle' in Nejma Kermele and Bernard Lavallé (eds.), *L'Amérique en Projet: Utopies, Controverses et Réformes dans l'Empire Espagnol, XVIe-XVIIIe Siècle* (Paris, 2008), pp. 213–227; Alejandra Osorio, *Inventing Lima. Baroque Modernity in Peru's South Sea Metropolis* (New York, 2008); Ralph Bauer and José Antonio Mazzotti 'Introduction: Creole Subjects in the Colonial Americas' in Ralph Bauer and José Antonio Mazzotti (eds.), *Creole Subjects in the Colonial Americas. Empires, Texts, Identities* (Williamsburg, VA, 2009); Mark Burkholder, *Spaniards in the Colonial Empire. Creoles vs. Peninsulars?* (Chichester and West Sussex, 2013).

seeing themselves as the 'conquered' subjects and began to represent themselves as 'restorers' of the Portuguese and Catholic rule. They rejected the notion of 'conquest' and adopted the same form of discourse that until the mid-seventeenth century had been limited to the peninsula, using it with greater frequency – and ability – as their demands to the king intensified.[66]

In essence, the Portuguese of America attempted to eliminate the idea of 'original conquest' by imposing a more honourable and horizontal understanding of its relationship with the Portuguese king. This gesture basically imitated what had been done for decades by the 'creole' elites of Spanish America,[67] but also by certain territories on the Iberian Peninsula: recall, for example, that some years earlier in Navarre, a kingdom which also had been conquered, García de Góngora y Torreblanca, in his *Historia apologetica y descripción del reino de Navarra* (1628), had argued that the time had come for Navarre to abandon the notion of being a 'conquest' and embrace the idea of 'restoration'. And as show throughout this essay, during the 60 year aggregation of Portugal to the Spanish monarchy, the allegedly status of 'conquest' was a motive of constant debate.

***

Despite the singularity of some of the arguments elaborated during the period analysed throughout this chapter, it became clear that the ties between Portugal and the monarchy of Philip II were established by a series of instruments that had emerged at the end of the fifteenth century and that were used to establish the union between several territories in the Iberian world. In fact, the mechanisms of aggregation put into practice in 1581 are in every way similar to those that previously had been adopted in other situations of territorial expansion: first in the context of the union between Castile and Aragon, and later under the Habsburgs.

As has been emphasised throughout this text, Philip II and his successors remained under permanent vigilance by his Portuguese subjects. The manner in which Portugal was incorporated into the Spanish monarchy was constantly a matter of debate during the next 60 years, but also after the rupture between Portugal and the Habsburgs. Many Portuguese 'discovered' that the compromise of 1581 was overlaid with ambiguities, and this allowed the controversial memory of this event to become

---

[66] Evaldo Cabral de Mello, *Olinda Restaurada. Guerra e Açúcar no Nordeste, 1630–1654*, 2ª edição revista e aumentada (Rio de Janeiro, 1998).

[67] Óscar Mazin, 'Architect of the New World: Juan de Solórzano Pereyra and the Status of the Americas' in Pedro Cardim, Tamar Herzog and José Javier Ruíz Ibáñez e Gaetano Sabatini (eds.), *Polycentric Monarchies. How Did Early Modern Spain and Portugal Achieve and Maintain a Global Hegemony?* (Eastbourne, 2012), pp. 27–42.

a 'weapon of resistance' against the reformist measures that were taken throughout the 60 years Portugal was ruled by the Habsburg, in particular under Philip III and Philip IV. Similarly, the defenders of royal prerogative also took advantage of the controversial memory of the events of 1580–1581 and used it to assert that Portugal had been 'conquered' by Philip II.[68]

It is important to stress that Portugal was not the only territory where this type of debate developed. In reality, and as this study has endeavoured to show, since the middle of the sixteenth century, all of the kingdoms within the Habsburg monarchy were simultaneously reflecting upon their own situation, their own history, and their own identity. And at the same time that this reflection took place, each member continued to scrutinise the activity of the monarch and to constantly evaluate whether the monarch was paying due respect to their status or not. Furthermore, and because reflecting on the political profile of a territory necessarily implicated rethinking its character and the faculties of the king within each territory, this reflection led to numerous debates over the 'constitutional role' of the king, both at the level of each kingdom as well as in the monarchy as a whole. And, in reality, it can be said that between 1500 and 1700, the majority of the debates across the Iberian Peninsula over the extent and limits of royal power stemmed from the situation of belonging to the Spanish Monarchy.

Portugal was deeply involved in this political environment, and the debates occurring in Portugal at the time were neither new nor unique. Much to the contrary, they followed the same patterns that simultaneously were emerging in all the territories that were then under the Habsburg rule, including – it should be noted – Castile. For this reason, to understand the full sense of the debates taking place in Portugal requires studying in tandem the debates transpiring in the other domains of the Habsburg Empire at the time. The interplay between these debates ultimately constitutes a fundamental quality that should be considered lest a form of exceptionalism be attributed to the Portuguese case, which, to a great extent, it did not have.

---

[68] José Javier Ruiz Ibáñez and Gaetano Sabatini, 'Monarchy as Conquest. Violence, Social Opportunity, and Political Stability in the Establishment of the Hispanic Monarchy', *The Journal of Modern History*, LXXXI:3 (2009), pp. 501–536.

9 In the Service of the Dynasty: Building a Career in the Habsburg Household, 1550–1650

Dries Raeymaekers

On 9 April 1611, Cardinal Franz von Dietrichstein, President of Emperor Rudolph II's Privy Council, wrote a letter to Archduke Albert of Austria, Rudolph's younger brother and sovereign ruler of the Habsburg Low Countries. In the letter, the Cardinal announced the death of his sibling Maximilian von Dietrichstein, who had once served Albert as *sumiller de corps* (Head of the Bedchamber) at the court of Brussels. Since Maximilian had never sired any children, the Cardinal had been appointed his brother's legitimate heir and would be taking over as head of the Dietrichstein family. He informed Albert that he had not only inherited Maximilian's estate, but also the latter's obligations, 'the most important of which is to serve Your Highness'. The Cardinal therefore wanted to profess his family's unwavering loyalty to the Archduke. At the same time, he urged Albert to continue to protect 'this House [of Dietrichstein], which is so [attached] to you'.[1] Upon receiving a favourable answer from the Archduke, the Cardinal, anxious to seize the opportunity, responded with two new letters in one day. In the first, he confirmed his loyalty once again, thanking Albert for 'the honour and favour Your Highness has bestowed (. . .) on me' and stating that this 'has added very strong links to the chain of obligations that I have towards Your Highness'.[2] In the second, he requested that his young nephew, also called Maximilian, be accepted as page at the court of Brussels.[3] This request was granted soon afterwards.[4]

The wording of Franz von Dietrichstein's letters may serve as a textbook example of the language of patronage that was commonly

---

[1] Brussels, Archives Généraux du Royaume de Belgique, Secrétairerie d'État et de Guerre [hereinafter AGRB, SEG] 494, s.f.: Cardinal Franz Seraph von Dietrichstein to Archduke Albert of Austria, 9 April 1611.

[2] AGRB, SEG 494, s.f.: Dietrichstein to Albert, 6 January 1612 (1).

[3] AGRB, SEG 494, s.f.: Dietrichstein to Albert, 6 January 1612 (2).

[4] Young Maximilian entered the household on 12 March 1612. See the household accounts in AGRB, Chambre des Comptes 1837, f. 40v.

used in early modern Europe.[5] Since the 1980s historians have become well aware of this specific type of letter and of their significance as written testimonies of interdependence.[6] What is striking about Dietrichstein's letters is thus not so much their wording as the fact that they were sent to Archduke Albert, who as long-time ruler of the Habsburg Low Countries seemed far removed from the patronage networks that were active in and around the Imperial court in Prague. Nevertheless, the Cardinal maintained a frequent correspondence with the Archduke, in which he never failed to mention the ancient *obligaciones* his family had towards Albert and that he considered his kinsmen to be the latter's *verdaderos servidores y criados* (true servants and creatures).[7] If anything, the fact that Franz von Dietrichstein – generally perceived as one of the most powerful men in the Empire – deliberately sought to maintain the support of a remote member of the ruling dynasty, offers food for thought about the nature and functioning of Habsburg patronage.

Even though the august House of Austria has received ample attention in both traditional and recent scholarship, its role as a distributor of patronage has never been systematically analysed. Research on the subject has hitherto been conducted on the distribution of patronage at a specific Habsburg court or by a specific Habsburg monarch, but it has never been done from the viewpoint of the dynasty as a whole.[8] This can partly be explained by its complex history. The facts are well known. When in 1555 Emperor Charles V decided to abdicate, his vast dominions 'upon which the sun never set' were split up between his brother Ferdinand, who already governed the Austrian possessions and would soon succeed him on the Imperial throne, and his son Philip, who inherited the Spanish hereditary lands as well as the Habsburg territories in Italy and the Low Countries. From that point forward the House of Austria would consist of two major branches, the establishment of which triggered the formation of two distinct political entities, each of which developed its own governmental structure, its own domestic and foreign policies, and its own political elites. However, what has often been

---

[5] See A. L. Herman, 'The Language of Fidelity in Early Modern France', *The Journal of Modern History* 67 (1995), pp. 1–24.

[6] The late Sharon Kettering in particular was among the first to systematically study such letters and to emphasize the role of patronage as a key element when it comes to understanding the complex meanderings of power in the period at hand. Seminal works include S. Kettering, *Patrons, Brokers and Clients in Seventeenth-Century France* (New York, 1986) and S. Kettering, *Patronage in Sixteenth and Seventeenth Century France* (Aldershot, 2002).

[7] This correspondence can be found in AGRB, SEG 494.

[8] See for example K. J. MacHardy, *War, Religion and Court Patronage in Habsburg Austria. The Social and Cultural Dimensions of Political Interaction, 1521–1622* (Basingstoke, 2003).

overlooked is the fact that the division of the dynasty did not automatically lead to the establishment of two separate patronage networks.

Ever since the accession of Maximilian I, the Habsburg dynasty had become one of the largest suppliers of patronage on the continent. Its vast resources – surpassed in quality and quantity only by those of the Roman Catholic Church – enabled the House of Austria to offer a wide range of favours to the elites of the realm, in return for which it received the political support it needed to sustain and legitimize itself. Obviously, this pan-European patronage network did not cease to exist after 1555. The overall impression is that the distribution of patronage even intensified as the dynasty further eroded, and several Habsburg 'subcourts' came into being. Indeed, whereas many scholars of Habsburg history tend to focus on either the royal court in Madrid or the Imperial court in Prague/Vienna, contemporaries were well aware that by the end of the sixteenth century the dynasty boasted an extensive network of courts, many of which served as powerbases for younger siblings and other members of the family. The best known among these were probably the courts of Graz and Innsbruck, but there were various others in cities such as Brussels in the Low Countries, Hall in Tyrol, Mergentheim in the lands of the Teutonic Order, and Saverne in the prince-bishopric of Strasburg.[9] Combined, this multitude of Habsburg courts and accompanying households constituted a seemingly infinite source of titles, honours, money and other favours for the aristocrats and lesser men and women who spent their lives serving the dynasty.

The distribution of patronage, of course, was a standard procedure at virtually all early modern courts.[10] However, what most of these Habsburg courts had in common is that they seem to have deliberately established and maintained patron/client-relationships with people hailing from all corners of the Habsburg possessions, indicating that the divide between the several dynastic branches was less clear-cut than is often assumed. Even after 1555 Habsburg patronage remained first and foremost a family business and was thus only mildly affected by the breakdown of the realm into separate political entities. A dynasty had an internal logic of its own, and this is especially true for the Habsburgs, whose dynastic logic happened to stretch across state borders and was

---

[9] This network of Habsburg courts and households has been studied in a recent volume by R. Vermeir, D. Raeymaekers and J. E. Hortal Muñoz (eds.), *A Constellation of Courts. The Courts and Households of Habsburg Europe, 1555–1665* (Leuven, 2014). Here, see the introduction by Muñoz, Raeymaekers and Vermeir, 'Courts and Households of the Habsburg Dynasty: History and Historiography', pp. 7–19.

[10] See the various chapters in J. Adamson (ed.), *The Princely Courts of Europe. Ritual, Politics and Culture under the Ancien Régime 1500–1750* (London, 1999).

thus prone to collide with the *raison d'état*.[11] It could be argued, then, that as the various Habsburg branches grew further apart and were increasingly identified with the respective territories they governed, the vast patronage network may have served as a means to bypass the emerging demands of the state and preserve the interests of the dynasty. As such, political patronage may have been the glue that held the crumbling House of Austria together. This hypothesis cannot be fully explored in the present chapter, but I seek to address some aspects of it by focusing on one specific form of patronage that was masterfully deployed by the Habsburg dynasty: the distribution of offices in its various households.

Taking the court of Brussels in the age of the Archdukes Albert and Isabella (1598–1621) as its starting point, this chapter aims to analyse how a 'typical' Habsburg court recruited its courtiers. To say that the archducal court may, indeed, serve as an example in this regard, may seem surprising, because it has been seen by historians first and foremost as a bulwark of the Spanish presence in the Low Countries, and therefore as a mere sub-court of the Royal court in Madrid. In other words, it is usually considered 'Spanish' rather than 'Habsburg'. To a certain extent, this is understandable. Luc Duerloo has argued that on the surface, the court of Albert and Isabella displayed many characteristics that can be said to have been cobbled from the Spanish model: the court ceremonial was Spanish, fashion was Spanish, the dominant language spoken was Spanish, and the devotional atmosphere was Spanish.[12] However, looking beyond the obvious, it is clear that the court incorporated elements derived from all corners of the Habsburg territories (including works of art, music, food, scientific instruments and exotic artefacts). In Duerloo's words, 'the culture of the archducal court was not so much Spanish as Habsburg. It appropriated elements from all the scattered possessions of the dynasty and as such materialized its universalist ambitions'.[13]

Going even further, I would argue that the court of Brussels shared with the other courts of the House of Austria a certain cultural ethos, which can be considered profoundly 'Habsburg' in nature. This ethos, I argue, extended to the recruitment of court personnel as well. By scrutinizing the job opportunities available to members of the nobility at the court of the Archdukes and discussing the criteria that were used to determine one's eligibility for office, this chapter seeks to demonstrate that the selection of courtiers for the archducal household reflected an approach that was characteristic for the dynasty. As such, the chapter argues that the division

---

[11] See the discussion in L. Duerloo, *Dynasty and Piety. Archduke Albert (1598–1621) and Habsburg Political Culture in an Age of Religious Wars* (Farnham, 2012), p. 12.

[12] Duerloo, *Dynasty and Piety*, pp. 90–93.   [13] Ibid., p. 92.

of the Habsburg possessions in 1555 had by the start of the seventeenth century not resulted in two separate patronage networks. On the contrary, it is clear that Habsburg patronage knew no geographical boundaries, as courtier's careers often led from one Habsburg household to another. And neither did it take heed of temporal confines, as household offices were often passed down from generation to generation.

Launching a Career

For noblemen and -women eager to pursue a career in the service of the Habsburg dynasty, possibilities were rife. Taken together, the amalgam of Habsburg courts offered a source of employment surpassed in size only by the Church. In that sense, it is important to note that during the final decades of the sixteenth century and the initial stages of the seventeenth century, many European courts were characterized by a marked increase in size.[14] Although for various reasons it is difficult to assess the exact size of a princely retinue, there is no doubt that this proliferation resulted in a substantial expansion of most Habsburg households as well. In the course of the reign of Rudolph II (1576–1612), for example, the court of Prague witnessed what could be called an inflation of offices: the number of courtiers rose from about 700 in 1580 to a rough estimate of 1,200 in 1611. Due to financial constraints, the *Hofstaat* was reduced to c. 785 persons during the reign of Rudolph's successor Matthias (1612–1619), but it was to expand again under Ferdinand II.[15] The court of Madrid was even bigger. In 1623, the combined households of King Philip IV and his wife Isabella of Bourbon employed an estimated 1,700 personnel.[16]

In Brussels, the household of Archduke Albert and his wife Isabella counted almost 600 permanent members of staff in 1618, a figure which includes the members of the guard and the court chapel.[17] Yet, even though there were many posts to fill, the number of applicants looking for employment was even higher. Acquiring a position in a princely household was deemed an excellent way to improve one's prospects in life, as it not only offered financial stability in the form of steady (albeit moderate)

---

[14] See the introduction in Adamson, *The Princely Courts of Europe*, pp. 7–42, at p. 12.

[15] J. Duindam, *Vienna and Versailles. The Courts of Europe's Dynastic Rivals, 1550–1780* (Cambridge, 2003), pp. 70–71.

[16] J. H. Elliott, 'The Court of the Spanish Habsburgs: A Peculiar Institution?', in P. Mack and M. C. Jacob (eds.), *Politics and Culture in Early Modern Europe: Essays in Honour of H.G. Koenigsberger* (Cambridge, 1987), p. 5–24.

[17] D. Raeymaekers, *One Foot in the Palace: The Habsburg Court of Brussels and the Politics of Access in the Reign of Albert and Isabella, 1598–1621* (Leuven, 2013), p. 105.

wages and all kinds of fiscal benefits and bonuses, but also – depending on the office – a chance to enjoy free meals and lodging at the ruler's expense. Apart from these privileges, employees enjoyed a unique form of social security: their health was being looked after by court doctors; their children were given scholarships to either study or enter a convent; they received pensions when old age forced them to quit work; and their families were provided for in the event of their death.[18] These and other emoluments ensured that competition for office was fierce, and court administrators had their hands full in trying to pick the best candidates. Obviously however, the nobility – who were in less need of material remuneration – had other, less straightforward motives for applying.

From time immemorial, the ruler's dwelling was a point of contact for all those who sought to partake in the government of the realm and a hub of political and diplomatic activity. It was the main forum on which power was brokered, favours were gained, and conflicting interests were fought over. For a nobleman to acquire an office, there was the ultimate acknowledgement of his status, as it proved that he belonged to the high and mighty and could be recognized as such. Furthermore, the opportunity to be close to the centre of patronage and have direct access to the ruler was an asset much coveted by most aristocrats. Access, it has been established, was often one of the principal reasons why they would seek office, as it allowed one to see and talk to the monarch at any given moment and to seek his favour at one's own instigation.[19] As one nobleman at the court of Brussels put it, 'Given the many things illustrious houses . . . require, it is . . . advantageous to always keep one foot inside the palace.'[20] Hence the noble elites, too, were eager to secure a position in the princely household.

In some cases, a career in the household could start off as early as childhood. As mentioned in the introduction, one of the first things Cardinal Franz von Dietrichstein did when he became the head of his family was request that his young nephew Maximilian be accepted as page at the court of Brussels. The request was granted, leaving the Cardinal much pleased, and with good reason. A tradition that stemmed from

---

[18] See the discussion in Raeymaekers, *One Foot in the Palace*, pp. 118–123.

[19] David Starkey was one of the first scholars to emphasise the importance of access in early modern politics. See his introduction in D. Starkey et al., *The English Court from the Wars of the Roses to the Civil War* (London and New York, 1987). The topic is studied from a variety of viewpoints in a volume edited by Dries Raeymaekers and Sebastiaan Derks (eds.), *The Key to Power? The Culture of Access in Princely Courts, 1400–1750* (Leiden, 2016).

[20] Enghien (Belgium), Archive and Cultural Centre Arenberg, Correspondance de Charles d'Arenberg [hereinafter ACA, CCA] 38/4, file 133, f. 5: Gaston Spínola, Count of Bruay, to Charles d'Arenberg, Princely Count of Arenberg and Duke of Aarschot, 16 March 1613.

medieval times, the system of pagehood was considered a respectable way to introduce one's children to the requirements of noble life and all it entailed. From the age of six or seven, sons of noble families could be invited to live at court and serve the Archduke as pages. Yet, places being scarce, it was not easy to get in. Those fortunate enough to secure a position were considered the pick of the future aristocracy.[21] Archduke Albert, for his part, would not have hesitated long before allowing young Maximilian to enter his service. From the viewpoint of the ruler, the system of pagehood was a useful form of patronage, not in the least because it offered him a chance to lure future noble generations to his court and acquaint them with such advantageous political virtues as loyalty, fidelity and commitment. When in 1595 Albert was getting ready to travel to Brussels and take up the post of governor-general of the Low Countries in the service of Philip II of Spain, one of his counsellors advised him to take on at least 24 pages with the purpose of strengthening the ties between the dynasty and the local nobility:

> Such a [large] number of pages is of greater concern than one can imagine, and it will be even more so when they are educated with as little cost for their parents as possible, and all this in view of the benefits one can expect from it, as [these pages] will be a true seedbed of virtue for the entire nobility, which at the moment is straying from the path and has little affection for its prince, and which is full of flaws, and far from any kind of virtue.[22]

The same counsellor proposed that, besides receiving training in the time-honoured chivalric arts, the pages would be taught 'virtue, piety and Christianity'. In order to explain the benefits of this education to the Archduke, he used a telling metaphor. According to the counsellor, it would 'serve as a fishing rod to fish [the boys] up and raise them as true subjects in the service of His Majesty [Philip II]'. After their graduation, the Archduke could order them to either join the army or enter the clergy, where they were expected to continue their services to the dynasty.[23]

Noble girls, too, could be invited to serve at court, usually as maids of honour or ladies-in-waiting in the household of Infanta Isabella. Like the pages, the maids of honour were taught skills that were deemed suitable for a future life as the wife of an aristocrat or – following the example of many pious Habsburg women – that of a nun in one of the many religious orders favoured by the dynasty, such as the Discalced Carmelites or the

---

[21] Raeymaekers, *One Foot in the Palace*, p. 86.

[22] Madrid, Instituto Valencia de Don Juan (hereinafter IVDJ), envío 47, caja 63, doc. 506: 'Autoridad absoluta sin eçesion alguna' (the author has been identified as Philippe de Croÿ, Count of Solre).

[23] Ibid.

Sisters of the Annunciation.[24] Here, too, a decent Catholic upbringing was deemed of paramount importance. According to Habsburg custom, women at court were generally kept behind closed doors and were not allowed to have unsupervised contacts with the outside world.[25] In Brussels, the maids of honour were carefully watched over by the lady chamberlain (the *camarera mayor*), who was responsible for their good behaviour.[26] By night, they were put under lock and key by a household officer referred to as the *guardadamas* so as to make sure that no one could pose a threat to their virtue and chastity. Perhaps it need not surprise, then, that an English nobleman who visited the court of Brussels in 1612 wrote in his diary that '[The Infanta's] ladies are kept up as if they were in a Nunnerie ....'[27]

Acquiring an Office

Few noble families would have declined the honour to send their children off to the court of the archdukes. Yet, what most of them were really after were the numerous steady positions in the household, the esteemed offices that enabled one to see and be seen at court. These were divided into several categories, some of which were considered more prestigious than others. For reasons of space, they cannot all be discussed here. The following overview is therefore limited to the offices that were generally considered to be the most desirable.

Male nobles of lesser status could hope to be admitted to the ranks of the middle-tier officers in the household, such as the *gentilhombres de la Casa* and the *gentilhombres de la Boca*.[28] Their presence at court was based on the ancient custom that the aristocrats of the realm were given positions in the ruler's household so as to confirm the traditional bond between the dynasty and the nobility. Over time however, these

---

[24] Cf. M. S. Sánchez, *The Empress, the Queen and the Nun: Women and Power at the Court of Philip III of Spain* (Johns Hopkins, 1998).

[25] M. J. Rodríguez-Salgado, '"Una perfecta princesa." Casa y vida de la reina Isabel de Valois (1559–1568). Primera parte', in C. Gómez-Centurión (ed.), *Monarquía y Corte en la España Moderna: Cuadernos de Historia Moderna* (Madrid, 2003), pp. 39–96.

[26] On the responsibilities of the *camarera mayor*, M. V. López-Cordón Cortezo, 'Entre damas anda el juego: las camareras mayores de Palacio en la edad moderna', in Gómez-Centurión (ed.), *Monarquía y Corte en la España Moderna*, pp. 123–152.

[27] M. G. Brennan (ed.), *The Travel Diary (1611–1612) of an English Catholic Sir Charles Somerset, edited from the manuscript in the Brotherton Collection University of Leeds* (Leeds, 1993), p. 288.

[28] For information on these offices, see R. Mayoral López, La Casa Real de Felipe III (1598–1621). Ordenanzas y Etiquetas, unpublished doctoral dissertation (Universidad Autónoma de Madrid, 2007). See also C. Hofmann, *Das Spanische Hofzeremoniell von 1500–1700* (Frankfurt, 1985).

once full-time offices had become mainly ceremonial in nature. The *gentilhombres de la Boca*, for example, were expected to serve Albert as carvers or cupbearers when he dined in public – a time-honoured ritual that reached back to Burgundian times.[29] The remainder of their duties consisted in accompanying the Archduke during public festivities and dazzling the onlookers with their magnificent attire. As such, these courtiers contributed in substantial measure to the visual spectacle of government and to the pomp and circumstance which the Habsburg dynasty chose to surround itself with. This is not, however, to say that their responsibilities were limited to their participation in the *representatio maiestatis*. In many cases, the obligation of these lesser nobles to aid the ruler could become very concrete in the sense that they often held offices in regional and local political institutions. Others served as administrators or as officers in the army, and many enjoyed good contacts with the clergy or the city guilds. In this way, the courtiers could play an important role as intermediaries between the central government and subaltern levels of society.

Whereas the middle-tier positions were usually sought by lesser noblemen aspiring to a career in the archducal household, members of the prominent aristocratic houses qualified for a wholly different category of court office. In terms of prestige, the position of chamberlain was considered one of the most desirable offices in the household. In theory, the duties of the *gentilhombres de la Cámara* consisted of making the ruler's bed and serving the sovereign when he dined in the privacy of his own apartments. In practice however, the position came to mean something entirely different. The dignity of the chamberlains was symbolized by a ceremonial golden key proudly worn on their costumes which signalled to everyone their right to open the door that led into the Archdukes's bedroom.[30] The message could not be clearer: these were men who enjoyed free access to Albert's personal living quarters and, hence, belonged to his most intimate circle of companions. They were the ones who had his ear, who could advise him on all matters, sway his decisions, seek his favour or convince him of certain views. It has been established that in the early modern age, the monarch's bedchamber was first and foremost a political entity and should be studied as such.[31] If anything,

---

[29] W. Paravicini, 'The Court of the Dukes of Burgundy. A Model for Europe?', in R. G. Asch and A. M. Birke (eds.), *Princes, Patronage and the Nobility: The Court at the Beginning of the Modern Age, c. 1450–1650* (Oxford, 1991), pp. 69–102.

[30] Raeymaekers, *One Foot in the Palace*, p. 76.

[31] David Starkey's doctoral dissertation has been instrumental in reassessing the importance of the private living quarters of the monarch: D. Starkey, The Development of the Privy Chamber, 1485–1547. Unpublished doctoral dissertation (Cambridge University, 1973).

the gilded key signified the ability of its bearer to enter the world of politics. Small wonder, then, that the office of chamberlain was much coveted by aristocrats who aspired to power and influence. Understandably, the competition that ensued from this was often extraordinarily fierce. Here too, Cardinal Franz von Dietrichstein was quick to take action. In 1613, merely one year after his nephew Maximilian von Dietrichstein had acquired the position of page at the court of Brussels, he wrote a letter to Archduke Albert in which he stated that his family had served the august House of Austria for so many years that it could claim certain favours '*por derecho de herencia*' (by right of inheritance).[32] The Cardinal therefore asked that Maximilian be given the office of *gentilhombre de la Cámara* as soon as the young man would finish his training, a request that was granted one year later.[33]

The anecdote demonstrates that 'reciprocity' was not considered a hollow term in the early modern system of patronage. There was a strong sense of entitlement involved, a feeling that one could rightfully claim certain offices in recompense for services rendered. In March 1613, three new *gentilhombres de la Cámara* were appointed at the court of Brussels.[34] The sudden round of promotions can be seen as a deliberate measure to soothe the local nobility at a time when the Habsburg dynasty found itself in dire straits. Archduke Albert had been dangerously ill for quite some time and no one knew how the population was going to react when he should die childless and sovereignty over the Low Countries would return to the King of Spain – as had been stipulated by Philip II in the Act of Cession of 1598. However, not everyone was pleased with the new appointments. Having heard the news, one of the other chamberlains, Philippe-Charles d'Arenberg, wrote an angry letter to his father Charles d'Arenberg, who as Duke of Aarschot was one of the principal aristocrats in the Low Countries. According to Philippe-Charles the gilded key should have been given to his younger brother Alexandre, 'to whom it cannot be refused'.[35] He urged his father to talk to Archduke Albert about this, stating that the household already employed two brothers and one uncle of another – unidentified – noble family, despite the fact that the merits of the Duke of Aarschot (who was also a chamberlain) were 'far greater than theirs'. Hence there was no reason why Alexandre should not get the office, 'since there might well be a father and two sons

---

[32] AGRB, SEG 494, s.f.: Dietrichstein to Albert, 13 February 1613.

[33] According to the household accounts, Maximilian was promoted in February 1614. AGRB, Chambres des Comptes 1837, f. 270r.

[34] Raeymaekers, *One Foot in the Palace*, 171.

[35] ACA, CCA 38/3, file 72, nr. 122: Philippe-Charles d'Arenberg to Charles d'Arenberg, s.d. [March 1613].

where there are two brothers and one uncle, and that is how the world is governed'.[36] It was a somewhat puzzling argument, but one that showed that Philippe-Charles considered his family to be *incontournable* at the court of Brussels. Whether or not the Duke of Aarschot agreed with his son, is unknown, but the fact of the matter is that Alexandre was never offered the gilded key. It was, however, presented to a third brother, Antoine d'Arenberg, who received it in 1615 in recompense for the good services of his father, who had to quit the office because of his failing health.[37] In a letter to the Duke, a proud Antoine described all the details of his reception at court. In the morning he had taken the required oath of loyalty in the hands of the *mayordomo mayor*, the high steward of the household, who had presented him with the gilded key. At noon, a group of courtiers had accompanied him to the bedchamber of the Archduke, who lectured him on the duties of the *gentilhombre de la Cámara*.

While I was sitting on one knee, he took the rapier that was hanging from my side (which is a sign of extraordinary favour) and tapped me three times on the shoulder. Afterwards he made me kiss the handle and embraced me, saying that I would be a good knight and that he hoped that the thought of my sword having belonged to such a fine prince [*this refers to Antoine's father, DR*] would urge me to wield it even better in his service.[38]

In Antoine's day, the office of chamberlain was still very hard to come by. However, later on in the seventeenth century it would lose much of its former exclusivity as a result of the rising number of nobles who would be given the gilded key in the various Habsburg households. For example, at the dawn of the seventeenth century, the Imperial household counted 12 or 13 chamberlains. This number continued to rise throughout the consecutive reigns of the Emperors Matthias and Ferdinand II, reaching a total of no less than 150 by the time of Ferdinand III's death in 1657.[39] This was only possible due to an elaborate system of *service par terme*, which allowed courtiers to serve in rotation: a *Kämmerer* or *gentilhombre* would actively serve in the household for short periods of time and afterwards return to his estate in the country.[40] Such an arrangement had a major advantage in that it enabled the Habsburgs to expand their patronage and take on many more courtiers at a time without having to pay them all at once. Over time however, it contributed to the erosion of

---

[36] Ibid.
[37] Raeymaekers, *One Foot in the Palace*, 171. On Antoine d'Arenberg, see F. Callaey [= Frédégand d'Anvers, Père O.M.F. Cap.], *La vie religieuse et familiale en Belgique au XVIIe siècle. Étude sur le Père Charles d'Arenberg, frère-mineur Capucin (1593–1669)* (Paris-Rome, 1919).
[38] ACA, CCA 38/1, file 32, f. 29: Antoine d'Arenberg to Charles d'Arenberg, s.d.
[39] Duindam, *Vienna and Versailles*, p. 72.   [40] Ibid., p. 49.

the office as its incumbents were increasingly subdivided into confused groups of serving and titular, ordinary and extraordinary chamberlains.

Be that as it may, the position of chamberlain remained highly desirable for anyone who aspired to be someone at court until well into the eighteenth century, as in many cases the prestigious office not only enabled one to receive many favours, but also to become a broker of patronage and establish a network of clients of one's own. Indeed, their connections with regional and local elites allowed the chamberlains to act as intermediaries between the centre and the periphery of the realm. In addition, the office often formed the springboard to other career opportunities and paved the way towards an active involvement in politics. Members of the household – and of the bedchamber in particular – could play a vital role as representatives of the dynasty on several strategic levels of society. The fact that many chamberlains also served as military commanders, for example, shows how strongly the Habsburg households were interwoven with the command structure in the Imperial and royal armies.[41] Furthermore, plenty of chamberlains were given lucrative posts in the governmental councils and institutions, where they were expected to support the political views of the monarch. Others served as diplomatic agents, representing the ruler at foreign courts or performing secret missions in his service. Here, too, the court of Brussels may serve as an example.

During the reign of Archduke Albert, practically all of the *gentilhombres de la Cámara* occupied a position in the renowned Army of Flanders.[42] In addition, nearly all of the provincial governors in the Low Countries were in some way connected to the archducal bedchamber, either directly or through their kinsmen.[43] It is also striking that even though Albert disposed of an entire army of diplomatic agents who were able to represent his views to other rulers, on certain occasions he chose to send one of his chamberlains instead. The impression is that whenever the wellbeing of the Habsburg dynasty was at stake, it was the *gentilhombres de la Cámara* who negotiated the matter, rather than the usual envoys. This, for example, was the case when the Marquess of Marnay, one of the Archduke's most trusted chamberlains, was sent on a secret mission to the Holy See in order to persuade the pope to grant the Archduke the long-lost title of King of Burgundy. Not even Herman van Ortenberg, Albert's resident diplomatic agent in Rome, was informed about the content of Marnay's instructions.[44] It was also the case during the famous *Brüderzwist*, in which Albert's *gentilhombres*, the Count of Solre and Ottavio Visconti,

---

[41] Raeymaekers, *One Foot in the Palace*, pp. 233–234. [42] Ibid., pp. 232–233.
[43] Ibid., p. 247. [44] Ibid., pp. 250–251.

played a significant but often overlooked role as mediators between Emperor Rudolph and his brothers.[45] All this leads to an interesting hypothesis: is it possible that the chamberlains, as intimate companions of the Archduke, were expected to act as the defenders of his personal interests and those of his dynasty in a political climate that was increasingly concerned with an emerging *raison d'état*? Further research is needed to substantiate this theory, but it seems plausible.

As far as proximity to the Archduke was concerned, the real top-tier offices were the ones whose incumbents directed the three major departments in the household: the *mayordomo mayor* as the formal head of the household; the *sumiller de corps* as the head of the bedchamber service; and the *caballerizo mayor* as the head of the stables. These offices were without a doubt the most prestigious ones in the household, and they were reserved for members of the high aristocracy only. However, it should not be forgotten that their incumbents were also highly influential. These men enjoyed virtually unlimited access to the Archduke and were considered his main political advisors. They held sway over the Archduke's agenda and decided who was to have access to him and who was not. More importantly, they were often responsible for the distribution of princely patronage, which – as can be expected – rendered them some of the most powerful men in the realm. Hence it cannot be stressed enough that these offices were first and foremost *political* offices. In many ways their incumbents were not only responsible for the upkeep of the household, but also for the smooth running of government. This, in turn, reminds us that the princely household and the princely government in the early modern age were by no means distinct spheres. If anything, they were inextricably bound up with each other.[46]

Finally, an overview of important offices in the archducal household should not omit the positions that were reserved for noble ladies. It may have resembled a nunnery, but this did not prevent the women's quarter in the archducal household from playing an important role at court. In recent years historians have identified the *Frauenzimmer* as an environment in which women were able to build their own networks of patronage, less visible perhaps than those of men, but hardly less

---

[45] Ibid., p. 252. On Albert's involvement in the *Brüderzwist*, see L. Duerloo, 'Der ehrgeizige Jüngste. Erzherzog Albrecht und die Nachfolge Rudolfs II', *Mitteilungen des Instituts für österreichische Geschichtsforschung* 118 (2010), pp. 103–139.

[46] In her essay on the court of Philip II, Mia Rodríguez concluded that making a division between household and government in the early modern era 'is not only difficult, it is false'. M. J. Rodríguez-Salgado, 'Honour and Profit in the Court of Philip II of Spain', in M. Aymard and M. Romani (eds.), *La cour comme institution économique. Actes du douzième congrès international d'histoire économique, Séville-Madrid, 24–28 août 1998* (Paris, 1998), pp. 67–86. See p. 76.

efficient.[47] As research on the subject has shown, some of the ladies-in-waiting could become highly influential and played an important role in procuring favours for themselves and their families.[48] This was the principal reason why in 1615 the Duke of Aarschot went out of his way to get his sister appointed as the new *camarera mayor* of Infanta Isabella. It was, we can assume, also the reason why other nobles at the court of Brussels strongly resented the appointment. But the Duke would not come to regret it. From the moment of her arrival in the household, Antonia-Wilhelmina d'Arenberg frequently used her position to actively promote and support the good fortunes of her brother's family.[49] Here, too, access was the keyword, as it was Antonia-Wilhelmina's proximity to the Infanta that allowed her to ask for favours directly and without delay.

Guidelines for Determining Eligibility

Now that we have established the available high offices in the household and the reasons why aristocrats coveted them, it is time to shift the focus from the demand side to the supply side and examine the criteria with which the Archdukes determined the eligibility of noble applicants. The question of who was eventually given an office and who was not is important, as the answer can teach us something about the expectations that were put on the courtiers and, hence, about the role the household was expected to play in the Habsburg political constellation. Obviously, in the early modern age the composition of a princely entourage was never detached from certain political realities. To a Habsburg prince, the establishment of a household was by definition a political matter. Apart from possible conflicting state and dynastic interests, he had to take into account a wide range of religious, social and even regional and local concerns, and all kinds of individual claims and counterclaims.

When in 1595 Philip II appointed Archduke Albert as governor-general of the Habsburg Low Countries, the establishment of his nephew's court in Brussels gave cause for concern. Torn apart by a civil war that had been going on for more than three decades, the state of affairs in the

---

[47] See for example K. Keller, *Hofdamen. Amtsträgerinnen im Wiener Hofstaat des 17. Jahrhunderts* (Vienna, 2005).

[48] See for example B. Houben, 'Intimacy and Politics: Isabel and Her Ladies-in-Waiting', in C. Van Wyhe (ed.), *Isabel Clara Eugenia. Female Sovereignty in the Courts of Madrid and Brussels* (London, 2012), pp. 312–338.

[49] B. Houben and D. Raeymaekers, 'Women and the Politics of Access at the Archducal Court of Brussels. The Infanta Isabella's Camareras Mayores', in N. Akkerman and B. Houben (eds.), *The Politics of Female Households: Ladies-in-Waiting across Early Modern Europe* (Leiden, 2013), pp. 123–145.

Netherlands was such that the arrival of a new Habsburg household was bound to stir up emotions. It was not for a lack of candidates however. The office that was to oversee the recruitment process – the *Bureo* – received numerous applications from Netherlandish nobles wishing to join the Archduke's household.[50] In order to separate the wheat from the chaff, the *Bureo's* president, Francisco de Mendoza, issued a document that summed up the pros and cons of each candidate. The introduction contained the following statement:

> Concerning the choice of servants from these lands which Your Highness will have to employ, many things need to be taken into account, namely their firmness and constancy in the Catholic Religion and in the service of His Majesty [Philip II]; the virtue and quality of their person; their experience and [financial] estate and their social skills; so as to make sure that those who possess all these qualities would be preferred above others, and that – in case the afore-mentioned qualities and virtues are not all found in one person – the best and the one with the least defects would be chosen from those who present themselves.[51]

Even though it was given with the political situation of the Low Countries in mind, I would argue that Mendoza's advice summarizes a number of dynastic concerns that influenced the selection of household officers in all Habsburg courts at the start of the seventeenth century. In a sense, the recruitment of courtiers reflected a common Habsburg philosophy, a shared ethos of norms and values endorsed by all members of the House of Austria, regardless of the individual territories they ruled. The first guideline speaks for itself: Habsburg courtiers had to be decent Catholics, in theory if not in practice. There were, of course, exceptions, but in general this seems to have been a *condition sine qua non* for any noble man or woman who aspired to a career at a Habsburg court. In some cases, it was even stipulated that the courtiers' own servants had to be Catholic so as to protect the pious character of the court.[52] A notable exception, it would appear, was the household of Archduke Maximilian III – Albert's brother – in Innsbruck, which showed a marked openness towards

---

[50] Raeymaekers, *One Foot in the Palace*, p. 161.

[51] 'Prosupuesto que para las ellectiones de los criados destos Payses de S[u] A[lteza] ha de meter en su casa se han de considerar muchas cosas, es a saber la firmeza y seguridad en la Religion Catholica y en el servicio de S[u] M[ajestad], la virtud y qualidad de la persona, la experiencia y hazienda y la apacibilidad de la condicion, paraque hallandose todos se prefieran los que les tuvieren a los demas, y faltando algunas se elixe lo mejor de lo que se offreciere y que menos inconvenientes tenga'. Madrid, Real Academia de la Historia (hereinafter RAH), Colección Salazar y Castro A-61, f. 20–31: *Relacion de las personas del Pays que pretenden servir a Su Alteza de Mayordomos.* See f. 30.

[52] Upon her appointment as *camarera mayor* at the court of Brussels, Antonia-Wilhelmina d'Arenberg was forbidden to bring servants 'who were not profoundly Catholic'. See ACA, CCA 36/17, s.f.: Antonio Suárez de Arguello to Charles d'Arenberg, 19 November 1615.

Protestants. Already at his court in Mergentheim – where he resided until 1602 as Grand Master of the Teutonic Order – Maximilian had employed a few Protestant servants, and this seems to have been the case when he moved to Innsbruck as well, despite several attempts by Rudolph II to make his brother dismiss them.[53] Nevertheless, these and other religious dissenters remained a distinct minority at the courts of the Habsburgs, which – following the principles of the *Pietas Austriaca* – were characterized by a profound Catholic piety and devotion.

Another criterion on the list was the 'quality' of a person. Combined with the suggestion that applicants should be financially well off, the message seems clear: ideally, potential courtiers had to be of good social standing. The Habsburg dynasty was profoundly aware that the presence of noblemen and -women in the entourage of its members could not only contribute to the maintenance of its good relationship with the elites of the realm, but also to the splendid appearance and the prestige of its courts. It is therefore no coincidence that the high aristocracy was well represented in the various Habsburg households. Consequently, there was also a certain apprehension towards people whose noble background was deemed suspicious or simply not prestigious enough. In that respect, there existed major differences between the two branches of the dynasty. Whereas on the Austrian side the requirements with regard to one's noble ancestry were fairly strict when it came to the appointment of a potential courtier, on the Spanish side they seem to have been less so. In 1615 Baltasar de Zúñiga, the Spanish ambassador in Prague, sent a letter to Archduke Albert in which he requested that one Iñigo de Brizuela, *gentilhombre de la Boca* at the court of Brussels, be given the office of *gentilhombre de la Cámara*.[54] Given that Brizuela was a nephew of Albert's personal confessor, Zúñiga hoped that the Archduke would endorse the promotion. The latter, however, flatly refused to do so because Brizuela was not of sufficient noble *qualidad*. Upon receiving this news, Zúñiga complained that Albert based his decision on rules that may have applied in the Austrian lands, but certainly not in Spain:

The House of Brizuela is one of the oldest and most prominent in … Burgos, and if the ears of Your Highness had not been so purely German, one could inform you that this family shares the blood of the Royal House of Castile, since according to my information the mistress of King Alonso XI (who is the ancestor of the Kings) was a daughter of Teresa de Brizuela. And although this may not be something that is valued in Germany, it is certainly prestigious in Castile and other countries.[55]

[53] Keller, *Hofdamen*, p. 36.
[54] AGRB, SEG 516, s.f.: Baltasar de Zúñiga to Albert, 17 October 1615.   [55] Ibid.

It seemed a reasonable argument. The Archduke, however, was inexorable, and Iñigo de Brizuela would never get his promotion.

An important obligation for applicants that is often overlooked in historiography on the early modern court, but which nevertheless made a lot of sense to contemporaries, was – quite simply – that they had to be decent workers and capable of doing the job for which they were applying. This seems strangely at odds with the perception most people have of early modern courtiers, but Mendoza's description of the pros and cons of the applicants makes clear that (at least in theory) the expectations did not differ much from those that are still valid today. The Duke of Aarschot's brother, for example, was described as 'a noble and rich knight and [a member of] a house that has always been loyal to His Majesty'. However, 'he knows little and drinks a lot, and has lived a licentious life' and was therefore not deemed a suitable candidate.[56] Another applicant, the Lord of Willerval, was 'old and talkative, careless and boisterous'.[57] A third courtier, the Count de Ligne, was 'a boy with few skills, and there are some who express doubt about his ability to serve in the household of His Highness, and some who believe he will do a good job'.[58] One candidate who did receive a positive appraisal was the Count of Sainte-Aldegonde, whose father had been *sumiller de corps* of Emperor Charles V and who was 'a virtuous man, quick-witted and in good health'.[59] The list goes on, and it demonstrates that being considered competent, smart and discreet was definitely an asset. Moreover, showing relevant experience did not hurt either. Speaking different languages was a must for stewards who had to receive foreign envoys. The keeper of the wardrobe had better have some knowledge of accountancy if he was to verify the accounts of his department, which was arguably one of the most expensive in the household. For a master of the horse, an aptitude for organizing long journeys was a useful talent. Disposing of a sound mind and a good deal of competence and social skills, it would seem, was a definite trump card for anyone who desired to serve in the Habsburg household.

Finally, the criterion of constancy in the service of the Crown was perhaps the most pressing one. Aspiring courtiers had to have a proven track record of loyalty towards the monarch, and by extension, towards the dynasty. If this was not the case, then they did not stand a chance. This seems logical enough. However, in recent decades the question of how loyalty was perceived in an early modern context has been much discussed. One of the problems appears to be that it is difficult for modern historians to dismiss the use of national labels when it comes to tackling

---

[56] RAH, Colección Salazar y Castro A-61, f. 30r.   [57] Ibid.   [58] Ibid.   [59] Ibid., f. 27.

the issue.[60] The general presumption is that contemporaries considered political affinity to be dependent on one's nation, which in turn depended on one's country of birth. To a certain extent, this is an understandable view. Rivalry among different nations at court was rife and 'national minorities' were frequently seen as disloyal and prone to treason.[61] The Habsburgs tried to deal with this by deliberately integrating courtiers hailing from 'underrepresented' regions in their households so as to give each part of the dynastic agglomerate its rightful share. The same councillor who told Archduke Albert to take on at least 24 pages also seemed to think that the ideal Habsburg household should reflect the diversity of the Habsburg possessions:

Much do I desire that the household of Your Highness should consist of several nations, vassals of His Majesty, and this in order to maintain the benevolence of all of them. In particular, it should be Spaniards, Netherlanders and Burgundians, and some Italian vassals of His Majesty, and Germans, all good Catholics and deserving persons.[62]

Whether or not Albert acted on the counsellor's advice, the fact of the matter is that the archducal household ended up consisting of many Netherlandish and Spanish courtiers, but also of Burgundians, Germans and Italians. The same pattern can be found at other Habsburg courts, albeit in varying numbers. The origin of potential courtiers, then, was thus clearly of some concern during the recruitment process. The idea was that a deliberate selection of nobles hailing from every part of the Habsburg realm would benefit the political stability of the Habsburg court in question.

Was this concern justified? Widespread though they may have been, it would appear that the feelings of rivalry and distrust between members of different nations were often based on perception – not necessarily on facts. More importantly, national labels themselves often gave cause for confusion. In September 1613, word reached the court of Brussels that Emperor Matthias had appointed Charles-Bonaventure de Longueval, Count of Buquoy, as the new commander of the Imperial Army. In a letter to his superiors in Paris, the French ambassador in Brussels reported that the Spanish nobles at court were over the moon when they heard the news. He explained that even though the Spaniards considered Buquoy to be *'alleman de naisanse'* (German by birth), they felt that he was

---

[60] On the concept of nation in the Spanish Monarchy, see the contributions in A. Álvarez-Ossorio Alvariño and B. J. García García (eds.), *La Monarquía de las naciones. Patria, nación y naturaleza en la Monarquía de España* (Madrid, 2004).

[61] For a discussion, see Raeymaekers, *One Foot in the Palace*, pp. 151–160.

[62] IVDJ, envío 47, caja 63, doc. 506: 'Autoridad absoluta sin eçesion alguna' (the author has been identified as Philippe de Croÿ, Count of Solre).

'*espaignol d'effect*' (Spanish in effect) and would thus be able to strengthen the influence of Spain in the Habsburg military.[63] Interestingly, the fact that Buquoy actually hailed from Arras in the county of Artois – then a province of the Habsburg Low Countries – did not seem to occur to them, and if it did, it was not deemed relevant.[64]

Clearly, early modern conceptions of 'nation' and 'loyalty' – and of the correlation between the two – were not as clear-cut as they are today. Nevertheless, throughout the nineteenth and twentieth centuries many historians have been quick to compare the early modern court to an arena of conflict in which 'nations' were necessarily interchangeable with political 'factions', each of which vied for its own interests. This is obviously erroneous. In the early modern age, political loyalty was based on factors that far surpassed the ratio of the concept of nation. 'Loyalty,' as Luc Duerloo has recently argued, 'was about serving. It rested on ancient feudal concepts and implied a traditional sense of honour ... Loyalty was by definition to the prince ... and such feelings were supported by a wider allegiance to the dynasty. It was only loosely defined by one's nation.'[65] Talking about the middle tier of courtiers at the court of Brussels, he goes on to explain that 'they were recruited from all corners of the Habsburg possessions and sometimes even beyond. Their loyalty was in part based on personal ties, in part sustained by notions of what Habsburg rule stood for. Their nation was something of an accident of birth; their loyalty was an acquired virtue.'[66]

According to Duerloo, the real test of loyalty – as contemporaries saw it – was one's record of service.[67] Indeed, to a certain extent loyalty could be measured by counting the number of years someone had served in the household; by looking at their *cursus honorum*; by taking into account the dedication they showed towards the monarch and the sacrifices they had made in order to support the dynasty. In some cases, loyalty to the Crown even became something of a family tradition, as court offices were passed down from generation to generation. Furthermore, even though most courtiers would focus their ambitions on one specific court, it was not uncommon for some people to serve in one Habsburg household for a number of years and then move on to another. Quite frequently this was the result of the death of the ruler, after which his household was dissolved and the members of his entourage had to find employment

---

[63] Paris, Bibliothèque Nationale, Manuscrits Français 16130, f. 178: Charles de l'Aubespinne-Chasteauneuf, abbot of Préaux, to Secretary of State Puisieux, 27 September 1613.
[64] His biography in O. Chaline, 'Charles-Bonaventure de Longueval, Comte de Buquoy (1571–1621)', *Dix-septième Siècle* 240 (2008), pp. 399–422.
[65] Duerloo, *Dynasty and Piety*, p. 100.   [66] Ibid.   [67] Ibid.

elsewhere.[68] At other times, they opted to move to a different Habsburg court in the hopes of securing better positions for themselves or their families. Some noble families even tried to perfect this strategy by 'branching out' and pursuing careers for its members in several Habsburg households. Here too, the House of Dietrichstein may serve as an example.

Hailing from the duchy of Carinthia, the Dietrichstein family rose to the fore in the early sixteenth century and quickly became one of the foremost noble houses in the Holy Roman Empire.[69] Baron Siegmund von Dietrichstein (1480–1533), the first *Freiherr* of his house, was appointed *Landeshauptmann* of Styria in 1515 and later became *Obersthofmeister* in the household of Empress Anna, the wife of Ferdinand I. Siegmund's son Adam von Dietrichstein (1527–1590) started his career in 1548 at the court of Vienna, where he served as *Kämmerer* in the household of Archduke Maximilian II, the later Emperor. In 1553 he married Margarita Folch de Cardona, a Spanish noblewoman from the entourage of Maximilian's wife, the Spanish infanta Maria. A scion of one of the foremost noble houses in Aragon, Margarita was a daughter of Antonio Folch de Cardona, Viceroy of Sardinia, and Maria de Requeséns, a descendant of King Ferdinand the Catholic. It was a match made in heaven. By marrying Margarita, Adam von Dietrichstein allied himself not only with the Spanish high aristocracy, but also with a descendant of Ferdinand of Aragon and hence – if only from afar – with the Habsburg dynasty itself. The marriage thus secured his place among the ranks of the high and mighty in both Vienna and Madrid. To a noble family that aspired to make its fortune in the service of the House of Austria, this acquaintance with both branches of the dynasty was a major advantage. It certainly worked for Adam, who was able to gain the special favour of the Emperor and was given the office of *Oberststallmeister* in the household of Empress Maria. A few years later, in 1563, his career reached its pinnacle when he was appointed as the Imperial ambassador in Madrid. One of his responsibilities here was to oversee the education of Maximilian's sons Rudolph and Ernest. The boys had been sent to live at the court of Philip II in order to complete their upbringing, and Adam served as their caretaker and *mayordomo mayor*.[70] In the meantime, Margarita too proved her worth for the House of Dietrichstein. She became a trusted confidante of Empress

---

[68] Duindam, *Vienna and Versailles*, p. 168.

[69] The family history can be found in F. Edelmayer (ed.), *Die Korrespondenz der Kaiser mit ihren Gesandten in Spanien*, vol. 1 (Oldenbourg, 1997) pp. 33–49.

[70] F. Edelmayer, 'Honor y dinero. Adam de Dietrichstein al servicio de la Casa de Austria', *Studia Histórica. Historia Moderna* 10:11 (1992/93), pp. 89–116.

Maria and did not fail to use her privileged position in order to strengthen the influence of her family at court.[71]

Margarita bore Adam 13 children: eight girls and five boys. As could be expected, the couple made good use of its connections in both branches of the Habsburg dynasty and saw to it that their offspring were able to follow in their parents' footsteps. At least four of their surviving daughters became ladies-in-waiting at the court of Madrid: Maria in the household of Queen Anna; Ana and Hipolita in that of Infantas Isabella and Catalina Micaela; and Beatriz in that of Queen Margarita.[72] Of the five sons, only three survived. Siegmund (1560–1602) succeeded his father as head of the Dietrichstein family. Maximilian (1569–1611) first entered the service of Rudolph II's younger brother Ernest. In 1593 he accompanied Ernest as *Oberststallmeister* to the Low Countries, where the latter had been appointed governor-general.[73] When Ernest died unexpectedly two years later, Maximilian remained at the court of Brussels as *sumiller de corps* of Ernest's brother and successor, Archduke Albert. He left Albert's service in 1598 and returned to the Empire, where he died in 1611. It was, however, the youngest brother Franz Seraph (1570–1636) who was to have the most brilliant career. As cardinal and bishop of Olomouc, he became one of the champions of the Counter Reformation in the Holy Roman Empire. He was appointed president of Rudolph II's Privy Council and would remain the most prominent figure at the Imperial court for years in a row. In 1624 he was elevated to the status of *Reichsfürst*, in 1635 to that of *Protector Germaniae*.[74] During all these years he acted as guardian to his nephew, Siegmund's son Maximilian (1596–1655), who – as we have seen – started his career at the court of Brussels and would move on to become *Obersthofmeister* in the household of Empress Eleonora Gonzaga in Vienna.[75] From that moment on, the Dietrichsteins had secured their place among the high and mighty in the Holy Roman Empire, and would remain there for decades to come.

[71] V. de Cruz Medina, 'Margarita de Cardona y sus hijas, damas entre la Corte madrileña y Bohemia', in J. Martínez Millán and M. P. Marçal Lourenço (eds.), *Las relaciones discretas entre las Monarquías Hispana y Portuguesa: Las casas de las Reinas (siglos XV-XIX)*, vol. 2 (Madrid, 2009), pp. 1267–1300.

[72] Ibid. See also J. Martínez Millán and S. Fernández Conti (eds.), *La Monarquía de Felipe II: La casa del Rey*, vol. 2 (Madrid, 2005) pp. 675 and 692.

[73] J. E. Hortal Muñoz, 'La casa del Archiduque Ernesto durante su gobierno en los Países Bajos (1593–1595)', in Álvarez-Ossorio Alvariño and García García (eds.), *La Monarquía de las Naciones*, pp. 193–205.

[74] His biography in W. Eberhard, 'Dietrischstein, Franz Seraph (seit 1623) Fürst von (1570–1636)', in E. Gatz (ed.) *Die Bischöfe des Heiligen Römischen Reiches, 1448 bis 1648: ein biographisches Lexikon* (Berlin, 1996), pp. 129–133.

[75] His biography can be found at http://www.univie.ac.at/Geschichte/wienerhof/wiener hof2/datenblaetter/dietrichstein_m1.htm (last consulted on 30 January 2016).

The Dietrichstein family may serve as a prime example of a noble house that rose to prominence because of its attachment to the Habsburg dynasty. Part of its rapid ascent can perhaps be explained by coincidence, as its members seem to have had a knack for being in the right place at the right time. Be that as it may, there is little doubt that the Dietrichsteins owe much of their success to their persistent dedication to the august House of Austria. Not only were they able to gain the particular favour of the consecutive Emperors, but they managed to do so without losing perspective and placing all their hopes in just one court. Indeed, it could be argued that the family deliberately opted for a wider 'spread of risks' by branching out to other Habsburg courts and making use of the entire range of possibilities Habsburg patronage had to offer. By launching the careers of its sons and daughters in several Habsburg households, the House of Dietrichstein avoided to put all of its eggs in one basket. In a sense, they chose to serve the entire dynasty, rather than a single member of that dynasty.

Conclusion

The distribution of patronage was a modus operandi in which the august House of Austria excelled. Contrary to what is often implied, the establishment of two separate Habsburg branches in 1555 did not automatically result in a division of the vast Habsburg patronage network. If anything, it became even more important for the dynasty to establish patron/client-relationships in other parts of the realm. One of the obvious ways to do this was for a Habsburg ruler to create positions in his household and deliberately seek out courtiers originating from other Habsburg regions. Indeed, by turning the amalgam of Habsburg courts into a gigantic source of employment and introducing a large-scale system of *service par terme*, the dynasty was able to provide noblemen and -women in all corners of the Habsburg possessions with a wide range of prestigious, lucrative and potentially influential offices. It could be argued that the vast network of households that were scattered across Europe was one of the House of Austria's main assets, as it enabled the dynasty to secure the continued support of the nobility and remain in power for centuries in a row.

To aristocrats looking for advancement, the prospect of exercising an office in one of the Habsburg households was obviously alluring. It not only facilitated their access to the court, which throughout the early modern age remained the main forum for policy-making, but it enabled them to stay close to the monarch and be first in line to receive his good graces. Nevertheless, the notion of reciprocity that characterized every early modern patron/client relationship implied that there was also a sense of entitlement involved when it came to the distribution of offices: some noble families considered it a hereditary right to claim certain positions, and this concern had to be dealt with appropriately. In some cases, this meant that offices were passed down from father to son, thus rendering this type of court service a form of patronage that could transcend generations. Nevertheless, acquiring an office in the household was usually easier said than done. Even though there were many local differences that need to be taken into account, it could be argued that the recruitment process in the various Habsburg courts followed certain guidelines that reflected a shared Habsburg ethos and distinguished it from that it in other European courts. The requirement that aspiring courtiers had to adhere to the Catholic creed was a *conditio sine qua non*, albeit one that was sometimes mollified. Another condition was the proven demonstration of loyalty to the dynasty. As we have seen, historians would do well to base their assessment of one's fidelity to the monarch on one's record of service, rather than on one's nation (insofar as this category is at all applicable in an early modern context).

Finally, this chapter has broached the subject of mobility between the various Habsburg courts and households by analysing the case of the noble House of Dietrichstein. All too often, we tend to assume that early modern courtiers were tied to a specific ruler and hence, to a specific court. In the case of the Habsburg dynasty however, we find several nobles whose career paths led them from one Habsburg household to the next. Further research is needed to detect if and how this mobility rendered the various courts more or less cosmopolitan, and to detect whether the factions operating at the various Habsburg courts were particular to each individual court or whether they on the contrary formed networks of their own.

10 Revolutionary Absolutism and the Elites of the Danish Monarchy in the Long Seventeenth Century

Gunner Lind

> IV. The king alone shall have the supreme power and authority to appoint and dismiss all officials, high and low, no matter what name or title they may have, according to his own free will and judgment, so that all offices and positions, no matter what authority they possess, shall have their first source, as from a spring, in the absolute power of the king.
> [...]
> VI. The king alone shall also have supreme power over the clergy from the highest to the lowest [...][1]

The Royal Law of 1665, the constitutional law defining royal absolute rule in the united kingdom of Denmark and Norway, left no room for ambiguity. The power to distribute offices, and thus to define a major part of the social elites, was asserted in the beginning, just after the power to create laws and before the power to wage war and collect taxes. Later on, in Section XXVI, the successors were admonished to keep a watchful eye 'since daily experience and the sorry examples of other countries accurately demonstrate how harmful it is when the mildness and piety of kings and lords are misused in such a fashion that their power and authority are, almost imperceptibly, taken from them by one person or another, indeed, even by their own nearest and most trusted servants'.[2]

It is not surprising that the famous 'absolutist constitution' testifies to such concern for the relations between elites and royal power. The political process leading to the revolutionary changes of 1660–1661, which were codified by the Royal Law, was to a large extent a matter of the definition of the elites of the state and their social and political rights. All over Europe, the development of the early modern monarchies implied changes in the relations between the elites and the monarchy. Characteristic changes affected personal and spatial relations to the ruler,

---

[1] Royal Law 1665, as translated in Ernst Ekman, 'The Danish Royal Law of 1665,' *Journal of Modern History* 29 (1957), pp. 102–107, at p. 106. The original consists of parallel Danish and Latin texts.
[2] Ibid., 106–107.

with the court of Versailles as the classical specimen: the mobilization of traditional elites as servants to their prince, especially military officers, where the service obligation of Russian nobles and the Prussian *Kadettenkorps* are well-known examples; giving broad segments of the landed and urban elite a share of public power, like it happened emblematically in Great Britain or the old Dutch Republic; and finally, in some cases, the expansion of traditional elites through massive integration of new men, as happened in Sweden.

Even if certain aspects of some national histories are famous, most elements could be found in some guise everywhere. The actual solutions, however, were evidently very different. Relations to changes in other fields – constitutional, military, fiscal, ideological – were anything but linear either. New, but rarely radically new, solutions were mixed with a considerable mass of traditional social and political elements, leading many scholars to question how much newness was really present in the 'new monarchies'. Compared with the changes in such areas as the military or the interpretation of government, the social patterns surrounding the elites appear in most current scholarship as a stable rather than a dynamic aspect of the early modern age.

Not so in the Danish monarchy. The Danish case demonstrates that radical change in this field might be realized by an early modern 'new monarchy'. It does also suggest why, and indirectly, why most other early modern societies avoided comparable radical change. Thus it is of special interest in any systematic and comparative approach to this phase of the history of monarchy and the elites in Europe.

The Rule of the Nobility

Absolute monarchy became formal and radical in Denmark partly because it succeeded a relatively formal and radical political order, which was also the product of a revolution. Danish historians have traditionally christened it 'the rule of the nobility', pointing to the most salient aspect. During this epoch, Danish kings were elected, even if election never did bypass a living son of a deceased king. The electing body was the Council of the Realm. This body of noblemen related to the king like the cardinals to the pope. They were selected by the ruler, selected his successor, and served as his counsellors in between. The election charters confirmed among other privileges that the new king intended to 'love and prefer' Danish noblemen and 'rule and govern the realm of Denmark with them', conferring an exclusive right to higher office on the noble order. The charters also made it unlawful for the 'unfree' to acquire noble land.[3] During the sixteenth century, the Crown, the nobility and others (freeholders, urban land, church property) shared the land in Denmark proper with 50, 40 and 10 per cent respectively. Proportions in Norway were 50, 15 and 35 per cent.[4]

The core of this system was old, but it had gotten a more radical twist at the great meeting of the Estates that ended the civil war of 1534–1536. Instituting the Lutheran Reformation removed the bishops from the council and the church as such from any political influence. The bulk of church land was taken over by the king. As the leading cities had backed one of the losing sides, burgess political power was much diminished, while the Lutheran faction among the lay nobility emerged as partners in victory with the king. The collective power of the noble estate was secured, and the Council as well as the noble order expanded their base when the rebellious Council of Norway was abolished. The few Norwegian noble families were either absorbed by the Danish nobility or lost their noble status.[5]

The only elements outside the unitary kingdom were the German lands of the king, mainly the duchies Schleswig and Holstein. The duchies had their own rich and independent-minded aristocracy. The *Ritterschaft* was a corporation separate from the Danish nobility. The duchies had a complicated system of rule. Power was shared between the royal house and the cadet line residing at the castle Gottorf; and Holstein was a fief of the German Empire, Schleswig of the Danish crown. The kingdoms and the duchies treated each other as foreign countries despite the personal link and despite treaties uniting them in perpetual political and military union since 1533.[6]

The corporative independence between the two nobilities was visible when a nobleman from the duchies moved to Denmark. He had to be naturalized by marriage, acquisition of land or even formal oath before he would be able to enter royal service outside the court. Quite

---

[3] *Samling af danske Kongers Haandfæstninger og andre lignende Acter* (Copenhagen, 1856; reprint, 1974), quoted from p. 84 (version 1536).

[4] Øystein Rian, *Den aristokratiske fyrstestaten 1536–1648 (Danmark-Norge 1380–1814)*, vol. 2 (Oslo, 1997), pp. 173, 180, 186.

[5] On the two revolutionary processes see Erling Ladewig Petersen and Knud J. V. Jespersen, 'Two Revolutions in Early Modern Denmark,' in E. I. Kouri and Tom Scott (ed.), *Politics and Society in Reformation Europe. Essays for Sir Geoffrey Elton* (London, 1987), pp. 473–501. On the sixteenth-century state see Paul Douglas Lockhart, *Denmark, 1513–1660: The Rise and Decline of a Renaissance Monarchy* (Oxford, 2007), pp. 30–54.

[6] On the union, Gunner Lind, 'Krig, udenrigspolitik og statsdannelse i Oldenborg-monarkiet, 1533–1658. En analyse af unionen mellem Danmark, Norge og Slesvig-Holsten,' in Knut P. Arstad (ed.), *Strategi, ledelse og samfunn 1588–1720*, Forsvarsmuseets småskrifter (Oslo, 2000), pp. 8–38.

a few did so, however, even sitting on the Council of the Realm.[7] They were part of a pattern of northward migration of elite men which persisted into the nineteenth century. Not only nobles, but also merchants, skilled artisans, clergymen, school and university educated men in general, moved from Denmark to Norway and Iceland, from Schleswig and Holstein to Denmark and sometimes farther north, and from the whole German area into all the lands of the king of Denmark. This reflected the pattern of urbanization, distribution of schools and universities and degree of economic development. It did also make German rather than Danish the lingua franca of the Danish state, even if Danish was the language of the political core.[8]

Elite migration was encouraged by the relatively small size of the native elite groups. The Danish-Norwegian nobility was a true aristocracy, counting only c. 2,000 persons out of a sixteenth-century population of about two million (in all the lands of the Crown). Between 500 to 700 of these can be counted as adult men. This can be compared with the 1536–1660 immigration of 131 nobles, of whom 32 came from Schleswig and Holstein and 77 from the rest of Germany.[9] Other elite groups were obviously much larger – the clergy counted in the thousands and urban population was 10–20 per cent of the total. But immigrants from Germany, the Netherlands and Scotland were prominent even in the cities.

Despite the antagonisms incorporated into the system, king and Council formed a quite strong central power likened to the standards of the age. Fast rotation of young noblemen made an old-fashioned masculine and warlike court a platform for making connections between the king and his nobility.[10] The administrative, military and financial resources of these partners enabled the Danish crown to dominate the immediate neighbourhood from the fifteenth century into the 1620s.

---

[7] Albert Fabritius, *Danmarks Riges Adel. Dens Tilgang og Afgang 1536–1936* (Copenhagen, 1946), Bilag [Appendix] B; Gunner Lind, *Hæren og magten i Danmark, 1614–1662* (Odense, 1994), p. 189.

[8] Vibeke Winge, *Dänische Deutsche, deutsche Dänen: Geschichte der deutschen Sprache in Dänemark 1300–1800 mit einem Ausblick auf das 19. Jahrhundert* (Heidelberg, 1992).

[9] Svend Aage Hansen, *Adelsvældens Grundlag.* Studier fra Københavns Universitets Økonomiske Institut, vol. 6 (Copenhagen, 1964), Bilagstabel 15, 19; Fabritius, *Danmarks Riges Adel*, Bilag B.

[10] Leon Jespersen, 'Court and Nobility in Early Modern Denmark,' *Scandinavian Journal of History* 27:3 (2002), pp. 129–142; Gunner Lind, 'The Friendship of Kings: Friendship and Clientelism around the Kings of Denmark, 1600–1750,' in Jón Viðar Sigurðsson and Thomas Småberg (eds.), *Friendship and Social Networks in Scandinavia, c. 1000–1800* (Turnhout, 2013), pp. 233–254.

New Militarization

The 1620s was the first decade of severe and mainly unsuccessful wars with the emperor, with Sweden, and with Sweden again. Sweden expanded as a *condottiere* state, marrying innovative and ambitious government with resources donated by France or extracted from Germany. Swedish power meant the loss of important provinces in 1645 and 1658. The Danish crown had to compete with the size and quality of the Swedish military. It did so quite ambitiously, but not quite successfully, as can be seen from the territorial loss. After 1658 Denmark became the aggressive and more successful part, a core partner in the alliances which finally reduced Sweden to manageable strength in 1718–1720.

Military growth was a continuous process spanning the political divide in 1660. The first permanent regiments were created in 1615. Subtracting the oscillations created by war, a stable growth trend in army size continued to around 1700. Armies of 80,000 to 100,000 were deployed during the following decades. The Danish crown was also an important naval power. Like in Sweden and later in Prussia, militarization was made possible by a considerable use of conscripts who were mostly kept demobilized as a part of rural society. It was still a remarkable effort for a society of 2 to 2.5 million inhabitants. As a British observer remarked, Denmark was 'all head and no body, all soldiers and no subjects'.[11]

The New Military Creates a New Elite

The stresses from war and military expansion destroyed the elective monarchy. They produced a cascade of political conflicts, starting when Christian IV went to war in Germany 1625 against the express will of the Council of the Realm, and ending at the meeting of the Estates in 1660. Everyday quarrels centred on the direction of foreign policy and the size and distribution of the rapidly rising tax burden. But military expansion did also raise the more fundamental question of the composition of the elite of society.

The growth of the armed forces and the associated bureaucracy created a question of capacity. The nobility could man the 100–200 leading positions of the existing central and local civilian administration; but the permanent army required more than 100 officers in peacetime soon after 1620, and double that in the 1640s. By mid-century, mobilization for war demanded more than a thousand.[12] Many of these positions were not

---

[11] Robert Molesworth, *An Account of Denmark as It Was in the Year 1692* (London, 1694), p. 224.
[12] Lind, *Hæren og magten*, pp. 485–503.

particularly well paid or powerful. Still they did not carry the subordinate stamp normally associated with commoners in royal service. Any officer is a leader of men; carrying arms was the traditional noble role, routinely extolled in word and image; and the new military soon acquired the potential to dominate any force which might be mobilized by private persons.

This challenge was met by several means. One of them was husbanding the resources. The percentage of Danish noblemen rose with each step in the military hierarchy. (As did the share of local nobles in the units of the duchies.) Special care was taken never to place a junior officer of noble descent under the command of a commoner. The political leverage of the noble estate was deployed to these ends, as was the patronage of the nobles at the head of the royal government – not least the Marshal of the Realm, transformed from a relic of the feudal levy to leader of the military administration. The Council openly demanded that new units 'must be formed by the Marshal of the Realm using Danish noblemen and other native born'. More confidentially we can find lists of noblemen put forward for promotion and letters from the patronage networks.[13]

Another element was the mobilization of resources. The nobility was re-militarized as modern officers and military enterprisers in both parts of the state. When the last war of the old regime started in the autumn of 1657, the military participation rate of the Danish nobility reached about 40 per cent, and most new regiments were organized by local noblemen. This mobilization did of course appeal to the old noble warrior identity. It did also involve action by the older generation. Young noblemen were encouraged to get military experience abroad, and the new Noble Academy in Sorø taught infantry drill (by a Spaniard part-timing from his regular job as army captain). A military career did also involve at least a certain cultural adaptation to the values of the international professional military. This might be controversial. 'Do not let your stay among those who shout "dulce bellum, dulce bellum" give you cause to add to their scream. Do not make it a pleasure to see blood,' ran the advice of an elder brother.[14] Still a growing number combined career stages at home with service in foreign armies; and the increasing stability and size of the Danish army and navy professionalized an increasing number at home through decades of service. An increasingly prominent discourse on 'the fatherland' and 'patriotism' gave respectability to this re-militarization and served as a platform for political demands.[15]

The last tool for fulfilling the demand for numbers was co-optation, especially immigration. Immigration of both soldiers and military officers

---

[13] Ibid., p. 232 (quotation); Chapter 3.   [14] Ibid., p. 193.   [15] Ibid., Chapter 3.

was minimal during the sixteenth century, but now became important, with a high point during the closing decades of the Thirty Years' War. Naturalization of officers of foreign noble lineage as Danish noblemen became quite common, allowing some Holsteiners and truly foreign Germans to rise in the army. A few commoner officers were also ennobled. Ennoblement was otherwise rare and mostly confined to learned men serving in the diplomacy.[16] Both kinds of co-optation were controversial in the eyes of the noble estate. Integration of necessary foreigners, however, still provided the Danish nobility with needed manpower and facilitated its dominance of the state service in general and the armed forces in particular. Such integration was increasingly sought by formal oath to the chancellor as joint representative of king, kingdom, council and noble estate.

The elites of the Danish kingdom seemed on the road to a transformation of the same kind as in Sweden. The Swedish rulers had met a parallel challenge by creating a vastly enlarged nobility of royal servants, mainly through ennoblement and naturalization but also through mobilization of the old noble order.[17] Such a transformation did also fit well with the political developments in Denmark during the crisis decades, where the political importance of the Estates increased enormously and recruitment to the Council of the Realm was subjected to pre-selection by the noble order instead of being a free royal choice.[18] The transformation of the nobility was not as speedy and thorough as in Sweden, however, where the army in Germany served as a transforming agent.

Noble Privilege under Attack

From the late 1620s, political propaganda harped on the military incompetence of the nobility and the near impossibility for commoners to be promoted. During two centuries Danish forces had mostly been victorious and mostly fought outside the borders. Now three wars in one generation were major defeats. Wallenstein's imperial army occupied the whole of Jutland 1628–1629. Even more provinces were occupied by the Swedes in 1644 and 1657–1658. Anger over defeat and foreign

---

[16] Fabritius, *Danmarks Riges Adel*, Bilag B.

[17] Ingvar Elmroth, *För kung och Fosterland: studier i den svenska adelns demografi och offentliga funktioner 1600–1900*. Bibliotheca historica Lundensis, vol. 50 (Lund, 1981), pp. 209–217.

[18] On this election see Leon Jespersen, 'En valghandling i 1600-tallet,' in Leon Jespersen and Asger Svane-Knudsen (eds.), *Stænder og magtstat: de politiske brydninger i 1648 og 1660, Odense University Studies in History and social Sciences* (Odense, 1989).

invasion strengthened and legitimized the long-standing resentment to noble privilege in the royal service, just like the necessity of new taxation created pressure for the reduction of noble tax privilege. The authors were anonymous, and this subversive literature only circulated in manuscript. The 'little elite' carrying this opposition was composite seen in relation to the old estates of society. Some might be classified as clergy or burgesses. Many evidently belonged to the substantial second layer in public and private service: bailiffs, bookkeepers, clerks, teachers, non-commissioned officers and so on. It was a heterogeneous class, but all highly dependent on noble bosses, employers or customers. Even if this had not been the case, most of the texts circulating were too strongly worded to be fit for print. This ballad written c. 1657 can serve as an example:

> If an honest Danish man appears
> A burgess or from the peasant estate
> And wants to offer his service
> To his Fatherland like a gentleman
> He will be regarded as a fool
> By our Danish nobility
> [...]
>
> It would be an insult to their noble rank
> If he should command or instruct them
> But that is why our country sees
> These mad expeditions on land and sea
> [...]
>
> Seize the wolf before it bites you
> King of Denmark, then you will act wisely
> Pray God for mercy, take the sword in your hand
> So beg the burgess and the farming man.[19]

The discourse of the leading nobles on patriotism and service to the fatherland was turned against the noble order itself. This must have resonated among many, as defence of the fatherland was a major theme in the popular literature carrying news or commenting on the wars.[20] It was recurrently argued that merits and competence ought to be preferred for noble birth, instead of the current system:

---

[19] C. F. Bricka, 'To Viser fra Svenskekrigen 1657–58,' *Danske Magazin* 4. rk. 6 (1886) pp. 64–65.

[20] Gunner Lind, 'Syndens straf og mandens ære: Danske tolkninger af krigen 1611–1660,' *Historisk Tidskrift [Stockholm]* 2008, no. 1 (2008), pp. 339–365; Sebastian Olden-Jørgensen, 'Krigens viser – pønitense, patriotisme og ironi i Trediveårskrigens danske skillingsviser,' in Lars Bisgaard, et al. (eds.), *Krig fra først til sidst. Festskrift til Knud J. V. Jespersen* (Odense, 2006), pp. 99–122.

Didn't Lucas Henriksen get shame and abuse in return for his manly deed, while Bjørn Ulfeldt was rewarded with the command of a squadron for surrendering Laholm? It is highly probable that there are privates under his command who are far more experienced than he will ever be [...] it is miserable and pathetic that this condition [nobility] ever became inheritable in Denmark. If not, then one might have taken care to select officers who had served in war before.[21]

A tough formal inquiry and informal reprisals from noble superiors hit those representatives of the burgess estate who raised the question of burgess military service politically in 1629. This episode was remembered, and not repeated.[22] Access to the service elite was a too controversial question to be part of normal politics.

The New Order

It reappeared 10 August 1658. Two days before, the king of Sweden had renewed war without warning. All Danish lands were controlled by the enemy, except parts of Norway and Copenhagen itself. Now king and Council found it wise to confer new privileges on the city. The inhabitants, clergy and secular, got privileges on par with the nobility with regard to landownership and taxation. And 'all private people, ecclesiastical or lay, now, and their children after them, shall enjoy equal access to *officia* and *honores* with the nobility, when they can make themselves competent and merit it through their capability and qualities'. The city itself was elevated as 'a free estate of the realm' with right to be heard in everything concerning the public benefit.[23]

The 'liberties of Copenhagen' were the political platform of clergy and burgesses uniting against noble privilege and the elective monarchy when the Estates met after the peace in 1660. The nobility adamantly refused to comply, but noble resistance was broken by declaring a state of emergency, closing the city and placing both city and country under military control. This was possible because the old army had been largely destroyed by the enemy in 1657/1658. A new one was created 1658–1660 in territory liberated from the Swedes, first by allies, then by the newly created forces themselves. It was controlled by strongly professional men: foreigners, Holsteiners, Danes and Norwegians, noble and

---

[21] S. Birket Smith, 'Tre satirisk-politiske småstykker fra Enevældens Dæmringstid,' *Danske Magazin* 4. rk. 6 (1886), p. 282. Ulfeldt came from a leading noble family.

[22] Rudi Thomsen, 'Den jyske borgerbevægelse 1629,' *Historisk Tidsskrift* 11. rk. 1 (1946); Leon Jespersen, 'Ryresolutionen og den jyske borgerbevægelse 1629,' *Historie Jyske Samlinger* Ny rk. 17, 1 (1987).

[23] V. A. Secher (ed.), *Corpus Constitutionum Daniæ. Forordninger, Recesser og andre kongelige Breve Danmarks Lovgivning vedrørende 1558–1660*, 6 vols. (Copenhagen: Selskabet for Udgivelse af Kilder til dansk Historie, 1887–1918), vol. 6, pp. 383–384.

commoners, but sharing a sceptical attitude towards the old system, the system of failure. Men like Hans von Ahlefeldt, who returned from years abroad '*n'ayant iamais eu une plus grande ambition, que de pouvoir seruir mon Roy, et sur tout dans la profession, que j'ay exercée durant quelques années, tant dans l'Empire que parmi les Nations estrangers.*'[24] He was a nobleman from Schleswig, but spoke about serving his lord and exercising his professional skills, not about his country. When the gates closed around the recalcitrant nobles in 1660 Lieutenant General Hans von Ahlefeldt commanded the Horse Guards.[25]

The pressures of war had thus modified the composition of the largest body of elite servants of the Crown, the army officers, already before 1660. The share of nobles and commoners, Danes and foreigners, had changed more than in previous wars. Foreigners and Holsteiners dominated at the key positions. The Marshal of the Realm died in action 1657 and was not replaced, and his successors in 1660 were immigrants with strong personal relations to the king. Members of the local aristocracy still in service tended to be men marked more by their profession than their class.[26]

This new army – and the support of the populace of Copenhagen, well armed after 21 months of siege – enabled the king to intimidate the nobility in 1660. 'The little army, which is the most real security for the royal hereditary house'[27] also stood by in early 1661, when it was revealed that the reformed monarchy was going to be absolute as well as hereditary, without any Council or Assemblies of the Estates.

Privilege and Merit

These further fundamental constitutional changes did not undermine, however, the alliance between the king and the lower orders. The Copenhagen privileges were confirmed in 1661. Then all estates got new privileges fitting the new order. The number of estates was now five. The burgesses of Copenhagen and the royal servants of the city were added to the three traditional privileged estates. Superficially a modest renewal with no changes beyond those promised 1658. Closer inspection revealed important details, however. The nobility lost all claims to political influence. The nobles could see their tax immunity and preeminent rank confirmed – but the first only 'unless the safety and wellbeing of Our

---

[24] Lind, *Hæren og magten*, pp. 245–246.
[25] Gunner Lind, 'Database of Danish Army Officers 1610–1665,' (Danish Data Archives, 1994).
[26] Lind, *Hæren og magten*, pp. 223–267.
[27] J. A. Fridericia (ed.), *Generallieutenant Jørgen Bjelkes Selvbiografi* (Copenhagen, 1890), pp. 175–176 (Hermann Meier, Secretary of the Council of War, 1662).

royal house or Our subjects makes [taxation] necessary' and the second with exemption of 'Our servants which are not of noble quality but still serve in important positions, on whom we will reserve the right to make a separate edict'.[28]

These ominous words did herald important and lasting changes. One element was the royal freedom to choose. It was confirmed in the strongest terms in the Royal Law. Another element was equality. This was realized e.g. in the new *Collegia* heading each administrative department. Each board must consist of an equal number of nobles and commoners. A third element was the emphasis on merit.

These changes had rapid and considerable practical results without turning the world upside down. Landowners without nobility soon became common, but still possessed less than a third of private land in Denmark around the middle of the eighteenth century.[29] Nobles became a small minority in the *Collegia* within a few decades – but the president was always noble, even if often an immigrant or recently ennobled. The old nobility suffered an economic and demographic crash as the new tax burdens forced many to sell their lands and (very often) live from modest charges in the army.[30] The disappearance of national restrictions had the most conspicuous results. Already in 1661 we find the viceroy in the duchies, Christian von Rantzau, as the first minister in Copenhagen. From then on, immigrants both from the duchies and the wider world were an important minority in all elite groups from the royal council downwards, and most of all at the top.[31]

The Table of Ranks

The new policy produced a slight increase in the number of new Danish noble families in the decades after 1660. Compared with the decades before, more new men were ennobled or naturalized.[32] Two much larger groups, however, were the product of more radical change. These were

---

[28] Nils G. Bartholdy, 'Adelsbegrebet under den ældre enevælde. Sammenhængen med privilegier og rang i tiden 1660–1730,' *Historisk Tidsskrift* 12. rk. 5 (1971), pp. 581.

[29] Axel Linvald, 'Hvem ejede Danmarks jord omkring midten af det 18. Aarhundrede?,' *Historisk Tidsskrift* 8. Rk. IV, tillæg (1913), p. 153.

[30] Hansen, *Adelsvældens Grundlag*, pp. 274–275.

[31] Erik Gøbel, *De styrede rigerne: Embedsmændene i den dansk-norske civile centraladministration 1660–1814* (Odense, 2000), pp. 42–45; Gunner Lind, 'Den heroiske tid? Administrationen under den tidlige enevælde 1660–1720,' in *Dansk Forvaltningshistorie I: Stat. Forvaltning og Samfund. Fra Middelalderen til 1901*, ed. Leon Jespersen and E. Ladewig Petersen (Copenhagen: Jurist- og Økonomforbundets Forlag, 2000), pp. 159–226, at pp. 180–183.

[32] 1660 October–1699: 86; 1620–1660 October: 61. Fabritius, *Danmarks Riges Adel*, Bilag B.

the noble immigrants who did not bother to get local recognition and the men who served the state in high positions without any kind of hereditary nobility at all. As an example, the king's colonels and generals 1670–1699 were 49 per cent of foreign nobility, 12 per cent nobles from Denmark and Holstein, and 3 per cent newly ennobled. The remaining 36 per cent did not have any kind of nobility.[33]

Their status was secured by a new instrument, the Table of Ranks, introduced in 1671,[34] and part of a packet of new policies towards the elites dating from the same year. Another was the introduction of counts and barons as high nobility within the traditionally undivided estate.[35] These new titles were conferred by the king on a chosen few, almost exclusively his close servants, some of them immigrants or recently ennobled, thus splitting the traditional unity of the noble estate. A third element was the 'resurrection' of the knightly Order of Dannebrog, enabling many more to become knighted than the old Order of the Elephant and creating a shared platform of social excellence for Danes, Holsteiners and immigrants.[36]

The first Table of Ranks was fairly innocent. It did mainly concern precedence at court, like so many others. But the scope expanded gradually during the following decades. This was an age of radical reform, including a new codification of the laws of Denmark and of Norway, new articles of war and a new statute for the church; a new uniform system of weights and measures; and a new land tax based on measurement and assessment of all land in the two kingdoms. Rank as organizing principle was linked with the new privileges of all royal servants, which confirmed that those with wives and children enjoyed full noble privilege, including

---

[33] Database on army officers. See Gunner Lind, 'Military and Absolutism. The Army Officers of Denmark-Norway as a Social Group and Political Factor, 1660–1848,' *Scandinavian Journal of History* 12 (1987), pp. 221–243, at pp. 242–243.

[34] The various versions of the Table are printed as: Casper Peter Rothe, ed. *Kong Christian den Femtes skrevne Befalinger og Anordninger eller Reskripter for Dannemark* (Copenhagen, 1776), pp. 111–119; *Forordning om Rangen 31. December A° 1680* (Copenhagen, 1680); *Forordning om Rangen 11. Februar A° 1693* (Copenhagen, 1693); *Forordning om Rangen 11 Februarii A° 1699* (Copenhagen, 1699); *Forordning om Rangen 11. Februarii Aar 1717 med sit Alfabets-Register etc* (Copenhagen, 1726); *Forordning om Rangen Copenhagen 13. Dec. 1730* (Copenhagen, 1730); *Forordning om Rangen 11. Febr. Anno 1734* (Copenhagen, 1734); *Forordning om Rangen 11. Febr. 1744* (Copenhagen, 1744); *Forordning om Rangen 14. Octobr. Anno 1746* (Copenhagen, 1746); *Den kgl. Danske Rangfølge* ([S.L.], 1784); *Kgl. Bekiendtgiørelse angaaende en Forandring i Rangforordningen, 12. Aug. 1808* (Copenhagen, 1808). Most have parallel editions in German.

[35] On these see Birgit Bjerre Jensen, 'Christian V's greve- og friherreprivilegier,' *Arkiv* 2 (1968), pp. 89–130.

[36] Knud J. V. Jespersen, 'For dyd, tro tjeneste og mandige bedrifter. De danske ridderordner og enevældens rangdelte samfund,' in Mogens Bencard and Tage Kaarsted (eds.), *Fra Korsridder til Ridderkors. Elefantordenens og Dannebrogordenens historie* (Odense, 1993), pp. 72–96.

equal access to office. This document polished the glory of the royal servants telling how they were rewarded for their combination of fidelity, patriotism and merit:

To encourage others to covet virtue and to desire what will make themselves and their fatherland famous, as well as to admonish them and their descendants of their duty and obligation by which they and their posterity are pledged to risk life, property and blood for the sovereignty, *absolutum dominium* and right of succession of the king and the transfer of these to his hereditary successors in government.[37]

Several of the documents were issued with the emblematic date of 11 February. This was the day of the failed Swedish storm of Copenhagen 1659, symbolically pointing to the alliance between burgesses and king forged during the siege. This fitted with two basic principles of the Tables: Rank followed exclusively from service, not from birth, except for the royal family and the counts and barons created by the king; and outside the Table the estates conserved their traditional ranking order – but below anybody in the Table of Ranks. A position – any position – in the table thus placed royal servants above even the oldest nobility (and their wives above mere noble ladies).

This became ever more important as more and more royal servants gained a slot in the Table. The lowest military rank in the table was major in 1671, captain in 1693 and ensign in 1717. Civilians were incorporated accordingly. The number of royal servants with rank must have grown from a few hundred to several thousand, outnumbering all other groups which could reasonably be included among the social elites.[38] The number swelled even more by the distribution of empty titles conferring rank without office. First real titles were used. It developed so rapidly that the Table from 1693 started to distinguish between real and titular incumbents in a number of cases. A real *'Etats-Raad'* ranked in Third Class subdivision 3, a titular *'Etats-Raad'* merely in Fourth Class subdivision 5; and so on. Later virtual office titles only used to confer rank began to appear. By such means most men of prestige and property might be included. Only the top of the clergy had a true rank as direct royal appointees (superintendents, professors, court chaplains), but other distinguished clergymen might be elevated with the title 'Ecclesiastic Councillor'. An important merchant might become 'Commercial Councillor'. And so on.

---

[37] Jacob Henric Schou and J. L. A. Kolderup-Rosenvinge (eds.), *Chronologisk Register over de kongelige Forordninger og aabne Breve*, 25 vols. (Copenhagen: Gyldendal, 1777–1850), vol. 1, p. 136.

[38] The army alone counted about 2000 officers qualifying by 1717. (Lind, 'Database of Danish Army Officers 1610–1665.')

The relationship between rank and hereditary nobility was complex. Everybody in the Table of Ranks enjoyed full noble rights and privileges. This followed from the 1679 privileges of the royal servants. Noble advantages were few, apart from the prestige, but there were some, especially when nobility was connected with landownership. From 1693 noble status was awarded to all descendants in perpetuity for those reaching Class III or higher. One might imagine that these families would struggle to get full recognition as nobility, but few did. Most did not even make use the offer of an officially recognized coat of arms. This royal grace thus created some further confusion concerning who enjoyed what kind of noble rights, but did not create a new class of inheritable quasi-nobility. The royal administration kept trace of nobility in the traditional sense, of the new high nobility, and of those serving with rank. These lists were the main content of the Calender of Court and State appearing annually from 1734. But the new hereditable status was lost in confusion, and abolished in 1730.[39]

A New Social Order

The basic principles spread to lesser areas of regulation. Meritocratic principles of advancement were conserved and even gained ground during the eighteenth century. It was e.g. explicitly prohibited to recommend for promotion according to 'naissance'; and the noble pages at court were replaced by the best students from the senior class of the Cadet Corps (1772).[40]

It is obvious that this policy potentially neutralized geographical distinctions. Danish, Schleswig-Holstein and foreign nobility were still different, commoner royal servants even more, but privilege and rank allowed them to act as one social group. Just as obvious that formal ennoblement should be less attractive than before. Royal servants did not need it at all; and for others empty rank titles were a simpler, cheaper and less politically suspect road to status. Old-fashioned ennoblement was now mainly attractive for commoners buying land.[41]

Still hereditary rank was not fully forgotten. This is clear at the very top of the system: The royal councillors were all noble until the nineteenth century. (Even if many were not noble born: 11 percent in the first

---

[39] Bartholdy, 'Adelsbegrebet.' This article is the main analysis of the complex relations between rank and noble status.

[40] *Des Reglements für Unsere Geworbene und National-Infanterie Dritter Theil* (Copenhagen, 1747), p. 71; Mogens Rosenløv, *Uddannelsen af Hærens linieofficerer 1713–1963* (Copenhagen, 1963), p. 36.

[41] Bartholdy, 'Adelsbegrebet'; Fabritius, *Danmarks Riges Adel*, Bilag B.

Geheime Conseil 1670, 50 per cent of those entering 1673–1700, 13 per cent 1700–1770, 26 per cent 1773–1848.)[42] In the army, where rank can be studied with precision, hereditary nobility (of any kind) conferred a career advantage among officer's sons until the middle of the eighteenth century. Rank was, however, a much stronger force than hereditary nobility much earlier. The son of a noble captain had fewer advantages than the son of a commoner colonel.[43] A local study of marriage and social networks indicate that middle-of-the-road landed nobility intermarried without any trouble with serving commoners already during the early decades of the eighteenth century. A few degrees of linkage could connect a wealthy count with modest infantry officers in a family network.[44]

It is easy to find statements depicting society as divided in the traditional four estates throughout the eighteenth century and beyond. For many, especially in the countryside, it must have seemed a reasonably realistic representation of the world. Paying war debt had reduced the Crown lands substantially, increasing the share of private large land-owners. These were also mobilized by the Crown as intermediaries in the collection of taxes and recruits. Most 'nobles', however, were not noble in the traditional sense; and in the upper echelons of society, the effects of royal policies produced a complex pattern of interference with the old ideas. The sparse studies on career and marriage patterns indicate that different forms of 'capital' (in Bourdieu's sense) were highly negotiable across a broad social range, hereditary nobility among them. The core of this social range was the men with a position in the Table of Ranks. The lower boundary probably ran along the lower boundary of the three traditional privileged estates, excluding the peasantry and the urban poor or dependent population. The higher boundary only excluded a very select group, 20 or 50 men and their families, at the top of society. Royal councillors, ambassadors, commanding generals and admirals and so on always belonged to an inner circle of the high nobility. The core of this aristocratic element consisted of the extended royal house: princely relatives from Germany and high noble families descending from seventeenth-century royal mistresses. Many were new men elevated by royal grace, but the great majority of these were born as German noblemen, not Danish or Norwegian commoners. In short, the Danish monarchy had moved from a traditional society of estates to one which was divided into three layers. In most contexts, the composite middle layer could be seen

---

[42] Gøbel, *De styrede rigerne*, p. 109.   [43] Lind, 'Military and Absolutism', pp. 231–232.
[44] Jesper Munk Andersen, 'Rangsyge eller standsbesættelse i Frederik von Lützows sociale netværk' (MA Thesis, University of Copenhagen, 2008).

as *the* elite of society; but the special status of the very few at the top was also quite visible and increasingly so during the first half of the eighteenth century.[45]

Ambiguous Ideas

The principles of equal access, advancement by merit etc. had very little influence at the pinnacle of monarchy and society. This ambiguity can be traced back to an ambiguity among the kings themselves. The testaments of Christian V (1670–1699) and Frederik IV (1699–1730) contain sharp warnings against the old nobility of Denmark and the Duchies.[46] But even Christian V, after recommending 'to open the door even to the highest charges and offices for everyone among our dear and faithful subjects' continues, 'this does not mean that those individuals ought not to be considered where, besides a sincere zeal for the advantage of the royal hereditary house, *naissance* and merits concur'.[47] In other words, good birth was still a quality. It was *just* to consider birth, and not only merit, even in the eyes of the man responsible for the most revolutionary steps in the transformation of the elite. At the core, of course, hereditary monarchy itself rested on descent. The bulk of the Royal Law consisted of a detailed regulation of succession. Heredity could not be abandoned as a principle.

This created a tension with the ideas natural to most of the servants of the king. In the revolutionary generation we can hear voices like Major General Georg Reichwein. A tailor's son, university dropout, and recently ennobled:

I can only answer that His Royal Majesty most graciously has ennobled me [. . .] furthermore saying, with the Roman general Marius in his speech in Sallust: My nobility is new. I cannot demonstrate the images, triumphs or consulates of my ancestors as proof; but if necessary, I can show lances, banners, corselets and

---

[45] Lind, 'Military and Absolutism'; Gøbel, *De styrede rigerne*; Gunner Lind, 'Officer! – men gentleman? Jævne mænd som officerer i enevældens Danmark-Norge,' in Lars Bisgaard, et al. (ed.), *Krig fra først til sidst. Festskrift til Knud J. V. Jespersen* (Odense, 2006), pp. 163–184; Fredrik Thisner, *Militärstatens arvegods: Officerstjänstens socialreproduktiva funktion i Sverige och Danmark, ca 1720–1800* (Uppsala, 2007), 197–260; Pernille Ulla Knudsen, *Lovkyndighed og vederhæftighed. Sjællandske byfogeder 1682–1801* (Copenhagen, 2001), pp. 23–232.

[46] These texts are discussed in Knud J. V. Jespersen, 'Welmeente Erindringer oc Maximer for Wore Kongelige Arfve-Successorer'. Christian 5.s testamenter – En fortolknings-kitse,' in Hans Jeppesen (ed.) *Søfart. Politik. Identitet. Tilegnet Ole Feldbæk*, Søhistoriske Skrifter (Copenhagen, 1996), pp. 127–142; Sebastian Olden-Jørgensen, 'Christian Vs og Frederik IVs politiske testamenter,' *Historisk Tidsskrift* 96 (1996), pp. 313–348.

[47] J. J. A. Worsaae (ed.), *Kong Christian den Vtes Testamenter som Tillæg til Kongeloven* (Copenhagen, 1860), pp. 17–18.

other military spoils, as well as the scars on my body. This is my lineage, this is my nobility, not inherited, but obtained by myself through much toil and many dangers.[48]

The ideology of equality and meritocracy was conserved among those concerned. During the early eighteenth century, Danish army officers started calling themselves and their colleagues 'von', the German indicator of nobility, regardless of their birth or nationality, obliterating all trace of inherited distinction.[49] In the late eighteenth century we can find statements like this by a colonel to a new ensign, a poor German promoted from the ranks: 'Together with the *port'épée* the king has given you noble rank [. . .] my house will always be open to you; on Sundays I give a party in alternation with the Provincial Governor and the Bishop. Turn up, all officers are welcome.'[50] In the early nineteenth century it was repeated in a handbook for young officers, written by serving military men: 'In the military hereditary nobility is ignored, as well as higher or lower noble rank. The service rank confers honour, not the lineage.'[51]

Public and potentially political statements about the system most of all stressed the magnificent qualities of the royal family and of absolute monarchy. From the 1760s onward we do however find public statements of a less innocent kind. When the centenary of the revolution arrived in 1760, some loyal subjects celebrated emphasizing the alliance between king and commoners and celebrating the anti-aristocratic and egalitarian aspects of the existing order.[52] It was also a theme among those who argued against Montesquieu (whose comments on the Royal Law had offended Danish sentiment). When a monarchy 'tightens the band' connecting it with the separate estates – wrote an anonymous author in 1766 – then 'immediately every distinction disappears, everything becomes Citizen – In a warlike monarchy all are citizens. Merit and not birth determines the estates. The state resembles a republic with the king as dictator'.[53]

The royal government was not amused when the old principles were ostensibly celebrated in 1760. Accentuating equality between subjects

---

[48] H. J. Huitfeldt-Kaas, 'Generalmajor Georg Reichwein (1593–1667),' *(Norsk) Historisk Tidsskrift* 3. rk. 5 (1899), pp. 337–426, at p. 405.

[49] H. F. Bilsted, 'Officers-Adel og "von",' *Militært Tidsskrift* XXXIII (1904).

[50] Ludvig Wagner, *Et Soldaterliv i forrige Aarhundrede* (Kolding, 1880), p. 59.

[51] F. von Sengespeik and C. von Schneider, *Der Officier. Eine Anleitung fur junge Leute, welche diese Benennung verdienen und im Militairstande Glück machen wollen* (Glückstadt, 1810), p. 152.

[52] Edvard Holm, *Danmark-Norges Historie fra den Store Nordiske Krigs Afslutning til Rigernes Adskillelse.* 3:2 (Copenhagen, 1898), pp. 485–486.

[53] *Militærisk Bibliothek.* 4 vols. Ed. by H. V. von Schmettow (Christiania, 1765–1766), vol. 2: p. 326.

with regard to the Crown, even in exquisitely loyal terms, contained an implicit critique and a political programme. The critique targeted the aristocratic predominance at the top, and implicitly the royal family itself. The programme did not only concern state service. The middle classes, to a large extent consisting of servants of the state, adopted the cause of agricultural reform. They demanded that the royal government should replace indirect administration in the countryside through the land-owners with direct state administration, and that the peasants now culti-vating rented land under the prevailing *Grundherrschaft* system should be transformed into independent freeholders. The state should enforce a massive reduction in the social and economic significance of the land-owning class, to the benefit of the peasants and of itself. Indirectly, of course, also of the many who derived their income and status from the royal service.[54]

The reformers won this struggle. Society in Denmark, and to a lesser extent Norway and the duchies, was transformed in a series of great reforms, starting with military conscription (1788) and ending with a reformed and compulsory school system (1814). This carried the revo-lutionary practice of the late seventeenth century – including the strong focus on the state – from the elites into the rural majority. The social, economic and political consequences shaped the nineteenth century and can be felt to this day.

The Danish Case: General Perspectives

The most salient trait of the Danish case is the brutal clarity with which the elite was transformed, matching the clarity of the change in political power distribution. The role and definition of the elites in the realm were explicit political questions, both before and after 1660, and closely linked to the constitutional question. Radical political change in 1660–1665 was followed by increasingly radical changes in the definition of the elites during the following decades. Extensive formal equality between the upper estates was followed by a formal meritocracy in royal service and

---

[54] On eighteenth century reformist opinion see Edvard Holm, *Om det Syn på Kongemagt, Folk og borgerlig Frihed, der udviklede sig i den dansk- norske Stat i Midten af 18. Aarhundrede* (Copenhagen, 1883); Edvard Holm, *Nogle Hovedtræk af Trykkefrihedens Historie 1770–1773* (Copenhagen, 1885); Edvard Holm, *Den offentlige Mening og Statsmagten i den dansk-norske Stat i Slutningen af det 18. Aarhundrede* (Copenhagen, 1888); Edvard Holm, *Kampen om Landboreformerne i Danmark i Slutningen af 18. Aarhundrede* (Copenhagen, 1888); Jens Arup Seip, 'Teorien om det opinionsstyrte enevelde,' *(Norsk) Historisk Tidsskrift* 38 (1957); John Christian Laursen, 'Luxdorph's Press Freedom Writings: Before the Fall of Struensee in Early 1770s Denmark- Norway,' *The European Legacy* 7:1 (2002), pp. 61–77.

the formal redefinition of elite status in society as primarily a function of non-hereditary relations to the Crown.

These were not dead letters. Practice and perceptions were really transformed, defining the ways in which this particular new monarchy related to the elites of society. Change can be observed in all the four typical areas mentioned in the introduction. The new policies directly shaped the personal relations between the elite and the ruler by submitting most of them to the rank system. They involved the mobilization of traditional elites as royal servants but inscribed it in a wider framework of broad access to office. They implied the sharing of public power with a wider circle than before but as minor shareholders in the well being of the Crown rather than actors with any substantial independence. Finally the new policies created a new, larger social elite along the way of military mobilization, itself enforced by competition with other crowns. It did so without transferring the political institutions and ideas of the old nobility, securing royal absolutism against the aristocratic challenge feared by the first absolute kings, but opening the gates to the influence of later enlightened public opinion. These policies thus drove a transition to a more fluid and flexible definition of the social elite, breaking with many traditions, but conserving and enhancing an extreme focus on the Crown and on service to the Crown. In the long run, the anti-aristocratic and crown-focused elements of official ideology opened the door for the transformation of rural society starting during the 1780s; and even later facilitated the transformation to democracy as constitutional monarchy. There were limits to the newness of the new monarchy, even in this extreme case; but Danish radical absolutism was definitely not a superficial phenomenon.

Why did the Danish case show such drastic traits? Mainly, it seems, for three reasons. One was quantity. The small strength of the traditional nobility combined with the extreme size of the army necessitated a massive change in the definition of the elite. Another reason was path dependency of a peculiar kind. The new monarchy in the Danish Realm was explicitly and radically new because the order it replaced – mainly the product of the Reformation crisis of the 1530s – had also been explicit and radical. Under such conditions, new formal rules had to replace the old; and the transformative assembly of the Estates 1536 was a pattern for that of 1660. These two traits meant that considerable change must come in one way or another. It took such sharp form because of the third factor, short-term contingency in the form of the wars 1657 to 1660. War opened for a solution with fewer elements of continuity than the reform path taken during the 1640s and 1650s, and it opened a window for influence from the lesser elite groups below the nobility. Compared with these three factors, traditional socioeconomic variables – the economic and demographic rise and fall of different estates or other groups – seem less relevant.

In a European context, one may note the strong coherence of these different aspects. Radical solutions encompassed constitutional, military, fiscal, ideological and social change; and change in one field was generally connected with change in another. This case came close to the ideal type of an early modern 'new monarchy', probably closer than any other. That such a case can be found is an argument in favour of this sometimes disputed idea. The Danish case does also reinforce classical proposals about the importance of absolute royal rule and the dynamic role of military competition between dynasties.

Seen in a European context, Denmark was part of a regional pattern. All the principal neighbours in the Nordic-Baltic area – Sweden, Prussia and Russia – shared the tendency to radical solutions. Local imitation probably played a role; but the region was otherwise shaped by the influence of the same two quantities which were so important in the Danish case. Extreme military competition was a shared condition promoting equivalent solutions in all four states. The other quantity, the small size of the traditional elite, was an exceptional transformative factor in Sweden as it was in Denmark. Many of the differences between the new monarchies of early modern Europe, differences which can make them difficult to recognize as one species, can probably be traced back to the influence of these same two quantities.

11 The 'New Monarchy' as Despotic Beast: The Perspective of the Lesser Nobility in France and Germany, 1630s to 1650s

Robert von Friedeburg

'Central to the new monarchies is the social cohesion of new elites.'[1] In the 'Holy Roman Empire of the German Nation' emerging from the second half of the fourteenth century onwards, the elite aristocracy were of course the emerging estates of electoral princes and princes who eventually gained privileged access to the new Imperial Diet. Soon divided by religious confession, they also developed very different political outlooks, in particular during the Thirty Years' War. Not least during that war, however, the very experience of war further strengthened the process of social cohesion among their own fiefholders, the lower nobility within the fiefs of the princes. As a consequence of that process, these noblemen stuck together and openly opposed their princes in order to defend themselves and their often tiny holdings against the destruction of war. In order to do that, they had to argue the existence of the fief as a clearly demarcated legal district in its own right, existing undisturbed for a long time, with its own laws, to which the prince himself was allegedly subject. The further development of the territorial state in Germany was not least rooted in this development.

During the second third of the seventeenth century, in both the kingdom of France and the Holy Roman Empire, pamphlets attacked the alleged profits of princely advisors and favourites gained from war and its burdens. Allegedly, favourites and financiers had persuaded princes to engage in war for the sole goal of profiting from the taxes and offices coming along with the pursuit of war, while the established nobility and common subjects were effectively deprived of their privileges and livelihood. To these pamphlets, monarchy had transformed during the course of the sixteenth and seventeenth century. The pursuit of war and the new offices that monarchy began to offer in its course had produced a new and illegitimate kind of rule. This new kind of rule was compared to the rule of Tiberius and his client Sejanus over the Roman senators and people, a rule addressed as 'despotic' in both France and

[1] See Chapter 2 by John Morrill (above, p.26).

Germany.[2] The French historian Jean Marie Constant addressed this sort of polemic as attacking 'war despotism',[3] though he was not aware that similar arguments, and partly with reference to French sources, were advanced in Germany at the same time. The focus of this contribution is the similarity of the pamphlet-rhetoric against 'war despotism' and how it played out against very different political, social and institutional circumstances in France and Germany. It is the argument of this contribution that the formation of the political attitude of Germany's lesser noblemen towards the 'war despotism' was shaped by three fundamental differences in comparison to France, by differences, however, that must be understood through the prism of the issues stressed in this book, rather than the argument of the princely 'state' subjecting elites.

One, the formation of an elite aristocracy in the German-speaking lands of the empire went along with the establishment of a privileged place in the emerging Imperial Diet and increasingly coherent territorial jurisdictions by this elite aristocracy, i.e. the German princes and electoral princes. In particular the group of the counts that had been important in Germany's higher nobility during the Higher Middle Ages was significantly reduced in size and landholding by dying out or by being raised to princes. Their lands went into princely hands.[4] For example, the formation of the lands of the House of Hesse between Eder and Werra was mainly due to their gathering and inheriting the lands of a number of families of counts, for example those of Ziegenhain and Nidda. A gaping hole developed between the princely dynasties on the one hand and the remaining groups of Germany's lesser nobility, on the other. Indeed, the large majority of lesser noblemen became in time legally subjected to those princes to which emerging jurisdiction they were counted. Up to this point, the older narrative of the emerging princely state – in Germany, the territorial state of German princes – and its subjections of local elites seems to be warranted. However, there were significantly more princely dynasties and branches of princely dynasties than branches of France's elite aristocracy of pairs and *ducs*.[5] These jurisdictions of the German

---

[2] Not only to attack for example Buckingham, the *topos* of Sejanus was also used in England. The issue of the rise of new classes of 'officeholders' is addressed in many works, among others in J. H. Elliott and L. W. B. Brockliss (eds.), *The World of the Favourite* (New Haven, 1998).

[3] The argument is indicative for the attack on the alleged 'war despotism' of Richelieu and Mazarin by members of the French nobility, see, Jean Marie Constant, 'Der Adel und die Monarchie in Frankreich', in Ronald Asch (ed.), *Der europäische Adel im Ancien Regime* (Köln, 2001), pp. 129–150, at p. 146.

[4] Ernst Schubert, *Fürstliche Herrschaft, Fürstliche Herrschaft und Territorium im späten Mittelalter* (München, 1996), p. 10.

[5] As discussed above by Hamish Scott in ch.3, at pp.66, 72–5, 84.

princes, the emerging 'territories', were considerably smaller (even Brandenburg had only about half a million inhabitants) and often also considerably poorer than French provinces such as Brittany or Burgundy. The noble bench of the estate assemblies of these emerging territories was made up primarily of lesser noblemen.[6] While these lesser noblemen were thus increasingly seen as (special) subjects to their princes, we will see that they were much more able to dominate business at the emerging territorial estate assemblies according to their own interests and wishes. Indeed, the very establishment of the princely territories provided these lesser noblemen in Germany with a political arena of their own that their French counterparts did not have. The emerging territories thus became, to an extent, a bulwark of their privileges and interests.

Two, the princes building up their territories were not anointed kings. German princes could variously expect the respect of their lesser vassals, and their rule was addressed as 'monarchy' since the mid-sixteenth century.[7] But at least during the sixteenth and seventeenth centuries they were never held in the esteem that the French monarchy was by the overwhelming majority of French noblemen.

Third and finally, whatever the burdens of war and plundering troops in France, for all we know the catastrophe of the Thirty Years' War in German lands remained an experience altogether more drastic than what most French provinces had to deal with (with the possible exception of Burgundy in 1636). As the livelihood of their lesser noble members seemed threatened by and during the Thirty Years' War, German territorial estate assemblies turned to open threats against their princes – they even had one prince deposed – and included princes in the hate rhetoric that. in France, only attacked advisors and financiers. A comparative look at the attacks on 'war despotism' in France and Germany is meant to highlight similarities

---

[6] Ronald Asch, *Nobilities in Transition* (London, 2003), pp. 126–133. A fairly typical case of small-scale German territorial nobility is described by Gregory W. Pedlow, *The Survival of the Hessian Nobility, 1770–1870* (Princeton, 1988). In Silesia, Moravia and Bohemia, all in a problematic relation to the Empire and not simply part of it, the situation was clearly different than in Brandenburg or Hesse-Cassel. Bohemian and Moravian magnates are sometimes described as quintessential examples of an elite aristocracy. But as Hamish Scott very kindly brought to my attention, even among the major noble families of Brandenburg, only the Arnheim-Boitzenburg was thought to be just wealthy enough to make it into the top 100 of the aristocratic elite in Bohemia or Hungary with around 50,000 to 100,000 per year in the later eighteenth century. See Peter Michael Hahn, 'Aristokratisierung und Professionalisierung. Der Aufstieg der Obristen zu einer militärischen und höfischen Elite in Brandenburg-Preussen von 1650–1725', in *Forschungen zur brandenburgischen und preussischen Geschichte* N.F. 1 (1991), pp. 161–208, at p. 165 on the absence of 'magnates' in the lands of the Berlin Hohenzollern.

[7] See Horst Dreitzel, *Monarchiebegriffe in der Fürstengesellschaft* (Vienna, 1991), 2 vols., vol. 1: Semantik der Monarchie, 58, with respect to Melchior von Osse and his 1552 'Politisches Testament'.

concerning points of contention towards 'war despotism' of a transformed monarchy, but also highlight that the emerging German territories, with their territorial estate assemblies, far from consolidating the entire subjection of the lesser nobility, and moving into their critical period of formation just as the Thirty Years' War was raging, proved much more apt to give such sentiments an institutional platform than French lesser noblemen ever had or were going to get. This contribution will first introduce the French and German arguments against 'war despotism' (I). It then compares the extent of the lesser nobility in France and Germany and its economic and social situation (II). It will provide examples for the attack on 'war despotism' in France (III). It finally provides examples of the attack on 'war despotism' in Germany (IV).

I

The 'Lettre d'Avis a Mess. du Parlement de Paris. Ecrit par un Provincial', published anonymously in Paris in 1649, like many other pamphlets, made Mazarin the focus of critique. But along that critique, the pamphlet argued that the venality of offices and the advantages for clients of Mazarin had led to an undermining of the actual constitution of France similar to the undermining of the Roman constitution by Tiberius and Sejanus, when Tiberius had filled the senate with his 'creatures'.[8] Mazarin kept the war against Spain going so his 'minions' could further profit from financing the war effort and from the offices they could buy.[9] French subjects had to pay the bill in taxes and other war-related burdens. War politics, pursued to allow Richelieu's and Mazarin's clients to profit from the financial practises generated by war, had transformed France into a *'Despotique Gouvernement'*, comparable to the *'gouvernement de Turc'*, for the total burdens of war had turned French subjects into slaves.[10]

---

[8] 'Lettre D'Avis a Mess. De Parlement de Paris. Ecrit par un Provincial', Bibliotheque Mazarine A 13942, 10.

[9] Ibid., pp. 6, 19–21.

[10] Ibid., pp. 21–22. The argument is indicative for the attack on the alleged 'war despotism' of Richelieu and Mazarin by members of the French nobility, see Constant, *Adel*, pp. 129–150. The secondary literature on the *Mazarinades* is considerable, see Christian Jouhard, 'Mazarinades', in Lucien Bély (ed.), *Dictionnaire de l Ancien Regime* (Paris, 2002), pp. 808–809; Christian Jouhard, *Mazarinades: La Frondes des mots* (Paris, 1985); on the analysis of the factual effects of war and its burdens in advantaging certain and disadvantaging other groups, amounting to a fundamental change in French society, see already Hubert Carrier, 'Machiavelli dans les pamphlets de la Fronde', in *L' Italienisme en France au XVII siècle. Akten des Kongresses der französischen Gesellschaft für vergleichende Literatur in Grenoble* (Turin, 1969), pp. 39–46, at pp. 43–44 on *Les Sentiments d' Aristide sur less affaires politiques* (Paris, 1649, Bibliotheque Mazarin M 13999).

Raging onslaughts on French crown financiers go back at least to the period between the meeting of the General Estates of 1614 and the killing of favourite Concini in 1617, when Condé and the queen mother struggled for control of the young king and pamphlet attacks on opponents were ripe with rhetoric of national, among them anti-Italian, stereotypes.[11] According to one such pamphlet, Jean Bourgoin's 1618 'La Chasse aux Larrons', royal government, rather than protecting the privileges and property of its subjects, had become a 'vassal and tributary of the financiers'. They had to be cleansed from the kingdom.[12] This very same pamphlet, though cited as published in Paris in 1625,[13] was cited in one of the most violent attacks on princely rule during the Thirty Years' War in Germany, an attack uncompromisingly condemning taxation for war and the profits of princely favourites gained from burdens imposed on subjects and noblemen alike.[14] In 1633, a year later, the same author published a thinly disguised handbook for rebellion and negotiation by force against princes who attempted to suppress their subjects by means of war. German estate assemblies took these attacks against princes and their corrupt advisors to heart. In the course of the conflicts between lesser noblemen and their princes in the duchies of Jülich-Berg, of Cleve-Mark or the landgraviate of Hesse-Cassel, they condemned the rule of these princes as Machiavellian and despotic, leading to the ruin of themselves and their people. Not least because in these cases, the leaders of local opposition were supported by substantial majorities among the lesser nobility, the large majority of estate-institutions in the emerging German territories established themselves successfully as part of the public constitution of these territories and kept representing, and if need be, defending the privileges of their overwhelmingly lesser and poorer noble members, primarily in terms of determining the burdens

---

[11] Lucien Bély, *La France au XVII siecle. Puissance de l'Etat, contrôle de la societe* (Paris, 2009), pp. 158–163. I do thank Jim Collins for making me aware how important anti-Italian stereotypes were, not least with respect to attacks on financiers, but also with respect to Catherine de Medici, already during the 1570s and 1580s, see J. -F. Dubost, *La France italienne. XVIe-XVIIe siècle* (Paris, 1997); see also David Parrott, *The Business of War: Military Enterprise and Military Revolution in Early Modern Europe* (Cambridge, 2012); Claude Dulong, *Mazarin et l'argent: banquiers et prête-noms* (Ecole de Chartes, 2002).

[12] Jean Bourgoin, *La chasse aux larrons ou avant coureur de l'histoire de la chambre de justice. Des livres du biens public, & autres oeuvres faits pour la recherche des financiers & de leurs fauteurs* (s.n. Paris, 1618), fol.8r, fol.54; quoted by Julien Dent, 'An Aspect of the Crisis of the Seventeenth Century: The Collapse of Financial Administration of the French Monarchy (1653–1661)', *Economic History Review* 20 (1967), pp. 241–256, at p. 241.

[13] This is a mistake: Jacques Le Long et al. (eds.), *Bibliotheque historique de la France* (Paris 1775), tome IV, 414, no. 21244, gives 1623.

[14] Johann Willhelm Neumair von Ramsla, *Von Schatzungen und Steuern sonderbarer Tractat,* Schlepfingen 1632, p. 32.

of their tenants, jurisdictional privileges, and participation in the administration of taxation.[15]

That German territorial estate assemblies were neither wiped out nor rendered irrelevant during the clashes of the seventeenth century is now well established.[16] Attitudes of their noble members or their relation towards the satirical and polemic tracts of the time are less well studied. Highly polemical attacks against 'war despotism' (Jean-Marie Constant)[17] were published in both France and Germany, and French works were cited in Germany. They addressed in particular the evolution of groups of princely officers and financiers profiting from the increasing burdens of taxes and of war, burdens that were negatively felt specifically by the poorer sections of the nobility that had little chance to profit from the accompanying spoils, but feared that the burdens on their tenants constituted a threat to their own income.

II

The kingdom of France and the Holy Roman Empire, however, provided very different environments to act on such sentiments. In France, estate assemblies providing a platform for protest only survived in the *pays d'états*, such as in Brittany, not the *pays d'élection* or the *pays d'imposition*. Even in a *pay d'état* such as Brittany, the estates did not primarily represent the lesser nobility, but, given the sheer scale of this large and rich principality of two million inhabitants, primarily magnate and commercial interests. Magnate families in Brittany profited from royal tax burdens imposed on Brittany's population by receiving the offices financed with these burdens. But not least because the province was not subjected to utter devastation by decades of continuing war and occupation, these profits from France's 'war despotism' did not preclude the needs of the lesser nobility from being taken care of, too. Their tenants were also protected against over-heavy direct taxes.[18] What is more, attacks on the 'war despotism' of France's New Monarchy never targeted the king himself, only counsellors or financiers.[19]

As Hamish Scott argues in his contribution to this volume, by the early eighteenth century, a European elite-aristocracy had emerged that was clearly distinguished from the lesser nobility in European lands. Their

---

[15] On the quantity and responsibilities of surviving estate assemblies see Kersten Krüger, *Die Landständische Verfassung* (München, 2003).

[16] See Section II.   [17] Constant, *Adel*, p. 146.

[18] See James Collins, *Classes, Estates, and Order in Early Modern Brittany* (Cambridge, 1994).

[19] See Constant, *Adel*, pp. 143–147.

considerable landed estates helped them to weather particular economic crises and their income from royal offices contributed significantly to their economic resilience. Even in comparatively poorer areas with less of a stark differentiation within the nobility, the Dohna, Dönhoff or Finckenstein in Eastern Prussia had still different opportunities and attitudes than the larger rest of the regional lower nobility.[20] Much more pronounced was the situation in France. In lifestyle opportunities for acquiring offices and preferment at court, aristocratic magnates such as the Guise[21] had little to do with, and would hardly intermarry with, noble families with only a few or even only a single estate held in trust for several branches.[22] For example, in late sixteenth-century France, there were only 46, in 1715 only 76 *ducs* and counts, with an income of at least 24,000 livres.[23] During the eighteenth century, only 150 to 250 families, the latter figure including ennobled financiers, had an income above 50,000 livre, about 3,500 an income from 10,000 to 50,000 livre, but 7,000 an income from 4,000 to 10,000. According to the survey of Ronald Asch, that still allowed a comfortable life in the province, but not membership in the international aristocratic elite. But below 4,000 livre, constraints began to become considerable. In Brittany, for example, about two-thirds of the relatively large provincial nobility did not pay more than 20 livres for the capitation, the minimum being 10 livres. During the sixteenth century, they did not profit from the rise in prices.[24] 'The overwhelming majority of nobles fell into the final two categories' of this tax.[25] The landed wealth of these lesser noblemen was often hardly more substantial than that of wealthy farmers.[26] Estimates on the total number of noble families in France assess approximately 30,000 to 40,000, with a relative low during the seventeenth century. While numerical estimates remain tricky, and do not in themselves even address the dynamics behind them, e.g. the issue of the rise of families into the nobility, changes of position within the nobility, and the

---

[20] Wolfgang Neugebauer, 'Der Adel in Preussen im 18. Jahrhundert', in Ronald Asch (ed.), *Der Europäische Adel im Ancien Regime* (Köln, 2001), pp. 49–76, at pp. 58–62; Hahn, Aristokratisierung, 188.

[21] Jonathan Spangler, *The Society of Princes. The Lorraine-Guise and the Conservation of Power in Seventeenth Century France* (Farnham, 2009).

[22] See for example Michel Nassiet, *Noblesse et Pauvrete. La petite noblesse en Bretagne, XV – XVIII siecle* (Paris, 1993).

[23] Lucien Bély, *La France au XVII siècle* (Paris, 2009), p. 447.

[24] Ronald Asch, *'Europäischer Adel in der frühen Neuzeit'* (Köln, 2008), p. 82. Lucien Bély, *La France au XVII siècle* (Paris, 2009), p. 82; Nassiet (based on the 1710 capitation), *Noblesse et Pauvreté*, pp. 145, 202–206.

[25] Collins, Classes, Estates, and Order, p. 9.

[26] Richard Bonney (ed.), *Society and Government in France under Richelieu and Mararin, 1624–1661* (London, 1988), p. 152; Nassiet, *Noblesse et Pauvreté*, pp. 171–210.

dying out of branches,[27] they do suggest how large the number of middling and poorer noble families with an income below 4,000 livres, the
'petite noblesse' below the *ducs et pairs* and also below the *'noblesse seconde'*
of marquesses, viscounts and barons, must have been. These lesser noblemen had not the resources to serve on their own as intermediaries
between crown and province, and they were, accordingly, hardly considered worth a royal office.[28] Indeed, among the lesser and poorer Breton
nobility, military careers remained rare.[29]

Research also agrees that these massive differences within each of the
European nobilities had considerable and varying consequences for the
ability of different sections within the nobility to profit from or at least to
adapt to the changes coming along with the transformation of monarchy
in the course of the sixteenth and seventeenth century. For Brandenburg
or the landgraviate of Hesse-Cassel, for example, the large majority of
noblemen with limited resources of a few or only one manor were hit hard
by the devastation and depopulation of the countryside in the course of
the Thirty Years' War. In Brandenburg, most of the about 250 noble
families had been profiting from the rise in grain prices throughout the
sixteenth century, but many manors were devastated during the war.
'In 1624, for example, the Arnim estate complex at Boitzenburg had
225 peasant households, by 1653, only twenty remained. On the
Stavenow estates, only 30 per cent of the pre-war peasant farmsteads
were occupied in 1647.'[30] After decades of recovery, the substantial
Stavenov estate in Brandenburg was meant to make between 2,300 and
4,500 taler. These were substantial rewards from a substantial estate,
though the latter estimate proved overoptimistic and grain prices and
labour cost had to develop in manners allowing such profit margins.
They allowed a comfortable noble life in the countryside, not membership to the aristocratic elite gathering in Vienna or other capitals.[31]

What is more, the Junkers' estate income depended not on the prince in
helping to enforce unlimited serfdom.[32] Rather, as the brilliant research

---

[27] See Bély, *France*, pp. 456–458; Roger Mettam, 'The French Nobility, 1610-1715', in
Hamish Scott (ed.), *The European Nobilities of the Seventeenth and Eighteenth Century.
Vol I: Western Europe* (London, 1995), pp. 114–141, at pp. 114–115, assesses between
260,000 and 400,000 *persons*, and opting for the lower estimate.

[28] Bély, *La France*, p. 438; J. H. M. Salmon, 'A Second Look at the Noblesse Seconde:
The Key to Noble Clientage and Power in Early Modern France?' *French Historical
Studies* 25 (2002), pp. 575–593, at p. 592; Mettam, 'Nobility', pp. 128–135.

[29] Nassiet, *Noblesse et Pauvreté*, pp. 138–146.

[30] Edgar Melton, 'The Prussian Junkers 1600-1786', in Scott (ed.), *The European Nobilities*,
vol. 2, pp. 71–109, at pp. 82–83.

[31] William W. Hagen, *Ordinary Prussians. Brandenburg Junkers and Villagers, 1500–1840*
(Cambridge, 2002), pp. 98–99.

[32] Ibid., pp. 648–649.

of William W. Hagen has shown, the income from Brandenburg noble estates stemmed primarily from the consolidation of viable economic units during the sixteenth century and from agricultural improvement during the eighteenth century, including the purchase of manual labour on the labour market, while extra enforcement of unpaid labour via the institution of serfdom remained quite limited.[33] As William Hagen and the research of Christoph Fürbringer have also shown, many Junkers resented the Calvinist Hohenzollern, but were curtailed in their political punch by the devastating economic situation of the 1630s to 1650s, and many eventually needed to rely on extra income from the slowly growing army of their Berlin prince.[34] In contrast, Wolfgang Neugebauer has noted a particular affinity of the larger and richer magnate aristocracy in Eastern Prussia to work together with the Berlin Hohenzollern throughout the seventeenth century.[35] Similarly, still in the eighteenth century, those few noble families from Hesse-Cassel that did send their offspring to universities chose only the immediate neighbourhood such as Marburg, Rinteln, Göttingen, Jena or Giessen.[36] The large majority of the noble members of German territorial estates, from Hesse to Saxony and from Bavaria to Brandenburg, belonged to this category of lesser nobility – not necessarily too poor to afford a provincial noble lifestyle, but ultimately dependent on the well being of the few tenants and villages belonging to their own estate, and with no contact or even realistic prospect to ever get into the world of the elite aristocracy with city palaces in Prague, Vienna, Paris or London.[37]

Characteristically, this type of lesser nobility did not dominate – as in German lands – but was in turn led by Brittany's elite aristocracy in the provinces' estate assemblies. Throughout the seventeenth century, the Breton estates remained institutionally vibrant and continued to do

---

[33] Ibid., pp. 69–122, 391–422.

[34] William W. Hagen, 'Two Ages of Seigneurial Economy in Brandenburg-Prussia: Structural Innovation in the Sixteenth Century, Productivity Gains in the Eighteenth Century', in Paul Janssens and Bartolomé Yun Casalilla (eds.), *European Aristocracies and Colonial Elites: Patrimonial Management Strategies and Economic Development, 15th–18th Centuries* (Aldershot, 2005), pp. 137–153.

[35] Neugebauer, 'Der Adel', pp. 60–62; many more members of the nobility might have wanted to join, for example the Defensionswerk, but the places were, at least until the 1660s, limited: See Ullrich Marwitz, *Staatsräson und Landesdefension. Untersuchungen zum Kriegswesen des Herzogtums Preussen 1640–1655* (Boppard, 1984), pp. 78–80: However, of the Samland 18 officers, 15 came from a non-noble background.

[36] Charles Ingrao, *The Hessian Mercenary State* (Cambridge, 1987), p. 29.

[37] See for example George W. Pedlow, 'The Landed Elite of Hesse Cassel in the Nineteenth Century', in Ralph Gibson and Martin Blinkhorn (eds.), *Landownership and Power in Modern Europe* (London, 1991), pp. 109–129, at p. 112, with evidence back into the eighteenth century: The large majority of estates had less than 500 hectares, over half of all estates less than 200 hectares.

everything they could to represent all the elite Breton interest, from urban merchants by defending commercial interests to the landed nobility of the sword by 'opposing the extension of hereditary nobility' to mere office-holders. The estates also tried to keep the direct tax load down to protect the tenants of both substantial and less substantial noble landholders. Indirect taxes increased massively, but in general, the tax burden of Brittany remained than in other French provinces. From the perspective of the Crown, this 'Breton solution', securing important regional elite privileges in exchange for cooperation with regard to taxation, loans and support for the king, organized and mediated by the institutionalized estates, 'worked well for both parties'.[38] From the provincial perspective, while the general common population suffered under indirect taxes, the more substantial peasants bore the brunt of direct taxes.[39] The 'lion's share of Breton tax money' transferred to Paris and returning into the province as spoils of the New Monarchy (offices, pensions) was received only by the very 'peak of the feudal hierarchy', the Breton magnate families, such as the Rohan and a few others to around 60 families with very significant estate incomes.[40] Despite this clear difference in relative advantages of the 'Breton solution', the total burden of direct taxes on the peasants remained limited enough to allow them to also shoulder the significant burdens imposed by their noble landlords, the magnates and the lesser ones.[41] Also, no war of decades of occupation and devastation ruined the agrarian income of the lesser nobility.

A rough and ready comparison of the general tax burden of the German territories of the elector of Brandenburg – including his western provinces – and Bavaria with Brittany suggests that the Brandenburg tax load was definitely higher than the Breton one, but still smaller than in most other French provinces. Burdens in Bavaria were even less than in Brittany. The elector of Brandenburg's income from all his lands rose from about one million Reichsthaler during the 1640s to 3.4 million in 1688, of which approximately 400,000 Reichsthaler came from taxes in the 1640s and 1.7 million in 1688. That is about 1.7 Reichsthaler per head (with approximately one million subjects), and equalling around 5 livres. That is significantly more than the approximate single livre estimated for Brittany for the rule of Henry IV, and still more than the approximate 2.5 to 4 livres for Brittany under Louis XIV, calculated by Jim Collins.[42] At the same time, the tax burden in Brittany was

---

[38] Collins, *Order*, pp. 24, 224–228.   [39] Ibid., pp. 232–233, 245.   [40] Ibid., pp. 276.
[41] Ibid., pp. 12–13, 246.
[42] Arndt, *Kurfürst*, p. 266: I base this estimate on his figures, but take into account that more than half of the income of 1688 was from the demesne, and only one half taxes; Collins,

exceptionally low compared with most other French provinces, varying from about 1.5 livres under Henry IV to 8 livres under Louis XIV per head of the population. While the lands of the Brandenburg elector were more heavily taxed than Brittany, they fared not so bad compared to the rest of France.[43] But in Bavaria, average payments ranged between 1619 and 1651 at about 446,000 fl. (Gulden), about one guilder per head of population p.a., given a relation of about 1 livre equalling about half a guilder, even less then in Brittany.[44] In these three cases of Brittany, Brandenburg and Bavaria, important legal privileges of provincial elites were successfully defended; at the same time, taxation to keep up armed forces had to be accepted. But while in Brandenburg the estates eventually submitted to the argument of the elector that paying for such forces cost less than allowing enemy occupation, the Breton estates also paid for offices and spoils only reaching a small part of the elite, a fact with hindsight acceptable by the nature of the 'Breton solution'. From the point of view of minimal peasant burdens for princely taxes and appropriate space for burdens imposed by local landlords, Bavaria seemed to be the ideal spot for lesser noblemen. On the whole, it seems that provincial estates, where they survived, did fulfil that function missed in provinces where there were none and defended the local elite's privileges similarly demanded at the 1651 assembly of the French nobility, such as own courts of jurisdiction and tax privileges.[45]

III

Scattered evidence also suggests that the economic and social differences among the nobility and the varying options to profit from war were reflected in differences in attitude to actively engaging in upheaval. For the British Civil Wars, it has been noted how reluctant middling and lower gentry could become to commit themselves to campaigns outside

---

Brittany, p. 208–209. With 90 Kreutzer equaling a single Reichsthaler, 1.7 Reichsthaler were about 2 gulden, 33 Kreutzer, equalling about 5 livres.

[43] I base this estimate on information given to me very kindly by Professor James Collins: Henri IV's income was about 30 million l., and he had about 20 million subjects, so 1.5; Louis XIV's income was more like 200 million l. for about 25 million subjects, so 8 l. a head. Breton taxation under Henry was probably 1.5 million a year, so indeed 1 l. each; under Louis XIV, the Bretons paid more like 5 million, and sometimes as much as 8 million, so between 2.5 and 4 l. each.

[44] Katrin Ellen Kummer, *Landstände und Landschaftsverordnung unter Maximilian I von Bayern, 1598 – 1651* (Berlin, 2006), pp. 152–155, though cf. pp. 218–219, Kummer reminds us that in Bavaria itself, these payments were seen as dramatic increases in comparison to earlier decades.

[45] Constant, *Adel*, 147.

their county regardless of what their cause might be and to submit to the flood of extraordinary burdens going along with financing campaigns. Their perspective was clearly different from major magnates such as Argyll in Scotland, the Marquis of Antrim in Ireland, or the Earl of Essex or the Barringtons in Essex, whose status and economic standing allowed and demanded to take an active role. In England, 'those at the tail of the gentry were far less likely to have been actively involved in the civil war then those at the top of the gentry'.[46]

Similarly, French noblemen of highly varying status viewed with suspicion the 'war-despotism' coming about under Richelieu and Mazarin. The flood of grievances produced during the *Fronde*, in particular the assemblies of noblemen in 1649 and 1651,[47] articulated bitter resentment of sections of the *noblesse petite* at the sale of offices and the emergence of a nobility of office, wealthy financiers, and new tax burdens on rural tenants.[48] They did not feel they profited from the offices and spoils paid by these taxes, but that a weakening of their own few tenants hurt them, too. The nobility of Perigord petitioned the Estates General (that were meant to meet) for general exemption of their tenants from the *taille* and other taxes;[49] the February 1649 *Cahiers* of remonstrances of the nobility of the Angoumois protested against taxes and commissions, but attacked in particular the alleged profits of financiers. The *Cahiers* also required the institution of some form of representative institution in provinces without own estate meeting, for the nobility – and here of course in particular the *noblesse petite* – had otherwise no means to make its voice heard at all. Lack of institutional channels to present grievances had allegedly led to insults and abuses from royal officers.[50] The grievances of the nobility of Champagne of July 1651 attacked the whole practice of the sale of offices and the alleged corruption in the judiciary as its consequence. A nobleman was not able any more to secure any offices for his own sons due to the rising price of these offices. In particular in the army, the grievances demanded, offices should no longer be venal. They complained against the abuses of – richer – purchasers of these offices and their growing numbers. They in particular

---

[46] John Morrill, *The Nature of the English Revolution* (London, 1993), pp. 179–242, quotation at p. 199; Aaron Graham, 'Finance, Localism, and Military Representation in the Army of the Earl of Essex', *The Historical Journal* 52 (2009), pp. 879–898; Jane H. Ohlmeyer, *Civil War and Restoration in the Three Stuart Kingdoms* (Cambridge, 2001).

[47] Constant, *Adel*, pp. 146–147.

[48] Bonney, *Society*, pp. 151–153. For a research overview see Constant, *Adel*, pp. 129–150.

[49] List of grievances of the nobility of Perigord to the Estates General called to meet at Tours on 8 September 1651, in Bonney, *Society*, p. 183.

[50] Cahier of remonstrances of the nobility of the Angoumois to the projected meeting of the Estates General, 22–24 February 1649, Bonney, *Society*, pp. 172–173.

pleaded for a decrease in taxes for their own tenants and the 'common people' in general, burdened by the 'inventions of financiers' and the 'monstrous and unbridled multitude of new and useless offices'.[51] Still in 1657 at Montauban, the intendant requested cavalry to be dispatched to Gascony to punish those refusing to pay taxes. The alleged emergence of a regional league of noblemen organized to resist royal orders made quick action particularly important.[52] A 'letter into the provinces to all the gentlemen of the kingdom' of May 1652 had already urged a 'union of the nobility' and an immediate meeting of the General Estates to address the 'license of the troops' (sic), their threat to property and the security of family women, and mentioned an 'act of union' among individuals within and between baillages, but also recognized that the 'nobility' was 'divided by the diversity of its private interests and lack of communication, to unite as a body'.[53] Still in 1658, an assembly at the forest of Conches in Perche mentioned a union of nobility allegedly forged in Paris in 1651.[54] In the wake of the self-dissolution of the 1651 assembly of the nobility, 1652 saw several regional associations on the basis of the *bailliages* to defend localities against plundering soldiers.[55]

These scattered observations should neither lead to a revival of speculations about the general rise or decline of a given social group nor about the alleged direct effect of social and economic considerations on religious and political attitudes.[56] They were rather made to stress that while the phenomenon of 'war despotism' offered different challenges and opportunities for different strata of the nobility, resentment against it was shared across different polities, political cultures and extremely different constitutional arrangements. The specific circumstances of the emerging German territorial state with regard to these resentments will now be examined.

---

[51] List of grievances of the nobility of Champagne, and particularly those of the bailliage of Troyes, July 1651, in Bonney, *Society*, pp. 182–183.

[52] Intendant of Montauban to Séguier, March 1657, in Bonney, *Society*, pp. 189–90.

[53] Letter sent into the provinces to all the gentlemen of the kingdom: a union of nobility to prevent the disorders, excesses and ravages of the troops and to obtain a general peace, May 1652, in Bonney, *Society*, p. 188.

[54] Referring to informal meetings of noblemen in Paris during 1651, when the 13-year-old child king was effectively imprisoned in Paris, the city being temporarily under the control of the Paris *Fronde*, and the various sources of the *Fronde* temporarily cooperating, see Bély, *La France*, pp. 311–312.

[55] Constant, *Adel*, pp. 144–145.

[56] See H. Trevor Roper, *The Crisis of the Seventeenth Century* (New York, 1999), assembling articles published between 1956 and 1967; G. Parker and L.M. Smith (eds.), *The General Crisis of the Seventeenth Century* (London, 1997); and the critical remarks by John Morrill, 'The Ecology of Allegiance in the English Civil Wars', in Morrill, *The Nature of the English Revolution*, pp. 224–242.

IV

During the Thirty Years' War, almost all German territorial estate assemblies feared involvement in war. Where war came, as to Württemberg, Hesse, Pomerania, Mecklenburg, Saxony, Julich-Berg-Cleve or, to a lesser extent, Bavaria, their fears proved generally well grounded. The economic backbone of the German territorial nobility, their relatively small estates and limited number of tenants, was badly shattered by war. But the accompanying conclusion, held until the 1980s, that this considerable economic weakening led to their political emaciation, measured as constitutional decline or even extinction of territorial estates, has proven incorrect.[57] Still in the mid-eighteenth century, roughly two-thirds of all territorial states in the Empire did have established territorial estates. Hardly anywhere did they rule the territory by themselves or had an influence comparable to the eighteenth-century English parliament. But neither is a useful benchmark of success. What they did do was to successfully shield the privileges of their noble members in terms of taxes, jurisdiction and participation in important ways in the administration of the country, not least by organizing tax administration for the prince.[58]

This often close cooperation between prince and territorial estates collapsed occasionally in spectacular clashes, not only during the seventeenth, but also still during the eighteenth century, such as in Württemberg and Mecklenburg. During the seventeenth century, though the specific circumstances varied enormously from case to case, a combination of meagre princely funds, of the intricacies of dynastic succession disputes among competing dynasties and competing branches of one dynasty, of Swedish, French, Spanish or Imperial military occupation during the Thirty Years' War, and of the emperor's eagerness to insert influence by hearing the complaints of territorial estates against their prince, conspired to stabilize the position of the territorial estates as part of the public law of the emerging territories (*ius publicum territoriale*). Under pressure of this combination of circumstances, most princes had eventually to find compromise with their local elites.[59]

Examples of the vicissitudes of German princely dynasties under the pressure of war abound. Ferdinand II deposed the dukes of Mecklenburg in 1628–1630 and gave the duchy to Wallenstein as a fief. The ecclesiastical holdings of the Dukes of Württemberg had been

---

[57] For this older thesis Volker Press, 'Formen des Ständewesens in den deutschen Territorialstaaten des 16. und 17. Jahrhunderts', in Peter Baumgart (ed.), *Ständetum und Staatsbildung in Brandenburg-Preussen* (Berlin, 1983), pp. 234–300.

[58] Krüger, *Landständische Verfassung*, pp. 12–31.

[59] Recent overview Gabriele Haug Moritz, *Württembergischer Ständekonflikt und deutscher Dualismus* (Stuttgart, 1992), pp. 17–26.

particularly hard hit by the 1629 edict of restitution, and Duke Eberhard III (1614–1674), who had sided with the Swedes, had to abandon his fief after the defeat at Nördlingen in 1634. The duchies of Jülich-Cleve-Berg were, after the extinction of their reigning house in 1609, claimed simultaneously by the Berlin Hohenzollern, by Pfalz-Neuburg and by other competitors. The Hohenzollern eventually secured Cleve and Mark, the Pfalz-Neuburg Jülich and Berg, but both had to reckon with the problems of the succession question and the influence of the Imperial courts when negotiating with the estates in these duchies, who in turn kept communicating with each other. The lesser nobility in Jülich, Cleve and Berg resisted continuously any attempt to be taxed or restrained in their room of manoeuvre by Pfalz-Neuburg or Hohenzollern. Dutch military backing for the regional elites also eventually forced princely concessions.[60] In Hesse-Cassel, the vassals refused from the 1610s any financial support for the landgrave's plans to build up armed forces, placed the blame for Spanish occupation in the 1620s squarely on the landgrave and his main advisor, and forced the resignation of the landgrave and the dismissal and then execution of the advisor in 1628–1629. His son Wilhelm V was, as ally of Sweden and Calvinist, excluded from the general pardon of the Peace of Prague in 1635, was banned and died in exile in Eastern Frisia in 1637. His widow built up, with French support, a large mercenary force that recovered the area in the mid-1640s. But eventually, her son had to compromise with the enraged territorial estates.[61] After the war, the rule of the Catholic Johann Friedrich over the Brunswick-Calenberg principality provided another theatre of conflict, culminating in 1674 with legal proceedings against the prince by the estates before the Imperial Aulic Court.[62] Quite independent of involvement in war, ongoing dynastic divisions of fiefs often led to a weakening of the princely position. For example, Duke Ernest the Pious 'failed' to capitalize on his 1672 inheritance of Saxony-Altenburg but declined, in his *nexus Gothanus*, to impose indivisibility and instead allowed all his seven sons the establishment of his own court, leading to seven different lines, each with their own bit of the land.[63]

[60] See Rainer Walz, *Stände und frühmoderner Staat. Die Landstände von Jülich und Berg im 16. und 17. Jahrhundert* (Neustadt, 1982).

[61] Armand Maruhn, *Necessitäres Regiment und fundamentalgesetzlicher Ausgleich. Der hessische Ständekonflikt 1646–1655* (Marburg, 2004).

[62] Annette von Stieglitz, *Landesherr und Stände zwischen Konfrontation und Kooperation. Die Innenpolitik Herzog Johann Friedrichs im Fürstentum Calenberg 1665–1679* (Hannover, 1994), pp. 106–240.

[63] Thomas Klein, 'Verpasste Staatsbildung? Die Wettinischen Landesteilungen in Spätmittelalter und früher Neuzeit', in Johannes Kunisch (ed.), *Der dynastische Fürstenstaat* (Berlin, 1982), pp. 89–114, see in particular pp. 89–95.

Even where political disaster and divisions of the fief for dynastic reasons were avoided and princes were not structurally weak themselves, many princes attempted to go along with their estates for their own good reasons. The arguable two strongest and largest emerging principalities of the period, the duchy of Bavaria and Electoral Saxony, saw, on the whole, and despite individual clashes, cooperation between prince and estates. Duke Maximilian of Bavaria managed to avoid open confrontation with his estates and let them participate in time in important issues of the country. While he succeeded with most of his tax claims, the right to collect taxes and the administration of them remained substantially in the hands of the estates.[64] In Electoral Saxony, in particular war expenses during the Thirty Years' War, but also costs of the court and of diplomacy forced the electors to negotiate with their estates for taxes. Disagreements were frequent, but the estates did not oppose princely claims in significant ways. The Electors kept consulting them and never denied their right to assent to taxes. More than that, negotiations with estates included almost all matters of foreign policy and constitutional issues, such as the 1657 negotiations about the will of Johann Georg I. In 1660–1661 the estates succeeded in abolishing the agreements among the four princely brothers in Electoral Saxony and the *Secundogenituren* regarding the establishment of independent tax administrations for each of the *Secundogenituren* and defended in March 1661 the old procedures regarding taxation. They also exerted massive influence on territorial legislation, such as in matter of *policey*. In general, the estates were prepared to grant considerable taxes and acted together with the prince, notwithstanding major disagreements in individual points, in running the country.[65] Neither part intended to eliminate the other. The Saxon elector even appealed explicitly for the cooperation with the estates and promised the defence of their privileges in return for cooperation.[66]

On the road to eventual constitutional establishment, however, the specific burdens of the Thirty Years' War and new ideas about princely

---

[64] Katrin Ellen Kummer, *Landstände und Landschaftsverordnung unter Maximilian I. von Bayern, 1598–1651* (Berlin, 2006), pp. 215–219.

[65] Nina Krüger, *Landesherr und Landstände in Kursachsen auf den Ständeversammlungen der zweiten Hälfte des 17. Jahrhunderts* (Frankfurt, 2006), pp. 299–309.

[66] Yv 2444 8 Helmstedt: Copia Dass Churfürstlich Sächsischen Original Versicherung ODER Revers, an Fürsten und Stände daselbst/Nemblich dass Sie hinferner mit einer solchen Contribution nicht mehr sollen bschwert werden/auch dass es nur eine freywillige Steuer so die Ritterschaft und die Gemeine dem Vaterlandt zu einem Defensionswerk herschiessen thun, Dresden 1631: the elector promised not to engage in any war or alliances without prior negotiation with the estates – 'wir wollen uns auch ohne gemein Landschafft in kein Krieg/Bündnis Religionshandlung und ander Sachen damit uns und unser Landt und Leuten Schaden und Nachthehil erfolgen möchte/einlassen'.

rule conspired to make particularly the 1620s to 1680s a crucial period of harsh conflict. While specific economic and war burdens on the nobility and their tenants were regularly the major and initial point of contention, confrontations also regularly led to the question whether the estates could meet on their own initiative, and whether they were allowed, as subjects, to debate matters of public relevance or whether such behaviour constituted a riot under the Imperial Capital Code. In each case, explicit political aims were not initially voiced by the estates, but in the course of confrontation, they were charged by advisors of the prince and in princely reactions to the legal steps of the estate to undermine order.[67] By the same token, no matter how hostile juridical and political rhetoric during these confrontations became, in most cases agreements were eventually found once the material grievances of the estates had been met to some degree. Possibly with the only exception of the confrontation in Jülich-Berg, where Dutch support and the specific succession problems led to an almost independent estate government for some time,[68] territorial estates actually wished to live under the rule of a prince. In the case of Hesse-Cassel, where Wilhelm V of the Calvinist Cassel branch of the House of Hesse had been excluded from the general pardon of the Peace of Prague and banned, and his hostile Lutheran cousins in Hesse-Darmstadt aimed hard to persuade the nobility to swear allegiance to them and abandon the Cassel branch, and where the nobility had thus every opportunity to help create a larger Hessian principality, leave the division of the lands among various branches of the House of Hesse behind them and join with the southern Hessian nobility, they explicitly refused to do that but swore allegiance to the son of Wilhelm V, the minor Wilhelm VI. Most realized that given their scarce resources, their best option was to become privileged subjects within an emerging princely territorial state. Just these privileges and the precise nature of that state needed to be negotiated, and sometime negotiated with the help of the imperial courts. Thus, most noble members of the estates were contend to style themselves 'patriots',[69] to defend more or less successfully certain rights and privileges,[70] and in doing this, defended a privileged place in particular for its lesser and poorer members in a world of rapid economic, social and

---

[67] Maruhn, *Necessitäres Regiment*, pp. 216–234.   [68] Walz, *Jülich Berg*, pp. 191–219.

[69] Robert von Friedeburg, 'The Making of Patriots: Love of Fatherland and Negotiating Monarchy in Seventeenth Century Germany', *The Journal of Modern History* 77 (2005), pp. 881–916; for the use of the rhetoric of fatherland and patriots see also Stiglietz, *Landesherr und Stände zwischen Konfrontation und Kooperation*, p. 117.

[70] In particular in electoral Saxony, see *Landesherr und Landstände in Kursachsen auf den Ständeversammlungen der zweiten Hälfte des 17. Jahrhunderts* (Frankfurt, 2006). The large majority of principalities had still estates in 1750, see Krüger, *landständische Verfassung*, pp. 16–35.

political change. If we abandon nineteenth-century back-projections on parliamentary dualism and sovereignty, the large majority of territorial estates successfully survived and managed to defend, by and large, their own privileges regarding taxation and jurisdiction, though with considerable and bitter conflicts with individual princes along the way. The overwhelming desire for cooperation must thus neither lead to underestimate the sharpness of anti-princely arguments used during these conflicts nor the importance of the willingness of estates to take a stand once that seemed necessary.

Satirical treatment of princely government in print was not entirely new. For example, in 1497 Johann von Morsheim (d. 1516) from a palatinate dynasty of knights had written his Mirror of Government (Spiegel des Regiments), published from 1515 in various editions right until 1637.[71] He satirized and criticized excesses of luxury at court in the tradition of Erasmus' Praise of Folly or Brandt's Ship of Fools. The narrator characterized himself not as 'scholasticus', but as 'homo politicus'. Successive chapters, entitled as 'warning', addressed the infidelity of councillors and courtiers. In particular life at court bred vice, avarice towards subjects and greed and allowed evil councillors to undermine good government by their quest for personal profit.[72] Quite in line with other later fifteenth and early sixteenth-century pamphlet attacks on the money economy, the Jews were singled out as evil perpetrators, but so were the 'Judengenossen', the friends of the Jews, such as *Hofmeister* and chancellors.[73] The sale of offices was explicitly attacked, for it allowed improper persons to acquire office and then exploit it for their own profit.[74] But also among subjects, lack of fidelity was frequent.[75] Such satires did thus anything but criticize princely government as such; they urged Christian moral reform in the broadest of senses and quoted a range of present manifestations of evil, such as Rome, the Turks or the Jews, in order to substantiate the cleansing necessary to reform society.[76] In particular in popular pamphlets during the Peasant War, the lower nobility, counts and ecclesiastical corporations were singled out as further targets for their suppression of the 'common men'. Hope was placed in the empire and the emperor as just a Christian ruler.[77] But in effect, it

---

[71] Hoffleben, 'Dessen Schlag und Händel wie untrue daselbsten von telichen gepflogen und gespüret wird; item, Ermahnung an die Obrogkeit und Richter' HAB 40–1-pol-35.

[72] Ibid., pp. 10, 15–23.   [73] Ibid., p. 24.

[74] Ibid., p. 25. See Heiko Obermann, *The Roots of Antisemitism in the Age of Renaissance and Reformation* (Philadelphia, 1984).

[75] Hoffleben, 'Dessen Schlag', p. 30.

[76] See Frank Ganseuer, *Der Staat des Gemeinen Mannes* (Frankfurt, 1985).

[77] Heinz Angermeier, 'Die Vorstellung des Gemeinen Mannes von Staat und Reich', in *Vierteljahrschrift für Sozial- und Wirtschaftsgeschichte*, 53 (1966), pp. 329–343.

proved to be the emerging princely territorial state and its university trained and often non-noble princely servants of the later fifteenth and sixteenth century that capitalized most successfully on the demand for a general reform for the sake of the common good.[78]

It is important to remember these characteristics, for the satirical attacks on courts and court life from the 1630s had a quite different focus. The air of religious zeal, the personification of evil by Rome, Turks and Jews, and the utopia of a good, Christian empire for the common men were all entirely absent in one of the most successful of these later satires, the anonymously published *Alamodische Politicus* of 1647. Instead, the princes themselves had moved to centre stage. This set of stories had developed from Johann Michael Moscherosch's satirical *Visiones de Don Quevedo. Gesichte Philanders von Sittewald*, a compilation of stories told as 'dreams' of the fictional Philander, published first at Strassburg in 1640 and then in Leipzig, Hamburg and Leiden in editions ranging into the 1660s.[79] The success and influence of the story was so significant that many prints, unauthorized by the author, appeared, including prints adding new stories or leaving out others.[80] Such an unauthorized print was the collection of satires entitled *Alamodischer Politicus*.[81] In its subtitle, it promised to reveal the *arcana status* of present day 'Machiavellists'. The dreaming narrator found himself at a ducal court, where applicants for advisory functions had to prove their (evil) ambition, their parental connections and their knowledge of and ability in 'cunning arts' ('chymisch Kunststücke'). Candidates who instead proved their love to fatherland and their piety were rejected. The candidate who was eventually taken had as fiancée the daughter of the vice chancellor and the prince, in turn, was sexually interested in her, too. Servants of the prince were introduced to use various 'coats' to hide their true ambition. Terms such as *'salus populi', 'bonum publicum', 'conservatio religionis', 'Zelus fidei', 'libertas Patriae'* and *'assertio privilegiorum'* addressed these 'coats' and the *'dissimulatio'* indicated by them.[82] Similarly, important for service to the prince were also masks stored in another room for the princely servants, addressed with names such as

[78] See William Bradford Smith, *Reformation and the German Territorial State. Upper Franconia 1300–1630* (Rochester, NY, 2008).

[79] Gerhard Dünnhaupt, Peronalbibliographien zu den Drucken des Barock, Stuttgart 1991, Vierter Teil, 2849–2858.

[80] Dünnhaupt, 2859. On the problem of authorship see Michael Wieczorrek, 'Review of Edit Grether', *Ius Commune* 22 (1995), pp. 410–413.

[81] Anon., *Alamodischer Politicus, samt Rent-Cammer und peinlicher Prozess in drei Theilen. Warinnen heutiger Statisten Machiavellistischer Griff und arcana status sonnenklar abgemahlt ...* (Hamburg, 1647).

[82] *Alamodischer Politicus*, pp. 11–24.

'*simulatio*' or '*calumnis*'. Among the instruments of *ratio status* were tools for torture, with which Sweden and France had tortured Germany over the past years.[83]

Major examples for cunning princes were Machiavelli himself, Tarquinius Superbus and Nero, but characteristically, also contemporary monarchs such as Louis XI of France, Philipp II of Spain and Henry III of France. The aim of the Machiavellian councillors was to make as much profit as possible while in office, not least by creating an own principality in the course of political turmoil and war.[84] Good networks among such councillors proved vital, and young princes needed to be manipulated into all sorts of political bargains, if possible involving debt, credit and the mortgaging of parts of the principality to get such credit. One specific case was further elaborated in the course of the dream. While the territorial estates urged to litigate against a neighbouring prince for illicit practices in relation to the mortgaging of land, the councillors paid by that very prince suggested to their hapless master to attempt military capture rather than peaceful negotiation. An army was built up, but the officers were primarily instructed to root out the liberties of the country. The satire described in detail the phraseology used to hide this true political motive for mobilizing troops, such as 'necessity' or the 'welfare' of the country. As a result of his war politics, the lands of the duke were invaded and captured; the towns and villages had to pay dearly to the invading enemy army, and the invading prince had himself praised as Joshua in the churches of the occupied.[85]

In terms of types of princes, subjects had either hapless naïve princes who found themselves ousted and their lands wasted, as the duke of the dream; or Machiavellian manipulators whose aim was to treat captured lands as possession by conquest and to get rid entirely of the estates in such a land. To that end, a propaganda campaign had to paint in particular the regional nobility in the darkest of colours to influence the feeble mind of common subjects. In order to provide clout, an occupational army was raised that lived of the land. Princely propaganda addressed this occupational army as 'soldiers of peace'.[86] The prince also began inquisitions against the most eminent members of the urban councils, declared them void of their privileges, confiscated their lands and gave their offices to his own 'creatures'.[87] 'Other true patriots, that the prince could not get a hand on, were sent away under any number of pretexts out of the country, or were given offices that led to their financial ruin; yet others he gave to mean members from the common multitude [*gemeiner Pöbel*]

---

[83] Ibid., pp. 30–32.   [84] Ibid., pp. 40–55.   [85] Ibid., pp. 93–115   [86] Ibid., p. 116.
[87] Ibid., p. 117.

who had to serve by plainly singing his song.'[88] Virtue gradually disintegrated among all ranks of the population, while the prince's physical body, falling sick, began to stink, ulcers covering him.[89]

Two comments must suffice. On the one hand, the satire clearly remained indebted to various literary tropes, including the metaphor of evilness of mind being displayed in the rotting away of the physical body. But, second, the utter violence of the description of princely rule, of the sexual exploitation of the daughters of the country and the population at large, of the systematic attack on the 'patriots' of the country, and the details of the use of religion and political thought as mere propaganda to cover up the ruthless exploitation of land and people had little precursors at least in German literature and was markedly different from sixteenth-century satires. While several individual measures of the evil prince could be found in Aristotle's analysis of undermining the *polis* by a tyrant, the satire's application to current politics as displayed allegedly by German princes of the 1630s and 1640s had no precursor. No case was made for the need of moral reform. Rather, the satire delivered an unqualified indictment of any and every princely rule and everything associated with war, politics, or taxes. Also, in particular in comparison to the *Spiegel des Regiments* and the critical evaluation of noble life in sixteenth century satires, the local nobility was virtually the only group not attacked. They delivered the 'patriots', they attempted to save the country, they were left out of office recruitment at the ducal court, they were the prime targets of the army of the tyrant.

It is significant that important elements of such satires did find their way also into more regular tracts on taxes and politics that were published under proper author name. Johann Wilhelm Neumair von Ramsla's *Von Schatzungen und Steuern sonderbarer Tractat*[90] is a prime example. Neumair was the son and grandson of non-noble servants of the dukes of Saxe-Weimar. His grandfather had also been a delegate for the dukes at the Imperial Diet in 1565–1566. His father was a leading servant in the ducal chancery and, based on substantial property he gained as princely servant, also creditor to the dukes. Neumair himself became princely advisor, received in 1617 by imperial patent noble title and belonged to the territorial estates of the duchy of Saxe Weimar, working for them in executive commissions. In this latter role he did probably oppose plans for armed intervention by the duke on behalf of the Bohemian crisis in 1620

---

[88] Ibid., p. 118   [89] Ibid., pp. 119–120.
[90] Wilhelm Neumair von Ramsla, *Von Schatzungen und Steuern sonderbarer Tractat* (Schlepfingen, 1632). Friedrich Ratzel, *Neumair von Ramsla, Allgemeine Deutsche Biographie*, 23 (Leizpig, 1886), p. 542.

and published a tract on neutrality in this very year. In this tract he argued that a prince should not act in any significant way politically without the consent of the estates. He also addressed the members of the estates as 'Eingessene des Vaterlands' (inhabitants of the fatherland).[91] Duke Johann Ernst the Younger had to listen and to transfer his rule to his brothers to keep his lands out of the trouble that he had brought over himself by supporting Frederick of the Palatinate against the emperor in 1620. Landgrave Moritz of Hesse-Cassel led his branch of the dynasty into a confrontation with the estates in which they eventually quoted Ramsla's most radical 1633 volume on rebellion on how a territory actually should be run, and what 'patriots' should do to resist a tyrannical prince.[92]

Ramsla's 1632 volume on taxes stressed the lack of legitimacy of any extraordinary burdens for subjects, for the prince was supposed to live entirely on his demesne income. Sixteenth-century princes such as elector Frederick the Wise of Saxony were praised for their economical politics and for their work for the welfare of the 'fatherland' by the 'patriots' of that 'fatherland'.[93] As opposed to these pious princes, other princes hired 'Press-und Fress Reuter' ('Force and divulge – horsemen') to take away whatever subjects had saved in 'the sweat of their work', instigated and led by 'Reichmacher' and 'evil councillors'.[94] But also in the text proper, he alleged that those who advised princes to tax and burden subjects received considerable profits from such endeavours, citing a letter by Oldenbarneveldt, until 1620 syndic to the states of Holland, that allegedly proved that he had advised to tax subjects to increase his own fortunes.[95] As Ramsla further claimed, tax officers did use tax money to run their own financial enterprises rather than to pay back debt or to carry interest.[96] To gain this possibility, certain offices had to be captured, and favourites competed for them. It is in the context of this argument that Ramsla quoted Bourgoin's *Chasse aux Larrons*.[97]

---

[91] Frank Boblenz, 'Johann Wilhelm Neumair von Ramsla und seine Beziehungen zum Weimarer Hof', in Jörg J. Berns et al. (eds.), *Frühneuzeitliche Hofkultur in Hessen und Thüringen* (Erlangen, 1993), pp. 200–232, at pp. 217–19 on to Ramsla and his von der Neutralität, Erfurt 1620, 144.

[92] On the context Robert von Friedeburg, 'Why Did Seventeenth Century Estates Address the Jurisdictions of Their Princes as Fatherlands? War, Territorial Absolutism and the Duties of Patriots in Seventeenth Century German Political Discourse', in Randolph C. Head and Daniel Christensen (eds.), *Orthodoxies and Heterodoxies in German-Speaking Lands: Religion, Politics and Culture 1500–1700* (Leiden, 2007), pp. 169–194, the quotation in State Archive Marburg Bestand 73 nr 1806 (but also StAM 5 19147, and 5 19158), 'Remonstratio', 1647, quoting Ramsla, *Vom Aufstand der Untern*, Chapter 4, p. 223.

[93] Ramsla, *Von Schatzungen*, preface, a iii–Aiiii.   [94] Ibid., preface a v.   [95] Ibid., p. 30

[96] Ibid., p. 30.   [97] Ibid., pp. 31–32.

On the detrimental effects of war, Ramsla did not need other sources. He had become himself the victim of repeated plundering during the 1630s and complained bitterly about them.[98] But for constructing the culprit as evil financier and princely officer, he arguably needed a source like Bourgoin. For the sale of offices and the range of financial business of German princes remained, at this point of time, rather negligible. To be sure, also in German lands there had been scandals about princely officeholders. Ronald Asch showed that the case of the favourite of the duke of Württemberg Matthäus Enzlin, executed at the instigation of the estates in 1613, was understood by German contemporaries against Tacitist ideas of corruption of government and evil courtiers, with Sejanus and Tiberius as classical examples and a host of contemporary cases against which to understand the case of Enzlin.[99] French pamphlets of the *Fronde* compared Richelieu and Mazarin with Sejanus, too.[100] Similarities in the use of classical sources notwithstanding, the income for German dukes and counts came primarily from their patrimonial demesne and to an extent from loans, not least from one's own inferior nobility. Elaborated financial markets in offices, loans and rents like in the kingdom of France with its large mercantile groups and rich cities, were alien to most rather agricultural German imperial fiefs and to its small town folk in towns like Stuttgart or Cassel.

But Ramsla, who had seen the wider world during several tours to Italy, Spain and France,[101] made little attempt in his work to differentiate between Saxe-Weimar or Hesse-Cassel on the one hand and the larger kingdom of France. He warned the reader that any over-taxation was counterproductive, since the love of subjects was lost. Historical examples ranged from Vespasian to John of England. Rebellions against unjust taxation, such as in Vienna 1462 and France 1464, but also in Luzern in 1627 and in Guyenne in 1629 proved that tyrannical rule ultimately always backfired.[102] But Ramsla went further. He stressed that it was the office of the estates to prevent the prince from exploiting his subjects.[103] By contrast, advisors only looking for favour with the prince

---

[98] Boppard, *Ramsla*, p. 225.

[99] See Ronald Asch, 'Der Sturz des Favoriten. Der Fall Matthäus Enzlin und die politische Kultur des deutschen Territorialstaates an der Wende vom 16, zum 17. Jahrhundert', *Zeitschrift für Württembergische Landesgeschichte* 57 (1998), pp. 37–63, on the fall of Enzlin, an advisor tot he Duke of Württemberg in 1613. Asch, 3, 7 refers to Georg Acasius Enenkel, *Sejanus seu de praepotentibus regum ac principum ministris commonefactio*, 1620.

[100] For example: *Lettre D'Avis a Mess. De Parlement de Paris Escrit par un Provincial* (Paris, 1649, 6–7, Bibliotheque Mazarin A 13942 10).

[101] Boblenz, 'Johann Wilhelm Neumair von Ramsla', pp. 206–209.

[102] Ramsla, *Von Schatzungen*, examples on pp. 32–68.   [103] Ibid., p .313.

had to be treated with suspicion.[104] Chapter VIII suggested measures for subjects should a prince ask for illegitimate burdens. Deliberations of the estates, though often prohibited by princes, but allowed in general, was a major institutional tool in order to organize resistance; another one was litigation towards superior courts. For more precise advise on further steps leading to open rebellion the reader was advised to consult his upcoming book 'on riot'.[105]

The latter appeared a year later and was no less critical of princely rule. Though couched as a scholarly treatise inquiring into the consequences of princely tyrannical rule, namely rebellion, it was a barely disguised manual how to organize such a rebellion. It is the only book this author knows that treats the terms 'Aufstand der Untern wider ihre Regenten' ('rebellion of the lower orders against their magistrates') without any qualification as neutral descriptive terms rather than as negatively charged terms. After all, rebellion was generally considered a mortal sin and, under the Imperial Statutary code, the Carolina, plainly a capital crime, to be punished by death penalty. Immediately in Chapter I, the use ('*Nutz*') and advantage ('*Vortheil*') of rebellion is discussed, alongside the timing, the organization, and the issue of allies. Reasons for rebellion are the introduction of any new procedures by the prince, any abrogation of privileges, any burden deemed too heavy, such as labour services, misadministration of justice, or new taxes, any abuse by princely servants, in a word – tyrannical treatment in the broadest of terms. The room of manoeuvre for any magistrate to do anything not precisely according to the spirit and letter of existing accords was virtually annihilated. Quoting Machiavelli, rebellion was advised by Ramsla to successfully enforce existing rules on magistrates.[106] Ramsla came up with a whole range of alleged historical examples for such successful rebellions, among them German urban rebellions against the city magistrates, late medieval English peasant uprisings, but also the Dutch Revolt against Philip of Spain.[107] It is in this context that Ramsla accused the Spanish to treat all subjects like animals and to rule in a particularly cruel and despotic manner.[108] Ramsla did also treat the punishment of rebels, but apart

---

[104] Ibid., pp. 314–15.

[105] Ibid., p. 576: The German title of this book on riot was *Vom Aufstand der Unteren wider ihre Regenten*. A short treatment is to be found in Winfried Schulze, Die veränderte Bedeutung sozialer Konflikte im 16. und 17. Jahrhundert, in H. -U. Wehler (ed.), *Der Deutsche Bauernkrieg 1524–1526* (Göttingen, 1975), pp. 277–302, see pp. 293–295, embedding Ramsla into other attempts to understand riot from a sociological point of view.

[106] Johann Wilhelm Neumair von Ramsla, *Vom Aufstand der Untern wieder ihre Regenten* (Jena, 1633), preface, pp. 2–76.

[107] Ibid., pp. 76–86.   [108] Ibid., pp. 86–88.

from Scotland's punishment at the hand of Edward III, the cruelty of punishment and the later misery of the punisher were stressed, from Darius of Persia to the House of Habsburg and the punishment of the 1626 Austrian peasant uprising.[109] Referring to Roman law post-glossarist Baldus, obedience to magistrates was only due once established accords were held, and the welfare of the fatherland – 'salus patriae' – demanded the defence of existing agreements.[110] Ramsla did consider the danger of the multitude and of the chaos regularly ensuing in the case of rebellion and civil war.[111] In considering a legal rationale for rebellion, he singled out the most respectable families within the land, the 'furnemb-sten'. Public order was not the office of the prince alone, but also of these respectable families. In his German context, these were plainly the petty nobility of the territorial estates. It was this particular claim on page 213 of his tract that found his way into the deliberations of territorial estates in actual rebellion against their prince.[112]

Not all princes proved prudent and listened to the warnings of their estates against the dangers of war. Many, such as landgrave Moritz of Hesse-Cassel, did not. Moritz paid eventually with his forced resignation.[113] As the war visited the landgraviate with devastating consequences, the estates had to run government after Moritz' son Wilhelm V, excluded from the Peace of Prague in 1635, banned in 1636 and died in exile in 1637, could not any more govern. After his widow had returned in 1644, conflicts between the estates and her about how to run the country began again. In the course of this confrontation, the estates, led by the knights, reiterated their claim to safe the country as 'patriots' from harm, if necessary using physical force against Amelie, and referred to Ramsla. The document in question was drafted in 1647 and signed by 34 knights, the better part of the local petty nobility. Some had provincial holdings substantial within the local economy of scale. All were middling to petty noblemen.[114] In a consideration written a year later possibly by a Speyer advocate in preparing further litigation, prevention of independent meetings of the estates is defamed as 'Machiavellist'.[115] In 1652, in another document prepared for litigation, such a government is deemed a 'regimen despoticum'.[116] As argued elsewhere, the unprecedented

---

[109] Ibid., p. 103.   [110] Ibid., pp. 150–151.   [111] Ibid., p. 121.   [112] Ibid., p. 213.

[113] Recent summary of the events leading to this spectacular event Friedeburg, 'Why', pp. 177–182; and in Robert von Friedeburg, *Luther's Legacy: The Thirty Years War and the Modern Notion of 'State' in the Empire, 1530s to 1790s* (Cambridge, 2016), Chapter 6.

[114] Friedeburg, 'Why', p. 185; the 1647 *remonstratio* is to be found in State Archive Marburg Bestand 73 no 1816. They quote the above argument as p. 223.

[115] StAM 304, 200. Survived as 'Beilage E' to the Imperial Chamber Court litigation.

[116] StAm Bestand 73 No 1816.

physical devastation of the country was contrasted with the responsibility of the prince to care for his subjects, and the existence of the principality as imperial fief translated into a historic fatherland, to which its patriots, the lesser noblemen, had responsibility to save it against any harm.[117]

Needless to say, the advocates of first Amelie and then of her son Wilhelm VI fought these notions, both in direct deliberations with the estates and in the ensuing litigation before the Imperial Chamber Court.[118] But the Imperial Chamber Court mandated the landgrave to stop infringing the estates' privileges.[119] No matter how constitutionally and legally problematic the claims of the knights and how outrageous the literature they were using, territorial estate assemblies could reckon on an Emperor and Imperial courts supporting subjects against individual princes in favour of neighbouring princes and the influence of the emperor. In the end, Wilhelm VI had to compromise and enshrine a number of privileges, including to be considered in vital matters of state, to the estates in the constitutional compromise of 1655.[120]

Attacks on 'war despotism' were not specific to this particular conflict. In the course of their clash with the princely successors Pfalz-Neuburg and Brandenburg, the estates of the duchies of Jülich, Berg, Cleve and Mark joined in 1647 into a corporate union, an *Einung*, recognized and protected by the emperor, committing the estates of the duchies to collective bargaining towards the princes. The princes in turn did not forge an alliance, but competed with each other. In a pamphlet written in the Netherlands, the support of the Dutch Republic for the estates was defended as a defence of written accords among princes and estates, their violation by the princes was described as 'barbarian Despotism' (*'barbarische Dominatien'*).[121] In another one, published by the Cleve estates in the Netherlands in 1647, the government of elector Friedrich Wilhelm was attacked for attempting to exercise *'Machiavellian Raison d' etat'*.[122] The estates of Jülich and Berg argued against claims for taxes, in that the claims of the princes would submit the country into slavery. Issues such as the princely defence of the country were nothing but pretexts in order to regularize taxes that could only be asked for in a real case of necessity, a case over which the estates had to decide whether it really existed.[123]

---

[117] Friedeburg, *Making of Patriots.*   [118] Maruhn, *Necessitäres Regiment*, pp. 50–51.
[119] StAM Bestand 304, I, 504.   [120] Maruhn, *Necessitäres Regiment*, pp. 81–96.
[121] Walz, *Jülich Berg*, pp. 68, 81.
[122] Ontdeckinge van den valschen Cleeffchen Patriot, Knuttel 5542, B2.
[123] Quoted after Walz, Jülich Berg, p. 94: ' ...aus diesen immerwährenden contributions extraordinariis eine libertas collectas ex absoluta potesate colligendi möge eingeführt, über der Stand und Untertanen leib, hab und Gut nach Wohlgefallen dominieret, selbige zu ewiger Dienstbarkeit und armut gestürzet werden, dadurch dann endlich

The rule of the Berlin Hohenzollern in Cleves and Mark, Brandenburg and Eastern Prussia was long seen to be an example of the general triumph of territorial absolutism over territorial estates. As Johannes Arndt's review of the research situation showed, the Hohenzollern princes were, if possibly even more than other German princes, constrained by lack of financial resources, involvement in too many conflicts at the same time, legal restraints to their rule by Imperial Feudal law (*Reichslehensrecht*) and severe limitations on the use of force (*Landfriedenspflicht*), and the general problems of enemy occupation of Brandenburg by the Swedes and part of the Western provinces by the Dutch. Despite occasional rough going in negotiating with the estates[124] the large majority of the poorer nobility remained primarily interested in peace and possible offices from the prince.[125] Despite considerable tensions between Elector Friedrich Wilhelm and the estates in particular in Brandenburg and Eastern Prussia, in particular about his attempt to recruit and pay troops to be able to be more than a hapless victim at the hand of Sweden (about 9,000 men, including militia), in general noble and estate privileges were rather preserved then monarchical absolutism introduced. Friedrich Wilhelm saw himself as defender of law and current legal procedure. The most significant estate meetings of 1652/1653 (Brandenburg), 1661 (Cleve) and 1661–1663 (Eastern Prussia) led into regular taxation for subjects, alignments with the local elites, and confirmed the general legal protection of privileges, for subjects and nobility alike.[126] The elector reacted extremely aggressively once estates sought foreign help, as did Catholic noblemen in Cleves in 1653, the town of Koenigsberg and nobles in 1661 and 1670. One of them secured clemency, two were executed for treason.[127] But on the whole, as Peter Michael Hahn and William W. Hagen have shown, subjects and noble's privileges were preserved and in particular the lower and poorer nobility did find new employment in the princes' forces, where already company command could bring income.[128]

alle sachen in confusione zergehen, der status regiminis intervenieret, die landständ extinguiert und ein absolutus dominatus ex sola principis voluntate . . . '.

[124] See on Brandenburg and the negotiations of the 1650s Christoph Fürbringer, *Necessitas und Libertas* (Frankfurt, 1985).

[125] Johannes Arndt, 'Der Grosse Kurfürst, ein Herrscher des Abslutismus?' in Ronald Asch and Heinz Duchhardt (eds.), *Der Absolutismus – ein Mythos?* (Köln, 1996), pp. 249–273.

[126] Ibid., pp. 262–263.   [127] Ibid., pp. 268–269.

[128] Peter Michael Hahn, 'Aristokratisierung und Professionalisierung. Der Aufstieg der Obristen zu einer militärischen und höfischen Elite in Brandenburg Preussen', in *Forschungen zur Brandenburgisch-Preussischen Geschichte* NF 1 (1991), pp. 161–208. Recent summary by Wolfgang Neugebauer, 'Brandenburg Preussen in der frühen Neuzeit', in Wolfgang Neugebauer (ed.), *Handbuch der preussischen Geschichte*, vol. I (Berlin, 2009), pp. 178–209, at pp. 182–191.

V

How did the lesser nobility fare? As Ronald Asch has stated, in some polities, such as Bohemia, Moravia and 'to a lesser extent in the Austrian duchies, the once politically important lower nobility had virtually disappeared by the end of the seventeenth century, leaving the field to a small class of magnates and wealthy noble landowners often closely connected to the imperial court'.[129] For Bohemia, Howard Louthan has now questioned the actual extent of prosecution of the nobility in general and stressed the continuing importance of aristocratic rule during the Habsburg Counter Reformation.[130] Indeed, as is the argument of this book, no dynastic agglomerate could do without its elite aristocracy, even if that elite was only developed or reshaped as the dynastic agglomerate developed. Thus, even captured kingdoms like Ireland and Bohemia were not run by an absolutist 'state', but by their elite aristocracy. And within this restructured nobility, the lower segments could find themselves comparatively diminished.

In Denmark, military disaster and enemy occupation led into a radical reconstruction of the older into a new service-nobility. Older noble families did partly join, lacking much alternative, the ranks of the new offices, but many of their sons did choose not to marry and a significant decline in the number of these older families was the consequence. In contrast, in Sweden and Brandenburg, both experiencing similar to Denmark extensive wars and in relation to their size and population a considerable build up of armed forced, but no comparative defeats, the lesser nobility moved into the evolving offices of the growing armies,[131] a process similar to the militarization of the French nobility between the 1580s and 1670s.[132]

Resentment against 'war despotism' led nowhere, neither in France nor in Germany, and arguable not even in England.[133] As John Morrill noted,

---

[129] Asch, *Nobilities in Transition*, p. 49.

[130] Howard Louthan, *Converting Bohemia. Force and Persuasion in the Catholic Reformation* (Cambridge, 2009).

[131] In Sweden, the number of nobles increased from about 500 to about 3,000 in the course of the seventeenth century. As Gunnar Lind argues, the ennoblement of military officers led to this considerable increase. In Denmark, by contrast, after 1660, noble members of the old nobility declined in numbers not least because those in military positions found their income too meager to warrant marriage.

[132] Guy Rowlands, *The Dynastic State and the Army under Louis XIV* (Cambridge 2002), pp. 151–260: The proportion of noble households having a member in the forces rose probably to about 50 per cent by 1670.

[133] Indeed, the majority of officers and regimental leaders in Germany's Thirty Years' War Armies came from the lower nobility, thus war and its 'despotism' did already provide an income for many a lesser nobleman in Germany: Michael Kaiser, 'Ist er vom Adel? Ja. Id satis videtur'. Adlige Standesqualität und militärische Leistung als Karrierefaktoren in

the considerable neutralism within county communities was not able to stem the lengthy civil war that actually emerged.[134] As it were, the networks and influences of the elite aristocracy (in France), the greater gentry and aristocracy in the three kingdoms of the British Isles and the princes in Germany overwhelmed the reluctance of lesser gentry and *noblesse petite*. Wars went on, taxes were not going to fall again, and beyond agricultural resources income had to be found even among the relatively meagre resources that lower officer positions in the evolving armies offered. The only major polity where the nobility successfully opposed fundamental features of the New Monarchy's 'war despotism' was arguably Poland Lithuania.

On second sight, however, the balance sheet for the lesser nobility looks more varied. In general, offices in army and administration were not for sale in German lands. While commissions in the army even on company-level could generate solid income,[135] not to mention prestige, the lesser nobility could remain at the top of regional society and occasionally even acquire wealth. In Prussian lands, offices on the level of colonel or general also opened later civil careers without the need to buy them. And the lesser nobility dominated all military charges, including the higher offices. Among colonels, the lesser nobility controlled about 70 per cent (1650–1725).[136] The broad development and then survival of territorial estate assemblies – or of regular meetings of commissions acting on their behalf – in core parts of the Holy Roman Empire helped to defend specific legal privileges and specific social interests of the lesser nobility, for they regularly dominated these institutions. For example, of the Brandenburg nobility, very few families realized towards the end of the eighteenth century an income comparable to Bohemian or Moravian magnates. But the lesser nobility secured with the help of estate-institutions and within the slowly emerging German territorial state, if not always a respectable provincial living, then definitely considerable societal prestige. Arguably, the comparable poverty and smallness of most German territories and their accompanying social make up remained a crucial factor for this outcome. The number of major merchant cities from which a wealthy elite could have come forward in order to translate

der Epoche des Dreissigjährigen Krieges, in Franz Bosbach, Keith Robbins and Karina Urbach (eds.), *Geburt oder Leistung? Elitenbildung im deutsch-britischen Vergleich*, pp. 73–90, at p. 79.

[134] Morrill, *Nature*, p. 186.

[135] Hahn, *Aristokratisierung*, p. 172; an exception are the Prussian Western provinces, see Horst Möller, 'Ämterkäuflichkeit in Brandenburg–Preussen im 17. und 18. Jahrhundert', in Klaus Malettke (ed.), *Ämterkäuflichkeit: Aspekte sozialer Mobilität im europäischen Vergleich* (Berlin, 1980), pp. 156–178, at p. 167.

[136] Hahn, *Aristokratisierung*, pp. 184, 190, 192.

their riches into offices, titles and income was significantly smaller than in France; in many a developing territory, they did not exist at all.[137] In contrast, in the vast kingdom of France, the higher echelons of the sword nobility, the emerging office nobility and finally also financiers began to engage in mutual social contact, leaving the lesser provincial nobility behind as a class noted to be clearly separated from the top by the later eighteenth century.[138]

Equally important, while the German onslaught on princely government owed examples and references from France, it turned against the princes themselves. The overwhelming royalism among most segments of the French nobility stands in marked contrast to the open spite of German local noblemen for their princes in many a clash.[139] Indeed, when, as Ronald Asch was kind enough to bring to my attention, Cardinal Retz, coadjutor of the Archbishop of Paris and himself a major conspirator against Mazarin, confronted the Paris parliament in 1649 whether they really wanted to challenge the authority of king and Crown in France, they declined. Neither they nor any section of the sword nobility could or wanted to run the kingdom without the authority and leadership of the person of the king to hold everything together.[140]

In contrast, while litigation before the Imperial Aulic and Imperial Chamber Court did use, of course, different repertoires than the slander of the *Alamodische Politicus* or Ramsla, it did challenge princely authority on basic levels. It addressed the prince as mere officeholder and translated the dignity of the lesser nobility in terms of specific responsibilities for the territorial state – that had to be envisioned for that very purpose – into a defence of vital privileges. At least in Jülich-Cleve-Berg, Hesse-Cassel, Pomerania and Mecklenburg, the vicissitudes of war had forced local elites to run the principality de facto on their own for many years during absences of a viable ruler and enemy occupation. For these comparatively small principalities, that was not what they wished for, but it had been done and could be done, in particular given the important legal and constitutional umbrella of the Empire. Indeed, while actual participation in open rebellion against Royal government (never against the king) concerned only a small minority of the French nobility, led by the

---

[137] Wolfgang Mager, Robert von Friedeburg, 'Learned Men and Merchants: The Rise of the "Bürgertum", 1648–1806', in Sheilagh Ogilvie and Robert Scribner (eds.), *Germany: A Social History 1300–1800*, vol. II (London, 1996), pp. 164–195.

[138] Mettam, 'French Nobility', p. 117.

[139] Constant, *Adel*, pp. 144–145; J. M. Smith, *The Culture of Merit: Nobility, Royal Service and the Making of Absolute Monarchy in France 1600–1789* (Ann Arbor, MI, 1996).

[140] Cardinal de Retz, *Memoires*, ed. Michel Pernot (Paris, 2003), p. 185. I owe this reference to Ronald Asch.

occasional daring personality of the French elite aristocracy,[141] the German lesser nobility acted quite collectively and with clear majorities during most conflicts with their princes. The consolidation of the formal institution of territorial estates, the regular backbone of protest, helped in that regard.[142]

Each of these developments provided a gulf to the late medieval situation; all of them constituted a specific 'path' into the future, a path considerable shaped by the varying experiences and reactions to the 'war despotism' of the 'New Monarchy', of the incessant warfare of Europe's evolving dynastic agglomerates. For the German case, incidentally, the successful entrenchment of Germany's lesser nobility within the emerging territorial state is another way to understand phenomena the 1950s and 1960s had associated with Rosenberg's Prussian militarization thesis,[143] the seventeenth and eighteenth century unholy alliance of the Junkers and their soldier–kings, suppressing first the peasants and then movements for modernization in Prussia and ultimately in all of Germany. The economic and social aspects of this argument have almost entirely been demolished by more recent research, not least by William Hagen. But the fact itself of this successful institutional and social entrenchment of Germany's lesser nobility in the emerging territorial state remains, at least when looking back from the eighteenth century. It will need to be squared with the evidence of the nobility's open hostility and spite towards the princes, and with tracts and satires that, while taking over French tropes, extended the attack from its original target, officers and financiers, to the princes themselves. As it were, the transformation of monarchy in conjunction with the particular opportunities of the emerging elite aristocracy let to considerable spite among lesser noblemen both in France and German lands. But while it also let in France to an if anything increasing orientation to the French king as source of patronage (the army) and of protection against the vicissitudes of change, loyalty in Germany rather went to the fief of the princes as imagined fatherland and arena of the smaller local

---

[141] Constant, *Adel*, p. 149. These daring personalities include Cesar de Vendome, governor of Brittany, convicted for his involvement in the 1626 Chalais conspiracy.

[142] Walz, *passim*.

[143] Hans Rosenberg, *Bureaucracy, Aristocracy and Autocracy: The Prussian Experience 1660–1815* (Boston, 1958); Gordon Craig, *The Politics of the Prussian Army, 1640–1945* (New York, 1955); see on them Neugebauer, 'Historiographie zur preussischen Geschichte seit 1945', in *Handbuch*, pp. 75–112, in particular pp. 81–84, 88–96. See for a modern treatment entirely beyond the issues of the 1950s and 1960s Frank Göse, *Rittergut – Garnison – Residenz. Studien zur Sozialstruktur und politischen Partizipation des brandenburgischen Adels 1648–1763* (Berlin, 2005); Hahn, *Aristokratisierung*, p. 163.

networks the petty nobility had at its hands. Neither in France nor in Germany, however, was the petty nobility transformed into obedient servants of a 'state'. Given its often marginal resources, it welcomed the opening up of new possibilities of employment, as in the evolving armies, but remained able to shift its allegiance, as it did in France as in Germany, as circumstances changed.

12 The Crisis of Sacral Monarchy in England in the Late Seventeenth Century in Comparative Perspective

Ronald G. Asch

The Problem

Both in England and in France the king could claim to be *rex et sacerdos* in the late Middle Ages and in the sixteenth and seventeenth centuries. In both countries the ability to heal the sick, or those who suffered from the scrofula, was ascribed to the monarch, although the priest-like position of the king manifested itself in other areas as well. On the other hand, the person of the monarch was under immediate threat in the late sixteenth and early seventeenth centuries. The assassinations of Henry III (1589) and Henry IV (1610) sent shockwaves into the political system. For Henry IV alone, 23 attempts on his life were counted by contemporaries before the last finally succeeded. The Gun Powder Plot added to James I's fears for his life in England. No matter how much political culture and political institutions differed in the two kingdoms and regardless of the different dynastic situation in the two countries (James VI of Scotland had two sons when he ascended the English throne in 1603, while Henry had no legitimate male heir until 1601), both monarchies reacted to the perceived threat posed by religious militants with a strong stress on the sacral nature of royal power.

This renewed emphasis on the priest-like position of the king and on the divine origins of his authority manifested itself not least in the practice of the Royal Touch, although this was more visible in France than in England before the second half of the seventeenth century. The monarchs themselves clearly understood the exercise of the Royal Touch as their prerogative and as a sign of their specific, divinely instituted office,[1] and

This chapter is partly based on the author's monograph, *Sacral Kingship between Disenchantment and Re-Enchantment. The French and English Monarchies, 1587–1688*, New York 2014, in particular pp. 128–153.
[1] Hermann Weber, 'Das "Tocher Royal" in Frankreich zur Zeit Heinrichs IV. und Ludwigs XIII', in Heinz Duchhardt et al. (eds.), *European Monarchy* (Stuttgart, 1992), pp. 155–170, at p. 157; David J. Sturdy, The Royal Touch in England, in Duchhardt et al. *European Monarchy*, pp. 171–184, esp. p. 173–174. Ronald Asch, *Jakob I (1566–1625). König von England und Schottland* (Stuttgart, 2005), pp. 114–132; Lucien Bély, *Murder*

such divine legitimation was important as a basis for a vision of kingship which ascribed a power to the king that was absolute in the sense that nobody in this world could call the king to account.

The rhetoric of absolutism, and also a political practice inspired by such a rhetoric, reached its apogee in France in the later seventeenth century, while in England, Stuart rule broke down and was replaced by a more sober form of kingship which largely lacked the sacral aura of divine right monarchy in its traditional form. What is indisputable is the fact that both in France and England, the confessional aspects of royal authority and its religious underpinnings had to be redefined in this period. What is equally clear is that the last decades of the seventeenth century, and in particular the 1680s, constitute a time of intense interaction between France and England. France provided at least potentially a model, which other kings and rulers in Europe were likely to emulate to a greater or lesser extent, and this was hardly anywhere of greater significance for the fate of monarchy as such than in later Stuart England, where the native monarchical tradition had been visibly shaken by the regicide of 1649 and the republican regime which replaced royal authority for 11 years after this momentous event. As a dynasty the Stuarts were in dire need of support from abroad both in terms of cultural and intellectual resources and of material, even perhaps military, support,[2] but on the other hand, such real or imagined attempts to remodel kingship in England on continental or in fact French lines were bound to be highly controversial, not least because of the association with 'popery' and despotism.[3]

Nevertheless, attempts to follow a real or imagined French example in redefining royal authority and the framework for the Crown's policies in

---

and Monarchy in France, in Robert von Friedeburg (ed.), *Murder and Monarchy. Regicide in European History* (Basingstoke, 2004), pp. 195–211.

[2] Ronald Hutton, 'The Making of the Secret Treaty of Dover', *Historical Journal* 29 (1986), pp. 97–318, esp. pp. 122–145, at p. 144, on Charles's repeated attempts to establish a firm alliance with France: 'What precisely he hoped to gain from it, is difficult to say [...] But the hegemonic position of France in European culture was a powerful influence and Charles's court was undoubtedly in cultural thrall to that of Louis XIV. Even more than that, though, Charles II, it might be surmised, had a desire to attach himself to the most powerful and energetic state in Europe in the expectation of being able to win military, as well as reflected, glory.' See also J. R. Jones, *Charles II: Royal Politician* (London, 1987), p. 81. Cf. Paul Seward, art. 'Charles II (1630–1685)', in *Oxford Dictionary of National Biography* (Oxford, 2004), online edn, http://www.oxforddnb.com/view/article/5144 (accessed 21 December 2011).

[3] One should, of course, not assume that either Charles II or his brother tried to imitate the example of Louis XIV slavishly. Moreover, as John Callow has rightly pointed out with regard to James II there were more than enough Protestant princes in Europe including William III of Orange who tried to emulate Versailles. See John Callow, *The Making of King James II. The Formative Years of a Fallen King* (Stroud, 2000), pp. 134–135.

England (and the two other Stuart kingdoms) were not as unrealistic or hopelessly misconceived as one might assume if one looks only at the outcome after 1688. In the 1680s in particular, and more specifically between the dissolution of the Oxford Parliament by Charles II (1681) and James II's disastrous decision to abandon his alliance with the Tories and the Tory clergymen dominating the church, the Stuarts seemed to be quite successful in establishing strong royal government and in transforming the court into the dominant centre of politics.[4] Given the more recent historical debates on the internal contradictions of absolutism and on the limitations to which royal government was subject almost everywhere in western and central Europe – even in France – it is a moot point whether we call the sort of regime Charles created after 1681 during his personal rule and which James tried to redesign in such a way that it was compatible with his religious convictions absolutism or not.[5] What is clear, is that the English monarchy despite its limited financial resources – which did increase however in the 1680s – was not as inherently weak as has sometimes been maintained. In some ways an English king (and that would be even more true for the King of Scotland or Ireland) had more political options and was less constrained by tradition and vested interests than his French counterpart. It is inconceivable to imagine that a French Dauphin or even the brother of the king could have become a Protestant in the way the Duke of York became a Catholic in the late 1660s. The Bourbons had subjected themselves once and for all in 1593–1594 to the principle that the ruler of France had to be a Catholic – the principle that only a Catholic could govern France was widely seen as one of the fundamental laws of the monarchy such as the Salic Law for the succession, which no king could ever change. It is almost equally inconceivable that a late-seventeenth-century French king would have tried to openly favour the Huguenots by dismissing Catholic officeholders and replacing them with Protestants. Louis XIV, as is well known, did just the opposite and his decision to suppress Protestantism was probably one of the most popular ones he ever took – at least as far as the reaction of the majority of the French population was concerned.[6] Thus if the French king's

---

[4] See for example J. R. Western, *Monarchy and Revolution. The English State in the 1680s* (Basingstoke, 1985); Grant Tapsell, *The Personal Rule of Charles II, 1681–85* (Woodbridge, 2007), as well as John Miller, *After the Civil Wars: English Politics and Government in the Reign of Charles II* (Harlow, 2000), pp. 272–295.

[5] Ronald G. Asch and Heinz Duchhardt (eds.), *Der Absolutismus – ein Mythos?* (Cologne, 1996); Richard Bonney, *The Limits of Absolutism in Ancien Régime France* (Aldershot, 1995); Fanny Cosandey and Robert Descimon, *L'absolutisme in France* (Paris, 2002); James B. Collins, *The State in Early Modern France* (2nd edn, Cambridge, 2009).

[6] Oliver Chaline, *Le Règne de Louis XIV* (Paris, 2005), pp. 143–147; see also Elisabeth Labrousse, *La révocation de l'Edit de Nantes: une foi, une loi, un roi?* (Paris,

authority was hardly ever openly challenged between 1660–1715, apart from a revolt in the Bretagne in 1675 and the war of the *Camisards* between 1702 and 1705 and minor provincial conflicts, this was at least partly due to the fact that Louis XIV knew very well what he could get away with and when it was wiser to refrain from actions which might seem provocative. This was true not only with regard to his religious policy, but it was also true for the king's relations with the social elite. As Jeroen Duindam and many other historians have pointed out, Louis was careful to do nothing which might be seen as an attack on the established social hierarchy.[7] To dismiss dozens or hundreds of officeholders, including judges, and to replace them with social outsiders and upstarts – as James did in his campaign to promote men who were absolutely loyal to him both in the army and in the judiciary as well as at the local level on the benches of the justices of the peace – would have been inconceivable in France as long as Louis XIV ruled.[8]

One might say that James II – and to a lesser extent Charles II in his campaign to cleanse the government of urban corporations of Whigs, crypto-Dissenters and other troublemakers – took such extreme and in some way desperate steps for the very reason that their position was so precarious but nevertheless neither judges nor justices of the peace held their positions in England by purchase or hereditary right,[9] so they could be much more easily removed than the *officiers* in France. Thus at least for the period of the 'Second Restoration'[10] between 1681 and the first years

---

1990); Janine Garrisson, *L'Edit des Nantes et sa révocation: histoire d'une intolérance* (Paris, 1985).

[7] Jeroen K. Duindam, *Vienna and Versailles: The Courts of Europe's Dynastic Rivals 1550–1780* (Cambridge, 2003), pp. 97–103; William Beik, *A Social and Cultural History of Early Modern France* (Cambridge, 2009), pp. 333–336; Joël Cornette, 'Figures politiques du Grand Siècle. Roi-État ou État-roi?', in Cornette (ed.), *La Monarchie entre Renaissance et Révolution* (Paris, 2000), pp. 137–278, at pp. 243–274; Leonhard Horowski, 'Das Erbe des Favoriten: Minister, Mätressen und Günstlinge am Hof Ludwigs XIV', in Jan Hirschbiegel and Werner Paravicini (eds.), *Der Fall des Günstlings. Hofparteien in Europa vom 13. Bis zum 17. Jahrhundert* (Ostfildern, 2004), pp. 77–126.

[8] For the justices of the peace see Lionel K. J. Glassey, *Politics and the Appointment of Justices of the Peace, 1675–1720* (Oxford, 1979), pp. 89–90; cf. for local government also Victor L. Stater, *Noble Government. The Stuart Lord Lieutenancy and the Transformation of English Politics* (Athens, Georgia, 1994), pp. 141–179.

[9] For the purchase of offices in France see most recently Jean Nagle, *Unorgueil Français. La venalité des offices sous l'ancien regime* (Paris, 2008); Beik, *A Social and Cultural History*, pp. 134–163.

[10] For the idea of a second restoration see Gary S. De Krey, *Restoration and Revolution in Britain. A Political History of the Era of Charles II and the Glorious Revolution* (Basingstoke, 2007), pp. 202–210; Philip Hart, *Pen for a Party: Dryden's Tory Propaganda in its Context* (Princeton, NJ, 1993), Chapter 5.

of James II's reign it would be wrong to assume that royal authority was inherently weaker in England than in France, although undoubtedly the potential for rebellion if not revolution remained always much greater. But then this was at least to a considerable extent due to the fact that political opposition in the Stuart kingdoms was so closely linked to religious grievances and could thus gain an edge and an aggressiveness which remained alien to the discontents of dissatisfied courtly aristocrats or even of over-taxed and half-starving peasants in France.

France 1660s–1700s: The King as Semi-Divine Hero and the Shift Back to Confessional Sacral Kingship

Whatever importance one might attribute to French influence in politics and culture, what was at stake in England in the Restoration period was ultimately the very nature of kingship itself and its religious foundations. Charles II never fully committed himself to any specific model of kingship after 1660. There was the option of representing the king as an almost Christ-like figure exercising an office that was sacred in nature and who ruled the country as the successor of an Anglican martyr and saint surrounded and guided by his spiritual counsellors, the bishops.[11] But there was also the alternative of a more secular, rationalistic idea of kingship, a sort of monarchy which was compatible with some degree of religious toleration but which could also – potentially – draw on Hobbesian notions of absolute royal sovereignty.[12] And finally Charles could – theoretically – have chosen to ally himself with those who wanted the king to act as a godly ruler in the Calvinist or Presbyterian mould, governing strictly within the framework provided by the Common Law and parliamentary statute and strenuously fighting against both popery and vice. Charles, with his all too visible aversion to conventional principles of sexual conduct and his seeming religious indifference was clearly not the right man for such a model of kingship, which was to appeal much more – after 1688 – to William III, but one should not forget that this option was favoured by an influential and

---

[11] For *Eikon Basilike*, which promoted this image, see below. For Charles's position see also Ronald Hutton, 'The Religion of Charles II', in R. Malcolm Smuts (ed.), *The Stuart Courts and Europe: Essays in Politics and Political Culture* (Cambridge, 1995), pp. 228–246; cf. Hutton, *Charles II, King of England, Scotland and Ireland* (Cambridge, 1989), pp. 455–458. For Charles's attitude towards Scottish Presbyterians in particular see also J. R. Jones, *Charles II: Royal Politician* (London, 1987), pp. 21–22.

[12] Jeffrey R. Collins, *The Allegiance of Thomas Hobbes* (Oxford, 2006), and Jon Parkin, *Taming the Leviathan: The Reception of the Political and Religious Ideas of Thomas Hobbes, 1640–1700* (Cambridge, 2007).

powerful minority among the elite in his three kingdoms, or at least in England and Scotland.[13]

Given these tensions between different models of kingship – each of them highly controversial – in the Restoration period, matters were bound to become even more complicated by the impact the French monarchy and its political culture had on England. This held even more true as the perception of France and its court changed considerably during the period under discussion here, a change which was partly due to a real reorientation of the French monarchy at the time, in particular with regard to the way kingship was presented by court culture and, even more importantly, regarding the religious and confessional framework of royal policy. As late as the early 1670s, France still seemed to be a reasonably tolerant country. Her king, although a Catholic, of course, did not define his role as a ruler primarily in religious or confessional terms, or so it could seem when seen from abroad. Certainly there were English Dissenters in the late 1660s who saw the combination of a strong monarchy with a reasonably high degree of religious toleration not as entirely unattractive, as Mark Goldie has pointed out.[14] Louis XIV's war against the Dutch Republic in 1672–1678, with its attempts to restore the dominant position of the Catholic church in those Dutch provinces which had been temporarily conquered early in the war, put paid to all that.[15] The increasing pressure the French crown put on Huguenots to convert during the 1670s also contributed to destroying this positive image of France among English Dissenters.

If for English Dissenters and other radical opponents of 'popery' in whatever form, France became a greater and more imminent threat to liberty and Protestantism in the 1670s and 1680s than in the past, the policies of those who saw the French monarchy for the very reason that it was strong and autocratic in a more positive light, such as Charles II and his brother, the Duke of York, were also bound to be affected by the real and perceived changes the French monarchy underwent in this period.

---

[13] Mark Goldie, *Roger Morrice and the Puritan Whigs* (= idem. [ed.], *The Entering Book of Roger Morrice, 1677–1691*, vol. I) (Woodbridge 2007), pp. 154–161.

[14] Mark Goldie, 'The Huguenot Experience and the Problem of Toleration in Restoration England', in C. E. J. Caldicott et al. (eds.), *The Huguenots and Ireland. Anatomy of an Emigration* (Dublin, 1987), pp. 175–203, at pp. 179–183.

[15] Steve C. A. Pincus, 'From Butterboxes to Wooden Shoes: The Shift in English Popular Sentiment from Anti-Dutch to Anti-French in the 1670s', *Historical Journal* 38 (1995), pp. 333–361, argues at p. 361: 'The public outcry against the third Anglo-Dutch war did represent a fundamental turning point in the fortunes of the restored monarchy. Its significance lay not in the revival of fear of Roman Catholicism, but rather in the conviction that only an English parliament could protect the nation from French universal dominion and a French style of government.'

The gradual transformation of French court culture and of the dominant style of monarchical representation were of particular importance in this respect.

Right from the beginning of his reign, Louis XIV had seen to it that art, poetry, history and official news reporting created an image of himself which presented him as a ruler who outshone all his rivals and was a true hero both in war and in peace. Court culture had always been about extolling the ruler as victorious, wise and virtuous, as both courageous and pious. However, Louis XIV went undoubtedly further than other rulers both past and present in having his own glory and greatness depicted and acclaimed by artists and poets. Whatever the reality of absolute monarchy, the rhetoric of absolutism was all too audible in French court culture, in the sermons of loyal preachers or the encomia of obsequious poets and members of the academy after 1660.[16] For Louis's enemies and critics this was just abject and relentless flattery, if not downright idolatry verging on the blasphemous.[17] What certainly gave court culture in France its special flavour was the fact that the office and institution of kingship was entirely conflated with the king's body natural. The man Louis XIV was not just king, he embodied the very idea of kingship. The tendency to let the king's *corps mystique* disappear behind his natural body had already been visible in the past and court ceremonial had even earlier begun to concentrate more on celebrating the actions of the individual king than the institution of monarchy which found its expression in the traditional rituals of state such as the *sacre*, the *funerailles* of even the royal entries into cities.[18] With Louis XIV, however, as Gerard Sabatier has put it: 'toute gémellité des deux corps a disparu. Tout l'État, toute la monarchie, tous les principes d'autorité, d'ordre, de souveraineté, d'unicité, sont contenus dans ce corps de ce roi.' What we see here is in Sabatier's opinion much more than a quest for glory and a limitless pride ('orgueil'), it is 'la formulation la plus achevée de l'absolutisme'.[19] In the representations of kingship Sabatier has examined – mainly works of art such as public monuments and sculptures (panegyric poems or sermons would yield a different result) – this fusion of the king's body natural with the idea of kingship often lacks a clear religious dimension, at least in the

---

[16] Cornette, 'Figures', pp. 229–235; Pierre Zoberman, *Les panégyriques du roi* (Paris, 1991); Peter Burke, *The Fabrication of Louis XIV* (New Haven, CT, 1992), pp. 61–106, and for the image of the king as military leader, Joël Cornette, *Le roi de guerre. Essai sur la souveraineté dans la France du Grand Siècle* (Paris, 2000), pp. 231–248.

[17] Hendrik Ziegler, *Der Sonnenkönig und seine Feinde. Die Bildpropaganda Ludwigs XIV. in der Kritik* (Petersberg, 2010).

[18] Michèle Fogel, *Les céremonies de l'information dans la France du XVIe au XVIIIe siècle* (Paris, 1989), pp. 198–205.

[19] Gérard Sabatier, *Versailles ou la figure du roi* (Paris, 1999), p. 565.

sense of a distinctly Christian as opposed to a mythological vocabulary. This holds true at least for the first decades of Louis's rule.[20] This was to a certain extent to change in later years but during the 1660s and 1670s the religious dimension of court culture was, if not absent, less prominent than in the more recent past. Louis XIV although himself conventionally religious and certainly conscious of the fact that his position as an anointed rulers conferred a special status on him stood at the centre of splendid baroque court which was not conspicuous for its excessive piety and high moral standards – as opposed to the Habsburg courts in Vienna and Madrid.[21]

The language which the king's artists used to glorify the ruler had primarily been the language of pagan mythology, or of ancient and contemporary (Louis's own victories and achievements) history, not that of the bible or of theology. The king was not just depicted as Apollo-Helios or Alexander the Great, he took part in dramatic performances such as the *ballets de cour* – where he played himself the role of the ancient god and the Greek military hero – and to some extent the theatrical culture of the court had a performative quality which really transformed the king from a mere human being holding high office into a superhuman heroic or semi-divine figure who belonged to a sphere which transcended the world of mere mortals.[22] Undoubtedly, however, the great frescoes in Versailles emphasized more the heroic virtues of the king (*magnanimitas* and *magnificentia*) and less the divine origin of royal authority in the sense of a Christian kingship *iure divino* and *dei gratia*.[23] This emphasis on the king as a heroic figure may be partly due to the fact that the language of mythology and ancient histories could be controlled entirely by the king and his artists, whereas the language of religion was ultimately controlled by the church.[24] The 1680s saw a culmination of this tendency to depict

[20] Sabatier, *Versailles*, p. 565: 'Et effectivement, dans cette figure de roi produite à Versailles et à Paris à la fin du XVIIe siècle, siècle de foi, qui a aussi été celui du début du désenchantement du monde, nulle sacralité de nature religieuse ne s'aperçoit. Mais elle resplendit dans ce qui est devenu le politique – soit, dans sa version d'alors, l'absolutisme fantasmé.'

[21] Bernard Hours, 'De la piété personelle de Louis XIV', in Gérard Sabatier and Margarita Torrione (eds.), *¿Louis XIV espagnol? Madrid et Versailles, images et modèles* (Versailles, 2009), pp. 237–254.

[22] Georgia J. Cowart, *The Triumph of Pleasure. Louis XIV and the Politics of Spectacle* (Chicago, 2008); see further Sabatier, *Versailles*, pp. 47–242 on the function of mythological images at Versailles and Jean-Pierre Néraudau, *L'olympe du roi-soleil. Mythologie et idéologie royale au Grand Siècle* (Paris, 1986), pp. 119–134.

[23] Nicolas Milanovic, *Du Louvre à Versailles. Lecture des grands décors monarchiques* (Paris, 2005), p. 179. See also Nicolas Milanovic and Alexandre Maral (eds.), *Louis XIV, l'homme et le roi* (Paris, 2009).

[24] Gérard Sabatier, 'Imagerie héroïque et sacralité monarchique', in Alain Boureau (ed.), *La royauté sacré dans le monde Chrétien* (Paris, 1995), pp. 115–128, at p. 118; cf. for the

the king as a semi-divine hero, ultimately superior to any other heroic figure even the great examples from antiquity such as Alexander the Great. Louis XIV who was now increasingly addressed as 'the Great' and his actions and his entire reign were praised not just as equal in greatness and splendour to the age of Augustus – the golden age of monarchy in antiquity – but as far superior to anything France or Europe had ever seen. As early as the mid 1670s the so-called '*modernes*' had asserted this superiority of the glorious present over the past.[25] But if royal panegyric in all its forms reached its apogee in the 1680s, a period marked by the greatest effort in promoting the royal image both at home and abroad France had ever seen, this decade was also marked by an incipient crisis of representation as has frequently been emphasized.

In Versailles, which now became the permanent residence of the king, not just one among many palaces in and around Paris where the king held court, works of art now dominated which tried to demonstrate that Louis was absolutely incomparable as has already been emphasized. There was no longer any need to depict him as Apollo or a new Augustus – he himself had set the standard for what it meant to be a great ruler, he had defined greatness itself. Or as Olivier Chaline has put it: 'Seul Louis est capable de rendre compte de Louis.'[26] Mythological stories continued to be used on occasion to decorate ballrooms, gardens and apartments but their political message was reduced in scope. They were now mere metaphors for glory and greatness, which could be used more or less at random, and ceased to be a means whereby a true metamorphosis of the man at the centre of all this glorification was effected.[27]

Historians have spoken of a crisis of representation for the 1680s because mythological and historical figures became mere signs and representations and lost their deeper symbolic quality whereby they not only invoked the presence of what they represented, but to some extent even embodied the higher order and transcendent truth they mysteriously

---

heroic image of the king Joël Cornette, 'La tente de Darius', in Alain Boureau and Henry Mechoulan (eds.), *L'État classique 1652–1715. Regards sur la pensée politique dans la France dans la seconde moitié XVIIe siècle* (Paris, 1996), pp. 9–42, and Thomas Kirchner, *Der epische Held. Historienmalerei und Kunstpolitik im Frankreich des 17. Jahrhunderts* (Munich, 2001), pp. 103–117, 272–317.

[25] Chaline, *Louis XIV*, p. 107, cf. p. 226; cf. Hans Kortum, *Charles Perrault und Nicolas Boileau. Der Antike-Streit im Zeitalter der klassischen französischen Literatur* (Berlin, 1966); Joan E. DeJean, *Ancientsagainst Moderns. Culture Wars and the Making of a fin de siècle* (Chicago, 1997).

[26] Chaline, *Louis XIV*, p. 229; Chaline continues: 'Divinités et héros ne sont là que pour orner les haut faits du règne. Ils n'en sont plus les modèles.'

[27] Sabatier, *Versailles*, pp. 547–566; Burke, *Fabrication*, pp. 125–135. See also Kirchner, *Held*, pp. 431–435.

hinted at.[28] In fact, by freeing himself from the constraints and limitations which the language of mythology and Greek and Roman history had imposed on him and having himself depicted as an absolutely incomparable figure, Louis XIV ultimately also laid the foundations for an increasing disenchantment of kingship itself, or so it may seem. This may partly explain – in conjunction with the fact that Louis now faced an ever stronger criticism from his opponents in other countries but also from French writers who had fled abroad – that in the later decades of Louis's reign the arms of discursive, and not merely panegyric, rhetoric as well as legal and political arguments became much more important in defending Louis's claims to authority than in the past.[29] Images were clearly no longer enough. However, with the vocabulary of mythology and of heroic history both in decline, the monarchy was also thrown back onto different languages to articulate its claim to authority and represent it to a wider public.

One of these languages, and one of the most important one was that of Christian religion and of theology. It was certainly no mere coincidence that the last great building which Louis XIV had constructed in Versailles from 1688 onwards was the magnificent chapel which was designed to celebrate the idea of Christian, Catholic monarchy. The chapel was a monument to the idea of sacerdotal kingship which influenced representations of the French monarchy from the mid 1680s onwards much more visibly than during the 1660s and 70s.[30] We can certainly discern a change in the predominant strategies of representation in this period as Nicolas Milanovic among others has pointed out. Buildings and works of art which served directly a religious purpose such as the royal chapel in Versailles or the Dome des Invalides in Paris become now much more important, and with this change in emphasis the role of the monarch as mediator between God and men also became more prominent. In the profane buildings, in Versailles, the Trianon, and Marly, the figure of the king in as far as he was depicted at all receded into the background. The King of Glory becomes almost a 'roi caché', a hidden king, as

---

[28] See Sabatier, *Versailles*, p. 560: 'on ne croit plus au système des ressemblances des analogies, des similitudes, qu'on ne croit plus à une substance idéelle du pouvoir qui s'incarnerait temporairement, une substance qui serait forcément plus réelle, dans son éternité, que son éphémère apparence charnelle. On ne croit plus aux deux corps du roi. Du moins ne les montre-t-on pas.'

[29] Joseph Klaits, *Printed Propaganda under Louis XIV. Absolute Monarchy and Public Opinion* (Princeton, NJ, 1976), p. 26.

[30] Martha Mel Stumberg Edmunds, *Piety and Politics. Imagining Divine Kingship in Louis XIV's Chapel at Versailles* (Newark, DE, 2002), p. 229. For the role of the chapel cf. Alexandre Maral, *La Chapelle Royale de Versaille sous Louis XIV: ceremonial, liturgie et musique* (Sprimont, 2002).

Milanovic has argued.[31] It was now clearly seen as increasingly difficult to invest the king with the attributes of a super-human, a divine nature outside a strictly Christian frame of reference which was centred less on promoting the king's glory and advertising his position as God's image on earth but on proclaiming his virtue and piety, if not in fact humility. There had already been an outcry against the cult of majesty which Louis XIV had promoted until the 1680s. French Protestants and foreign critics of the French monarchy alike had denounced the statues and paintings which celebrated the French king as a hero and semi-divine figure as mere idolatry, and as ultimately blasphemous.[32] French artists and writers had tried to respond to such criticism, either by arguing that statues represented the king only in legal sense, taking his place when he could not be present in person, or by actually claiming that kings were justly venerated as almost divine beings because they presented a visible image of God's majesty on earth.[33] Bossuet had already strongly emphasized this aspect in his *Politique tirée des propres paroles de l'écriture sainte* at the end of the 1670s, where he had compared the king sitting in his cabinet and giving orders to his servants and officers to God ruling the entire world.[34]

But much as Bossuet emphasized that the king's throne was God's own throne and the monarch God's image on earth,[35] he was nevertheless an implicit opponent of the theological assumptions which provided such analogies with more solid foundations, which made them more than mere figures of speech. For Bossuet was critical of the religious mysticism which had one of its sources in a neo-platonic philosophy, which tried to establish an analogy between the celestial hierarchies of angels and saints and the order of this world. Mystics who favoured such a view took their inspiration not least form the works of St. Dionysius the Areopagite (or rather the works written in the fifth century which went under his name), who in France was often identified until the late seventeenth

---

[31] Milanovic, *Du Louvre à Versailles*, pp. 230–231, cf. Burke, *Fabrication*, pp. 125–131.

[32] Pierre Jurieu, *La Religion des Jesuites* (The Hague, 1689), p. 6, had emphasized that kings were in the presence of God not more than mere shadows ('que le personage qu'ils jouent sur la terre n'est qu'un roolle [sic] de Comédie'), and strongly rejected the idolatry which he saw in the veneration of the sun king.

[33] Ziegler, *Der Sonnenkönig*, pp. 101–103. Cf. François Lemée, *Traité des statues* (Paris, 1688), p. 422–425, against the Protestant Pierre Moulin's *De imaginibus*.

[34] Quoted by Sabatier, *Versailles*, p. 429. See Jacques-Bénigne Bossuet, *Politique tirée des propres parole de l'écriture sainte*, ed. Jacques Le Brun (Geneva, 1967), p. 178. Bossuet had written the first draft of the *Politique* in the late 1670s, but did not complete the work until shortly before his death in 1704. For Bossuet cf. Lothar Schilling 'Bossuet, Die Bibel und der "Absolutismus"', in Kai Trampedachand Andreas Pečar (ed.), *Die Bibel als Politisches Argument* (HZ, Beiheft 43, Munich, 2007), pp. 349–370.

[35] Bossuet, *Politique*, p. 65.

century with the martyr and first bishop of Paris, Saint Denis. There are historians who have found an echo of this neo-platonic mysticism even in the *Mémoires* of Louis XIV and in particular in the reasons Louis gives for having adopted the image of the sun as the symbol of his power and majesty.[36] But influential as this neo-platonic philosophy may have been until the second third of the seventeenth century, the authenticity of the corpus of writings attributed to Saint Denis, the identification of the Eastern Saint with the French national martyr, and not least Neo-platonic mysticism itself were increasingly attacked by influential theologians and historians in the later seventeenth century. Thus a cult of majesty built on such foundations and on the analogy between celestial and earthly hier-archies – which was at the core of the Dionysian theology – gradually lost its persuasiveness.[37]

These changes in the general intellectual climate were bound to have an effect on the political theology of kingship and ultimately on the prevailing representations of monarchy. It was certainly true that from the 1680s onwards works of art which celebrated and extolled Louis XIV became more subdued in style and also more conventionally Christian, as Niclas Milanovic has pointed out: 'il ya dans le même temps une *disparition* ou plutôt une *dissolution* du portrait du roi, qui peut être également interpretée dans le context de l'impossibilité d'une véritable sacralité du roi dans les monarchies occidentales: Le souverain n'y est pas divinisé, il tient seulement une position intermédiare entres ses sujets et Dieu.'[38]

At the same time the style of monarchical representation changed in other aspects as well. One might say that the spoken or printed word became now comparatively more important than the symbolic language of paintings and other works of art. For the young Louis XIV words and texts had been of comparatively limited significance as a means for projecting an image of his own person and of kingship in general onto a wider world.[39] To the extent that this image of the king's body was at

---

[36] Yves Durand, *L'Ordre du monde. Idéal politique et valeurs sociales en France du XVIe au XVIIIe siècle* (Paris, 2001), pp. 136–137; cf. Louis XIV, *Mémoires suivis de Manière de montrer les jardins de Versailles*, ed. Joël Cornette (Paris, 2007), p. 172. See also Yves Durand, 'Mystique et politique au XVIIe siècle. L'influence du pseudo-Denys', *Dix-septième siècle* 173 (1991), pp. 323–350, at pp. 344–345.

[37] For the attack on Pseudo-Dionysios and Dionysian mysticism see Durand, *Ordre du Monde*, pp. 135–136, and much more extensively, Jean-Marie Le Gall, *Le Mythe de Saint Denis entre Renaissance et Révolution* (Seyssel, 2007), pp. 205–314, in particular 216. See also Louis Cognet, *Crépuscule des mystiques. Bossuet-Fénelon*, ed. J. R. Armogathe (2nd edn, Paris, 1991).

[38] Milanovic, *Du Louvre*, p. 229.

[39] Paul Kléber Monod, *The Power of Kings: Monarchy and Religion in Europe, 1589–1715* (New Haven, CT, 1999), p. 216: cf. ibid.: 'Jean-Pierre Néraudau has perceived in such public performances a "devaluation of the word", a deliberate avoidance of verbal

least partially disenchanted, other strategies of representation superseded
or complemented it. This change in representational strategies was also
influenced by the fact that the king seemingly forever victorious and
glorious was after about 1690 confronted by the experience of defeat.
To the extent that Louis suffered a number of setbacks in his fight against
his enemies in Europe in the 1690s and much more so after 1701 he
allowed himself to be depicted increasingly as a Christian ruler who
followed Christ in his sufferings.[40] In fact James II of England who had
lost his crowns and fled to France as an exile may have offered Louis XIV
an example of a monarch who represented the sacred character of kingship through his sufferings and his piety if not in fact through his martyrdom. In 1690 when it had become clear that it would take the Stuarts
a long time to regain their crowns – should they in fact ever succeed in
doing so – a court preacher at Louis's court invoked the example of Josias
the pious king of the Jews in a sermon. Josias had been overthrown and
succumbed to his enemies in the same way in which James II has suffered
a terrible defeat so that now France and Catholic Europe witnessed the
spectacle of 'la piété détrônée, fugitive, abandonée, la révolte au contraire
et la perfidie coronnées.'[41] Thus, whereas Louis XIV in all his power and
glory as a militantly Catholic king became to some extent a model for
James II before 1688,[42] so the exiled James II as a saintly ruler seems to
have become increasingly a figure which influenced the way Louis XIV
saw himself and his mission as a king, or at least the way this mission was
represented by his chaplains and by the artists working in the *chapelle
royale* in Versailles. A few years before Louis died a preacher in Versailles
could exclaim that through his sufferings Louis demonstrated that he was
the true heir of his predecessors who since Saint Louis held their crown
'en dépôt à l'ombre des épines de celle des Jésus-Christ.'[43] The allegedly
original crown of thorns was of course one of the most precious relics

---

expression so that language would not be seen to encompass the person of the king.' See
Jean-Pierre Néraudau, *L'olympe du roi-soleil. Mythologie et idéologie royale au Grand Siècle*
(Paris, 1986), pp. 80–84.

[40] Stumberg Edmunds, *Piety*, p. 228: 'Like the close association between Louis XIV and the
theme of the battle against heresy, the theme of martyrdom repeated throughout the
chapel corresponds to arguments developed by royal preachers that the king's misfor-
tunes were an earthly martyrdom that would lead to his salvation.'

[41] Jacques-Paul de Migne (ed.), *Collection intégral et universelle des orateurs sacrés, du premier
ordre*, vol. XXVIII (Paris, 1847), sermon by Charles de la Rue S. J., Second Sunday in
Advent 1690, cols. 301ff., 301 and 314. For the impact James II's life as a penitent sinner
and his death had in France see also Migne, *Collection*, vol. XXI, cols. 179–204, sermon
on the death of James II by Père Antoine Anselme, 8 November 1702; cf. John Callow,
King in Exile. James II: Warrior, King and Saint (Stroud, 2004), pp. 378–384.

[42] Callow, *The Making of King James II*, pp. 134–135.

[43] Migne, *Collection*, vol. XXVIII, col. 243, sermon by Charles de la Rue, Tous les Saints
1709.

which the French kings had owned since the Middle Ages and was kept in the Saint Chapelle in Paris. All this lay of course still in the future in the early 1680s when Louis was at the height of his power but what was already visible at the time was a turn towards a more sacerdotal and more militantly Catholic concept of kingship.

There were a number of reasons for the gradual transformation of the dominant idea of kingship in this period. Apart from the comparative devaluation of mythological metaphors and of the language of heroism there had always been a competition between Versailles and the Habsburg courts in Vienna and Madrid, but this competition took on a new dimension in the 1680s. With the victory over the Ottoman army besieging Vienna in 1683 the Emperor Leopold emerged as the victorious leader of a new crusade against the enemies of Christendom and could reclaim the pre-eminent position among the Catholic princes of Europe to which his imperial status had – in his own opinion at least – always entitled him.[44] At the same time the likelihood that the last Spanish Habsburg ruler, Charles II, would die childless within the foreseeable future created vast new prospects for the Bourbons as a dynasty. Louis XIV's descendants had a reasonably good claim to the Spanish crown but it was almost self-evident that it would be difficult for a Bourbon prince whose credentials as a fervent Catholic were not absolutely unimpeachable to become king of Spain.[45] Thus Louis's decision to pursue a policy which was in some sense more devout but at the same time more aggressively anti-Protestant in the 1680s must also be seen as an attempt to make his dynasty more acceptable to those Catholics in Spain and elsewhere who had always rejected the least compromise with Protestantism.[46]

England: The Reign of Charles II

The French monarchy to which Charles II and even more so his brother might look both as an ally and as a model for their own kingship in the 1680s was thus much more aggressively Catholic and in some ways 'Hispanized' than in the past. Spanish kings had always tried to promote

---

[44] Cf. Jean Orcibal, 'Les "supercroisades" de Louis XIV (1683–1689)', in J. van Bavel and M. Schrama (eds.), *Jansénius et le Jansénisme dans les Pays-Bas* (Louvaine, 1982), pp. 138–147.

[45] For the strong religious dimension of the War of the Spanish succession see for example David González Cruz, *Une Guerre de Religion entre princes catholiques. La succession de Charles II dans l'Empire espagnol* (Paris, 2006).

[46] For the impact the Spanish connection had on France see Jean-Frédéric Schaub, *La France espagnole: les racines hispaniques de l'absolutisme français* (Paris, 2003); and Sabatier and Torrione, *¿Louis XIV espagnol?*. See also Emmanuel Le Roy Ladurie, *L'AncienRègime, vol. I: 1610–1715* (Paris, 1991), pp. 305–306.

an image of themselves as crusaders, fighting both Muslims and heretics. French monarchs on the other hand, had in the past frequently cooperated with protestant powers (and of course with the Ottoman Empire). Louis XIV, however, broke with that tradition, and pursued a policy which gained him a reputation as the scourge of Protestantism both in France and on the European stage.[47] This could not fail to have a marked impact on the persuasiveness and acceptability of this French vision of kingship in England. The religious basis of monarchy was in any case more fragile in England than in France. Whereas before 1640 it had seemed self-evident to most that church and nation were largely co-extensive and that the secular community of ruler and subjects was in many ways identical with the ecclesiastical community of the faithful, this unity had been shattered by the breakdown of the established church in the late 1640s and the 1650s. The failure of a religious settlement, which could form a basis for a truly comprehensive church in the 1660s, was bound to provoke calls for toleration and consequently for some degree of separation between church and state, be it ever so limited. From such a perspective there could no longer be one church as a divinely ordained institution but different competing churches which were essentially associations created by men and women who shared the same religious convictions; a view which John Locke was to advocate in his *Essay Concerning Toleration* (1667), and more forcefully in his *Letter Concerning Toleration* (1685).[48]

Without depicting the decades after 1660 as a period of inexorable secularization, there can be little doubt that those who wanted to defend the full panoply of traditional Christian dogma and metaphysics against its critics increasingly faced an uphill struggle.[49] We would look in vain in England for the *Crépuscule des mystiques* which we find in France at the end of the seventeenth century, because English Protestantism was little given to mysticism as such anyhow in comparison to Counter-Reformation Catholicism in France, but a more moralistic, more

---

[47] See Hours, 'De la piété personelle', who sees the conspicuous piety of the aging king only as pose. See, however, also Sylvène Édouard, 'Le messianisme de Louis XIV: un modèle espagnol?', in Sabatier and Torrione, ¿*Louis XIV espagnol?*, pp. 255–270. See also more recently Alexandre Maral, *Le Roi-Soleil et Dieu* (Paris, 2012), pp. 223–288.

[48] John Locke, *Political Writings*, ed. David Wootton (London, 1993), p. 396: 'A church then I take to be a voluntary society of men, joining themselves together' (*An Essay Concerning Toleration*). See also John Locke, *An Essay Concerning Toleration and Other Writings on Law and Politics, 1667–1683*, eds. J. R. Milton and Philip Milton (Oxford, 2006); and John Marshall, *John Locke, Toleration and Early Enlightenment Culture. Religious Intolerance and Arguments for Religious Toleration in Early Modern and 'Early Enlightenment' Europe* (Cambridge, 2006).

[49] lair Worden, 'The Question of Secularisation', in Alan Houston and Steve Pincus (eds.), *A Nation Transformed: England after the Restoration* (Cambridge, 2001), pp. 40–60.

individualistic and one might say more pragmatic, less metaphysical concept of religion certainly posed problems for the very idea of sacral kingship in England in the late seventeenth century. Among the educated the first signs of a theological rationalism became visible at this stage which developed a tendency to reduce Christianity to a 'providential deism' based more on 'natural' religion than on scripture and its teachings.[50] Such a rational religion clearly left little place for traditional divine right kingship and its sacerdotal aspects, although the ruler might ultimately still play an important, possibly even providential role as the heroic champion of spiritual freedom in the fight against prelacy, superstition and 'priest-craft'.[51]

Of course the re-established Church of England provided a bulwark against any attempts to subject faith to individual judgement and reason and to disenchant the world in this way, but its hold on society as a whole remained always – even before 1688 – somewhat tenuous and it was itself at times influenced, not to say infected, by the rationalism which it claimed to combat.[52] In any case it was by no means always an easy let alone submissive ally of the Restoration monarchy. Many convinced royalists had sought to re-establish a close cooperation between divine right kingship and a church governed by bishops who derived their own authority from God after 1660. Only such a partnership could in their opinion guarantee that England did not succumb once more to the forces of disorder and rebellion.[53] But this alliance had its price. The old royalists who had been forced to lie low after 1649 wanted a king who accepted the legacy his father had left him and ruled church and state accordingly. Moreover the representatives of the restored Church of England, such as Gilbert Sheldon who acted as Archbishop of Canterbury from 1663 to

---

[50] Charles Taylor, *A Secular Age* (Cambridge, MA, 2007), pp. 221–234, for a general account of these changes in the late seventeenth and early eighteenth century affecting both England and France.

[51] Mark Goldie, 'Priestcraft and the Birth of Whiggism', in Nicholas Phillipson and Quentin Skinner (eds.), *Political Discourse in Early Modern Britain* (Cambridge, 1993), pp. 209–231.

[52] John Spurr, 'Religion in Restoration England', in Lionel K. J. Glassey (ed.), *The Reigns of Charles II and James VII & II* (Basingstoke, 1997), pp. 90–124; John Spurr, *The Restoration Church of England, 1646–1689* (New Haven, CT, 1991), pp. 249–269; Stefan Weyer, *Die Cambridge Platonists. Religion und Freiheit in England im 17. Jahrhundert* (Frankfurt, 1993), pp. 137–154.

[53] For the Anglican Church after 1660 see Spurr, *The Restoration Church*; cf. for the Restoration settlement also Paul Seaward, *The Cavalier Parliament and the Reconstruction of the Old Regime, 1661–1667* (Cambridge, 1989), and I. M. Green, *The Re-Establishment of the Church of England, 1660–1663* (Oxford, 1978). For theories of church government see now the important work by Jacqueline Rose, *Godly Kingship in Restoration England: The Politics of the Royal Supremacy 1660–1688* (Cambridge, 2011).

1677 were not reluctant to tell the king what they expected of him and to thwart his plans in parliament when their advice went unheeded.[54]

The 'Lambeth model' of monarchy, if we are to call the version of sacral kingship based on a firm alliance with a powerful episcopal estate whose members enjoyed their authority iure divino, thus, therefore had a number of drawbacks for the Crown after 1660. However, given the impact Charles I's death as a martyr and the book which had extolled this martyrdom, *Eikon Basilike*, had after the Restoration, it was difficult to escape from such a vision of kingship entirely. Whoever had written *Eikon Basilike*, the king himself or his chaplain John Gauden, had tried to ensure that Charles I's heir could never really abandon the Church of England let alone commit himself to an alliance with the Presbyterians or other non-Anglican Protestants without betraying the memory of his father.[55]

After the Restoration there might still have been a chance to reach a lasting *modus vivendi* with the Dissenters and in particular with the more moderate English Presbyterians who had after all made the Restoration possible in the first place. But such attempts were undermined again and again by the memory of Charles I's death on the scaffold enshrined in *Eikon Basilike*. Thus *Eikon Basilike* contradicted Charles II's attempts to appear as tolerant king and as the ruler of all Englishmen (and women) and possibly even the crypto-Presbyterian Scots and Catholic Irish as well, regardless of their religious convictions, and not just the head of a royalist party which after many defeats had finally proved victorious, or as Sean Kelsey has put it: 'Eikon Basilike [. . .] contributed powerfully to the growing crisis of representation that beset the political discourse of the age.'[56]

Charles II must have been aware of the pitfalls of committing himself too much to the cult of his martyred father. In any case, he clearly felt uneasy about the more fulsome aspects of sacral monarchy and sacerdotal kingship despite his enthusiasm for healing the scrofula. At least the way he conducted his private life could be seen as a permanent denial of the idea that the royal body was in some sense sacred. Other kings had mistresses as well of course, not least Louis XIV before 1683, but the way Charles II paraded the less salubrious aspects of his sex life in

---

[54] Victor D. Sutch, *Gilbert Sheldon Architect of Anglican Survival* (The Hague, 1973); and Jones, *Royal Politician*, pp. 47–50.

[55] Sean Kelsey, 'The King's Book: Eikon Basilike and the English Revolution', in Nicholas Tyacke (ed.), *The English Revolution, c. 1540–1720: Politics, Religion and Communities* (Manchester, 2007), pp. 150–169. It is significant that the Duke of York, the later James II, rejected the authenticity of *Eikon Basilike*: Callow, *The Making*, p. 153.

[56] Kelsey, 'Eikon Basilike', p. 163.

public remained nevertheless remarkable. In some sense debauchery, serial fornication and the culture of pornography some of Charles's courtiers indulged in could be seen as the strongest antidotes to religious fanaticism. Unfortunately they also undermined what was left of the sacred aura of kingship after the regicide and presented a version of kingship which was not easily acceptable to the Anglican royalists who provided the bedrock of support for the restored monarchy in 1660 as much as during the Exclusion Crisis 1678–1681.[57]

With all his self-indulgence and his cynicism Charles was, however, on other occasions quite capable of appreciating the value of ceremony and state ritual for the prestige of the monarchy. Although personally rather easy going and affable and no great friend of the over precise ceremonial practised at other courts, in Spain in particular,[58] he could at times use the language of ceremony deliberately to enhance his authority and to snub his opponents. This became particularly visible during the last years of his reign when the king became also less accessible as stricter rulers were enforced at court. Thus recent research has demonstrated that England – at least towards the end of Charles's reign – was much more of a dynamic baroque monarchy than historians have often admitted.[59] What is more, having overcome the threat to monarchy which the Exclusion Crisis posed, Charles left a crown to his brother and heir, which seemed to give the king an almost undisputed authority in most matters both secular and ecclesiastical.

James II of England: Sacral Authority Reasserted

When James II ascended the throne both the power of the Stuart dynasty and the authority of the Church of England were more firmly established than ever since 1660. In retrospect James's real achievement seems to have been to have destroyed everything his brother had built and obtained since 1678 within less than four years, the alliance with the hierarchy of the Church of England, the loyalty of the Tories, and the widespread

---

[57] Julia Marciari Alexander (ed.), *Politics, Transgression and Representation at the Court of Charles II* (New Haven, CT, 2007).

[58] Paul Hammond, 'The King's Two Bodies: Representations of Charles II', in Jeremy Black and Jeremy Gregory (eds.), *Culture, Politics and Society in Britain, 1660–1800* (Manchester, 1991), pp. 13–48, at p. 22.

[59] Anna Keay, *The Magnificent Monarch: Charles II and the Ceremonies of Power* (London, 2008), pp. 171–206; cf. Brian Weiser, *Charles II and the Politics of Access* (Woodbridge, 2003), pp. 74–87; and Matthew Jenkinson, *Culture and Politics at the Court of Charles II, 1660–1685* (Woodbridge, 2010). See also Kevin Sharpe, *Rebranding Rule: The Restoration and Revolution Monarchy, 1660-1714* (London, 2013).

support which he enjoyed both in England and Scotland among all those who were prepared to pay a high price to avoid another civil war.

In fact James's keenest defenders could hardly argue that he was a clever and astute politician. The question, however, is what his vision of kingship was? Clearly this vision cannot be easily separated from his faith as a Catholic. About 15 years before he became king he had converted to Catholicism. Given the fact that most of his subjects outside Ireland were Protestants and that anti-Popery was such a crucial ingredient in both English and Scottish political culture this move can only explained by a deep personal conviction. James seems to have been genuinely convinced that loyalty to Rome was the only way to save his soul. His most recent biographer has written: 'it seems as if the Duke's conversion was undertaken with little thought to political dogma, or to finding the religion best suited to the propagation of a foreign brand of absolutism. It was instead a uniquely individual response to a basic quest for truth and scriptural authority that was totally in keeping with James's serious nature and rather crude conception of all human relationships.'[60] However, the same author in a later book on James in exile asserts that James deliberately committed himself to a vision of sacral and indeed 'theocratic kingship' in which Catholicism and the notion of the divine right monarchy became fused. Callow speaks of a 'commitment to an explicitly Roman Catholic vision of the Stuart dynasty, which bound the theory of a divinely ordained kingship passed on from father to son to an unbreakable commitment to the Church of Rome'.[61] Of course, to some extent this attempt to present himself both as a king and as a would-be saint was a reaction to the experience of defeat and motivated by a feeling of personal sinfulness – which he now strove to overcome. But clearly life in exile gave James a chance to indulge in a religious vision of his own life and role as a king, which had already been present although in a more subdued form before 1688. For many historians this obsession with his own salvation and with the religious aspects of his role as a monarch shows that James was a man governed by bigotry and quixotic ideas of kingship as a religious mission. Sacral monarchy in this perspective had really come to an end with the execution of Charles I and all attempts to revive it, in particular if undertaken with such unmitigated fervour as James II showed – and not with the self-conscious irony Charles II displayed –, could only end in failure.[62] Other historians like Steve

[60] Callow, *Making*, p. 151.

[61] Callow, *King in Exile*, p. 307, and for the theocratic vision of kingship p. 309.

[62] See for example Monique and Bernard Cottret, 'La Sainteté de Jacques II et les miracles d'un roi defunt', in Edward Corp (ed.), *L'autre exil: Les Jacobites en France* (Paris, 1993), pp. 79–106, and Bernard Cottret, 'Ecce Homo. La crise de l'incarnation royale en

Pincus take James II's attempt to create a new model of Catholic kingship more seriously. If we follow Pincus James II was not such a bad politician after all. His policies were 'neither foolish nor unrealistic'. Rather they provided at core a realistic model of a sort of 'catholic modernity' which had found its apogee in Louis XIV's France.[63] 'Modern' for Pincus means primarily rational, efficient, with the capacity to create new structures of power and authority not hampered by mere tradition.

However, at closer examination this was not the driving force behind James's vision of kingship and government. What was really at the core of his self-perception but also to some extent of his political agenda was an ideal, which had been quite alien to his brother: sincerity. James was convinced that sacral monarchy – and he certainly did see his role as a king as one which was divinely sanctioned and which was similar in some ways to that of a priest – could only work when it was based on the personal religious commitment and piety of the ruler.[64] His brother had played with the trappings of sacral monarchy, he had submitted himself to all the rituals which were part of this vision of kingship, the regular attendance at church and the healing of the scrofula for example, but he remained convinced that ritual was enough and could stand on its own. As long as he did not openly disavow the teachings of the Church of England – and he was careful not to do so until the very end of his life – these rituals had an innate force which need not be reaffirmed by displays of personal piety; in fact, to lead the cheerful life of an unrepentant sinner was for Charles not in contradiction to his role as a sacred monarch. But to some extent this was a model of kingship, which no longer quite worked in the late seventeenth century, certainly not in England where religious sensibilities even outside the communities of Dissenters had been so much shaped by the legacy of Puritanism. Ritual had to be founded in some sort of sincere and visible conviction otherwise it lost its credibility and could all too easily be undermined as mere show and playacting.[65]

Angleterre (1649-1688-1701)', in Maria-Christian Pitassi (ed.), *Le Christ entre Orthodoxie et Lumières* (Geneva, 1994), pp. 77–99.

[63] Steve C. A. Pincus, *1688: The First Modern Revolution* (New Haven, CT, 2009), p. 122.

[64] James's personal piety is not that easy to fathom for the years before he went into exile but it was certainly inspired by contemporary French Catholicism, see Steve Pincus, 'The European Catholic Context of the Revolution of 1688–89: Gallicanism, Innocent XI and Catholic Opposition', in Alan I. Macinnes and Arthur H. Williamson (eds.), *Shaping the Stuart World, 1603–1714* (Leiden, 2006), pp. 79–114, at p. 93; on Bossuet as an author who had great influence in England; cf. John Miller, *James II: A Study in Kingship* (London, 1978), pp. 58–60. For James's piety and devotions in exile see Edward T. Corp, *A Court in Exile: The Stuarts in France, 1689–1718* (Cambridge, 2004), pp. 234–243.

[65] On the relationship between ritual and sincerity see Adam B. Seligman, Robert P. Weller, Michael J. Puett and Bennett Simon, *Ritual and Its Consequences. An Essay on the Limits of*

If kings wanted to give legitimacy to their authority endowing it with a specific religious aura, they had to fashion themselves as exemplary Christians, as both Louis XIII and Charles I had done at least when they were about to die and in moments of crisis long before. This was a lesson even Louis XIV was to learn in the 1680s although his real personal piety was probably never a very deep one, but at least he now played the role of the personally devout ruler, including a family life which was (after 1683) by and large in harmony with the teachings of the church.[66]

Louis XIV became more intolerant to the extent that he became more devout. This was not the case with James II. Because of his emphasis on sincerity in religion and his more individualistic piety his commitment to toleration seems to have been largely genuine,[67] although he did hope and assume that religious freedom would favour the church with the better arguments, in his opinion Rome. The real problem with James's religious fervour and his conviction that sacral kingship had to be founded in personal piety was that the personal religious commitment which was to give credibility and coherence to his role as a sacerdotal king was not an Anglican but a Catholic one and, thus, to all intents and purposes incompatible with the creed of the church by law established. But then the faith of the Church of England with its many fudged compromises in theology and regarding its ecclesiastical structure did not necessarily foster or even value the religious sincerity and straightforwardness which James so cherished, and so his conversion was in some ways a natural consequence of his highly individualized conception of what religion was about.

Moreover, James II was convinced that he was both *rex et sacerdos*, that he had – almost – priestly powers and could, although a Catholic, use his position as head of the Church of England not just to appoint his clients and supporters as bishops and to transform university colleges into Catholic seminaries but also to impose a policy of toleration without reference to parliamentary statutes. He felt entirely entitled to force Anglican clergy to comply with this policy due to his exalted

Sincerity (Oxford, 2008), in particular p. 118. On the need for the individual to develop an '*eingeübte Selbstbeschreibung*' (the equivalent of sincerity in many ways) under the constraints of a confessionalised faith see also Niklas Luhmann, *Gesellschaftsstruktur und Semantik. Studien zur Wissenssoziologie der modernen Gesellschaft*, vol. III (2nd edn, Frankfurt, 1998), p. 252.
[66] Hours, 'La piété personelle'.
[67] Miller, *James II*, pp. 144–145; cf. idem, 'James II and Toleration', in Eveline Cruickshanks (ed.), *By Force or by Default? The Revolution of 1688–89* (Edinburgh, 1989), pp. 8–27, and for the period after 1689, Corp, *Court in Exile*, pp. 156–157, 234–248. For a different interpretation Pincus, *1688*, pp. 163–178; see also Michael Mullett, *James II and English Politics, 1678–1688* (London, 1994).

semi-sacerdotal position. Official and semi-official publications justifying his Declarations of Indulgence in 1687 and 1688 are highly revealing for this vision of kingship.

In one of the semi-official tracts which were disseminated in 1687–1688 to justify James's decision to suspend all laws against recusants and Dissenters the author argued that the 'King of England is not only a *mixt* Person, but in some sense he may be termed a Spiritual Person'. The very fact that the king was not just crowned but anointed demonstrated 'a kind of Sacredness'. To prove this the author even quoted a commentary on the Pragmatical Sanction of France – on the assumption that the kings of France and England who were both equally anointed shared the same character of being more than mere laymen. But then 'if our King (as undoubtedly he is) be a spiritual person it is not improper for him to grant Indulgence in matters Spiritual'.[68]

If, however, the character of the king as a spiritual person were denied, then 'he could not so properly be Head of the Church in England'. What is more, being head of the church the king must be presumed to have the same power to grant indulgences as the Pope had before the Reformation, and so it was only up to him to decide to what extent individuals or entire communities and churches should enjoy liberty of conscience.[69] It is somewhat surprising to see supporters of a Catholic monarch acting as head of a Protestant church, claiming the same powers for the king which some of Henry VIII's theologians, including Cranmer, had claimed for the Tudor monarch in rebellion against Rome: that is the capacity to act both as prince and priest and as a sort of lay patriarch with the full panoply of powers which the Pope had enjoyed in the past. However, it was just such a Caesaro-papism which was at the heart of James's concept of kingship, at least as far as his church policy was concerned. Such an approach may seem so self-contradictory that it was bound to fail, and fail it did indeed. However, there was a vociferous minority of Anglican divines who were prepared to supply the king with all the arguments he needed to underpin this sacerdotal kingship[70] and given enough time

[68] *The King's Right of Indulgence in Spiritual Matters, with the Equity Thereof, Asserted, by a Person of Honour and Eminent Minister of State Lately Deceased* (London, 1688), p. 37. The tract had originally been written – but not published – by Bulstrode Whitelocke for Charles II in 1663. For the context see Jacqueline Rose, *Godly Kingship in Restoration England: The Politics of the Royal Supremacy 1660–1688* (Cambridge, 2011), pp. 169–170, 185.

[69] *The King's Right of Indulgence*, p. 38.

[70] On supporters of James policy, in particular Thomas Pierce and Samuel Parker, see Rose, *Godly Kingship*, pp. 139–140, 228, and Gordon J. Schochet, 'Between Lambeth and Leviathan: Samuel Parker on the Church of England and Political Order', in Nicholas Phillipson and Quentin Skinner (eds.), *Political Discourse in Early Modern Britain* (Cambridge, 1993), pp. 189–208.

James could promote these men within the church and make sure that they would govern the more important episcopal sees. This was probably one of the reasons William Sancroft as Archbishop of Canterbury and many of his brethren raised the standard of (passive) resistance against the king in spring 1688. In refusing to read the king's Declaration of Indulgence from the pulpits and in instructing the inferior clergy to act accordingly they directly attacked the legitimacy of the king's rule.[71]

In attacking James's policies the seven bishops who openly protested against the king's reissued Declaration of Indulgence in May 1688 tried to stage a virtual Anglican revolution, a revolution not in the sense that James was replaced by another monarch but in the sense that the king was forced to consult his *consiliarii nati* in matters of ecclesiastical policy and to renew the alliance with the Tory Anglicans which had provided the basis of royal authority in the years 1681–1686.[72] The king from a High Anglican point of view may have been God's anointed but he had no real sacerdotal power and had to govern the church in accordance with the doctrines taught by its hierarchy. Otherwise he risked being confronted by a massive wave of passive disobedience as he was in 1688.[73]

Of course, what ultimately proved to be James's undoing was not just the attack on his authority orchestrated from Lambeth Palace by Archbishop Sancroft but also his perceived subservience to France. The fact that Louis XIV decided to abrogate the Edict of Nantes in the same year in which James came to power had a devastating effect. In some sense Louis's crusade against the Protestants and James's campaign for toleration in England were two faces of the same coin, not in the sense that both James and Louis were proponents of Catholic absolutism who wanted to extirpate heresy at all costs, as many contemporaries and a number of historians, most recently Steve Pincus, have argued, but in a more complicated way.[74] To the extent that Louis became more

---

[71] Spurr, *Restoration Church*, pp. 88–95.

[72] For the seven bishops, Sancroft of Canterbury and the bishops of Bath and Wells, Ely, Chichester, Peterborough, St. Asaph, and Bristol, see Tim Harris, *Revolution: The Great Crisis of the British Monarchy, 1685–1720* (London, 2006), pp. 260–264; also Mark Goldie, 'The Political Thought of the Anglican Revolution', in R. Beddard (ed.), *The Revolutions of 1688* (Oxford, 1991), pp. 103–136, and William Gibson, *James II and the Trial of the Seven Bishops* (Basingstoke, 2009).

[73] Rose, *Godly Kingship*, pp. 157–162.

[74] For Pincus's position see his statement: 'French Gallicanism provoked more papally inclined Catholics to enunciate an alternative vision for the Church and society at large. Just as the court Catholicism in the 1680s cannot be properly understood without appreciating its continental context, so the opposition to the French-tinged Catholicism had continental roots.' See Steve Pincus, 'The European Catholic Context', p. 114.

ostentatiously devout as a king and came to embrace a vision of sacerdotal kingship he became more intolerant, whereas for James his vision of sacerdotal kingship founded in personal piety led – at least for the time being – to a programme of religious toleration; partly for the simple reasons that James's co-religionists were hitherto a persecuted religious minority but probably also because James's faith, which was after all the faith of a convert, was more individualist and less conventional than that of his French counterpart and put greater emphasis on personal religious experience.[75] Moreover, as we have seen, for James the clearest expression of his power as supreme governor of the church and as a king in the tradition of David, Solomon and Constantine was his right to grant indulgences to religious minorities – for Louis it was the opposite: it was his ability to unite all his subject behind him and have them all to subscribe to one creed.

In 1688 James II was replaced by a king who claimed with sufficient plausibility in the eyes of many observers to be the Godly prince, acting in the name of providence to save both Protestantism and English liberty from the French tyrant and his English henchman, very much in the tradition of Elizabeth I. His vision of monarchy was definitely not a predominantly secular one, but it lacked the elements of sacerdotal kingship which had been so important to James II and were to become even more important when he lived in exile in France during the last 12 years of his life. Moreover, William III's model of monarchy was more easily compatible with an Erastian and radically Protestant anti-clericalism, which had gained ground in the 1670s and 80s, than James's vision of sacral monarchy.[76]

Conclusion: The Rise and Fall of Sacral Kingship

In France Louis XIV reinforced the sacral and the confessional elements in the representation of the French monarchy from the 1680s onwards. Being the successor of Saint Louis became more important to him now than being a modern Alexander or a new incarnation of Emperor Augustus, let alone a royal Apollo. This tendency to re-confessionalize monarchy became even more pronounced to the extent that political and military victories proved to be elusive after about 1690, as we have seen.

---

[75] On James's policy of toleration see most recently Scott Sowerby, 'Of Different Complexion: Religious Diversity and National Identity in James II's Toleration Campaign', *English Historical Review* 124 (2009), pp. 29–52. See also idem., 'James II's Revolution. The Politics of Religious Toleration in England, 1685-1689' (PhD thesis Harvard, 2006).

[76] Tony Claydon, *William III and the Godly Revolution* (Cambridge, 1996).

There-confessionalization of the Bourbon monarchy, partly perhaps even an imitation of Habsburg models of monarchical culture and certainly developed in competition with Vienna, was successful enough for the time being at least as far as domestic policy was concerned despite the revolt of the *Camisards*. But undoubtedly it posed a major obstacle to all attempts to achieve an accommodation between the monarchy and a secularizing Enlightenment in the eighteenth century. Louis XIV had irrevocably committed himself to a revived model of sacral monarchy which found it difficult to withstand the test of time after his death, but could no longer be abandoned either without destroying the foundations of royal authority.

England came, at least at first glance, much nearer than in the past to the French model of government during the personal rule of Charles II in the years 1681–1685. The king finally after many vacillations decided to ally himself without visible reservations with the Anglican Church and those among its clergy who rejected all calls for toleration as much as any attempts for a more comprehensive approach to church government, which would have allowed the more moderate Dissenters to find some sort of home within the Church of England. In the same way in which Louis XIV emphasized the unity between church and crown more forcefully than ever in the 1680s to the detriment both of the Protestants and of the papal supremacy, Charles committed himself, though perhaps for merely tactical reasons, to a state church which tended to emphasize that loyalty to the king and allegiance to the established church were largely interchangeable and synonymous.

But the legacy of the Reformation was not easy to combine with any consistent model of monarchy. There was the idea of the king as a new Constantine, a truly godly ruler, trampling under his feet not just the Pope but all lordly prelates. This essentially anti-clerical model of kingship had in the past been invoked to justify the rejection of the papal supremacy as much as the fight against the theocratic variety of Calvinism which Scottish Presbyterianism represented. But such a model was at odds with a Tory vision of church and monarchy for which episcopacy *iure divino* and the autonomy of the church were so important. On the other hand, there was the option of sacerdotal kingship, with the ruler playing to some extent the role of a priest-king inspired by the example of the saint-like Charles I (and perhaps more distant examples such as Edward the Confessor as well).[77] and guided by his episcopal councillors whose role

---

[77] See for example Henry Keepe, *True and Perfect Narrative of the Strange and Unexpected Finding the Crucifix and the Gold Chain of the Pious Prince St. Edward the King [. . .] presented to [. . .] King James the Second* (London, 1688).

was ultimately indispensable in giving credibility to this vision of monarchy, which had found its expression in *Eikon Basilike*. Such a model, however, imposed enormous constraints on the freedom of action the monarch had in all matters of ecclesiastical policy, not to mention the fact that even among high Anglicans many theologians were increasingly inclined to down play the quasi sacerdotal powers of a king whose support for the church was not beyond doubt. What is more, this model encountered the growing resistance not only of those who preferred other varieties of Protestantism to the – in their eyes – Popish ceremonialism of Tory Anglicans but also of those who had become increasingly sceptical about any sort of church dominated by an authoritarian clergy. In the late seventeenth century the traditional anti-clericalism and Erastianism of English Protestantism became partly transformed into a more general rejection of 'priestcraft' and religious intolerance in any form.[78] One may consider this opposition against an intolerant national church and all it entailed as part of a much more wide-ranging process of secularization affecting politics society and culture or one may discern here a move towards a more individualized, subjective form of non-doctrinal religion, but in any case the fight against priestcraft was opposed to a vision of kingship which saw the king himself as a honorary member of the clergy and certainly not as a mere lay-man. James II, as we have seen, nevertheless tried to combine both models of kingship, the Constantinian one and the sacerdotal clerical one, albeit in its Catholic version, but this combination failed to create a lasting religious foundation for monarchy. Moreover it was tainted by its association with French power and ambitions and the crusading Counter-Reformation Catholicism which Louis XIV seemed to have embraced in the 1680s, at a time when the confessional and sacral aspects of French monarchical culture were visibly re-enforced to the detriment of other languages of representation which might more easily have an appeal even in Protestant countries Although James II's Gallican leanings entailed by no means – as Steve Pincus seems to assume in his recent account of the Revolution of 1688 – a slavish submission to France as such,[79] James's alliance with Louis XIV was seen as a grave error even by many Catholics in Europe.[80]

---

[78] Mark Goldie, 'Priestcraft and the Birth of Whiggism'; cf. Justin A. I. Champion, *Republican Learning: John Toland and the Crisis of Christian Culture, 1696–1722* (Manchester, 2003), and idem, *The Pillars of Priestcraft Shaken: The Church of England and its Enemies, 1160–1730* (Cambridge, 1992).

[79] See the review by Scott Sowerby, 'Pantomime History', *Parliamentary History* 30/2 (2011), pp. 236–258.

[80] *The Spirit of France and the Politick Maxims of Lewis XIV Laid Open to the World* (London, 1689), p. 43. The original tract was probably written in Dutch, then translated into

James's flight from England in 1688 largely ended the tradition of sacerdotal kingship in England – although his daughter Anne continued to heal the scrofula as Queen until her death in 1714 – but it would be a mistake to assume that it therefore amounted to a full-scale secularization of kingship and politics in Britain. It remains, however, true that after 1688 kingship in England and in France developed in opposite directions and that the medieval legacy, which they had had in common in the past, receded now more and more into the background. Both monarchies had attempted to reemphasize the sacral nature of royal power, but both were going to enter the eighteenth century on very different paths.

French and only subsequently into English. For James's somewhat fraught relations with Rome before 1688 see also Eoin Lorcan Devlin, 'English Encounters with Papal Rome in the Late Counter-Reformation c. 1685-1697' (PhD thesis, Cambridge University, 2010), pp. 91–98. – For the mistrust which James's reliance on France provoked in England itself among Protestants see Roger Morrice, *The Entring Book of Roger Morrice, 1677–1691*, 7 vols., ed. Mark Goldie (London, 2007), vol. IV, p. 5 (April 1687), and vol. III, pp. 273 and 336 (January 1687).

Afterword

13   Rethinking the Relations of Elites and Princes in Europe, from the 1590s to the 1720s

Nicholas Canny

The chapters in this volume range extensively over the monarchies, principalities and empires of Europe during the early modern centuries, and one chapter on France also traces developments there as far back as the fourteenth century. Collectively they confirm that during the early modern centuries, a growing tension developed in most jurisdictions throughout Europe between the demands of rulers for extra revenue to defend their inheritances both from external threat and internal subversion, and the belief of the heads of great noble houses that they were honour-bound to defend their patrimonies and to protect their dependents and subordinates in the regions where they were socially dominant from interference by the agents of any centralizing authority. These tensions, as we have long known from the extensive literature published from the 1950s to the 1970s on the so-called General Crisis of the Seventeenth Century, frequently spilled over into open conflict whenever rulers sought to involve themselves with new-style, large-scale warfare of long duration. When this occurred, central rulers sometimes mandated officials, without sanction from the provincial elites, either to recruit soldiers for the royal army directly within the regions or to collect taxes within the provinces to support the war effort. The General Crisis literature makes it abundantly clear that resistance also manifested itself whenever a king, queen or regent sought to curtail privileges (especially exemption from taxes) or to reduce sources of income that elite groups had come to consider as entitlements.[1] Opposition to royal intervention in the localities could be even more trenchant whenever central authorities appointed agents to survey, or otherwise estimate the wealth of, the territories over which they ruled. In France, for example, it was common for provincial estates to

---

[1] Hamish Scott has provided bibliographic details on the General Crisis debate in his chapter in this volume; see pp. 45–6 at nn.4–6; see also J. H. Elliott, 'The General Crisis: A Debate without End', in J.H. Elliott, *Spain, Europe and the Wider World, 1500–1800* (New Haven, CT, 2009), pp. 52–73, and the subject has been given a completely new life in Geoffrey Parker, *Global Crisis: War, Climate Change and Catastrophe in the Seventeenth Century* (New Haven, CT, 2013).

hinder the attempts by central government to map their regions.[2] Similarly in Ireland many provincial proprietors of the late sixteenth and early seventeenth centuries obstructed the endeavours of English surveyors and cartographers who had been assigned by the government to ascertain and delineate the ownership of land in the provinces as a preliminary to plantation. Such opposition did not prevent Ireland acquiring the doubtful distinction, by the late seventeenth century, of having been surveyed and mapped more comprehensively than any other jurisdiction in Europe.[3]

The fact that tensions between centres and peripheries seemed chronic and that frequent inter – and intra-jurisdictional conflicts flowed from them, means that there is no justification for assuming, as Ranke and Burckhardt did, that an abstract, impersonal state, such as was comprehended by those familiar with balance-of-power diplomacy in the nineteenth century, had been in embryo since early modern times.[4] Scholars of the 1950s and 1960s who wrote of 'New Monarchies' in Europe at the close of the fifteenth or the outset of the sixteenth centuries were addressing something more tangible because they could identify a cluster of potent and literate rulers (Henry VIII of England, Francis I of France and the Emperor Charles V were cited by some, while others went back to Henry VII of England, Louis XII of France, and Ferdinand and Isabella of Aragon and Castile) who came to power at roughly the same time.[5] However the evidence cited in the several chapters of this volume collectively make it clear that the survival of none of the jurisdictions governed by these rulers was assured. France, for example, which was ruled over by forceful kings in the persons of Francis I and Henry II, came close to being

---

[2] David Buisseret, *Sully and the Growth of Centralized Government in France, 1598–1610* (London, 1968), p. 195

[3] Nicholas Canny, *Making Ireland British, 1580–1650* (Oxford, 2001), p. 138; *Cal. State Papers Ireland, 1608–10* (London, 1874), p. 280; the scientific mapping of Ireland was the achievement of Sir William Petty in the aftermath of the Cromwellian re-conquest of Ireland, on which see Ted McCormick, *William Petty and the Ambitions of Political Arithmetic* (Oxford, 2009).

[4] Jacob Burckhardt, 'The State as a Work of Art', Chapter 1 of *The Civilization of the Renaissance in Italy* (first published 1860; London, 1944 edition), pp. 1–80. See for example the compilation of texts from Leopold von Ranke, Heinrich Treitschke, et al., *Weltgeschichte der Neuzeit, in ihren leitenden Ideen* (Berlin 1939), ed. Kurt L. Walter-Schomburg.

[5] One popular collection of essays on the subject aimed at undergraduate audiences was Arthur J. Slavin (ed.), *The 'New Monarchies' and Representative Assemblies: Medieval Constitutionalism or Modern Absolutism?* (Boston, 1964); Robert von Friedeburg and John Morrill, citing another edition of this work, mentions a cluster of rulers of a previous generation that Slavin, and his contributors, also considered innovative; see Chapter 1 of this volume, p. 1.

dismembered during the Wars of Religion of the later sixteenth century when the Catholic League, which enjoyed the support of the royally connected Guise family, conspired with the Spanish monarchy to frustrate the efforts of the French crown to achieve an accommodation between Protestant and Catholic factions.

When we think more broadly, we can appreciate that even apparently secure states continued to face an uncertain future until well into the eighteenth century. For example, Brandenburg-Prussia, which had been nurtured and developed as a kingdom by Frederick the Great (and by his father before him) to become a European power of the first rank, might well have been dismembered by competing powers, as befell some neighbouring jurisdictions, were it not for some lucky breaks that Frederick achieved on the field of battle when defeat by his opponents seemed imminent.[6] Moreover, while the more effective rulers of the early modern centuries promoted more efficient administrative instruments both for raising and managing armies and for collecting the taxes that covered the cost of these armies, their ambitions were not necessarily to develop a 'nation state' within recognizable 'borders' that nineteenth-century authors had come to consider the natural order of things. Thus while Cardinal Richelieu has frequently been credited with defining natural boundaries for France behind defensible military lines, and while he and Cardinal Mazarin, as Lucien Bély has detailed, dramatically accelerated the growth in the size of the French bureaucracy from having one royal agent for every 2,000 inhabitants, as had been the case in 1515, to having one for every 250 subjects in 1661, the guiding ambition of Louis XIV, whose authority had benefited from the stewardship of the two cardinals, remained that of pursuing his dynastic claims regardless of where that might lead. This exposed him to the charge of his foreign rivals that his ultimate ambition was universal monarchy. Therefore, the determination of others to frustrate any such outcome remained a live issue in the minds of rulers of the early modern centuries for longer than is frequently acknowledged.[7]

Succeeding chapters in this volume challenge the teleological assumptions concerning the evolution of the European state system that have distorted previous understanding of the nature of politics during the early modern centuries. They demonstrate that almost every polity of that time was composite in nature either because of conquest or because of planned, or unanticipated, outcomes of matrimonial

---

[6] Tim Blanning, *Frederick the Great; King of Prussia* (London, 2015).
[7] Anthony Pagden, *Lords of All the World; Ideologies of Empire in Spain, Britain and France, c.1500–c.1800* (New Haven, CT, 1995).

entanglements entered upon by succeeding generations or rulers.[8] Among the unanticipated outcomes was that which resulted from the marriage negotiated by King Henry VII for his daughter Margaret Tudor with King James IV of Scotland. This was favoured by the English king of the time in the belief that it would result in the English monarchy becoming more influential over affairs in Scotland.[9] The unanticipated outcome was that King James VI of Scotland succeeded to the throne of England in 1603, which, apart from the 11 years of Interregnum 1649–1660, and the shared monarchy of King William III, a Stuart would occupy from 1603 until 1714.[10]

The Portuguese royal house initiated similar strategic marriage alliances with their Castilian neighbours with a view to enhancing their prestige within the Iberian Peninsula. The unanticipated outcome there also was that a Castilian monarch, in the person of Philip II of Spain, became one of three claimants to the disputed Portuguese throne in 1580. Then, as Pedro Cardim has shown, Philip made good his claim by sending a Castilian army into the neighbouring kingdom where it exercised a 'swift and intimidating military campaign' that made it possible for Philip to add the Crown of Portugal to the several crowns he already held.[11] The resulting Iberian monarchy consisting of the Crowns of Castile, Aragon and Portugal (and also the kingdom of Navarre that had been acquired by Castile through conquest[12]) ruled also over several jurisdictions in Italy and over vice royalties throughout the world. It was therefore a monarchy in the real sense of that term where, in the words of Pedro Cardim, its ruler had become a 'king of kings', even if the Crowns of all those kings rested on one forehead.[13] Several families at the upper reaches of Portuguese society welcomed the broader horizons and the possibilities for foreign employment that this new political arrangement provided. However, many members of the wider Portuguese political nation came to resent being marginalized within what was, in effect, a universal dispensation operated from Madrid, and they seized the opportunity that presented itself in 1640 to re-establish Portugal as an

---

[8] On composite monarchies see the chapter 'A Europe of Composite Monarchies', in J. H. Elliott, *Spain, Europe and the Wider World, 1500–1800*, pp. 3–24.

[9] John Morrill in his chapter explains how English ambitions to secure Scotland through even more complex dynastic entanglements remained alive into the reign of Edward VI; see Chapter 2 in this volume, pp. 18–19, 25.

[10] The initial Union of Crowns of 1603 was achieved because the Scottish King James VI, a great grandson of Margaret Tudor, succeeded Queen Elizabeth, second daughter to King Henry VIII, to become also King James I of England and Ireland.

[11] See Chapter 8 by Pedro Cardim, p. 217.

[12] Alfredo Floristán ed., *1512: Conquista e incorporación de Navarra* (Barcelona, 2012).

[13] See Chapter 8 by Pedro Cardim, pp. 220–1.

independent kingdom, this time with the Duke of Braganza, who was declared King John IV, as their leader. This opportunity happened when first Catalonia and then Portugal challenged the authority of Castile in a dual revolution that resulted in Portugal, but not Catalonia, breaking away from Castilian rule.[14]

The Union of Crowns effected between England and Scotland in 1603 also gave no assurance of permanency, and even the seemingly secure Parliamentary Union of 1707, sanctioned in both England and Scotland, was disputed by Scottish supporters of the exiled Stuart dynasty when, after the death in 1714 of Queen Anne (the last reigning Stuart monarch), the Elector of Hanover (grandson of Elizabeth the Winter Queen of Bohemia who had been a daughter of King James VI and 1) ascended the British throne as King George I. Significant Scottish opposition to the Hanoverian succession persisted until 1746 when the forces raised largely in the Scottish Highlands to support the Stuart pretender and the soldiers who had accompanied 'Bonny Prince Charlie' from the Continent, were defeated comprehensively at the Battle of Culloden by a second largely-Scottish army fighting in the service of the British crown. This intervention might have led to a Scottish secession or to a civil war in Scotland had the Pretender's army concentrated on making him King of Scotland rather than on ousting King George II from the British throne.[15]

These examples, and others that have been cited by John Morrill is his chapter, show that unifications resulting from dynastic alliances and successions did not necessarily provide secure foundations on which to build a 'nation state'. Indeed John Morrill argues that almost all 'super states' that resulted from dynastic alliances were so unstable that he thinks it more appropriate to refer to them as 'dynastic agglomerates' rather than composite monarchies.[16] If we might look more optimistically at some dynastic arrangements that were negotiated, it strikes me that they became easier to manage, and had therefore a better chance of enduring, when the inheritances in question were contiguous to each other, and when rulers abided by their pledges and those of their predecessors, to uphold the administrative, fiscal, legal, linguistic or cultural peculiarities of the multiple jurisdictions that were being brought together under a single head. However bids to undo these unifications were also almost invariably triggered whenever monarchs, in the interest of bringing greater fiscal, legal, religious or administrative coherence to a composite jurisdiction, disregarded the pledges that had been agreed upon with the

[14] Geoffrey Parker, *Global Crisis*, pp. 267–76.
[15] On Scottish divisions over the Jacobite cause in 1745 see Linda Colley, *Britons: Forging the Nation, 1707–1837* (New Haven, CT, 1992), pp. 79–85
[16] Morrill, Chapter 2, pp. 17–43, esp. at 19–20.

Estates of the various constituent elements of the amalgamations over which they ruled.[17]

Unifications, or extensions of authority, achieved by military conquest could prove more enduring because these usually resulted both in the destruction of elites who might have fostered memories of previous 'liberties', and in the imposition of the administrative, fiscal, legal, religious and cultural norms of the conquering monarchy upon the newly acquired jurisdictions.[18] However, as would be shown in the case of Sweden after the death from a bullet wound of King Charles XII in 1718, territories acquired by force could be lost to rivals as readily as they had been acquired if a ruler suffered an unexpected setback in either war or diplomacy. This proved especially true when any unanticipated reverse occurred before the conquering rulers had reshaped society in the jurisdictions they had conquered.

The chapters in this volume, and the conferences that preceded it, also illustrate how the future of any monarchical jurisdiction was almost always uncertain because it relied on reigning kings or queens leaving an heir, usually a male heir, to succeed to the throne. To reduce uncertainty, increasing care was taken by royal advisors in some monarchies of the early modern period to protect the person of the monarch from the dangers of the battlefield, and to have them meet their obligations to be seen to be warrior kings or queens symbolically rather than actually. When their military campaigns proved successful this could be done most readily by having rulers appear at battle sites on carefully managed ceremonial occasions, such as when accepting the surrender of fortified positions after terms had been negotiated. However political crises sometimes meant that it became more important for rulers to be seen to be militarily active than to be cautious. Thus even women rulers such as Queen Mary I of England, during Wyatt's rebellion in 1554, and her half-sister Queen Elizabeth I, when the Spanish Armada was within sight off the English coast in 1588, cast caution to the wind and appeared before their troops in full public view, and in view of the enemy, to exhort their supporters to greater exertion in defence of the Crown.[19] Also many monarchs (we have already mentioned Charles XII of Sweden and Frederick II of Prussia, to whom we could add Henry IV of France,

---

[17] Elliott, 'A Europe of Composite Monarchies'.

[18] The most single-minded enforcement of dominant norms within a composite jurisdiction was, perhaps, that pursued by the Austrian Habsburgs on which see R. J. W. Evans, *The Making of the Habsburg Monarchy, 1550–1700. An Interpretation* (Oxford, 1979).

[19] On Mary see D. M Loades, *Two Tudor Conspiracies* (Cambridge, 1965), pp. 66–67; on Elizabeth see Garrett Mattingly, *The Defeat of the Spanish Armada* (London, 1959), pp. 290–297.

Christian IV of Denmark and Gustavus Adolphus of Sweden, as well as King James II of Britain and his rival son-in-law Prince William of Orange, who ousted James to become King William III) chose, or had no option but, to participate actively in war. And while Louis XIV, unlike Queen Mary and Queen Elizabeth in England, was careful to remain out of danger when battle was underway, he wanted his French subjects to think of him as a warrior king. His effort to cultivate this image is illustrated by the portrait of Louis, astride a grey horse, leading his army of 120,000 men across the frontier into the Netherlands at the commencement of the Dutch War in 1672, when, in fact, he was sheltering in the security of a monastery some miles from where the action was taking place.[20]

Because kings and queens continued to be sometimes exposed to military hazards, and because life expectation in early modern times was, in any event, altogether more unpredictable than in the western world today, monarchical dynasties (and the jurisdictions that had come to be associated with them) could be optimistic that their line would endure only when the reigning monarch had at least one, and ideally several, potential heirs; usually legitimate sons or brothers. However not even a plenitude of heirs saved the ancient French House of Valois from having to give way to the Bourbons in 1589. When the forceful King Henry II had died following an accident on the jousting field in 1559, the survival of the Valois line had seemed assured because Henry had left several surviving sons, albeit minors. These did succeed as kings of France in rapid succession from 1559 to 1589, but all were to die over the span of 30 years without leaving legitimate heirs. The last Valois was King Henry III who was assassinated in 1589 in one of the more infamous acts of the French Wars of Religion.

While every monarch in every jurisdiction hoped to have many children as an assurance against dynastic failure, fulfilment of their wishes could also be a source of instability because discontented subjects frequently looked to the sons (including even the natural sons) or brothers (even bastard brothers) of a monarch to lend a semblance of legitimacy to their actions whenever they took up arms to oppose unpopular government

---

[20] The canvas, by Adam-Frans van der Meulen entitled 'Louis XIV Crossing into the Netherlands at Lobith', or 'Le Passage du Rhin' or 'Lodewijk XIV trekt bij het Lobith de Rijn over, 12 juni 1672' is on display in the Rijksmuseum, Amsterdam, room 2.22; for discussion of a related subject see E. Croft Murray, 'A Drawing by Charles Le Brun for the Passage Du Rhin in the Grande Galerie at Versailles', in *British Museum Quarterly*, vol. 19 (1954), pp. 58–60, at pp. 58–59; I wish to thank Robert von Friedeburg and the staff of the Rijksmuseum for assistance with this reference regarding the painting in the Rijksmuseum.

policies. There are several well-known examples in the French historical experience of such opposition being led by Princes of the Blood to which Lucien Bély makes reference.[21] Similarly in England a Protestant faction solicited support in July 1553 for Lady Jane Grey (great-grand-daughter of King Henry VII) to pre-empt the succession of the Catholic Queen Mary (the eldest surviving daughter of King Henry VIII) to the English throne.[22] Then between 1679 and 1685 James, Duke of Monmouth, a natural son of King Charles II (the king himself having no legitimate children to succeed him), offered himself as a potential king to the Protestant English Whig faction that was anxious to prevent the Catholic James Duke of York from succeeding his brother Charles as king.[23]

Experience from previous centuries had shown that opposition coun-tenanced by people carrying royal blood in their veins could be even more threatening to established authority whenever the blood relative of the royal house was connected through marriage with nobles from within a particular realm. It was possibly to reduce the likelihood of factional conflict in England that Queen Elizabeth decided against marrying Robert Dudley, earl of Leicester, and she then remained a 'virgin queen' because no royal suitor chosen from abroad was found to meet both her liking and that of her closest advisors.[24] However in not marrying a foreign prince Elizabeth was defying the European norm as an increas-ing number of royal dynasties during the early modern centuries, and including Elizabeth's own sister Mary who had married King Philip II of Spain, found marriage partners among members of other royal houses. In France, for example, the Bourbons proved altogether more reluctant than their Valois predecessors to have royal princes and princesses marry with the high nobility. Such stratagems created the complex dynastic inheritances we have discussed, but also produced a fresh threat to survival because, as Geoffrey Parker has detailed with particular reference to the Habsburg dynasty, inbreeding and crossbreeding between a limited number of royal houses both fostered genetic weaknesses and reduced the chances of procreation.[25]

Monarchies that became entitled to accretions of power and inheri-tances as a by-product of royal intermarriage usually considered

---

[21] See Bély's Chapter 6, pp. 165–6.

[22] Eric Ives, *Lady Jane Grey: a Tudor Mystery* (Oxford, 2009).

[23] John Miller, 'Politics in Restoration Britain', in Barry Coward, (ed.), *A Companion to Stuart Britain* (Oxford, 2003), pp. 399–415.

[24] On debates concerning the Elizabethan succession see Wallace MacCaffrey, *Elizabeth I* (London, 1993).

[25] This point is also made by John Morrill in Chapter 2, pp. 32–6, and is detailed, in the case of the Habsburgs, in Geoffrey Parker, *Global Crisis*, p. 48.

themselves honour-bound to accept and defend such legacies. When they did so, it frequently hindered the fashioning of geographically defined 'nation states', because inheritances could be remote from the core realm of the beneficiary and might include populations who professed different religions or spoke different languages from their new monarch. The Habsburgs (Austrian as well as Spanish) strove to overcome some such difficulties by creating secondary courts where the elite of newly acquired jurisdictions might attend upon the representatives of monarchs, or upon monarchs themselves should they visit these distant domains. This stratagem has been exemplified here by the chapter by Antonio Álvarez-Ossorio Alvariño on the Court of the State of Milan maintained by the King of Spain in his capacity as Duke of Milan.[26] Another is the study by Dries Raeymaekers on the Court and household maintained at Brussels by the Archduke Albert of Austria and his wife and cousin, the Spanish Infanta the Archduchess Isabel Clara Eugenia. While the Habsburgs had devised what seemed reasonable ways of managing such accretions, and usually assured the elites or estates of each new jurisdiction being brought under their authority that they would retain their customary privileges and distinctiveness, this did not always convince rival powers that they should desist from blocking such acquisitions. Such concerns provoked the War of the Spanish Succession, 1702–1713, when the traditional rivals to King Louis XIV of France, other than Spain, opposed the notion of the inheritances of both France and Spain being ruled by Bourbon monarchs.

The concern of rulers over the issue of universal monarchy remained a live issue for longer than is usually thought because, as B. J. García García has demonstrated in his chapter, successive Spanish monarchs actively fostered such an ambition from the time that King Charles I of Spain had become Emperor Charles V to the end of the reign of King Philip IV.[27] They were encouraged to do so in the first instance because dynastic accidents, which supporters of the Habsburgs liked to consider providential, had decreed that a King of Spain should become Emperor at the very moment that forceful leadership was required to halt the advance of Protestantism. Then as Charles V, and later his son, who succeeded him as King Philip II of Spain, set about their task of halting the spread of Protestantism they were seen to be emulating their progenitors who had ousted Islam from Spain. The argument that this had been divinely ordained was all the more persuasive because circumstances had also decreed that Charles V and Philip II became the prime defenders of Christianity, including the Papacy itself, against Turkish naval expansion

[26] See pp. 183–211.   [27] See pp. 127–63.

in the Mediterranean because the army of Spain had prevailed over the forces of the French monarchy in the Italian Wars that had concluded but some decades previously. And another convincing proof that the Spanish monarchy had been specially chosen to fulfil a divine purpose was that Spanish mariners and adventurers had been more successful than those of their rivals in bringing under Christian domination large tracts of the world that had been previously unknown to them. Thus, in the words of B. J. García García, the kings of Spain became champions from quite an early stage of what he describes as 'a fervent "Catholic" confessional militancy', that they made manifest in America and Asia as well as in Europe.[28]

Some of the territories over which the Habsburgs ruled had been acquired by conquest, but most had fallen to Spain by rightful succession to the point where, as Antonio Álvarez-Ossorio Alvariño has phrased it, the King of Spain was 'monarch of the twenty-two kingdoms'.[29] We noted that as the Kings of Spain assembled this portfolio of jurisdictions they usually (but not, for example, so in the case of Navarre) entered into compacts with the Estates of inherited kingdoms assuring them that they would uphold their customary rights. To this extent the agglomeration that emerged was partly the product of negotiation, which resulted also in the creation of a sequence of Councils, located in Castile, to manage the discrete and heterogeneous political entities from which the Spanish monarchy was composed, and to the appointment of officials to administer justice in what continued to be distinct dominions. The elites of these dominions, as has been demonstrated by Antonio Álvarez-Ossorio Alvariño in the case of Milan, wished to control appointment to whatever administrative positions were created.[30] However one underlying characteristic of rule by both the Spanish and Austrian Habsburgs was their concern to circulate the most senior officials regularly between their many and various dominions, including to Spanish Vice Royalties in America. In so far as the Spanish authorities used the word 'state' it was to designate the power exercised by the Crown in each particular dominion rather than to the umbrella 'imperial' structure that held the disparate pieces together. However other rulers considered the expanding authority of the Habsburgs to be threatening and especially so when there seemed no limit to their ability to increase the size of their army and navy because of their ready access to precious metals in Mexico and Peru. For this reason the rulers of other polities, or at least Protestant militants within those jurisdictions, became ever more determined to establish Atlantic

[28] See p. 127.   [29] See p. 183.   [30] See pp. 183–211.

colonies of their own and, while they awaited progress in this respect, they encouraged coalitions to hinder the threatening authority of Spain.[31]

Historians have been attributing so many political developments of the early modern centuries to contingency, that we are forced to ask if we can associate any long-term political change or trends with this period? The chapters in this volume, added to what has been published on the subject over the past half century, confirm that the character of monarchy underwent change everywhere because of the escalating scale and the increasing expense of long-term warfare, which was now usually entered upon either to promote, or to halt, territorial expansion. The sheer cost of engaging in war and the hazards that were consequent upon defeat meant that there were fewer fully sovereign and more extensive political entities in Europe in 1720 than there had been 200 years previously, and there would be fewer still in 1789. This reduction was both a consequence of the many agglomerations, both by conquest and inheritance, that had occurred in the intervening years and of a decline also in the tendency, that had been so apparent throughout the medieval centuries, of provinces or principalities to hive off from a core monarchy to become independent political entities. Breakaways did not cease entirely during the early modern centuries as can be witnessed in the case of the United Provinces which, after a prolonged struggle, finally won international recognition (including recognition from both the Austrian and Spanish Habsburg houses) as an independent polity following the Peace of Westphalia in 1648.[32] And while some new independent entities came into being during these years they were few in number and as in the case of Ireland, which was declared a kingdom within the Crown of England in 1541, many had their seeming independence circumscribed in some way.

Authors in this volume, like those from the 1950s to the 1970s who wrote of the General Crisis of the Seventeenth Century, allude to the frequency with which the attempts by rulers to increase both their military capability and the taxes required to meet the costs of escalating military expenditure, provoked challenges to the 'innovations' that were necessary to the attainment of such ambitions. However, where the original participants in the debate over the existence and character of a General Crisis drew attention to the political and social polarization that resulted from the crisis, the contributors to this volume make repeated reference to the fact that noble elites achieved considerable success either in keeping the

---

[31] Nicholas Canny, 'Confessional Divisions and the Writing of Natural History', in *Proceedings of the British Academy*, vol. 181 (2012), pp. 83–121, esp. 84–104; Geoffrey Parker, *Spain and the Netherlands, 1559–1659. Ten Studies* (2nd edn, London, 1990).

[32] Parker, *Spain and the Netherlands*.

intruding power of central government at arm's length, or in ensuring that they too would benefit from the accretions to monarchical power. Attention is being drawn therefore to the accommodations that were regularly negotiated between monarchs and their more substantial noble subjects. Lucien Bély, speaking from the French experience, explains how those at the upper reaches of society who were opposed to being ruled by regents or favourites, always appreciated that any significant weakening of the authority of monarchy could leave themselves exposed to attack from people beneath them on the social scale. For this reason they, no less than monarchs and their advisors, agreed ultimately to resolve whatever difficulties arose between them through negotiation and compromise rather than through continued confrontation.[33] Therefore, if war, and the cost or war, was the principal occasion for the tensions that developed between kings and nobility, the evidence cited in this volume makes it clear that families from the highest ranks of the nobility usually became reconciled to innovation when they were given the opportunity to become parties to the changes that were being promoted, usually by purchasing commissions in the royal army. Such investment both increased their opportunity to achieve honour and reputation – the prerequisites to being noble – and enhanced their standing within the provinces where their estates were located because they could now recruit soldiers and junior officers into the regiments they had been assigned.

Members of the High Nobility in France, as Lucien Bély makes clear, were interested also in purchasing (and therefore controlling) newly created offices that had been designed to increase crown authority in the provinces, and they took an interest also in influencing crown appointments to local ecclesiastical benefices not least because they wished to see their own younger sons become bishops or abbots.[34] However these very real gains by the higher nobility did not come without cost. In several European monarchies, besides France, it became essential for those nobles who wished to exert any influence over policy to attend upon the person of the monarch at the royal court, given that it was those who were thus positioned to make a favourable impression on monarchs or their closest advisors who stood the best chance of sharing in royal patronage. While all nobles could, theoretically, benefit from royal munificence it was only the wealthiest noble families who could afford to maintain a presence at court. This meant that, in almost all European countries, lesser nobles who had little income besides what came from their rents had perforce to remain in the provinces and fade into political obscurity.

---

[33] Chapter 6 by Bély, pp. 164–179.   [34] Chapter 6 by Bély, pp. 168–70.

The French court culture that was elaborated at Versailles was initially imitative of the culture that had been fostered at the main Habsburg courts at Madrid and Vienna.[35] However Louis XIV sought from an early stage to have his court more magnificent and less pious than the courts maintained by his Habsburg cousins and rivals. His success was such that other monarchs throughout Europe sought to emulate Versailles. This court, and the pale imitations of it that were established elsewhere, served also to facilitate intermarriage between families at the apex of noble society. In seems in the case of France, that while those who carried royal blood in their veins strove to keep it from being diluted by confining their choice of marriage partners for their children to other princely families, those at the top echelons of the French nobility were equally concerned not to marry beneath their rank. Therefore, as they were being denied the possibility of marrying above their station, members of the high nobility strove to forge marriage alliances with lineages of equal rank, and they would contemplate marrying a younger sibling to the daughter of a 'robe' family usually only when such an alliance proved necessary to uphold a family fortune. This meant that families who held positions in the *parlement* in Paris or in the various provincial *parlements*, enjoyed few opportunities to establish links through marriage with noble families of ancient lineage. Despite this, they too could establish a vested interest in the on-going expansion of government both through the purchase of offices that would both yield a return to them in fees and make them part of a service nobility, and by associating themselves with merchants who secured contracts to supply military and naval supplies to the government. Thus, as already mentioned, those of the elite who gained least, or even lost out, from the caste-like society that was emerging in France, were the lesser provincial who became increasingly isolated. Their position was all the more precarious because the peasants who paid rent for the farms they leased from the landowners were being compelled to pay increased taxes to maintain the king's army and the administration. Therefore the most glaring social reconfiguration that resulted from the expansion in the size of government that happened in France and throughout Europe during the early modern centuries was the clearer distinction that emerged between aristocratic families who became associated with courts and the wars that preoccupied these courts, and the families of lesser nobles who suffered a decline in income

---

[35] This point was emphasized at the Rotterdam conference by Jeroen Duindam and a continued comparison between the courts at Versailles and Vienna has been developed in Jeroen Duindam, *Vienna and Versailles: The Courts of Europe's Dynastic Rivals* (Cambridge, 2007).

as well as in status and reputation. Circumstances also continued to be difficult for peasants whose precarious existence was further challenged because young men were being constantly drawn from their villages to serve in the ranks of the army. Another hazard was that village communities frequently fell prey to the depredations of marauding soldiers both when they deserted their posts or were de-mobilized at the close of each of the recurring wars of the period.

While the French kingdom continued to be a conglomerate of provinces and estates which owed allegiance to a common sovereign,[36] it became more centralized over the course of the seventeenth century both because a greatly expanded bureaucracy exerted varying degrees of influence in the several provinces, and because the more prominent families from each province had been brought together in the king's court where, as Lucien Bély has explained, they began to establish friendships and alliances between themselves.[37] Also, while King Louis XIV asserted claim to all inheritances beyond the confines of France to which he, or his wife, or his heirs could show plausible title, the wars that Louis XIV pursued did much to identify boundaries for the kingdom of France. Therefore, while respecting John Morrill's reservations concerning the permanency of any frontier, it became difficult, following the reign of Louis XIV, to imagine an early modern Europe that did not have a kingdom of France located roughly within the frontiers that existed following the Wars of Louis XIV and that were frequently marked by the fortifications Vauban had designed.

Most authors in this volume have identified the establishment of a stable working relationship between monarchs and elites, and the benefits that elites derived from the expansion of the army and the bureaucracy, as the essential guard against political fission. They see that the establishment of stability was also a prerequisite for the development and maintenance of an extensive jurisdiction, which, in the sixteenth and early seventeenth centuries, was best exemplified by the Castilian monarchy, and, then in the later seventeenth century by the France of Louis XIV. For this reason these authors, like those of previous generations, look closely at the political crises that occurred during the minorities of each of Louis XIII and Louis XIV, in the belief that the accommodations then negotiated between incoming kings and the various branches of the nobility was the principal positive outcome of breakdowns that had brought France to the point of implosion.

[36] Though between the fourteenth and the sixteenth century it became increasingly legally enshrined that no king could alienate its provinces anymore from the possessions of the Crown of France, see the contribution of James Collins in Chapter 4, pp. 111–26.
[37] Chapter 6 by Bély, pp. 171–7.

James Collins does not demur from the idea that political innovation in France was the product of crisis, and he too believes that concern that the kingdom would fall apart or be subjected to 'foreign' rule was a major driver of change. For him, however, the fundamental departures from customary practice happened first in the fourteenth century, and again towards the conclusion of the French Wars of Religion of the sixteenth century. Moreover, he contends that the innovative political ideas that changed the character of the monarchy in France emanated not from the great noble families but rather from the educated literate advisors to the monarchy some of whom served as preceptors to future rulers. Some also, he claims, became the principal beneficiaries of the multiplicity of administrative offices that were created by successive monarchs.[38]

For James Collins the chronic uncertainty relating to royal succession was more acute in the fourteenth than in subsequent centuries because royal daughters, who were then usually married to powerful provincial nobles or foreign monarchs, could assert claims to all, or part, of the royal inheritance. Uncertainty was carried even to the point where it seemed for a time that King Edward III of England would succeed to the throne of France, thus creating the possibility that France would become but one of several dominions ruled from London. The response to such challenges, according to James Collins, was that the advisors to the French crown formulated the notion of 'the common good' with the added suggestion that the well-being of crown and commonwealth together were more important than the claims of any one person. On this basis, he contends, they won agreement from the Estates to what became three fundamental laws of the kingdom; the Salic Law by which succession to the throne followed only in the male line; a law decreeing that the royal demesne was inalienable, meaning that it became the responsibility of each monarch to transfer the royal inheritance intact to his successor; and the law giving the king the exclusive right to make public law. Collins acknowledges that these innovations did not prevent the eruption of further succession disputes whenever a reigning king died without leaving a direct male heir. However he believes that the laws did reduce the number of rival claimants on such occasions, saved the kingdom of France from dismemberment, and thus enhanced the reputation of the monarchy.

For James Collins this explains how the French monarchy remained a potent force until the middle of the sixteenth century when it met fresh challenges during the course of the Wars of Religion. The most acute of these, claims Collins, was when Henry of Navarre – a cousin and brother-in-law to the reigning monarch – became the strongest claimant to

[38] On this and subsequent paragraphs see Chapter 4 by James Collins, pp. 124-7.

succeed the childless King Henry III. This occasioned objection because Henry of Navarre was not then a Catholic and had, for long, been a champion and protector of the Protestant cause. The prospect of such a person succeeding to the throne, which became a reality in 1589 after King Henry III had been assassinated, was anathema to the leaders of the Catholic League who argued that the good of the Commonwealth required that the king of France be a committed Catholic who would be ready to uphold Catholicism as the religion of the kingdom in the same way that the king of Spain upheld Catholicism in his dominions. When most advisors to the monarchy were confronted with this challenge they backed the claims of Henry of Navarre who duly became King Henry IV of France despite the fact that supporters of the Catholic League withheld their allegiance. These latter identified themselves instead as defenders of the commonwealth, with the implication that a French commonwealth could exist independently of the king. In response, as James Collins portrays it, the advisors to the monarchy called upon subjects to profess loyalty to the king and state rather than, as previously, to the king and commonwealth. This call for support for king and state, according to James Collins, won general acceptance from most within the elite groups in France who were both weary of internecine conflict and appalled by the chaos into which the kingdom had fallen. Hope was thus fostered that order could be restored by a forceful king with assistance from the state, by which was meant the royal officialdom that held the kingdom together.

This contribution of James Collins dovetails with the others in this volume to the extent that it proceeds from the presumption that the French monarchy was precocious, and to some degree exemplary, in the matter of state formation, and that realignment between the rulers and elites in that jurisdiction proved essential to such development. He also agrees with the other authors in the volume in arguing that the prospect of the monarchy falling apart was a major factor in bringing people to promote, or acquiesce in, change. In so far as he differs from his fellow authors on France, it is in tracing the more significant innovations to episodes that long pre-dated the General Crisis of the Seventeenth Century, and in associating a much broader spread of the social elite, and not the great nobles alone, with the political realignment that saved the monarchy. James Collins also attaches more importance than do his fellow authors, to ideas – speech acts – in promoting change, and he thus gives credit to the role of educated officials in fostering the ideas that led to the development of a French state. And at the same time he attaches less importance than does Lucien Bély to the true bureaucratization of the French state accomplished by Mazarin.

Events in France have received more attention in this volume than those in any other country, which is reflective of scholarly writing on the development of the modern state published over the past half century. This seems reasonable given the wealth and population of France relative to its neighbours during early modern times. However, this emphasis presents the authors in this volume with the challenge of estimating how developments in France were replicated in other jurisdictions of Europe, because this alone would justify generalizations being advanced from the French case.

Hamish Scott, who has taken a more extensive chronological and geographic brief than any other author, is impressed by how monarchies throughout Europe became more stable over the course of the seventeenth century, and how this greater stability was, in almost every instance, related to the 'consolidation of the status and strength of leading families' within the particular jurisdictions. He contends that this 'consolidation of the social elite' was usually, as had been the case in France, related both to the development of royal courts with their associated court cultures, and to the tendency of rulers throughout Europe to assign members of the traditional noble families the responsibility to form the officer corps of the enlarged armies that most monarchs considered vital to their well-being and survival. He finds that those nobles who were appointed to military and diplomatic positions became, in effect, an aristocracy within the ranks of nobility, who conserved and enhanced their positions by strategic marriage alliances, by restrictive inheritance practices aimed at conserving landed inheritances for one male heir, and by accepting gifts of landed estates from their monarchs in return for the services they had rendered. Scott finds that rulers who proved most successful in consolidating their authority within their domains were usually those who came into possession of 'windfall properties', which they could then distribute among those noble families who enjoyed their favour. Some such windfalls resulted from the confiscation of church property, but more became available to rulers when the estates of rebellious subjects were declared confiscate to the Crown, or when rulers acquired control over territories as the fruits of military victory.[39]

The two most extensive land reallocations made during this period were the reassignment by the Austrian Habsburgs of the lands in Bohemia that had belonged to those noble families who, in 1618, had invited the Protestant Prince Frederick of the Palatinate to become their king, and the Cromwellian plantation of Ireland that followed upon the victory of the English Parliamentary army over all in Ireland who had

[39] On this and the subsequent paragraphs see Chapter 3 by Hamish Scott pp. 56-98.

challenged their authority. While these reassignments of property were exceptional, Hamish Scott finds that, during our period, monarchs from almost every jurisdiction throughout Europe ranging from France to Russia to Sweden, gained control of some landed property with which to reward loyal noble families. And, as he details the assignment of landed property by monarchs to families belonging to the ranks of Europe's high nobility, he also traces the close co-operative alliances that successive groups of benefiting aristocracies established with their respective monarchies. Moreover, Hamish Scott finds that those who lost most from such reassignments, both in relative and absolute terms, were the families of the lesser nobility who did not have the opportunity to attract royal favour and whose incomes were being challenged by inflationary forces. And he concurs also that another group whose standard of living was most adversely affected by these Europe-wide developments were the cultivators of the soil who were forced to bear the principal costs (including the human costs) of the wars that were initiated by their betters.

It is clear from what has been said of Portugal by Pedro Cardim that it conformed to that general configuration during the interlude, 1580–1640, when Portugal was ruled from Madrid.[40] Then the high nobility of that kingdom, like their counterparts in Catalonia, worked studiously to become fluent in Spanish as well as Portuguese and grasped the career opportunities that came their way when they attended at the metropolitan court in Madrid. However, in Portugal the lesser nobility preserved some of their vitality, and it was they, in association with the towns, and against the wishes on their social betters, who re-established Portugal in 1640 as a kingdom independent from that of Spain. This suggests that Portugal was more akin to France as that kingdom has been depicted by James Collins, with a broader constituency than that of the great nobles playing a part in the political realignment with monarchy that gave stability to the country. The break with Spain also made it possible for the new Portuguese government to establish alliances with those – notably Britain and France – who had been hostile to Portuguese interests while it had remained part of a pan-Iberian monarchy. Comparison with the English/British experience, as this has been depicted by John Morrill, appears more difficult because it seems to have been only in that case that the Crown encouraged marriages between the nobility in the three jurisdictions that produced a truly 'British' aristocracy at a time when the subjects of the monarchy continued to identify themselves variously as English, Scots or Irish.[41]

---

[40] See Chapter 8 by Pedro Cardim, pp. 212–33.
[41] See Chapter 2 by John Morrill pp. 23–6; most of the examples that Morrill cites to sustain this point relate to the reigns of James VI and I and of Charles I. However the experience of serving at a court in exile on the Continent, 1649–1660, also facilitated the forging of

Developments in the kingdom of Denmark, as these have been depicted by Gunner Lind, resembled those in Portugal to the extent that, following a period of civil turmoil in the early sixteenth century, the great nobility constituted a real aristocracy who, theoretically, elected their king from within the royal family and governed with the king in council. In this respect the nobles were more powerful and independent than their Portuguese counterparts during the interlude 1580–1640. Also, because Denmark was almost constantly at war, the king interacted with his nobles in what Gunner Lind describes as 'an old-fashioned masculine and warlike court'. This was made up of 500–700 male heads of households out of a total population of two million people, and expanded in size down to the third quarter of the seventeenth century as 131 nobles immigrated, 32 from Schleswig and Holstein and 77 from various parts of Germany. The social distance between king and nobility and the population at large was accentuated when, after the addition of the foreigners, German rather than Danish became the language of a court dedicated principally to the pursuit of war at land and sea and within the Baltic and in Germany. In their bilingualism the Danish nobility resembled their Portuguese counterparts but in the Danish case it was the language of the periphery rather than of the core that had become the esteemed one.[42]

Given their indispensability to the Danish war effort, the nobility were able to negotiate an exemption of their own property from taxes and secured for themselves appointment to the senior posts in both the military services and the bureaucracy that was necessary to support them. Those excluded from a place in government seemed reconciled to their lot, until after the military campaign of 1657–1658 that resulted in the effective destruction of the Danish army by their Swedish opponents and the occupation by Swedish troops, of most of the kingdom other than Norway and the city of Copenhagen. Then, the long simmering discontent over the aloofness of the aristocracy gave way to popular outrage and an assault upon the privileges of the nobles who had been shown to be ineffectual in war. Under these circumstances, the clergy and the burgesses of Copenhagen supported the Crown in creating a new Danish army, composed largely of foreigners and officered by professionals,

---

cross jurisdictional alliances between some noble families from the three kingdoms of England, Scotland and Ireland that held good at least during the early reign of King Charles II; this has been touched upon in Mark R. F. Williams, *The Irish in the Exiled Court of Charles II, 1649–1660* (Woodbridge, 2014); see also Williams, 'The Devotional Landscape of the Royalist Exile, 1649-1660', in *Journal of British Studies*, vol.53 (2014), pp. 909–933.

[42] See Chapter 10 by Gunner Lind, pp. 265–286.

which quickly recovered from the Swedes most of what had been lost. These events also enabled the king to free himself from the stranglehold of his nobles and, in 1665, he declared himself an absolute ruler with power to choose his officers and officials on the basis of capability and merit rather than rank. Then, to satisfy his new supporters, the king ended the exemption from taxation that nobles had previously enjoyed and decreed equality between nobles and commoners in the officer corps. This 'revolution of 1665', as Gunner Lind interprets it, brought an end not only to 'the rule of the nobility' but to the beginning also of an economic decline of many aristocratic families once they had lost their tax-free status. The state and society that developed in Denmark after its revolution of 1665 therefore proved even more egalitarian than what had emerged in Portugal after 1640 under the rule of the house of Braganza. Comparisons between what transpired in Denmark with what happened in other jurisdictions in northern Europe that also suffered from endemic warfare would seem more fruitful than comparison with Portugal, or with France for that matter. In this respect, Gunner Lind suggests that, in its persistent warlike character and in its openness to accepting people of talent, including foreigners, into the ranks of its new service nobility, the Danish monarchy came to fit a Baltic model that had been first exemplified in Sweden.

The consideration given by Robert von Friedeburg to developments in Germany shows that there it was the lesser nobility, rather than the burgesses and the clergy, who persisted as a vital force, and continued to assert a moral influence in all principalities through their various estate assemblies. He, like James Collins, also takes account of the role of ideas in shaping developments and finds that the minor nobles were inspired to assert themselves in the various principalities of Germany by the popular literature produced in France during the minority years of both Louis XIII and of Louis XIV that was critical of rule by regents. However, where the French pamphlets had defamed whatever Queen Mother or favourite was considered to be usurping the authority of the ruler, the literature in Germany tended to criticise the Princes themselves together with the 'war despotism' their several governments were pursuing. Robert von Friedeburg explains this departure from what had been the experience in France to a variety of factors. First was the intimate character of the various principalities in Germany, which were small in size and low in population density compared even with provinces in France. Second, German princes, unlike French kings, were not anointed individuals. And third – and here the Danish experience comes to mind – the devastating and continuous character of warfare in many parts of Germany during the Thirty Years' War, 1618–1648, had eroded the credibility of princes and the higher nobles who were thought to have persisted with the fighting longer than was necessary. Von Friedeburg also finds that, even when the fighting had ended, most German principalities were slow to recover their wealth and previous population levels, and that moral authority rested, for a considerable time, with those who aspired to no more than 'a comfortable noble life in the countryside', which would allow them the opportunity to educate their sons in universities within, or close to, the neighbourhoods where they resided. He also finds that, largely due to the straitened circumstances in which they found themselves, German princes found a new moral purpose in becoming champions of the well-being of the tenants and villages on their estates. Poverty and deprivation were, of course, not spread evenly across Germany and some principalities (notably Bavaria) that had suffered but minor military incursions during the War, were reasonably prosperous and with tax burdens lower even than in the more lightly taxed provinces of France. However, according to von Friedeburg, the Estates continued to flourish even in such principalities.[43]

As he describes this situation, Robert von Friedeburg finds that while disputes between princes and Estates occurred regularly across Germany (right until the 1680s), the Estates, and with them the lesser nobility, maintained their constitutional position relative to that of the princes to the middle of the eighteenth century. Besides the previously mentioned factors that contributed to the survival of the Estates, von Friedeburg identifies the occasional succession disputes between different branches of princely families, sometimes sharpened by religious difference. And the Estates also benefited because emperors tended to adjudicate in favour of Estates whenever there were constitutional disputes between Princes and Estates.

As memories of the Thirty Years' War dimmed and as some German princes, notably the Hohenzollerns of Brandenburg-Prussia, sought to become involved in large-scale warfare, Robert von Friedeburg finds that right down to 1740 and the succession to power of Frederick the Great, princes could win support for their military undertakings only when their declared purpose was to protect their territories from invasion. Such restraint meant that the rulers of Brandenburg-Prussia could mobilise for war only when they could enter into agreements with the lesser nobility who were rewarded for their support by being appointed as officers in the armies that the Hohenzollern princes raised and trained for battle. And the earlier Hohenzollern rulers had argued that they

---

[43] On this and the following paragraphs see Chapter 11 by Robert von Friedeburg, pp. 285–318.

wished to become involved with the War of the Spanish Succession primarily to secure the subsidies that would enable them to build up the army for self-defence.

Robert von Friedeburg consistently contrasts this German experience with that of France, and also with developments in Spain and Austria. In doing so, he is making the case that the marginalization of lesser nobles and the forging of an alliance between the courts of kings and the higher nobility that proved essential to the consolidation of monarchical power in Spain, Austria and France did not happen in Germany because of the moral authority enjoyed by the Estates in all German polities after the Princes had become discredited as promoters of wasteful war. As he argues his case, Robert von Friedeburg uses the evidence, which he and the other researchers whose investigations underpin his study have assembled, to challenge 'the Prussian militarization thesis' formulated by Hans Rosenberg and others in the mid-twentieth century. This thesis, not unlike what Hamish Scott advances in this volume, held that the 'unholy alliance' forged in the seventeenth and the eighteenth centuries between Prussian Junkers and their soldier-kings at the expense of the peasants and the lesser nobles, underpinned the military might of Germany down to the First World War.[44]

Another difference between the French and German experiences, which Robert von Friedeburg alludes to, is that while princes in Germany were theoretically bound to uphold the religion that had been designated as the official religion of their principalities by the terms of the Peace of Westphalia of 1648 they were not always dedicated to doing so. Deviations from the norm occurred most frequently when the rulers of jurisdictions where Lutheranism was established converted to Reformed confessions not provided for under what was essentially a Lutheran/ Catholic peace. Also, more unusually, religious differences between princes and the populations over which they ruled crossed the Protestant/Catholic divide. Where confessional differences of whatever kind occurred, princes or members of the princely family frequently maintained chaplains from their preferred religion within their house-holds, or constructed court chapels or burial places where services to their liking might be held, and left it to bishops to uphold the official religion of the principality.

Protestants in France, including Henry of Navarre before he became King of France in 1589, frequently favoured such local and social discretion, and one of the terms of the Edict of Nantes that brought the French Wars of Religion to an end in 1598, allowed Protestant nobles, when they

---

[44] As cited by Robert von Friedeburg, pp. 306–7.

had occasion to visit Paris on official business, to hold Protestant services in the privacy of their residences within the capital. Such tolerance did not extend to the King however, and even Henry IV considered it necessary that he be seen to uphold Catholicism as the exclusive religion of the kingdom, other than in the particular fortified towns and regions where Protestant worship was permitted by the settlement made in 1598. Moreover, he took to making use of the supposed royal touch to cure scrofula as proof that he was indeed the true king. Such demonstration of the sacral nature of kingship would have been despised by France's Protestants who supported Henry consistently, yet did not convince more committed Catholics that he was their legitimate sovereign. Few therefore can have been surprised when Henry was assassinated in 1610 given that there had been 23 previous attempts on his life.[45] However, despite consistent Catholic opposition to Henry IV, his reign and to a much greater extent those of his son Louis XIII and his grandson Louis XIV, provided the Catholic church with the opportunity to consolidate its position in France after the devastation of the religious wars.

As this consolidation proceeded, the limited tolerance that had been conceded to Protestants in 1598 was, with the agreement of Kings Louis XIII and Louis XIV, gradually eroded until 1685 when, with the Revocation of the Edict of Nantes, Protestants were given the choice between conforming with the dominant Catholic religion or going into exile from France. The Revocation, which was welcomed enthusiastically in Catholic France, earned Louis the reputation throughout Protestant Europe of being a tyrant, and as Ronald G. Asch has phrased it, associated Louis XIV with 'a more sacerdotal and more militantly Catholic concept of kingship'. At this point the moral difference that had previously separated the French from the Spanish monarchy was diminished, and France rather than Spain was now identified as the aggressive power in Europe.[46]

Even before this, successive Bourbon kings, and certainly Louis XIII and Louis XIV, had tacitly accepted that as kings of France they were obliged to promote Catholicism within the kingdom. Then what Asch has described as the 'more aggressively Catholic' pose adopted by Louis XIV during the later decades of his reign, was partly to prepare the way for a Bourbon prince to become king of Spain. However whatever freedom of action had previously been enjoyed by French kings in religious matters had been circumscribed long before then, and none of them could have contemplated professing any religion besides Catholicism, or in

---

[45] Denis Crouzet, *Les guerriers de Dieu: la violence au temps des troubles de religion, vers 1525-vers 1610* (Seyssel, 1990), pp. 463–520.
[46] On this and subsequent paragraphs see Chapter 12 by Ronald Asch, pp. 319–57, at p. 332.

permitting Protestant services to take place at court. In this respect they enjoyed less freedom of action than Princes in Germany, or monarchs in Sweden where Queen Christina had converted to Catholicism before she abdicated voluntarily. More to the point, as Ronald Asch demonstrates, the French kings were more restricted also than their counterparts on the British throne where three of the Stuart monarchs (Charles I, Charles II and James II) had had Catholic wives, and where one of them, James II, had let it be known publicly in 1673 that he had embraced Catholicism, a full 12 years before he would succeed his brother Charles II as king.[47]

This suggests that the French kingdom, as well as the French monarchy, like its Spanish and Austrian counterparts, was defined as Catholic at quite an early stage. However, if we follow the line of argument pursued by Ronald Asch, the British monarchy and state continued, for a long time, to be religiously permissive notwithstanding the existence in both England and Scotland of majority Protestant populations who worried constantly that Catholic conspirators would subvert their dominions.[48] Despite such fears, the British monarchy was not defined as Protestant until after the Glorious Revolution of 1688 that had brought William of Orange and his Stuart wife Mary to the throne in place of the Catholic King James II and VII. Even then, it was only the birth of a male heir to the throne, and with it the prospect that the kingdom would have to contend into the future with a Catholic Stuart dynasty, that made it necessary for the interested parties to formulate a strict Protestant definition for the British monarchy under the 1702 Act of Settlement.[49]

* * * *

This summation of the chapters in this volume makes it clear that anybody aspiring to propose generalizations concerning state formation in early modern Europe, or on how evolving relationships between monarchs and nobilities impacted on this development, will experience difficulty in moving from conclusions that hold true for particular case studies to those that remain valid for state formation in all countries or regions of Europe. The complexity of the subject was even more apparent at the Conferences in Rotterdam where there were presentations on other European polities besides those represented in this volume including the Austrian Habsburg Monarchy and the Polish-Lithuanian Commonwealth. And those present at Rotterdam were encouraged by

---

[47] J. Miller, *James II; A Study in Kingship* (revised edn, New Haven, Ct., 2000).

[48] T. Harris, M. Goldie and P. Seaward, eds., *The Politics of Religion in Restoration England* (Oxford, 1991).

[49] On this point see John Morrill in Chapter 2, p. 42.

Geoffrey Parker to take account also of state formation in Asia. Because of the diversity of experience, contributors to this volume have limited themselves, as John Morrill and Robert von Friedeburg have stated in their introduction, to describing the changes that contemporaries believed were occurring in their own lifetimes.[50]

It was my understanding when I was invited to serve as joint rapporteur with Geoffrey Parker to the Rotterdam conference, that my role was to serve as impartial witness, since I am no authority on the subject of state formation and had not been involved with the 'state formation' conferences that had preceded the Rotterdam meeting. It is in this same spirit that I am seeking in this afterword to posit some general conclusions on the process of state formation in early modern Europe drawn from both the essays in the collection and from discussions at the Rotterdam conferences.

The first obvious conclusion is that the political map of Europe was revised dramatically during the course of the early modern centuries. Moreover, regardless of where in Europe they resided, people would have been more aware than their predecessors of the existence of a centralized government authority that was an extension of the power of the sovereign. While at the end of the period under discussion, government institutions existed in almost every European country to protect the lives and property of the subjects residing within that jurisdiction, these institutions also intruded upon the lives of subjects, not only by waging war and raising taxes to meet the costs of warfare but also by monitoring international trade. Classically educated Europeans of whatever jurisdiction would have found a precedent in Ancient Rome for a militarized state whose costs were borne by the community. However, while some rulers were inspired by the Roman ambition to become lords of all the world, these quickly discovered that universal monarchy was no longer attainable because any move in that direction was invariably countered by rulers of rival states working in consort to prevent its achievement. Another obstacle in the way of pursuing any geographical extension of power was that in a Europe that was becoming increasingly riven by confessional division, Protestant publicists were decrying the very concept of universal monarchy as a secular counterpart to the universal rule that the Papacy aspired after in the spiritual realm.

As the dream of extending authority by force was proving to be increasingly difficult, rulers in Europe seem to have concentrated instead on deepening their control over the polities they held, usually in

---

[50] John Morrill and Robert von Friedeburg, Chapter 1, pp. 4–5.

collaboration with local elites of various compositions. These latter – and the chapters here show that these might include nobles, great and small, and representatives of towns – had usually conceded to the sovereign the conditional entitlement to wage war and to exercise justice within a designated domain provided the monarch guaranteed them specified privileges. This had the consequence of making them also part of the state. The populations of most larger political entities were multilingual and multicultural, and some states, notably Spain and Austria, held dominion over satellite jurisdictions each with a court of its own where the elites of peripheral jurisdictions had the opportunity to attend upon monarchs or their representatives. Their multicultural character of such polities suggests that we should refrain from describing the political entities that were developing as nation-states even if historians of previous generations used that term glibly.

The territorial boundaries to the more potent states in western Europe – and this was certainly so in the cases of the British, French and Spanish monarchies towards the end of our period – were described precisely on maps and atlases which implied that the frontiers of these states were immutable. The several chapters show that dynastic accident or defeat in war could still bring about boundary changes, but after our terminal date of 1720 and even before then, conflict usually erupted only when particular rulers sought to assert their authority beyond such conventionally accepted demarcation lines, or when the failure of a lineage gave rise to successions that threatened the established order. However even here it is difficult to generalize because matters were altogether more fluid in the Baltic region and in Eastern Europe where political boundaries continued to undergo more significant change than in western Europe, and where rulers were sometimes elected by elites. Yet another variation in state type was the sequence of relatively compact principalities that occupied the German-speaking heartland of Europe. The rulers of these jurisdictions were usually constitutionally subservient to the emperor and the privileged few took pride in being electors of emperors. Some princes aspired to greater independence and a few (notably Brandenburg and Saxony) assumed kingly titles from areas outside the empire but with the agreement of the ruling emperor. Despite such apparent bids for independence the moral authority of the empire achieved what Peter. H. Wilson has described as a 'recovery' both because it played an important role in the working out of the various settlements and military demobilization that had been agreed upon at Westphalia, and because Emperors Ferdinand III and Leopold I worked closely to govern by consent and to enhance the reputation of imperial institutions particularly the judicial ones that now acted independently of the emperor.[51] Whatever consolidation of princely authority occurred was, as has been made clear by the chapter by Robert von Friedeburg, enabled by accommodations negotiated between princes and the principal landowners within each principality who usually held noble titles. These arrangements contributed greatly to boundary stability, as did the powers enjoyed by revitalized imperial institutions. The new reality was symbolized by the modest princely courts, universities and libraries that princes maintained and patronized to indicate their dedication both to learning and culture and the welfare of their subjects as well as to the exercise of power.

Each principality, kingdom or polity under one government that existed in Europe at 1720 had to some degree been challenged and/or shaped by the confessional differences that came to divide European society as first the Protestant Reformation and then the Catholic Counter-Reformation promoted evangelization drives, sometimes encouraged, or enabled, by secular rulers. The Spanish monarchy was among the first dominions to be affected politically by these developments because Protestants were prominent among those in the Low Countries who rejected Spanish governance of the provinces that Philip II had inherited from his father, Emperor Charles V. These rebels cited religious oppression as one of their prime justifications for withdrawing their allegiance to Philip, and the ensuing struggle became even more confessional as some Protestant rulers of contiguous states, and some Protestant factions from various countries, gave military assistance to the dissidents in the Low Countries. This development, in turn, motivated successive Spanish Habsburg rulers and their Austrian cousins to become strident opponents of the spread of Protestantism, particularly within their own jurisdictions.

Because of this stand taken by Habsburg rulers, both Spain and Austria can be described as confessional states in that the rulers of each assumed responsibility to champion Catholicism in their own jurisdictions and internationally. Other rulers sought for a time to accommodate confessional diversity within their dominions rather than incur the ignominy of fanaticism and tyranny that was attached to rulers in Spain and Austria by Protestant propagandists. However, most attempts by rulers to accommodate a plurality of confessions within their realms proved more difficult than originally appreciated, and the bitterness of the Wars of Religion in France alerted rulers to the threat that diversity in religion presented to

---

[51] Peter H. Wilson, *Europe's Tragedy: A New History of the Thirty Years' War* (London, paperback edn, 2010), pp. 773–778; idem, *The Holy Roman Empire, 1595–1806* (2nd edn, London, 2011), pp. 50–59.

social order in any realm. Moreover, persistent difficulty over reaching a religious settlement for the empire that would satisfy both Protestant and Catholic interests, alerted rulers to the political tensions that would inevitably arise if diversity of religion was to be permitted within more compact jurisdictions. Consequently, in the aftermath of prolonged destructive warfare that usually had a confessional dimension, rulers throughout Europe became reconciled to the resolution formulated at the Peace of Westphalia in 1648 whereby princes would determine whether Lutheranism or Catholicism, and now also Calvinism, would prevail as the religion of the realm that they governed. Religious minorities persisted in many jurisdictions of Europe and while formal toleration and informal tolerance often made their lives easier they were frequently aggrieved, persecuted or discriminated against. However the general application of the convention agreed at Westphalia meant that, by the close of the seventeenth century, almost every polity in Europe had defined what the official religion of that jurisdiction should be. Such definition tended to strengthen the position of rulers both because their powers of patronage could be extended to include church appointments, and because the clergy in officially designated state churches could be counted upon to exhort their congregations to show loyalty to their political leaders where, previously, religious diversity had fostered political division.

The chapters in this volume suggest that by 1720 most polities in Western Europe, and this would include the United Provinces as well as the British, French and Spanish monarchies, had assumed modes of governance and even boundaries that would persist to the time of the French Revolution and even beyond. Furthermore, they show that accommodations between kings and nobles had also been negotiated in the Baltic states, which had developed courts where established nobles attended and who, over time, were joined by foreigners of talent, particularly military talent, who were admitted to the ranks of nobility. Members of the political nation in the several states whose territories abutted the shores of the Baltic were far from agreed on what should be the frontiers of any given jurisdiction, and the supposition that boundaries would be finally resolved only by might presented rulers with a persistent challenge to prove their prowess on the field of battle. The essays also show that what appeared to be a viable working arrangement had also been negotiated between princes, estates and imperial institutions in the German-speaking core of Europe. It appeared in 1720 that this area was destined to remain segmented into a series of moderately sized states governed by princes whose authority would continue to be restricted by constitutional constraints.

The common feature of government in all jurisdictions (except arguably in the United Provinces and in the cantons of Switzerland) was that it derived any permanence it had from monarchical or princely title and from negotiated working relationships between monarchs and elites. These latter were both concerned with how men and money should be raised for the conduct of war, which remained the principal business of almost every state. This, in turn, raised the question of who would meet the costs of war and this also usually called for negotiations between kings and elites because the previous options available to monarchs to default on their debts, or to devalue their currencies, or to leave their soldiers unpaid, or to billet their armies on the lands of their opponents, had all been discredited as short-term expedients that were unsuited to supporting prolonged warfare. Such stratagems had also either fostered indiscipline, which could not be countenanced in standing armies, or threatened the standing and wealth of elites. Under the changing circumstances and after some early hesitation, elites tended to seize upon whatever opportunities presented themselves to retain, or enhance, their status or wealth and they found that they could do so most readily by establishing a vested interest in the smooth functioning of the state in which they lived either by lending it money, or purchasing government office, or by securing commissions in armies and navies for themselves or their sons.

Authors of the chapters in this volume have, for the most part, not detailed the tax raising and credit mechanisms used by different states to meet their obligations. However, specialists who have addressed this subject have concluded that the only states that succeeded in freeing themselves from the constraints on their tax raising ability imposed the natural resources of the countries over which they ruled, were either those who could mobilize long-term credit to cover the immediate cost of their military undertakings, or those who found other states ready to meet the costs of their military pursuits.

In the case of Britain it proved both imaginative and successful in persuading creditors, mostly from within Britain itself, to extend it long-term loans at assured interest rates. This exercise in financial mobilization goes some way to explain why, from that point forward, Britain was able to play an altogether more prominent role in the politics of mainland Europe than it had done previously.[52] However, while more imaginative fiscal devices undoubtedly helped Britain in becoming a creditor state from a relatively early date, the fundamental reason why the state there came to be regarded as a good credit risk was because, by the late

---

[52] John Brewer, *The Sinews of Power: War, Money and the English State, 1688–1783* (New York, 1989).

seventeenth century, Britain had actually become dramatically more wealthy and more populous than previously. Economic historians are not of one mind in explaining precisely how this economic transformation had been achieved, but one major factor was England's success in exploiting the resources of parts of the world beyond its shores, particularly in America, to increase its wealth by foreign trade, which also contributed generously (and disproportionately) to state taxes.[53] In doing so the British were consciously emulating the Dutch who they had regarded as their principal trading rivals, and with whom they went to war on three occasions during the second half of the seventeenth century.

The British and the Dutch were not, of course, the first European peoples to exploit extra-European resources to facilitate state development, and I will argue in these concluding paragraphs that one major oversight in this collection of essays, as in the discussion of European state formation more generally, has been in explaining how the engagement of Europeans with the world outside impacted upon state formation within Europe.

We already noted the manoeuvres of the Portuguese monarchy of the fifteenth century to play a more prominent role within the politics of the Iberian Peninsula, and this aspiration of the ruler of what, from the perspective of the twenty-first century, would be thought of as a relatively poor jurisdiction, to be treated as an equal with the ruler of Castile makes sense only when we take account of Portugal's previous success in exploiting trading opportunities along the west coast of Africa. This had not only made Portugal a significant trader in gold, textiles and slaves, but it had led also to Portuguese mariners discovering an all-water route to Asia with the benefits that accrued from that, and access also to the coast of Brazil which, over time, would bring considerable wealth to Portugal.[54] These overseas successes explain why Portuguese monarchs could aspire to playing a more active role in Iberian and European politics even if their first strategy towards that end resulted, largely as a consequence of dynastic accident, in Portugal being absorbed into the Castilian monarchy in 1580. However, the lesser nobility and burgesses of Portugal never became reconciled to this subservience, and they, as Pedro Cardim has detailed, took advantage of the opportunity that presented itself in 1640 to recover the independence of the Portuguese monarchy from Spanish dominion. And, as Pedro Cardim has also explained, one of the prime causes of the dissatisfaction of these groups was that rule from Spain

---

[53] Nuala Zahedieh, *The Capital and the Colonies, 1660–1700* (Cambridge, 2012).

[54] Daviken Studnicki-Gizbert, *A Nation Upon the Ocean Sea: Portugal's Atlantic Diaspora and the Crisis of the Spanish Empire, 1492–1640* (Oxford, 2007).

meant that Portugal's overseas empire became exposed to attack by the enemies of Spain which was then not able to defend these Portuguese interests. Another reason for Portuguese dissatisfaction, as Cardim also explains, was that once they became overlords of Portugal the Spanish took credit for having conquered the world for Christianity and disregarded that Portugal had led the way.[55]

At the moment of Portugal's liberation in 1640, the Spanish monarchy seemed still to be the prime military power in Europe. We know, with the benefit of hindsight, that the period of Spain's ascendancy was over, but contemporaries continued to be mesmerized by the fact that the military capacity of Spain far exceeded its human and material resources. The secret of Spain's ability to pay for its armies and navies was that it could negotiate loans from northern European bankers on the strength of the regular inflow of precious metal from the New World that it had enjoyed for more than a century. Therefore those who were jealous of Spain's position in the world set their sights on emulating its New World successes. The most prominent in doing so were Protestant radicals from England, France and the Low Countries whose propaganda and attacks upon Spanish interests in the Atlantic, resulted ultimately in each of England, the United Provinces and France possessing considerable New World settlements by the mid seventeenth century. None of these colonies produced the precious metals that the propagandists had hoped for, and what the French acquired in the sixteenth and seventeenth centuries led to but to an incremental increase in the wealth of what was already the richest and most populous country in Europe.[56]

However in the case of England, which, apart from London, had always been a poor and thinly inhabited dominion, the New World possessions it acquired, populated, and exploited proved economically transformative. They did so both by providing England with commodities (principally tobacco and sugar) that boosted its re-export trade, and by creating a demand for provisions and for mundane manufactured goods to meet the needs of the white and black settler populations in their colonies. The trade that English merchants promoted with Asia provided them with luxury goods which, like commodities from America, boosted re-exports, and, with the passage of time, Asian trade became ever more consequential.[57]

The increase in wealth and population which was evident first in England and later extended to Scotland and Ireland, not only enabled

[55] See Chapter 8 by Pedro Cardim, pp. 221–2.
[56] Canny, 'A Protestant or Catholic Atlantic World?'
[57] Zahedieh, *The Capital and the Colonies*.

the British state to raise direct and indirect taxes but also, as we noted, to offer this wealth as security on long-term loans. The money thus raised was used to cover the immediate costs of its armies and navies in wartime. However, what had initially promised to be a short-term involvement of Britain with the military effort to curb the power of Louis XIV of France became a long-term engagement with the politics and military affairs of Continental Europe. This happened partly because after 1714, when the Elector of Hanover became King George I of Great Britain, the British monarch, and his successor, continued to have a German interest and responsibility.[58] This obligation on Britain to uphold its interest in Hanover was to be met ultimately by Britain entering into an alliance with Frederick the Great of Brandenburg Prussia who, in the middle of the eighteenth century, had become the most capable military ruler in the region. That monarch, like all rulers of German principalities, was constricted by his Estates in what he might spend on war. However Britain helped resolve his problem for him, and thereby exerted a major influence on state development in Germany, by using its own wealth to become a significant paymaster of the army of Frederick the Great during much of the Seven Years' War, 1756–1763.

When they pursued this policy Britain was following a precedent established by France when, during the course of the Thirty Years' War, it had provided subsidies first to King Christian IV of Denmark and then to King Gustavus Adolphus of Sweden to enable them to keep armies in the field to confront the forces of the Austrian Habsburgs in Germany. What was being done in that instance was also with the intention of overcoming the limitations placed on the power of monarchs by their Estates. Therefore France in the 1630s was providing a fillip to the development of absolute rule in the Baltic region, in the same way that Britain's eighteenth-century support for Frederick the Great would enable the emergence of more forceful state power in Germany.

These realities would suggest that the phenomenon of state formation in Europe with which the contributors to this volume are concerned was not a spontaneous development and was in the first instance primarily a Western European phenomenon. Then, over time, the rulers of the various western dominions transmitted their models of governance to other countries of Europe both by example and by direct influence. Most has been written on how better working relations were established between elites and monarchs in France, which, as authors agree, was the key to the establishment there of greater political stability and of agreed

[58] Brendan Simms, *Three Victories and a Defeat: The Rise and Fall of the First British Empire, 1714–1783* (London, 2007).

principles of government. What is less frequently stated is that the France of Louis XIII and of Louis XIV was to an extent emulating developments that had already been achieved in Spain. When we thus allow for change that resulted from imitation and emulation we are left wondering the extent to which, as European rulers gained greater knowledge of Asia during these centuries and as they were brought, by experience, to recognize the potency of Ottoman power, they were being persuaded by these extra European examples that they would have to increase the scope of their authority if they wished to survive. While this must remain speculative, I would contend that the accomplishments of the Spanish monarch, and the achievements also of some of the other western European powers – notably Britain and the United Provinces – who proved themselves capable of developing coherent states and pursuing systematic policies, were greatly facilitated by the increase in the wealth of these dominions that had resulted from the acquisitions they had made in the wider Atlantic world.

Index